Dictionary of World Biography

Index

Dictionary of World Biography

The Ancient World
The Middle Ages
The Renaissance
The 17th and 18th Centuries
The 19th Century, 2 volumes
The 20th Century, 3 volumes
Index

Frank N. Magill, *editor*

Christina J. Moose, *managing editor*

Alison Aves, *researcher and bibliographer*

Mark Rehn, *acquisitions editor*

Dictionary of World Biography

Volume 10
Index

Steve Seddon, Indexer

FITZROY DEARBORN PUBLISHERS
CHICAGO • LONDON

SALEM PRESS
PASADENA • HACKENSACK, NJ

©Copyright 2000 by Salem Press, Inc.

All rights in this book are reserved. No part of this work may be used or reproduced in any manner whatso-ever or transmitted in any form or by any means, electronic or mechanical, including photocopy, recording, or any information storage and retrieval system, without written permission from the copyright owner except in the case of brief quotations embodied in critical articles and reviews.

Dictionary of World Biography is a copublication of Salem Press, Inc. and Fitzroy Dearborn Publishers

For information, write to:

SALEM PRESS, INC.
P.O. Box 50062
Pasadena, California 91115

or

FITZROY DEARBORN PUBLISHERS
919 North Michigan Avenue, Suite 760
Chicago, Illinois 60611
USA

or

FITZROY DEARBORN PUBLISHERS
310 Regent Street
London W1R 5AJ
England

The paper used in this volume conforms to the American National Standard for Permanence of Paper for Printed Library Materials, Z39.48-1992.

Library of Congress Cataloging-in-Publication Data
Dictionary of world biography / editor, Frank N. Magill ; managing editor, Christina J. Moose ; researcher and bibliographer, Alison Aves ; acquisitions editor, Mark Rehn.
    v. cm.
    A revision and reordering, with new entries added, of the material in the thirty vols. comprising the various subsets designated "series" published under the collective title: Great lives from history, 1987-1995.
    Includes bibliographical references and indexes.
    Contents: v.10. Index.
    ISBN 0-89356-324-2 (v. 10: alk. paper)
    ISBN 0-89356-273-4 (v. 1-10 set: alk paper)
    1. Biography. 2. World history. I. Magill, Frank Northen, 1907-1997. II. Moose, Christina J., 1952- . III. Aves, Alison. IV. Great lives from history.
CT104.D54 1998
920.02—dc21
                                                  97-51154
                                                    CIP

British Library Cataloguing-in-Publication Data is available.
Fitzroy Dearborn ISBN 1-57958-049-1
First Published in the U.K. and U.S., 2000
    Printed by Braun-Brumfield, Inc.

Cover design by Peter Aristedes.

First Printing

CONTENTS

AREA OF ACHIEVEMENT INDEX

ABOLITIONISM. *See* **CIVIL RIGHTS;
SOCIAL REFORM**

ACTING. *See* **THEATER AND
ENTERTAINMENT**

AERONAUTICS. *See* **AVIATION AND SPACE
EXPLORATION; ENGINEERING**

AGRICULTURE. *See also* **BOTANY;
HORTICULTURE**
Tull, Jethro, **IV:**1345

ALCHEMY. *See* **CHEMISTRY**

AMERICAN INDIAN AFFAIRS. *See* **NATIVE
AMERICAN AFFAIRS**

ANTHROPOLOGY
Baer, Karl Ernst von, **V:**109
Benedict, Ruth, **VII:**255
Boas, Franz, **VII:**339
Breuil, Henri-Édouard-Prosper, **VII:**456
Dunham, Katherine, **VII:**984
Frobenius, Leo, **VII:**1242
Heyerdahl, Thor, **VIII:**1658
Leakey, L.S.B., **VIII:**2145
Le Bon, Gustave, **VIII:**2134
Lévi-Strauss, Claude, **VIII:**2164
Mead, Margaret, **VIII:**2468
Morgan, Lewis Henry, **VI:**1584
Rasmussen, Knud Johan Victor, **IX:**3121
Teilhard de Chardin, Pierre, **IX:**3626
Virchow, Rudolf, **VI:**2312

ARCHAEOLOGY
Ballard, Robert Duane, **VII:**180
Heyerdahl, Thor, **VIII:**1658
Raphael, **III:**642
Schliemann, Heinrich, **VI:**1980
Winckelmann, Johann Joachim, **IV:**1460

ARCHITECTURE
Aalto, Alvar, **VII:**1
Adam, James and Robert, **IV:**7
Alberti, Leon Battista, **III:**8
Arnolfo di Cambio, **II:**82
Ashurbanipal, **I:**105
Ashurnasirpal II, **I:**109

Barry, Sir Charles, **V:**138
Bernini, Gian Lorenzo, **IV:**118
Boffrand, Germain, **IV:**151
Borromini, Francesco, **IV:**167
Bramante, Donato, **III:**81
Brunelleschi, Filippo, **III:**89
Bulfinch, Charles, **V:**349
Burnham, Daniel Hudson, **V:**365
Candela, Felix, **VII:**557
Cimabue, **II:**272
Fischer von Erlach, Johann Bernhard, **IV:**473
Freyssinet, Eugène, **VII:**1228
Fuller, R. Buckminster, **VII:**1265
Garnier, Tony, **VII:**1308
Gaudí, Antonio, **VII:**1315
Giotto, **II:**388
Greenway, Francis, **V:**990
Gropius, Walter, **VIII:**1486
Guarini, Guarino, **IV:**583
Hardouin-Mansart, Jules, **IV:**901
Hawksmoor, Nicholas, **IV:**635
Hildebrandt, Johann Lucas von, **IV:**655
Imhotep, **I:**443
Jones, Inigo, **IV:**735
Latrobe, Benjamin Henry, **VI:**1327
Le Corbusier, **VIII:**2137
Lescot, Pierre, **III:**428
Lin, Maya Ying, **VIII:**2185
Mansart, François, **IV:**898
Mendelsohn, Erich, **VIII:**2487
Michelangelo, **III:**517
Mies van der Rohe, Ludwig, **VIII:**2520
Morris, William, **VI:**1588
Nash, John, **IV:**1012
Nervi, Pier Luigi, **VIII:**2720
Niemeyer, Oscar, **VIII:**2739
Oud, J.J.P., **IX:**2859
Palladio, Andrea, **III:**580
Pei, I.M., **IX:**2946
Perret, Auguste, **IX:**2976
Pugin, Augustus Welby Northmore, **VI:**1821
Raphael, **III:**642
Richardson, Henry Hobson, **VI:**1882
Sansovino, Jacopo, **III:**664
Scott, Sir George Gilbert, **VI:**2002
Siloé, Diego de, **III:**696
Street, George Edmund, **VI:**2160
Suger, **II:**859
Sullivan, Louis, **VI:**2167

Vanbrugh, Sir John, **IV:**1351
Vasari, Giorgio, **III:**743
Wren, Sir Christopher, **IV:**1480
Wright, Frank Lloyd, **IX:**4060
Xenakis, Iannis, **IX:**4075
Xerxes I, **I:**962
Zoser, **I:**978

ART. *See also* **PATRONAGE OF THE ARTS;
  PHOTOGRAPHY**
Andrea del Sarto, **III:**24
Angelico, Fra, **III:**28
Arnolfo di Cambio, **II:**82
Ashurbanipal, **I:**105
Ashurnasirpal II, **I:**109
Audubon, John James, **V:**86
Beardsley, Aubrey, **V:**161
Bellini, Giovanni, **III:**58
Bernini, Gian Lorenzo, **IV:**118
Bierstadt, Albert, **V:**233
Bingham, George Caleb, **V:**236
Blake, William, **IV:**137
Boccioni, Umberto, **VII:**342
Bonnard, Pierre, **VII:**362
Bosch, Hieronymus, **III:**70
Botticelli, Sandro, **III:**74
Brancusi, Constantin, **VII:**414
Braque, Georges, **VII:**431
Bruegel, Pieter (the Elder), **III:**85
Brunelleschi, Filippo, **III:**89
Calder, Alexander, **VII:**538
Canaletto, **IV:**242
Canova, Antonio, **V:**408
Carracci Family, The, **III:**125
Cartier-Bresson, Henri, **VII:**594
Cassatt, Mary, **V:**434
Catlin, George, **V:**443
Cellini, Benvenuto, **III:**151
Cézanne, Paul, **V:**453
Chagall, Marc, **VII:**639
Chardin, Jean Siméon, **IV:**275
Claude Lorrain, **IV:**317
Cocteau, Jean, **VII:**721
Constable, John, **V:**547
Copley, John Singleton, **IV:**356
Correggio, **III:**184
Courbet, Gustave, **V:**565
Cranach, Lucas (the Elder), **III:**200
Dalí, Salvador, **VII:**827
David, Jacques-Louis, **V:**610
Degas, Edgar, **V:**641
Delacroix, Eugène, **V:**645

Delaunay, Robert, **VII:**888
Denis, Maurice, **VII:**909
Donatello, **III:**220
Duccio di Buoninsegna, **II:**305
Duchamp, Marcel, **VII:**972
Dürer, Albrecht, **III:**230
Eakins, Thomas, **V:**732
Epstein, Sir Jacob, **VII:**1087
Ernst, Max, **VII:**1098
Eyck, Jan van, and Hubert van Eyck, **III:**250
Fragonard, Jean-Honoré, **IV:**488
Frankenthaler, Helen, **VII:**1208
Fry, Roger, **VII:**1253
Gainsborough, Thomas, **IV:**515
Gauguin, Paul, **V:**888
Geisel, Theodor Seuss, **VII:**1329
Géricault, Théodore, **V:**910
Ghiberti, Lorenzo, **III:**302
Giacometti, Alberto, **VII:**1359
Giorgione, **III:**305
Giotto, **II:**388
Gogh, Vincent van, **V:**944
Goya, Francisco de, **IV:**569
Greco, El, **III:**311
Gris, Juan, **VIII:**1483
Grünewald, Matthias, **III:**322
Hals, Frans, **IV:**604
Hiroshige, **V:**1117
Hockney, David, **VIII:**1711
Hogarth, William, **IV:**668
Hokusai, **V:**1120
Holbein, Hans, the Younger, **III:**358
Homer, Winslow, **V:**1133
Hopper, Edward, **VIII:**1740
Hsia Kuei, **II:**479
Hunt, William Holman, **V:**1168
Ingres, Jean-Auguste-Dominique, **V:**1183
Jacopo della Quercia, **III:**389
Jōchō, **II:**537
John, Augustus, **VIII:**1854
Jones, Inigo, **IV:**735
Kandinsky, Wassily, **VIII:**1903
Kauffmann, Angelica, **IV:**765
Kirchner, Ernst Ludwig, **VIII:**1991
Klee, Paul, **VIII:**2005
Kokoschka, Oskar, **VIII:**2012
Kollwitz, Käthe, **VIII:**2016
Krasner, Lee, **VIII:**2023
Kupka, František, **VIII:**2036
Lawrence, Sir Thomas, **IV:**808
Léger, Fernand, **VIII:**2154
Leonardo da Vinci, **III:**423

Lescot, Pierre, **III:**428
Lipchitz, Jacques, **VIII:**2199
Lorenzetti, Pietro, and
    Ambrogio Lorenzetti, **II:**595
Lysippus, **I:**515
Ma Yüan, **II:**612
Magritte, René, **VIII:**2349
Manet, Édouard, **VI:**1471
Mantegna, Andrea, **III:**460
Marc, Franz, **VIII:**2404
Martin, Agnes, **VIII:**2437
Martini, Simone, **II:**632
Masaccio, **III:**483
Matisse, Henri, **VIII:**2452
Mi Fei, **II:**639
Michelangelo, **III:**517
Miró, Joan, **VIII:**2546
Mondrian, Piet, **VIII:**2575
Monet, Claude, **VIII:**2579
Moore, Henry, **VIII:**2609
Morris, William, **VI:**1588
Moses, Grandma, **VIII:**2633
Munch, Edvard, **VIII:**2658
Nash, Paul, **VIII:**2689
Nast, Thomas, **VI:**1627
Nevelson, Louise, **VIII:**2728
Nicholson, Ben, **VIII:**2732
Nordau, Max, **VIII:**2766
Ogata Kōrin, **IV:**1041
O'Keeffe, Georgia, **IX:**2800
Orcagna, Andrea, **II:**698
Orozco, José Clemente, **IX:**2836
Pater, Walter, **VI:**1749
Peale, Charles Willson, **IV:**1070
Phidias, **I:**624
Picasso, Pablo, **IX:**2997
Piero della Francesca, **III:**606
Pisano, Andrea, **II:**744
Pisano, Nicola and Giovanni, **II:**747
Pissarro, Camille, **VI:**1779
Pollock, Jackson, **IX:**3048
Polygnotus, **I:**676
Potter, Beatrix, **IX:**3063
Poussin, Nicolas, **IV:**1118
Praxiteles, **I:**690
Pucelle, Jean, **II:**762
Raeburn, Sir Henry, **VI:**1836
Raphael, **III:**642
Redon, Odilon, **VI:**1854
Rembrandt, **IV:**1152
Remington, Frederic, **VI:**1861
Renoir, Pierre-Auguste, **VI:**1869

Reynolds, Sir Joshua, **IV:**1160
Rivera, Diego, **IX:**3184
Rockwell, Norman, **IX:**3198
Rodin, Auguste, **VI:**1900
Romney, George, **IV:**1187
Ross, Betsy, **IV:**1191
Rouault, Georges, **IX:**3251
Rousseau, Henri, **VI:**1921
Rubens, Peter Paul, **IV:**1198
Ruskin, John, **VI:**1925
Saint-Gaudens, Augustus, **VI:**1940
Sansovino, Jacopo, **III:**664
Sargent, John Singer, **VI:**1961
Schmidt-Rottluff, Karl, **IX:**3354
Scopas, **I:**764
Sendak, Maurice, **IX:**3387
Sesshū, 679
Seurat, Georges, **VI:**2033
Siloé, Diego de, **III:**696
Sluter, Claus, **II:**832
Sōtatsu, **IV:**1257
Stuart, Gilbert, **IV:**1289
Su Tung-p'o, **II:**855
Sung Dynasty, **II:**866
Sutherland, Graham Vivian, **IX:**3587
Taine, Hippolyte-Adolphe, **VI:**2182
Thomson, Tom, **IX:**3665
Thurber, James, **IX:**3677
Tiepolo, Giovanni Battista, **IV:**1323
Tintoretto, **III:**717
Titian, **III:**721
Toulouse-Lautrec, Henri de, **VI:**2247
Turner, J.M.W., **VI:**2272
Unkei, **II:**924
Vasari, Giorgio, **III:**743
Velázquez, Diego, **IV:**1364
Vermeer, Jan, **IV:**1368
Veronese, Paolo, **III:**747
Verrocchio, Andrea del, **III:**750
Vigée-Lebrun, Élisabeth, **IV:**1376
Vuillard, Édouard, **IX:**3826
Wang Hsi-chih, **I:**946
Wang Wei, **II:**965
Warhol, Andy, **IX:**3884
Watteau, Antoine, **IV:**1413
Wedgwood, Josiah, **IV:**1421
Weyden, Rogier van der, **III:**778
Whistler, James McNeill, **VI:**2363
Whitney, Gertrude Vanderbilt, **IX:**3969
Wood, Grant, **IX:**4045
Wyeth, Andrew, **IX:**4072
Yen Li-pen, **II:**1015

ASTRONAUTICS. *See* **AVIATION AND SPACE EXPLORATION**

ASTROPHYSICS. *See* **PHYSICS**

ASTRONOMY. *See also* **NATURAL HISTORY; PHYSICS**
Abul Wefa, **II:**20
Alhazen, **II:**63
Ambartsumian, Viktor A., 63
Anaximander, **I:**50
Apollonius of Perga, **I:**72
Aryabhata, **II:**89
Avicenna, **II:**106
Banneker, Benjamin, **IV:**88
Battani, al-, **II:**121
Bernoulli, Jakob I, **IV:**122
Bessel, Friedrich Wilhelm, **V:**215
Brahe, Tycho, **III:**77
Brahmagupta, **II:**181
Bruno, Giordano, **III:**96
Copernicus, Nicolaus, **III:**176
Danjon, André-Louis, **VII:**837
Eudoxus of Cnidus, **I:**310
Fracastoro, Girolamo, **III:**270
Galileo, **IV:**519
Gauss, Carl Friedrich, **V:**893
Halley, Edmond, **IV:**600
Hawking, Stephen W., **VIII:**1580
Hipparchus, **I:**407
Huygens, Christiaan, **IV:**695
Kepler, Johannes, **IV:**772
Khwarizmi, al-, **II:**563
Langley, Samuel Pierpont, **VI:**1313
Laplace, Pierre-Simon, **VI:**1319
Lemaître, Georges, **VIII:**2157
Nabu-rimanni, **I:**566
Nostradamus, **III:**567
Oort, Jan Hendrik, **IX:**2827
Ptolemy, **I:**712
Pythagoras, **I:**727
Sagan, Carl, **IX:**3292
Schmidt, Bernhard Voldemar, **IX:**3351
Schwarzschild, Karl, **IX:**3366
Sosigenes, **I:**811
Tombaugh, Clyde William, **IX:**3699
Wolf, Max, **IX:**4039

ATHLETICS. *See* **SPORTS**

AUTO RACING. *See* **SPORTS**

AVIATION AND SPACE EXPLORATION
Armstrong, Neil, **VII:**110
Blériot, Louis, **VII:**325
Braun, Wernher von, **VII:**440
Byrd, Richard E., **VII:**534
Cayley, Sir George, **V:**450
Earhart, Amelia, **VII:**992
Eckener, Hugo, **VII:**1011
Gagarin, Yuri Alekseyevich, **VII:**1270
Glenn, John H., Jr., **VII:**1387
Goddard, Robert H., **VII:**1396
Heinkel, Ernst Heinrich, **VIII:**1614
Korolev, Sergei, **VIII:**2019
Langley, Samuel Pierpont, **VI:**1313
Lindbergh, Charles A., **VIII:**2193
Montgolfier, Jacques-Étienne and Joseph-Michel, **IV:**995
Oberth, Hermann, **IX:**2777
Piccard, Auguste and Jean-Felix, **IX:**3002
Prandtl, Ludwig, **IX:**3073
Ride, Sally, **IX:**3178
Santos-Dumont, Alberto, **IX:**3320
Shepard, Alan, **IX:**3405
Tereshkova, Valentina, **IX:**3639
Tsiolkovsky, Konstantin, **IX:**3749
Tupolev, Andrei Nikolayevich, **IX:**3764
Whittle, Sir Frank, **IX:**3972
Wright, Wilbur and Orville, **IX:**4064
Zeppelin, Ferdinand von, **IX:**4108

BALLET. *See* **DANCE**

BANKING AND FINANCE. *See also* **BUSINESS AND INDUSTRY; ECONOMICS**
Biddle, Nicholas, **V:**225
Bottomley, Horatio W., **VII:**382
Cooke, Jay, **V:**551
Gallatin, Albert, **V:**861
Medici, Lorenzo de', **III:**495
Morgan, J.P., **VI:**1579
Morris, Robert, **IV:**999
Necker, Jacques, **IV:**1016

BASEBALL. *See* **SPORTS**

BASKETBALL. *See* **SPORTS**

BIBLICAL FIGURES. *See also* **RELIGION AND THEOLOGY**
Aaron, **I:**1
Abraham, **I:**5

Darius the Great, **I:**236
David, **I:**241
Deborah, **I:**246
Ezekiel, **I:**326
Ezra, **I:**330
Herod the Great, **I:**390
Isaiah, **I:**452
Jeremiah, **I:**459
Jesus Christ, **I:**467
John the Apostle, **I:**475
John the Baptist, **I:**479
Moses, **I:**561
Nebuchadnezzar II, **I:**569
Paul, Saint, **I:**604
Peter, Saint, **I:**614
Pilate, Pontius, **I:**640
Samuel, **I:**746
Solomon, **I:**798
Stephen, Saint, **I:**822
Thomas, Saint, **I:**880
Virgin Mary, **I:**939

BIOCHEMISTRY. *See also* **BIOLOGY;**
CHEMISTRY
Bayliss, Sir William Maddock, **VII:**217
Domagk, Gerhard, **VII:**951
Jacob, François, **VIII:**1827
Macleod, John J.R., **VIII:**2329
Oparin, Aleksandr Ivanovich, **IX:**2830
Theorell, Axel Hugo Teodor, **IX:**3654

BIOLOGY. *See also* **BOTANY; GENETICS;**
ZOOLOGY
Baer, Karl Ernst von, **V:**109
Buffon, Comte de, **IV:**215
Calmette, Albert, **VII:**546
Cohn, Ferdinand Julius, **V:**534
Cousteau, Jacques-Yves, **VII:**778
Crick, Francis, **VII:**797
Cuvier, Georges, **V:**589
Darwin, Charles, **V:**606
Fleming, Sir Alexander, **VII:**1166
Florey, Baron, **VII:**1172
Haeckel, Ernst, **V:**1018
Harvey, William, **IV:**626
Hevesy, Georg von, **VIII:**1654
Houssay, Bernardo Alberto, **VIII:**1759
Jacob, François, **VIII:**1827
Leeuwenhoek, Antoni van, **IV:**825
Oparin, Aleksandr Ivanovich, **IX:**2830
Pasteur, Louis, **VI:**1744
Pauling, Linus, **IX:**2926

Piaget, Jean, **IX:**2990
Smith, Theobald, **IX:**3450
Spallanzani, Lazzaro, **IV:**1260
Waksman, Selman Abraham, **IX:**3833
Watson, James D., **IX:**3897
Weismann, August, **VI:**2348

BOTANY. *See also* **HORTICULTURE**
Bligh, William, **IV:**143
Cohn, Ferdinand Julius, **V:**534
Humboldt, Alexander von, **V:**1159
Kämpfer, Engelbert, **IV:**754
Linnaeus, **IV:**846
Malpighi, Marcello, **IV:**891
Oparin, Aleksandr Ivanovich, **IX:**2830
Vavilov, Nikolai Ivanovich, **IX:**3801

BOXING. *See* **SPORTS**

BROADCAST JOURNALISM. *See*
JOURNALISM; RADIO; TELEVISION

BUSINESS AND INDUSTRY. *See also*
BANKING AND FINANCE; ECONOMICS
Astor, John J., **V:**82
Boulton, Matthew, **IV:**182
Carnegie, Andrew, **V:**420
Chanel, Coco, **VII:**648
Citroën, André-Gustave, **VII:**695
Duke, James Buchanan, **V:**704
Du Pont, Eleuthère Irénée, **V:**718
Eads, James Buchanan, **V:**729
Eastman, George, **VII:**996
Ferrari, Enzo, **VII:**1150
Field, Marshall, **V:**783
Ford, Henry, **VII:**1184
Gadsden, James, **V:**858
Geddes, Norman Bel, **VII:**1319
Guggenheim, Daniel, **VIII:**1498
Hill, James Jerome, **IV:**659
Honda, Soichiro, **VIII:**1724
Krupp, Alfred, **VI:**1301
Lesseps, Ferdinand de, **VI:**1355
Lumière, Auguste and Louis, **VIII:**2276
Matsushita, Konosuke, **VIII:**2457
Mellon, Andrew, **VIII:**2480
Michelin, André and Édouard, **VIII:**2514
Morita, Akio, **VIII:**2622
Owen, Robert, **VI:**1708
Paterson, William, **IV:**1066
Perot, H. Ross, **IX:**2973
Pirelli Family, The, **IX:**3020

Revere, Paul, **IV:**1156
Rhodes, Cecil, **VI:**1873
Rockefeller, John D., **VI:**1896
Rolls, Charles Stewart, **IX:**3209
Rothschild Family, The, **VI:**1916
Royce, Sir Frederick Henry, **IX:**3209
Slater, Samuel, **VI:**2074
Stanford, Leland, **VI:**2096
Taylor, Frederick Winslow, **IX:**3618
Toyoda, Eiji, **IX:**3719
Vanderbilt, Cornelius, **VI:**2296
Walker, Madam C.J., **IX:**3853
Ward, Montgomery, **VI:**2331
Wedgwood, Josiah, **IV:**1421
Wilkinson, John, **IV:**1443
Winfrey, Oprah, **IX:**4029

Lomonosov, Mikhail Vasilyevich, **IV:**860
Mendeleyev, Dmitry Ivanovich, **VI:**1529
Monge, Gaspard, **IV:**975
Natta, Giulio, **VIII:**2698
Nernst, Walther Hermann, **VIII:**2713
Ostwald, Wilhelm, **IX:**2855
Paracelsus, **III:**584
Pasteur, Louis, **VI:**1744
Pauling, Linus, **IX:**2926
Spallanzani, Lazzaro, **IV:**1260
Stahl, Georg Ernst, **IV:**1268
Staudinger, Hermann, **IX:**3497
Volta, Alessandro, **IV:**1387
Weizmann, Chaim, **IX:**3930
Wöhler, Friedrich, **VI:**2403
Woodward, Robert Burns, **IX:**4052

CAESARS. *See* **ROMAN CAESARS**

CARTOGRAPHY. *See also* **GEOGRAPHY**
Lavoisier, Antoine-Laurent, **IV:**805
Mercator, Gerardus, **III:**513
Vespucci, Amerigo, **III:**758

CARTOON ILLUSTRATION. *See* **ART**

CHEMISTRY. *See also* **BIOCHEMISTRY**
Arrhenius, Svante August, **VII:**114
Avogadro, Amedeo, **V:**98
Becquerel Family, The, **V:**166
Bergius, Friedrich, **VII:**275
Bohr, Niels, **VII:**345
Boyle, Robert, **IV:**185
Cavendish, Henry, **IV:**261
Claude, Georges, **VII:**699
Curie, Pierre and Marie, **VII:**811
Dalton, John, **V:**602
Davy, Sir Humphry, **V:**621
Diels, Otto Paul Hermann, **VII:**927
Ehrlich, Paul, **VII:**1032
Faraday, Michael, **V:**767
Gay-Lussac, Joseph-Louis, **V:**897
Gibbs, Josiah Willard, **V:**923
Haber, Fritz, **VIII:**1509
Hahn, Otto, **VIII:**1513
Hevesy, Georg von, **VIII:**1654
Jabir ibn Hayyan, **II:**522
Joliot, Frédéric, and Irène Joliot-Curie,
    VIII:1870
Lavoisier, Antoine-Laurent, **IV:**805
Leblanc, Nicolas, **IV:**813
Liebig, Justus von, **VI:**1366

CHURCH GOVERNMENT. *See also* **CHURCH
    REFORM; GOVERNMENT AND
    POLITICS; MONASTICISM; POPES;
    RELIGION AND THEOLOGY**
Boniface VIII, **II:**171
Gregory VII, **II:**395

CHURCH REFORM. *See also* **CHURCH
    GOVERNMENT; MONASTICISM;
    RELIGION AND THEOLOGY; SOCIAL
    REFORM**
Bernard of Clairvaux, Saint, **II:**143
Boleyn, Anne, **III:**66
Brunner, Emil, **VII:**475
Bucer, Martin, **III:**101
Catherine of Aragon, **III:**136
Clement VII, **III:**166
Colet, John, **III:**169
Fulbert of Chartres, Saint, **II:**373
Hus, Jan, **II:**487
John XXIII, **VIII:**1858
John of the Cross, Saint, **III:**401
John Paul II, **VIII:**1862
Leo XIII, **VI:**1347
Luther, Martin, **III:**443
Marguerite of Navarre, **III:**467
Menno Simons, **III:**510
Nicholas V, **III:**559
Niemöller, Martin, **VIII:**2742
Paul VI, **IX:**2919
Philip the Magnanimous, **III:**603
Pius V, **III:**616
Ridley, Nicholas, **III:**654
Teresa of Ávila, Saint, **III:**713
Torquemada, Tomás de, **III:**725

Zinzendorf, Graf von, **IV:**1488
Zwingli, Huldrych, **III:**791

CIVIL RIGHTS. *See also* **SOCIAL REFORM;**
    WOMEN'S RIGHTS
Abernathy, Ralph David, **VII:**9
Beauvoir, Simone de, **VII:**230
Bunche, Ralph, **VII:**501
Buxton, Sir Thomas Fowell, **V:**378
Chase, Salmon P., **V:**477
Douglass, Frederick, **V:**695
du Bois, W.E.B., **VII:**963
Forten, Charlotte, **V:**807
Gandhi, Mahatma, **VII:**1282
Garvey, Marcus, **VII:**1311
Jackson, Jesse L., **VIII:**1824
Kennedy, Robert F., **VIII:**1932
King, Martin Luther, Jr., **VIII:**1971
Lincoln, Abraham, **VI:**1380
Lutuli, Albert, **VIII:**2281
Malcolm X, **VIII:**2373
Mandela, Nelson, **VIII:**2384
Parks, Rosa, **IX:**2888
Randolph, A. Philip, **IX:**3112
Robeson, Paul, **IX:**3187
Robinson, Jackie, **IX:**3193
Sakharov, Andrei, **IX:**3296
Scott, Dred, **VI:**1999
Stevens, Thaddeus, **VI:**2136
Sumner, Charles, **VI:**2170
Truth, Sojourner, **VI:**2255
Tubman, Harriet, **VI:**2264
Turner, Nat, **VI:**2276
Tutu, Desmond, **IX:**3775
Wells-Barnett, Ida B., **IX:**3941
White, Walter, **IX:**3961
Wiesel, Elie, **IX:**3980

COLONIAL ADMINISTRATION. *See also*
    EXPLORATION AND COLONIZATION
Carleton, Guy, **IV:**246
Césaire, Aimé, **VII:**631
Éboué, Félix, **VII:**1004
Faidherbe, Louis, **V:**763
Goldie, Sir George, **V:**953
Las Casas, Bartolomé de, **III:**413
Lawrence, First Baron, **VI:**1331
Outram, Sir James, **VI:**1705
Rhodes, Cecil, **VI:**1873

COLONIZATION. *See* **EXPLORATION AND**
    COLONIZATION

COMPUTER SCIENCE
Babbage, Charles, **V:**101
Neumann, John von, **VIII:**2724
Turing, Alan Mathison, **IX:**3768

CONQUEST. *See* **EXPLORATION AND**
    COLONIZATION; WARFARE AND
    CONQUEST

CONSERVATION AND
    ENVIRONMENTALISM
Carson, Rachel, **VII:**585
Lindbergh, Charles A., **VIII:**2193
Muir, John, **VI:**1608
Roosevelt, Theodore, **IX:**3228
Ward, Montgomery, **VI:**2331

COSMOLOGY. *See* **ASTRONOMY;**
    NATURAL HISTORY; PHYSICS

DANCE. *See also* **THEATER AND**
    ENTERTAINMENT
Astaire, Fred, **VII:**125
Balanchine, George, **VII:**155
Danilova, Alexandra, **VII:**832
de Mille, Agnes, **VII:**874
Diaghilev, Sergei, **VII:**919
Duncan, Isadora, **VII:**980
Dunham, Katherine, **VII:**984
Fonteyn, Dame Margot, **VII:**1175
Fuller, Loie, **VII:**1261
Graham, Martha, **VIII:**1455
Laban, Rudolf, **VIII:**2058
Lifar, Serge, **VIII:**2182
Massine, Léonide, **VIII:**2448
Nijinsky, Vaslav, **VIII:**2746
Pavlova, Anna, **IX:**2937
Tallchief, Maria, **IX:**3607

DENTISTRY. *See* **MEDICINE**

DIPLOMACY. *See also* **GOVERNMENT AND**
    POLITICS
Abbas, Ferhat, **VII:**5
Acheson, Dean, **VII:**16
Albright, Madeleine, **VII:**49
Alva, Duke of, **III:**18
Angell, Norman, **VII:**74
Bancroft, George, **V:**124
Beust, Friedrich von, **V:**222
Bevin, Ernest, **VII:**313
Bodley, Sir Thomas, **III:**62

Botha, Louis, **VII:**376
Boutros-Ghali, Boutros, **VII:**399
Bülow, Bernhard von, **VII:**494
Bunche, Ralph, **VII:**501
Burton, Sir Richard Francis, **V:**374
Castlereagh, Viscount, **V:**438
Chou En-lai, **VII:**676
Conant, James Bryant, **VII:**748
Coubertin, Pierre de, **VII:**774
Covilhã, Pêro da, **III:**197
Cushing, Caleb, **V:**581
Dulles, John Foster, **VII:**976
Eban, Abba, **VII:**1000
Eden, Anthony, **VII:**1015
Evatt, Herbert Vere, **VII:**1109
Gadsden, James, **V:**858
Hammarskjöld, Dag, **VIII:**1529
Hardenberg, Karl von, **V:**1033
Harriman, William Averell, **VIII:**1560
Hay, John, **V:**1068
Hein, Piet, **IV:**644
Herzl, Theodor, **V:**1102
Hiss, Alger, **VIII:**1683
Holstein, Friedrich von, **V:**1130
Hughes, Charles Evans, **VIII:**1766
Hull, Cordell, **VIII:**1779
Irving, Washington, **V:**1192
Kirkpatrick, Jeane, **VIII:**1994
Kissinger, Henry A., **VIII:**1998
La Fontaine, Henri-Marie, **VIII:**2051
Lesseps, Ferdinand de, **VI:**1355
Litvinov, Maksim Maksimovich, **VIII:**2208
Marlborough, First Duke of, **IV:**922
Marshall, George C., **VIII:**2429
Medici, Lorenzo de', **III:**495
Metternich, **VI:**1544
Molotov, Vyacheslav Mikhailovich, **VIII:**2571
Monnet, Jean, **VIII:**2583
Mornay, Philippe de, **III:**537
Nicholas V, **III:**559
O'Kelly, Seán T., **IX:**2804
Oldenbarnevelt, Johan van, **III:**574
Palmerston, Lord, **VI:**1719
Pandit, Vijaya Lakshmi, **IX:**2867
Pérez de Cuéllar, Javier, **IX:**2957
Perry, Matthew C., **VI:**1760
Pius XI, **IX:**3026
Pius XII, **IX:**3030
Pocahontas, **IV:**1106
Rabi, Isidor Isaac, **IX:**3101
Root, Elihu, **IX:**3232

Salisbury, First Earl of, **III:**660
Seward, William H., **VI:**2037
Stanhope, First Earl, **IV:**1277
Stimson, Henry L., **IX:**3537
Thant, U, **IX:**3646
Waldheim, Kurt, **IX:**3841
Webster, Daniel, **VI:**2344
Yamani, Ahmad Zaki, **IX:**4079

DRAMA. *See* **THEATER AND ENTERTAINMENT**

ECONOMICS. *See also* **BANKING AND FINANCE; BUSINESS AND INDUSTRY**
Beveridge, Lord, **VII:**308
Erhard, Ludwig, **VII:**1094
George, Henry, **V:**906
Greenspan, Alan, **VIII:**1471
Keynes, John Maynard, **VIII:**1952
Lassalle, Ferdinand, **VI:**1323
Malthus, Thomas Robert, **VI:**1467
Marx, Karl, **VI:**1492
Mendès-France, Pierre, **VIII:**2491
Mill, James, **VI:**1556
Mill, John Stuart, **VI:**1559
Monnet, Jean, **VIII:**2583
Myrdal, Gunnar, **VIII:**2671
Proudhon, Pierre-Joseph, **VI:**1817
Ricardo, David, **VI:**1878
Smith, Adam, **IV:**1249
Turgot, Anne-Robert-Jacques, **IV:**1348
Veblen, Thorstein, **IX:**3805
Walras, Léon, **IX:**3865
Webb, Beatrice and Sidney, **IX:**3905

EDUCATION. *See also* **HISTORIOGRAPHY; SCHOLARSHIP**
'Abduh, Muhammad, **V:**4
Adler, Alfred, **VII:**30
Adler, Felix, **V:**26
Agassiz, Louis, **V:**30
Ahmad Khan, Sir Sayyid, **V:**34
Albertus Magnus, Saint, **II:**37
Alcott, Bronson, **V:**37
Alcuin, **II:**44
Anthony of Padua, Saint, **II:**76
Arnold, Thomas, **V:**74
Arthur, Chester A., **V:**77
Bacon, Roger, **II:**110
Balch, Emily Greene, **VII:**160
Barnard, Henry, **V:**130
Barton, Clara, **V:**142

Basedow, Johann Bernhard, **IV**:92
Beale, Dorothea, **V**:157
Beecher, Catharine, **V**:170
Bell, Alexander Graham, **V**:185
Beneš, Edvard, **VII**:259
Beveridge, Lord, **VII**:308
Bodley, Sir Thomas, **III**:62
Brougham, Henry, **V**:314
Bunche, Ralph, **VII**:501
Butler, Nicholas Murray, **VII**:524
Butler, R.A., **VII**:529
Carver, George Washington, **VII**:602
Chang Chih-tung, **V**:466
Chu Hsi, **II**:265
Colet, John, **III**:169
Conant, James Bryant, **VII**:748
Condorcet, Marquis de, **IV**:348
Confucius, **I**:222
Dawidowicz, Lucy S., **VII**:847
Dewey, Melvil, **V**:660
Dunham, Katherine, **VII**:984
Eliot, Charles William, **V**:748
Erasmus, Desiderius, **III**:246
Fisher, Saint John, **III**:264
Flexner, Abraham, **VII**:1169
Forster, William Edward, **V**:804
Forten, Charlotte, **V**:807
Froebel, Friedrich, **V**:845
Fulbert of Chartres, Saint, **II**:373
Gentile, Giovanni, **VII**:1336
Green, Thomas Hill, **V**:987
Harper, William Rainey, **V**:1044
Howe, Samuel Gridley, **V**:1150
Hutchins, Robert M., **VIII**:1800
Isidore of Seville, Saint, **II**:518
Jiménez de Cisneros, Francisco, **III**:392
Jordan, Barbara, **VIII**:1887
Kay-Shuttleworth, First Baronet, **VIII**:1917
Keller, Helen, **VIII**:1924
Lancaster, Joseph, **VI**:1309
Langer, Susanne K., **VIII**:2087
Laski, Harold J., **VIII**:2093
Lyon, Mary, **VI**:1423
McGuffey, William Holmes, **VI**:1440
Mackinder, Sir Halford John, **VIII**:2321
Mann, Horace, **IV**:894
Mather, Increase, **IV**:938
Maurice, Frederick Denison, **VI**:1503
Melanchthon, Philipp, **III**:503
Millikan, Robert Andrews, **VIII**:2539
Montessori, Maria, **VIII**:2596
Naidu, Sarojini, **VIII**:2683

Natta, Giulio, **VIII**:2698
Neckam, Alexander, **II**:663
Palmer, Alice Freeman, **VI**:1715
Pestalozzi, Johann Heinrich, **VI**:1767
Piaget, Jean, **IX**:2990
Protagoras, **I**:705
Raman, Sir Chandrasekhara Venkata, **IX**:3109
Rousseau, Jean-Jacques, **IV**:1194
Sagan, Carl, **IX**:3292
Seaborg, Glenn Theodore, **IX**:3375
Seton, Saint Elizabeth Ann Bayley, **VI**:2029
Sidgwick, Henry, **VI**:2062
Spock, Benjamin, **IX**:3478
Stanford, Leland, **VI**:2096
Steinmetz, Charles Proteus, **VI**:2121
Stone, Harlan Fiske, **IX**:3546
Sylvester II, **II**:869
Talbot, Marion, **IX**:3603
Thayer, Sylvanus, **VI**:2223
Thorndike, Edward L., **IX**:3669
Verrius Flaccus, Marcus, **I**:930
Vincent de Paul, Saint, **IV**:1380
Webster, Noah, **IV**:1417
Willard, Emma, **VI**:2384
Willard, Frances, **VI**:2388
Wise, Isaac Mayer, **VI**:2400
Witherspoon, John, **IV**:1467

ELECTRONICS. *See* **COMPUTER SCIENCE; INVENTION AND TECHNOLOGY**

EMPERORS. *See* **ROMAN EMPERORS**

EMPIRE-BUILDING. *See* **COLONIAL ADMINISTRATION; EXPLORATION AND COLONIZATION; GOVERNMENT AND POLITICS; WARFARE AND CONQUEST**

ENGINEERING. *See also* **AVIATION AND SPACE EXPLORATION; INVENTION AND TECHNOLOGY**
Bergius, Friedrich, **VII**:275
Braun, Wernher von, **VII**:440
Brindley, James, **IV**:201
Brunel, Isambard Kingdom, **V**:335
Brunel, Marc Isambard, **V**:339
Citroën, André-Gustave, **VII**:695
Cousteau, Jacques-Yves, **VII**:778
Daimler, Gottlieb, **V**:597

Eads, James Buchanan, **V:**729
Ferrari, Enzo, **VII:**1150
Fitch, John, **IV:**476
Freyssinet, Eugène, **VII:**1228
Fuller, R. Buckminster, **VII:**1265
Fulton, Robert, **V:**854
Gadsden, James, **V:**858
Goethals, George Washington, **VIII:**1408
Hounsfield, Godfrey Newbold, **VIII:**1751
Latrobe, Benjamin Henry, **VI:**1327
Monge, Gaspard, **IV:**975
Nasmyth, James, **VI:**1624
Newcomen, Thomas, **IV:**1022
Picard, Émile, **IX:**2994
Popov, Aleksandr Stepanovich, **VI:**1806
Prandtl, Ludwig, **IX:**3073
Roebling, John Augustus, **VI:**1904
Rolls, Charles Stewart, **IX:**3209
Royce, Sir Frederick Henry, **IX:**3209
Steinmetz, Charles Proteus, **VI:**2121
Stephenson, George, **VI:**2132
Telford, Thomas, **VI:**2207
Tesla, Nikola, **VI:**2219
Thayer, Sylvanus, **VI:**2223
Trevithick, Richard, **VI:**2251
Vauban, Sébastien Le Prestre de, **IV:**1358
Whittle, Sir Frank, **IX:**3972
Xenakis, Iannis, **IX:**4075

ENTERTAINMENT. *See* **THEATER AND ENTERTAINMENT**

ENVIRONMENTALISM. *See* **CONSERVATION AND ENVIRONMENTALISM**

ETHICS. *See* **PHILOSOPHY; RELIGION AND THEOLOGY**

EXPLORATION AND COLONIZATION. *See also* **AVIATION AND SPACE EXPLORATION; COLONIAL ADMINISTRATION; WARFARE AND CONQUEST**
Alvarado, Pedro de, **III:**21
Amundsen, Roald, **VII:**66
Austin, Stephen Fuller, **V:**94
Balboa, Vasco Núñez de, **III:**45
Bering, Vitus Jonassen, **IV:**111
Bligh, William, **IV:**143
Boone, Daniel, **IV:**163
Bougainville, Louis-Antoine de, **IV:**179

Bruce, James, **IV:**208
Burton, Sir Richard Francis, **V:**374
Byrd, Richard E., **VII:**534
Cabot, John, **III:**113
Calamity Jane, **V:**390
Carpini, Giovanni da Pian del, **II:**206
Carson, Kit, **V:**429
Cartier, Jacques, **III:**129
Cavendish, Thomas, **III:**140
Champlain, Samuel de, **IV:**271
Cheng Ho, **II:**253
Citroën, André-Gustave, **VII:**695
Clark, William, **VI:**1358
Columbus, Christopher, **III:**172
Cook, Captain James, **IV:**351
Coronado, Francisco Vásquez de, **III:**180
Cortés, Hernán, **III:**188
Covilhã, Pêro da, **III:**197
Crockett, David, **V:**578
Dampier, William, **IV:**389
Davis, John, **III:**212
Dias, Bartolomeu, **III:**215
Drake, Sir Francis, **III:**224
Frémont, John C., **V:**839
Gama, Vasco da, **III:**287
Hanno, **I:**368
Hayden, Ferdinand Vandeveer, **V:**1072
Henry the Navigator, Prince, **III:**354
Heyerdahl, Thor, **VIII:**1658
Hillary, Sir Edmund, **VIII:**1662
Hsüan-tsang, **II:**482
Hudson, Henry, **IV:**680
Ibn Battutah, **II:**495
Jolliet, Louis, **IV:**732
La Salle, Sieur de, **IV:**793
Leif Eriksson, **II:**577
Lewis, Meriwether, **VI:**1358
Livingstone, David, **VI:**1399
Lugard, Lord, **VIII:**2269
Mackenzie, Sir Alexander, **IV:**879
Magellan, Ferdinand, **III:**453
Mas'udi, al-, **II:**636
Messner, Reinhold, **VIII:**2506
Muir, John, **VI:**1608
Nansen, Fridtjof, **VIII:**2686
Oglethorpe, James Edward, **IV:**1043
Park, Mungo, **VI:**1723
Peary, Robert Edwin, **IX:**2941
Pike, Zebulon Montgomery, **IV:**1094
Pinzon Brothers, The, **III:**610
Pizarro, Francisco, **III:**620
Polo, Marco, **II:**750

Ponce de Léon, Juan, **III:**629
Powell, John Wesley, **VI:**1810
Pytheas, **I:**731
Raleigh, Sir Walter, **III:**638
Rasmussen, Knud Johan Victor, **IX:**3121
Ross, Sir James Clark, **VI:**1907
Sacagawea, **VI:**1933
Smith, Jedediah Strong, **VI:**2077
Smith, John, **IV:**1253
Soto, Hernando de, **III:**699
Speke, John Hanning, **VI:**2083
Standish, Miles, **IV:**1273
Stanley, Henry Morton, **VI:**2101
Tasman, Abel Janszoon, **IV:**1313
Vancouver, George, **IV:**1355
Vespucci, Amerigo, **III:**758
Wilkes, Charles, **VI:**2381
Wilkins, Sir George Hubert, **IX:**3999
William of Rubrouck, **II:**987
Workman, Fanny Bullock, **VI:**2410

FASHION
Chanel, Coco, **VII:**648

FILM. *See also* **TELEVISION; THEATER
    AND ENTERTAINMENT**
Arzner, Dorothy, **VII:**117
Astaire, Fred, **VII:**125
Ball, Lucille, **VII:**176
Bergman, Ingmar, **VII:**278
Brando, Marlon, **VII:**424
Buñuel, Luis, **VII:**505
Chaplin, Charles, **VII:**653
Cocteau, Jean, **VII:**721
Coward, Noël, **VII:**783
Davis, Bette, **VII:**843
Demille, Cecil B., **VII:**896
Dietrich, Marlene, **VII:**930
Disney, Walt, **VII:**938
Dreyer, Carl Theodor, **VII:**959
Eisenstein, Sergei, **VII:**1047
Ephron, Nora, **VII:**1083
Fellini, Federico, **VII:**1141
Gance, Abel, **VII:**1274
Garbo, Greta, **VII:**1286
Garland, Judy, **VII:**1304
Gish, Lillian, **VII:**1383
Godard, Jean-Luc, **VII:**1391
Goldwyn, Samuel, **VIII:**1415
Griffith, D.W., **VIII:**1478
Hayworth, Rita, **VIII:**1596
Hellman, Lillian, **VIII:**1620

Henie, Sonja, **VIII:**1629
Hepburn, Katharine, **VIII:**1637
Hitchcock, Alfred, **VIII:**1687
King, Stephen, **VIII:**1977
Kurosawa, Akira, **VIII:**2043
Lang, Fritz, **VIII:**2077
Loos, Anita, **VIII:**2231
Monroe, Marilyn, **VIII:**2587
Olivier, Sir Laurence, **IX:**2808
Pickford, Mary, **IX:**3006
Ray, Satyajit, **IX:**3132
Renoir, Jean, **IX:**3157
Stewart, James, **IX:**3528
Truffaut, François, **IX:**3736
Visconti, Luchino, **IX:**3818
Wayne, John, **IX:**3901
Welles, Orson, **IX:**3934
West, Mae, **IX:**3949
Winfrey, Oprah, **IX:**4029
Zanuck, Darryl F., **IX:**4100

FINANCE. *See* **BANKING AND FINANCE**

GENETICS
Crick, Francis, **VII:**797
Galton, Francis, **V:**867
Jacob, François, **VIII:**1827
Mendel, Gregor Johann, **VI:**1526
Morgan, Thomas Hunt, **VIII:**2618
Muller, Hermann Joseph, **VIII:**2651
Vavilov, Nikolai Ivanovich, **IX:**3801
Watson, James D., **IX:**3897
Weismann, August, **VI:**2348

GEOGRAPHY. *See also* **CARTOGRAPHY**
Anaximander, **I:**50
Benjamin of Tudela, **II:**140
Braudel, Fernand, **VII:**436
Covilhã, Pêro da, **III:**197
Eratosthenes of Cyrene, **I:**303
Hipparchus, **I:**407
Humboldt, Alexander von, **V:**1159
Idrisi, al-, **II:**506
Khwarizmi, al-, **II:**563
Mackinder, Sir Halford John, **VIII:**2321
Mas'udi, al-, **II:**636
Maury, Matthew Fontaine, **VI:**1507
Mercator, Gerardus, **III:**513
Rasmussen, Knud Johan Victor, **IX:**3121
Strabo, **I:**828
Tasman, Abel Janszoon, **IV:**1313
Workman, Fanny Bullock, **VI:**2410

GEOLOGY
Agricola, Georgius, **III:**1
Baer, Karl Ernst von, **V:**109
Lyell, Sir Charles, **VI:**1418
Spallanzani, Lazzaro, **IV:**1260
Teilhard de Chardin, Pierre, **IX:**3626
Wegener, Alfred, **IX:**3918

GOLF. *See* **SPORTS**

GOVERNMENT AND POLITICS. *See also*
    CHURCH GOVERNMENT; COLONIAL
    ADMINISTRATION; DIPLOMACY; HOLY
    ROMAN EMPERORS; LAW; MILITARY
    AFFAIRS; MONARCHY; PHARAOHS;
    PUBLIC ADMINISTRATION; ROMAN
    CAESAR; ROMAN EMPERORS;
    WARFARE AND CONQUEST
Abahai, **IV:**1
Abbas, Ferhat, **VII:**5
'Abbās the Great, **IV:**4
'Abd al-Mu'min, **II:**4
'Abd-al-Rahman III al-Nasir, **II:**7
Abdelkader, **V:**1
'Abduh, Muhammad, **V:**4
Acheson, Dean, **VII:**16
Adams, John, **IV:**16
Adams, John Quincy, **V:**20
Adams, Samuel, **IV:**21
Adenauer, Konrad, **VII:**26
Afonso I, **II:**30
Agesilaus II, **I:**16
Agrippa, Marcus Vipsanius, **I:**20
Akhenaton, **I:**23
Akiba ben Joseph, **I:**27
Akihito, **VII:**41
Alboin, **II:**41
Albright, Madeleine, **VII:**49
Albuquerque, Afonso de, **III:**11
Alcibiades, **I:**31
Alexander I, **V:**44
Alexander II, **V:**48
Alexander VI, **III:**14
Alexander Nevsky, **II:**52
Alexander the Great, **I:**38
Alfonso X, **II:**56
Alp Arslan, **II:**67
Altgeld, John Peter, **V:**54
Ambrose, Saint, **I:**43
Antigonus I Monophthalmos, **I:**60
Antony, Marc, **I:**69
Aquino, Corazon, **VII:**86

Arafat, Yasir, **VII:**90
Árpád, **II:**86
Arthur, Chester A., **V:**77
Ashikaga Takauji, **II:**97
Ashurbanipal, **I:**105
Ashurnasirpal II, **I:**109
Aśoka the Great, **I:**112
Aspasia, **I:**115
Asquith, H.H., **VII:**121
Astor, Nancy, **VII:**129
Atatürk, Kemal, **VII:**133
Attila, **I:**124
Attlee, Clement, **VII:**137
Augustus, **I:**132
Aurangzeb, **IV:**69
Aurobindo, Sri, **VII:**141
Austin, Stephen Fuller, **V:**94
Azikiwe, Nnamdi, **VII:**144
Bābur, **III:**36
Bacon, Francis, **III:**41
Bacon, Nathaniel, **IV:**80
Baldwin, Robert, **V:**116
Baldwin, Stanley, **VII:**168
Balfour, Arthur, **VII:**172
Bancroft, George, **V:**124
Banerjea, Surendranath, **VII:**183
Barton, Sir Edmund, **V:**147
Basil the Macedonian, **II:**117
Baybars I, **II:**124
Bayezid II, **III:**51
Beaverbrook, Lord, **VII:**234
Begin, Menachem, **VII:**243
Ben-Gurion, David, **VII:**251
Beneš, Edvard, **VII:**259
Benton, Thomas Hart, **V:**195
Besant, Annie, **V:**211
Beust, Friedrich von, **V:**222
Bevan, Aneurin, **VII:**304
Bevin, Ernest, **VII:**313
Bismarck, Otto von, **V:**240
Blaine, James G., **V:**255
Blake, Robert, **IV:**132
Blanc, Louis, **V:**259
Blum, Léon, **VII:**335
Bolingbroke, First Viscount, **IV:**157
Bolívar, Simón, **V:**267
Bondfield, Margaret, **VII:**353
Boniface VIII, **II:**171
Borah, William E., **V:**279
Borden, Robert Laird, **VII:**365
Boris I of Bulgaria, **II:**175
Botha, Louis, **VII:**376

Bottomley, Horatio W., **VII:**382
Bourguiba, Habib, **VII:**391
Boutros-Ghali, Boutros, **VII:**399
Bradford, William, **IV:**189
Brandt, Willy, **VII:**427
Brezhnev, Leonid Ilich, **VII:**459
Bright, John, **V:**306
Brougham, Henry, **V:**314
Brown, George, **V:**318
Bruni, Leonardo, **III:**93
Brutus, Marcus Junius, **I:**140
Bryan, William Jennings, **VII:**479
Buchanan, James, **V:**346
Buckingham, First Duke of, **IV:**211
Bukharin, Nikolai Ivanovich, **VII:**491
Bulfinch, Charles, **V:**349
Bülow, Bernhard von, **VII:**494
Burgh, Hubert de, **II:**190
Burr, Aaron, **V:**369
Bush, George, **VII:**520
Butler, R.A., **VII:**529
Caesar, Julius, **I:**147
Calhoun, John C., **V:**394
Caligula, **I:**152
Calles, Plutarco Elías, **VII:**542
Cambacérès, Jean-Jacques-Régis de, **V:**398
Campbell, Kim, **VII:**549
Canning, George, **V:**405
Cárdenas, Lázaro, **VII:**571
Carlos, Don, **V:**413
Carroll, Charles, **IV:**250
Carter, Jimmy, **VII:**589
Casimir the Great, **II:**210
Cassiodorus, **II:**215
Cassius (Longinus), **I:**159
Castlereagh, Viscount, **V:**438
Castro, Fidel, **VII:**617
Catherine de Médicis, **III:**132
Catherine of Siena, Saint, **II:**218
Cato the Censor, **I:**162
Cato the Younger, **I:**166
Cavour, Count, **V:**446
Cecil, William, **III:**147
Chamberlain, Joseph, **V:**462
Chamberlain, Neville, **VII:**643
Chang Chih-tung, **V:**466
Charles V, **III:**159
Charles XIV John, **V:**474
Charles d'Orléans, **II:**232
Charles Martel, **II:**242
Charles the Bold, **III:**163
Chartier, Alain, **II:**245

Chase, Salmon P., **V:**477
Ch'en Tu-hsiu, **VII:**660
Cheng Ch'eng-kung, **IV:**297
Cheng Ho, **II:**253
Chiang Kai-shek, **VII:**664
Ch'ien-lung, **IV:**300
Ch'in Shih Huang-ti, **I:**176
Chisholm, Shirley, **VII:**668
Chou En-lai, **VII:**676
Chrétien, Jean, **VII:**680
Christophe, Henri, **V:**501
Chu Hsi, **II:**265
Chu Teh, **VII:**687
Ch'ü Yüan, **I:**187
Churchill, Sir Winston, **VII:**691
Cicero, **I:**194
Cimon, **I:**198
Claudius I, **I:**203
Clay, Henry, **V:**507
Cleisthenes of Athens, **I:**207
Clemenceau, Georges, **VII:**702
Cleomenes, **I:**214
Cleopatra VII, **I:**218
Cleveland, Grover, **V:**512
Clinton, Bill, **VII:**707
Clinton, DeWitt, **V:**517
Clinton, Hillary Rodham, **VII:**713
Clovis, **II:**274
Cobbett, William, **V:**522
Cobden, Richard, **V:**526
Collins, Michael, **VII:**733
Constantine, Baron, **VII:**759
Constantine the Great, **I:**226
Coolidge, Calvin, **VII:**762
Cornwallis, First Marquess, **IV:**367
Cosgrave, William T., **VII:**770
Croce, Benedetto, **VII:**801
Crockett, David, **V:**578
Cromwell, Oliver, **IV:**378
Cromwell, Thomas, **III:**208
Curtin, John, **VII:**816
Curzon, Lord, **VII:**819
Cushing, Caleb, **V:**581
Cyrus the Great, **I:**233
Dalhousie, First Marquess of, **V:**600
Dandolo, Enrico, **II:**282
Danton, Georges, **IV:**393
Darius the Great, **I:**236
Davis, Jefferson, **V:**614
Dayan, Moshe, **VII:**854
Deák, Ferenc, **V:**625
Deakin, Alfred, **V:**630

Debs, Eugene V., **VII:**880
de Gasperi, Alcide, **VII:**862
de Gaulle, Charles, **VII:**866
de Klerk, F.W., **VII:**870
Demosthenes, **I:**253
Deng Xiaoping, **VII:**905
Derby, Fourteenth Earl of, **V:**652
de Valera, Eamon, **VII:**877
Diocletian, **I:**263
Disraeli, Benjamin, **V:**675
Djilas, Milovan, **VII:**944
Dole, Robert J., **VII:**947
Dorgon, **IV:**421
Douglas, Stephen A., **V:**692
Draco, **I:**280
Dubcek, Alexander, **VII:**968
Dulles, John Foster, **VII:**976
Durham, First Earl of, **V:**721
Eban, Abba, **VII:**1000
Éboué, Félix, **VII:**1004
Eden, Anthony, **VII:**1015
Edward VII, **VII:**1020
Eisenhower, Dwight D., **VII:**1043
Elizabeth II, **VII:**1062
Engels, Friedrich, **V:**760
Enver Pasha, **VII:**1078
Epaminondas, **I:**290
Erhard, Ludwig, **VII:**1094
Erzberger, Matthias, **VII:**1102
Evatt, Herbert Vere, **VII:**1109
Fabius Maximus, Quintus, **I:**334
Fahd, **VII:**1115
Fairfax, Third Baron, **IV:**446
Faisal, **VII:**1118
Faisal I, **VII:**1122
Fawkes, Guy, **III:**257
Feinstein, Dianne, **VII:**1137
Ferdinand II and Isabella I, **III:**260
Ferraro, Geraldine, **VII:**1153
Fillmore, Millard, **V:**792
Ford, Gerald R., **VII:**1180
Forster, William Edward, **V:**804
Fox, Charles James, **IV:**479
Francis Ferdinand, **VII:**1197
Francis Joseph I, **V:**829
Franco, Francisco, **VII:**1200
Franklin, Benjamin, **IV:**492
Frederick William, the Great Elector, **IV:**508
Frémont, John C., **V:**839
Fujiwara Michinaga, **II:**370
Gallatin, Albert, **V:**861
Gambetta, Léon, **V:**871

Gandhi, Indira, **VII:**1278
Gandhi, Mahatma, **VII:**1282
Gardiner, Stephen, **III:**291
Garfield, James A., **V:**875
Genghis Khan, **II:**376
Genseric, **I:**342
Gentile, Giovanni, **VII:**1336
George IV, **V:**902
George V, **VII:**1339
George VI, **VII:**1343
Ghazan, Mahmud, **II:**381
Gioberti, Vincenzo, **V:**932
Gladstone, William Ewart, **V:**935
Glenn, John H., Jr., **VII:**1387
Godolphin, First Earl of, **IV:**552
Godunov, Boris Fyodorovich, **III:**308
Goebbels, Joseph, **VIII:**1404
Gorbachev, Mikhail, **VIII:**1423
Gore, Albert, **VIII:**1431
Göring, Hermann, **VIII:**1438
Gracchi, The, **I:**345
Gramsci, Antonio, **VIII:**1459
Grant, Ulysses S., **V:**975
Greenspan, Alan, **VIII:**1471
Gregory the Great, **II:**407
Grey, Second Earl, **V:**994
Grey, Sir George Edward, **V:**998
Guevara, Che, **VIII:**1494
Hadrian, **I:**356
Haile Selassie I, **VIII:**1517
Halide Edib Adivar, **VIII:**1522
Hamilton, Alexander, **IV:**608
Hammurabi, **I:**360
Hancock, John, **IV:**613
Hanna, Marcus A., **V:**1029
Hardenberg, Karl von, **V:**1033
Hardie, James Keir, **V:**1036
Harding, Warren G., **VIII:**1550
Harmsworth, Alfred and Harold, **VIII:**1554
Harriman, William Averell, **VIII:**1560
Harrison, Benjamin, **V:**1053
Harrison, William Henry, **V:**1061
Harsha, **II:**430
Harun al-Rashid, **II:**437
Hastings, Warren, **IV:**631
Hatoyama Ichiro, **VIII:**1574
Hatshepsut, **I:**371
Hatta, Mohammad, **VIII:**1577
Haya de la Torre, Víctor Raúl, **VIII:**1584
Hayes, Rutherford B., **V:**1075
Heath, Edward, **VIII:**1606
Henry IV, **III:**333

Henry, Patrick, **IV**:647

Henry the Lion, **II**:466

Heraclius, **II**:470

Herod the Great, **I**:390

Herriot, Édouard, **VIII**:1644

Himmler, Heinrich, **VIII**:1666

Hindenburg, Paul Von, **VIII**:1674

Hirohito, **VIII**:1678

Hitler, Adolf, **VIII**:1692

Hobby, Oveta Culp, **VIII**:1703

Ho Chi Minh, **VIII**:1698

Hoover, Herbert, **VIII**:1727

Hoover, J. Edgar, **VIII**:1732

Hopkins, Harry, **VIII**:1736

Houphouët-Boigny, Félix, **VIII**:1754

Houston, Sam, **V**:1137

Howe, Admiral Richard, **IV**:672

Hughes, Charles Evans, **VIII**:1766

Hughes, William Morris, **VIII**:1775

Hull, Cordell, **VIII**:1779

Humphrey, Hubert H., **VIII**:1783

Hung Hsiu-ch'üan, **V**:1165

Hunyadi, János, **III**:374

Hussein I, **VIII**:1791

Hutchinson, Thomas, **IV**:691

Ii Naosuke, **V**:1180

Ikeda, Hayato, **VIII**:1809

Innocent III, **II**:509

Innocent IV, **II**:514

İnönü, İsmet, **VIII**:1812

Itzcóatl, **III**:377

Ivan the Great, **III**:381

Ivan the Terrible, **III**:385

Jackson, Andrew, **V**:1196

Jackson, Jesse L., **VIII**:1824

Jamāl al-Dīn al-Afghānī, **V**:1207

James I, **IV**:699

James I the Conqueror, **II**:529

James II, **IV**:703

Jaurès, Jean, **V**:1221

Jefferson, Thomas, **IV**:716

Jiménez de Cisneros, Francisco, **III**:392

Jinnah, Mohammed Ali, **VIII**:1847

Joan of Arc, **III**:396

Johnson, Andrew, **V**:1232

Johnson, Lyndon B., **VIII**:1866

Jordan, Barbara, **VIII**:1887

Joséphine, **V**:1246

Juárez, Benito, **V**:1250

Justinian I, **II**:553

Kamehameha I, **VI**:1255

K'ang-Hsi, **IV**:757

Kanishka, **I**:494

Kennedy, John F., **VIII**:1928

Kennedy, Robert F., **VIII**:1932

Kenyatta, Jomo, **VIII**:1936

Kerensky, Aleksandr Fyodorovich, **VIII**:1941

Khomeini, Ruhollah, **VIII**:1957

Khosrow I, **II**:559

Khrushchev, Nikita S., **VIII**:1961

Kidd, William, **IV**:777

King, William Lyon Mackenzie, **VIII**:1981

Kirkpatrick, Jeane, **VIII**:1994

Kissinger, Henry A., **VIII**:1998

Kohl, Helmut, **VIII**:2009

Kublai Khan, **II**:566

Kuo Mo-jo, **VIII**:2033

La Follette, Robert M., **VIII**:2047

La Fontaine, Henri-Marie, **VIII**:2051

La Guardia, Fiorello Henry, **VIII**:2054

Lambert, John, **IV**:789

Lansdowne, Fifth Marquess of, **VIII**:2090

László I, Saint, **II**:574

Lathrop, Julia C., **VIII**:2096

Laurier, Sir Wilfrid, **VIII**:2100

Laval, Pierre, **VIII**:2105

Law, Bonar, **VIII**:2112

Lee Kuan Yew, **VIII**:2150

Leeds, First Duke of, **IV**:821

Lenin, Vladimir Ilich, **VIII**:2160

Leo X, **III**:419

Li Hung-chang, **VI**:1362

Li Peng, **VIII**:2178

Liebknecht, Wilhelm, **VI**:1369

Liliuokalani, **VI**:1372

Lin Piao, **VIII**:2189

Lin Tse-hsü, **VI**:1376

Lincoln, Abraham, **VI**:1380

Liu Shao-ch'i, **VIII**:2212

Liverpool, Second Earl of, **VI**:1395

Lloyd George, David, **VIII**:2216

Lodge, Henry Cabot, **VIII**:2219

Long, Huey, **VIII**:2227

Louis IX, **II**:603

Louis XI, **III**:434

Lu Hsün, **VIII**:2252

Luce, Clare Boothe, **VIII**:2256

Lugard, Lord, **VIII**:2269

Lutuli, Albert, **VIII**:2281

Lyons, Dame Enid Muriel, **VIII**:2289

Lyons, Joseph Aloysius, **VIII**:2292

Macaulay, Thomas Babington, **VI**:1427

McCarthy, Joseph R., **VIII**:2300

MacDonald, Ramsay, **VIII**:2312

Macdonald, Sir John Alexander, **VI**:1435

Machel, Samora Moisès, **VIII**:2317

Mackenzie, William Lyon, **VI**:1447

Mackinder, Sir Halford John, **VIII**:2321

McKinley, William, **VI**:1453

Macmillan, Harold, **VIII**:2340

Madero, Francisco, **VIII**:2345

Madison, Dolley, **VI**:1464

Madison, James, **IV**:886

Maecenas, Gaius, **I**:519

Mahfouz, Naguib, **VIII**:2355

Major, John, **VIII**:2369

Malenkov, Georgi M., **VIII**:2377

Malraux, André, **VIII**:2380

Mankiller, Wilma P., **VIII**:2389

Mannerheim, Carl Gustaf, **VIII**:2396

Mannix, Daniel, **VI**:1480

Mansa Mūsā, **II**:623

Mao Tse-tung, **VIII**:2400

Marat, Jean-Paul, **IV**:910

Marcos, Ferdinand E., **VIII**:2420

Marcus Aurelius, **I**:523

Margaret of Denmark, Norway, and Sweden, **II**:626

Marius, Gaius, **I**:528

Marshall, George C., **VIII**:2429

Masaryk, Tomáš, **VIII**:2440

Masinissa, **I**:535

Mason, George, **IV**:926

Massey, Vincent, **VI**:1496

Massey, William Ferguson, **VIII**:2444

Matthias I Corvinus, **III**:487

Maximilian I, **III**:491

Mazzini, Giuseppe, **VI**:1514

Medici, Lorenzo de', **III**:495

Mehmed II, **III**:499

Meir, Golda, **VIII**:2472

Melbourne, Second Viscount, **VI**:1517

Menander (Indian king), **I**:541

Mendès-France, Pierre, **VIII**:2491

Menelik II, **VI**:1537

Menes, **I**:547

Menzies, Robert Gordon, **VIII**:2497

Messalina, Valeria, **I**:550

Metternich, **VI**:1544

Miltiades the Younger, **I**:553

Mirabeau, Comte de, **IV**:963

Mithradates the Great, **I**:557

Mitterrand, François, **VIII**:2558

Mobutu Sese Seko, **VIII**:2562

Mohammad Reza Shah Pahlavi, **VIII**:2566

Mohammed I Askia, **III**:521

Molotov, Vyacheslav Mikhailovich, **VIII**:2571

Monmouth, Duke of, **IV**:980

Monnet, Jean, **VIII**:2583

Monroe, James, **VI**:1570

Montaigne, Michel de, **III**:524

Montfort, Simon V de, **II**:642

More, Sir Thomas, **III**:533

Mornay, Philippe de, **III**:537

Morris, William, **VI**:1588

Mosca, Gaetano, **VIII**:2630

Mountbatten, Louis, **VIII**:2641

Mugabe, Robert, **VIII**:2647

Muhammad, **II**:651

Muhammad 'Alī Pasha, **VI**:1604

Mulroney, Brian, **VIII**:2655

Mussolini, Benito, **VIII**:2667

Naidu, Sarojini, **VIII**:2683

Napoleon I, **VI**:1616

Napoleon III, **VI**:1620

Nasser, Gamal Abdel, **VIII**:2693

Nast, Thomas, **VI**:1627

Nebuchadnezzar II, **I**:569

Necker, Jacques, **IV**:1016

Nefertiti, **I**:573

Nehru, Jawaharlal, **VIII**:2709

Nero, **I**:577

Nezahualcóyotl, **III**:555

Nicholas I, **VI**:1650

Nikon, **IV**:1030

Nixon, Richard M., **VIII**:2758

Nizam al-Mulk, **II**:677

Nkrumah, Kwame, **VIII**:2762

Nordau, Max, **VIII**:2766

North, Lord, **IV**:1034

Nostradamus, **III**:567

Nyerere, Julius, **VIII**:2773

Oates, Titus, **IV**:1038

Obregón, Álvaro, **IX**:2781

O'Connell, Daniel, **VI**:1680

O'Connor, Sandra Day, **IX**:2789

O'Connor, Thomas Power, **IX**:2793

Oda Nobunaga, **III**:570

Odoacer, **II**:685

O'Kelly, Seán T., **IX**:2804

Olaf, Saint, **II**:691

Oldenbarnevelt, Johan van, **III**:574

Onassis, Jacqueline Kennedy, **IX**:2815

O'Neill, Thomas Philip, Jr., **IX**:2824

Orleans, Duc d', **IV**:1048

Ortega, Katherine Davalos, **IX**:2840

Osman, **II**:702

Ou-yang Hsiu, **II**:709

Oxenstierna, Axel, **IV:**1052
Pachacuti, **III:**577
Palmerston, Lord, **VI:**1719
Pandit, Vijaya Lakshmi, **IX:**2867
Papen, Franz von, **IX:**2876
Parkes, Sir Henry, **VI:**1731
Parnell, Charles Stewart, **VI:**1740
Patel, Vallabhbhai Jhaverbhai, **IX:**2903
Peel, Sir Robert, **VI:**1752
Pelham, Henry, **IV:**1074
Penn, William, **IV:**1078
Pérez de Cuéllar, Javier, **IX:**2957
Pericles, **I:**609
Perkins, Frances, **IX:**2961
Perón, Eva, **IX:**2965
Perón, Juan, **IX:**2969
Perot, H. Ross, **IX:**2973
Pétain, Philippe, **IX:**2987
Philip II of France, **II:**732
Philip II of Macedonia, **I:**628
Philip II of Spain, **III:**599
Philip IV the Fair, **II:**736
Philip the Good, **II:**740
Phillip, Arthur, **IV:**1091
Piankhi, **I:**636
Pierce, Franklin, **VI:**1775
Pilate, Pontius, **I:**640
Pirelli Family, The, **IX:**3020
Pisistratus, **I:**648
Pitt the Elder, William, **IV:**1098
Pitt the Younger, William, **IV:**1102
Pittacus of Mytilene, **I:**651
Pius II, **III:**613
Place, Francis, **VI:**1786
Pobedonostsev, Konstantin Petrovich, **VI:**1790
Poincaré, Raymond, **IX:**3044
Polk, James K., **VI:**1801
Pompey the Great, **I:**679
Pompidou, Georges, **IX:**3052
Pride, Thomas, **IV:**1126
Psamtik I, **I:**709
Psellus, Michael, **II:**758
Ptolemy Philadelphus, **I:**716
Ptolemy Soter, **I:**720
Pym, John, **IV:**1141
Qaddafi, Muammar al-, **IX:**3098
Rabanus Maurus, **II:**766
Ramses II, **I:**734
Rankin, Jeannette, **IX:**3117
Rasputin, Grigori Yefimovich, **VI:**1842
Reagan, Ronald, **IX:**3136
Reno, Janet, **IX:**3153

Revere, Paul, **IV:**1156
Rhee, Syngman, **IX:**3165
Richards, Ann, **IX:**3169
Richelieu, Cardinal de, **IV:**1165
Rienzo, Cola di, **II:**790
Robespierre, **IV:**1170
Rodney, George, **IV:**1178
Rollo, **II:**793
Roosevelt, Franklin D., **IX:**3222
Roosevelt, Theodore, **IX:**3228
Root, Elihu, **IX:**3232
Ross, Nellie Tayloe, **IX:**3243
Rurik, **II:**803
Russell, Bertrand, **IX:**3264
Russell, Lord John, **VI:**1930
Sadat, Anwar el-, **IX:**3289
Saigō Takamori, **VI:**1936
Saint-Just, Louis de, **IV:**1205
Sakharov, Andrei, **IX:**3296
Saladin, **II:**809
Salisbury, First Earl of, **III:**660
Salisbury, Third Marquess of, **VI:**1943
Samuel, **I:**746
Santa Anna, Antonio López de, **VI:**1955
Sargon II, **I:**754
Sato, Eisaku, **IX:**3336
Sauvé, Jeanne, **IX:**3344
Savonarola, Girolamo, **III:**667
Schurz, Carl, **VI:**1996
Scipio Aemilianus, **I:**757
Scipio Africanus, **I:**760
Seddon, Richard John, **VI:**2017
Seleucus I Nicator, **I:**767
Seneca the Younger, **I:**770
Senghor, Léopold, **IX:**3391
Sesostris III, **I:**774
Seward, William H., **VI:**2037
Sforza, Ludovico, **III:**682
Shaftesbury, First Earl of, **IV:**1228
Shah Jahan, **IV:**1232
Shays, Daniel, **IV:**1239
Sherman, Roger, **IV:**1242
Shōtoku Taishi, **II:**826
Sihanouk, Norodom, **IX:**3417
Sinclair, Upton, **IX:**3426
Śivajī, **IV:**1246
Smith, Alfred E., **IX:**3439
Smith, Margaret Chase, **IX:**3446
Smuts, Jan Christian, **IX:**3453
Solomon, **I:**798
Solon, **I:**803

Solzhenitsyn, Aleksandr, **IX:**3459
Spaak, Paul-Henri, **IX:**3475
Speransky, Mikhail Mikhaylovich, **VI:**2089
Ssu-ma Kuang, **II:**840
Staël, Madame de, **VI:**2092
Stalin, Joseph, **IX:**3482
Standish, Miles, **IV:**1273
Stanford, Leland, **VI:**2096
Stanhope, First Earl, **IV:**1277
Stanton, Edwin M., **VI:**2106
Stefan Du?an, **II:**843
Stein, Freiherr vom, **VI:**2115
Stephen I, **II:**851
Stephens, Alexander H., **VI:**2129
Stevens, Thaddeus, **VI:**2136
Stevenson, Adlai E., **IX:**3523
Stimson, Henry L., **IX:**3537
Strafford, First Earl of, **IV:**1285
Stresemann, Gustav, **IX:**3563
Stuyvesant, Peter, **IV:**1294
Su Tung-p'o, **II:**855
Sukarno, **IX:**3570
Süleyman the Magnificent, **III:**707
Sulla, Lucius Cornelius, **I:**833
Sumner, Charles, **VI:**2170
Sun Yat-sen, **IX:**3578
Sundjata, **II:**863
Sung Dynasty, **II:**866
Sylvester II, **II:**869
Tacitus, Cornelius, **I:**837
Taft, Robert A., **IX:**3590
Taft, William Howard, **IX:**3594
T'ai Tsung, **II:**876
Taira Kiyomori, **II:**881
Talleyrand, **VI:**2185
Tamerlane, **II:**884
Taylor, Zachary, **VI:**2194
Tereshkova, Valentina, **IX:**3639
Thatcher, Margaret, **IX:**3649
Themistocles, **I:**857
Theodora, **II:**890
Theodoric the Great, **II:**894
Theodosius the Great, **I:**868
Thiers, Adolphe, **VI:**2226
Thomas, Clarence, **IX:**3657
Thomas, Norman, **IX:**3660
Thutmose III, **I:**889
Tiberius, **I:**892
Tigranes the Great, **I:**896
Tilak, Bal Gangadhar, **IX:**3681
Tito, **IX:**3692
Tokugawa Ieyasu, **IV:**1327

Torquemada, Tomás de, **III:**725
Touré, Ahmed Sékou, **IX:**3711
Toussaint-Louverture, **IV:**1338
Toyotomi Hideyoshi, **III:**728
Trajan, **I:**899
Trotsky, Leon, **IX:**3726
Trudeau, Pierre Elliott, **IX:**3730
Truman, Harry S, **IX:**3740
Tseng Kuo-fan, **VI:**2260
Tshombe, Moïse, **IX:**3745
Tubman, William V. S., **IX:**3757
Turgot, Anne-Robert-Jacques, **IV:**1348
Tutankhamen, **I:**904
Tweed, William Marcy, **VI:**2284
Tyler, John, **VI:**2288
Ulbricht, Walter, **IX:**3779
Urban II, **II:**928
Valdemar II, **II:**932
Van Buren, Martin, **VI:**2292
Venizélos, Eleuthérios, **IX:**3808
Vercingetorix, **I:**922
Vespasian, **I:**933
Victoria, Queen, **VI:**2307
Virchow, Rudolf, **VI:**2312
Vladimir I, **II:**952
Vo Nguyen Giap, **IX:**3821
Wakefield, Edward Gibbon, **VI:**2321
Waldheim, Kurt, **IX:**3841
Walesa, Lech, **IX:**3844
Wallace, George C., **IX:**3857
Wallace, Henry A., **IX:**3860
Wallenstein, Albrecht Wenzel von, **IV:**1396
Walpole, Sir Robert, **IV:**1400
Wang An-shih, **II:**962
Wang Ching-wei, **IX:**3877
Wang Wei, **II:**965
Wang Yang-ming, **III:**771
Washington, George, **IV:**1405
Webster, Daniel, **VI:**2344
Weizmann, Chaim, **IX:**3930
Wellington, Duke of, **VI:**2351
Wentworth, W.C., **VI:**2355
Widukind, **II:**973
Wilkes, John, **IV:**1439
William II, **IX:**4003
William IV, **VI:**2392
William the Silent, **III:**781
Williams, George Washington, **VI:**2396
Wilson, Sir Harold, **IX:**4016
Wilson, Woodrow, **IX:**4020
Winthrop, John, **IV:**1463
Witherspoon, John, **IV:**1467

Władysław II Jagiełło and Jadwiga, **II:**1001
Wolsey, Cardinal Thomas, **III:**785
Yamani, Ahmad Zaki, **IX:**4079
Yeltsin, Boris N., **IX:**4082
Ypsilanti, Alexander and Demetrios, **VI:**2417
Yung-lo, **II:**1021
Zaghlūl, Sa'd, **IX:**4093
Zetkin, Clara, **IX:**4112
Zhukov, Georgy Konstantinovich, **IX:**4116
Zoser, **I:**978

HISTORIOGRAPHY. *See also* **EDUCATION;
  SCHOLARSHIP**
Acton, Lord, **V:**10
Adams, Henry, **V:**15
Alfonso X, **II:**56
Arnold, Thomas, **V:**74
Athanasius, Saint, **I:**119
Bancroft, George, **V:**124
Bayle, Pierre, **IV:**103
Beard, Charles A., **VII:**221
Bede the Venerable, Saint, **II:**132
Biruni, al-, **II:**147
Bossuet, Jacques-Bénigne, **IV:**170
Braudel, Fernand, **VII:**436
Bruni, Leonardo, **III:**93
Burckhardt, Jacob, **V:**358
Carlyle, Thomas, **V:**416
Carpini, Giovanni da Pian del, **II:**206
Cassiodorus, **II:**215
Cassirer, Ernst, **VII:**614
Celsus, Aulus Cornelius, **I:**173
Comte, Auguste, **V:**543
Croce, Benedetto, **VII:**801
Dawidowicz, Lucy S., **VII:**847
Eusebius of Caesarea, **I:**322
Froissart, Jean, **II:**366
Gibbon, Edward, **IV:**545
Gilson, Étienne, **VII:**1374
Gregory of Tours, **II:**403
Guicciardini, Francesco, **III:**325
Herodotus, **I:**394
Ibn Khaldun, **II:**502
Irving, Washington, **V:**1192
Joachim of Fiore, **II:**534
Josephus, Flavius, **I:**483
Livy, **I:**504
Lomonosov, Mikhail Vasilyevich, **IV:**860
Macaulay, Thomas Babington, **VI:**1427
Machiavelli, Niccolò, **III:**448
Mas'udi, al-, **II:**636
Michelet, Jules, **VI:**1548

Mill, James, **VI:**1556
Mommsen, Theodor, **VI:**1566
Niebuhr, Barthold Georg, **VI:**1654
Pan Ku, **I:**589
Parkman, Francis, **VI:**1735
Parrington, Vernon L., **IX:**2892
Pirenne, Henri, **IX:**3023
Polybius, **I:**673
Prescott, William Hickling, **VI:**1814
Psellus, Michael, **II:**758
Pushkin, Alexander, **VI:**1832
Ranke, Leopold von, **VI:**1839
Sallust, **I:**742
Sandburg, Carl, **IX:**3308
Saxo Grammaticus, **II:**815
Scaliger, Joseph Justus, **III:**671
Snorri Sturluson, **II:**836
Ssu-ma Ch'ien, **I:**818
Ssu-ma Kuang, **II:**840
Strabo, **I:**828
Tabari, al-, **II:**873
Tacitus, Cornelius, **I:**837
Taine, Hippolyte-Adolphe, **VI:**2182
Theophanes the Confessor, **II:**903
Thiers, Adolphe, **VI:**2226
Thucydides, **I:**885
Toynbee, Arnold, **IX:**3715
Troeltsch, Ernst, **IX:**3722
Tuchman, Barbara, **IX:**3760
Turner, Frederick Jackson, **IX:**3771
Vico, Giambattista, **IV:**1372
Villani, Giovanni, **II:**938
Vincent of Beauvais, **II:**946
Webb, Beatrice and Sidney, **IX:**3905
Williams, George Washington, **VI:**2396
Winckelmann, Johann Joachim, **IV:**1460
Yaqut, **II:**1013

HOLY ROMAN EMPERORS
Charlemagne, **II:**226
Charles IV, **II:**235
Charles V, **III:**159
Charles the Bald, **II:**239
Frederick I Barbarossa, **II:**357
Frederick II, **II:**362
Henry II the Saint, **II:**449
Henry IV (of Germany), **II:**461
Louis II the German, **II:**599
Maximilian I, **III:**491
Otto the Great, **II:**706
Rudolf I, **II:**796
Wenceslaus, **II:**969

HORTICULTURE. *See also* **BOTANY; LANDSCAPE ARCHITECTURE**
Appleseed, Johnny, **V:**66
Burbank, Luther, **V:**353

IMMUNOLOGY. *See* **MEDICINE**

INDIAN AFFAIRS. *See* **NATIVE AMERICAN AFFAIRS**

INDUSTRY. *See* **BUSINESS AND INDUSTRY**

INVENTION AND TECHNOLOGY. *See also* **AVIATION AND SPACE EXPLORATION; COMPUTER SCIENCE; ENGINEERING**
Archimedes, **I:**76
Arkwright, Richard, **IV:**59
Armstrong, Edwin H., **VII:**102
Babbage, Charles, **V:**101
Baskerville, John, **IV:**95
Bell, Alexander Graham, **V:**185
Benz, Carl, **V:**199
Bergius, Friedrich, **VII:**275
Bessemer, Sir Henry, **V:**218
Braille, Louis, **V:**303
Brunelleschi, Filippo, **III:**89
Carlson, Chester F., **VII:**579
Cayley, Sir George, **V:**450
Claude, Georges, **VII:**699
Colt, Samuel, **V:**540
Cooke, William Fothergill, **V:**555
Ctesibius of Alexandria, **I:**231
Daguerre, Jacques, **V:**592
Daimler, Gottlieb, **V:**597
Darby, Abraham, **IV:**396
Davy, Sir Humphry, **V:**621
de Forest, Lee, **VII:**858
Diesel, Rudolf, **V:**672
Eads, James Buchanan, **V:**729
Eastman, George, **VII:**996
Edison, Thomas Alva, **V:**743
Eupalinus of Megara, **I:**314
Fitch, John, **IV:**476
Fuller, R. Buckminster, **VII:**1265
Fulton, Robert, **V:**854
Goodyear, Charles, **V:**960
Grove, Sir William Robert, **V:**1010
Guericke, Otto von, **IV:**586
Gutenberg, Johann, **III:**328
Hargreaves, James, **IV:**623
Holland, John Philip, **V:**1123
Hounsfield, Godfrey Newbold, **VIII:**1751

Howe, Elias, **V:**1141
Huygens, Christiaan, **IV:**695
Kapitsa, Pyotr Leonidovich, **VIII:**1906
Kay, John, **IV:**769
Krupp, Alfred, **VI:**1301
Lanchester, Frederick William, **VIII:**2069
Langley, Samuel Pierpont, **VI:**1313
Lenoir, Étienne, **VI:**1343
Lippershey, Hans, **IV:**850
Lumière, Auguste and Louis, **VIII:**2276
McCormick, Cyrus Hall, **VI:**1431
Marconi, Guglielmo, **VIII:**2415
Mergenthaler, Ottmar, **VI:**1541
Michelin, André and Édouard, **VIII:**2514
Montgolfier, Jacques-Étienne and Joseph-Michel, **IV:**995
Morse, Samuel F. B., **VI:**1592
Murdock, William, **IV:**1008
Nasmyth, James, **VI:**1624
Natta, Giulio, **VIII:**2698
Newcomen, Thomas, **IV:**1022
Niépce, Nicéphore, **VI:**1657
Nobel, Alfred, **VI:**1673
Otto, Nikolaus August, **VI:**1702
Papin, Denis, **IV:**1059
Pirelli Family, The, **IX:**3020
Popov, Aleksandr Stepanovich, **VI:**1806
Roebuck, John, **IV:**1182
Rolls, Charles Stewart, **IX:**3209
Royce, Sir Frederick Henry, **IX:**3209
Santos-Dumont, Alberto, **IX:**3320
Schmidt, Bernhard Voldemar, **IX:**3351
Siemens Family, The, **VI:**2066
Swan, Joseph Wilson, **VI:**2179
Swedenborg, Emanuel, **IV:**1302
Torricelli, Evangelista, **IV:**1331
Tull, Jethro, **IV:**1345
Wankel, Felix, **IX:**3881
Watt, James, **IV:**1409
Westinghouse, George, **VI:**2358
Wheatstone, Charles, **V:**555
Whitney, Eli, **IV:**1431
Wiener, Norbert, **IX:**3976
Wright, Wilbur and Orville, **IX:**4064
Zworykin, Vladimir, **IX:**4125

IRONMAKING. *See* **INVENTION AND TECHNOLOGY**

JOURNALISM. *See also* **PUBLISHING**
'Abduh, Muhammad, **V:**4
Addison, Joseph, **IV:**26

Angell, Norman, **VII:**74
Beaverbrook, Lord, **VII:**234
Bennett, James Gordon, **V:**190
Bierce, Ambrose, **V:**230
Bottomley, Horatio W., **VII:**382
Bourke-White, Margaret, **VII:**395
Brown, George, **V:**318
Bryant, William Cullen, **V:**343
Cather, Willa, **VII:**621
Cobbett, William, **V:**522
Collins, Norman, **VII:**737
Day, Dorothy, **VII:**850
du Bois, W.E.B., **VII:**963
Ellis, Havelock, **VII:**1070
Ephron, Nora, **VII:**1083
Fuller, Margaret, **V:**849
Godkin, Edwin Lawrence, **VIII:**1400
Graham, Katharine, **VIII:**1451
Greeley, Horace, **V:**982
Hale, Sarah Josepha, **V:**1022
Harmsworth, Alfred and Harold,
    VIII:1554
Hearst, William Randolph,
    VIII:1601
Herzl, Theodor, **V:**1102
Jeffrey, Lord, **V:**1224
Johnson, Samuel, **IV:**728
Lippmann, Walter, **VIII:**2203
Luce, Clare Boothe, **VIII:**2256
Luce, Henry R., **VIII:**2260
Luxemburg, Rosa, **VIII:**2285
McCarthy, Mary, **VIII:**2304
Mackenzie, William Lyon, **VI:**1447
Marat, Jean-Paul, **IV:**910
Mencken, H. L., **VIII:**2483
Murrow, Edward R., **VIII:**2662
O'Connor, Thomas Power, **IX:**2793
Ortega y Gasset, José, **IX:**2843
Pulitzer, Joseph, **VI:**1825
Reith of Stonehaven, First Baron,
    IX:3146
Rogers, Will, **IX:**3204
Scripps, Edward Wyllis, **VI:**2014
Steinem, Gloria, **IX:**3519
Tarbell, Ida, **IX:**3614
Trotsky, Leon, **IX:**3726
Wallace, Henry A., **IX:**3860
Walter, John, II, **VI:**2324
Walters, Barbara, **IX:**3868
Wells-Barnett, Ida B., **IX:**3941
Wilkes, John, **IV:**1439
Zenger, John Peter, **IV:**1484

JURISPRUDENCE. *See* **LAW**

LABOR MOVEMENT. *See also* **SOCIAL REFORM**
Bevin, Ernest, **VII:**313
Bondfield, Margaret, **VII:**353
Debs, Eugene V., **VII:**880
Gompers, Samuel, **V:**956
Hardie, James Keir, **V:**1036
Hernandez, Aileen Clarke, **VIII:**1641
Huerta, Dolores, **VIII:**1762
Jones, Mary Harris "Mother," **VIII:**1879
Lewis, John L., **VIII:**2170
Randolph, A. Philip, **IX:**3112
Reuther, Walter P., **IX:**3161
Walesa, Lech, **IX:**3844
Zetkin, Clara, **IX:**4112

LANDSCAPE ARCHITECTURE. *See also* **HORTICULTURE**
Brown, Lancelot, **IV:**204
Farrand, Beatrix Jones, **VII:**1130
Le Nôtre, André, 834
Olmsted, Frederick Law, **VI:**1691

LANGUAGE AND LINGUISTICS. *See also* **PHILOLOGY**
Avicenna, **II:**106
Barthes, Roland, **VII:**207
Chomsky, Noam, **VII:**673
Cyril, Saint, **II:**278
Derrida, Jacques, **VII:**912
Grimm, Jacob and Wilhelm, **V:**1006
Jahiz, al-, **II:**526
Jakobson, Roman, **VIII:**1831
Lacan, Jacques, **VIII:**2061
Lévi-Strauss, Claude, **VIII:**2164
Methodius, Saint, **II:**278
Priscian, **II:**755
Saussure, Ferdinand de, **IX:**3340
Sequoyah, **VI:**2025

LAW. *See also* **GOVERNMENT AND POLITICS**
Abu Hanifah, **II:**16
Ahmad ibn Hanbal, **II:**33
Alfonso X, **II:**56
Arthur, Chester A., **V:**77
Avicenna, **II:**106
Barton, Sir Edmund, **V:**147
Basil the Macedonian, **II:**117
Black, Hugo L., **VII:**321

Blackstone, William, **IV:**129
Borden, Lizzie, **V:**283
Boutros-Ghali, Boutros, **VII:**399
Bracton, Henry de, **II:**178
Brandeis, Louis D., **VII:**419
Brougham, Henry, **V:**314
Burger, Warren E., **VII:**509
Burr, Aaron, **V:**369
Cambacérès, Jean-Jacques-Régis de, **V:**398
Capone, Alphonse, **VII:**563
Cardozo, Benjamin Nathan, **VII:**575
Carroll, Charles, **IV:**250
Cassin, René, **VII:**610
Chase, Salmon P., **V:**477
Chase, Samuel, **IV:**293
Ch'in Shih Huang-ti, **I:**176
Cicero, **I:**194
Cleisthenes of Athens, **I:**207
Clinton, Hillary Rodham, **VII:**713
Coke, Sir Edward, **IV:**329
Cushing, Caleb, **V:**581
Darius the Great, **I:**236
Darrow, Clarence, **VII:**839
Demosthenes, **I:**253
Draco, **I:**280
Earp, Wyatt, **V:**735
Ehrlich, Eugen, **VII:**1029
Erskine, First Baron, **IV:**439
Evatt, Herbert Vere, **VII:**1109
Field, Stephen J., **V:**787
Fortescue, Sir John, **III:**267
Frankfurter, Felix, **VII:**1212
Gentili, Alberico, **III:**295
Grotius, Hugo, **IV:**579
Grove, Sir William Robert, **V:**1010
Hale, Matthew, **IV:**596
Hammurabi, **I:**360
Hand, Learned, **VIII:**1541
Hickok, Wild Bill, **V:**1107
Hiss, Alger, **VIII:**1683
Holmes, Oliver Wendell, Jr., **VIII:**1720
Hotman, François, **III:**362
Hughes, Charles Evans, **VIII:**1766
James I the Conqueror, **II:**529
Jay, John, **IV:**711
Jeffrey, Lord, **V:**1224
Jordan, Barbara, **VIII:**1887
Justinian I, **II:**553
Kent, James, **VI:**1277
La Fontaine, Henri-Marie, **VIII:**2051
Littleton, Sir Thomas, **III:**431
Lockwood, Belva A., **VI:**1406

MacKinnon, Catharine A., **VIII:**2325
Mansfield, First Earl of, **IV:**904
Marshall, John, **VI:**1487
Marshall, Thurgood, **VIII:**2433
Nader, Ralph, **VIII:**2679
O'Connell, Daniel, **VI:**1680
O'Connor, Sandra Day, **IX:**2789
Olaf, Saint, **II:**691
Pufendorf, Samuel von, **IV:**1133
Rehnquist, William H., **IX:**3142
Reno, Janet, **IX:**3153
Sacco, Nicola, **IX:**3281
Savigny, Friedrich Karl von, **VI:**1966
Sewall, Samuel, **IV:**1225
Solon, **I:**803
Speransky, Mikhail Mikhaylovich, **VI:**2089
Stone, Harlan Fiske, **IX:**3546
Story, Joseph, **VI:**2147
Süleyman the Magnificent, **III:**707
Taft, William Howard, **IX:**3594
Taney, Roger Brooke, **VI:**2189
Van Buren, Martin, **VI:**2292
Vitoria, Francisco de, **III:**768
Warren, Earl, **IX:**3888
Webster, Daniel, **VI:**2344
Webster, Noah, **IV:**1417
Wiesenthal, Simon, **IX:**3984
Wilson, James, **IV:**1455

LINGUISTICS. *See* **LANGUAGE AND LINGUISTICS**

LITERATURE. *See also* **LANGUAGE AND LINGUISTICS; ORATORY; PHILOLOGY**

Achebe, Chinua, **VII:**13
Adam de la Halle, **II:**23
Adams, Henry, **V:**15
Addison, Joseph, **IV:**26
Aesop, **I:**13
Ahmad Khan, Sir Sayyid, **V:**34
Akhmatova, Anna, **VII:**37
Alcott, Louisa May, **V:**40
Alcuin, **II:**44
Alfonso X, **II:**56
Alger, Horatio, **V:**51
Andersen, Hans Christian, **V:**58
Angelou, Maya, **VII:**79
Apollinaire, Guillaume, **VII:**82
Ariosto, Ludovico, **III:**32
Arnold, Matthew, **V:**69
Ashurbanipal, **I:**105
Austen, Jane, **V:**90

Bakhtin, Mikhail, **VII:**152
Baldwin, James, **VII:**164
Balzac, Honoré de, **V:**120
Barnes, Djuna, **VII:**199
Barthes, Roland, **VII:**207
Baudelaire, Charles, **V:**150
Baum, L. Frank, **V:**154
Beauvoir, Simone de, **VII:**230
Beckett, Samuel, **VII:**238
Bede the Venerable, Saint, **II:**132
Bellow, Saul, **VII:**247
Benét, Stephen Vincent, **VII:**263
Benjamin, Walter, **VII:**267
Bierce, Ambrose, **V:**230
Black Hawk, **V:**247
Blake, William, **IV:**137
Blok, Aleksandr, **VII:**332
Boccaccio, Giovanni, **II:**150
Boethius, **II:**155
Böll, Heinrich, **VII:**349
Borges, Jorge Luis, **VII:**371
Bossuet, Jacques-Bénigne, **IV:**170
Boswell, James, **IV:**174
Bradstreet, Anne, **IV:**193
Brecht, Bertolt, **VII:**444
Breton, André, **VII:**448
Brontë Sisters, The, **V:**310
Browning, Elizabeth Barrett, **V:**327
Bruni, Leonardo, **III:**93
Bryant, William Cullen, **V:**343
Buber, Martin, **VII:**483
Buck, Pearl S., **VII:**486
Bunyan, John, **IV:**218
Burnett, Frances Hodgson, **V:**361
Burns, Robert, **IV:**229
Burroughs, Edgar Rice, **VII:**516
Burton, Sir Richard Francis, **V:**374
Byron, Lord, **V:**381
Caesar, Julius, **I:**147
Callimachus, **I:**156
Camões, Luís de, **III:**122
Camus, Albert, **VII:**553
Capek, Karel, **VII:**560
Capote, Truman, **VII:**567
Carlyle, Thomas, **V:**416
Carroll, Lewis, **V:**425
Carson, Rachel, **VII:**585
Casanova, Giovanni Giacomo, **IV:**254
Cather, Willa, **VII:**621
Catullus, **I:**169
Cavalcanti, Guido, **II:**223
Cædmon, **II:**198

Cellini, Benvenuto, **III:**151
Cervantes, Miguel de, **IV:**265
Césaire, Aimé, **VII:**631
Chapman, George, **III:**155
Charles d'Orléans, **II:**232
Chartier, Alain, **II:**245
Chateaubriand, **V:**481
Chaucer, Geoffrey, **II:**248
Chekhov, Anton, **V:**485
Ch'en Tu-hsiu, **VII:**660
Child, Lydia Maria, **V:**489
Chopin, Kate, **V:**497
Chrétien de Troyes, **II:**257
Christie, Agatha, **VII:**683
Christine de Pizan, **II:**260
Chuang-tzu, **I:**190
Churchill, Sir Winston, **VII:**691
Ch'ü Yüan, **I:**187
Cicero, **I:**194
Clarendon, First Earl of, **IV:**308
Cocteau, Jean, **VII:**721
Coleridge, Samuel Taylor, **V:**537
Colette, **VII:**729
Conrad, Joseph, **VII:**753
Cooper, James Fenimore, **V:**560
Crane, Hart, **VII:**789
Crane, Stephen, **V:**569
Crockett, David, **V:**578
Cruz, Sor Juana Inés de la, **IV:**382
cummings, e.e., **VII:**804
Cyrano de Bergerac, Savinien de, **IV:**385
Dante, **II:**286
Deborah, **I:**246
Defoe, Daniel, **IV:**399
Derrida, Jacques, **VII:**912
Dickens, Charles, **V:**663
Dickinson, Emily, **V:**667
Diderot, Denis, **IV:**412
Disraeli, Benjamin, **V:**675
Djilas, Milovan, **VII:**944
Donne, John, **IV:**416
Dostoevski, Fyodor, **V:**687
Doyle, Sir Arthur Conan, **V:**700
Dreiser, Theodore, **VII:**954
Dryden, John, **IV:**424
Dumas, Alexandre, *père*, **V:**708
Dunbar, Paul Laurence, **V:**714
Ehrenfels, Christian Von, **VII:**1026
Eliade, Mircea, **VII:**1055
Eliot, George, **V:**751
Eliot, T.S., **VII:**1058
Éluard, Paul, **VII:**1074

Emerson, Ralph Waldo, **V:**755
Ennius, Quintus, **I:**287
Erasmus, Desiderius, **III:**246
Eratosthenes of Cyrene, **I:**303
Erdrich, Louise, **VII:**1091
Faulkner, William, **VII:**1133
Fielding, Henry, **IV:**469
Firdusi, **II:**350
Fitzgerald, F. Scott, **VII:**1161
Flaubert, Gustave, **V:**796
Forester, C.S., **VII:**1189
Forster, E.M., **VII:**1193
Forten, Charlotte, **V:**807
Fracastoro, Girolamo, **III:**270
France, Anatole, **V:**725
Frank, Anne, **VII:**1204
Frazer, Sir James George, **VII:**1220
Frisch, Max, **VII:**1238
Frost, Robert, **VII:**1250
Fugard, Athol, **VII:**1257
García Lorca, Federico, **VII:**1290
García Márquez, Gabriel, **VII:**1293
Gardner, Erle Stanley, **VII:**1297
Geisel, Theodor Seuss, **VII:**1329
Genet, Jean, **VII:**1333
Gide, André, **VII:**1367
Giraudoux, Jean, **VII:**1379
Godwin, William, **IV:**555
Goethe, Johann Wolfgang von, **IV:**560
Gogol, Nikolai, **V:**949
Goldsmith, Oliver, **IV:**564
Gordimer, Nadine, **VIII:**1427
Gorky, Maxim, **VIII:**1442
Gottfried von Strassburg, **II:**392
Grass, Günter, **VIII:**1463
Greene, Graham, **VIII:**1467
Gregory of Nazianzus, **I:**349
Grimm, Jacob and Wilhelm, **V:**1006
H.D., **VIII:**1505
Hafiz, **II:**417
Hale, Sarah Josepha, **V:**1022
Halide Edib Adivar, **VIII:**1522
Hamsun, Knut, **VIII:**1537
Hansberry, Lorraine, **VIII:**1545
Hardy, Thomas, **V:**1040
Harris, Joel Chandler, **V:**1049
Hartmann von Aue, **II:**433
Hawthorne, Nathaniel, **V:**1064
Hayslip, Le Ly, **VIII:**1593
Heine, Heinrich, **V:**1085
Hellman, Lillian, **VIII:**1620
Hemingway, Ernest, **VIII:**1624

Henry, O., **V:**1096
Herder, Johann Gottfried, **IV:**651
Herzen, Aleksandr, **V:**1099
Hesiod, **I:**402
Hesse, Hermann, **VIII:**1650
Higginson, Thomas Wentworth, **V:**1110
Hildegard von Bingen, **II:**474
Holmes, Oliver Wendell, **V:**1126
Homer, **I:**420
Horace, **I:**424
Howe, Julia Ward, **V:**1145
Hsieh Ling-yün, **I:**429
Hsüan-tsang, **II:**482
Hughes, Langston, **VIII:**1771
Hugo, Victor, **V:**1154
Hurston, Zora Neale, **VIII:**1787
Huxley, Aldous, **VIII:**1804
Ibn Gabirol, **II:**498
Ionesco, Eugène, **VIII:**1816
Irving, Washington, **V:**1192
Isidore of Seville, Saint, **II:**518
Jackson, Helen Hunt, **V:**1200
Jahiz, al-, **II:**526
Jakobson, Roman, **VIII:**1831
James I the Conqueror, **II:**529
James, Henry, **V:**1211
Jewett, Sarah Orne, **V:**1228
John of Damascus, **II:**544
Johnson, Samuel, **IV:**728
Jonson, Ben, **IV:**744
Joyce, James, **VIII:**1891
Judah ha-Levi, **II:**548
Juvenal, **I:**488
Kafka, Franz, **VIII:**1900
Kālidāsa, **I:**491
Kämpfer, Engelbert, **IV:**754
Kawabata, Yasunari, **VIII:**1913
Kazantzakis, Nikos, **VIII:**1920
Keats, John, **VI:**1264
Kerouac, Jack, **VIII:**1945
King, Stephen, **VIII:**1977
Kipling, Rudyard, **VI:**1288
Kleist, Heinrich von, **VI:**1294
Kuo Mo-jo, **VIII:**2033
La Fontaine, Jean de, **IV:**781
Lagerlöf, Selma, **VIII:**2065
Lawrence, D.H., **VIII:**2115
Lawrence, T.E., **VIII:**2125
Laxness, Halldór, **VIII:**2131
Lazarus, Emma, **VI:**1334
Lermontov, Mikhail, **VI:**1351
Lessing, Gotthold Ephraim, **IV:**842

Lewis, C.S., **VIII**:2167
Lewis, Sinclair, **VIII**:2174
Li Ch'ing-chao, **II**:588
Li Po, **II**:591
Lomonosov, Mikhail Vasilyevich, **IV**:860
London, Jack, **VIII**:2223
Longfellow, Henry Wadsworth, **VI**:1414
Loos, Anita, **VIII**:2231
Lowell, Amy, **VIII**:2249
Lu Hsün, **VIII**:2252
Lucian, **I**:507
Lucretius, **I**:511
Lukács, György, **VIII**:2272
Lull, Raymond, **II**:608
Macaulay, Thomas Babington, **VI**:1427
McCarthy, Mary, **VIII**:2304
McCullers, Carson, **VIII**:2308
Machado de Assis, Joaquim Maria, **VI**:1444
Machaut, Guillaume de, **II**:615
Machiavelli, Niccolò, **III**:448
Maecenas, Gaius, **I**:519
Mahfouz, Naguib, **VIII**:2355
Mailer, Norman, **VIII**:2365
Malory, Sir Thomas, **III**:457
Malraux, André, **VIII**:2380
Mann, Thomas, **VIII**:2392
Manzoni, Alessandro, **VI**:1483
Marcel, Gabriel, **VIII**:2407
Marcus Aurelius, **I**:523
Marie de France, **II**:629
Martial, **I**:532
Matsuo Bashō, **IV**:942
Maupassant, Guy de, **VI**:1500
Mayakovsky, Vladimir, **VIII**:2461
Medici, Lorenzo de', **III**:495
Melville, Herman, **VI**:1520
Michener, James A., **VIII**:2517
Millay, Edna St. Vincent, **VIII**:2529
Milne, A.A., **VIII**:2543
Milton, John, **IV**:958
Mishima, Yukio, **VIII**:2551
Montagu, Mary Wortley, **IV**:983
Montaigne, Michel de, **III**:524
Montale, Eugenio, **VIII**:2592
Moore, Marianne, **VIII**:2614
Morris, William, **VI**:1588
Morrison, Toni, **VIII**:2626
Murasaki Shikibu, **II**:657
Nabokov, Vladimir, **VIII**:2675
Naidu, Sarojini, **VIII**:2683
Nashe, Thomas, **III**:548
Neruda, Pablo, **VIII**:2716

Nietzsche, Friedrich Wilhelm, **VI**:1662
Nordau, Max, **VIII**:2766
Nostradamus, **III**:567
O'Connor, Flannery, **IX**:2785
Omar Khayyám, **II**:695
Orwell, George, **IX**:2846
Ou-yang Hsiu, **II**:709
Ovid, **I**:585
Parker, Dorothy, **IX**:2884
Parrington, Vernon L., **IX**:2892
Pasternak, Boris, **IX**:2899
Pater, Walter, **VI**:1749
Paton, Alan, **IX**:2907
Petrarch, **II**:726
Phaedrus, **I**:618
Pindar, **I**:644
Pirandello, Luigi, **IX**:3013
Plath, Sylvia, **IX**:3036
Pléiade, La, **III**:623
Plutarch, **I**:670
Poe, Edgar Allan, **VI**:1794
Poggio, **III**:626
Pope, Alexander, **IV**:1115
Porter, Katherine Anne, **IX**:3059
Potter, Beatrix, **IX**:3063
Propertius, Sextus, **I**:702
Proust, Marcel, **IX**:3089
Pushkin, Alexander, **VI**:1832
Rabelais, François, **III**:633
Raleigh, Sir Walter, **III**:638
Ratramnus, **II**:773
Remarque, Erich Maria, **IX**:3150
Rilke, Rainer Maria, **IX**:3181
Rimbaud, Arthur, **VI**:1886
Ronsard, Pierre de, **III**:657
Rousseau, Jean-Jacques, **IV**:1194
Rukeyser, Muriel, **IX**:3257
Rumi, Jalal al-Din, **II**:800
Sachs, Nelly, **IX**:3285
Sa'di, **II**:806
Salimbene, **II**:812
Salinger, J.D., **IX**:3301
Sand, George, **VI**:1951
Sandburg, Carl, **IX**:3308
Santayana, George, **IX**:3317
Sappho, **I**:750
Sarraute, Nathalie, **IX**:3324
Sartre, Jean-Paul, **IX**:3327
Saxo Grammaticus, **II**:815
Scaliger, Joseph Justus, **III**:671
Schiller, Friedrich, **IV**:1217
Scott, Sir Walter, **VI**:2005

Seneca the Younger, **I:**770
Senghor, Léopold, **IX:**3391
Sexton, Anne, **IX:**3395
Shakespeare, William, **III:**686
Shaw, George Bernard, **IX:**3399
Shelley, Mary Wollstonecraft, **VI:**2048
Shelley, Percy Bysshe, **VI:**2052
Sidney, Sir Philip, **III:**691
Simonides, **I:**787
Sinclair, Upton, **IX:**3426
Skinner, B.F., **IX:**3431
Snorri Sturluson, **II:**836
Solon, **I:**803
Solzhenitsyn, Aleksandr, **IX:**3459
Sophocles, **I:**807
Soyinka, Wole, **IX:**3471
Spenser, Edmund, **III:**703
Ssu-ma Kuang, **II:**840
Staël, Madame de, **VI:**2092
Stein, Gertrude, **IX:**3511
Steinbeck, John, **IX:**3515
Stendhal, **VI:**2125
Stevenson, Robert Louis, **VI:**2139
Strindberg, August, **IX:**3566
Su Tung-p'o, **II:**855
Sung Dynasty, **II:**866
Suttner, Bertha von, **VI:**2175
Swift, Jonathan, **IV:**1305
Tagore, Rabindranath, **IX:**3598
Taine, Hippolyte-Adolphe, **VI:**2182
Tanizaki, Jun'ichiro, **IX:**3611
T'ao Ch'ien, **I:**841
Tasso, Torquato, **III:**710
Teasdale, Sara, **IX:**3622
Tennyson, Alfred, Lord, **VI:**2211
Terence, **I:**844
Tertullian, **I:**848
Theophrastus, **I:**873
Thoreau, Henry David, **VI:**2234
Thurber, James, **IX:**3677
Tolkien, J.R.R., **IX:**3696
Tolstoy, Leo, **VI:**2242
Tsvetayeva, Marina, **IX:**3753
Tu Fu, **II:**917
Turgenev, Ivan, **VI:**2268
Twain, Mark, **VI:**2279
Unamuno y Jugo, Miguel de, **IX:**3783
Valéry, Paul, **IX:**3791
Vasari, Giorgio, **III:**743
Vega Carpio, Lope de, **IV:**1361
Venette, Jean de, **II:**935
Vergil, **I:**926

Verne, Jules, **VI:**2303
Villehardouin, Geoffroi de, **II:**942
Villon, François, **III:**763
Vincent of Beauvais, **II:**946
Vitry, Philippe de, **II:**949
Voltaire, **IV:**1392
Walker, Alice, **IX:**3849
Walther von der Vogelweide, **II:**959
Wang Wei, **II:**965
Warren, Robert Penn, **IX:**3893
Wells, H.G., **IX:**3938
Wharton, Edith, **IX:**3953
Whitman, Walt, **VI:**2368
Whittier, John Greenleaf, **VI:**2374
Wiesel, Elie, **IX:**3980
Wilde, Oscar, **VI:**2377
Wilder, Laura Ingalls, **IX:**3992
Williams, Tennessee, **IX:**4007
Wilson, Edmund, **IX:**4012
Wolfe, Thomas, **IX:**4041
Wolfram von Eschenbach, **II:**1005
Wollstonecraft, Mary, **IV:**1475
Woolf, Virginia, **IX:**4056
Wordsworth, William, **VI:**2406
Xenophanes, **I:**955
Xenophon, **I:**958
Yeats, William Butler, **IX:**4082
Zola, Émile, **VI:**2420

MANUFACTURING. *See* **BUSINESS AND INDUSTRY; ENGINEERING; INVENTION AND TECHNOLOGY**

MATHEMATICS. *See also* **STATISTICS**
Abel, Niels Henrik, **V:**7
Abul Wefa, **II:**20
Alembert, Jean le Rond d', **IV:**30
Alhazen, **II:**63
Apollonius of Perga, **I:**72
Archimedes, **I:**76
Aryabhata, **II:**89
Babbage, Charles, **V:**101
Banneker, Benjamin, **IV:**88
Bernoulli, Daniel, **IV:**122
Bernoulli, Jakob I, **IV:**122
Bernoulli, Johann I, **IV:**122
Bessel, Friedrich Wilhelm, **V:**215
Brahmagupta, **II:**181
Carroll, Lewis, **V:**425
Condorcet, Marquis de, **IV:**348
Dedekind, Richard, **V:**638
Descartes, René, **IV:**403

Diophantus, **I:**272
Eratosthenes of Cyrene, **I:**303
Euclid, **I:**307
Eudoxus of Cnidus, **I:**310
Euler, Leonhard, **IV:**443
Fermat, Pierre de, **IV:**458
Fourier, Joseph, **V:**819
Frege, Gottlob, **V:**836
Galois, Èvariste, **V:**864
Gauss, Carl Friedrich, **V:**893
Hamilton, Sir William Rowan, **V:**1025
Hero of Alexandria, **I:**387
Hipparchus, **I:**407
Hypatia, **I:**436
Khwarizmi, al, **II:**563
Lagrange, Joseph-Louis, **IV:**785
Laplace, Pierre-Simon, **VI:**1319
Leibniz, Gottfried Wilhelm, **IV:**829
Lemaître, Georges, **VIII:**2157
Leonardo of Pisa, **II:**585
Lobachevsky, Nikolay Ivanovich, **VI:**1403
Maclaurin, Colin, **IV:**882
Mersenne, Marin, **IV:**949
Monge, Gaspard, **IV:**975
Napier, John, **III:**544
Neumann, John von, **VIII:**2724
Omar Khayyám, **II:**695
Pappus, **I:**593
Pascal, Blaise, **IV:**1062
Picard, Émile, **IX:**2994
Piero della Francesca, III-**III:**606
Poincaré, Henri, **VI:**1798
Ptolemy, **I:**712
Pythagoras, **I:**727
Russell, Bertrand, **IX:**3264
Sosigenes, **I:**811
Steiner, Jakob, **VI:**2118
Torricelli, Evangelista, **IV:**1331
Turing, Alan Mathison, **IX:**3768
Whitehead, Alfred North, **IX:**3965
Wiener, Norbert, **IX:**3976
Xenakis, Iannis, **IX:**4075

MEDICINE. *See also* **NURSING;
    PHYSIOLOGY; PUBLIC HEALTH; SEX
    RESEARCH**
Abano, Pietro d', **II:**1
Adler, Alfred, **VII:**30
Alcmaeon, **I:**34
Alhazen, **II:**63
Aretaeus of Cappadocia, **I:**81
Arnold of Villanova, **II:**79

Asclepiades of Bithynia, **I:**101
Avicenna, **II:**106
Banting, Sir Frederick Grant, **VII:**187
Barnard, Christiaan, **VII:**195
Behring, Emil von, **V:**182
Bernard, Claude, **V:**207
Bernoulli, Daniel, **IV:**122
Blackwell, Elizabeth, **V:**251
Breuer, Josef, **VII:**452
Burnet, Sir Macfarlane, **VII:**512
Calmette, Albert, **VII:**546
Celsus, Aulus Cornelius, **I:**173
Curie, Pierre and Marie, **VII:**811
Cushing, Harvey Williams, **VII:**823
Diocles of Carystus, **I:**260
Dioscorides, Pedanius, **I:**276
Domagk, Gerhard, **VII:**951
Egas Moniz, António, **VII:**1023
Ehrlich, Paul, **VII:**1032
Einthoven, Willem, **VII:**1039
Erasistratus, **I:**299
Fleming, Sir Alexander, **VII:**1166
Florey, Baron, **VII:**1172
Fowler, Lydia Folger, **V:**822
Fracastoro, Girolamo, **III:**270
Freud, Sigmund, **VII:**1224
Galen, **I:**338
Gesner, Conrad, **III:**298
Guy de Chauliac, **II:**414
Hahnemann, Samuel, **IV:**593
Harvey, William, **IV:**626
Herophilus, **I:**398
Hevesy, Georg von, **VIII:**1654
Hippocrates, **I:**411
Holmes, Oliver Wendell, **V:**1126
Hounsfield, Godfrey Newbold, **VIII:**1751
Houssay, Bernardo Alberto, **VIII:**1759
Imhotep, **I:**443
Jaspers, Karl, **VIII:**1843
Jenner, Edward, **IV:**721
Kämpfer, Engelbert, **IV:**754
Koch, Robert, **VI:**1297
Le Bon, Gustave, **VIII:**2134
Lister, Joseph, **VI:**1388
Lorenz, Konrad, **VIII:**2238
Maimonides, Moses, **II:**619
Mayo, William J. and Charles H., **VIII:**2465
Montagu, Mary Wortley, **IV:**983
Montessori, Maria, **VIII:**2596
Morton,William Thomas Green, **VI:**1596
Nostradamus, **III:**567
Osler, Sir William, **VI:**1698

Paracelsus, **III:**584
Pauling, Linus, **IX:**2926
Paul of Aegina, **II:**712
Pavlov, Ivan Petrovich, **IX:**2933
Picotte, Susan La Flesche, **IX:**3010
Razi, al-, **II:**779
Reed, Walter, **VI:**1857
Ross, Ronald, **IX:**3247
Rush, Benjamin, **IV:**1202
Salk, Jonas Edward, **IX:**3305
Santorio, Santorio, **IV:**1209
Schweitzer, Albert, **IX:**3370
Semmelweis, Ignaz Philipp, **VI:**2021
Servetus, Michael, **III:**675
Smith, Theobald, **IX:**3450
Spock, Benjamin, **IX:**3478
Stahl, Georg Ernst, **IV:**1268
Starling, Ernest Henry, **IX:**3494
Sydenham, Thomas, **IV:**1310
Vesalius, Andreas, **III:**754
Virchow, Rudolf, **VI:**2312
Waksman, Selman Abraham, **IX:**3833
Whipple, George Hoyt, **IX:**3957
Wilkins, Maurice H.F., **IX:**3995

METALLURGY
Hadfield, Sir Robert Abbott, **V:**1015

METEOROLOGY
Bjerknes, Vilhelm, **VII:**318
Dalton, John, **V:**602
Geiger, Rudolf Oskar Robert Williams, **VII:**1326
Humboldt, Alexander von, **V:**1159
Maury, Matthew Fontaine, **VI:**1507
Wilkins, Sir George Hubert, **IX:**3999

MICROBIOLOGY. *See* **BIOLOGY**

MILITARY AFFAIRS. *See also*
EXPLORATION AND COLONIZATION;
GOVERNMENT AND POLITICS;
WARFARE AND CONQUEST
Abahai, **IV:**1
Abdelkader, **V:**1
Alanbrooke, First Viscount, **VII:**45
Albuquerque, Afonso de, **III:**11
Allen, Ethan, **IV:**34
Allenby, Lord, **VII:**58
Alva, Duke of, **III:**18
André, John, **IV:**42
Anson, Lord, **IV:**55
Arafat, Yasir, **VII:**90

Arnold, Benedict, **IV:**64
Atatürk, Kemal, **VII:**133
Bābur, **III:**36
Baden-Powell, Sir Robert Stephenson Smyth, **V:**105
Bayard, Chevalier de, **III:**48
Bayezid II, **III:**51
Bligh, William, **IV:**143
Blücher, Gebhard Leberecht von, **V:**263
Bolívar, Simón, **V:**267
Botha, Louis, **VII:**376
Bougainville, Louis-Antoine de, **IV:**179
Bradley, Omar N., **VII:**403
Calamity Jane, **V:**390
Carleton, Guy, **IV:**246
Carlos, Don, **V:**413
Carson, Kit, **V:**429
Charles XIV John, **V:**474
Cheng Ch'eng-kung, **IV:**297
Chu Teh, **VII:**687
Clark, George Rogers, **IV:**312
Clausewitz, Carl von, **V:**503
Clinton, Sir Henry, **IV:**321
Clive, Robert, **IV:**325
Condé, The Great, **IV:**341
Cornwallis, First Marquess, **IV:**367
Cortés, Hernán, **III:**188
Crockett, David, **V:**578
Custer, George A., **V:**585
Cyrano de Bergerac, Savinien de, **IV:**385
Dayan, Moshe, **VII:**854
Decatur, Stephen, **V:**634
de Gaulle, Charles, **VII:**866
Dewey, George, **V:**656
Dorgon, **IV:**421
Eisenhower, Dwight D., **VII:**1043
Enver Pasha, **VII:**1078
Faidherbe, Louis, **V:**763
Fairfax, Third Baron, **IV:**446
Farnese, Alessandro, **III:**254
Farragut, David G., **V:**772
Ferdinand II and Isabella I, **III:**260
Frederick Henry, **IV:**500
Gadsden, James, **V:**858
Gage, Thomas, **IV:**511
Gama, Vasco da, **III:**287
Garibaldi, Giuseppe, **V:**879
Gneisenau, August von, **V:**940
Gordon, Charles George, **V:**964
Göring, Hermann, **VIII:**1438
Grant, Ulysses S., **V:**975
Greene, Nathanael, **IV:**574
Grenville, Sir Richard, **III:**315

Guderian, Heinz, **VIII**:1490
Guevara, Che, **VIII**:1494
Halsey, William F., **VIII**:1525
Harrison, William Henry, **V**:1061
Hein, Piet, **IV**:644
Henry the Navigator, Prince, **III**:354
Hickok, Wild Bill, **V**:1107
Higginson, Thomas Wentworth, **V**:1110
Himmler, Heinrich, **VIII**:1666
Hindenburg, Paul Von, **VIII**:1674
Howe, Admiral Richard, **IV**:672
Howe, General William, **IV**:676
Huáscar, **III**:371
Hunyadi, János, **III**:374
Jackson, Andrew, **V**:1196
Jackson, Stonewall, **V**:1204
Joffre, Joseph-Jacques-Césaire, **VIII**:1851
Jones, John Paul, **IV**:738
Julius II, **III**:405
Kamehameha I, **VI**:1255
Kesselring, Albert, **VIII**:1949
Kidd, William, **IV**:777
Kitchener, Lord, **VIII**:2002
Kutuzov, Mikhail Illarionovich, **VI**:1305
Lawrence, T.E., **VIII**:2115
Lee, Robert E., **VI**:1338
Li Hung-chang, **VI**:1362
Lin Piao, **VIII**:2189
Louvois, Marquis de, **IV**:871
Ludendorff, Erich, **VIII**:2265
MacArthur, Douglas, **VIII**:2295
Machel, Samora Moisès, **VIII**:2317
Mannerheim, Carl Gustaf, **VIII**:2396
Mao Tse-tung, **VIII**:2400
Marlborough, First Duke of, **IV**:922
Marshall, George C., **VIII**:2429
Matthias I Corvinus, **III**:487
Mehmed II, **III**:499
Metacomet, **IV**:954
Mitchell, William, **VIII**:2554
Mobutu Sese Seko, **VIII**:2562
Monck, George, **IV**:971
Monmouth, Duke of, **IV**:980
Montgomery, Bernard Law, **VIII**:2601
Mornay, Philippe de, **III**:537
Mountbatten, Louis, **VIII**:2641
Muhammad 'Alī Pasha, **VI**:1604
Napoleon I, **VI**:1616
Nasser, Gamal Abdel, **VIII**:2693
Nelson, Lord, **VI**:1634
Ney, Michel, **VI**:1646
Nimitz, Chester W., **VIII**:2750

Obregón, Álvaro, **IX**:2781
Oda Nobunaga, **III**:570
O'Higgins, Bernardo, **VI**:1688
Osceola, **VI**:1695
Outram, Sir James, **VI**:1705
Pachacuti, **III**:577
Papen, Franz von, **IX**:2876
Patton, George S., **IX**:2911
P'eng Te-huai, **IX**:2954
Perry, Matthew C., **VI**:1760
Perry, Oliver Hazard, **VI**:1764
Pershing, John J., **IX**:2983
Pétain, Philippe, **IX**:2987
Phillip, Arthur, **IV**:1091
Pike, Zebulon Montgomery, **IV**:1094
Powell, Colin L., **IX**:3070
Pride, Thomas, **IV**:1126
Revere, Paul, **IV**:1156
Rickover, Hyman G., **IX**:3171
Rochambeau, Comte de, **IV**:1174
Rodney, George, **IV**:1178
Rommel, Erwin, **IX**:3213
Root, Elihu, **IX**:3232
Rundstedt, Gerd von, **IX**:3260
San Martín, José de, **VI**:1947
Santa Anna, Antonio López de, **VI**:1955
Saragossa, La, **VI**:1958
Scharnhorst, Gerhard Johann David von, **VI**:1969
Scott, Winfield, **VI**:2009
Seeckt, Hans von, **IX**:3380
Shaka, **VI**:2041
Shays, Daniel, **IV**:1239
Sherman, William Tecumseh, **VI**:2057
Śivajī, **IV**:1246
Slim, First Viscount, **IX**:3435
Smuts, Jan Christian, **IX**:3453
Standish, Miles, **IV**:1273
Stanton, Edwin M., **VI**:2106
Stimson, Henry L., **IX**:3537
Sucre, Antonio José de, **VI**:2164
Suvorov, Aleksandr Vasilyevich, **IV**:1298
Taylor, Zachary, **VI**:2194
Thayer, Sylvanus, **VI**:2223
Tirpitz, Alfred von, **IX**:3688
Tito, **IX**:3692
Tokugawa Ieyasu, **IV**:1327
Torstenson, Lennart, **IV**:1335
Toussaint-Louverture, **IV**:1338
Toyotomi Hideyoshi, **III**:728
Tromp, Cornelius and Maarten, **IV**:1342
Trotsky, Leon, **IX**:3726

Tseng Kuo-fan, **VI:**2260
Vauban, Sébastien Le Prestre de, **IV:**1358
Villa, Pancho, **IX:**3811
Vo Nguyen Giap, **IX:**3821
Wallenstein, Albrecht Wenzel von, **IV:**1396
Warwick, Earl of, **III:**774
Wellington, Duke of, **VI:**2351
Wolfe, James, **IV:**1471
Zapata, Emiliano, **IX:**4104
Zhukov, Georgy Konstantinovich, **IX:**4116

MINISTRY. *See* **RELIGION AND THEOLOGY**

MOLECULAR BIOLOGY. *See* **BIOLOGY**

MONARCHY. *See also* **GOVERNMENT AND POLITICS; PHARAOHS; ROMAN EMPERORS**
Akbar, **III:**5
Alfred the Great, **II:**59
Anne, Queen, **IV:**50
Boleyn, Anne, **III:**66
Bruce, Robert, **II:**184
Canute the Great, **II:**201
Catherine of Aragon, **III:**136
Catherine the Great, **IV:**257
Charles I, **IV:**279
Charles II, **IV:**283
Charles III, **IV:**287
Charles XII, **IV:**290
Charles XIV John, **V:**474
Christina, **IV:**304
David I, **II:**291
David II, **II:**294
Diana, Princess of Wales, **VII:**923
Edward I, **II:**322
Edward II, **II:**326
Edward III, **II:**329
Edward IV, **III:**234
Edward VI, **III:**237
Edward VII, **VII:**1020
Edward the Confessor, **II:**315
Edward the Elder, **II:**319
Egbert, **II:**333
Eleanor of Aquitaine, **II:**336
Elizabeth I, **III:**241
Elizabeth II, **VII:**1062
Ethelred II, the Unready, **II:**344
Ferdinand II of Austria, **IV:**450
Ferdinand II of Spain, **III:**260
Francis I, **III:**274

Francis Joseph I, **V:**829
Frederick I, **IV:**497
Frederick the Great, **IV:**504
George I, **IV:**531
George II, **IV:**535
George III, **IV:**539
George IV, **V:**902
George V, **VII:**1339
George VI, **VII:**1343
Grey, Lady Jane, **III:**318
Gustavus II Adolphus, **IV:**589
Harold II, **II:**426
Henry I, **II:**443
Henry II, **II:**446
Henry III, **II:**453
Henry IV of England, **II:**457
Henry IV of France, **III:**333
Henry V, **III:**337
Henry VI, **III:**341
Henry VII, **III:**345
Henry VIII, **III:**349
Howard, Catherine, **III:**367
Huáscar, **III:**371
Isabella I, **III:**260
John, King, **II:**540
John III Sobieski, **IV:**725
Joseph II, **IV:**750
Leopold I, **IV:**838
Louis XIII, **IV:**863
Louis XIV, **IV:**866
Manuel I, **III:**464
Marguerite of Navarre, **III:**471
Maria Theresa, **IV:**914
Marie-Antoinette, **IV:**918
Mary, Queen of Scots, **III:**475
Mary I, **III:**479
Matthias I Corvinus, **III:**487
Menelik II, **VI:**1537
Mohammed I Askia, **III:**521
Montezuma II, **III:**528
Parr, Catherine, **III:**592
Peter III, **IV:**1087
Peter the Great, **IV:**1082
Philip the Magnanimous, **III:**603
Richard I, **II:**782
Richard II, **II:**786
Richard III, **III:**647
Shaka, **VI:**2041
Stephen, King, **II:**847
Tudor Family, The, **III:**732
Victoria, Queen, **VI:**2304
William III, **IV:**1447

William IV, **VI:**2392
William the Conqueror, **II:**997
Windsor, Duke of, **IX:**4025

MONASTICISM. *See also* **RELIGION AND THEOLOGY; SAINTS**
Anthony of Egypt, Saint, **I:**56
Benedict of Nursia, Saint, **II:**136
Buddha, **I:**144
Cassiodorus, **II:**215
Chuang-tzu, **I:**190
Dominic, Saint, **II:**301
Francis of Assisi, Saint, **II:**354
Gregory the Great, **II:**407
Ibn al-'Arabi, **II:**491
Jerome, Saint, **I:**463
Rabanus Maurus, **II:**766
Vardhamāna, **I:**915

MOTION PICTURES. *See* **FILM**

MUSIC. *See also* **THEATER AND ENTERTAINMENT**
Adam de la Halle, **II:**23
Alembert, Jean le Rond d', **IV:**30
Anderson, Marian, **VII:**70
Aristoxenus, **I:**98
Armstrong, Louis, **VII:**105
Bach, Johann Sebastian, **IV:**76
Barber, Samuel, **VII:**191
Bartók, Béla, **VII:**210
Beatles, The, **VII:**226
Beethoven, Ludwig van, **V:**178
Berg, Alban, **VII:**271
Berlin, Irving, **VII:**287
Berlioz, Hector, **V:**202
Bernstein, Leonard, **VII:**295
Bizet, Georges, **V:**244
Boccherini, Luigi, **IV:**147
Borodin, Aleksandr, **V:**286
Boulez, Pierre, **VII:**386
Brahms, Johannes, **V:**299
Britten, Benjamin, **VII:**466
Bruckner, Anton, **V:**331
Burney, Charles, **IV:**226
Byrd, William, **III:**105
Caruso, Enrico, **VII:**598
Casals, Pablo, **VII:**606
Charles, Ray, **VII:**657
Chopin, Frédéric, **V:**493
Coltrane, John, **VII:**741
Copland, Aaron, **VII:**766

Corelli, Arcangelo, **IV:**360
Couperin, François, **IV:**374
Coward, Noël, **VII:**783
Debussy, Claude, **VII:**884
Delibes, Léo, **V:**649
Delius, Frederick, **VII:**892
Donizetti, Gaetano, **V:**684
Dunstable, John, **III:**227
Dvořák, Antonín, **V:**725
Elgar, Sir Edward, **VII:**1051
Ellington, Duke, **VII:**1066
Falla, Manuel de, **VII:**1127
Fitzgerald, Ella, **VII:**1157
Foster, Stephen Collins, **V:**810
Franck, César, **V:**832
Franklin, Aretha, **VII:**1216
Gabrieli, Andrea, **III:**281
Gabrieli, Giovanni, **III:**284
Gershwin, George, **VII:**1347
Gershwin, Ira, **VII:**1352
Gilbert, W.S., **V:**927
Gillespie, Dizzy, **VII:**1370
Gluck, Christoph, **IV:**549
Goodman, Benny, **VIII:**1419
Gounod, Charles, **V:**967
Grieg, Edvard, **V:**1002
Guido d'Arezzo, **II:**411
Handel, George Frideric, **IV:**619
Haydn, Franz Joseph, **IV:**639
Henze, Hans Werner, **VIII:**1633
Hildegard von Bingen, **II:**474
Hindemith, Paul, **VIII:**1670
Holiday, Billie, **VIII:**1715
Horowitz, Vladimir, **VIII:**1747
Humperdinck, Engelbert, **V:**1162
Ives, Charles, **VIII:**1820
Janácek, Leoš, **VIII:**1835
Joplin, Janis, **VIII:**1883
Joplin, Scott, **V:**1239
Karajan, Herbert von, **VIII:**1910
Key, Francis Scott, **VI:**1281
Landini, Francesco, **II:**570
Lang, K.D., **VIII:**2080
Lind, Jenny, **VI:**1385
Liszt, Franz, **VI:**1391
Machaut, Guillaume de, **II:**615
Mahler, Gustav, **VIII:**2359
Mendelssohn, Felix, **VI:**1534
Menotti, Gian Carlo, **VIII:**2494
Mersenne, Marin, **IV:**949
Messiaen, Olivier, **VIII:**2503
Milhaud, Darius, **VIII:**2525

Monteverdi, Claudio, **IV:**990
Mozart, Wolfgang Amadeus, **IV:**1003
Muris, Johannes de, **II:**660
Mussorgsky, Modest, **VI:**1611
Norman, Jessye, **VIII:**2769
Offenbach, Jacques, **VI:**1684
Paganini, Niccolò, **VI:**1711
Parker, Charlie, **IX:**2880
Parton, Dolly, **IX:**2896
Pavarotti, Luciano, **IX:**2930
Pérotin, **II:**723
Pindar, **I:**644
Porter, Cole, **IX:**3055
Poulenc, Francis, **IX:**3066
Presley, Elvis, **IX:**3076
Price, Leontyne, **IX:**3081
Prokofiev, Sergei, **IX:**3085
Puccini, Giacomo, **IX:**3093
Purcell, Henry, **IV:**1137
Pythagoras, **I:**727
Rachmaninoff, Sergei, **IX:**3105
Rameau, Jean-Philippe, **IV:**1148
Ravel, Maurice, **IX:**3129
Rimsky-Korsakov, Nikolay, **VI:**1889
Robeson, Paul, **IX:**3187
Rossini, Gioacchino, **VI:**1913
Satie, Erik, **IX:**3331
Scarlatti, Alessandro, **IV:**1213
Schoenberg, Arnold, **IX:**3357
Schubert, Franz, **VI:**1988
Schumann, Robert, **VI:**1992
Schütz, Heinrich, **IV:**1221
Schweitzer, Albert, **IX:**3370
Segovia, Andrés, **IX:**3383
Shostakovich, Dmitri, **IX:**3409
Sibelius, Jean, **IX:**3413
Sinatra, Frank, **IX:**3422
Smith, Bessie, **IX:**3442
Sousa, John Philip, **IX:**3466
Stockhausen, Karlheinz, **IX:**3541
Stradivari, Antonio, **IV:**1281
Strauss, Johann, **VI:**2155
Strauss, Richard, **IX:**3555
Stravinsky, Igor, **IX:**3559
Sullivan, Sir Arthur, **V:**927
Tchaikovsky, Peter Ilich, **VI:**2198
Telemann, Georg Philipp, **IV:**1319
Thomas, Theodore, **VI:**2230
Toscanini, Arturo, **IX:**3707
Varèse, Edgard, **IX:**3794
Vaughan Williams, Ralph, **IX:**3798
Verdi, Giuseppe, **VI:**2299

Villa-Lobos, Heitor, **IX:**3815
Vitry, Philippe de, **II:**949
Vivaldi, Antonio, **IV:**1383
Wagner, Richard, **VI:**2316
Walton, Sir William, **IX:**3872
Wang Wei, **II:**965
Weber, Carl Maria von, **VI:**2340
Webern, Anton von, **IX:**3914
Weill, Kurt, **IX:**3926
Xenakis, Iannis, **IX:**4075
Zwilich, Ellen Taaffe, **IX:**4121

NATION-BUILDING. *See* **COLONIAL ADMINISTRATION; EXPLORATION AND COLONIZATION; GOVERNMENT AND POLITICS; WARFARE AND CONQUEST**

NATIVE AMERICAN AFFAIRS
Black Hawk, **V:**247
Brant, Joseph, **IV:**196
Carson, Kit, **V:**429
Catlin, George, **V:**443
Clark, William, **VI:**1358
Crazy Horse, **V:**573
Geronimo, **V:**915
Joseph, Chief, **V:**1242
McGillivray, Alexander, **IV:**875
Massasoit, **IV:**930
Metacomet, **IV:**954
Osceola, **VI:**1695
Pocahontas, **IV:**1106
Pontiac, **IV:**1110
Powhatan, **IV:**1122
Red Cloud, **VI:**1850
Ross, John, **VI:**1910
Sequoyah, **VI:**2025
Sitting Bull, **VI:**2070
Tecumseh, **VI:**2203
Tekakwitha, Kateri, **IV:**1316

NATURAL HISTORY. *See also* **ASTRONOMY; BIOLOGY; BOTANY; GENETICS; GEOLOGY; OCEANOGRAPHY; ORNITHOLOGY; PHYSICS; ZOOLOGY**
Agassiz, Louis, **V:**30
Anaxagoras, **I:**47
Anaximander, **I:**50
Aristotle, **I:**94
Bacon, Francis, **III:**41
Banks, Sir Joseph, **IV:**83
Buffon, Comte de, **IV:**215

Darwin, Charles, **V:**606
Empedocles, **I:**282
Gesner, Conrad, **III:**298
Haeckel, Ernst, **V:**1018
Hayden, Ferdinand Vandeveer, **V:**1072
Lankester, Sir Edwin Ray, **VI:**1316
Linnaeus, **IV:**846
Lucretius, **I:**511
Morgan, Lewis Henry, **VI:**1584
Peale, Charles Willson, **IV:**1070
Pliny the Elder, **I:**662
Spallanzani, Lazzaro, **IV:**1260
Weismann, August, **VI:**2348

NAVAL SERVICE. *See also* **MILITARY AFFAIRS**

NAVIGATION. *See* **EXPLORATION AND COLONIZATION**

NAVY. *See* **MILITARY AFFAIRS**

NURSING. *See also* **MEDICINE**
Barton, Clara, **V:**142
Nightingale, Florence, **VI:**1667
Tubman, Harriet, **VI:**2264
Wald, Lillian D., **IX:**3837

OCEANOGRAPHY
Ballard, Robert Duane, **VII:**180
Bjerknes, Vilhelm, **VII:**318
Maury, Matthew Fontaine, **VI:**1507
Piccard, Auguste and Jean-Felix, **IX:**3002

ORATORY. *See also* **LITERATURE**
Chrysostom, Saint John, **I:**184
Cicero, **I:**194
Gregory of Nazianzus, **I:**349

ORNITHOLOGY
Audubon, John James, **V:**86

PAINTING. *See* **ART**

PATRONAGE OF THE ARTS. *See also* **PHILANTHROPY**
'Abd al-Mu'min, **II:**4
Colbert, Jean-Baptiste, **IV:**336
Diaghilev, Sergei, **VII:**919
Francis I, **III:**274
Gardner, Isabella Stewart, **VII:**1300
Julius II, **III:**405

Kanishka, **I:**494
Leo X, **III:**419
Matthias I Corvinus, **III:**487
Mazarin, Jules, **IV:**945
Nero, **I:**577
Nicholas V, **III:**559
Pisistratus, **I:**648
Scipio Aemilianus, **I:**757
Sforza, Ludovico, **III:**682
Shah Jahan, **IV:**1232
Tamerlane, **II:**884
Whitney, Gertrude Vanderbilt, **IX:**3969

PEACE ADVOCACY. *See also* **SOCIAL REFORM**
Angell, Norman, **VII:**74
Balch, Emily Greene, **VII:**160
Cassin, René, **VII:**610
La Fontaine, Henri-Marie, **VIII:**2051
Niemöller, Martin, **VIII:**2742
Pauling, Linus, **IX:**2926
Rankin, Jeannette, **IX:**3117
Roosevelt, Eleanor, **IX:**3217
Russell, Bertrand, **IX:**3264
Sakharov, Andrei, **IX:**3296
Schweitzer, Albert, **IX:**3370
Söderblom, Nathan, **IX:**3456
Teresa, Mother, **IX:**3635
Tutu, Desmond, **IX:**3775
Wiesel, Elie, **IX:**3980

PHARAOHS
Akhenaton, **I:**23
Hatshepsut, **I:**371
Menes, **I:**547
Nefertiti, **I:**573
Psamtik I, **I:**709
Ptolemy Philadelphus, **I:**716
Ramses II, **I:**734
Sesostris III, **I:**774
Thutmose III, **I:**889
Tutankhamen, **I:**904
Zoser, **I:**978

PHILANTHROPY
Carnegie, Andrew, **V:**420
Eastman, George, **VII:**996
Field, Marshall, **V:**783
Guggenheim, Daniel, **VIII:**1498
Howe, Samuel Gridley, **V:**1150
McCormick, Cyrus Hall, **VI:**1431
Morgan, J.P., **VI:**1579

Nobel, Alfred, **VI**:1673
Rockefeller, John D., **VI**:1896

PHILOLOGY. *See also* **LANGUAGE AND LINGUISTICS**
Gesner, Conrad, **III**:298
Niebuhr, Barthold Georg, **VI**:1654

PHILOSOPHY. *See also* **RELIGION AND THEOLOGY**
Abano, Pietro d', **II**:1
Abelard, Peter, **II**:10
Alberti, Leon Battista, **III**:8
Alcmaeon, **I**:34
Alcott, Bronson, **V**:37
Alembert, Jean le Rond d', **IV**:30
Anaxagoras, **I**:47
Anaximenes of Miletus, **I**:53
Antisthenes, **I**:66
Arendt, Hannah, **VII**:98
Aristippus, **I**:85
Aristotle, **I**:94
Ash'ari, al-, **II**:93
Aspasia, **I**:115
Augustine, Saint, **I**:128
Aurobindo, Sri, **VII**:141
Averroës, **II**:100
Avicenna, **II**:106
Bacon, Francis, **III**:41
Bacon, Roger, **II**:110
Baeck, Leo, **VII**:148
Bakunin, Mikhail, **V**:112
Balfour, Arthur, **VII**:172
Bayle, Pierre, **IV**:103
Beauvoir, Simone de, **VII**:230
Bentham, Jeremy, **IV**:107
Bergson, Henri, **VII**:283
Berkeley, George, **IV**:114
Blanc, Louis, **V**:259
Boethius, **II**:155
Böhme, Jakob, **IV**:154
Bonhoeffer, Dietrich, **VII**:358
Bradley, F.H., **V**:290
Bruno, Giordano, **III**:96
Buber, Martin, **VII**:483
Buddha, **I**:144
Buridan, Jean, **II**:194
Camus, Albert, **VII**:553
Carnap, Rudolf, **VII**:582
Cassirer, Ernst, **VII**:614
Cato the Younger, **I**:166
Chu Hsi, **II**:265

Chuang-tzu, **I**:190
Cicero, **I**:194
Clausewitz, Carl von, **V**:503
Comte, Auguste, **V**:543
Condillac, Étienne Bonnot de, **IV**:344
Condorcet, Marquis de, **IV**:348
Confucius, **I**:222
Croce, Benedetto, **VII**:801
Davy, Sir Humphry, **V**:621
Democritus, **I**:249
Derrida, Jacques, **VII**:912
Descartes, René, **IV**:403
Dewey, John, **VII**:916
Diderot, Denis, **IV**:412
Diogenes, **I**:268
Djilas, Milovan, **VII**:944
Duns Scotus, John, **II**:309
Ehrenfels, Christian Von, **VII**:1026
Ehrlich, Eugen, **VII**:1029
Empedocles, **I**:282
Epicurus, **I**:295
Eucken, Rudolf Christoph, **VII**:1106
Fechner, Gustav Theodor, **V**:780
Ferguson, Adam, **IV**:454
Fichte, Johann Gottlieb, **IV**:465
Fracastoro, Girolamo, **III**:270
Galen, **I**:338
Gentile, Giovanni, **VII**:1336
Gilson, Étienne, **VII**:1374
Gioberti, Vincenzo, **V**:932
Godwin, William, **IV**:555
Green, Thomas Hill, **V**:987
Haeckel, Ernst, **V**:1018
Harrison, Frederic, **V**:1057
Hartmann, Nicolai, **VIII**:1571
Hegel, Georg Wilhelm Friedrich, **V**:1080
Heidegger, Martin, **VIII**:1610
Heraclitus of Ephesus, **I**:382
Herder, Johann Gottfried, **IV**:651
Hippolytus of Rome, **I**:415
Hobhouse, Leonard T., **VIII**:1707
Hsieh Ling-yün, **I**:429
Hsün-tzu, **I**:433
Hume, David, **IV**:683
Husserl, Edmund, **VIII**:1797
Huxley, Thomas Henry, **V**:1172
Hypatia, **I**:436
Ibn al-'Arabi, **II**:491
Ibn Gabirol, **II**:498
Isocrates, **I**:456
Jamāl al-Dīn al-Afghānī, **V**:1207
James, William, **V**:1216

Jaspers, Karl, **VIII**:1843
Judah ha-Levi, **II**:548
Kant, Immanuel, **IV**:761
Kierkegaard, Søren, **VI**:1284
Lacan, Jacques, **VIII**:2061
Langer, Susanne K., **VIII**:2087
Lao-tzu, **I**:498
Leibniz, Gottfried Wilhelm, **IV**:829
Lessing, Gotthold Ephraim, **IV**:842
Locke, John, **IV**:854
Lucretius, **I**:511
Lukács, György, **VIII**:2272
Lull, Raymond, **II**:608
Luria, Isaac ben Solomon, **III**:440
Luther, Martin, **III**:443
Luxemburg, Rosa, **VIII**:2285
Maimonides, Moses, **II**:619
Marcel, Gabriel, **VIII**:2407
Maritain, Jacques, **VIII**:2425
Marx, Karl, **VI**:1492
Masaryk, Tomáš, **VIII**:2440
Mazzini, Giuseppe, **VI**:1514
Mencius, **I**:543
Merleau-Ponty, Maurice, **VIII**:2500
Mersenne, Marin, **IV**:949
Michelet, Jules, **VI**:1548
Mill, James, **VI**:1556
Mill, John Stuart, **VI**:1559
Montaigne, Michel de, **III**:524
Montesquieu, **IV**:986
Moore, G.E., **VIII**:2605
Moses de León, **II**:648
Nicholas of Autrecourt, **II**:669
Nicholas of Cusa, **III**:563
Niebuhr, Reinhold, **VIII**:2735
Nietzsche, Friedrich Wilhelm, **VI**:1662
Nishida, Kitaro, **VIII**:2754
Ockham, William of, **II**:681
Ortega y Gasset, José, **IX**:2843
Ostwald, Wilhelm, **IX**:2855
Paracelsus, **III**:584
Parmenides, **I**:596
Pascal, Blaise, **IV**:1062
Peirce, Charles Sanders, **VI**:1756
Philo of Alexandria, **I**:632
Piaget, Jean, **IX**:2990
Planck, Max, **IX**:3033
Plato, **I**:655
Plotinus, **I**:666
Porphyry, **I**:683
Posidonius, **I**:686
Priestley, Joseph, **IV**:1129

Proclus, **I**:698
Protagoras, **I**:705
Proudhon, Pierre-Joseph, **VI**:1817
Psellus, Michael, **II**:758
Pufendorf, Samuel von, **IV**:1133
Pyrrhon of Elis, **I**:724
Pythagoras, **I**:727
Razi, al-, **II**:779
Renan, Ernest, **VI**:1865
Royce, Josiah, **IX**:3254
Russell, Bertrand, **IX**:3264
Santayana, George, **IX**:3317
Sartre, Jean-Paul, **IX**:3327
Scheler, Max, **IX**:3347
Schelling, Friedrich Wilhelm Joseph, **VI**:1972
Schiller, Friedrich, **IV**:1217
Schleiermacher, Friedrich, **VI**:1976
Schopenhauer, Arthur, **VI**:1984
Schrödinger, Erwin, **IX**:3362
Schweitzer, Albert, **IX**:3370
Seneca the Younger, **I**:770
Sidgwick, Henry, **VI**:2062
Siger of Brabant, **II**:829
Smith, Adam, **IV**:1249
Socrates, **I**:793
Sorel, Georges, **IX**:3463
Spencer, Herbert, **VI**:2086
Spinoza, Baruch, **IV**:1264
Staël, Madame de, **VI**:2092
Stein, Edith, **IX**:3506
Sung Dynasty, **II**:866
Taine, Hippolyte-Adolphe, **VI**:2182
Teilhard de Chardin, Pierre, **IX**:3626
Thales of Miletus, **I**:852
Theophrastus, **I**:873
Thomas Aquinas, Saint, **II**:911
Tillich, Paul, **IX**:3685
Troeltsch, Ernst, **IX**:3722
Valentinus, **I**:911
Valla, Lorenzo, **III**:739
Vico, Giambattista, **IV**:1372
Vitoria, Francisco de, **III**:768
Voltaire, **IV**:1392
Wang Ch'ung, **I**:943
Wang Pi, **I**:949
Wang Yang-ming, **III**:771
Weil, Simone, **IX**:3922
Whitehead, Alfred North, **IX**:3965
Wiesel, Elie, **IX**:3980
William of Auvergne, **II**:976
William of Auxerre, **II**:981
Wittgenstein, Ludwig, **IX**:4036

Xanthippe, **I:**952
Xenophanes, **I:**955
Xenophon, **I:**958
Zeno of Citium, **I:**967
Zeno of Elea, **I:**972

PHOTOGRAPHY. *See also* **ART**
Arbus, Diane, **VII:**95
Bourke-White, Margaret, **VII:**395
Brady, Mathew B., **V:**294
Carroll, Lewis, **V:**425
Cunningham, Imogen, **VII:**808
Daguerre, Jacques, **V:**592
Eastman, George, **VII:**996
Lange, Dorothea, **VIII:**2083
Steichen, Edward, **IX:**3501
Stieglitz, Alfred, **IX:**3532
Wilkins, Sir George Hubert, **IX:**3999

PHYSICS. *See also* **ASTRONOMY; NATURAL HISTORY**
Alembert, Jean le Rond d', **IV:**30
Alhazen, **II:**63
Arrhenius, Svante August, **VII:**114
Avogadro, Amedeo, **V:**98
Basov, Nikolay Gennadiyevich, **VII:**214
Becquerel Family, The, **V:**166
Bernoulli, Daniel, **IV:**122
Bernoulli, Jakob I, **IV:**122
Bethe, Hans Albrecht, **VII:**300
Bjerknes, Vilhelm, **VII:**318
Bohr, Niels, **VII:**345
Bothe, Walther, **VII:**379
Boyle, Robert, **IV:**185
Bragg, Sir Lawrence, **VII:**410
Bridgman, Percy Williams, **VII:**463
Broglie, Louis de, **VII:**472
Buridan, Jean, **II:**194
Chadwick, James, **VII:**635
Compton, Arthur Holly, **VII:**745
Curie, Pierre and Marie, **VII:**811
Dalton, John, **V:**602
Einstein, Albert, **VII:**1035
Euler, Leonhard, **IV:**443
Faraday, Michael, **V:**767
Fechner, Gustav Theodor, **V:**780
Fermi, Enrico, **VII:**1145
Fourier, Joseph, **V:**819
Galvani, Luigi, **IV:**523
Gauss, Carl Friedrich, **V:**893
Gay-Lussac, Joseph-Louis, **V:**897
Gibbs, Josiah Willard, **V:**923

Grove, Sir William Robert, **V:**1010
Guericke, Otto von, **IV:**586
Guillaume, Charles-Édouard, **VIII:**1502
Hahn, Otto, **VIII:**1513
Hamilton, Sir William Rowan, **V:**1025
Hawking, Stephen W., **VIII:**1580
Heisenberg, Werner, **VIII:**1617
Helmholtz, Hermann von, **V:**1089
Hertz, Gustav, **VIII:**1647
Hevesy, Georg von, **VIII:**1654
Huygens, Christiaan, **IV:**695
Kapitsa, Pyotr Leonidovich, **VIII:**1906
Kelvin, Lord, **VI:**1269
Kepler, Johannes, **IV:**772
Kurchatov, Igor Vasilyevich, **VIII:**2039
Landau, Lev Davidovich, **VIII:**2073
Laplace, Pierre-Simon, **VI:**1319
Lawrence, Ernest Orlando, **VIII:**2121
Lemaître, Georges, **VIII:**2157
Lockyer, Sir Joseph Norman, **VI:**1410
Lomonosov, Mikhail Vasilyevich, **IV:**860
Lorentz, Hendrik Antoon, **VIII:**2235
Maclaurin, Colin, **IV:**882
McMillan, Edwin Mattison, **VIII:**2336
Maxwell, James Clerk, **VI:**1511
Meitner, Lise, **VIII:**2476
Mersenne, Marin, **IV:**949
Michelson, Albert A., **VI:**1551
Millikan, Robert Andrews, **VIII:**2539
Monge, Gaspard, **IV:**975
Néel, Louis-Eugène-Félix, **VIII:**2705
Neumann, John von, **VIII:**2724
Newton, Sir Isaac, **IV:**1025
Oppenheimer, J. Robert, **IX:**2833
Ostwald, Wilhelm, **IX:**2855
Pauli, Wolfgang, **IX:**2923
Peregrinus de Maricourt, Petrus, **II:**719
Picard, Émile, **IX:**2994
Piccard, Auguste and Jean-Felix, **IX:**3002
Planck, Max, **IX:**3033
Poincaré, Henri, **VI:**1798
Prandtl, Ludwig, **IX:**3073
Rabi, Isidor Isaac, **IX:**3101
Raman, Sir Chandrasekhara Venkata, **IX:**3109
Rutherford, Ernest, **IX:**3277
Sakharov, Andrei, **IX:**3296
Schmidt, Bernhard Voldemar, **IX:**3351
Schrödinger, Erwin, **IX:**3362
Stark, Johannes, **IX:**3490
Teller, Edward, **IX:**3631
Torricelli, Evangelista, **IV:**1331
Volta, Alessandro, **IV:**1387

Wegener, Alfred, **IX:**3918
Wilkins, Maurice H. F., **IX:**3995
Yukawa, Hideki, **IX:**4090

PHYSIOLOGY. *See also* **MEDICINE**
Bayliss, Sir William Maddock, **VII:**217
Bernard, Claude, **V:**207
Breuer, Josef, **VII:**452
Eccles, Sir John Carew, **VII:**1008
Egas Moniz, António, **VII:**1023
Einthoven, Willem, **VII:**1039
Helmholtz, Hermann von, **V:**1089
Houssay, Bernardo Alberto, **VIII:**1759
Krogh, August, **VIII:**2027
Lorenz, Konrad, **VIII:**2238
Macleod, John J.R., **VIII:**2329
Malpighi, Marcello, **IV:**891
Pavlov, Ivan Petrovich, **IX:**2933
Raman, Sir Chandrasekhara Venkata,
 IX:3109
Spallanzani, Lazzaro, **IV:**1260
Swedenborg, Emanuel, **IV:**1302
Vesalius, Andreas, **III:**754
Whipple, George Hoyt, **IX:**3957
Wundt, Wilhelm, **IX:**4069

POETRY. *See* **LITERATURE**

POLITICAL SCIENCE. *See also*
GOVERNMENT AND POLITICS
Beard, Charles A., **VII:**221
Burke, Edmund, **IV:**222
Clarendon, First Earl of, **IV:**308
Dickinson, John, **IV:**408
Godwin, William, **IV:**555
Gramsci, Antonio, **VIII:**1459
Hobbes, Thomas, **IV:**662
Hobhouse, Leonard T., **VIII:**1707
Hotman, François, **III:**362
Laski, Harold J., **VIII:**2093
Lassalle, Ferdinand, **VI:**1323
Lippmann, Walter, **VIII:**2203
Machiavelli, Niccolò, **III:**448
Marx, Karl, **VI:**1492
Montesquieu, **IV:**986
Mosca, Gaetano, **VIII:**2630
Paine, Thomas, **IV:**1055
Rousseau, Jean-Jacques, **IV:**1194
Tocqueville, Alexis de, **VI:**2238

POLITICS. *See* **GOVERNMENT AND
POLITICS**

POPES
Adrian IV, **II:**27
Alexander III, **II:**48
Alexander VI, **III:**14
Boniface VIII, **II:**171
Clement I, **I:**210
Clement VII, **III:**166
Gregory VII, **II:**395
Gregory IX, **II:**399
Gregory the Great, **II:**407
Innocent III, **II:**509
Innocent IV, **II:**514
Julius II, **III:**405
Leo IX, **II:**581
Leo X, **III:**419
Nicholas V, **III:**559
Nicholas the Great, **II:**673
Paul III, **III:**595
Pius II, **III:**613
Pius V, **III:**616
Sergius I, Saint, **II:**823
Sylvester II, **II:**869
Urban II, **II:**928

PRINTING AND TYPEFOUNDING. *See*
INVENTION AND TECHNOLOGY

PSYCHIATRY AND PSYCHOLOGY
Bleuler, Eugen, **VII:**328
Breuer, Josef, **VII:**452
Dewey, John, **VII:**916
Ehrenfels, Christian Von,
 VII:1026
Freud, Sigmund, **VII:**1224
Fromm, Erich, **VII:**1246
Gesell, Arnold, **VII:**1356
Horney, Karen, **VIII:**1744
James, William, **V:**1216
Janet, Pierre, **VIII:**1839
Jung, Carl, **VIII:**1896
Kübler-Ross, Elisabeth, **VIII:**2030
Lacan, Jacques, **VIII:**2061
Lorenz, Konrad, **VIII:**2238
Rorschach, Hermann, **IX:**3236
Skinner, B.F., **IX:**3431
Sullivan, Harry Stack, **IX:**3575
Thorndike, Edward L., **IX:**3669
Wertheimer, Max, **IX:**3945
Wundt, Wilhelm, **IX:**4069

PSYCHOLOGY. *See* **PSYCHIATRY AND
PSYCHOLOGY**

PUBLIC ADMINISTRATION
Kay-Shuttleworth, First Baronet, **VIII:**1917

PUBLIC HEALTH. *See also* **MEDICINE;
    NURSING; SEX RESEARCH**
Gorgas, William Crawford, **VIII:**1434
Sanger, Margaret, **IX:**3313

PUBLISHING. *See also* **JOURNALISM;
    LITERATURE**
Armstrong, Edwin H., **VII:**102
Bennett, James Gordon, **V:**190
Brown, George, **V:**318
Caxton, William, **III:**143
Collins, Norman, **VII:**737
Graham, Katharine, **VIII:**1451
MacMillan, Daniel and Alexander,
    VI:1457
Morris, William, **VI:**1588
Newbery, John, **IV:**1019
O'Connor, Thomas Power, **IX:**2793

RADIO
Reith of Stonehaven, First Baron, **IX:**3146
Scripps, Edward Wyllis, **VI:**2014
Walter, John, II, **VI:**2324

RELIGION AND THEOLOGY. *See also*
    **BIBLICAL FIGURES; CHURCH
    GOVERNMENT; CHURCH REFORM;
    MONASTICISM; PHILOSOPHY; POPES;
    SAINTS**
Aaron, **I:**1
Abelard, Peter, **II:**10
Abraham, **I:**5
Abu Hanifah, **II:**16
Adrian IV, **II:**27
Ahmad ibn Hanbal, **II:**33
Ahmad Khan, Sir Sayyid, **V:**34
Akhenaton, **I:**23
Akiba ben Joseph, **I:**27
Alcuin, **II:**44
Alexander III, **II:**48
Alexander VI, **III:**14
Ambrose, Saint, **I:**43
Andrewes, Lancelot, **IV:**46
Anselm, Saint, **II:**72
Anthony of Egypt, Saint, **I:**56
Anthony of Padua, Saint, **II:**76
Arnold of Villanova, **II:**79
Ash'ari, al-, **II:**93
Aśoka the Great, **I:**112

Athanasius, Saint, **I:**119
Augustine, Saint, **I:**128
Aurobindo, Sri, **VII:**141
Ba'al Shem Tov, **IV:**73
Baeck, Leo, **VII:**148
Ball, John, **II:**114
Barth, Karl, **VII:**203
Becket, Thomas, **II:**128
Beecher, Henry Ward, **V:**174
Benedict of Nursia, Saint, **II:**136
Berkeley, George, **IV:**114
Bernard of Clairvaux, Saint, **II:**143
Besant, Annie, **V:**211
Biddle, John, **IV:**126
Boethius, **II:**155
Böhme, Jakob, **IV:**154
Bonaventure, Saint, **II:**163
Bonhoeffer, Dietrich, **VII:**358
Boniface, Saint, **II:**167
Boniface VIII, **II:**171
Booth, William, **V:**275
Boris I of Bulgaria, **II:**175
Bossuet, Jacques-Bénigne, **IV:**170
Brunner, Emil, **VII:**475
Buber, Martin, **VII:**483
Bucer, Martin, **III:**101
Buddha, **I:**144
Bultmann, Rudolf, **VII:**498
Bunyan, John, **IV:**218
Cabrini, Frances Xavier, **V:**386
Calvin, John, **III:**117
Cameron, Richard, **IV:**239
Campbell, Alexander, **V:**401
Carpini, Giovanni da Pian del, **II:**206
Catherine of Siena, Saint, **II:**218
Channing, William Ellery, **V:**470
Charlemagne, **II:**226
Charles V, **III:**159
Christopher, Saint, **I:**180
Chrysostom, Saint John, **I:**184
Clement I, **I:**210
Clement VII, **III:**166
Clovis, **II:**274
Colet, John, **III:**169
Comte, Auguste, **V:**543
Constantine the Great, **I:**226
Cotton, John, **IV:**371
Coverdale, Miles, **III:**193
Cranmer, Thomas, **III:**204
Cyril, Saint, **II:**278
David, **I:**241
Deborah, **I:**246

Denis, Saint, **I**:257
Diogenes, **I**:268
Dionysius Exiguus, **II**:298
Dominic, Saint, **II**:301
Duns Scotus, John, **II**:309
Eddy, Mary Baker, **V**:738
Edwards, Jonathan, **IV**:428
Eliade, Mircea, **VII**:1055
Elijah ben Solomon, **IV**:432
Eliot, John, **IV**:435
Elizabeth of Hungary, Saint, **II**:340
Erasmus, Desiderius, **III**:246
Eusebius of Caesarea, **I**:322
Ezekiel, **I**:326
Ezra, **I**:330
Fakhr al-Din al-Razi, **II**:347
Ferrar, Nicholas, **IV**:462
Fisher, Saint John, **III**:264
Fox, George, **IV**:484
Francis of Assisi, Saint, **II**:354
Gandhi, Mahatma, **VII**:1282
Gardiner, Stephen, **III**:291
Ghazzali, al-, **II**:385
Gibbons, James, **V**:919
Gilson, Étienne, **VII**:1374
Gioberti, Vincenzo, **V**:932
Graham, Billy, **VIII**:1447
Gregory VII, **II**:395
Gregory IX, **II**:399
Gregory of Nazianzus, **I**:349
Gregory of Nyssa, **I**:352
Gregory the Great, **II**:407
Hallaj, al-, **II**:421
Harnack, Adolf von, **VIII**:1557
Harsha, **II**:430
Hasan al-Basri, al-, **II**:440
Helena, Saint, **I**:375
Hildegard von Bingen, **II**:474
Hippolytus of Rome, **I**:415
Hsüan-tsang, **II**:482
Hung Hsiu-ch'üan, **V**:1165
Hus, Jan, **II**:487
Hutchinson, Anne, **IV**:687
Ibn al-'Arabi, **II**:491
Ignatius of Antioch, **I**:440
Innocent III, **II**:509
Innocent IV, **II**:514
Irenaeus, Saint, **I**:447
Isaiah, **I**:452
Isidore of Seville, Saint, **II**:518
James, William, **V**:1216
Jansen, Cornelius Otto, **IV**:707

Jeremiah, **I**:459
Jesus Christ, **I**:467
Jiménez de Cisneros, Francisco, **III**:392
Joachim of Fiore, **II**:534
Joan of Arc, **III**:396
Johanan ben Zakkai, **I**:471
John of Damascus, **II**:544
John of the Cross, Saint, **III**:401
John the Apostle, **I**:475
John the Baptist, **I**:479
Julius II, **III**:405
Kanishka, **I**:494
Khomeini, Ruhollah, **VIII**:1957
Kierkegaard, Søren, **VI**:1284
Las Casas, Bartolomé de, **III**:413
László I, Saint, **II**:574
Latimer, Hugh, **III**:416
Laud, William, **IV**:797
Laval, François, **IV**:801
Lee, Ann, **IV**:817
Leo IX, **II**:581
Leo X, **III**:419
Leo XIII, **VI**:1347
Lewis, C.S., **VIII**:2167
Livingstone, David, **VI**:1399
Louis IX, **II**:603
Loyola, Saint Ignatius of, **III**:437
Lull, Raymond, **II**:608
Luria, Isaac ben Solomon, **III**:440
Luther, Martin, **III**:443
Maimonides, Moses, **II**:619
Manning, Henry Edward, **VI**:1476
Maritain, Jacques, **VIII**:2425
Mather, Cotton, **IV**:934
Mather, Increase, **IV**:938
Maurice, Frederick Denison, **VI**:1503
Melanchthon, Philipp, **III**:503
Menander, **I**:541
Menno Simons, **III**:510
Mersenne, Marin, **IV**:949
Methodius, Saint, **II**:278
Moody, Dwight L., **VI**:1575
More, Sir Thomas, **III**:533
Mornay, Philippe de, **III**:537
Moses de León, **II**:648
Moses, **I**:561
Mott, John R., **VIII**:2637
Muhammad, **II**:651
Nānak, **III**:540
Napier, John, **III**:544
Neckam, Alexander, **II**:663

Nefertiti, **I:**573
Neri, Saint Philip, **III:**551
Newman, John Henry, **VI:**1641
Nichiren, **II:**666
Nicholas of Autrecourt, **II:**669
Nicholas of Cusa, **III:**563
Nicholas the Great, **II:**673
Niebuhr, Reinhold, **VIII:**2735
Nikon, **IV:**1030
Nishida, Kitaro, **VIII:**2754
Ockham, William of, **II:**681
Olaf, Saint, **II:**691
Olaf I, **II:**688
Origen, **I:**581
Parker, Matthew, **III:**588
Parker, Theodore, **VI:**1727
Pascal, Blaise, **IV:**1062
Patrick, Saint, **I:**600
Paul III, **III:**595
Paul VI, **IX:**2919
Pecham, John, **II:**715
Peter, Saint, **I:**614
Philip II, **III:**599
Pilate, Pontius, **I:**640
Pius II, **III:**613
Pius V, **III:**616
Pius IX, **VI:**1782
Pius XI, **IX:**3026
Pius XII, **IX:**3030
Planck, Max, **IX:**3033
Priestley, Joseph, **IV:**1129
Priscillian, **I:**694
Psellus, Michael, **II:**758
Pusey, E.B., **VI:**1828
Rabanus Maurus, **II:**766
Rāmānuja, **II:**770
Rasputin, Grigori Yefimovich, **VI:**1842
Ratramnus, **II:**773
Rauschenbusch, Walter, **IX:**3125
Ray, Rammohan, **VI:**1846
Raymond of Peñafort, **II:**776
Renan, Ernest, **VI:**1865
Ridley, Nicholas, **III:**654
Ritschl, Albrecht, **VI:**1892
Rumi, Jalal al-Din, **II:**800
Saladin, **II:**809
Samuel, **I:**746
Savonarola, Girolamo, **III:**667
Scheler, Max, **IX:**3347
Schleiermacher, Friedrich, **VI:**1976
Schweitzer, Albert, **IX:**3370
Sergius I, **II:**819

Sergius I, Saint, **II:**823
Servetus, Michael, **III:**675
Seton, Saint Elizabeth Ann Bayley, **VI:**2029
Sewall, Samuel, **IV:**1225
Shōtoku Taishi, **II:**826
Simeon Stylites, Saint, **I:**783
Siricius, Saint, **I:**790
Smith, Joseph, **VI:**2080
Söderblom, Nathan, **IX:**3456
Solomon, **I:**798
Stein, Edith, **IX:**3506
Stephen, Saint, **I:**822
Stephen I, **II:**851
Sunday, Billy, **IX:**3582
Swedenborg, Emanuel, **IV:**1302
Tabari, al-, **II:**873
Teilhard de Chardin, Pierre, **IX:**3626
Tekakwitha, Kateri, **IV:**1316
Teresa, Mother, **IX:**3635
Teresa of Ávila, Saint, **III:**713
Tertullian, **I:**848
Theodore of Mopsuestia, **I:**861
Theodoret of Cyrrhus, **I:**865
Theoleptus of Philadelphia, **II:**899
Thomas, Saint, **I:**880
Thomas à Kempis, **II:**906
Thomas Aquinas, Saint, **II:**911
Tillich, Paul, **IX:**3685
Torquemada, Tomás de, **III:**725
Troeltsch, Ernst, **IX:**3722
Turner, Nat, **VI:**2276
Tutu, Desmond, **IX:**3775
Tyndale, William, **III:**735
Ulfilas, **I:**908
Urban II, **II:**928
Valentinus, **I:**911
Valla, Lorenzo, **III:**739
Vardhamāna, **I:**915
Venette, Jean de, **II:**935
Vincent de Paul, Saint, **IV:**1380
Vincent of Lérins, Saint, **I:**936
Virgin Mary, **I:**939
Vitoria, Francisco de, **III:**768
Vladimir I, **II:**952
Wach, Joachim, **IX:**3829
Weil, Simone, **IX:**3922
Wesley, John, **IV:**1426
Widukind, **II:**973
Wiesel, Elie, **IX:**3980
William of Auxerre, **II:**981
William of Saint-Amour, **II:**990
William of Saint-Thierry, **II:**994

Williams, Roger, **IV:**1451
Wise, Isaac Mayer, **VI:**2400
Wise, Stephen Samuel, **IX:**4033
Witherspoon, John, **IV:**1467
Władysław II Jagiełło and Jadwiga, **II:**1001
Wyclif, John, **II:**1009
Xavier, Saint Francis, **III:**788
Xenophanes, **I:**955
Young, Brigham, **VI:**2414
Zoroaster, **I:**975
Zwingli, Huldrych, **III:**791

ROCKETRY. *See* AVIATION AND SPACE EXPLORATION

ROMAN CAESARS

Augustus, **I:**132
Caesar, Julius, **I:**147
Caligula, **I:**152
Claudius I, **I:**203
Tiberius, **I:**892
Vespasian, **I:**933

ROMAN EMPERORS

Constantine the Great, **I:**226
Diocletian, **I:**263
Hadrian, **I:**356
Justinian I, **II:**553
Marcus Aurelius, **I:**523
Nero, **I:**577
Theodosius the Great, **I:**868
Trajan, **I:**899

SAINTS

Albertus Magnus, Saint, **II:**37
Ambrose, Saint, **I:**43
Anselm, Saint, **II:**72
Anthony of Egypt, Saint, **I:**56
Anthony of Padua, Saint, **II:**76
Athanasius, Saint, **I:**119
Augustine, Saint, **I:**128
Bede the Venerable, Saint, **II:**132
Benedict of Nursia, Saint, **II:**136
Bernard of Clairvaux, Saint, **II:**143
Bonaventure, Saint, **II:**163
Boniface, Saint, **II:**167
Catherine of Siena, Saint, **II:**218
Christopher, Saint, **I:**180
Chrysostom, Saint John, **I:**184
Clement I, **I:**210
Cyril, Saint, **II:**278
Denis, Saint, **I:**257
Dominic, Saint, **II:**301
Elizabeth of Hungary, Saint, **II:**340
Francis of Assisi, Saint, **II:**354
Fulbert of Chartres, Saint, **II:**373
Gregory VII, **II:**395
Gregory of Nazianzus, **I:**349
Gregory of Nyssa, **I:**352
Gregory the Great, **II:**407
Helena, Saint, **I:**375
Henry II the Saint, **II:**449
Hildegard von Bingen, **II:**474
Hippolytus of Rome, **I:**415
Ignatius of Antioch, **I:**440
Irenaeus, Saint, **I:**447
Isidore of Seville, Saint, **II:**518
Jerome, Saint, **I:**463
John of Damascus, **II:**544
John the Apostle, **I:**475
John the Baptist, **I:**479
László I, Saint, **II:**574
Leo IX, **II:**581
Louis IX, **II:**603
Methodius, Saint, **II:**278
Nicholas the Great, **II:**673
Olaf, Saint, **II:**691
Patrick, Saint, **I:**600
Paul, Saint, **I:**604
Peter, Saint, **I:**614
Raymond of Peñafort, **II:**776
Sergius I, Saint, **II:**823
Simeon Stylites, Saint, **I:**783
Siricius, Saint, **I:**790
Stephen, Saint, **I:**822
Stephen I, **II:**851
Thomas, Saint, **I:**880
Vincent of Lérins, Saint, **I:**936
Vladimir I, **II:**952

SCHOLARSHIP. *See also* EDUCATION; HISTORIOGRAPHY

Averroës, **II:**100
Baeck, Leo, **VII:**148
Boccaccio, Giovanni, **II:**150
Evatt, Herbert Vere, **VII:**1109
Gregory IX, **II:**399
Harnack, Adolf von, **VIII:**1557
Jerome, Saint, **I:**463
Josephus, Flavius, **I:**483
Porphyry, **I:**683
Varro, Marcus Terentius, **I:**918
William of Moerbeke, **II:**985

SCIENCE. *See also* **ANTHROPOLOGY; ASTRONOMY; AVIATION AND SPACE EXPLORATION; BIOLOGY; CHEMISTRY; COMPUTER SCIENCE; ENGINEERING; GENETICS; GEOLOGY; HORTICULTURE; INVENTION AND TECHNOLOGY; MATHEMATICS; MEDICINE; METEOROLOGY; NATURAL HISTORY; OCEANOGRAPHY; ORNITHOLOGY; PHYSICS; PHYSIOLOGY; ZOOLOGY**

Abano, Pietro d', **II:**1
Abul Wefa, **II:**20
Albertus Magnus, Saint, **II:**37
Alcmaeon, **I:**34
Alhazen, **II:**63
Anaxagoras, **I:**47
Anaximander, **I:**50
Anaximenes of Miletus, **I:**53
Apollonius of Perga, **I:**72
Archimedes, **I:**76
Aretaeus of Cappadocia, **I:**81
Aristotle, **I:**94
Arnold of Villanova, **II:**79
Aryabhata, **II:**89
Asclepiades of Bithynia, **I:**101
Avicenna, **II:**106
Bacon, Roger, **II:**110
Battani, al-, **II:**121
Bell, Alexander Graham, **V:**185
Berkeley, George, **IV:**114
Biruni, al-, **II:**147
Brahmagupta, **II:**181
Bridgman, Percy Williams, **VII:**463
Buridan, Jean, **II:**194
Carver, George Washington, **VII:**602
Celsus, Aulus Cornelius, **I:**173
Conant, James Bryant, **VII:**748
Diocles of Carystus, **I:**260
Diophantus, **I:**272
Dioscorides, Pedanius, **I:**276
Empedocles, **I:**282
Erasistratus, **I:**299
Eratosthenes of Cyrene, **I:**303
Euclid, **I:**307
Eudoxus of Cnidus, **I:**310
Galen, **I:**338
Gallatin, Albert, **V:**861
Gray, Asa, **V:**979
Guy de Chauliac, **II:**414
Henry, Joseph, **V:**1093
Hero of Alexandria, **I:**387

Herophilus, **I:**398
Hipparchus, **I:**407
Hippocrates, **I:**411
Huxley, Thomas Henry, **V:**1172
Hypatia, **I:**436
Imhotep, **I:**443
Jabir ibn Hayyan, **II:**522
Jahiz, al-, **II:**526
Khwarizmi, al-, **II:**563
Leonardo of Pisa, **II:**585
Lockyer, Sir Joseph Norman, **VI:**1410
Lucretius, **I:**511
Maimonides, Moses, **II:**619
Nabu-rimanni, **I:**566
Neckam, Alexander, **II:**663
Newcomb, Simon, **VI:**1638
Omar Khayyám, **II:**695
Pappus, **I:**593
Paul of Aegina, **II:**712
Peregrinus de Maricourt, Petrus, **II:**719
Pliny the Elder, **I:**662
Powell, John Wesley, **VI:**1810
Priestley, Joseph, **IV:**1129
Ptolemy, **I:**712
Pythagoras, **I:**727
Pytheas, **I:**731
Razi, al-, **II:**779
Seaborg, Glenn Theodore, **IX:**3375
Sosigenes, **I:**811
Thales of Miletus, **I:**852
Theophrastus, **I:**873
Urey, Harold C., **IX:**3787

SCREENWRITING. *See* **FILM; TELEVISION**

SCULPTURE. *See* **ART**

SEX RESEARCH
Ellis, Havelock, **VII:**1070
Kinsey, Alfred Charles, **VIII:**1986
Stopes, Marie, **IX:**3551

SOCIAL REFORM. *See also* **CHURCH REFORM; CIVIL RIGHTS; LABOR MOVEMENT; PEACE ADVOCACY; WOMEN'S RIGHTS**
Abernathy, Ralph David, **VII:**9
Addams, Jane, **VII:**21
Adler, Felix, **V:**26
Angell, Norman, **VII:**74
Astor, Nancy, **VII:**129
Baden-Powell, Sir Robert Stephenson Smyth, **V:**105

Bakunin, Mikhail, **V**:112

Balch, Emily Greene, **VII**:160

Ball, John, **II**:114

Barton, Clara, **V**:142

Baxter, Richard, **IV**:98

Beale, Dorothea, **V**:157

Beauvoir, Simone de, **VII**:230

Bernstein, Eduard, **VII**:291

Besant, Annie, **V**:211

Bevan, Aneurin, **VII**:304

Beveridge, Lord, **VII**:308

Bondfield, Margaret, **VII**:353

Booth, William, **V**:275

Braille, Louis, **V**:303

Brandeis, Louis D., **VII**:419

Brown, John, **V**:321

Butler, R.A., **VII**:529

Buxton, Sir Thomas Fowell, **V**:378

Cabrini, Frances Xavier, **V**:386

Cassin, René, **VII**:610

Cayley, Sir George, **V**:450

Chadwick, Edwin, **V**:457

Child, Lydia Maria, **V**:489

Chomsky, Noam, **VII**:673

Constantine, Baron, **VII**:759

Day, Dorothy, **VII**:850

Dewey, John, **VII**:916

Diana, Princess of Wales, **VII**:923

Dix, Dorothea, **V**:680

Douglass, Frederick, **V**:695

Dunant, Jean-Henri, **V**:711

Engels, Friedrich, **V**:760

Fawcett, Dame Millicent Garrett, **V**:776

Fourier, Charles, **V**:814

Fuller, Margaret, **V**:849

Gandhi, Mahatma, **VII**:1282

Garrison, William Lloyd, **V**:883

George, Henry, **V**:906

Goldman, Emma, **VIII**:1411

Gorky, Maxim, **VIII**:1442

Greeley, Horace, **V**:982

Harrison, Frederic, **V**:1057

Hayslip, Le Ly, **VIII**:1593

Hernandez, Aileen Clarke, **VIII**:1641

Herzen, Aleksandr, **V**:1099

Higginson, Thomas Wentworth, **V**:1110

Hill, Octavia, **V**:1113

Howe, Julia Ward, **V**:1145

Hutchins, Robert M., **VIII**:1800

Jackson, Helen Hunt, **V**:1200

Jones, Mary Harris "Mother," 1879

Keller, Helen, **VIII**:1924

Kemble, Fanny, **VI**:1273

La Follette, Robert M., **VIII**:2047

Lange, Dorothea, **VIII**:2083

Las Casas, Bartolomé de, **III**:413

Lathrop, Julia C., **VIII**:2096

Lazarus, Emma, **VI**:1334

Lockwood, Belva A., **VI**:1406

Low, Juliette Gordon, **VIII**:2246

Lutuli, Albert, **VIII**:2281

Luxemburg, Rosa, **VIII**:2285

Mahfouz, Naguib, **VIII**:2355

Malcolm X, **VIII**:2373

Mandela, Nelson, **VIII**:2384

Mann, Horace, **IV**:894

Manning, Henry Edward, **VI**:1476

Montessori, Maria, **VIII**:2596

Mott, Lucretia, **VI**:1600

Nader, Ralph, **VIII**:2679

Nation, Carry, **VI**:1630

Niemöller, Martin, **VIII**:2742

O'Connell, Daniel, **VI**:1680

O'Higgins, Bernardo, **VI**:1688

Olmsted, Frederick Law, **VI**:1691

Osborne, Thomas Mott, **IX**:2852

Owen, Robert, **VI**:1708

Pankhurst, Emmeline, **IX**:2871

Paton, Alan, **IX**:2907

Phillips, Wendell, **VI**:1771

Picotte, Susan La Flesche, **IX**:3010

Pire, Dominique, **IX**:3017

Place, Francis, **VI**:1786

Potter, Beatrix, **IX**:3063

Rankin, Jeannette, **IX**:3117

Rauschenbusch, Walter, **IX**:3125

Ray, Rammohan, **VI**:1846

Reuther, Walter P., **IX**:3161

Robeson, Paul, **IX**:3187

Roosevelt, Eleanor, **IX**:3217

Ruskin, John, **VI**:1925

Sakharov, Andrei, **IX**:3296

Sanger, Margaret, **IX**:3313

Sartre, Jean-Paul, **IX**:3327

Sewall, Samuel, **IV**:1225

Sharp, Granville, **IV**:1236

Shaw, George Bernard, **IX**:3399

Sinclair, Upton, **IX**:3426

Smith, Alfred E., **IX**:3439

Söderblom, Nathan, **IX**:3456

Solzhenitsyn, Aleksandr, **IX**:3459

Sorel, Georges, **IX**:3463

Spock, Benjamin, **IX**:3478

Stanton, Elizabeth Cady, **VI**:2110

Stein, Freiherr vom, **VI:**2115
Stone, Lucy, **VI:**2143
Stopes, Marie, **IX:**3551
Stowe, Harriet Beecher, **VI:**2151
Suttner, Bertha von, **VI:**2175
Teresa, Mother, **IX:**3635
Theodora, **II:**890
Thomas, Norman, **IX:**3660
Tolstoy, Leo, **VI:**2242
Truth, Sojourner, **VI:**2255
Tutu, Desmond, **IX:**3775
Tyler, Wat, **II:**921
Vincent de Paul, Saint, **IV:**1380
Wakefield, Edward Gibbon, **VI:**2321
Wald, Lillian D., **IX:**3837
Washington, Booker T., **VI:**2335
Webb, Beatrice and Sidney, **IX:**3905
Wilberforce, William, **IV:**1435
Willard, Frances, **VI:**2388
Wise, Stephen Samuel, **IX:**4033
Zapata, Emiliano, **IX:**4104
Zetkin, Clara, **IX:**4112

SOCIAL SCIENCES. *See also*
    ANTHROPOLOGY; ECONOMICS;
    EDUCATION; GEOGRAPHY;
    HISTORIOGRAPHY; POLITICAL
    SCIENCE; SEX RESEARCH;
    SOCIOLOGY
Adler, Alfred, **VII:**30
Arendt, Hannah, **VII:**98
Braudel, Fernand, **VII:**436
Ellis, Havelock, **VII:**1070
Frazer, Sir James George, **VII:**1220
Kinsey, Alfred Charles, **VIII:**1986
McLuhan, Marshall, **VIII:**2332
Veblen, Thorstein, **IX:**3805

SOCIOLOGY
Comte, Auguste, **V:**543
Durkheim, Émile, **VII:**988
Hobhouse, Leonard T., **VIII:**1707
Le Bon, Gustave, **VIII:**2134
Myrdal, Gunnar, **VIII:**2671
Scheler, Max, **IX:**3347
Talbot, Marion, **IX:**3603
Tocqueville, Alexis de, **VI:**2238
Tönnies, Ferdinand Julius, **IX:**3703
Troeltsch, Ernst, **IX:**3722
Ward, Lester Frank, **VI:**2328
Webb, Beatrice and Sidney, **IX:**3905
Weber, Max, **IX:**3910

SPACE EXPLORATION. *See* **AVIATION AND**
    SPACE EXPLORATION

SPORTS
Ali, Muhammad, **VII:**53
Borg, Björn, **VII:**368
Bradman, Donald G., **VII:**407
Cobb, Ty, **VII:**717
Coe, Sebastian, **VII:**725
Constantine, Baron, **VII:**759
Coubertin, Pierre de, **VII:**774
Dempsey, Jack, **VII:**900
Dimaggio, Joe, **VII:**934
Evert, Chris, **VII:**1112
Ferrari, Enzo, **VII:**1150
Gehrig, Lou, **VII:**1322
Gibson, Althea, **VII:**1363
Grace, William Gilbert, **V:**971
Henie, Sonja, **VIII:**1629
Jones, Bobby, **VIII:**1874
Killy, Jean-Claude, **VIII:**1965
King, Billie Jean, **VIII:**1968
Laver, Rod, **VIII:**2109
Louis, Joe, **VIII:**2241
Marciano, Rocky, **VIII:**2411
Messner, Reinhold, **VIII:**2506
Navratilova, Martina, **VIII:**2702
Oakley, Annie, **VI:**1677
Oh, Sadaharu, **IX:**2796
Owens, Jesse, **IX:**2862
Pelé, **IX:**2950
Perry, Fred, **IX:**2979
Player, Gary, **IX:**3040
Robinson, Jackie, **IX:**3193
Rose, Pete, **IX:**3239
Russell, Bill, **IX:**3268
Ruth, Babe, **IX:**3273
Thorpe, Jim, **IX:**3672
Wightman, Hazel Hotchkiss, **IX:**3989
Woods, Tiger, **IX:**4049
Zaharias, "Babe" Didrikson, **IX:**4096

STATECRAFT. *See* **DIPLOMACY;**
    GOVERNMENT AND POLITICS;
    WARFARE AND CONQUEST

STATISTICS
Galton, Francis, **V:**867

SUFFRAGE. *See* **WOMEN'S RIGHTS**

SWIMMING. *See* **SPORTS**

TECHNOLOGY. *See* **INVENTION AND TECHNOLOGY**

TELEVISION. *See also* **THEATER AND ENTERTAINMENT**
Ball, Lucille, **VII:**176
Collins, Norman, **VII:**737
Disney, Walt, **VII:**938
Winfrey, Oprah, **IX:**4029
Zworykin, Vladimir, **IX:**4125

TENNIS. *See* **SPORTS**

THEATER AND ENTERTAINMENT. *See also* **LITERATURE; MUSIC**
Aeschylus, **I:**9
Akalaitis, Joanne, **VII:**34
Aristophanes, **I:**88
Barnum, P.T., **V:**133
Beatles, The, **VII:**226
Beaumont, Francis, **III:**54
Beckett, Samuel, **VII:**238
Bergman, Ingmar, **VII:**278
Booth, Edwin, **V:**271
Brando, Marlon, **VII:**424
Burnett, Frances Hodgson, **V:**361
Calderón de la Barca, Pedro, **IV:**235
Chapman, George, **III:**155
Chekhov, Anton, **V:**485
Cody, William Frederick, **V:**530
Corneille, Pierre, **IV:**363
Coward, Noël, **VII:**783
Crawford, Cheryl, **VII:**793
Davis, Bette, **VII:**843
Disney, Walt, **VII:**938
Dumas, Alexandre, *père*, **V:**708
Euripides, **I:**317
Fletcher, John, **III:**54
Forrest, Edwin, **V:**800
Garland, Judy, **VII:**1304
Garrick, David, **IV:**527
Geddes, Norman Bel, **VII:**1319
Gilbert, W.S., **V:**927
Gish, Lillian, **VII:**1383
Goethe, Johann Wolfgang von, **IV:**560
Hammerstein, Oscar, II, **VIII:**1533
Harsha, **II:**430
Hart, Lorenz, **VIII:**1566
Hayes, Helen, **VIII:**1588
Hellman, Lillian, **VIII:**1620
Ibsen, Henrik, **V:**1175
Irving, Henry, **V:**1187

Jonson, Ben, **IV:**744
Kean, Edmund, **VI:**1259
Kemble, Fanny, **VI:**1273
Kleist, Heinrich von, **VI:**1294
Le Gallienne, Eva, **VIII:**2141
Lessing, Gotthold Ephraim, **IV:**842
Macready, William Charles, **VI:**1460
Marlowe, Christopher, **III:**471
Menander (dramatist), **I:**538
Meyerhold, Vsevolod Yemilyevich, **VIII:**2510
Miller, Arthur, **VIII:**2533
Molière, **IV:**966
Nashe, Thomas, **III:**548
Oakley, Annie, **VI:**1677
Olivier, Sir Laurence, **IX:**2808
O'Neill, Eugene, **IX:**2819
Plautus, **I:**659
Racine, Jean, **IV:**1144
Robeson, Paul, **IX:**3187
Rodgers, Richard, **IX:**3201
Rogers, Will, **IX:**3204
Schiller, Friedrich, **IV:**1217
Shakespeare, William, **III:**686
Shaw, George Bernard, **IX:**3399
Stanislavsky, Konstantin, **IX:**3486
Stewart, James, **IX:**3528
Sullivan, Sir Arthur, **V:**927
Terry, Ellen, **VI:**2215
Terry, Megan, **IX:**3642
Thespis, **I:**877
Thurber, James, **IX:**3677
Vanbrugh, Sir John, **IV:**1351
Vega Carpio, Lope de, **IV:**1361
Visconti, Luchino, **IX:**3818
Wagner, Richard, **VI:**2316
Welles, Orson, **IX:**3934
West, Mae, **IX:**3949
Wilde, Oscar, **VI:**2377
Zeami Motokiyo, **II:**1025

THEOLOGY. *See* **RELIGION AND THEOLOGY**

TRACK AND FIELD. *See* **SPORTS**

TRADE UNIONISM. *See* **LABOR MOVEMENT**

URBAN DEVELOPMENT. *See also* **ARCHITECTURE**
Burnham, Daniel Hudson, **V:**365

VIROLOGY. *See* **MEDICINE**

WARFARE AND CONQUEST. *See also* **GOVERNMENT AND POLITICS; MILITARY AFFAIRS**

'Abd al-Mu'min, **II:**4
Agesilaus II, **I:**16
Agrippa, Marcus Vipsanius, **I:**20
Alboin, **II:**41
Alcibiades, **I:**31
Alexander Nevsky, **II:**52
Alexander the Great, **I:**38
Alp Arslan, **II:**67
Antigonus I Monophthalmos, **I:**60
Antiochus the Great, **I:**63
Antony, Marc, **I:**69
Árpád, **II:**86
Ashikaga Takauji, **II:**97
Ashurnasirpal II, **I:**109
Attila, **I:**124
Boadicca, **I:**136
Bohemond I, **II:**159
Brutus, Marcus Junius, **I:**140
Caesar, Julius, **I:**147
Cassius (Longinus), **I:**159
Charlemagne, **II:**226
Charles Martel, **II:**242
Ch'in Shih Huang-ti, **I:**176
Cid, El, **II:**268
Cimon, **I:**198
Cleomenes, **I:**214
Clovis, **II:**274
Constantine the Great, **I:**226
Cyrus the Great, **I:**233
Deborah, **I:**246
Egbert, **II:**333
Epaminondas, **I:**290
Fabius Maximus, Quintus, **I:**334
Genghis Khan, **II:**376
Genseric, **I:**342
Ghazan, Mahmud, **II:**381
Hannibal, **I:**364
Harold II, **II:**426
Harsha, **II:**430
Harun al-Rashid, **II:**437
Hengist, **I:**378
Heraclius, **II:**470
James I the Conqueror, **II:**529
Khosrow I, **II:**559
Kublai Khan, **II:**566
Leonidas, **I:**501
Marius, Gaius, **I:**528

Masinissa, **I:**535
Miltiades the Younger, **I:**553
Nebuchadnezzar II, **I:**569
Odoacer, **II:**685
Olaf I, **II:**688
Osman, **II:**702
Pheidippides, **I:**621
Philip II of Macedonia, **I:**628
Piankhi, **I:**636
Pompey the Great, **I:**679
Regulus, Marcus Atilius, **I:**739
Rollo, **II:**793
Rurik, **II:**803
Sargon II, **I:**754
Scipio Aemilianus, **I:**757
Scipio Africanus, **I:**760
Seleucus I Nicator, **I:**767
Shapur II, **I:**778
Spartacus, **I:**814
Stilicho, Flavius, **I:**825
Sulla, Lucius Cornelius, **I:**833
Tancred, **II:**887
Themistocles, **I:**857
Trajan, **I:**899
Valdemar II, **II:**932
Vercingetorix, **I:**922
Villehardouin, Geoffroi de, **II:**942
Vladimir I, **II:**952
Wallace, Sir William, **II:**955
Widukind, **II:**973
Xerxes I, **I:**962
Yo Fei, **II:**1018
Žižka, Count Jan, **II:**1030

WOMEN'S RIGHTS. *See also* **SOCIAL REFORM**

Adams, Abigail, **IV:**12
Anthony, Susan B., **V:**61
Beauvoir, Simone de, **VII:**230
Beecher, Catharine, **V:**170
Catt, Carrie Chapman, **VII:**627
Fawcett, Dame Millicent Garrett, **V:**776
Fowler, Lydia Folger, **V:**822
Friedan, Betty, **VII:**1231
Halide Edib Adivar, **VIII:**1522
Hernandez, Aileen Clarke, **VIII:**1641
Higginson, Thomas Wentworth, **V:**1110
Kirkpatrick, Jeane, **VIII:**1994
Lockwood, Belva A., **VI:**1406
MacKinnon, Catharine A., **VIII:**2325
Millett, Kate, **VIII:**2536

Montagu, Mary Wortley, **IV:**983
Mott, Lucretia, **VI:**1600
Naidu, Sarojini, **VIII:**2683
Paul, Alice, **IX:**2915
Shaw, Anna Howard, **VI:**2044
Stanton, Elizabeth Cady, **VI:**2110
Stein, Edith, **IX:**3506
Steinem, Gloria, **IX:**3519
Stone, Lucy, **VI:**2143
Stowe, Harriet Beecher, **VI:**2151
Talbot, Marion, **IX:**3603
Theodora, **II:**890
Wells-Barnett, Ida B., **IX:**3941
Willard, Frances, **VI:**2388

Wollstonecraft, Mary, **IV:**1475
Workman, Fanny Bullock, **VI:**2410
Zetkin, Clara, **IX:**4112

ZOOLOGY. *See also* **NATURAL HISTORY**
Cousteau, Jacques-Yves, **VII:**778
Frisch, Karl von, **VII:**1235
Haeckel, Ernst, **V:**1018
Kinsey, Alfred Charles, **VIII:**1986
Krogh, August, **VIII:**2027
Lankester, Sir Edwin Ray, **VI:**1316
Lorenz, Konrad, **VIII:**2238
Malpighi, Marcello, **IV:**891
Weismann, August, **VI:**2348

GEOGRAPHICAL LOCATION INDEX

AFRICA. *See* ALEXANDRIA; ALGERIA;
CARTHAGE; EAST AFRICA; EGYPT;
ETHIOPIA; GABON; GHANA; GUINEA;
IVORY COAST; KENYA; LIBERIA;
LIBYA; MALI; MOROCCO;
MOZAMBIQUE; NIGERIA; NORTH
AFRICA; NUMIDIA; OTTOMAN
EMPIRE; SENEGAL; SONGHAI EMPIRE;
SOUTH AFRICA; TANZANIA; TUNISIA;
WEST AFRICA; ZAIRE; ZIMBABWE;
ZULU EMPIRE

ALEXANDRIA. *See also* **EGYPT**
Athanasius, Saint, **I:**119
Callimachus, **I:**156
Ctesibius of Alexandria, **I:**231
Eratosthenes of Cyrene, **I:**303
Hero of Alexandria, **I:**387
Herophilus, **I:**398
Hypatia, **I:**436
Origen, **I:**581
Pappus, **I:**593
Philo of Alexandria, **I:**632
Ptolemy, **I:**712
Ptolemy Philadelphus, **I:**716
Ptolemy Soter, **I:**720
Valentinus, **I:**911

ALGERIA. *See also* **OTTOMAN EMPIRE**
Abbas, Ferhat, **VII:**5

ARABIA. *See also* **ASSYRIA; IRAN; IRAQ;**
MESOPOTAMIA; SYRIA
Alp Arslan, **II:**67
Hasan al-Basri, al-, **II:**440
Lucian, **I:**507
Muhammad, **II:**651

ARGENTINA
Borges, Jorge Luis, **VII:**371
Guevara, Che, **VIII-**1494
Houssay, Bernardo Alberto, **VIII:**1759
Perón, Eva, **IX:**2965
Perón, Juan, **IX:**2969
San Martín, José de, **VI:**1947

ARMENIA
Tigranes the Great, **I:**896

ASIA. *See* ARABIA; ARMENIA; ASIA
MINOR; ASSYRIA; BABYLONIA;
BITHYNIA; BURMA; BYZANTINE
EMPIRE; CAMBODIA; CAPPADOCIA;
CENTRAL ASIA; CHINA; CILICIA;
INDIA; INDONESIA; IRAN; IRAQ;
ISRAEL; JAPAN; JORDAN; KHWARIZM;
KOREA; MESOPOTAMIA;
MOPSUESTIA; OTTOMAN EMPIRE;
PAKISTAN; PERGA; PHILIPPINES;
PONTUS; RUSSIA; SINGAPORE;
SOVIET UNION; SYRIA; TAIWAN;
TURKEY; VIETNAM

ASIA MINOR. *See also* **ASSYRIA;**
BITHYNIA; CAPPADOCIA; CILICIA;
CNIDUS; COS; GREECE; MILUTUS;
MOPSUESTIA; PERGA; PONTUS
Anaxagoras, **I:**47
Aspasia, **I:**115
Christopher, Saint, **I:**180
Diogenes, **I:**268
Galen, **I:**338
Helena, Saint, **I:**375
Herodotus, **I:**394
Homer, **I:**420
Irenaeus, Saint, **I:**447
Osman, **II:**702
Rumi, Jalal al-Din, **II:**800
Theoleptus of Philadelphia, **II:**899

ASSYRIA
Ashurbanipal, **I:**105
Ashurnasirpal II, **I:**109
Sargon II, **I:**754

AUSTRALIA
Barton, Sir Edmund, **V:**147
Bradman, Donald G., **VII:**407
Bragg, Sir Lawrence, **VII:**410
Burnet, Sir Macfarlane, **VII:**512
Curtin, John, **VII:**816
Deakin, Alfred, **V:**630
Eccles, Sir John Carew, **VII:**1008
Evatt, Herbert Vere, **VII:**1109
Florey, Baron, **VII:**1172
Greenway, Francis, **V:**990
Hughes, William Morris, **VIII:**1775

Laver, Rod, **VIII:**2109
Lyons, Dame Enid Muriel, **VIII:**2289
Lyons, Joseph Aloysius, **VIII:**2292
Mannix, Daniel, **VI:**1480
Menzies, Robert Gordon, **VIII:**2497
Parkes, Sir Henry, **VI:**1731
Wentworth, W.C., **VI:**2355
Wilkins, Sir George Hubert, **IX:**3999

AUSTRIA
Adler, Alfred, **VII:**30
Berg, Alban, **VII:**271
Beust, Friedrich von, **V:**222
Breuer, Josef, **VII:**452
Bruckner, Anton, **V:**331
Buber, Martin, **VII:**483
Ehrenfels, Christian Von, **VII:**1026
Ehrlich, Eugen, **VII:**1029
Ferdinand II, **IV:**450
Fischer von Erlach, Johann Bernhard,
    IV:473
Francis Ferdinand, **VII:**1197
Francis Joseph I, **V:**829
Freud, Sigmund, **VII:**1224
Gluck, Christoph, **IV:**549
Haydn, Franz Joseph, **IV:**639
Hildebrandt, Johann Lucas von, **IV:**655
Joseph II, **IV:**750
Kafka, Franz, **VIII:**1900
Karajan, Herbert von, **VIII:**1910
Kokoschka, Oskar, **VIII:**2012
Lang, Fritz, **VIII:**2077
Leopold I, **IV:**838
Lorenz, Konrad, **VIII:**2238
Mahler, Gustav, **VIII:**2359
Maria Theresa, **IV:**914
Marie-Antoinette, **IV:**918
Maximilian I, **III:**491
Meitner, Lise, **VIII:**2476
Mendel, Gregor Johann, **VI:**1526
Metternich, **VI:**1544
Mozart, Wolfgang Amadeus, **IV:**1003
Schoenberg, Arnold, **IX:**3357
Schrödinger, Erwin, **IX:**3362
Schubert, Franz, **VI:**1988
Strauss, Johann, **VI:**2155
Suttner, Bertha von, **VI:**2175
Vivaldi, Antonio, **IV:**1383
Waldheim, Kurt, **IX:**3841
Wallenstein, Albrecht Wenzel von, **IV:**1396
Webern, Anton von, **IX:**3914
Wiesenthal, Simon, **IX:**3984

AUSTRO-HUNGARIAN EMPIRE. *See*
    AUSTRIA; BOHEMIA; DALMATIA;
    HUNGARY

AZERBAIJAN
Landau, Lev Davidovich, **VIII:**2073

BABYLONIA
Abraham, **I:**5
Hammurabi, **I:**360
Nabu-rimanni, **I:**566
Nebuchadnezzar II, **I:**569

BAVARIA. *See* **GERMANY**

BELGIUM
Bruegel, Pieter, the Elder, **III:**85
Eyck, Jan van, and Hubert van Eyck, **III:**250
La Fontaine, Henri-Marie, **VIII:**2051
Lemaître, Georges, **VIII:**2157
Lévi-Strauss, Claude, **VIII:**2164
Magritte, René, **VIII:**2349
Mercator, Gerardus, **III:**513
Pire, Dominique, **IX:**3017
Pirenne, Henri, **IX:**3023
Rubens, Peter Paul, **IV:**1198
Spaak, Paul-Henri, **IX:**3475
Vesalius, Andreas, **III:**754
Weyden, Rogier van der, **III:**778

BELORUSSIA
Chagall, Marc, **VII:**639

BERMERSHEIM BEI ALZEY. *See* **GERMANY**

BITHYNIA
Asclepiades of Bithynia, **I:**101
Hipparchus, **I:**407

BOHEMIA. *See also* **CZECHOSLOVIA;**
    GERMANY
Dvořák, Antonín, **V:**725

BOSNIA-HERZEGOVINA. *See*
    YUGOSLAVIA

BRAZIL
Machado de Assis, Joaquim Maria, **VI:**1444
Niemeyer, Oscar, **VIII:**2739
Pelé, **IX:**2950
Santos-Dumont, Alberto, **IX:**3320
Villa-Lobos, Heitor, **IX:**3815

BRITAIN. *See also* **GREAT BRITAIN**
Boadicca, **I:**136
Hengist, **I:**378
Patrick, Saint, **I:**600

BULGARIA
Boris I of Bulgaria, **II:**175

BURMA
Thant, U, **IX:**3646

BYZANTINE EMPIRE
Constantine the Great, **I:**226
Cyril, Saint, **II:**278
Gregory of Nyssa, **I:**352
Heraclius, **II:**470
Justinian I, **II:**553
Methodius, Saint, **II:**278
Paul of Aegina, **II:**712
Priscian, **II:**755
Proclus, **I:**698
Psellus, Michael, **II:**758
Sergius I, **II:**819
Stilicho, Flavius, **I:**825
Theodora, **II:**890
Theophanes the Confessor, **II:**903
Ulfilas, **I:**908

CAMBODIA
Sihanouk, Norodom, **IX:**3417

CANAAN. *See* **ISRAEL**

CANADA
Baldwin, Robert, **V:**116
Banting, Sir Frederick Grant, **VII:**187
Borden, Robert Laird, **VII:**365
Brown, George, **V:**318
Carleton, Guy, **IV:**246
Chrétien, Jean, **VII:**680
Clinton, Sir Henry, **IV:**321
Durham, First Earl of, **V:**721
Jolliet, Louis, **IV:**732
King, William Lyon Mackenzie,
    VIII:1981
Lansdowne, Fifth Marquess of,
    VIII:2090
Laurier, Sir Wilfrid, **VIII:**2100
Laval, François, **IV:**801
Macdonald, Sir John Alexander, **VI:**1435
Mackenzie, William Lyon, **VI:**1447
McLuhan, Marshall, **VIII:**2332

Massey, Vincent, **VI:**1496
Mulroney, Brian, **VIII:**2655
Osler, Sir William, **VI:**1698
Tekakwitha, Kateri, **IV:**1316
Thomson, Tom, **IX:**3665
Trudeau, Pierre Elliott, **IX:**3730

CAPPADOCIA
Aretaeus of Cappadocia, **I:**81
Gregory of Nazianzus, **I:**349
Heraclius, **II:**470

CARTHAGE
Genseric, **I:**342
Hannibal, **I:**364
Hanno, **I:**368
Masinissa, **I:**535
Tertullian, **I:**848

CENTRAL ASIA. *See also* **KHWARIZM**
Attila, **I:**124
Genghis Khan, **II:**376
Kublai Khan, **II:**570
Tamerlane, **II:**884

CHALDEA. *See* **BABYLONIA**

CHILE
Neruda, Pablo, **VIII:**2716
O'Higgins, Bernardo, **VI:**1688

CHINA. *See also* **TAIWAN**
Abahai, **IV:**1
Chang Chih-tung, **V:**466
Ch'en Tu-hsiu, **VII:**660
Cheng Ch'eng-kung, **IV:**297
Cheng Ho, **II:**253
Chiang Kai-shek, **VII:**664
Ch'ien-lung, **IV:**300
Ch'in Shih Huang-ti, **I:**176
Chou En-lai, **VII:**676
Chu Hsi, **II:**265
Chu Teh, **VII:**687
Ch'ü Yüan, **I:**187
Chuang-tzu, **I:**190
Confucius, **I:**222
Deng Xiaoping, **VII:**905
Dorgon, **IV:**421
Hsia Kuei, **II:**479
Hsieh Ling-yün, **I:**429
Hsüan-tsang, **II:**482
Hsün-tzu, **I:**433

Hung Hsiu-ch'üan, **V:**1165
K'ang-Hsi, **IV:**757
Kuo Mo-jo, **VIII:**2033
Lao-tzu, **I:**498
Li Ch'ing-chao, **II:**588
Li Hung-chang, **VI:**1362
Lin Piao, **VIII:**2189
Lin Tse-hsü, **VI:**1376
Li Peng, **VIII:**2178
Li Po, **II:**591
Liu Shao-ch'i, **VIII:**2212
Lu Hsün, **VIII:**2252
Mao Tse-tung, **VIII:**2400
Ma Yüan, **II:**612
Mencius, **I:**543
Mi Fei, **II:**639
Ou-yang Hsiu, **II:**709
Pan Ku, **I:**589
Peary, Robert Edwin, **IX:**2941
P'eng Te-huai, **IX:**2954
Ssu-ma Ch'ien, **I:**818
Ssu-ma Kuang, **II:**840
Sung Dynasty, **II:**866
Su Tung-p'o, **II:**855
Sun Yat-sen, **IX:**3578
T'ai Tsung, **II:**876
T'ao Ch'ien, **I:**841
Tseng Kuo-fan, **VI:**2260
Tu Fu, **II:**917
Wang An-shih, **II:**962
Wang Ching-wei, **IX:**3877
Wang Ch'ung, **I:**943
Wang Hsi-chih, **I:**946
Wang Pi, **I:**949
Wang Wei, **II:**965
Wang Yang-ming, **III:**771
Yen Li-pen, **II:**1015
Yo Fei, **II:**1018
Yung-lo, **II:**1021

CILICIA
Dioscorides, Pedanius, **I:**276
Paul, Saint, **I:**604

CNIDUS
Eudoxus of Cnidus, **I:**310

COLOMBIA
Bolívar, Simón, **V:**267
García Márquez, Gabriel, **VII:**1293

CONGO. *See* **ZAIRE**

COS
Hippocrates, **I:**411

CROATIA. *See* **YUGOSLAVIA**

CUBA
Castro, Fidel, **VII:**617
Guevara, Che, **VIII**-1494

CZECHOSLOVAKIA. *See also* **BOHEMIA**
Beneš, Edvard, **VII:**259
Capek, Karel, **VII:**560
Dubcek, Alexander, **VII:**968
Janácek, Leoš, **VIII:**1835
Kupka, František, **VIII:**2036
Laban, Rudolf, **VIII:**2058
Masaryk, Tomáš, **VIII:**2440
Wenceslaus, **II:**969

DALMATIA
Diocletian, **I:**263

DENMARK
Andersen, Hans Christian, **V:**58
Bering, Vitus Jonassen, **IV:**111
Bohr, Niels, **VII:**345
Brahe, Tycho, **III:**77
Dreyer, Carl Theodor, **VII:**959
Kierkegaard, Søren, **VI:**1284
Krogh, August, **VIII:**2027
Margaret of Denmark, Norway, and
    Sweden, **II:**626
Rasmussen, Knud Johan Victor, **IX:**3121
Saxo Grammaticus, **II:**815
Valdemar II, **II:**932

EAST AFRICA
Piankhi, **I:**636

EAST AFRICA PROTECTORATE. *See*
    KENYA

EAST GERMANY. *See also* **GERMANY**
Ulbricht, Walter, **IX:**3779

EGYPT. *See also* **ALEXANDRIA**
'Abduh, Muhammad, **V:**4
Akhenaton, **I:**23
Anthony of Egypt, Saint, **I:**56
Baybars I, **II:**124
Boutros-Ghali, Boutros, **VII:**399
Cleopatra VII, **I:**218

Hatshepsut, **I:**371
Imhotep, **I:**443
Mahfouz, Naguib, **VIII:**2355
Maimonides, Moses, **II:**619
Menes, **I:**547
Muhammad 'Alī Pasha, **VI:**1604
Nasser, Gamal Abdel, **VIII:**2693
Nefertiti, **I:**573
Plotinus, **I:**666
Psamtik I, **I:**709
Ramses II, **I:**734
Sadat, Anwar el-, **IX:**3289
Sesostris III, **I:**774
Thutmose III, **I:**889
Tutankhamen, **I:**904
Zaghlūl, Sa'd, **IX:**4093
Zoser, **I:**978

ELEA
Parmenides, **I:**596
Zeno of Elea, **I:**972

ENGLAND. *See also* **BRITAIN; GREAT BRITAIN**
Adrian IV, **II:**27
Alfred the Great, **II:**59
Anselm, Saint, **II:**72
Bacon, Francis, **III:**41
Bacon, Roger, **II:**110
Ball, John, **II:**114
Beaumont, Francis, **III:**54
Becket, Thomas, **II:**128
Bede the Venerable, Saint, **II:**132
Bodley, Sir Thomas, **III:**62
Boleyn, Anne, **III:**66
Bracton, Henry de, **II:**178
Burgh, Hubert de, **II:**190
Byrd, William, **III:**105
Cabot, John, **III:**113
Canute the Great, **II:**201
Catherine of Aragon, **III:**136
Cavendish, Thomas, **III:**140
Caxton, William, **III:**143
Cædmon, **II:**198
Cecil, William, **III:**147
Chapman, George, **III:**155
Chaucer, Geoffrey, **II:**248
Colet, John, **III:**169
Coverdale, Miles, **III:**193
Cranmer, Thomas, **III:**204
Cromwell, Thomas, **III:**208
Davis, John, **III:**212

Drake, Sir Francis, **III:**224
Dunstable, John, **III:**227
Edward I, **II:**322
Edward II, **II:**326
Edward III, **II:**329
Edward IV, **III:**234
Edward VI, **III:**237
Edward the Confessor, **II:**315
Edward the Elder, **II:**319
Egbert, **II:**333
Eleanor of Aquitaine, **II:**336
Elizabeth I, **III:**241
Ethelred II, the Unready, **II:**344
Fawkes, Guy, **III:**257
Fisher, Saint John, **III:**264
Fletcher, John, **III:**54
Fortescue, Sir John, **III:**267
Gardiner, Stephen, **III:**291
Grenville, Sir Richard, **III:**315
Grey, Lady Jane, **III:**318
Harold II, **II:**426
Henry I, **II:**443
Henry II, **II:**446
Henry III, **II:**453
Henry IV, **II:**457
Henry V, **III:**337
Henry VI, **III:**341
Henry VII, **III:**345
Henry VIII, **III:**349
Howard, Catherine, **III:**367
John, King, **II:**540
Latimer, Hugh, **III:**416
Littleton, Sir Thomas, **III:**431
Malory, Sir Thomas, **III:**457
Marlowe, Christopher, **III:**471
Mary, Queen of Scots, **III:**475
Mary I, **III:**479
Montfort, Simon V de, **II:**642
More, Sir Thomas, **III:**533
Nashe, Thomas, **III:**548
Ockham, William of, **II:**681
Parker, Matthew, **III:**588
Parr, Catherine, **III:**592
Pecham, John, **II:**715
Raleigh, Sir Walter, **III:**638
Richard I, **II:**782
Richard II, **II:**786
Richard III, **III:**647
Ridley, Nicholas, **III:**654
Salisbury, First Earl of, **III:**660
Shakespeare, William, **III:**686
Sidney, Sir Philip, **III:**691

Spenser, Edmund, **III**:703
Stephen, King, **II**:847
Tudor Family, The, **III**:732
Tyler, Wat, **II**:921
Tyndale, William, **III**:735
Warwick, Earl of, **III**:774
William the Conqueror, **II**:997
Wolsey, Cardinal Thomas, **III**:785
Wyclif, John, **II**:1009

ESTONIA. *See* **GERMANY; SOVIET UNION**

ETHIOPIA
Haile Selassie I, **VIII**:1517
Menelik II, **VI**:1537

FINLAND
Aalto, Alvar, **VII**:1
Mannerheim, Carl Gustaf, **VIII**:2396
Sibelius, Jean, **IX**:3413

FLANDERS. *See* **BELGIUM**

FLORENCE, REPUBIC OF. *See* **ITALY**

FRANCE
Abelard, Peter, **II**:10
Adam de la Halle, **II**:23
Alcuin, **II**:44
Alembert, Jean le Rond d', **IV**:30
Apollinaire, Guillaume, **VII**:82
Arnold of Villanova, **II**:79
Balzac, Honoré de, **V**:120
Barthes, Roland, **VII**:207
Baudelaire, Charles, **V**:150
Bayard, Chevalier de, **III**:48
Bayle, Pierre, **IV**:103
Beauvoir, Simone de, **VII**:230
Beckett, Samuel, **VII**:238
Becquerel Family, The, **V**:166
Benjamin, Walter, **VII**:267
Bergson, Henri, **VII**:283
Berlioz, Hector, **V**:202
Bernard, Claude, **V**:207
Bernard of Clairvaux, Saint, **II**:143
Bizet, Georges, **V**:244
Blanc, Louis, **V**:259
Blériot, Louis, **VII**:325
Blum, Léon, **VII**:335
Boffrand, Germain, **IV**:151
Bonnard, Pierre, **VII**:362
Bossuet, Jacques-Bénigne, **IV**:170

Bougainville, Louis-Antoine de, **IV**:179
Boulez, Pierre, **VII**:386
Braille, Louis, **V**:303
Brancusi, Constantin, **VII**:414
Braque, Georges, **VII**:431
Braudel, Fernand, **VII**:436
Breton, André, **VII**:448
Breuil, Henri-Édouard-Prosper, **VII**:456
Broglie, Louis de, **VII**:472
Buffon, Comte de, **IV**:215
Buridan, Jean, **II**:194
Calmette, Albert, **VII**:546
Calvin, John, **III**:117
Cambacérès, Jean-Jacques-Régis de, **V**:398
Camus, Albert, **VII**:553
Cartier, Jacques, **III**:129
Cartier-Bresson, Henri, **VII**:594
Cassin, René, **VII**:610
Catherine de Médicis, **III**:132
Césaire, Aimé, **VII**:631
Cézanne, Paul, **V**:453
Chagall, Marc, **VII**:639
Chanel, Coco, **VII**:648
Chardin, Jean Siméon, **IV**:275
Charlemagne, **II**:226
Charles XIV John, **V**:474
Charles d'Orléans, **II**:232
Charles Martel, **II**:242
Charles the Bald, **II**:239
Charles the Bold, **III**:163
Chartier, Alain, **II**:245
Chateaubriand, **V**:481
Chrétien de Troyes, **II**:257
Christine de Pizan, **II**:260
Citroën, André-Gustave, **VII**:695
Claude, Georges, **VII**:699
Claude Lorrain, **IV**:317
Clemenceau, Georges, **VII**:702
Clovis, **II**:274
Cocteau, Jean, **VII**:721
Colbert, Jean-Baptiste, **IV**:336
Colette, **VII**:729
Comte, Auguste, **V**:543
Condé, The Great, **IV**:341
Condillac, Étienne Bonnot de, **IV**:344
Condorcet, Marquis de, **IV**:348
Coubertin, Pierre de, **VII**:774
Couperin, François, **IV**:374
Courbet, Gustave, **V**:565
Cousteau, Jacques-Yves, **VII**:778
Curie, Pierre and Marie, **VII**:811
Cuvier, Georges, **V**:589

Cyrano de Bergerac, Savinien de, **IV**:385
Daguerre, Jacques, **V**:592
Danjon, André-Louis, **VII**:837
Danton, Georges, **IV**:393
David, Jacques-Louis, **V**:610
Debussy, Claude, **VII**:884
Degas, Edgar, **V**:641
de Gaulle, Charles, **VII**:866
Delacroix, Eugène, **V**:645
Delaunay, Robert, **VII**:888
Delibes, Léo, **V**:649
Denis, Maurice, **VII**:909
Denis, Saint, **I**:257
Derrida, Jacques, **VII**:912
Descartes, René, **IV**:403
Diderot, Denis, **IV**:412
Duchamp, Marcel, **VII**:972
Dumas, Alexandre, *père*, **V**:708
Durkheim, Émile, **VII**:988
Éluard, Paul, **VII**:1074
Ernst, Max, **VII**:1098
Faidherbe, Louis, **V**:763
Fermat, Pierre de, **IV**:458
Flaubert, Gustave, **V**:796
Fourier, Charles, **V**:814
Fourier, Joseph, **V**:819
Fragonard, Jean-Honoré, **IV**:488
France, Anatole, **V**:825
Francis I, **III**:274
Franck, César, **V**:832
Freyssinet, Eugène, **VII**:1228
Froissart, Jean, **II**:366
Fulbert of Chartres, Saint, **II**:373
Galois, Èvariste, **V**:864
Gambetta, Léon, **V**:871
Gance, Abel, **VII**:1274
Garnier, Tony, **VII**:1308
Gauguin, Paul, **V**:888
Gay-Lussac, Joseph-Louis, **V**:897
Genet, Jean, **VII**:1333
Géricault, Théodore, **V**:910
Gide, André, **VII**:1367
Gilson, Étienne, **VII**:1374
Giraudoux, Jean, **VII**:1379
Godard, Jean-Luc, **VIII**:1391
Gounod, Charles, **V**:967
Gregory of Tours, **II**:403
Gris, Juan, **VIII**-1483
Guy de Chauliac, **II**:414
Hahnemann, Samuel, **IV**:593
Hardouin-Mansart, Jules, **IV**:901
Henry IV, **III**:333

Herriot, Édouard, **VIII**:1644
Hotman, François, **III**:362
Hugo, Victor, **V**:1154
Ingres, Jean-Auguste-Dominique, **V**:1183
Ionesco, Eugène, **VIII**:1816
Jacob, François, **VIII**:1827
Janet, Pierre, **VIII**:1839
Jaurès, Jean, **V**:1221
Joan of Arc, **III**:396
Joffre, Joseph-Jacques-Césaire, **VIII**:1851
Joliot, Frédéric, and Irène Joliot-Curie, **VIII**:1870
Jolliet, Louis, **IV**:732
Joséphine, **V**:1246
Killy, Jean-Claude, **VIII**:1965
Lacan, Jacques, **VIII**:2061
La Fontaine, Jean de, **IV**:781
Lagrange, Joseph-Louis, **IV**:785
Laplace, Pierre-Simon, **VI**:1319
La Salle, Sieur de, **IV**:793
Laval, Pierre, **VIII**:2105
Lavoisier, Antoine-Laurent, **IV**:805
Leblanc, Nicolas, **IV**:813
Le Bon, Gustave, **VIII**:2134
Le Corbusier, **VIII**:2137
Léger, Fernand, **VIII**:2154
Lenoir, Étienne, **VI**:1343
Le Nôtre, André, **IV**:834
Lescot, Pierre, **III**:428
Lesseps, Ferdinand de, **VI**:1355
Lévi-Strauss, Claude, **VIII**:2164
Lifar, Serge, **VIII**:2182
Lipchitz, Jacques, **VIII**:2199
Louis IX, **II**:603
Louis XI, **III**:434
Louis XIII, **IV**:863
Louis XIV, **IV**:866
Louvois, Marquis de, **IV**:871
Lumière, Auguste and Louis, **VIII**:2276
Machaut, Guillaume de, **II**:615
Malraux, André, **VIII**:2380
Manet, Édouard, **VI**:1471
Mansart, François, **IV**:898
Marat, Jean-Paul, **IV**:910
Marcel, Gabriel, **VIII**:2407
Marguerite of Navarre, **III**:467
Marie-Antoinette, **IV**:918
Marie de France, **II**:629
Maritain, Jacques, **VIII**:2425
Matisse, Henri, **VIII**:2452
Maupassant, Guy de, **VI**:1500
Mazarin, Jules, **IV**:945
Mendès-France, Pierre, **VIII**:2491

Merleau-Ponty, Maurice, **VIII:**2500
Mersenne, Marin, **IV:**949
Messiaen, Olivier, **VIII:**2503
Michelet, Jules, **VI:**1548
Michelin, André and Édouard, **VIII:**2514
Milhaud, Darius, **VIII:**2525
Mirabeau, Comte de, **IV:**963
Mitterrand, François, **VIII:**2558
Molière, **IV:**966
Monet, Claude, **VIII:**2579
Monge, Gaspard, **IV:**975
Monnet, Jean, **VIII:**2583
Montaigne, Michel de, **III:**524
Montesquieu, **IV:**986
Montgolfier, Jacques-Étienne and
    Joseph-Michel, **IV:**995
Mornay, Philippe de, **III:**537
Muris, Johannes de, **II:**660
Napoleon I, **VI:**1616
Napoleon III, **VI:**1620
Neckam, Alexander, **II:**663
Necker, Jacques, **IV:**1016
Néel, Louis-Eugène-Félix, **VIII:**2705
Ney, Michel, **VI:**1646
Nicholas of Autrecourt, **II:**669
Niépce, Nicéphore, **VI:**1657
Nordau, Max, **VIII:**2766
Nostradamus, **III:**567
Offenbach, Jacques, **VI:**1684
Orleans, Duc d', **IV:**1048
Papin, Denis, **IV:**1059
Pascal, Blaise, **IV:**1062
Pasteur, Louis, **VI:**1744
Peregrinus de Maricourt, Petrus, **II:**719
Pérotin, **II:**723
Perret, Auguste, **IX:**2976
Pétain, Philippe, **IX:**2987
Philip II, **II:**732
Philip the Good, **II:**740
Picard, Émile, **IX:**2994
Picasso, Pablo, **IX:**2997
Pissarro, Camille, **VI:**1779
Pléiade, La, **III:**623
Poincaré, Henri, **VI:**1798
Poincaré, Raymond, **IX:**3044
Pompidou, Georges, **IX:**3052
Poulenc, Francis, **IX:**3066
Poussin, Nicolas, **IV:**1118
Proudhon, Pierre-Joseph, **VI:**1817
Proust, Marcel, **IX:**3089
Pucelle, Jean, **II:**762
Pytheas, **I:**731

Rabanus Maurus, **II:**766
Rabelais, François, **III:**633
Racine, Jean, **IV:**1144
Rameau, Jean-Philippe, **IV:**1148
Ratramnus, **II:**773
Ravel, Maurice, **IX:**3129
Redon, Odilon, **VI:**1854
Renan, Ernest, **VI:**1865
Renoir, Jean, **IX:**3157
Renoir, Pierre-Auguste, **VI:**1869
Richelieu, Cardinal de, **IV:**1165
Rimbaud, Arthur, **VI:**1886
Robespierre, **IV:**1170
Rochambeau, Comte de, **IV:**1174
Rodin, Auguste, **VI:**1900
Rollo, **II:**793
Ronsard, Pierre de, **III:**657
Rouault, Georges, **IX:**3251
Rousseau, Henri, **VI:**1921
Rousseau, Jean-Jacques, **IV:**1194
Saint-Just, Louis de, **IV:**1205
Sand, George, **VI:**1951
Sarraute, Nathalie, **IX:**3324
Sartre, Jean-Paul, **IX:**3327
Satie, Erik, **IX:**3331
Scaliger, Joseph Justus, **III:**671
Seurat, Georges, **VI:**2033
Sluter, Claus, **II:**832
Sorel, Georges, **IX:**3463
Staël, Madame de, **VI:**2092
Stendhal, **VI:**2125
Suger, **II:**859
Taine, Hippolyte-Adolphe, **VI:**2182
Talleyrand, **VI:**2185
Teilhard de Chardin, Pierre, **IX:**3626
Thiers, Adolphe, **VI:**2226
Tocqueville, Alexis de, **VI:**2238
Toulouse-Lautrec, Henri de, **VI:**2247
Toussaint-Louverture, **IV:**1338
Truffaut, François, **IX:**3736
Turgot, Anne-Robert-Jacques, **IV:**1348
Valéry, Paul, **IX:**3791
Varèse, Edgard, **IX:**3794
Vauban, Sébastien Le Prestre de, **IV:**1358
Venette, Jean de, **II:**935
Vercingetorix, **I:**922
Verne, Jules, **VI:**2303
Vigée-Lebrun, Élisabeth, **IV:**1376
Villehardouin, Geoffroi de, **II:**942
Villon, François, **III:**763
Vincent de Paul, Saint, **IV:**1380
Vincent of Beauvais, **II:**946

Vincent of Lérins, Saint, **I**:936
Vitry, Philippe de, **II**:949
Voltaire, **IV**:1392
Vuillard, Édouard, **IX**:3826
Walras, Léon, **IX**:3865
Watteau, Antoine, **IV**:1413
Weil, Simone, **IX**:3922
Wiesel, Elie, **IX**:3980
William of Auvergne, **II**:976
William of Auxerre, **II**:981
William of Moerbeke, **II**:985
William of Rubrouck, **II**:987
William of Saint-Amour, **II**:990
William of Saint-Thierry, **II**:994
Xenakis, Iannis, **IX**:4075
Zola, Émile, **VI**:2420

FRANCONIA. *See* **GERMANY**

FRENCH EQUATORIAL AFRICA. *See*
   GABON

FRENCH GUIANA
Éboué, Félix, **VII**:1004

GABON
Schweitzer, Albert, **IX**:3370

GAUL. *See* **FRANCE**

GERMANY. *See also* **EAST GERMANY;**
   WEST GERMANY
Agricola, Georgius, **III**:1
Albertus Magnus, Saint, **II**:37
Bach, Johann Sebastian, **IV**:76
Baeck, Leo, **VIII**-148
Baer, Karl Ernst von, **V**:109
Basedow, Johann Bernhard, **IV**:92
Beethoven, Ludwig van, **V**:178
Behring, Emil von, **V**:182
Benjamin, Walter, **VII**:267
Benz, Carl, **V**:199
Bergius, Friedrich, **VII**:275
Bernstein, Eduard, **VII**:291
Bessel, Friedrich Wilhelm, **V**:215
Bethe, Hans Albrecht, **VII**:300
Bismarck, Otto von, **V**:240
Blücher, Gebhard Leberecht von, **V**:263
Boas, Franz, **VII**:339
Böhme, Jakob, **IV**:154
Böll, Heinrich, **VII**:349
Bonhoeffer, Dietrich, **VII**:358

Boniface, Saint, **II**:167
Bothe, Walther, **VII**:379
Brahms, Johannes, **V**:299
Braun, Wernher von, **VII**:440
Brecht, Bertolt, **VII**:444
Bucer, Martin, **III**:101
Bülow, Bernhard von, **VII**:494
Bultmann, Rudolf, **VII**:498
Carnap, Rudolf, **VII**:582
Cassirer, Ernst, **VII**:614
Charles IV, **II**:235
Clausewitz, Carl von, **V**:503
Cohn, Ferdinand Julius, **V**:534
Copernicus, Nicolaus, **III**:176
Cranach, Lucas, the Elder, **III**:200
Daimler, Gottlieb, **V**:597
Dedekind, Richard, **V**:638
Diels, Otto Paul Hermann, **VII**:927
Diesel, Rudolf, **V**:672
Domagk, Gerhard, **VII**:951
Dürer, Albrecht, **III**:230
Eckener, Hugo, **VII**:1011
Ehrenfels, Christian Von, **VII**:1026
Ehrlich, Paul, **VII**:1032
Einstein, Albert, **VII**:1035
Elizabeth of Hungary, Saint, **II**:340
Engels, Friedrich, **V**:760
Ernst, Max, **VII**:1098
Erzberger, Matthias, **VII**:1102
Eucken, Rudolf Christoph, **VII**:1106
Fechner, Gustav Theodor, **V**:780
Fichte, Johann Gottlieb, **IV**:465
Frank, Anne, **VII**:1204
Frederick I, **IV**:497
Frederick I Barbarossa, **II**:357
Frederick the Great, **IV**:504
Frederick William, the Great Elector, **IV**:508
Frege, Gottlob, **V**:836
Frisch, Karl von, **VII**:1235
Frobenius, Leo, **VII**:1242
Froebel, Friedrich, **V**:845
Fromm, Erich, **VII**:1246
Gauss, Carl Friedrich, **V**:893
Geiger, Rudolf Oskar Robert Williams, **VII**:1326
Gneisenau, August von, **V**:940
Goebbels, Joseph, **VIII**-1404
Goethe, Johann Wolfgang von, **IV**:560
Göring, Hermann, **VIII**-1438
Gottfried von Strassburg, **II**:392
Grass, Günter, **VIII**-1463
Grimm, Jacob and Wilhelm, **V**:1006
Gropius, Walter, **VIII**-1486

Grünewald, Matthias, **III**:322

Guderian, Heinz, **VIII**-1490

Guericke, Otto von, **IV**:586

Gutenberg, Johann, **III**:328

Haber, Fritz, **VIII**:1509

Haeckel, Ernst, **V**:1018

Hahn, Otto, **VIII**:1513

Hahnemann, Samuel, **IV**:593

Hardenberg, Karl von, **V**:1033

Harnack, Adolf von, **VIII**:1557

Hartmann, Nicolai, **VIII**:1571

Hartmann von Aue, **II**:433

Hegel, Georg Wilhelm Friedrich, **V**:1080

Heidegger, Martin, **VIII**:1610

Heine, Heinrich, **V**:1085

Heinkel, Ernst Heinrich, **VIII**:1614

Heisenberg, Werner, **VIII**:1617

Helmholtz, Hermann von, **V**:1089

Henry II the Saint, **II**:449

Henry IV, **II**:461

Henry the Lion, **II**:466

Henze, Hans Werner, **VIII**:1633

Herder, Johann Gottfried, **IV**:651

Hertz, Gustav, **VIII**:1647

Hesse, Hermann, **VIII**:1650

Hildegard von Bingen, **II**:474

Himmler, Heinrich, **VIII**:1666

Hindemith, Paul, **VIII**:1670

Hindenburg, Paul Von, **VIII**:1674

Hitler, Adolf, **VIII**:1692

Holbein, Hans, the Younger, **III**:358

Holstein, Friedrich von, **V**:1130

Humboldt, Alexander von, **V**:1159

Humperdinck, Engelbert, **V**:1162

Husserl, Edmund, **VIII**:1797

Jaspers, Karl, **VIII**:1843

Kämpfer, Engelbert, **IV**:754

Kant, Immanuel, **IV**:761

Kepler, Johannes, **IV**:772

Kesselring, Albert, **VIII**:1949

Kirchner, Ernst Ludwig, **VIII**:1991

Kleist, Heinrich von, **VI**:1294

Koch, Robert, **VI**:1297

Kohl, Helmut, **VIII**:2009

Kollwitz, Käthe, **VIII**:2016

Krupp, Alfred, **VI**:1301

Laban, Rudolf, **VIII**:2058

Lang, Fritz, **VIII**:2077

Lassalle, Ferdinand, **VI**:1323

Leibniz, Gottfried Wilhelm, **IV**:829

Lessing, Gotthold Ephraim, **IV**:842

Liebig, Justus von, **VI**:1366

Liebknecht, Wilhelm, **VI**:1369

Louis II the German, **II**:599

Ludendorff, Erich, **VIII**:2265

Luther, Martin, **III**:443

Luxemburg, Rosa, **VIII**:2285

Mann, Thomas, **VIII**:2392

Marc, Franz, **VIII**:2404

Marx, Karl, **VI**:1492

Melanchthon, Philipp, **III**:503

Mendelsohn, Erich, **VIII**:2487

Mendelssohn, Felix, **VI**:1534

Mies Van Der Rohe, Ludwig, **VIII**:2520

Mommsen, Theodor, **VI**:1566

Nernst, Walther Hermann, **VIII**:2713

Nicholas of Cusa, **III**:563

Niebuhr, Barthold Georg, **VI**:1654

Niemöller, Martin, **VIII**:2742

Nietzsche, Friedrich Wilhelm, **VI**:1662

Oberth, Hermann, **IX**:2777

Odoacer, **II**:685

Ostwald, Wilhelm, **IX**:2855

Otto, Nikolaus August, **VI**:1702

Otto the Great, **II**:706

Papen, Franz von, **IX**:2876

Pauli, Wolfgang, **IX**:2923

Peter III, **IV**:1087

Philip the Good, **II**:740

Philip the Magnanimous, **III**:603

Planck, Max, **IX**:3033

Prandtl, Ludwig, **IX**:3073

Pufendorf, Samuel von, **IV**:1133

Ranke, Leopold von, **VI**:1839

Remarque, Erich Maria, **IX**:3150

Rilke, Rainer Maria, **IX**:3181

Ritschl, Albrecht, **VI**:1892

Rommel, Erwin, **IX**:3213

Rothschild Family, The, **VI**:1916

Rudolf I, **II**:796

Rundstedt, Gerd von, **IX**:3260

Sachs, Nelly, **IX**:3285

Savigny, Friedrich Karl von, **VI**:1966

Scharnhorst, Gerhard Johann David von, **VI**:1969

Scheler, Max, **IX**:3347

Schelling, Friedrich Wilhelm Joseph, **VI**:1972

Schleiermacher, Friedrich, **VI**:1976

Schliemann, Heinrich, **VI**:1980

Schmidt, Bernhard Voldemar, **IX**:3351

Schmidt-Rottluff, Karl, **IX**:3354

Schopenhauer, Arthur, **VI**:1984

Schumann, Robert, **VI**:1992

Schütz, Heinrich, **IV**:1221

Schwarzschild, Karl, **IX**:3366

Schweitzer, Albert, **IX:**3370
Seeckt, Hans von, **IX:**3380
Siemens Family, The, **VI:**2066
Stahl, Georg Ernst, **IV:**1268
Stark, Johannes, **IX:**3490
Staudinger, Hermann, **IX:**3497
Stein, Edith, **IX:**3506
Stein, Freiherr vom, **VI:**2115
Stockhausen, Karlheinz, **IX:**3541
Strauss, Richard, **IX:**3555
Stresemann, Gustav, **IX:**3563
Telemann, Georg Philipp, **IV:**1319
Thomas à Kempis, **II:**906
Tillich, Paul, **IX:**3685
Tirpitz, Alfred von, **IX:**3688
Tönnies, Ferdinand Julius, **IX:**3703
Troeltsch, Ernst, **IX:**3722
Virchow, Rudolf, **VI:**2312
Wach, Joachim, **IX:**3829
Wagner, Richard, **VI:**2316
Walther von der Vogelweide, **II:**959
Wankel, Felix, **IX:**3881
Weber, Carl Maria von, **VI:**2340
Weber, Max, **IX:**3910
Wegener, Alfred, **IX:**3918
Weill, Kurt, **IX:**3926
Weismann, August, **VI:**2348
Wertheimer, Max, **IX:**3945
Widukind, **II:**973
William II, **IX:**4003
Winckelmann, Johann Joachim, **IV:**1460
Wöhler, Friedrich, **VI:**2403
Wolf, Max, **IX:**4039
Wolfram von Eschenbach, **II:**1005
Wundt, Wilhelm, **IX:**4069
Zeppelin, Ferdinand von, **IX:**4108
Zetkin, Clara, **IX:**4112
Zinzendorf, Graf von, **IV:**1488
Žižka, Count Jan, **II:**1030

GHANA
Nkrumah, Kwame, **VIII:**2762

GOLD COAST. *See* **GHANA**

GREAT BRITAIN. *See also* **BRITAIN;**
ENGLAND; IRELAND; SCOTLAND;
WALES
Acton, Lord, **V:**10
Adam, James and Robert, **IV:**7
Addison, Joseph, **IV:**26
Alanbrooke, First Viscount, **VII:**45

Allenby, Lord, **VII:**58
Amherst, Lord, **IV:**37
André, John, **IV:**42
Andrewes, Lancelot, **IV:**46
Angell, Norman, **VII:**74
Anne, Queen, **IV:**50
Anson, Lord, **IV:**55
Arkwright, Richard, **IV:**59
Arnold, Matthew, **V:**69
Arnold, Thomas, **V:**74
Asquith, H.H., **VII:**121
Astor, Nancy, **VII:**129
Attlee, Clement, **VII:**137
Austen, Jane, **V:**90
Babbage, Charles, **V:**101
Bacon, Nathaniel, **IV:**80
Baden-Powell, Sir Robert Stephenson Smyth, **V:**105
Baldwin, Stanley, **VII:**168
Balfour, Arthur, **VII:**172
Banks, Sir Joseph, **IV:**83
Barry, Sir Charles, **V:**138
Baskerville, John, **IV:**95
Baxter, Richard, **IV:**98
Bayliss, Sir William Maddock, **VII:**217
Beale, Dorothea, **V:**157
Beardsley, Aubrey, **V:**161
Beatles, The, **VII:**226
Beaverbrook, Lord, **VII:**234
Bentham, Jeremy, **IV:**107
Besant, Annie, **V:**211
Bessemer, Sir Henry, **V:**218
Bevan, Aneurin, **VII:**304
Beveridge, Lord, **VII:**308
Bevin, Ernest, **VII:**313
Biddle, John, **IV:**126
Blackstone, William, **IV:**129
Blake, Robert, **IV:**132
Blake, William, **IV:**137
Bligh, William, **IV:**143
Bolingbroke, First Viscount, **IV:**157
Bondfield, Margaret, **VII:**353
Booth, William, **V:**275
Bottomley, Horatio W., **VII:**382
Boulton, Matthew, **IV:**182
Boyle, Robert, **IV:**185
Bradley, F.H., **V:**290
Bright, John, **V:**306
Brindley, James, **IV:**201
Britten, Benjamin, **VII:**466
Brontë Sisters, The, **V:**310
Brown, Lancelot, **IV:**204
Browning, Elizabeth Barrett, **V:**327

Brunel, Isambard Kingdom, **V:**335
Brunel, Marc Isambard, **V:**339
Buckingham, First Duke of, **IV:**211
Bunyan, John, **IV:**218
Burke, Edmund, **IV:**222
Burnett, Frances Hodgson, **V:**361
Burney, Charles, **IV:**226
Burton, Sir Richard Francis, **V:**374
Butler, R.A., **VII:**529
Buxton, Sir Thomas Fowell, **V:**378
Byron, Lord, **V:**381
Canning, George, **V:**405
Carleton, Guy, **IV:**246
Carlyle, Thomas, **V:**416
Carroll, Lewis, **V:**425
Castlereagh, Viscount, **V:**438
Cavendish, Henry, **IV:**261
Cayley, Sir George, **V:**450
Chadwick, Edwin, **V:**457
Chadwick, James, **VII:**635
Chamberlain, Joseph, **V:**462
Chamberlain, Neville, **VII:**643
Chaplin, Charles, **VII:**653
Charles I, **IV:**279
Charles II, **IV:**283
Christie, Agatha, **VII:**683
Churchill, Sir Winston, **VII:**691
Clarendon, First Earl of, **IV:**308
Clinton, Sir Henry, **IV:**321
Clive, Robert, **IV:**325
Cobbett, William, **V:**522
Cobden, Richard, **V:**526
Coe, Sebastian, **VII:**725
Coke, Sir Edward, **IV:**329
Coleridge, Samuel Taylor, **V:**537
Collins, Norman, **VII:**737
Conrad, Joseph, **VII:**753
Constable, John, **V:**547
Cook, Captain James, **IV:**351
Cooke, William Fothergill, **V:**555
Cornwallis, First Marquess, **IV:**367
Coward, Noël, **VII:**783
Crick, Francis, **VII:**797
Cromwell, Oliver, **IV:**378
Curzon, Lord, **VII:**819
Dalton, John, **V:**602
Dampier, William, **IV:**389
Darby, Abraham, **IV:**396
Darwin, Charles, **V:**606
Davy, Sir Humphry, **V:**621
Defoe, Daniel, **IV:**399
Delius, Frederick, **VII:**892

Derby, Fourteenth Earl of, **V:**652
Diana, Princess of Wales, **VII:**923
Dickens, Charles, **V:**663
Disraeli, Benjamin, **V:**675
Donne, John, **IV:**416
Doyle, Sir Arthur Conan, **V:**700
Dryden, John, **IV:**424
Durham, First Earl of, **V:**721
Eden, Anthony, **VII:**1015
Edward VII, **VII:**1020
Elgar, Sir Edward, **VII:**1051
Eliot, George, **V:**751
Eliot, John, **IV:**435
Eliot, T.S., **VII:**1058
Elizabeth II, **VII:**1062
Ellis, Havelock, **VII:**1070
Epstein, Sir Jacob, **VII:**1087
Fairfax, Third Baron, **IV:**446
Faraday, Michael, **V:**767
Fawcett, Dame Millicent Garrett, **V:**776
Ferrar, Nicholas, **IV:**462
Fielding, Henry, **IV:**469
Fonteyn, Dame Margot, **VII:**1175
Forester, C.S., **VII:**1189
Forster, E.M., **VII:**1193
Forster, William Edward, **V:**804
Fox, Charles James, **IV:**479
Fox, George, **IV:**484
Fry, Roger, **VII:**1253
Gage, Thomas, **IV:**511
Gainsborough, Thomas, **IV:**515
Galton, Francis, **V:**867
Garrick, David, **IV:**527
George I, **IV:**531
George II, **IV:**535
George III, **IV:**539
George IV, **V:**902
George V, **VII:**1339
George VI, **VII:**1343
Gibbon, Edward, **IV:**545
Gilbert, W.S., **V:**927
Gladstone, William Ewart, **V:**935
Godolphin, First Earl of, **IV:**552
Godwin, William, **IV:**555
Goldie, Sir George, **V:**953
Goldsmith, Oliver, **IV:**564
Gordon, Charles George, **V:**964
Grace, William Gilbert, **V:**971
Green, Thomas Hill, **V:**987
Greene, Graham, **VIII-**1467
Grey, Second Earl, **V:**994
Grey, Sir George Edward, **V:**998

Grove, Sir William Robert, **V:**1010
Hadfield, Sir Robert Abbott, **V:**1015
Hale, Matthew, **IV:**596
Halley, Edmond, **IV:**600
Handel, George Frideric, **IV:**619
Hardy, Thomas, **V:**1040
Hargreaves, James, **IV:**623
Harmsworth, Alfred and Harold, **VIII:**1554
Harrison, Frederic, **V:**1057
Harvey, William, **IV:**626
Hastings, Warren, **IV:**631
Hawking, Stephen W., **VIII:**1580
Hawksmoor, Nicholas, **IV:**635
Heath, Edward, **VIII:**1606
Hill, Octavia, **V:**1113
Hitchcock, Alfred, **VIII:**1687
Hobbes, Thomas, **IV:**662
Hobhouse, Leonard T., **VIII:**1707
Hockney, David, **VIII:**1711
Hogarth, William, **IV:**668
Hounsfield, Godfrey Newbold, **VIII:**1751
Howe, Admiral Richard, **IV:**672
Howe, General William, **IV:**676
Hudson, Henry, **IV:**680
Hunt, William Holman, **V:**1168
Huxley, Aldous, **VIII:**1804
Huxley, Thomas Henry, **V:**1172
Irving, Henry, **V:**1187
James I, **IV:**699
James II, **IV:**703
Jenner, Edward, **IV:**721
John, Augustus, **VIII:**1854
Johnson, Samuel, **IV:**728
Jones, Inigo, **IV:**735
Jonson, Ben, **IV:**744
Kay, John, **IV:**769
Kay-Shuttleworth, First Baronet, **VIII:**1917
Kean, Edmund, **VI:**1259
Keats, John, **VI:**1264
Keynes, John Maynard, **VIII:**1952
Kidd, William, **IV:**777
Kipling, Rudyard, **VI:**1288
Kitchener, Lord, **VIII:**2002
Lambert, John, **IV:**789
Lancaster, Joseph, **VI:**1309
Lanchester, Frederick William, **VIII:**2069
Lankester, Sir Edwin Ray, **VI:**1316
Lansdowne, Fifth Marquess of, **VIII:**2090
Laski, Harold J., **VIII:**2093
Laud, William, **IV:**797
Law, Bonar, **VIII:**2112
Lawrence, First Baron, **VI:**1331
Lawrence, D.H., **VIII:**2115
Lawrence, T.E., **VIII:**2125
Lawrence, Sir Thomas, **IV:**808
Leeds, First Duke of, **IV:**821
Lewis, C.S., **VIII:**2167
Lister, Joseph, **VI:**1388
Liverpool, Second Earl of, **VI:**1395
Lloyd George, David, **VIII:**2216
Locke, John, **IV:**854
Lockyer, Sir Joseph Norman, **VI:**1410
Lugard, Lord, **VIII:**2269
Lyell, Sir Charles, **VI:**1418
Macaulay, Thomas Babington, **VI:**1427
MacDonald, Ramsay, **VIII:**2312
Mackinder, Sir Halford John, **VIII:**2321
MacMillan, Daniel and Alexander, **VI:**1457
Macmillan, Harold, **VIII:**2340
Macready, William Charles, **VI:**1460
Major, John, **VIII:**2369
Malthus, Thomas Robert, **VI:**1467
Manning, Henry Edward, **VI:**1476
Mansfield, First Earl of, **IV:**904
Marlborough, First Duke of, **IV:**922
Maurice, Frederick Denison, **VI:**1503
Melbourne, Second Viscount, **VI:**1517
Mill, James, **VI:**1556
Mill, John Stuart, **VI:**1559
Milne, A.A., **VIII:**2543
Milton, John, **IV:**958
Monck, George, **IV:**971
Monmouth, Duke of, **IV:**980
Montagu, Mary Wortley, **IV:**983
Montgomery, Bernard Law, **VIII:**2601
Moore, G.E., **VIII:**2605
Moore, Henry, **VIII:**2609
Morris, William, **VI:**1588
Mountbatten, Louis, **VIII:**2641
Murdock, William, **IV:**1008
Nash, John, **IV:**1012
Nash, Paul, **VIII:**2689
Nelson, Lord, **VI:**1634
Newbery, John, **IV:**1019
Newcomen, Thomas, **IV:**1022
Newman, John Henry, **VI:**1641
Newton, Sir Isaac, **IV:**1025
Nicholson, Ben, **VIII:**2732
Nightingale, Florence, **VI:**1667
North, Lord, **IV:**1034
Oates, Titus, **IV:**1038
O'Connor, Thomas Power, **IX:**2793
Olivier, Sir Laurence, **IX:**2808
Orwell, George, **IX:**2846

Outram, Sir James, **VI:**1705
Palmerston, Lord, **VI:**1719
Pankhurst, Emmeline, **IX:**2871
Pater, Walter, **VI:**1749
Paterson, William, **IV:**1066
Pavlova, Anna, **IX:**2937
Peel, Sir Robert, **VI:**1752
Pelham, Henry, **IV:**1074
Perry, Fred, **IX:**2979
Phillip, Arthur, **IV:**1091
Pitt the Elder, William, **IV:**1098
Pitt the Younger, William, **IV:**1102
Place, Francis, **VI:**1786
Pope, Alexander, **IV:**1115
Potter, Beatrix, **IX:**3063
Pride, Thomas, **IV:**1126
Priestley, Joseph, **IV:**1129
Pugin, Augustus Welby Northmore, **VI:**1821
Purcell, Henry, **IV:**1137
Pusey, E.B., **VI:**1828
Pym, John, **IV:**1141
Reynolds, Sir Joshua, **IV:**1160
Rhodes, Cecil, **VI:**1873
Ricardo, David, **VI:**1878
Rodney, George, **IV:**1178
Roebuck, John, **IV:**1182
Rolls, Charles Stewart, **IX:**3209
Romney, George, **IV:**1187
Ross, Sir James Clark, **VI:**1907
Ross, Ronald, **IX:**3247
Royce, Sir Frederick Henry, **IX:**3209
Ruskin, John, **VI:**1925
Russell, Lord John, **VI:**1930
Salisbury, Third Marquess of, **VI:**1943
Scott, Sir George Gilbert, **VI:**2002
Shaftesbury, First Earl of, **IV:**1228
Sharp, Granville, **IV:**1236
Shaw, George Bernard, **IX:**3399
Shelley, Mary Wollstonecraft, **VI:**2048
Shelley, Percy Bysshe, **VI:**2052
Sidgwick, Henry, **VI:**2062
Slim, First Viscount, **IX:**3435
Speke, John Hanning, **VI:**2083
Spencer, Herbert, **VI:**2086
Stanhope, First Earl, **IV:**1277
Starling, Ernest Henry, **IX:**3494
Stephenson, George, **VI:**2132
Stopes, Marie, **IX:**3551
Strafford, First Earl of, **IV:**1285
Street, George Edmund, **VI:**2160
Sullivan, Sir Arthur, **V:**927
Sutherland, Graham Vivian, **IX:**3587

Swan, Joseph Wilson, **VI:**2179
Swift, Jonathan, **IV:**1305
Sydenham, Thomas, **IV:**1310
Tennyson, Alfred, Lord, **VI:**2211
Terry, Ellen, **VI:**2215
Thatcher, Margaret, **IX:**3649
Tolkien, J.R.R., **IX:**3696
Toynbee, Arnold, **IX:**3715
Trevithick, Richard, **VI:**2251
Tull, Jethro, **IV:**1345
Turing, Alan Mathison, **IX:**3768
Turner, J.M.W., **VI:**2272
Vanbrugh, Sir John, **IV:**1351
Vancouver, George, **IV:**1355
Vaughan Williams, Ralph, **IX:**3798
Victoria, Queen, **VI:**2307
Wakefield, Edward Gibbon, **VI:**2321
Walpole, Sir Robert, **IV:**1400
Walter, John, II, **VI:**2324
Walton, Sir William, **IX:**3872
Webb, Beatrice and Sidney, **IX:**3905
Wedgwood, Josiah, **IV:**1421
Wellington, Duke of, **VI:**2351
Wells, H.G., **IX:**3938
Wesley, John, **IV:**1426
Wheatstone, Charles, **V:**555
Whitehead, Alfred North, **IX:**3965
Whittle, Sir Frank, **IX:**3972
Wilberforce, William, **IV:**1435
Wilkes, John, **IV:**1439
Wilkins, Maurice H.F., **IX:**3995
Wilkinson, John, **IV:**1443
William III, **IV:**1447
William IV, **VI:**2392
Wilson, Sir Harold, **IX:**4016
Windsor, Duke of, **IX:**4025
Wittgenstein, Ludwig, **IX:**4036
Wolfe, James, **IV:**1471
Wollstonecraft, Mary, **IV:**1475
Woolf, Virginia, **IX:**4056
Wordsworth, William, **VI:**2406
Wren, Sir Christopher, **IV:**1480

GREECE. *See also* **ALEXANDRIA; ASIA MINOR; CNIDUS; COS; ELEA; MACEDONIA; MILETUS; THRACE**
Aeschylus, **I:**9
Aesop, **I:**13
Agesilaus II, **I:**16
Alcibiades, **I:**31
Alcmaeon, **I:**34
Alexander the Great, **I:**38

Anaxagoras, **I:**47
Antisthenes, **I:**66
Aristippus, **I:**85
Aristophanes, **I:**88
Aristotle, **I:**94
Aristoxenus, **I:**98
Cimon, **I:**198
Cleisthenes of Athens, **I:**207
Cleomenes, **I:**214
Cyril, Saint, **II:**278
Demosthenes, **I:**253
Diocles of Carystus, **I:**260
Diogenes, **I:**268
Diophantus, **I:**272
Draco, **I:**280
Empedocles, **I:**282
Epaminondas, **I:**290
Epicurus, **I:**295
Erasistratus, **I:**299
Euclid, **I:**307
Eupalinus of Megara, **I:**314
Euripides, **I:**317
Heraclitus of Ephesus, **I:**382
Hesiod, **I:**402
Homer, **I:**420
Isocrates, **I:**456
Kazantzakis, Nikos, **VIII:**1920
Leonidas, **I:**501
Lysippus, **I:**515
Menander (dramatist), **I:**538
Methodius, Saint, **II:**278
Miltiades the Younger, **I:**553
Paul of Aegina, **II:**712
Pericles, **I:**609
Pheidippides, **I:**621
Phidias, **I:**624
Pindar, **I:**644
Pisistratus, **I:**648
Pittacus of Mytilene, **I:**651
Plato, **I:**655
Plotinus, **I:**666
Plutarch, **I:**670
Polybius, **I:**673
Polygnotus, **I:**676
Posidonius, **I:**686
Praxiteles, **I:**690
Protagoras, **I:**705
Pyrrhon of Elis, **I:**724
Pythagoras, **I:**727
Sappho, **I:**750
Scopas, **I:**764
Simonides, **I:**787

Socrates, **I:**793
Solon, **I:**803
Sophocles, **I:**807
Themistocles, **I:**857
Theophrastus, **I:**873
Thespis, **I:**877
Thucydides, **I:**885
Venizélos, Eleuthérios, **IX:**3808
Xanthippe, **I:**952
Xenakis, Iannis, **IX:**4075
Xenophanes, **I:**955
Xenophon, **I:**958
Ypsilanti, Alexander and Demetrios, **VI:**2417
Zeno of Citium, **I:**967

GUINEA
Touré, Ahmed Sékou, **IX:**3711

HAITI
Christophe, Henri, **V:**501

HUNGARY
Árpád, **II:**86
Bartók, Béla, **VII:**210
Deák, Ferenc, **V:**625
Elizabeth of Hungary, Saint, **II:**340
Herzl, Theodor, **V:**1102
Hevesy, Georg von, **VIII:**1654
Hunyadi, János, **III:**374
László I, Saint, **II:**574
Liszt, Franz, **VI:**1391
Lukács, György, **VIII:**2272
Matthias I Corvinus, **III:**487
Neumann, John von, **VIII:**2724
Nordau, Max, **VIII:**2766
Semmelweis, Ignaz Philipp, **VI:**2021
Stephen I, **II:**851

ICELAND
Laxness, Halldór, **VIII:**2131
Leif Eriksson, **II:**577
Snorri Sturluson, **II:**836

INDIA
Ahmad Khan, Sir Sayyid, **V:**34
Akbar, **III:**6
Aryabhata, **II:**89
Aśoka the Great, **I:**112
Aurangzeb, **IV:**69
Aurobindo, Sri, **VIII-**141
Bābur, **III:**36
Banerjea, Surendranath, **VII:**183

Brahmagupta, **II:**181
Buddha, **I:**144
Curzon, Lord, **VII:**819
Gandhi, Indira, **VII:**1278
Gandhi, Mahatma, **VII:**1282
Harsha, **II:**430
Jinnah, Mohammed Ali, **VIII:**1847
Kālidāsa, **I:**491
Kanishka, **I:**494
Lansdowne, Fifth Marquess of, **VIII:**2090
Menander (Indian king), **I:**541
Mountbatten, Louis, **VIII:**2641
Naidu, Sarojini, **VIII:**2683
Nānak, **III:**540
Nehru, Jawaharlal, **VIII:**2709
Pandit, Vijaya Lakshmi, **IX:**2867
Patel, Vallabhbhai Jhaverbhai, **IX:**2903
Raman, Sir Chandrasekhara Venkata, **IX:**3109
Rāmānuja, **II:**770
Ray, Rammohan, **VI:**1846
Ray, Satyajit, **IX:**3132
Shah Jahan, **IV:**1232
Śivajī, **IV:**1246
Tagore, Rabindranath, **IX:**3598
Teresa, Mother, **IX:**3635
Thomas, Saint, **I:**880
Tilak, Bal Gangadhar, **IX:**3681
Vardhamāna, **I:**915

INDOCHINA. *See* **BURMA; CAMBODIA; VIETNAM**

INDONESIA
Hatta, Mohammad, **VIII:**1577
Sukarno, **IX:**3570

IONIA. *See* **ASIA MINOR; GREECE**

IRAN. *See also* **ARABIA; ASSYRIA; IRAQ; MESOPOTAMIA; SYRIA**
'Abbās the Great, **IV:**4
Abul Wefa, **II:**20
Avicenna, **II:**106
Cyrus the Great, **I:**233
Darius the Great, **I:**236
Fakhr al-Din al-Razi, **II:**347
Firdusi, **II:**350
Ghazan, Mahmud, **II:**381
Ghazzali, al-, **II:**385
Hafiz, **II:**417
Hallaj, al-, **II:**421
Harun al-Rashid, **II:**437

Jabir ibn Hayyan, **II:**522
Jamāl al-Dīn al-Afghānī, **V:**1207
Khomeini, Ruhollah, **VIII:**1957
Mohammad Reza Shah Pahlavi, **VIII:**2566
Nizam al-Mulk, **II:**677
Omar Khayyám, **II:**695
Razi, al-, **II:**779
Sa'di, **II:**806
Shapur II, **I:**778
Tabari, al-, 873
Xerxes I, **I:**962
Zoroaster, **I:**975

IRAQ. *See also* **ARABIA; ASSYRIA; BABYLONIA; IRAN; MESOPOTAMIA; SYRIA**
Abu Hanifah, **II:**16
Abul Wefa, **II:**20
Ahmad ibn Hanbal, **II:**33
Alhazen, **II:**63
Ash'ari, al-, **II:**93
Battani, al-, **II:**121
Faisal I, **VII:**1122
Jabir ibn Hayyan, **II:**522
Jahiz, al-, **II:**526
Khwarizmi, al-, **II:**563
Mas'udi, al-, **II:**636
Tabari, al-, **II:**873

IRELAND
Beckett, Samuel, **VII:**238
Berkeley, George, **IV:**114
Campbell, Alexander, **V:**401
Castlereagh, Viscount, **V:**438
Charles I, **IV:**279
Charles II, **IV:**283
Collins, Michael, **VII:**733
Cornwallis, First Marquess, **IV:**367
Cosgrave, William T., **VII:**770
de Valera, Eamon, **VII:**877
George I, **IV:**531
George II, **IV:**535
George III, **IV:**539
Goldsmith, Oliver, **IV:**564
Hamilton, Sir William Rowan, **V:**1025
Holland, John Philip, **V:**1123
Joyce, James, **VIII:**1891
Kelvin, Lord, **VI:**1269
Lansdowne, Fifth Marquess of, **VIII:**2090
Mannix, Daniel, **VI:**1480
O'Connell, Daniel, **VI:**1680
O'Connor, Thomas Power, **IX:**2793

O'Kelly, Seán T., **IX:**2804
Parnell, Charles Stewart, **VI:**1740
Patrick, Saint, **I:**600
Shaw, George Bernard, **IX:**3399
Swift, Jonathan, **IV:**1305
Wilde, Oscar, **VI:**2377
Yeats, William Butler, **IX:**4082

ISRAEL. *See also* **JUDAEA; PALESTINE**
Aaron, **I:**1
Abraham, **I:**5
Begin, Menachem, **VII:**243
Ben-Gurion, David, **VII:**251
Buber, Martin, **VII:**483
David, **I:**241
Dayan, Moshe, **VII:**854
Deborah, **I:**246
Eban, Abba, **VII:**1000
Eusebius of Caesarea, **I:**322
Ezekiel, **I:**326
Ezra, **I:**330
Jerome, Saint, **I:**463
John the Apostle, **I:**475
John the Baptist, **I:**479
Josephus, Flavius, **I:**483
Judah ha-Levi, **II:**548
Lipchitz, Jacques, **VIII:**2199
Meir, Golda, **VIII:**2472
Moses, **I:**561
Peter, Saint, **I:**614
Pilate, Pontius, **I:**640
Samuel, **I:**746
Solomon, **I:**798
Stephen, Saint, **I:**822
Thomas, Saint, **I:**880
Virgin Mary, **I:**939
Weizmann, Chaim, **IX:**3930

ITALY. *See also* **ELEA**
Abano, Pietro d', **II:**1
Agrippa, Marcus Vipsanius, **I:**20
Alberti, Leon Battista, **III:**8
Alboin, **II:**41
Alcmaeon, **I:**34
Alexander III, **II:**48
Alexander VI, **III:**14
Ambrose, Saint, **I:**43
Andrea del Sarto, **III:**24
Angelico, Fra, **III:**28
Anthony of Padua, Saint, **II:**76
Antony, Marc, **I:**69
Archimedes, **I:**76

Ariosto, Ludovico, **III:**32
Arnold of Villanova, **II:**79
Arnolfo di Cambio, **II:**82
Asclepiades of Bithynia, **I:**101
Attila, **I:**124
Augustus, **I:**132
Avogadro, Amedeo, **V:**98
Bellini, Giovanni, **III:**58
Benedict of Nursia, Saint, **II:**136
Bernini, Gian Lorenzo, **IV:**118
Boccaccio, Giovanni, **II:**150
Boccherini, Luigi, **IV:**147
Boccioni, Umberto, **VII:**342
Boethius, **II:**155
Bohemond I, **II:**159
Bonaventure, Saint, **II:**163
Boniface VIII, **II:**171
Borromini, Francesco, **IV:**167
Botticelli, Sandro, **III:**74
Bramante, Donato, **III:**81
Brunelleschi, Filippo, **III:**89
Bruni, Leonardo, **III:**93
Bruno, Giordano, **III:**96
Brutus, Marcus Junius, **I:**140
Cabot, John, **III:**113
Caesar, Julius, **I:**147
Caligula, **I:**152
Canaletto, **IV:**242
Canova, Antonio, **V:**408
Carpini, Giovanni da Pian del, **II:**206
Carracci Family, The, **III:**125
Caruso, Enrico, **VII:**598
Casanova, Giovanni Giacomo, **IV:**254
Cassiodorus, **II:**215
Cassius, **I:**159
Catherine of Siena, Saint, **II:**218
Cato the Censor, **I:**162
Cato the Younger, **I:**166
Catullus, **I:**169
Cavalcanti, Guido, **II:**223
Cavour, Count, **V:**446
Cellini, Benvenuto, **III:**151
Celsus, Aulus Cornelius, **I:**173
Cicero, **I:**194
Cimabue, **II:**272
Claudius I, **I:**203
Clement I, **I:**210
Clement VII, **III:**166
Constantine the Great, **I:**226
Corelli, Arcangelo, **IV:**360
Correggio, **III:**184
Croce, Benedetto, **VII:**801

Dandolo, Enrico, **II**:282
Dante, **II**:286
de Gasperi, Alcide, **VII**:862
Denis, Saint, **I**:257
Diocletian, **I**:263
Dionysius Exiguus, **II**:298
Donatello, **III**:220
Donizetti, Gaetano, **V**:684
Duccio di Buoninsegna, **II**:305
Ennius, Quintus, **I**:287
Fabius Maximus, Quintus, **I**:334
Farnese, Alessandro, **III**:254
Fellini, Federico, **VII**:1141
Fermi, Enrico, **VII**:1145
Ferrari, Enzo, **VII**:1150
Fracastoro, Girolamo, **III**:270
Francis of Assisi, Saint, **II**:354
Frederick II, **II**:362
Gabrieli, Andrea, **III**:281
Gabrieli, Giovanni, **III**:284
Galileo, **IV**:519
Galvani, Luigi, **IV**:523
Garibaldi, Giuseppe, **V**:879
Gentile, Giovanni, **VII**:1336
Gentili, Alberico, **III**:295
Ghiberti, Lorenzo, **III**:302
Gioberti, Vincenzo, **V**:932
Giorgione, **III**:305
Giotto, **II**:388
Gracchi, The, **I**:345
Gramsci, Antonio, **VIII**-1459
Gregory VII, **II**:395
Gregory IX, **II**:399
Gregory the Great, **II**:407
Guarini, Guarino, **IV**:583
Guicciardini, Francesco, **III**:325
Guido d'Arezzo, **II**:411
Hadrian, **I**:356
Hannibal, **I**:364
Hippolytus of Rome, **I**:415
Horace, **I**:424
Hus, Jan, **II**:487
Innocent III, **II**:509
Innocent IV, **II**:514
Irenaeus, Saint, **I**:447
Jacopo della Quercia, **III**:389
Jerome, Saint, **I**:463
Joachim of Fiore, **II**:534
John XXIII, **VIII**:1858
Josephus, Flavius, **I**:483
Julius II, **III**:405
Juvenal, **I**:488

Landini, Francesco, **II**:570
Leo IX, **II**:581
Leo X, **III**:419
Leo XIII, **VI**:1347
Leonardo da Vinci, **III**:423
Leonardo of Pisa, **II**:585
Livy, **I**:504
Lorenzetti, Pietro, and
    Ambrogio Lorenzetti, **II**:595
Lucian, **I**:507
Lucretius, **I**:511
Machiavelli, Niccolò, **III**:448
Maecenas, Gaius, **I**:519
Malpighi, Marcello, **IV**:891
Mantegna, Andrea, **III**:460
Manzoni, Alessandro, **VI**:1483
Marconi, Guglielmo, **VIII**:2415
Marcus Aurelius, **I**:523
Marius, Gaius, **I**:528
Martial, **I**:532
Martini, Simone, **II**:632
Masaccio, **III**:483
Mazzini, Giuseppe, **VI**:1514
Medici, Lorenzo de', **III**:495
Menotti, Gian Carlo, **VIII**:2494
Messalina, Valeria, **I**:550
Messner, Reinhold, **VIII**:2506
Michelangelo, **III**:517
Montale, Eugenio, **VIII**:2592
Montessori, Maria, **VIII**:2596
Monteverdi, Claudio, **IV**:990
Mosca, Gaetano, **VIII**:2630
Mussolini, Benito, **VIII**:2667
Natta, Giulio, **VIII**:2698
Neri, Saint Philip, **III**:551
Nero, **I**:577
Nervi, Pier Luigi, **VIII**:2720
Nicholas V, **III**:559
Nicholas the Great, **II**:673
Oberth, Hermann, **IX**:2777
Orcagna, Andrea, **II**:698
Ovid, **I**:585
Paganini, Niccolò, **VI**:1711
Palladio, Andrea, **III**:580
Paul III, **III**:595
Paul VI, **IX**:2919
Pavarotti, Luciano, **IX**:2930
Petrarch, **II**:726
Phaedrus, **I**:618
Philip IV the Fair, **II**:736
Piero della Francesca, **III**:606
Pirandello, Luigi, **IX**:3013

Pirelli Family, The, **IX**:3020
Pisano, Andrea, **II**:744
Pisano, Nicola and Giovanni, **II**:747
Pius II, **III**:613
Pius V, **III**:616
Pius IX, **VI**:1782
Pius XI, **IX**:3026
Pius XII, **IX**:3030
Plautus, **I**:659
Pliny the Elder, **I**:662
Plutarch, **I**:670
Poggio, **III**:626
Polo, Marco, **II**:750
Pompey the Great, **I**:679
Porphyry, **I**:683
Posidonius, **I**:686
Propertius, Sextus, **I**:702
Puccini, Giacomo, **IX**:3093
Raphael, **III**:642
Regulus, Marcus Atilius, **I**:739
Rienzo, Cola di, **II**:790
Rossini, Gioacchino, **VI**:1913
Salimbene, **II**:812
Sallust, **I**:742
Sansovino, Jacopo, **III**:664
Santorio, Santorio, **IV**:1209
Savonarola, Girolamo, **III**:667
Scarlatti, Alessandro, **IV**:1213
Scipio Aemilianus, **I**:757
Scipio Africanus, **I**:760
Seneca the Younger, **I**:770
Sergius I, Saint, **II**:823
Sforza, Ludovico, **III**:682
Siricius, Saint, **I**:790
Sosigenes, **I**:811
Spallanzani, Lazzaro, **IV**:1260
Spartacus, **I**:814
Stilicho, Flavius, **I**:825
Stradivari, Antonio, **IV**:1281
Sulla, Lucius Cornelius, **I**:833
Sylvester II, **II**:869
Tacitus, Cornelius, **I**:837
Tancred, **II**:887
Tasso, Torquato, **III**:710
Terence, **I**:844
Theodoret of Cyrrhus, **I**:865
Theodoric the Great, **II**:894
Theodosius the Great, **I**:868
Thomas Aquinas, Saint, **II**:911
Tiberius, **I**:892
Tiepolo, Giovanni Battista, **IV**:1323
Tintoretto, **III**:717
Titian, **III**:721
Torricelli, Evangelista, **IV**:1331
Toscanini, Arturo, **IX**:3707
Trajan, **I**:899
Urban II, **II**:928
Valentinus, **I**:911
Valla, Lorenzo, **III**:739
Varro, Marcus Terentius, **I**:918
Vasari, Giorgio, **III**:743
Verdi, Giuseppe, **VI**:2299
Vergil, **I**:926
Veronese, Paolo, **III**:747
Verrius Flaccus, Marcus, **I**:930
Verrocchio, Andrea del, **III**:750
Vespasian, **I**:933
Vespucci, Amerigo, **III**:758
Vico, Giambattista, **IV**:1372
Villani, Giovanni, **II**:938
Visconti, Luchino, **IX**:3818
Volta, Alessandro, **IV**:1387

IVORY COAST
Houphouët-Boigny, Félix, **VIII**:1754

JAPAN
Akihito, **VII**:41
Ashikaga Takauji, **II**:97
Fujiwara Michinaga, **II**:370
Hatoyama Ichiro, **VIII**:1574
Hirohito, **VIII**:1678
Hiroshige, **V**:1117
Hokusai, **V**:1120
Honda, Soichiro, **VIII**:1724
Ii Naosuke, **V**:1180
Ikeda, Hayato, **VIII**:1809
Jōchō, **II**:537
Kawabata, Yasunari, **VIII**:1913
Kurosawa, Akira, **VIII**:2043
Matsuo Bashō, **IV**:942
Matsushita, Konosuke, **VIII**:2457
Mishima, Yukio, **VIII**:2551
Morita, Akio, **VIII**:2622
Murasaki Shikibu, **II**:657
Nichiren, **II**:666
Nishida, Kitaro, **VIII**:2754
Oda Nobunaga, **III**:570
Ogata Kōrin, **IV**:1041
Oh, Sadaharu, **IX**:2796
Saigō Takamori, **VI**:1936
Sato, Eisaku, **IX**:3336
Sesshū, **III**:679
Shōtoku Taishi, **II**:826

Sōtatsu, **IV:**1257
Taira Kiyomori, **II:**881
Tanizaki, Jun'ichiro, **IX:**3611
Tokugawa Ieyasu, **IV:**1327
Toyoda, Eiji, **IX:**3719
Toyotomi Hideyoshi, **III:**728
Unkei, **II:**924
Yukawa, Hideki, **IX:**4090
Zeami Motokiyo, **II:**1025

JERUSALEM. *See* **ISRAEL**

JORDAN
Hussein I, **VIII:**1791

JUDAEA. *See also* **ISRAEL; PALESTINE**
Herod the Great, **I:**390
Isaiah, **I:**452
Jeremiah, **I:**459
Jesus Christ, **I:**467
Johanan ben Zakkai, **I:**471
Pilate, Pontius, **I:**640
Virgin Mary, **I:**939

JUDAH. *See* **JUDAEA**

KAMPUCHEA. *See* **CAMBODIA**

KAZAKHSTAN. *See* **SOVIET UNION**

KENYA
Kenyatta, Jomo, **VIII:**1936
Leakey, L.S.B., **VIII:**2145

KHWARIZM
Alp Arslan, **II:**67
Biruni, al-, **II:**147

KIEV
Rurik, **II:**803
Vladimir I, **II:**952

KIRGIZIA. *See* **SOVIET UNION**

KOREA
Rhee, Syngman, **IX:**3165

LATVIA. *See also* **SOVIET UNION**
Ostwald, Wilhelm, **IX:**2855

LIBERIA
Tubman, William V. S., **IX:**3757

LIBYA
Qaddafi, Muammar al-, **IX:**3098

LIMBURG-IM BREISGAU. *See* **GERMANY**

LITHUANIA. *See also* **SOVIET UNION**
Elijah ben Solomon, **IV:**432
Lipchitz, Jacques, **VIII:**2199
Władysław II Jagiełło and Jadwiga, **II:**1001

LOW COUNTRIES. *See* **NETHERLANDS,
THE**

MACEDONIA. *See also* **GREECE;
YUGOSLAVIA**
Alexander the Great, **I:**38
Antigonus I Monophthalmos, **I:**60
Basil the Macedonian, **II:**117
Phaedrus, **I:**618
Philip II of Macedonia, **I:**628
Seleucus I Nicator, **I:**767

MALI
Mansa Mūsā, **II:**623

MARTINIQUE
Césaire, Aimé, **VII:**631

MESOPOTAMIA. *See also* **ARABIA;
ASSYRIA; BABYLONIA; IRAN; IRAQ;
SYRIA**
Khosrow I, **II:**559
Lucian, **I:**507
Mas'udi, al-, 636

MEXICO
Calles, Plutarco Elías, **VII:**542
Candela, Felix, **VII:**557
Cárdenas, Lázaro, **VII:**571
Cruz, Sor Juana Inés de la, **IV:**382
Itzcóatl, **III:**377
Juárez, Benito, **V:**1250
Madero, Francisco, **VIII:**2345
Montezuma II, **III:**528
Nezahualcóyotl, **III:**555
Obregón, Álvaro, **IX:**2781
Orozco, José Clemente, **IX:**2836
Rivera, Diego, **IX:**3184
Santa Anna, Antonio López de,
    VI:1955
Villa, Pancho, **IX:**3811
Zapata, Emiliano, **IX:**4104

MIDDLE EAST. *See* ALEXANDRIA;
  ARABIA; ARMENIA; ASIA MINOR;
  ASSYRIA; BABYLONIA; BITHYNIA;
  BYZANTINE EMPIRE; CAPPADOCIA;
  CILICIA; CNIDUS; COS; EGYPT; IRAN;
  IRAQ; ISRAEL; JORDAN; JUDAEA;
  MESOPOTAMIA; MOPSUESTIA;
  OTTOMAN EMPIRE; PALESTINE;
  PERGA; PHOENICIA; PONTUS; SYRIA;
  TURKEY

MILAN, REPUBLIC OF. *See* ITALY

MILETUS
Anaximander, **I:**50
Anaximenes of Miletus, **I:**53
Thales of Miletus, **I:**852

MODENA, REPUBLIC OF. *See* ITALY

MOLDAVIA. *See* SOVIET UNION

MONGOLIA. *See* CENTRAL ASIA; CHINA;
  SOVIET UNION

MOPSUESTIA
Theodore of Mopsuestia, 861

MOROCCO
Averroës, **II:**100
Ibn Battutah, **II:**495
Idrisi, al-, **II:**506

MOZAMBIQUE
Machel, Samora Moisès, **VIII:**2317

MUGHAL EMPIRE. *See* INDIA

MYANMAR. *See* BURMA

NAPLES, KINGDOM OF. *See* ITALY

NETHERLANDS, THE
Bosch, Hieronymus, **III:**70
Einthoven, Willem, **VII:**1039
Erasmus, Desiderius, **III:**246
Frank, Anne, **VII:**1204
Frederick Henry, **IV:**500
Gogh, Vincent van, **V:**944
Grotius, Hugo, **IV:**579
Hals, Frans, **IV:**604
Hein, Piet, **IV:**644

Huygens, Christiaan, **IV:**695
Jansen, Cornelius Otto, **IV:**707
Leeuwenhoek, Antoni van, **IV:**825
Lippershey, Hans, **IV:**850
Lorentz, Hendrik Antoon, **VIII:**2235
Menno Simons, **III:**510
Mondrian, Piet, **VIII:**2575
Oldenbarnevelt, Johan van, **III:**574
Oort, Jan Hendrik, **IX:**2827
Oud, J.J.P., **IX:**2859
Rembrandt, **IV:**1152
Siger of Brabant, **II:**829
Sluter, Claus, **II:**832
Spinoza, Baruch, **IV:**1264
Tasman, Abel Janszoon, **IV:**1313
Tromp, Cornelius and Maarten, **IV:**1342
Vermeer, Jan, **IV:**1368
Weyden, Rogier van der, **III:**778
William the Silent, **III:**781

NEW ZEALAND
Hillary, Sir Edmund, **VIII:**1662
Massey, William Ferguson, **VIII:**2444
Rutherford, Ernest, **IX:**3277
Seddon, Richard John, **VI:**2017
Wakefield, Edward Gibbon, **VI:**2321
Wilkins, Maurice H.F., **IX:**3995

NIGERIA
Achebe, Chinua, **VII:**13
Azikiwe, Nnamdi, **VIII**-144
Soyinka, Wole, **IX:**3471

NORTH AFRICA. *See also* CARTHAGE;
  MOROCCO; NUMIDIA; TUNISIA
'Abd al-Mu'min, **II:**4
Masinissa, **I:**535

NORTH VIETNAM. *See* VIETNAM

NORWAY
Abel, Niels Henrik, **V:**7
Amundsen, Roald, **VII:**66
Bjerknes, Vilhelm, **VII:**318
Grieg, Edvard, **V:**1002
Hamsun, Knut, **VIII:**1537
Henie, Sonja, **VIII:**1629
Heyerdahl, Thor, **VIII:**1658
Ibsen, Henrik, **V:**1175
Margaret of Denmark, Norway, and Sweden, **II:**626
Munch, Edvard, **VIII:**2658
Nansen, Fridtjof, **VIII:**2686

Olaf I, **II**:688
Olaf, Saint, **II**:691
Rollo, **II**:793

NUMIDIA
Augustine, Saint, **I**:128
Masinissa, **I**:535

OTTOMON EMPIRE. *See also* **ALGERIA;
EGYPT; IRAQ; PALESTINE; SAUDI
ARABIA; SYRIA; TURKEY**
Abdelkader, **V**:1
Bayezid II, **III**:51
Mehmed II, **III**:499
Süleyman the Magnificent, **III**:707

PAKISTAN
Jinnah, Mohammed Ali, **VIII**:1847

PALESTINE. *See also* **ISRAEL; JORDAN;
JUDAEA**
Akiba ben Joseph, **I**:27
Arafat, Yasir, **VII**:90
Herod the Great, **I**:390
Luria, Isaac ben Solomon,
    III:440
Pilate, Pontius, **I**:640
Thomas, Saint, **I**:880
Virgin Mary, **I**:939

PAPAL STATES. *See* **ITALY**

PEOPLE'S REPUBLIC OF CHINA. *See*
CHINA

PERGA
Apollonius of Perga, **I**:72

PERSIA. *See* **IRAN**

PERSIAN EMPIRE. *See* **IRAN**

PERU
Bolívar, Simón, **V**:267
Haya de la Torre, Víctor Raúl, **VIII**:1584
Huáscar, **III**:371
Pachacuti, **III**:577
Pérez de Cuéllar, Javier, **IX**:2957

PHILIPPINES
Aquino, Corazon, **VII**:86
Marcos, Ferdinand E., **VIII**:2420

PHOENICIA
Porphyry, **I**:683

POLAND
Casimir the Great, **II**:210
Chopin, Frédéric, **V**:493
Conrad, Joseph, **VII**:753
Copernicus, Nicolaus, **III**:176
Curie, Marie, **VII**:811
John III Sobieski, **IV**:725
John Paul II, **VIII**:1862
Luxemburg, Rosa, **VIII**:2285
Walesa, Lech, **IX**:3844
Władysław II Jagiełło and Jadwiga, **II**:1001
Wiesenthal, Simon, **IX**:3984

PONTUS
Chrysostom, Saint John, **I**:184
Mithradates the Great, **I**:557
Strabo, **I**:828

PORTUGAL
Afonso I, **II**:30
Albuquerque, Afonso de, **III**:11
Anthony of Padua, Saint, **II**:76
Camões, Luís de, **III**:122
Covilhã, Pêro da, **III**:197
Dias, Bartolomeu, **III**:215
Egas Moniz, António, **VII**:1023
Gama, Vasco da, **III**:287
Henry the Navigator (Prince of Portugal),
    III:354
Magellan, Ferdinand, **III**:453
Manuel I, **III**:464

PORTUGUESE EAST AFRICA. *See*
MOZAMBIQUE

PRUSSIA. *See* **GERMANY**

PUERTO RICO
Casals, Pablo, **VII**:606

RHODESIA. *See* **ZIMBABWE**

ROMAN EMPIRE. *See* **ITALY**

ROMANIA
Brancusi, Constantin, **VII**:414
Eliade, Mircea, **VII**:1055

ROME. *See* **ITALY**

RUPERTSBERG BEI BINGEN. *See* **GERMANY**

RUSSIA. *See also* **KIEV; KHWARIZM; SOVIET UNION; VLADIMIR-SUZDAL**
Alexander I, **V:**44
Alexander II, **V:**48
Bakunin, Mikhail, **V:**112
Balanchine, George, **VII:**155
Bering, Vitus Jonassen, **IV:**111
Borodin, Aleksandr, **V:**286
Catherine the Great, **IV:**257
Chekhov, Anton, **V:**485
Diaghilev, Sergei, **VII:**919
Dostoevski, Fyodor, **V:**687
Godunov, Boris Fyodorovich, **III:**308
Gogol, Nikolai, **V:**949
Herzen, Aleksandr, **V:**1099
Horowitz, Vladimir, **VIII:**1747
Ivan the Great, **III:**381
Ivan the Terrible, **III:**385
Jakobson, Roman, **VIII:**1831
Kutuzov, Mikhail Illarionovich, **VI:**1305
Lermontov, Mikhail, **VI:**1351
Lifar, Serge, **VIII:**2182
Lobachevsky, Nikolay Ivanovich, **VI:**1403
Lomonosov, Mikhail Vasilyevich, **IV:**860
Mendeleyev, Dmitry Ivanovich, **VI:**1529
Mussorgsky, Modest, **VI:**1611
Nabokov, Vladimir, **VIII:**2675
Nicholas I, **VI:**1650
Nijinsky, Vaslav, **VIII:**2746
Nikon, **IV:**1030
Pavlova, Anna, **IX:**2937
Peter III, **IV:**1087
Peter the Great, **IV:**1082
Pobedonostsev, Konstantin Petrovich, **VI:**1790
Popov, Aleksandr Stepanovich, **VI:**1806
Pushkin, Alexander, **VI:**1832
Rachmaninoff, Sergei, **IX:**3105
Rasputin, Grigori Yefimovich, **VI:**1842
Rimsky-Korsakov, Nikolay, **VI:**1889
Speransky, Mikhail Mikhaylovich, **VI:**2089
Stravinsky, Igor, **IX:**3559
Suvorov, Aleksandr Vasilyevich, **IV:**1298
Tchaikovsky, Peter Ilich, **VI:**2198
Tolstoy, Leo, **VI:**2242
Turgenev, Ivan, **VI:**2268
Yeltsin, Boris N., **IX:**4082
Zworykin, Vladimir, **IX:**4125

RUSSIAN FEDERATION. *See* **RUSSIA; SOVIET UNION**

SAUDI ARABIA
Fahd, **VII:**1115
Faisal, **VII:**1118
Yamani, Ahmad Zaki, **IX:**4079

SAXONY. *See* **GERMANY**

SCOTLAND
Bell, Alexander Graham, **V:**185
Boswell, James, **IV:**174
Brougham, Henry, **V:**314
Bruce, James, **IV:**208
Bruce, Robert, **II:**184
Burns, Robert, **IV:**229
Cameron, Richard, **IV:**239
Carlyle, Thomas, **V:**416
Dalhousie, First Marquess of, **V:**600
David I, **II:**291
David II, **II:**294
Doyle, Sir Arthur Conan, **V:**700
Duns Scotus, John, **II:**309
Erskine, First Baron, **IV:**439
Ferguson, Adam, **IV:**454
Fleming, Sir Alexander, **VII:**1166
Frazer, Sir James George, **VII:**1220
Hardie, James Keir, **V:**1036
Hume, David, **IV:**683
Jeffrey, Lord, **V:**1224
Kelvin, Lord, **VI:**1269
Kidd, William, **IV:**777
Livingstone, David, **VI:**1399
MacDonald, Ramsay, **VIII:**2312
Mackenzie, Sir Alexander, **IV:**879
Maclaurin, Colin, **IV:**882
Macleod, John J. R., **VIII:**2329
MacMillan, Daniel and Alexander, **VI:**1457
Maxwell, James Clerk, **VI:**1511
Mill, James, **VI:**1556
Napier, John, **III:**544
Nasmyth, James, **VI:**1624
Park, Mungo, **VI:**1723
Raeburn, Sir Henry, **VI:**1836
Reith of Stonehaven, First Baron, **IX:**3146
Scott, Sir Walter, **VI:**2005
Smith, Adam, **IV:**1249
Stevenson, Robert Louis, **VI:**2139
Telford, Thomas, **VI:**2207
Wallace, Sir William, **II:**955

Watt, James, **IV:**1409
Witherspoon, John, **IV:**1467

SENEGAL
Senghor, Léopold, **IX:**3391

SERBIA. *See also* **YUGOSLAVIA**
Stefan Dušan, **II:**843

SIENA, REPUBLIC OF. *See* **ITALY**

SILESIA. *See* **GERMANY**

SINGAPORE
Lee Kuan Yew, **VIII:**2150

SLOVENIA. *See* **YUGOSLAVIA**

SONGHAI EMPIRE
Mohammed I Askia, **III:**521

SOUTH AFRICA
Barnard, Christiaan, **VII:**195
Botha, Louis, **VII:**376
de Klerk, F.W., **VII:**870
Fugard, Athol, **VII:**1257
Gordimer, Nadine, **VIII**-1427
Lutuli, Albert, **VIII:**2281
Mandela, Nelson, **VIII:**2384
Paton, Alan, **IX:**2907
Player, Gary, **IX:**3040
Rhodes, Cecil, **VI:**1873
Smuts, Jan Christian, **IX:**3453
Tutu, Desmond, **IX:**3775

SOUTH AMERICA. *See* **ARGENTINA;
BRAZIL; CHILE; COLOMBIA; FRENCH
GUIANA; PERU**

SOUTH KOREA. *See* **KOREA**

SOVIET UNION. *See also* **ARMENIA;
AZERBAIJAN; BELORUSSIA; KIEV;
LATVIA; LITHUANIA; RUSSIA;
TAJIKISTAN; UKRAINE**
Akhmatova, Anna, **VII:**37
Ambartsumian, Viktor A., **VII:**63
Bakhtin, Mikhail, **VII:**152
Basov, Nikolay Gennadiyevich, **VII:**214
Blok, Aleksandr, **VII:**332
Brezhnev, Leonid Ilich, **VII:**459
Bukharin, Nikolai Ivanovich, **VII:**491

Chagall, Marc, **VII:**639
Eisenstein, Sergei, **VII:**1047
Gagarin, Yuri Alekseyevich, **VII:**1270
Gorbachev, Mikhail, **VIII**-1423
Gorky, Maxim, **VIII**-1442
Kandinsky, Wassily, **VIII:**1903
Kapitsa, Pyotr Leonidovich, **VIII:**1906
Kerensky, Aleksandr Fyodorovich, **VIII:**1941
Khrushchev, Nikita S., **VIII:**1961
Korolev, Sergei, **VIII:**2019
Kurchatov, Igor Vasilyevich, **VIII:**2039
Landau, Lev Davidovich, **VIII:**2073
Lenin, Vladimir Ilich, **VIII:**2160
Litvinov, Maksim Maksimovich, **VIII:**2208
Malenkov, Georgi M., **VIII:**2377
Massine, Léonide, **VIII:**2448
Mayakovsky, Vladimir, **VIII:**2461
Meyerhold, Vsevolod Yemilyevich, **VIII:**2510
Molotov, Vyacheslav Mikhailovich, **VIII:**2571
Oparin, Aleksandr Ivanovich, **IX:**2830
Pasternak, Boris, **IX:**2899
Pavlov, Ivan Petrovich, **IX:**2933
Prokofiev, Sergei, **IX:**3085
Sakharov, Andrei, **IX:**3296
Shostakovich, Dmitri, **IX:**3409
Solzhenitsyn, Aleksandr, **IX:**3459
Stalin, Joseph, **IX:**3482
Stanislavsky, Konstantin, **IX:**3486
Tereshkova, Valentina, **IX:**3639
Trotsky, Leon, **IX:**3726
Tsiolkovsky, Konstantin, **IX:**3749
Tsvetayeva, Marina, **IX:**3753
Tupolev, Andrei Nikolayevich, **IX:**3764
Vavilov, Nikolai Ivanovich, **IX:**3801
Yeltsin, Boris N., **IX:**4082
Zhukov, Georgy Konstantinovich, **IX:**4116

SPAIN
'Abd-al-Rahman III al-Nasir, **II:**7
Alfonso X, **II:**56
Alva, Duke of, **III:**18
Alvarado, Pedro de, **III:**21
Arnold of Villanova, **II:**79
Averroës, **II:**100
Balboa, Vasco Núñez de, **III:**45
Benjamin of Tudela, **II:**140
Buñuel, Luis, **VII:**505
Calderón de la Barca, Pedro, **IV:**235
Candela, Felix, **VII:**557
Carlos, Don, **V:**413
Casals, Pablo, **VII:**606
Catherine of Aragon, **III:**136

Cervantes, Miguel de, **IV:**265
Charles III, **IV:**287
Charles V, **III:**159
Cid, El, **II:**268
Columbus, Christopher, **III:**172
Coronado, Francisco Vásquez de, **III:**180
Cortés, Hernán, **III:**188
Dalí, Salvador, **VII:**827
Dominic, Saint, **II:**301
Falla, Manuel de, **VII:**1127
Ferdinand II and Isabella I, **III:**260
Franco, Francisco, **VII:**1200
García Lorca, Federico, **VII:**1290
Gaudí, Antonio, **VII:**1315
Goya, Francisco de, **IV:**569
Greco, El, **III:**311
Gris, Juan, **VIII**-1483
Ibn al-'Arabi, **II:**491
Ibn Gabirol, **II:**498
Isidore of Seville, Saint, **II:**518
James I the Conqueror, **II:**529
Jiménez de Cisneros, Francisco,
   III:392
John of the Cross, Saint, **III:**401
Las Casas, Bartolomé de, **III:**413
Loyola, Saint Ignatius of, **III:**437
Lull, Raymond, **II:**608
Maimonides, Moses, **II:**619
Martial, **I:**532
Miró, Joan, **VIII:**2546
Moses de León, **II:**648
Ortega y Gasset, José, **IX:**2843
Philip II, **III:**599
Picasso, Pablo, **IX:**2997
Pinzón Brothers, The, **III:**610
Pizarro, Francisco, **III:**620
Ponce de Léon, Juan, **III:**629
Priscillian, **I:**694
Raymond of Peñafort, **II:**776
Saragossa, La, **VI:**1958
Segovia, Andrés, **IX:**3383
Servetus, Michael, **III:**675
Siloé, Diego de, **III:**696
Soto, Hernando de, **III:**699
Teresa of Ávila, Saint, **III:**713
Theodosius the Great, **I:**868
Torquemada, Tomás de, **III:**725
Unamuno y Jugo, Miguel de, **IX:**3783
Vega Carpio, Lope de, **IV:**1361
Velázquez, Diego, **IV:**1364
Vitoria, Francisco de, **III:**768
Xavier, Saint Francis, **III:**788

SWABIA. *See* **GERMANY**

SWEDEN
Arrhenius, Svante August, **VII:**114
Bergman, Ingmar, **VII:**278
Borg, Björn, **VII:**368
Charles XII, **IV:**290
Charles XIV John, **V:**474
Christina, **IV:**304
Gustavus II Adolphus, **IV:**589
Hammarskjöld, Dag, **VIII:**1529
Lagerlöf, Selma, **VIII:**2065
Lind, Jenny, **VI:**1385
Linnaeus, **IV:**846
Margaret of Denmark, Norway, and Sweden,
   II:626
Meitner, Lise, **VIII:**2476
Myrdal, Gunnar, **VIII:**2671
Nobel, Alfred, **VI:**1673
Oxenstierna, Axel, **IV:**1052
Sachs, Nelly, **IX:**3285
Söderblom, Nathan, **IX:**3456
Strindberg, August, **IX:**3566
Swedenborg, Emanuel, **IV:**1302
Theorell, Axel Hugo Teodor, **IX:**3654
Torstenson, Lennart, **IV:**1335

SWITZERLAND
Barth, Karl, **VII:**203
Bernoulli Family, The, **IV:**122
Bleuler, Eugen, **VII:**328
Brunner, Emil, **VII:**475
Burckhardt, Jacob, **V:**358
Dunant, Jean-Henri, **V:**711
Euler, Leonhard, **IV:**443
Frisch, Max, **VII:**1238
Gesner, Conrad, **III:**298
Giacometti, Alberto, **VII:**1359
Guillaume, Charles-Édouard, **VIII:**1502
Jung, Carl, **VIII:**1896
Kauffmann, Angelica, **IV:**765
Klee, Paul, **VIII:**2005
Le Corbusier, **VIII:**2137
Mann, Thomas, **VIII:**2392
Marat, Jean-Paul, **IV:**910
Paracelsus, **III:**584
Pauli, Wolfgang, **IX:**2923
Pestalozzi, Johann Heinrich, **VI:**1767
Piaget, Jean, **IX:**2990
Piccard, Auguste and Jean-Felix, **IX:**3002
Rorschach, Hermann, **IX:**3236
Saussure, Ferdinand de, **IX:**3340

Steiner, Jakob, **VI:**2118
Zwingli, Huldrych, **III:**791

SYRIA. *See also* **ARABIA; ASSYRIA; IRAN;**
 IRAQ; MESOPOTAMIA
Antiochus the Great, **I:**63
Battani, al-, **II:**121
Chrysostom, Saint John, **I:**184
Ibn al-'Arabi, **II:**491
Ignatius of Antioch, **I:**440
John of Damascus, **II:**544
Lucian, **I:**507
Saladin, **II:**809
Seleucus I Nicator, **I:**767
Simeon Stylites, Saint, **I:**783
Theodoret of Cyrrhus, **I:**865
Yaqut, **II:**1013

TAIWAN
Chiang Kai-shek, **VII:**664

TAJIKISTAN
Enver Pasha, **VII:**1078

TANGANYIKA. *See* **TANZANIA**

TANZANIA
Nyerere, Julius, **VIII:**2773

TENOCHTITLÁN. *See* **MEXICO**

TEXCOCO. *See* **MEXICO**

THRACE
Democritus, **I:**249

THURINGIA. *See* **GERMANY**

TRANSJORDAN. *See* **JORDAN**

TUNISIA. *See also* **CARTHAGE**
Bourguiba, Habib, **VII:**391
Ibn Khaldun, **II:**502

TURKEY. *See also* **ASIA MINOR; BITHYNIA;**
 BYZANTINE EMPIRE; CAPPADOCIA;
 CILICIA; MOPSUESTIA; OTTOMAN
 EMPIRE; PERGA; PONTUS
Atatürk, Kemal, **VII:**133
Enver Pasha, **VII:**1078
Halide Edib Adivar, **VIII:**1522
İnönü, İsmet, **VIII:**1812

TURKMENISTAN. *See* **SOVIET UNION**

UKRAINE
Ba'al Shem Tov, **IV:**73

UNITED STATES
Abernathy, Ralph David, **VII:**9
Acheson, Dean, **VII:**16
Adams, Abigail, **IV:**12
Adams, Henry, **V:**15
Adams, John, **IV:**16
Adams, John Quincy, **V:**20
Adams, Samuel, **IV:**21
Addams, Jane, **VII:**21
Adler, Felix, **V:**26
Agassiz, Louis, **V:**30
Akalaitis, Joanne, **VII:**34
Albright, Madeleine, **VII:**49
Alcott, Bronson, **V:**37
Alcott, Louisa May, **V:**40
Alger, Horatio, **V:**51
Ali, Muhammad, **VII:**53
Allen, Ethan, **IV:**34
Altgeld, John Peter, **V:**54
Anderson, Marian, **VII:**70
Angelou, Maya, **VII:**79
Anthony, Susan B., **V:**61
Appleseed, Johnny, **V:**66
Arbus, Diane, **VII:**95
Arendt, Hannah, **VII:**98
Armstrong, Edwin H., **VII:**102
Armstrong, Louis, **VII:**105
Armstrong, Neil, **VII:**110
Arnold, Benedict, **IV:**64
Arthur, Chester A., **V:**77
Arzner, Dorothy, **VII:**117
Astaire, Fred, **VII:**125
Astor, John J., **V:**82
Audubon, John James, **V:**86
Austin, Stephen Fuller, **V:**94
Balanchine, George, **VII:**155
Balch, Emily Greene, **VII:**160
Baldwin, James, **VII:**164
Ball, Lucille, **VII:**176
Ballard, Robert Duane, **VII:**180
Bancroft, George, **V:**124
Banneker, Benjamin, **IV:**88
Barber, Samuel, **VII:**191
Barnard, Henry, **V:**130
Barnes, Djuna, **VII:**199
Barnum, P.T., **V:**133
Barton, Clara, **V:**142

Baum, L. Frank, **V:**154
Beard, Charles A., **VII:**221
Beecher, Catharine, **V:**170
Beecher, Henry Ward, **V:**174
Bell, Alexander Graham, **V:**185
Bellow, Saul, **VII:**247
Benedict, Ruth, **VII:**255
Benét, Stephen Vincent, **VII:**263
Bennett, James Gordon, **V:**190
Benton, Thomas Hart, **V:**195
Berlin, Irving, **VII:**287
Bernstein, Leonard, **VII:**295
Bethe, Hans Albrecht, **VII:**300
Biddle, Nicholas, **V:**225
Bierce, Ambrose, **V:**230
Bierstadt, Albert, **V:**233
Bingham, George Caleb, **V:**236
Black, Hugo L., **VII:**321
Black Hawk, **V:**247
Blackwell, Elizabeth, **V:**251
Blaine, James G., **V:**255
Boas, Franz, **VII:**339
Boone, Daniel, **IV:**163
Booth, Edwin, **V:**271
Borah, William E., **V:**279
Borden, Lizzie, **V:**283
Bourke-White, Margaret, **VII:**395
Bradford, William, **IV:**189
Bradley, Omar N., **VII:**403
Bradstreet, Anne, **IV:**193
Brady, Mathew B., **V:**294
Brandeis, Louis D., **VII:**419
Brando, Marlon, **VII:**424
Brant, Joseph, **IV:**196
Braun, Wernher von, **VII:**440
Bridgman, Percy Williams, **VII:**463
Brown, John, **V:**321
Bryan, William Jennings, **VII:**479
Bryant, William Cullen, **V:**343
Buchanan, James, **V:**346
Buck, Pearl S., **VII:**486
Bulfinch, Charles, **V:**349
Bunche, Ralph, **VII:**501
Burbank, Luther, **V:**353
Burger, Warren E., **VII:**509
Burnett, Frances Hodgson, **V:**361
Burnham, Daniel Hudson, **V:**365
Burr, Aaron, **V:**369
Burroughs, Edgar Rice, **VII:**516
Bush, George, **VII:**520
Butler, Nicholas Murray, **VII:**524
Byrd, Richard E., **VII:**534

Cabrini, Frances Xavier, **V:**396
Calamity Jane, **V:**390
Calder, Alexander, **VII:**538
Calhoun, John C., **V:**394
Campbell, Alexander, **V:**401
Campbell, Kim, **VII:**549
Capone, Alphonse, **VII:**563
Capote, Truman, **VII:**567
Cardozo, Benjamin Nathan, **VII:**575
Carlson, Chester F., **VII:**579
Carnap, Rudolf, **VII:**582
Carnegie, Andrew, **V:**420
Carroll, Charles, **IV:**250
Carson, Kit, **V:**429
Carson, Rachel, **VII:**585
Carter, Jimmy, **VII:**589
Carver, George Washington, **VII:**602
Cassatt, Mary, **V:**434
Cather, Willa, **VII:**621
Catlin, George, **V:**443
Catt, Carrie Chapman, **VII:**627
Champlain, Samuel de, **IV:**271
Channing, William Ellery, **V:**470
Chaplin, Charles, **VII:**653
Charles, Ray, **VII:**657
Chase, Salmon P., **V:**477
Chase, Samuel, **IV:**293
Child, Lydia Maria, **V:**489
Chisholm, Shirley, **VII:**668
Chomsky, Noam, **VII:**673
Chopin, Kate, **V:**497
Clark, George Rogers, **IV:**312
Clark, William, **VI:**1358
Clay, Henry, **V:**507
Cleveland, Grover, **V:**512
Clinton, Bill, **VII:**707
Clinton, DeWitt, **V:**517
Clinton, Hillary Rodham, **VII:**713
Cobb, Ty, **VII:**717
Cody, William Frederick, **V:**530
Colt, Samuel, **V:**540
Coltrane, John, **VII:**741
Compton, Arthur Holly, **VII:**745
Conant, James Bryant, **VII:**748
Cooke, Jay, **V:**551
Coolidge, Calvin, **VII:**762
Cooper, James Fenimore, **V:**560
Copland, Aaron, **VII:**766
Copley, John Singleton, **IV:**356
Cotton, John, **IV:**371
Crane, Hart, **VII:**789
Crane, Stephen, **V:**569

Crawford, Cheryl, **VII:**793
Crazy Horse, **V:**573
Crockett, David, **V:**578
cummings, e.e., **VII:**804
Cunningham, Imogen, **VII:**808
Cushing, Caleb, **V:**581
Cushing, Harvey Williams, **VII:**823
Custer, George A., **V:**585
Danilova, Alexandra, **VII:**832
Darrow, Clarence, **VII:**839
Davis, Bette, **VII:**843
Davis, Jefferson, **V:**614
Dawidowicz, Lucy S., **VII:**847
Day, Dorothy, **VII:**850
Debs, Eugene V., **VII:**880
Decatur, Stephen, **V:**634
de Forest, Lee, **VII:**858
de Mille, Agnes, **VII:**874
Demille, Cecil B., **VII:**896
Dempsey, Jack, **VII:**900
Derrida, Jacques, **VII:**912
Dewey, George, **V:**656
Dewey, John, **VII:**916
Dewey, Melvil, **V:**660
Dickinson, Emily, **V:**667
Dickinson, John, **IV:**408
Dietrich, Marlene, **VII:**930
Dimaggio, Joe, **VII:**934
Disney, Walt, **VII:**938
Dix, Dorothea, **V:**680
Dole, Robert J., **VII:**947
Douglas, Stephen A., **V:**692
Douglass, Frederick, **V:**695
Dreiser, Theodore, **VII:**954
du Bois, W.E.B., **VII:**963
Duke, James Buchanan, **V:**704
Dulles, John Foster, **VII:**976
Dunbar, Paul Laurence, **V:**714
Duncan, Isadora, **VII:**980
Dunham, Katherine, **VII:**984
Du Pont, Eleuthère Irénée, **V:**718
Eads, James Buchanan, **V:**729
Eakins, Thomas, **V:**732
Earhart, Amelia, **VII:**992
Earp, Wyatt, **V:**735
Eastman, George, **VII:**996
Eddy, Mary Baker, **V:**738
Edison, Thomas Alva, **V:**743
Edwards, Jonathan, **IV:**428
Einstein, Albert, **VII:**1035
Eisenhower, Dwight D., **VII:**1043
Eliade, Mircea, **VII:**1055

Eliot, Charles William, **V:**748
Eliot, John, **IV:**435
Eliot, T.S., **VII:**1058
Ellington, Duke, **VII:**1066
Emerson, Ralph Waldo, **V:**755
Ephron, Nora, **VII:**1083
Epstein, Sir Jacob, **VII:**1087
Erdrich, Louise, **VII:**1091
Evert, Chris, **VII:**1112
Farragut, David G., **V:**772
Farrand, Beatrix Jones, **VII:**1130
Faulkner, William, **VII:**1133
Feinstein, Dianne, **VII:**1137
Fermi, Enrico, **VII:**1145
Ferraro, Geraldine, **VII:**1153
Field, Marshall, **V:**783
Field, Stephen J., **V:**787
Fillmore, Millard, **V:**792
Fitch, John, **IV:**476
Fitzgerald, Ella, **VII:**1157
Fitzgerald, F. Scott, **VII:**1161
Flexner, Abraham, **VII:**1169
Ford, Gerald R., **VII:**1180
Ford, Henry, **VII:**1184
Forrest, Edwin, **V:**800
Forten, Charlotte, **V:**807
Foster, Stephen Collins, **V:**810
Fowler, Lydia Folger, **V:**822
Frankenthaler, Helen, **VII:**1208
Frankfurter, Felix, **VII:**1212
Franklin, Aretha, **VII:**1216
Franklin, Benjamin, **IV:**492
Frémont, John C., **V:**839
Friedan, Betty, **VII:**1231
Frost, Robert, **VII:**1250
Fuller, Loie, **VII:**1261
Fuller, Margaret, **V:**849
Fuller, R. Buckminster, **VII:**1265
Fulton, Robert, **V:**854
Gadsden, James, **V:**858
Gallatin, Albert, **V:**861
Garbo, Greta, **VII:**1286
Gardner, Erle Stanley, **VII:**1297
Gardner, Isabella Stewart, **VII:**1300
Garfield, James A., **V:**875
Garland, Judy, **VII:**1304
Garrison, William Lloyd, **V:**883
Garvey, Marcus, **VII:**1311
Geddes, Norman Bel, **VII:**1319
Gehrig, Lou, **VII:**1322
Geisel, Theodor Seuss, **VII:**1329
George, Henry, **V:**906

Geronimo, **V:**915
Gershwin, George, **VII:**1347
Gershwin, Ira, **VII:**1352
Gesell, Arnold, **VII:**1356
Gibbons, James, **V:**919
Gibbs, Josiah Willard, **V:**923
Gibson, Althea, **VII:**1363
Gillespie, Dizzy, **VII:**1370
Gish, Lillian, **VII:**1383
Glenn, John H., Jr., **VII:**1387
Goddard, Robert H., **VIII:**1396
Godkin, Edwin Lawrence, **VIII**-1400
Goethals, George Washington, **VIII**-1408
Goldman, Emma, **VIII**-1411
Goldwyn, Samuel, **VIII**-1415
Gompers, Samuel, **V:**956
Goodman, Benny, **VIII**-1419
Goodyear, Charles, **V:**960
Gore, Albert, **VIII**-1431
Gorgas, William Crawford, **VIII**-1434
Graham, Billy, **VIII**-1447
Graham, Katharine, **VIII**-1451
Graham, Martha, **VIII**-1455
Grant, Ulysses S., **V:**975
Gray, Asa, **V:**979
Greeley, Horace, **V:**982
Greene, Nathanael, **IV:**574
Greenspan, Alan, **VIII**-1471
Griffith, D.W., **VIII**-1478
Gropius, Walter, **VIII**-1486
Guggenheim, Daniel, **VIII**-1498
Hale, Sarah Josepha, **V:**1022
Halsey, William F., **VIII:**1525
Hamilton, Alexander, **IV:**608
Hammerstein, Oscar, II, **VIII:**1533
Hancock, John, **IV:**613
Hand, Learned, **VIII:**1541
Hanna, Marcus A., **V:**1029
Hansberry, Lorraine, **VIII:**1545
Harding, Warren G., **VIII:**1550
Harper, William Rainey, **V:**1044
Harriman, William Averell, **VIII:**1560
Harris, Joel Chandler, **V:**1049
Harrison, Benjamin, **V:**1053
Harrison, William Henry, **V:**1061
Hart, Lorenz, **VIII:**1566
Hawthorne, Nathaniel, **V:**1064
Hay, John, **V:**1068
Hayden, Ferdinand Vandeveer, **V:**1072
Hayes, Helen, **VIII:**1588
Hayes, Rutherford B., **V:**1075
Hayslip, Le Ly, **VIII:**1593

Hayworth, Rita, **VIII:**1596
H.D., **VIII:**1505
Hearst, William Randolph, **VIII:**1601
Hellman, Lillian, **VIII:**1620
Hemingway, Ernest, **VIII:**1624
Henry, Joseph, **V:**1093
Henry, O, **V:**1096
Henry, Patrick, **IV:**647
Hepburn, Katharine, **VIII:**1637
Hernandez, Aileen Clarke, **VIII:**1641
Hickok, Wild Bill, **V:**1107
Higginson, Thomas Wentworth, **V:**1110
Hill, James Jerome, **IV:**659
Hiss, Alger, **VIII:**1683
Hitchcock, Alfred, **VIII:**1687
Hobby, Oveta Culp, **VIII:**1703
Holiday, Billie, **VIII:**1715
Holland, John Philip, **V:**1123
Holmes, Oliver Wendell, **V:**1126
Holmes, Oliver Wendell, Jr., **VIII:**1720
Homer, Winslow, **V:**1133
Hoover, Herbert, **VIII:**1727
Hoover, J. Edgar, **VIII:**1732
Hopkins, Harry, **VIII:**1736
Hopper, Edward, **VIII:**1740
Horney, Karen, **VIII:**1744
Horowitz, Vladimir, **VIII:**1747
Houston, Sam, **V:**1137
Howe, Elias, **V:**1141
Howe, Julia Ward, **V:**1145
Howe, Samuel Gridley, **V:**1150
Huerta, Dolores, **VIII:**1762
Hughes, Charles Evans, **VIII:**1766
Hughes, Langston, **VIII:**1771
Hull, Cordell, **VIII:**1779
Humphrey, Hubert H., **VIII:**1783
Hurston, Zora Neale, **VIII:**1787
Hutchins, Robert M., **VIII:**1800
Hutchinson, Anne, **IV:**687
Hutchinson, Thomas, **IV:**691
Irving, Washington, **V:**1192
Ives, Charles, **VIII:**1820
Jackson, Andrew, **V:**1196
Jackson, Helen Hunt, **V:**1200
Jackson, Jesse L., **VIII:**1824
Jackson, Stonewall, **V:**1204
Jakobson, Roman, **VIII:**1831
James, Henry, **V:**1211
James, William, **V:**1216
Jay, John, **IV:**711
Jefferson, Thomas, **IV:**716
Jewett, Sarah Orne, **V:**1228

Johnson, Andrew, **V:**1232
Johnson, Lyndon B., **VIII:**1866
Jones, Bobby, **VIII:**1874
Jones, John Paul, **IV:**738
Jones, Mary Harris "Mother," 1879
Joplin, Janis, **VIII:**1883
Joplin, Scott, **V:**1239
Jordan, Barbara, **VIII:**1887
Joseph, Chief, **V:**1242
Kamehameha I, **VI:**1255
Keller, Helen, **VIII:**1924
Kemble, Fanny, **VI:**1273
Kennedy, John F., **VIII:**1928
Kennedy, Robert F., **VIII:**1932
Kent, James, **VI:**1277
Kerouac, Jack, **VIII:**1945
Key, Francis Scott, **VI:**1281
King, Billie Jean, **VIII:**1968
King, Martin Luther, Jr., **VIII:**1971
King, Stephen, **VIII:**1977
Kinsey, Alfred Charles, **VIII:**1986
Kirkpatrick, Jeane, **VIII:**1994
Kissinger, Henry A., **VIII:**1998
Krasner, Lee, **VIII:**2023
Kübler-Ross, Elisabeth, **VIII:**2030
La Follette, Robert M., **VIII:**2047
La Guardia, Fiorello Henry, **VIII:**2054
Lang, Fritz, **VIII:**2077
Lang, K.D., **VIII:**2080
Lange, Dorothea, **VIII:**2083
Langer, Susanne K., **VIII:**2087
Langley, Samuel Pierpont, **VI:**1313
Lathrop, Julia C., **VIII:**2096
Latrobe, Benjamin Henry, **VI:**1327
Lawrence, Ernest Orlando, **VIII:**2121
Lazarus, Emma, **VI:**1334
Lee, Ann, **IV:**817
Lee, Robert E., **VI:**1338
Le Gallienne, Eva, **VIII:**2141
Lewis, John L., **VIII:**2170
Lewis, Meriwether, **VI:**1358
Lewis, Sinclair, **VIII:**2174
Liliuokalani, **VI:**1372
Lin, Maya Ying, **VIII:**2185
Lincoln, Abraham, **VI:**1380
Lindbergh, Charles A., **VIII:**2193
Lippmann, Walter, **VIII:**2203
Lockwood, Belva A., **VI:**1406
Lodge, Henry Cabot, **VIII:**2219
London, Jack, **VIII:**2223
Long, Huey, **VIII:**2227
Longfellow, Henry Wadsworth, **VI:**1414

Loos, Anita, **VIII:**2231
Louis, Joe, **VIII:**2241
Low, Juliette Gordon, **VIII:**2246
Lowell, Amy, **VIII:**2249
Luce, Clare Boothe, **VIII:**2256
Luce, Henry R., **VIII:**2260
Lyon, Mary, **VI:**1423
MacArthur, Douglas, **VIII:**2295
MacKinnon, Catharine A., **VIII:**2325
McCarthy, Joseph R., **VIII:**2300
McCarthy, Mary, **VIII:**2304
McCormick, Cyrus Hall, **VI:**1431
McCullers, Carson, **VIII:**2308
McGillivray, Alexander, **IV:**875
McGuffey, William Holmes, **VI:**1440
McKinley, William, **VI:**1453
McMillan, Edwin Mattison, **VIII:**2336
Madison, Dolley, **VI:**1464
Madison, James, **IV:**886
Mailer, Norman, **VIII:**2365
Malcolm X, **VIII:**2373
Mankiller, Wilma P., **VIII:**2389
Mann, Horace, **IV:**894
Marciano, Rocky, **VIII:**2411
Marshall, George C., **VIII:**2429
Marshall, John, **VI:**1487
Marshall, Thurgood, **VIII:**2433
Martin, Agnes, **VIII:**2437
Mason, George, **IV:**926
Massasoit, **IV:**930
Mather, Cotton, **IV:**934
Mather, Increase, **IV:**938
Maury, Matthew Fontaine, **VI:**1507
Mayo, William J. and Charles H., **VIII:**2465
Mead, Margaret, **VIII:**2468
Mellon, Andrew, **VIII:**2480
Melville, Herman, **VI:**1520
Mencken, H.L., **VIII:**2483
Mendelsohn, Erich, **VIII:**2487
Mergenthaler, Ottmar, **VI:**1541
Metacomet, **IV:**954
Michelson, Albert A., **VI:**1551
Michener, James A., **VIII:**2517
Mies Van Der Rohe, Ludwig, **VIII:**2520
Millay, Edna St. Vincent, **VIII:**2529
Miller, Arthur, **VIII:**2533
Millett, Kate, **VIII:**2536
Millikan, Robert Andrews, **VIII:**2539
Mitchell, William, **VIII:**2554
Monroe, James, **VI:**1570
Monroe, Marilyn, **VIII:**2587
Moody, Dwight L., **VI:**1575

Moore, Marianne, **VIII:**2614
Morgan, J.P., **VI:**1579
Morgan, Lewis Henry, **VI:**1584
Morgan, Thomas Hunt, **VIII:**2618
Morris, Robert, **IV:**999
Morrison, Toni, **VIII:**2626
Morse, Samuel F.B., **VI:**1592
Morton, William Thomas Green, **VI:**1596
Moses, Grandma, **VIII:**2633
Mott, John R., **VIII:**2637
Mott, Lucretia, **VI:**1600
Muir, John, **VI:**1608
Muller, Hermann Joseph, **VIII:**2651
Murrow, Edward R., **VIII:**2662
Nabokov, Vladimir, **VIII:**2675
Nader, Ralph, **VIII:**2679
Nast, Thomas, **VI:**1627
Nation, Carry, **VI:**1630
Navratilova, Martina, **VIII:**2702
Neumann, John von, **VIII:**2724
Nevelson, Louise, **VIII:**2728
Newcomb, Simon, **VI:**1638
Niebuhr, Reinhold, **VIII:**2735
Nimitz, Chester W., **VIII:**2750
Nixon, Richard M., **VIII:**2758
Norman, Jessye, **VIII:**2769
Oakley, Annie, **VI:**1677
O'Connor, Flannery, **IX:**2785
O'Connor, Sandra Day, **IX:**2789
Oglethorpe, James Edward, **IV:**1043
O'Keeffe, Georgia, **IX:**2800
Olmsted, Frederick Law, **VI:**1691
Onassis, Jacqueline Kennedy, **IX:**2815
O'Neill, Eugene, **IX:**2819
O'Neill, Thomas Philip, Jr., **IX:**2824
Oppenheimer, J. Robert, **IX:**2833
Ortega, Katherine Davalos, **IX:**2840
Osborne, Thomas Mott, **IX:**2852
Osceola, **VI:**1695
Owens, Jesse, **IX:**2862
Paine, Thomas, **IV:**1055
Palmer, Alice Freeman, **VI:**1715
Parker, Charlie, **IX:**2880
Parker, Dorothy, **IX:**2884
Parker, Theodore, **VI:**1727
Parkman, Francis, **VI:**1735
Parks, Rosa, **IX:**2888
Parrington, Vernon L., **IX:**2892
Parton, Dolly, **IX:**2896
Patton, George S., **IX:**2911
Paul, Alice, **IX:**2915
Pauling, Linus, **IX:**2926

Peale, Charles Willson, **IV:**1070
Peary, Robert Edwin, **IX:**2941
Pei, I.M., **IX:**2946
Peirce, Charles Sanders, **VI:**1756
Penn, William, **IV:**1078
Perkins, Frances, **IX:**2961
Perot, H. Ross, **IX:**2973
Perry, Matthew C., **VI:**1760
Perry, Oliver Hazard, **VI:**1764
Pershing, John J., **IX:**2983
Phillips, Wendell, **VI:**1771
Pickford, Mary, **IX:**3006
Picotte, Susan La Flesche, **IX:**3010
Pierce, Franklin, **VI:**1775
Pike, Zebulon Montgomery, **IV:**1094
Plath, Sylvia, **IX:**3036
Pocahontas, **IV:**1106
Poe, Edgar Allan, **VI:**1794
Polk, James K., **VI:**1801
Pollock, Jackson, **IX:**3048
Pontiac, **IV:**1110
Porter, Cole, **IX:**3055
Porter, Katherine Anne, **IX:**3059
Powell, Colin L., **IX:**3070
Powell, John Wesley, **VI:**1810
Powhatan, **IV:**1122
Prescott, William Hickling, **VI:**1814
Presley, Elvis, **IX:**3076
Price, Leontyne, **IX:**3081
Pulitzer, Joseph, **VI:**1825
Rabi, Isidor Isaac, **IX:**3101
Rachmaninoff, Sergei, **IX:**3105
Randolph, A. Philip, **IX:**3112
Rankin, Jeannette, **IX:**3117
Rauschenbusch, Walter, **IX:**3125
Reagan, Ronald, **IX:**3136
Red Cloud, **VI:**1850
Reed, Walter, **VI:**1857
Rehnquist, William H., **IX:**3142
Remington, Frederic, **VI:**1861
Reno, Janet, **IX:**3153
Reuther, Walter P., **IX:**3161
Revere, Paul, **IV:**1156
Richards, Ann, **IX:**3169
Richardson, Henry Hobson, **VI:**1882
Rickover, Hyman G., **IX:**3171
Ride, Sally, **IX:**3178
Robeson, Paul, **IX:**3187
Robinson, Jackie, **IX:**3193
Rockefeller, John D., **VI:**1896
Rockwell, Norman, **IX:**3198
Rodgers, Richard, **IX:**3201

Roebling, John Augustus, **VI**:1904
Rogers, Will, **IX**:3204
Roosevelt, Eleanor, **IX**:3217
Roosevelt, Franklin D., **IX**:3222
Roosevelt, Theodore, **IX**:3228
Root, Elihu, **IX**:3232
Rose, Pete, **IX**:3239
Ross, Betsy, **IV**:1191
Ross, John, **VI**:1910
Ross, Nellie Tayloe, **IX**:3243
Royce, Josiah, **IX**:3254
Rukeyser, Muriel, **IX**:3257
Rush, Benjamin, **IV**:1202
Russell, Bill, **IX**:3268
Ruth, Babe, **IX**:3273
Sacagawea, **VI**:1933
Sacco, Nicola, **IX**:3281
Sagan, Carl, **IX**:3292
Saint-Gaudens, Augustus, **VI**:1940
Salinger, J.D., **IX**:3301
Salk, Jonas Edward, **IX**:3305
Sandburg, Carl, **IX**:3308
Sanger, Margaret, **IX**:3313
Santayana, George, **IX**:3317
Sargent, John Singer, **VI**:1961
Sauvé, Jeanne, **IX**:3344
Schoenberg, Arnold, **IX**:3357
Schurz, Carl, **VI**:1996
Scott, Dred, **VI**:1999
Scott, Winfield, **VI**:2009
Scripps, Edward Wyllis, **VI**:2014
Seaborg, Glenn Theodore, **IX**:3375
Sendak, Maurice, **IX**:3387
Sequoyah, **VI**:2025
Seton, Saint Elizabeth Ann Bayley,
    VI:2029
Sewall, Samuel, **IV**:1225
Seward, William H., **VI**:2037
Sexton, Anne, **IX**:3395
Shaw, Anna Howard, **VI**:2044
Shays, Daniel, **IV**:1239
Shepard, Alan, **IX**:3405
Sherman, Roger, **IV**:1242
Sherman, William Tecumseh, **VI**:2057
Sinatra, Frank, **IX**:3422
Sinclair, Upton, **IX**:3426
Sitting Bull, **VI**:2070
Skinner, B.F., **IX**:3431
Slater, Samuel, **VI**:2074
Smith, Alfred E., **IX**:3439
Smith, Bessie, **IX**:3442
Smith, Jedediah Strong, **VI**:2077

Smith, John, **IV**:1253
Smith, Joseph, **VI**:2080
Smith, Margaret Chase, **IX**:3446
Smith, Theobald, **IX**:3450
Sousa, John Philip, **IX**:3466
Spock, Benjamin, **IX**:3478
Standish, Miles, **IV**:1273
Stanford, Leland, **VI**:2096
Stanton, Edwin M., **VI**:2106
Stanton, Elizabeth Cady, **VI**:2110
Steichen, Edward, **IX**:3501
Stein, Gertrude, **IX**:3511
Steinbeck, John, **IX**:3515
Steinem, Gloria, **IX**:3519
Steinmetz, Charles Proteus, **VI**:2121
Stephens, Alexander H., **VI**:2129
Stevens, Thaddeus, **VI**:2136
Stevenson, Adlai E., **IX**:3523
Stewart, James, **IX**:3528
Stieglitz, Alfred, **IX**:3532
Stimson, Henry L., **IX**:3537
Stone, Harlan Fiske, **IX**:3546
Stone, Lucy, **VI**:2143
Story, Joseph, **VI**:2147
Stowe, Harriet Beecher, **VI**:2151
Stravinsky, Igor, **IX**:3559
Stuart, Gilbert, **IV**:1289
Stuyvesant, Peter, **IV**:1294
Sullivan, Harry Stack, **IX**:3575
Sullivan, Louis, **VI**:2167
Sumner, Charles, **VI**:2170
Sunday, Billy, **IX**:3582
Taft, Robert A., **IX**:3590
Taft, William Howard, **IX**:3594
Talbot, Marion, **IX**:3603
Tallchief, Maria, **IX**:3607
Taney, Roger Brooke, **VI**:2189
Tarbell, Ida, **IX**:3614
Taylor, Frederick Winslow, **IX**:3618
Taylor, Zachary, **VI**:2194
Teasdale, Sara, **IX**:3622
Tecumseh, **VI**:2203
Tekakwitha, Kateri, **IV**:1316
Teller, Edward, **IX**:3631
Terry, Megan, **IX**:3642
Tesla, Nikola, **VI**:2219
Thayer, Sylvanus, **VI**:2223
Thomas, Clarence, **IX**:3657
Thomas, Norman, **IX**:3660
Thomas, Theodore, **VI**:2230
Thoreau, Henry David, **VI**:2234
Thorndike, Edward L., **IX**:3669

Thorpe, Jim, **IX**:3672
Thurber, James, **IX**:3677
Tillich, Paul, **IX**:3685
Tombaugh, Clyde William, **IX**:3699
Truman, Harry S, **IX**:3740
Truth, Sojourner, **VI**:2255
Tubman, Harriet, **VI**:2264
Tuchman, Barbara, **IX**:3760
Turner, Frederick Jackson, **IX**:3771
Turner, Nat, **VI**:2276
Twain, Mark, **VI**:2279
Tweed, William Marcy "Boss", **VI**:2279
Tyler, John, **VI**:2288
Urey, Harold C., **IX**:3787
Van Buren, Martin, **VI**:2292
Vanderbilt, Cornelius, **VI**:2296
Varèse, Edgard, **IX**:3794
Veblen, Thorstein, **IX**:3805
Wach, Joachim, **IX**:3829
Waksman, Selman Abraham, **IX**:3833
Wald, Lillian D., **IX**:3837
Walker, Alice, **IX**:3849
Walker, Madam C.J., **IX**:3853
Wallace, George C., **IX**:3857
Wallace, Henry A., **IX**:3860
Walters, Barbara, **IX**:3868
Ward, Lester Frank, **VI**:2328
Ward, Montgomery, **VI**:2331
Warhol, Andy, **IX**:3884
Warren, Earl, **IX**:3888
Warren, Robert Penn, **IX**:3893
Washington, Booker T., **VI**:2335
Washington, George, **IV**:1405
Watson, James D., **IX**:3897
Wayne, John, **IX**:3901
Webster, Daniel, **VI**:2344
Webster, Noah, **IV**:1417
Weill, Kurt, **IX**:3926
Welles, Orson, **IX**:3934
Wells-Barnett, Ida B., **IX**:3941
West, Mae, **IX**:3949
Westinghouse, George, **VI**:2358
Wharton, Edith, **IX**:3953
Whipple, George Hoyt, **IX**:3957
Whistler, James McNeill, **VI**:2363
White, Walter, **IX**:3961
Whitman, Walt, **VI**:2368
Whitney, Eli, **IV**:1431
Whitney, Gertrude Vanderbilt, **IX**:3969
Whittier, John Greenleaf, **VI**:2374
Wiener, Norbert, **IX**:3976
Wiesel, Elie, **IX**:3980

Wightman, Hazel Hotchkiss, **IX**:3989
Wilder, Laura Ingalls, **IX**:3992
Wilkes, Charles, **VI**:2381
Willard, Emma, **VI**:2384
Willard, Frances, **VI**:2388
Williams, George Washington, **VI**:2396
Williams, Roger, **IV**:1451
Williams, Tennessee, **IX**:4007
Wilson, Edmund, **IX**:4012
Wilson, James, **IV**:1455
Wilson, Woodrow, **IX**:4020
Winfrey, Oprah, **IX**:4029
Winthrop, John, **IV**:1463
Wise, Isaac Mayer, **VI**:2400
Wise, Stephen Samuel, **IX**:4033
Witherspoon, John, **IV**:1467
Wolfe, Thomas, **IX**:4041
Wood, Grant, **IX**:4045
Woods, Tiger, **IX**:4049
Woodward, Robert Burns, **IX**:4052
Workman, Fanny Bullock, **VI**:2410
Wright, Frank Lloyd, **IX**:4060
Wright, Wilbur and Orville, **IX**:4064
Wyeth, Andrew, **IX**:4072
Young, Brigham, **VI**:2414
Zaharias, "Babe" Didrikson, **IX**:4096
Zanuck, Darryl F., **IX**:4100
Zenger, John Peter, **IV**:1484
Zwilich, Ellen Taaffe, **IX**:4121
Zworykin, Vladimir, **IX**:4125

UZBEKISTAN. *See* **SOVIET UNION**

VENEZUELA
Bolívar, Simón, **V**:267
Sucre, Antonio José de, **VI**:2164

VENICE, REPUBLIC OF. *See* **ITALY**

VIETNAM
Ho Chi Minh, **VIII**:1698
Vo Nguyen Giap, **IX**:3821

VLADIMIR-SUZDAL
Alexander Nevsky, **II**:52

WALES
Diana, Princess of Wales, **VII**:923
Grove, Sir William Robert, **V**:1010
Owen, Robert, **VI**:1708
Russell, Bertrand, **IX**:3264
Stanley, Henry Morton, **VI**:2101

WEST AFRICA. *See also* **MALI**
Sundjata, **II:**863

WEST GERMANY. *See also* **GERMANY**
Adenauer, Konrad, **VII:**26
Brandt, Willy, **VII:**427
Erhard, Ludwig, **VII:**1094

WEST INDIES
Constantine, Baron, **VII:**759

YUGOSLAVIA. *See also* **DALMATIA; SERBIA**
Djilas, Milovan, **VII:**944

Teresa, Mother, **IX:**3635
Tito, **IX:**3692

ZAIRE
Mobutu Sese Seko, **VIII:**2562
Tshombe, Moïse, **IX:**3745

ZIMBABWE
Mugabe, Robert, **VIII:**2647
Rhodes, Cecil, **VI:**1873

ZULU EMPIRE
Shaka, **VI:**2041

SUBJECT INDEX

Aalto, Alvar, **VII:1-4**
  Turan Sanomat, VII:1
Aaron, **I:1-4**
Aaron, Hank, IX:2797, 2798
Abahai, **IV:1-3,** 421, 423
Abailard, Pierre. *See* Abelard, Peter
Abano, Pietro d', **II:1-3**
  *Conciliator differentiarum philosophorum et
    praecipue medicorum,* II:1
  De venenis eorumque remediis, II:1
Abaqa, II:381
Abbas, Ferhat, **VII:5-8**
'Abbasid empire, II:18, 67-69, 124, 126, 437-439,
    522, 678
'Abbas the Great, **IV:4-6**
Abbott, Grace, VIII:2098, 2099
Abbott, Jack Henry, VIII:2367
ABC News, IX:3870
'Abd al-Mu'min, **II:4-6**
'Abd al-Qadirdir. *See* Abdelkader
'Abd-al-Rahman III al-Nasir, **II:7-9**
Abdelkader, **V:1-3**
Abdera, I:705
'Abduh, Muhammad, **V:4-6**
Abdülaziz, V:1207
Abdullah, King, VIII:1791
Abel, Niels Henrik, **V:7-9**
Abelard, Peter, **II:10-15,** 28, 50, 144, 995
  Apologia, II:14
  *Dialogue of a Philosopher with a Jew and a
    Christian,* II:14
  Ethics, II:13
  Sic et Non, II:13
  Story of My Misfortunes, The, II:13
  Tractatus de unitate et trinitate divina, II:13
Abe Masahiro, V:1181
Abercromby, Sir James, IV:37
Abernathy, Ralph David, **VII:9-12**
Abetz, Otto, VIII:2106
Abjuration, Act of, III:575
abolitionism
  Adams, V:23, 24
  Alcott, V:40
  Anthony, V:62
  Arthur, V:77
  Banneker, IV:88, 90, 91
  Beecher, Catharine, V:171
  Beecher, Henry Ward, V:174, 175

Benton, V:196
Brougham, V:314
Brown, V:321, 322, 324, 325
Bryant, V:344
Buchanan, V:347
Burr, V:369
Buxton, V:378-380
Channing, V:472
Chase, V:477-479
Child, V:489-491
Clay, V:508
Cushing, V:582, 583
Derby, V:654
Douglass, V:697
Dred Scott decision, VI:1999-2001, 2189,
    2191, 2192
Dunbar, V:714
Fillmore, V:792, 793
Forten, V:807-809
Fox, IV:482
Frémont, V:840
Garfield, V:876
Garibaldi, V:881
Garrison, V:883-886
Greeley, V:984, 985
Grey, V:996
Higginson, V:1110-1112
Howe, V:1151
Kemble, VI:1275
Lincoln, VI:1380, 1382, 1383
Mason, IV:926, 927
Mott, VI:1600-1602
Oglethorpe, IV:1045
Olmsted, VI:1691
Parker, VI:1727-1730
Phillips, VI:1771-1773
Sewall, IV:1225-1227
Seward, VI:2037-2039
Sharp, IV:1236-1238
Sinclair's *Manassas,* IX:3428
Stanton, VI:2110-2112
Stevens, VI:2137
Stone, VI:2143
Story, VI:2148, 2149
Stowe, VI:2151, 2152
Sumner, VI:2170-2173
Toussaint-Louverture, IV:1338-1340
Truth, VI:2255, 2257, 2258

Tubman, VI:2264-2267
Turner, VI:2276-2278
Van Buren, VI:2294
Whittier, VI:2374, 2375
Wilberforce, IV:1435-1438
William IV, VI:2394
Abominations, Tariff of, VI:2288, 2289
abortion
    Blackwell, V:252
    Campbell, VII:549
    Ferraro, VII:1154
    Herophilus, I:400
    John Paul II, VIII:1864
    O'Connor, IX:2790
    Reno, IX:3155
    Roe v. Wade, VII:511; IX:3143, 3144
    Sanger, IX:3313, 3314
    Steinem, IX:3519
Abraham, **I:5-8,** 564
Abraham of Beja, III:198
Absalom, I:243; II:815, 816
absolute monarchy
    Cameron, IV:240
    Colbert, IV:336
    Fortescue, III:268
    Frederick II, II:362
    Frobisher, III:275, 286
    Great Condé, IV:341-343
    Hobbes, IV:664, 665
    Richelieu, IV:1168
    Saint-Just, IV:1205, 1206
Abstract Expressionism. *See* Expressionism
Absurd, Theater of the, VIII:1816-1819
Absurdism, VII:240
Abu 'Abd Allah al-Shafi'i, II:33
Abu 'Ali al-Husain ibn 'Abdallah ibn Sina.
        See Avicenna
Abu 'Ali Hasan ibn 'Ali. *See* Nizam al-Mulk
Abu al-Qasim, II:714
Abu Hanifah, **II:16-19,** 33
Abu Hayyan al-Tawhidi, II:20
Abu Inan, II:502
Abu Ishaq al-Sahili, II:624
Abul Wefa, **II:20-22**
    Zij al-wadih, II:21
Abu Nidal, VII:92
Abu Simbel, I:737
Abu 'Ubaid al-Juzjani, II:106, 107
Abu Ya'qub Yusuf, II:100, 102
Abydos, I:736
Abyssinia, III:197-199
Academic Defense Corps, VIII:2742

Acamapichtli, III:528
Acatziri, I:125
Accademia Reale, IV:304
Acciaiuoli, Niccolò, II:150, 152
Acerbo Law, VIII:2668
Achaean League, I:215, 216, 673
Achaemenian dynastic empire, I:233-236, 238
Achaeus, I:63
Achamoth, I:912, 913
Achebe, Chinua, **VII:13-15**
    Anthills of the Savannah, VII:14
    Arrow of God, VII:13
    Beware, Soul-Brother and Other Poems, VII:14
    Chike and the River, VII:14
    Girls at War, VII:14
    Man of the People, A, VII:13
    No Longer at Ease, VII:13
    Sacrificial Egg and Other Short Stories, The,
        VII:13
    Things Fall Apart, VII:13, 14
Acheson, Dean, **VII:16-20**
Acheson-Lillienthal Report, IX:3102
Achilles asteroid, IX:4039
Achilli, Giacinto, VI:1643
ACLU. *See* American Civil Liberties Union
Acosta, Mercedes de
    Jeanne d'Arc, VIII:2142
acquired immune deficiency syndrome. *See* AIDS
Acre, Isaac de, II:649
Acre, siege of, II:782
Acropolis, I:280, 625, 962, 964
ACS. *See* American Colonization Society
Acte additionnel, V:611, 612
Action Committee for the United States of Europe,
        VIII:2585
Action Française, VIII:2425, 2427
Actium, Battle of, I:21, 133, 220
Acton, Lord, **V:10-14**
    "History of Liberty," V:11
Actors Studio, VII:424
Acts, Book of, I:243
Acts of the Apostles, I:822
adab culture, II:526, 527
Adad-nirari II, I:109
Adalbert, Saint, II:851
Adam, Adolphe-Charles, V:649
Adam, James and Robert, **IV:7-11**
    Works in Architecture, The, IV:10
Adam, William, IV:7
Adam and Eve, III:72; IV:961, 962
Adam de la Halle, **II:23-26**
    Jeu d' Adam ou de la feuillée, II:23-25

Jeu de Robin et de Marion, Le, II:24, 25
Nécrologe de la Confrérie des jongleurs et de bourgeois d' Arras, II:23
Roi de Secile, Le, II:23
Adamites, II:1031
Adam Kadmon, III:440
Adams, Abigail, **IV:12-14,** 16
Adams, Ansel, VII:809
Adams, Charles F., VI:2171
Adams, Henry, **V:15-19;** VI:1738; VIII:2219, 2220
   Democracy, V:16
   Education of Henry Adams, The, V:15, 16, 18
   Esther, V:16
   History of the United States of America, V:15, 16, 18
   Mont-Saint-Michel and Chartres, II:374; V:15, 16, 18
Adams, Herbert Baxter, IX:3773
Adams, John, IV:12-14, **16-20,** 295, 315, 615, 616, 718, 719, 999
   Defense of the Constitutions of Government of the United States of America, A, IV:18
   Dissertation upon Parties, A, IV:161
Adams, John Quincy, **V:20-25**
   Canning, V:406
   Clay, V:508
   Jackson, V:1197, 1198
   Monroe, VI:1571, 1573
   Mayflower Compact, IV:189
   Polk, VI:1801
   Van Buren, VI:2293
Adams, Samuel, **IV:21-25,** 691
Addams, Jane, **VII:21-25;** VIII:2097; IX:3838
   Democracy and Social Ethics, VII:24
   Spirit of Youth and the City Streets, The, VII:24
   Twenty Years at Hull House, VII:23
   Women at the Hague, VII:161
Addington, Henry, IV:1104
Addis Ababa, Treaty of, VI:1539
Addison, Joseph, **IV:26-29**
   Berkeley, IV:114
   Campaign, The, IV:26
   Freeholder, The, IV:27
   Guardian, The, IV:27, 114
   Old Whig, The, IV:27
   Spectator, The, IV:26-28, 566
   Tatler, The, IV:26, 27
Addled Parliament, IV:1285
Adelphi scheme, IV:9
Adenauer, Konrad, **VII:26-29;** VIII:2009

Adler, Alfred, **VII:30-33,** 1226
   Neurotic Constitution, The, VII:30, 31
   Social Interest: A Challenge to Mankind, VII:30, 31
   Study of Organ Inferiority and It's Psychical Compensation, VII:30, 31
   Understanding Human Nature, VII:30
   What Life Should Mean to You, VII:30
Adler, Dankmar, VI:2167, 2168
Adler, Felix, **V:26-29**
Adler, Kurt, VII:928
Admetus, I:317, 318
Administration of Justice Act, IV:616
Admirals' Revolt, VIII:2752
Admiralty Range, VI:1908
Adonijah, I:798
Adoula, Cyrille, IX:3746
Adrian II, II:279
Adrian IV, **II:27-29,** 48, 358
   Laudabiliter, II:29
Adrian VI, III:166, 325
Adrianople, battle of, I:825
Adult Suffrage Society, VII:353, 354
Advancement of Women, Association for the, V:1146
Adventure Galley, IV:777, 779
Adversaria, III:673
AEA. *See* Aerial Experiment Association
AEG, VIII:2520
Aegina, Island of, I:611
Aegospotami, Battle of, I:32
Aeken, Jeroen van. *See* Bosch, Hieronymus
Aelst, Pieter Coecke van, III:85
Aenesidemus, I:725
Aerial Experiment Association, V:186
aerodynamics
   Geddes, VII:1320
   Lanchester, VIII:2071
   Langley, VI:1313-1315
   Prandtl, IX:3073-3075
   Wright brothers, IX:4064-4067
aeronautics
   Blériot, VII:325-327
   Byrd, VII:534-536
   Eckener, VII:1011-1013
   Guggenheim, VIII:1500
   Heinkel, VIII:1614
   Korolev, VIII:2019
   Santos-Dumont, IX:3320-3322
   Tupolev, IX:3764-3766
   Whittle, IX:3972-3974
   Zeppelin, IX:4108-4110

Aeschines, I:254, 255
Aeschylus, **I:9-12,** 91, 807
  Aetnae, I:10
  Eumenides, I:10, 11
  Glaucus Potnieus, I:10
  Oresteia, I:10, 624; VIII:2525
  Persians, The, I:10, 624
  Phineus, I:10
  Prometheus Bound, I:11
  Suppliants, The, I:10, 11, 878
Aesop, **I:13-15,** 618
  Fables, I:13-15; IV:857
  "Frogs Who Asked for a King, The,"
    I:14
Aetius, I:126
Aetolia, I:64
Afer, Publius Terentius. *See* Terence
Affinity Laws, V:1170
affirmative action, VII:511; IX:2790, 3143
AFL-CIO. *See* American Federation of Labor;
  Congress of Industrial Organizations
Afonso I, **II:30-32**
Afonso V, III:197
African American Post, VII:144
African Association, VI:1723, 1724
African Intelligence Department, VIII:2146
African National Congress
  de Klerk, VII:871, 872
  Lutuli, VIII:2281-2283
  Machel, VIII:2318, 2319
  Mandela, VIII:2384, 2386, 2387
  Nyerere, VIII:2774
African Unity, Organization of, VIII:1520, 2763;
  IX:3758
Afrika Korps, IX:3213, 3215
Afzal Khan, IV:1246, 1247
Agakar, Gopal Ganesh, IX:3682
Agassiz, Louis, **V:30-33**
  *Contributions to the Natural History of the
    United States,* V:31
  Methods of Study in Natural History, V:32
Agathocles, I:716
Ageladas, I:624
Agesilaus II, **I:16-19**
Agis IV, I:215, 216
Agnadello, Battle of, III:48, 406
Agnes of Poitou, II:461
Agnew, Spiro, VIII:2759, 2760
Agnus Dei, II:823, 825
Agramonte, Aristides, VI:1858, 1859
Agram Treason Trials, VIII:2441
Agra palace-fort, IV:1234

Agricola, Georgius, **III:1-4**
  Bermannus sive de re metallica dialogus, III:2
  De natura fossilium, III:2
  De ortu et causis subterraneorum, III:2
  De re metallica libri XII, III:2
Agricultural Adjustment Act of 1933, IX:3860
Agriculture, United States Department of, VII:604
Agricus, I:377
Agrippa, Marcus Vipsanius, **I:20-22**
Agrippina, I:152, 206, 577, 772
Agrippina minor, I:550
Aguinaldo, Emiliano, V:657
Agustina, Maria. *See* Saragosa, La
Aha, I:548
Ahaz, I:453
Ahmad ibn Hanbal, **II:33-36**
  Musnad, II:34
Ahmad Khan, Sir Sayyid, **V:34-36**
  Asar-oos-sunnadeed, V:34
Ahmadu Tal, V:764
Ahmed ibn Arabshah, II:884
Ahmose, I:371
Ahna, Pauline de, IX:3556
Ahriman, I:976, 977
Ahura Mazda, I:237, 238
  Avesta, I:975, 976
Aidh, VII:1118
Aidit, Dipa Nusantara, IX:3572
AIDS, VIII:2031, 2032; IX:3637
Aikido, IX:2797
Ailly, Pierre d', III:172
Aitken, William Maxwell. *See* Beaverbrook, Lord
Aix-la-Chappelle, Treaty of, IV:1076
Akalaitis, Joanne, **VII:34-36**
  Balcony, The, VII:35
  Cascando, VII:34
  Cymbeline, VII:35
  Dead End Kids, VII:35
  Dressed Like an Egg, VII:35
  Endgame, VII:35
  Green Card, VII:35
  Photographer, The, VII:35
  Request Concert, VII:35
  Screams, The, VII:35
  Southern Exposure, VII:35
  Through the Leaves, VII:35
Akbar, **III:5-7**
Akechi Mitsuhide, III:571
Akhenaton, **I:23-26,** 573, 575, 734, 904
Akhmatova, Anna, **VII:37-40**
  Anno Domini, VII:38
  "By the Seashore," VII:38

Chetki, VII:38
"Courage," VII:38
Evening, VII:37
Flight of Time, The, VII:38
Plantain, VII:38
Poem without a Hero, A, VII:38, 39
Reed, The, VII:38
Requiem, VII:38
Rosary, VII:38
Seventh Book, The, VII:38
V khvale mira, VII:38
Akiba ben Joseph, **I:27-30**
Akihito, **VII:41-44**
Akins, Zoë, VII:117, 119
Akwe clan, VIII:1754
ALA. *See* American Library Association
'Alam Khan, III:38
Alamo, Battle of the, V:578, 579
Alanbrooke, First Viscount, **VII:45-48**
Alans, I:126, 342, 343
Alarcón, Hernando de, III:180
Alaric, I:342, 826
Alaric II, II:276
Alaska
    Alexander II, V:49
    Arthur, V:80
    Bering, IV:111, 112
    Canadian boundary, V:1070
    mining, VIII:1499
    purchase, V:1237; VI:2172
    Seward, VI:2038, 2039
    Taft, IX:3596
Alaskan Boundary Tribunal, VIII:2221
Alaska Syndicate, VIII:1499
Alba, Duke of. *See* Alva, Duke of
Albanian Crisis, IX:2877
Albany Academy, V:1093
Albatenius. *See* Battani, al-
Albemarle, Duke of, IV:511
Albergati, Niccoló, III:559
Albert II, III:374
Albert, Prince, VI:2308, 2309; VII:1020
Alberti, Leon Battista, **III:8-10**, 28, 81
    Architecture, The, III:9
    Della tranquillità dell' anima, III:8
    Family in Renaissance Florence, The, III:8, 9
    Of Painting, III:8
    Of Sculpture, III:8
    Theogenius, III:8
    Trivia Senatoria, III:9
Albert of Saxe-Coburg-Gotha, VI:1518
Albert the Bear, II:466

Albertus Magnus, Saint, **II:37-40**
    Book of Minerals, II:38
    De animalibus, II:38
    De causis proporietatum elementorum, II:38
    De vegetablilibus et plantis, II:38
Albigensian Crusade. *See* Catharist movement
Alboin, **II:41-43**
Albrecht V, III:281
Albrecht of Brandenburg, III:178
Albright, Madeleine, **VII:49-52**, 400
Albuquerque, Afonso de, **III:11-13**
Alcaeus, I:651, 652
alchemy
    Agricola, III:2
    Bosch, III:70
    Boyle, IV:187
    Jabir ibn Hayyan, II:522-524
    Lavoisier, IV:805
    Mersenne, IV:950
    Razi, II:781
    Stahl, IV:1268, 1271
Alcibiades, **I:31-33**, 795
Alcmaeon, **I:34-37**
Alcmaeonids, I:649, 803
ALCOA. *See* Aluminum Company of America
Alcott, Bronson, **V:37-39**, 40
    Conversations with Children on the Gospels, V:38
    Record of a School, V:38
Alcott, Louisa May, V:39, **40-43**
    Eight Cousins, V:41
    Flower Fables, V:40
    Little Men, V:41
    Little Women, V:41
    Modern Mephistopheles, V:41
    Old-Fashioned Girl, An, V:41
    Rose in Bloom, V:41
Alcuin, **II:44-47**, 756, 766
    On the Bishops, Kings, and Saints of York, II:44, 46
Aldhelm, II:824
Aldona, II:210
Aldrin, Edwin E., Jr., VII:112
Alekseyev, Konstantin Sergeyevich. *See* Stanislavsky, Konstantin
Alekseyev Circle, IX:3486
Alembert, Jean le Rond d', **IV:30-33**, 413; VI:1319
    Account of the Destruction of the Jesuits in France, An, IV:32
    Eléméns de musique théorique et practique suivant les principes de M. Rameau, IV:33
    Essai sur les gens de lettres, IV:32

Opuscules mathématiques, IV:32
Preliminary Discourse to the Encyclopedia of Diderot, IV:31
Traité de dynamique, IV:30
Alencar, José de, VI:1445
Alenquer, Pedro de, III:217
Alesia, I:924
Aleuads, I:787
Alexander I (of Russia), **V:44-47;** VI:1306, 1307, 2089, 2307
Alexander II (of Macedonia), I:628
Alexander II (of Russia), **V:48-50;** VI:1651, 1652, 1790, 1791
Alexander III (Pope), **II:48-51**
    Becket, II:128, 129
    Bruce, II:184, 185
    Frederick I Barbarossa, II:359
Alexander III (of Russia), VI:1790-1792; VIII:2160
Alexander IV (Pope), II:991, 992
Alexander VI (Pope), **III:14-17,** 406, 668, 669
Alexander VIII (Pope), IV:119
Alexander, Comso, IV:1289
Alexander, Franz, VIII:1745
Alexander, James, IV:1484, 1486
Alexander Nevsky, **II:52-55**
Alexander the Great, **I:38-42**
    Antigonus I Monohthalmos, I:60, 61
    Aristotle, I:95, 96
    Demosthenes, I:255
    Diogenes, I:270
    Lysippus, I:515, 516
    Philip II of Macedonia, I:630
    Pompey the Great, I:680
    Ptolemy Philadelphus, I:717
    Ptolemy Soter, I:720-722
    Pyrrhon of Elis, I:724, 725
    Seleucus I Nicator, I:767, 768
Alexandria, Egypt
    anti-Semitism, I:632
    Callimachus, I:156
    Cleopatra VII, I:218, 220, 221
    Eratosthenes of Cyrene, I:303-305
    Hypatia, I:436-438
    museum, I:307
    Origen, I:581
    Paul of Aegina, II:712
    Ptolemy Soter, I:722
    Sosigenes, I:811
    vivisection, I:398
Alexandria, Library of, I:303-305
Alexandrian Donations, I:70

Alexandrine War, I:149, 218
Alexis I, IV:1030, 1032
Alexius, II:159, 160
Alexius IV, II:942
Alexius V, II:429
Alfa Romeo Company, VII:1150
Alfonso X, **II:56-58**
    Cántigas de Santa María, II:57
    Crónica general, II:57
    Siete Partidas, Las, II:57
Alfred the Great, **II:59-62,** 319, 334
Alfthryth, II:344
Algarotti, Count Francesco, IV:1324
algebra
    Abel, V:7-9
    Aryabhata, II:90
    Diophantus, I:272-274
    Galois, V:864-866
    Gauss, V:893-895
    Hamilton, V:1025-1027
    Khwarizmi, II:563-565
    Lagrange, IV:786
    Leonardo of Pisa, II:586
    Picard, IX:2994, 2995
    Whitehead, IX:3966
Algeciras Conference of 1906, V:1131; VII:704
Alger, Horatio, **V:51-53**
    Bertha's Christmas, V:51
    Luck and Pluck, V:51
    Paul Prescott's Charge, V:51
    Ragged Dick, V:51
    Tattered Tom, V:51
Algerian People, Manifesto of the, VII:5, 6
Algerian People's Union, VII:5
Algirdas, II:1001
Algonquin Round Table, IX:2884, 2885
Algren, Nelson, VII:231
Alhazen, **II:63-66**
    Hay' at al-'alan, II:65
    Optics, II:63-66
Ali, Muhammad, **VII:53-57;** VIII:2413
Alianza Popular Revolucionaria Americana, VIII:1584-1586
Alien and Sedition Acts
    Adams, IV:19
    Chase, IV:295
    Jefferson, IV:718
    Madison, IV:888
Alien Enemies Bureau, VIII:1732
Allahbad Municipal Board, IX:2869
Allegemeine Deutsche Erziehungsanstalt, V:845, 846

Allegheny Observatory, VI:1313, 1314
Allegri, Antonio. *See* Correggio
Allen, Ethan, **IV:34-36,** 64
    Essay on the Universal Plentitude of Being, An,
      IV:36
    Narrative of Colonel Ethan Allen's Captivity, A,
      IV:35
    Reason the Only Oracle of Man, IV:34, 36
Allen, William Francis, IX:3772
Allenby, Lord, **VII:58-62;** IX:4094
Allende, Salvador, VIII:2718, 2759
Alliance and Friendship, Treaty of, VII:260
Alliance Israélite, VII:610, 611
All-India Conference, VII:184; IX:2867
Allison, Wilmer, IX:2981
Allouez, Father Claude-Jean, IV:732
Almanza, Battle of, IV:157
Almeida, Dom Francisco de, III:12
Almohad empire, II:4-6, 100
Almoravid dynasty, II:4, 30, 100, 268-270
Alp Arslan, **II:67-71,** 677
Alphege, Archbishop of Canterbury, II:202
Alpine skiing. *See* skiing
Alsace and Lorraine, III:164, 165; V:872, 873;
    VI:1622
Altenberg, Peter, VIII:2012
Alte Veste, Battle of the, IV:591
Altgeld, John Peter, **V:54-57;** VIII:2096
    Our Penal Machinery and Its Victims, V:54
Altmark, Truce of, IV:590
Aluminum Company of America, VIII:2480
Alva, Duke of, III:**18-20,** 537, 782
Alvarado, Hernando de, III:181, 182
Alvarado, Pedro de, **III:21-23**
Alvares, Francisco, III:198
Aly Khan, Prince, VIII:1597
Amadism. *See* Pure Land Buddhism
Amalgamation Party, V:346
Amal kings, II:894
Amalric I, II:809
Amarna Age, I:24
Amar Quartet, VIII:1670
Amati, Nicolò, IV:1281
Ambaridi, I:755
Ambartsumian, Viktor A., **VII:63-65**
Ambrose, Saint, **I:43-46,** 416, 791, 870, 871
    De fide, I:44
Ameinias, I:596
Amenhotep II, I:23, 891
Amenhotep III, I:23
Amenhotep IV. *See* Akhenaton
Amerbach, Bonifacius, III:358

American Academy of Tropical Medicine,
    IX:3452
American Anti-Slavery Society, V:490, 885, 886;
    VI:1773, 2110
American Art-Union, V:237
American Association of Petroleum Geologists,
    IX:3919, 3920
American Association of Social Workers, VIII:1736
American Ballet, School of, VII:835
American Ballet Company, VII:156, 296
American Bar Association, VII:421
American Biograph Studios, VIII:1480
American Civil Liberties Union, IX:3660
American Colonization Society, V:884, 885;
    VI:1490
American Enterprise Institute, VIII:1995
American Ethnological Society, V:861, 862
American Expeditionary Forces, VIII:1437, 2555;
    IX:2893-2895
American Federation of Labor, V:956-958;
    VII:881; VIII:2170-2172; IX:3163
American Federation of Radio Artists, VII:898
American Foundation for the Blind, VIII:1926
American Freedmen's Inquiry Commission,
    V:1151
American Fur Company, V:84
American Hebrew Congregations, Union of,
    VI:2400, 2401
American Historical Association, VII:223
American Independent Party, IX:3859
American Indians. *See* Native Americans
American Jewish Congress, IX:4034
American Journal of Sociology, The, IX:3603
American Library Association, V:660
American Magazine, The, IX:3616
American Newspaper Publishers Associatiion,
    VI:1542
American Party. *See* Know-Nothing Party
American Popular Revolutionary Alliance. *See*
    Alianza Popular Revolucionaria Americana
American Psychological Association, VIII:1989
American Railway Union, VII:881
American Red Cross, V:142, 143, 145; IX:3205,
    3839
American Revolution. *See* American War of
    Independence
American Revolution, Daughters of the, VII:23, 72
Americans for Democratic Action, VIII:1783;
    IX:3162, 3163
American Smelting and Refining Company,
    VIII:1499, 1500
American Sociology Society, VI:2329

American States, Organization of, IX:2959
American Telephone and Telegraph Company.
    See AT&T
American Tobacco Company, V:704-706
American Type Founders Company, VI:1542
American War of Independence
    Acton, V:12
    Adams, John, IV:16, 18, 19
    Adams, Samuel, IV:21-24
    Allen, IV:34-36
    André, IV:42-44
    Arnold, IV:64, 66, 67
    Bacon, IV:80-82
    Bancroft, V:126
    Blackstone, IV:130
    Bolingbroke, IV:161
    Boone, IV:164
    Brant, IV:196, 198
    Burke, IV:223, 224
    Charles III, IV:288
    Clark, IV:312, 314, 315
    Clinton, IV:321-323
    Cornwallis, IV:367
    Dickinson, IV:408-411
    Ferguson, IV:457
    Fox, IV:481
    Franklin, IV:494
    Gage, IV:513
    George III, IV:541, 542
    Greene, IV:574-577
    Hamilton, IV:608-611
    Hancock, IV:617
    Henry, IV:649
    Howe, IV:677, 678
    Hutchinson, IV:691-694
    Jay, IV:711
    Lewis, VI:1358
    Marshall, VI:1487
    Monroe, VI:1570
    Morris, IV:999-1001
    North, IV:1034-1036
    Paine, IV:1055-1057
    Peale, IV:1072
    Pitt the Younger, IV:1102
    Pontiac's Rebellion, IV:39, 40
    Revere, IV:1156-1159
    Rochambeau, IV:1174-1176
    Rodney, IV:1178
    Shays, IV:1239-1241
    Sherman, IV:1242-1244
    Washington, IV:1405-1407
    Wilson, IV:1456-1458
    Witherspoon, IV:1470
    Wolfe, IV:1473
American Woman Suffrage Association, V:62, 64;
    VI:2044, 2045, 2112, 2389
American Women's Education Association, V:172
Ames Monument, VI:1883
AM-FM broadcasting, VII:102, 103
Amherst, Lord, **IV:37-41,** 512, 513, 1472
Amida, I:779, 780
Amiens, Mise of, II:454, 645
Amiens, Treaty of, IV:1104; VI:2187
Amini, Ali, VIII:2568
Amistad case, V:24, 344; VI:2148
Amman Summit, VIII:1794
Ammonites, I:748
Amon, I:23, 24, 371, 636-638, 734, 889
Amos, I:468
Amphipolis, I:629, 630
Amphitheus, I:88, 90
Amritsar Massacres, IX:2867
Amsterdam Stock Exchange, IX:2859
Amundsen, Roald, **VII:66-69,** 534; IX:3020
Amyntas, I:628
Anabaptists, III:510-512, 793
Anaconda Plan, VI:2012
anarchism
    Altgeld, V:55, 56
    Bakunin, V:112-114
    Goldman, VIII:1411-1413
    Jaurès, V:1221
    Proudhon, VI:1818, 1820
    Sacco and Vanzetti, IX:3281-3283
Anastasius the Librarian, II:675, 904
Anatolius, treaty of, I:124, 125
anatomy
    Alcmaeon, I:35
    Aretaeus of Cappadocia, I:81, 82
    Brancusi, VII:414
    Celsus, I:174
    Cuvier, V:589-591
    Diocles of Carystus, I:260-262
    Eakins, V:732, 733
    Empedocles, I:284
    Erasistratus, I:299-302
    Galen, I:338-340
    Guy de Chauliac, II:414-416
    Harvey, IV:628
    Herophilus, I:398-400
    Lankester, VI:1317
    Malpighi, IV:891-893
    Michelangelo, III:517, 519, 520
    Vesalius, III:754-757

Anaxagoras, **I:47-49,** 609, 624
   Nature, I:47
Anaxandrides, I:501
Anaximander, **I:50-52,** 53, 382
Anaximenes of Miletus, **I:53-55,** 955,
   956, 972
Anazarbus, I:276
ANC. *See* African National Congress
Andersen, Hans Christian, **V:58-60**
   "Emperor's New Clothes," V:59
   Eventyr, V:59
   Improvisatore, V:58
   Little Match Girl, IX:3157
   "Little Mermaid," V:59
   "Nightingale," V:59
   Only a Fiddler, V:58
   O.T., V:58
   Poet's Bazaar, V:59
   "Princess and the Pea," V:59
   Story of My Life, V:60
   "Thumbelina," V:59
   "Tinder Box," V:59
   "Ugly Duckling," V:59
Anderson, Marian, **VII:70-73**
Anderson, Maxwell, IX:3928
Andersonn, Bibi, VII:278
Anderson School of Natural History, V:32
André, John, **IV:42-45,** 66
Andrea d'Agnolo. *See* Andrea del Sarto
Andrea del Sarto, **III:24-27**
   Birth of the Virgin, III:24
   Charity, III:26
   Death of the Saint, The, III:24
   Last Supper, The, III:26
   Madonna and Child with Saints, III:26
   Madonna del Sacco, III:26
   Madonna of the Harpies, III:26
   Miracles Performed by the Relics of the Saint,
     III:24
   Saint Curing the Possessed Woman, III:24
   Andrewes, Lancelot, **IV:46-49**
   Manual of Private Devotions, The, IV:48
   Responsio Matthaei Torti, IV:47, 48
Andrews, Samuel, VI:1897
Andronicus III, II:844
Andropov, Yuri, VIII:1423
Andros, Edmund, IV:934, 939
Angelico, Fra, **III:28-31,** 223
   Altarpiece, III:28
   Annunciation, The, III:28
   Christ on the Cross Adored by Saint Dominic,
     III:29

   Christ Scorned, III:29
   Crucifixion, The, III:29
   Presentation in the Temple, The, III:29
   St. Jerome Penitent, III:28
   Transfiguration, The, III:29
Angell, Norman, **VII:74-78**
   After All, VII:77
   Great Illusion, The, VII:74, 75, 77
   Patriotism Under Three Flags, VII:74
Angelou, Maya, **VII:79-81**
   Blacks, Blues, Black, VII:80
   Gather Together in My Name, VII:79
   I Know Why the Caged Bird Sings, VII:79, 80
   Just Give Me a Cool Drink of Water 'fore I Diiie,
     VII:80
   Oh Pray My Wings Are Gonna Fit Me Well,
     VII:80
   "On the Pulse of Morning," VII:80
   Roots, VII:80
   Singin', Swingin', and Gettin' Merry Like
     Christmas, VII:79
Angerstein, John Julius, IV:810
Angevin Empire, II:540, 733, 849
Anglican Church. *See* England, Church of
Anglo-Dutch Wars
   Blake, IV:134, 135
   Monck, IV:972
   Stuyvesant, IV:1296
   Tromp, IV:1343, 1344
Anglo-Iranian Oil Company, VIII:2566
Anglo-Irish Agreement of 1938, VII:878
Anglo-Japanese Treaty of 1902, VIII:2091
Anglo-Saxon Chronicle, The
   Alfred the Great, II:59, 60, 62
   Edward the Elder, II:319, 320
   Egbert, II:333, 334
   Ethelred II, the Unready, II:345
   Hengist, I:378, 380, 381
   Olaf I, II:688
Anglo-Saxons, II:167-169, 202, 204, 333, 334
Angora, Treaty of, VII:134
Angouleme, Marguerite d'. *See* Marguerite of
   Navarre
Anik-C satellite, IX:3179
animal behavior. *See* ethology
Animal Industry, Bureau of, IX:3450, 3451
Anjou, Count of, II:847-849
Anjou, Duke of, III:783
An Lu-shan, II:966, 967
Annam, II:1023, 1024
Annan, Khofi, VII:400
Anna O., VII:453, 454

Annapolis, IV:293

Annapolis Convention, IV:609

Anne, Queen of England, **IV:50-54,** 531-533, 620, 922-924

Anne of Austria, IV:864, 865, 899, 945, 946, 1166

Anne of Cleves, III:205, 360

Anne of Saxony, III:781, 782

Anniceris, I:87

Annual Register, The, IV:222

Annunciation, I:941; III:28

Anselm, Saint, II:10, **72-75**
  Monologion, II:72, 74
  On the Procession of the Holy Spirit, II:73
  Proslogion, II:72, 74
  Why God Became Man, II:73

Anshan, I:236

Anshe Emet, VI:2400

Anson, Lord, **IV:55-58**

Antarctica, VI:1908, VII:66-69, 534-536

Anthanasius, Saint, **I:119-123**

Anthony, Susan B., **V:61-65;** VI:1602, 2045, 2112, 2113; VII:880; IX:2919
  History of Woman Suffrage, VI:2112

Anthony of Egypt, Saint, **I:56-59,** 122

Anthony of Padua, Saint, **II:76-78**

Antichrist, II:535

Anti-Corn Law League, V:306, 307, 526-528; VI:1754

Antigonas I Monophthalmos, **I:60-62,** 721

Anti-Masonic Party, V:792; VI:2037, 2136

Antinomians, IV:688

Antioch, I:440; II:159-161, 887, 888

Antiochene school, I:861, 865, 866

Antiochus I Soter, I:299

Antiochus the Great, **I:63-65**

Anti-Party Group, VIII:2573

Anti-Pass Day, VIII:2282

Antipater, I:60, 255, 390, 392, 721

anti-Semitism
  Alexandria, I:632
  Ambrose, I:44
  Arendt, VII:98-100
  Bernstein, VII:293
  Brandeis, VII:422
  Butler, VII:526
  Chagall, VII:641
  Dewey, V:661
  Dreyfus affair, VIII:2767
  Goebbels, VIII:1404
  Herzl, V:1104, 1105
  Hitler, VIII:1692, 1694-1696
  Luxemburg, VIII:2285
  Malenkov, VIII:2378
  Mussolini, VIII:2669
  Pius XII, IX:3031
  Rickover, IX:3173
  Stein, IX:3508, 3509
  Suttner, VI:2177
  Waldheim, IX:3842, 3843
  William of Auvergne, II:977, 978
  See also Holocaust

Antisthenes, **I:66-68,** 270

Antonelli, Giacomo, VI:1348

Antony, Marc, **I:69-71**
  Augustus, I:20, 132, 133
  Brutus, I:141, 142, 160
  Cicero, I:196
  Cleopatra VII, I:220, 221
  Dryden, IV:425
  Herod the Great, I:391
  Varro, I:919

Antwerp, III:85, 86

Anwendung, VII:1244

Apache Indians, V:915, 917, 918

Apama, I:767

apartheid
  de Klerk, VII:870-872
  Fugard, VII:1259
  Gordimer, VIII:1427, 1429
  Lutuli, VIII:2281-2283
  Mandela, VIII:2384, 2386, 2387
  Mugabe, VIII:2649
  Nyerere, VIII:2774, 2775
  Player, IX:3042
  Rhodes, VI:1876
  Tutu, IX:3775-3777
  United Nations, IX:2958

Aphrodite, I:318

Apollinaire, Guillaume, VI:1922, 1923; **VII:82-85,** 448, 889; VIII:2037; IX:3066, 3067
  Alcools, VII:83, 84
  Breasts of Tiresias, The, VII:83
  Calligrammes, VII:83, 84
  Case d'armons, VII:83
  "Chanson du mal-aimé, La," VII:82
  Cubist Painters: Aesthetic Meditations, The, VII:83
  Heresiarch and Co., The, VII:82
  "Jolie Rousse, La," VII:83, 84
  "Mirabeau Bridge," VII:83
  Poet Assassinated, The, VII:83
  "Zone," VII:83

Apollo missions
    Apollo 11, VII:110-113; VIII:2022, 2624;
      IX:2779
    Apollo 13, IX:3406
    Apollo 14, IX:3407
    photography, VII:781
Apollonius of Perga, **I:72-75,** 437
    Conics, I:72-75
    Epaphai, I:73
    Neyseis, I:73
    Topoi epipedoi, I:73
Apollo of Delos, I:649
Apostles
    Clement I, I:210-212
    Irenaeus, I:447, 449, 450
    Jesus Christ, I:468
    John the Apostle, I:475, 477
    Paul, I:604-606
    Peter, I:614-616
    Stephen, I:822-824
    Thomas, I:880, 882, 883
Apostles, Acts of the, I:605
Apostles Club, VI:1503, 2062
Apostles' Creed, I:449, 450
Apostolic Fathers, I:210-212, 442
Apostolic Tradition, I:415
Appian, I:160
Appleseed, Johnny, **V:66-68**
Appleton, Frances "Fanny," VI:1416
April Laws, V:626
Aqaba, Gulf of, VII:855
Aqiba ben Joseph. *See* Akiba ben Joseph
aqualung. *See* SCUBA
Aquila, I:28
Aquillus, Manius, I:558
Aquinas, Saint Thomas. *See* Thomas Aquinas,
    Saint
Aquino, Benigno, VII:86, 87; VIII:2422
Aquino, Corazon, **VII:86-89;** VIII:2422, 2423
Aquitaine, II:239, 782
Arab Defense Council, VIII:1793
Arabian American Oil Company, IX:4079,
    4080
Arab-Israeli Wars, VIII:1791, 1794
Arab Legion, VIII:1793
Arab Socialist Union, VIII:2694, 2696
Arafat, Yasir, **VII:90-94**
    Faisal, VIII:1120
    Hussein I, VIII:1794
    Intifada, VII:92
    Nasser, VIII:2696
    Pérez de Cuéllar, IX:2958

Aragon, Louis, VIII:2351
Arakawa, Hiroshi, IX:2796, 2797
ARAMCO. *See* Arabian American Oil Company
Arango, Doroteo. *See* Villa, Pancho
Arap Moi, Daniel, VIII:1939
Aratus, I:216
Arbenz, Jacobo, VIII:1494
Arboath, Declaration of, II:188
Arbogast, I:871
Arbolancha, Don Pedro de, III:46
Arbues, Pedro, III:726
Arbus, Diane, **VII:95-97**
    "New Documents," VII:96
    "Recent Acquisitions," VII:96
    "Twins, The," VII:96
Arbuthnot, Dr. John, IV:158
Arcades Project, VII:268
Arcadia, I:293
Arcadius, I:871
Archer, William, IX:3399, 3400
Archimedes, **I:76-80**
    Equilibrium of Planes, The, I:79
    Measurement of the Circle, I:79
    Method of Mechanical Theorems, I:78
    On Conoids and Spheroids, I:78
    On Floating Bodies, I:79
    On Spirals, I:78
    On the Sphere and Cylinder, I:78
    Quadrature of the Parabola, I:78
    Sand-Reckoner, The, I:79
Arctic exploration
    Amundsen, VII:66-69
    Byrd, VII:534
    Rasmussen, IX:3121-3123
    Ross, VI:1907, 1908
    Wegener, IX:3918-3920
    Wilkins, IX:3999-4001
    See also North Pole
Ardashir I, I:778
Ardashir II, I:781
Arena Chapel, II:388, 390, 748
Arendt, Hannah, **VII:98-101**
    Between Past and Future, VII:99
    Eichmann in Jerusalem, VII:99, 100
    Human Condition, The, VII:98, 99
    Idea of Love in St. Augustine, The, VII:98
    Jew as Pariah, The, VII:100
    Life of the Mind, The, VII:100
    Men in Dark Times, VII:100
    On Revolution, VII:100
    Origins of Totalitarianism, The, VII:98, 100
Areopagus, I:199, 200, 609

Aretaeus of Cappadocia, **I:81-84**
    Book on the Treatment of Acute and Chronic Diseases, I:82
    On the Causes and Symptoms of Acute and Chronic Diseases, I:82
Arezzo, Guido d'. *See* Guido d'Arezzo
Argall, Captain Samuel, IV:1106, 1107
Argentine National Library, VII:374
Arghun, II:381
Argos, I:214
Argyle, Earl of, IV:283
Arianism
    Ambrose, I:44
    Athanasius, I:121, 122
    Bruno, III:96
    Clovis, II:274
    Constantine the Great, I:228
    Genseric, I:343
    Gregory of Nyssa, I:352-354
    Gregory the Great, II:408
    Theodoric the Great, II:896, 897
    Theodosius the Great, I:869, 870
    Ulfilas, I:908-910
Ariaramnes, I:236
Ariete Division, IX:3214
Arikara tribe, VI:2077
Ariosto, Ludvico, **III:32-35**
    Cinque canti, III:33
    Coffer, The, III:32, 33
    Lena, III:33
    Necromancer, The, III:33
    Orlando furioso, III:32, 33
    Pretenders, The, III:33
Arispe, Miguel Ramos, V:95
Aristarchus, I:308, 409, 712
Aristippus, **I:85-87**
Ariston of Chios, I:303, 970
Aristophanes, **I:88-93**
    Acharnians, The, I:88, 115
    Babylonioi, I:88
    Birds, The, I:88, 90
    Clouds, The, I:90
    Daitaleis, I:88
    Ecclesiazusae, I:91, 92
    Frogs, The, I:11, 91, 808, 809
    Knights, The, I:90
    Kokalos, I:92
    Lysistrata, I:91; V:162
    Plutus, I:91, 92
    Thesmophoriazusae, I:91
    Wasps, I:14, 90

Aristotle, **I:94-97**
    Albertus Magnus, II:37-39
    Alcmaeon, I:34, 36
    Alexander the Great, I:38
    Anaxagoras, I:48
    Antisthenes, I:68
    Averroës, II:102
    Buridan, II:194-196
    Categoriae, I:683, 685
    Diocles of Carystus, I:260, 261
    Ethics, VI:173
    Fracastoro, III:270-272
    Galen, I:339
    Metaphysics, I:312, 597, 727; II:106, 983, 985
    natural philosophy, II:400
    Nicholas of Autrecourt, II:669-671
    On the Heavens, II:195
    On the Soul, I:94, 698
    Poetics, I:809, 878
    Politics, II:985
    Polygnotus, I:677
    Protreptics, I:95
    Psellus, II:759
    Razi, II:781
    Rhetoric, I:15
    Scaliger, III:671
    Secretum secretorum, II:110
    Solon, I:803
    space, nature of, IV:586
    Thales of Miletus, I:852, 854
    Theophrastus, I:873-875
    Thomas Aquinas, II:911, 913, 914
    Valla, III:740
    William of Auvergne, II:976, 978
    William of Auxerre, II:981-983
    William of Moerbeke, II:985, 986
    Xanthippe, I:952
    Zeno of Elea, I:972
Aristoxenus, **I:98-100**
    Harmonics, The, I:98
Ari the Learned, II:837
Arius, I:323
Arkwright, Richard, **IV:59-63;** VI:2074, 2075
Armageddon, I:890
Armed Neutrality, League of, VI:1636
Armenia
    Basil the Macedonian, II:117
    Shapur II, I:779
    Theodosius the Great, I:869
    Tigranes the Great, I:896-898
    Trajan, I:901
Arminians. *See* Remonstrants

Armory Show, VI:1855; VII:416, 973; VIII:1740
Armour, Jean, IV:231, 232
Armstrong, Duff, VI:1382
Armstrong, Louis, **VII:105-109**
   "Chimes Blues," VII:105
   "I Wish I Could Shimmy Like My Sister Kate,"
     VII:105
   "Mabel's Dream," VII:105
Armstrong, Neil, **VII:110-113,** 1271; IX:3766
Armstrong, Samuel C., VI:2335
Arnaz, Desi, VII:176-178
Arnim, Count Harry von, V:1130
Arnold, Benedict, IV:42-44, **64-68**
Arnold, Matthew, **V:69-73**
   Culture and Anarchy, V:71
   Discourses in America, V:72
   Empedocles on Etna, V:71
   Essays in Criticism, V:71
   On Translating Homer, V:71
   "Rugby Chapel," V:76
   Strayed Reveller and Other Poems, The, V:70
Arnold, Thomas, V:69, **74-76**
   History of Rome, V:75
Arnold of Brescia, II:28
Arnold of Villanova, **II:79-81**
   Aphorismi de granibus, II:80
   Regimen sanitatis, II:80
Arnolfo di Cambio, **II:82-85**
Aroostook War, VI:2011
Arouet, François-Marie. *See* Voltaire
ARPA. *See* Alianza Popular Revolucionaria
   Americana
Arpad, **II:86-88**
Arpinum, I:194
Arrabbiata, III:668
Arrhenius, Svante August, **VII:114-116;**
   VIII:2713; IX:2855
   Destinies of the Stars, The, VII:116
   Erde and Weltall, VII:116
   Immunochemistry, VII:115
   Lehrbuch der kosmischen Physik, VII:115
   *Life of the Universe as Conceived by Man from
     Earliest Ages to the Present Time, The,* VII:115
   Quantitative Laws in Biological Chemistry,
     VII:115, 116
   Text-book of Electrochemistry, VII:115
   Theories of Chemistry, VII:115
   Theories of Solutions, VII:115
Arsames, I:236
Arshak II, I:780
Arsinoe II, I:716-718
Artabanus, I:962-964

Artaxerxes, I:331
Artek Company, VII:2
Artemidorus, I:159
Artemisium, I:764
Arthur, Chester A., **V:77-81**
Arthurian legends
   Chrétien de Troyes, II:257-259
   Hartmann von Aue, II:433-435
   Malory, III:457, 458; V:161; VI:2213
   Tennyson, VI:2213
Arthur of Wales, Prince, III:136
Articles of Confederation. *See* Confederation,
   Articles of
Artisans' and Laborers' Dwelling Act of 1875,
   V:678
Art Nouveau, VII:1263; VIII:1903
Artusi, Giovanni Mari, IV:991
Arundel, Thomas, II:787
Arverni, I:922
Arvey, Jacob M., IX:3524
Aryabhata, **II:89-92,** 181, 182
   Aryabhatiya, The, II:89-91
Aryans, I:618
Arzner, Dorothy, **VII:117-120**
   Anybody's Woman, VII:117, 119
   Bride Wore Red, The, VII:119
   Christopher Strong, VII:119
   Craig's Wife, VII:119
   Dance, Girl, Dance, VII:118
   Fashions for Women, VII:117
   First Comes Courgage, VII:118
   Get Your Man, VII:117
   Honor Among Lovers, VII:119
   Manhattan Cocktail, VII:117
   Merrily We Go to Hell, VII:119
   Nana, VII:119
   Sarah and Son, VII:117
   Ten Modern Commandments, VII:117
   Wild Party, VII:117
   Working Girls, VII:119
ASARCO. *See* American Smelting and Refining
   Company
asceticism
   Ba'al Shem Tov, IV:74, 75
   Chrysostom, I:184
   Diogenes, I:268
   Elijah ben Solomon, IV:432
   Schopenhauer, VI:1986
   Simeon Stylites, I:783-785
Ascham, Roger, III:241
Asclepiades of Bithynia, **I:101-104,** 807
   Concerning Common Aids, I:101

Enemata, I:101
Method of Giving Wine in Sickness, I:101
Asclepieions, I:338, 411, 445
Asdings, I:342
ASEAN. *See* Southeast Asian Nations,
    Association of
Ash'ari, al-, **II:93-96,** 348
Book of Highlights, II:93
Discourses of the Muslims, II:93
Elucidation of Islam's Foundation, The, II:93
Incitement to Investigation, II:93
Ashburn, Joseph, IV:1192, 1193
Ashdod, siege of, I:755
Ashdown, Battle of, II:59
Ashikaga Tadayoshi, II:97, 98
Ashikaga Takauji, **II:97-99**
Ashikaga Yoshiaki, III:571
Ashikaga Yoshimitsu, II:1025, 1026
Ashikaga Yoshimochi, II:1026
Ashikaga Yoshinori, II:1026, 1027
Ashley, Edwina, VIII:2642
Ashley, John, VI:1786
Ashley, William, VI:2077, 2078
Ashton, Frederick, VII:1175, 1177; IX:2939, 2940
Ashurbanipal, **I:105-108,** 709
Ashurnasirpal II, **I:109-111**
Asiatic Society of Bengal, VI:1846
Asoka the Great, **I:112-114**
Aspasia, **I:115-118**
Asquith, H.H., **VII:121-124;** VIII:1952, 2217
Asquith, Margot, VII:121
Associated Television Corporation, VII:739
Assumption, Church of the, I:376
Astaire, Fred, **VII:125-128**
Band Wagon, The, VII:125, 127, 128
Barkleys of Broadway, The, VII:127
Broadway Melody of 1940, VII:127
Daddy Long Legs, VII:127
Dancing Lady, VII:125
Easter Parade, VII:127
Evening with Fred Astaire, An, VII:127
Flying Down to Rio, VII:125
Funny Face, VII:127
Gay Divorcee, The, VII:125; IX:3057
Holiday Inn, VII:127, 289
Lady Be Good, VII:125, 1352
"Night and Day," VII:125
Notorious Landlady, The, VII:127
On the Beach, VII:127
Royal Wedding, VII:127, 128
Shall We Dance, VII:125, 1352
Swing Time, VII:125, 127

That's Entertainment, VII:127
Top Hat, VII:125, 127, 288
You'll Never Get Rich, VIII:1597
Astor, John J., **V:82-85**
Astor, Nancy, **VII:129-132**
Astor, Waldorf, VII:129-131
Astor House, V:84, 294
Astor Place Riot, V:802
astrology
    Abano, II:1
    'Abbas the Great, IV:5
    Copernicus, III:179
    Jabir ibn Hayyan, II:524
    Hippolytus of Rome, I:415
    Hypatia, I:437
    Kepler, IV:772
    Nostradamus, III:567, 568
    Ptolemy, I:713, 714
    Santorio, IV:1209, 1211
    Servetus, III:676
    Wallenstein, IV:1396
Astrup, Eivind, IX:2942
Aswan High Dam, VIII:2695
AT&T, VII:102, 103, 859
Atahualpa, III:371-373, 699
Atatürk, Kemal, **VII:133-136;** VIII:1812, 1813
Atenism, I:573, 575
Athalaric, II:896
Athanaric, I:908
Athanasius, Saint, I:58, **119-122**
Apology Against the Arians, An, I:122
History of the Arians, I:122
Athena Alea, temple of, I:764
Athena the Maiden, I:625, 649
Athenian Empire
    Aeschylus, I:9, 10
    Alcibiades, I:32
    Alexander the Great, I:38
    Antigonus I Monohthalmos, I:60
    Aristophanes, I:90, 91
    Aristotle, I:95
    Cimon, I:198-201
    Cleisthenes of Athens, I:207, 208
    Demosthenes, I:253-255
    Draco, I:280, 281
    Euripides, I:317
    Lysippus, I:515
    Miltiades the Younger, I:553-555
    Olympic Games, VII:774, 775
    Pericles, I:609, 611, 612
    Pheidippides, I:621-623
    Phidias, I:624

Pisistratus, I:648-650
Polygnotus, I:676, 677
Socrates, I:793-796
Solon, I:803-805
Sophocles, I:809
Themistocles, I:857-859
Thucydides, I:885-887
Xanthippe, I:952-954
Xenophon, I:958-960
Atlantic Charter, VIII:2257
Atlantic Monthly, The, V:1111, 1127, 1211, 1228;
    VI:2375
Atlantic Records, VII:1217, 1218
Atlee, Clement, VIII:2644
Atmospheric Nuclear Test Ban Treaty, VII:302;
    VIII:1963
atom
    Aretaeus of Cappadocia, I:81
    Avogadro, V:98-100
    Becquerel, V:167
    Dalton, V:602-604
    Einstein, VII:1035
    elementary-particle physics, IX:4091
    local molecular fields, VIII:2705
    Lockyer, VI:1411, 1412
    Ostwald, IX:2856
    plastics, VIII:2698
    splitting of the, VIII:1871
    structure of the, VII:379; VIII:2040;
        IX:2923
    See also nuclear physics
atom bomb
    Bethe, VII:300-303
    Bothe, VII:380
    Chadwick, VII:637
    Compton, VII:745-747
    Conant, VII:750
    Einstein, VII:1036
    Fermi, VII:1145, 1147, 1148
    Hertz, VIII:1647, 1648
    Kurchatov, VIII:2039-2041
    Lawrence, VIII:2121-2123
    Stimson, IX:3539
    Oppenheimer, IX:2833-2835
    Rabi, IX:3102
    Sato, IX:3337
    Seaborg, IX:3376
    Teller, IX:3631, 3632
    Truman, IX:3742
    University of Chicago, VIII:1801
    Urey, IX:3789
    See also nuclear weapons

Atomic Energy Commission, VII:750; VIII:2123,
    2338, 2726; IX:2834, 3377
Atomic Energy Committee, IX:3102
Aton, I:734
Attainder, Act of, III:593
Attalus III, I:346
Attianus, I:356
Attila, **I:124-127**
Attlee, Clement, **VII:137-140,** 304, 305, 310,
    315, 1345
Attrition, War of, VIII:2696
Auburn Prison, IX:2853, 2854
Auckland National Association, VIII:2444
Auden, W.H., VII:466, 468, 469, 608
Audion, VII:858-860
Audran, Claude III, IV:1413
Audubon, John James, **V:86-89**
    Birds of America, The, V:87, 88
    Ornithological Biography, V:87
    Viviparous Quadrupeds of North America, V:87
Audubon Society, V:88
Augsburg, Diet of, III:160, 505
Augsburg, League of, IV:840, 873, 1447
Augsburg, Peace of, III:161; IV:450
Augsburg Confession, III:503, 505; IV:1489
Augsburg Interim, III:103, 161
Augusta National Golf Club, VIII:1876, 1877
Augustine, Saint, **I:128-131**
    Anthony of Padua, II:76
    astrology, III:676
    City of God, The, I:128, 129; II:726; III:533
    Confessions, I:128
    Jansenism, IV:707-709
    On the Trinity, I:128
    Plotinus, I:667
    Vincent of Lérins, I:936, 937
    William of Auvergne, II:976
Augustine of Hippo, Saint, II:137, 138
Augustus, **I:132-135**
    Agrippa, I:20-22
    Antony, I:70, 71
    Brutus, I:141, 142
    Caligula, I:152, 153
    Cassius, I:160
    Claudius I, I:203
    Cleopatra VII, I:218, 220
    Diocletian, I:265
    Herod the Great, I:391
    Horace, I:426
    Livy, I:504
    Maecenas, I:519, 521
    Ovid, I:585-587

Phaedrus, I:618
Propertius, I:702-704
Tiberius, I:892-894
Vergil, I:926-928
Verrius Flaccus, I:930
Aulic Council, III:492, 493
Aurangzeb, **IV:69-72,** 1233, 1234, 1247
Aurobindo, Sri, **VII:141-143**
    Arya, VII:142
    Ausgleich, V:625, 627, 628, 830; VII:1197
Austen, Jane, **V:90-93**
    Emma, V:92
    Mansfield Park, V:92
    Northanger Abbey, V:91
    Persuasion, V:91, 92, 560
    Pride and Prejudice, V:90-92; VIII:2544
    Sense and Sensibility, V:90-92
    Watsons, The, V:91
Austerlitz, Battle of, V:45, 475; VI:1306,
    1307, 1616
Austin, James T., VI:1772
Austin, Stephen Fuller, **V:94-97**
Australian Open, VII:1112
Australopithecus boisei, VIII:2148
Austrian Baroque, IV:473, 655-657
Austrian Succession, War of
    Amherst, IV:37
    Carleton, IV:246
    Clive, IV:325
    Frederick the Great, IV:504
    George II, IV:536, 537
    Jenkins' Ear, IV:55
    Maria Theresa, IV:914, 915
    Pelham, IV:1074, 1075
    Pontiac, IV:1110
    Rochambeau, IV:1174
    Venice, IV:243
    Wolfe, IV:1471
    See also Jenkins' Ear, War of
Austro-Prussian War of 1866, V:762
automobile industry
    Benz, V:199-201
    Citroën, VII:695-697
    Daimler, V:200, 201, 597-599; IX:3881
    Diesel, V:672-674
    dymaxion car, VII:1266
    Ferrari, VII:1150-1152
    Ford, VII:1184, 1186, 1187
    Geddes, VII:1321
    General Motors, VII:1321; VIII:2679, 2680;
        IX:2974, 3162, 3881
    Honda, VIII:1724-1726
    Lanchester, VIII:2069-2071
    Lenoir, VI:1344
    Maybach, V:597-599
    Michelin brothers, VIII:2514-2516
    Otto, VI:1702-1704
    Pirelli family, IX:3020, 3021
    Rolls-Royce Limited, IX:3209-3211
    Toyota Motor Company, IX:3719-3721
    union labor, VIII:2171; IX:3161-3164
    Wankel engine, IX:3881, 3882
Auxentius, I:909
Avars, II:41, 42, 228, 470, 471, 820
Averroes, II:1, **100-105,** 491, 830, 913
    Incoherence of the Incoherence, The, II:103
    Incoherence of the Philosophers, The, II:103
    On the Harmony of Religion and Philosophy,
        II:103
Avery, Oswald, VII:797
Avicenna, II:1, **106-109**
    Birr wa al-ithm, al-, II:106
    Canon of Medicine, II:107
    Hasil wa al-mahsul, al-, II:106
    Lisan al-'Arab, II:107
    Majmu, al-, II:106
Avogadro, Amedeo, **V:98-100**
Avril, Jane, VI:2248
AWSA. *See* American Woman Suffrage
    Association
Axis Pact, VIII:2669
Ay, I:904
Aya, I:25
Aye, I:573
Aymer of Valence. *See* Pembroke, Earl of
Ayyubid Dynasty, II:124
Azcapotzalco, III:377, 378, 555, 556
Azeglio, Massimo d', V:446
Azikiwe, Nnamdi, **VII:144-147;** VIII:2762
Aztec Empire
    Alvarado, III:21-23
    Cortés, III:188-191
    Itzcóatl, III:377-379
    Montezuma II, III:528, 529, 531
    Nezahualcóyotl, III:555-557
    Prescott, VI:1815
Azuma Kagami, IV:1328
Azzolino, Cardinal Decio, IV:305, 306

Baader-Meinhof group, VII:350
Ba'al Shem Tov, **IV:73-75**
Babbage, Charles, **V:101-104**
Babeuf, Grachus, IV:912
Babor, Karl, IX:3985

Babrius, I:15
Babur, **III:36-40,** 541
Babylonian Captivity, II:487, 1009
Bach, Johann Sebastian, **IV:76-79,** 227, 1321,
    1383, 1385; VI:1535
  Before Thy Throne I Now Appear, IV:78
  Brandenburg Concertos, IV:77
  Christmas Oratorio, IV:78
  For Thou Wilt Not Leave My Soul in Hell,
    IV:76
  God Is My King, IV:76
  Jesu, Joy of Man's Desiring, IV:78
  Pastorale in F Major, IV:76
  Saint Matthew Passion, The, IV:78; VI:1534
  Sheep May Safely Graze, IV:78
  Well-Tempered Clavier, IV:77
Bach, Karl Philipp Emanuel, IV:227
Bachman, Richard. *See* King, Stephen
Bacon, Francis, **III:41-44,** 296, 451; IV:185, 187,
    331, 332, 662, 1310
  Magna Instauratio, III:43
  New Atlantis, III:43
  Novum Organum, III:43
  Two Bookes of Francis Bacon, III:41
Bacon, Nathaniel, **IV:80-82**
Bacon, Roger, **II:110-113,** 977
  Opus majus, II:112, 988
  Opus tertium, II:112, 719
Bacon's Rebellion, IV:81
bacteriology
  Behring, V:182-184
  Burnet, VII:512-514
  chromosomes, VIII:1828
  Cohn, V:534, 535
  Leeuwenhoek, IV:827
  Koch, VI:1297-1299
  Pasteur, VI:1746, 1747
  Smith, IX:3450-3452
  Watson, IX:3897, 3898
Bactria, I:64, 494, 541, 779
Bad Axe, Battle of, VI:2195
Baden-Powell, Sir Robert Stephenson Smyth,
    V:105-108; VIII:2246, 2247
  Scouting for Boys, V:106, 107
Bad Faces, VI:1850
Badooglio, Marshal Pietro, VIII:2669
Baeck, Leo, **VII:148-151**
  Essence of Judaism, The, VII:148
  Pharisees, and Other Essays, The, VII:150
  Romantische Religion, VII:148
  This People Israel, VII:150
  What Is Christianity?, VII:148

Baer, Karl Ernst von, **V:109-111**
  Über Entwickelungsgeschichte der Thiere, V:110
Baffin Island, III:279
Baghdad
  Benjamin of Tudela, II:141
  Nizam al-Mulk, II:678
  Razi, II:779
  Sa'di, II:807
  Tabari, II:873
Baghdad Summit Conference, VIII:1794
Bagot, Sir Charles, V:118
Bahadur Shah, IV:71
Bailey, James Anthony, V:136
Baillie, Thomas, IV:439
Bain, Alexander, V:557
Baines, Sir Edward, IV:59, 62
Baker v. Carr, VII:1214; IX:3889
Bakhtin, Mikhail, **VII:152-154**
  Dialogic Imagination, The, VII:153
  Problems of Dostoevsky's Poetics, VII:153
  Rabelais and His World, VII:153
bakufu. *See* Tokugawa shogunate
Bakunin, Mikhail, **V:112-115,** 1100
  Appeal to the Slavs, An, V:112
Balakirev, Mily, V:287; VI:1889, 2200
Balanchine, George, **VII:155-159,** 835, 921;
    VIII:1568, 2182, 2183; IX:3607, 3608
  Agon, VII:158
  Apollo, VII:156
  Coppelia, VII:158
  Danses Concertantes, VII:833
  Don Quixote, VII:158
  Four Temperaments, The, VII:156
  Gods Go A-Begging, The, VII:833
  Harlequinade, VII:158
  Ivesiana, VII:156
  Jewels, VII:158
  Metamorphoses, VII:156
  Midsummer Night's Dream, A, VII:158
  Mozartiana, VII:833
  Nutcracker, The, VII:158
  Opus, VII:156
  Orpheus, VII:156
  Prodigal Son, The, VII:156, 833
  Serenade, VII:156
  Sleeping Beauty, The, VII:155
  Tombeau de Couperin, Le, VII:158
  Triumph of Neptune, The, VII:833
  Valse, La, VII:156
  Vienna Waltzes, VII:158
  Western Symphony, VII:156, 158
Balboa, Vasco Núñez, de, **III:45-47**

Balch, Emily Greene, **VII:160-163**
  Approaches to the Great Settlement, VII:161
  Manual for Use in Cases of Juvenile Offenders and Other Minors in Massachusetts, VII:160
  Miracle of Living, The, VII:162
  Our Slavic Fellow Citizens, VII:160-162
  Public Assistance of the Poor in France, VII:160
  Women at the Hague, VII:160, 161
Baldwin, James, **VII:164-167**
  Amen Corner, The, VII:164
  Another Country, VII:165
  Blues for Mr. Charlie, VII:164
  Devil Finds Work, The, VII:166
  Dialogue, A, VII:166
  Evidence of Things Not Seen, The, VII:166
  Fire Next Time, The, VII:166
  Giovanni's Room, VII:164, 165
  Going to Meet the Man, VII:166
  Go Tell It on the Mountain, VII:164
  Just Above My Head, VII:166
  Nobody Knows My Name, VII:165
  Notes of a Native Son, VII:164, 165
  Price of the Ticket, The, VII:166
  Rap on Race, A, VII:166
  Tell Me How Long the Train's Been Gone, VII:166
Baldwin, Robert, **V:116-119;** VI:1451
Baldwin, Stanley, **VII:168-171,** 235, 304, 821; IX:4026
Baldwin of Flanders, II:943
Balfour, Arthur James, V:46; **VII:172-175**
  Defence of Philosophic Doubt, A, VII:172
Balfour Declaration
  Balfour, VII:174
  Ben-Gurion, VII:251, 252
  Faisal I, VII:1124
  Herzl, V:1105
  King, VIII:1982
  Lawrence, VIII:2127
  Weizmann, IX:3931
Balian de Adam. *See* Salimbene
Baline, Israel. *See* Berlin, Irving
Baliol, Edward de, II:294, 295
Baliol, John de, II:185, 294, 324, 956
Balkan Defense Pact, VII:134
Ball, John, **II:114-116,** 786, 921, 922
Ball, Lucille, VII:119, **176-179**
  I Love Lucy, VII:176, 178
  Lucy Show, The, VII:178
  Mame, VII:178
Ballance, John, VI:2018
Ballantyne, James and John, VI:2005, 2006

Ballard, Robert Duane, **VII:180-182**
Balleroy, Château de, IV:898
ballet
  Balanchine, VII:155-159
  Danilova, VII:832-835
  Degas, V:643
  Delibes, V:649-651
  de Mille, VII:874-876
  Diaghilev, VII:919-921
  Duncan, VII:980-982
  Fonteyn, VII:1175-1178
  Graham, VIII:1455-1458
  Laban, VIII:2059
  Lifar, VIII:2182-2184
  Massine, VIII:2448-2450
  musical comedy, VIII:1568
  Nijinsky, VIII:2746-2749
  Pavlova, IX:2937-2940
  Poulenc, IX:3066
  Prokofiev, IX:3085-3087
  Satie, IX:3333
  Shostakovich, IX:3409
  Stravinsky, IX:3559, 3560
  Tallchief, IX:3607-3609
  Zwilich, IX:4123
Ballet Russes
  Balanchine, VII:156
  Danilova, VII:833, 835
  Debussy, VII:885
  Diaghliev, VII:919-921
  Lifar, VIII:2182, 2183
  Massine, VIII:2448-2450
  Nijinsky, VIII:2746, 2748
  Pavlova, IX:2937
  Poulenc, IX:3066
  Satie, IX:3333
Ballinger, Richard, V:280; IX:3596
Ballot Act of 1872, V:804, 805
Ballou, Hosea, V:472
Ballou's Pictorial, V:1133
Baltimore Sermon of 1819, V:471
Baltimore *Sun,* VIII:2483, 2484
Balzac, Honoré de, **V:120-123;** VI:1901
  Chouans, Les, V:120
  Cousin Bette, V:121
  Droll Tales, V:827
  Eugénie Grandet, V:121
  Father Goriot, V:121
  Human Comedy, The, V:120, 122; VI:2183
  Magic Skin, The, V:120
  Peau de chagrin, La, V:121
  "Sarrasine," VII:208

Bancroft, George, **V:124-129**
    History of the United States, V:126, 127
    Martin Van Buren to the End of His Political
      Career, V:127
Banda, Hastings, VIII:2319
Bandinelli, Roland. *See* Alexander III (Pope)
Banerjea, Surendranath, **VII:183-186**
    Bengalee, VII:183, 184
Banks, Sir Joseph, **IV:83-87,** 353; VI:1723,
    1724
Banks, Nathaniel, V:1205
Banneker, Benjamin, **IV:88-91**
    Pennsylvania, Delaware, Maryland and Virginia
      Almanack, IV:89, 90, 91
Bannockburn, Battle of, II:326
Banting, Sir Frederick Grant, **VII:187-190;**
    VIII:2329, 2330
Bantu Education Act, IX:3775
baptism
    Anabaptists, III:510-512
    Campbell, V:401-403
    John the Baptist, I:478-481
    Maurice, VI:1504
    Pusey, VI:1829
    Servetus, III:676, 677
    Theodosius the Great, I:869
Barak, I:246, 247
Barbari, Jacopo de', III:201
Barbarossa, Frederick I. *See* Frederick I
    Barbarossa
Barbary Wars, V:634-636
Barber, Samuel, **VII:191-194**
    Antony and Cleopatra, VII:191, 193; IX:3083
    Canzonetta, VII:193
    Hermit Songs, The, VII:193; IX:3083
    Knoxville: Summer of 1915, Opus 24, VII:193
    School for Scandal, The, VII:191
    Vanessa, VII:193
Barbosa, Diogo, III:453
Barca, Hamilcar, I:364
Barclay, Robert H., VI:1764
Bardas, II:674
Bardot, Brigitte, VIII:1392
Barebones Parliament, IV:380, 790, 1228
Baret, Jeanne, IV:180
Barezzi, Antonio, VI:2299
Barlaam of Calabria, II:901
Barlow, Joel, V:854, 855
Barmakids, II:437, 522, 524
Barmen Confession, VII:204
Barnard, Christiaan, **VII:195-198**
Barnard, George G., VI:2284

Barnard, Henry, **V:130-132**
Barnato, Barney, VI:1874, 1875
Barner, Jacob, IV:1268
Barnes, Djuna, **VII:199-202**
    Antiphon, The, VII:201
    Book, A, VII:199
    Book of Repulsive Women, The, VII:199, 202
    Ladies Almanack, A, VII:199, 201, 202
    Night Among the Horses, A, VII:199
    Nightwood, VII:201, 202
    "Quarry," VII:202
    Ryder, VII:199, 201
    Spillwax, VII:199, 201
    "Walking Mort, The," VII:202
Barnes, Robert, III:193
Barnes, Thomas, VI:2325
Barnes v. Costle, VIII:2325
Barnet, Battle of, III:234, 235, 343, 649
Barnum, P.T., **V:133-137;** VI:1386, 1387
    Art of Money Getting, The, V:135
Barons' Cause, II:644, 645
Barron, James, V:635, 636
Barron, Moses, VII:187
Barry, Sir Charles, **V:138-141;** VI:1823
Barth, Karl, **VII:203-206,** 358, 476
    Church Dogmatics, VII:204, 205
    Dogmatics in Outline, VII:204
    Epistle to the Romans, The, VII:204
Barthes, Roland, **VII:207-209**
    Camera Lucida: Reflections on Photography,
      VII:209
    Empire of Signs, VII:209
    Lover's Discourse: Fragments, A, VII:208
    Michelet, VII:207
    Mythologies, VII:208
    On Racine, VII:207
    Pleasure of the Text, The, VII:208
    Roland Barthes by Roland Barthes,
      VII:208
    S/Z, VII:207-209
    Writing Degree Zero, VII:207
Bartholomew of Cremona, II:987
Bartlett, Bob, IX:2944
Bartók, Béla, **VII:210-213**
    Bagatelles, VII:211
    Concerto for Orchestra, VII:211
    Duke Bluebeard's Castle, VII:211
    Empire of Signs, VII:210
    Hungarian Folksongs, VII:211
    Kossuth Symphony, VII:210
    Mikrokosmos, VII:211
    Miraculous Mandarin, The, VII:211

Music for Strings, Percussion, and Celesta, VII:211
    Wooden Prince, The, VII:211
Barton, Clara, **V:142-146**
Barton, Sir Edmund, **V:147-149**
Barton, Elizabeth, III:265
baseball
    Cobb, VII:717-720
    DiMaggio, VII:934-937
    Gehrig, VII:1322-1324
    Oh, IX:2796-2798
    Robinson, IX:3193-3197
    Rose, IX:3239-3241
    Ruth, IX:3273-3276
    Thorpe, IX:3675
Basedow, Johann Bernhard, **IV:92-94**
    Elementarwerks erster Band, Des, IV:92
    Vorstellung an Menschemfreunde und vermögende Manner über Schulen, Studien, und ihren Enfluss in die öffentliche Wohlfahrt, IV:92
Basel, Council of, III:559, 563, 564
Bashkent, Battle of, III:500
Basil of Caesarea, I:349, 350, 352
Basil the Macedonian, **II:117-120**
    Basilics, II:118
Baskerville, John, **IV:95-97**
basketball, IX:3268, 3270, 3271
Basoalto, Neftali Ricardo Reyes. *See* Neruda, Pablo
Basov, Nikolay Gennadiyevich, **VII:214-216**
Bassus, Aufidius, I:663
Bastides, Don Pedro de, III:45
Bates, Edward, V:729
Bateson, Gregory, VIII:2469
Bathsheba, I:243, 798
Batista y Zaldivar, Fulgencio, VII:617, 618
Battani, al-, **II:121-123**
    De scientia stellarum, II:122
Battelle Memorial Institute, VII:579, 580
Batu Khan, II:987, 988
Baudelaire, Charles, **V:150-153;** VI:1472; VII:268; IX:3792
    Artificial Paradises, V:152
    Fanfarlo, La, V:150
    Flowers of Evil, V:150, 152; VI:1855; VIII:2530
    Paris Spleen, V:152
Bauer, Georg. *See* Agricola, Georgius
Bauhaus, the
    Gropius, VIII:1486-1488
    Klee, VIII:2006
    Marc, VIII:2406

    Mies van der Rohe, VIII:2522
    Pei, IX:2946, 2947
    Pugin, VI:1822
Baum, L. Frank, **V:154-156**
    Aunt Jane's Nieces, V:155
    Dorothy and the Wizard of Oz, V:156
    Dot and Tot of Merryland, V:155
    Emerald City of Oz, The, V:156
    Fairylogue and Radio-Plays, V:156
    Father Goose, His Book, V:155
    Glinda of Oz, V:156
    Marvelous Land of Oz, The, V:155
    Mother Goose in Prose, V:154
    Ozma of Oz, V:155
    Patchwork Girl, The, V:156
    Road to Oz, The, V:156
    Scarecrow of Oz, The, V:156
    Tik-Tok Man, The, V:156
    Wonderful Wizard of Oz, The, V:154-156
Baur, Ferdinand Christian, VI:1892, 1893
Bavaria, II:228, 358, 706
Baxter, Richard, **IV:98-102**
Bayard, Chevalier de, **III:48-50**
Baybars I, **II:124-127**
Baydu, II:381
Bayeu, Francisco, IV:569
Bayezid II, **III:51-53**
Bayle, Pierre, **IV:103-106**
    Historical and Critical Dictionary, An, IV:104, 105
    Miscellaneous Reflections Occasion'd by the Comet Which Appear'd in December, 1680, IV:103
    Nouvelles de la République des Lettres, IV:103
    Philosophical Commentary on These Words in the Gospel, Luke XIV, 23, IV:103
Bayliss, Sir William Maddock, **VII:217-220;** IX:3494
    Nature of Enzyme Action, The, VII:219
    Physiology of Food and Economy of Diet, The, VII:219
    Principles of General Physiology, VII:219
Bay of Islands rebellion, V:998
Bay of Pigs invasion, VIII:1930; IX:3525
Bayram Khan, III:5
Bazille, Jean Frédéric, VI:1869
Bazin, André, VIII:1391; IX:3736, 3737
BBC. *See* British Broadcasting Corporation
Beale, Dorothea, **V:157-160**
Beanes, William, VI:1281, 1282
Beard, Charles A., **VII:221-225,** 526; IX:2893, 3762

American Foreign Policy in the Making, 1932-1940, VII:224
American Government and Politics, VII:221
American Leviathan, VII:223
American Spirit, VII:224
Balkan Pivot, VII:223
Basic History of the United States, A, VII:224
Contemporary American History, 1877-1913, VII:222
Cross Currents in Europe To-day, VII:223
Development of Modern Europe, VII:221
Economic Interpretation of the Constitution of the United States, VII:222
Economic Origins of Jeffersonian Democracy, VII:222
Idea of National Interest, The, VII:223
Industrial Revolution, The, VII:221
Open Door at Home, The, VII:223
President Roosevelt and the Coming of the War 1941, VII:224
Republic, The, VII:224
Rise of American Civilization, The, VII:222, 224
Supreme Court and the Constitution, The, VII:222
Toward Civilization, VII:223
Whither Mankind, VII:223
Beardsley, Aubrey, **V:161-165**
Story of Venus and Tannhäuser, The, V:164
Beatles, the, **VII:226-239,** 658
Abbey Road, VII:228
Beatles for Sale, VII:227
Hard Days Night, A, VII:227
Help!, VII:227
"I Want to Hold Your Hand," VII:227
Let it Be, VII:228
Magical Mystery Tour, VII:228
"Norwegian Wood," VII:228
"Penny Lane," VII:228
Please, Please Me, VII:226
Revolver, VII:228
Rubber Soul, VII:228
Sgt. Pepper's Lonely Hearts Club Band, VII:228
"Strawberry Fields Forever," VII:228
"White Album, The," VII:228
With the Beatles, VII:227
Yellow Submarine, VII:228
Beat movement, VIII:1945-1947; IX:2883
Beatrice, II:288
Beatrix, II:357
Beaufort, Henry, III:338, 341
Beaufort, Margaret, III:345, 651
Beaufort, Thomas, III:337

Beauharnais, Viscount Alexandre de, V:1246
Beauharnais v. Illinois, VII:322
Beaujeu, Sieur de, IV:794
Beaumont, Élie de, VI:1419
Beaumont, Francis, **III:54-57,** 689
Captain, The, III:56
Coxcomb, The, III:56
Cupid's Revenge, III:56
King and No King, A, III:55, 689
Knight of the Burning Pestle, The, III:54, 689
Maid's Tragedy, The, III:55
Masque of the Inner Temple and Grayes Inn, The, III:56
Philaster, III:55, 689
Salmacis and Hermaphroditus, III:54
Scornful Lady, The, III:56
Tragedy of Thierry, King of France and His Brother Theodoret, III:56
Woman Hater, The, III:54
Beaumont, George, IV:1161; V:547
Beaumont, Gustave de, VI:2238
Beauvais, Vincent of. *See* Vincent of Beauvais
Beauvoir, Simone de, **VII:230-233;** IX:3327, 3328
Adieux: A Farewell to Sartre, VII:232
Belles Images, Les, VII:232
Blood of Others, The, VII:231
Coming of Age, The, VII:232
Ethics of Ambiguity, VII:231
Mandarins, The, VII:231
Memoirs of a Dutiful Daughter, VII:230
Second Sex, The, VII:231
She Came to Stay, VII:230, 231
Woman Destroyed, The, VII:232
Beaux-Arts, École des, IX:2976, 2977
Beaverbrook, Lord, VII:76, 169, **234-237**
Bebel, August
Woman Under Socialism, VIII:2016; IX:4112
bebop, VII:1370, 1371, 1373; VIII:1718; IX:2880, 2882, 2883
Beccaria, Cesare
Essay on Crimes and Punishments, An, VI:1483
Beccaria, Giambatista, IV:523
Beccaria, Giovanni, IV:1387
Becher, Johann Joachim, IV:1269
Physica subterranea, IV:1270
Bechuanaland, VI:1874, 1876
Becker, Lydia, V:778
Becket, Thomas, **II:128-131**
Clarendon Constitutions, II:49
Eleanor of Aquitaine, II:338
Henry II, II:446, 447

Beckett, Samuel, VII:34, 201, **238-242,** 1360,
    1361; IX:3091
    Breath, VII:241
    Cascando, VII:34
    Come and Go: Dramaticule, VII:241
    "Dante and the Lobster," VII:239
    Endgame, VII:35, 241
    Happy Days, VII:241
    Krapp's Last Tape, VII:241
    Malone Dies, VII:240
    Molloy, VII:240
    More Pricks than Kicks, VII:239
    Murphy, VII:239
    Not I, VII:241
    Play, VII:241
    Proust, VII:238
    Unnamable, The, VII:240, 1361
    Waiting for Godot, VII:240, 241, 1361
    Watt, VII:240
    Whoroscope, VII:238
Becquerel, Henry, VII:811, 812
Becquerel family, **V:166-169**
Bede the Venerable, Saint, **II:132-135,** 756, 825
    Ecclesiastical History of the English People,
        II:132, 133, 198, 199, 378
    *Lives of the First Abbots of Wearmouth and
        Jarrow,* II:133
Bedford, Earl of, IV:1141, 1142
Beecher, Catharine, **V:170-173**
    American Woman's Home, The, V:172
    Treatise on Domestic Economy, V:171, 172
Beecher, Harriet. *See* Stowe, Harriet Beecher
Beecher, Henry Ward, **V:174-177;** VI:2279, 2281
    Yale Lectures on Preaching, V:176
Beer Hall Putsch, VIII:1694, 2266
Beethoven, Ludwig van, **V:178-181**
    Boccherini, IV:149
    Brahms, V:301
    Choral, V:179
    Creatures of Prometheus, VIII:2182
    Eroica, V:179
    Fidelio, V:179, 181
    Haydn, IV:641
    Liszt, VI:1391
    Mahler, VIII:2363
    Missa Solemnis, V:179, 181
    Pastoral, V:179
    Schiller, IV:1219
Beghards, II:906
Begin, Menachem, **VII:243-246,** 253; IX:3290
Beguines, II:906
behavior, animal. *See* ethology

behavior, human
    Benedict, VII:257
    Freud, VII:1226
    Janet, VIII:1841
    Lorenz, VIII:2239, 2240
    Merleau-Ponty, VIII:2500
    Muller, VIII:2652
    Pavlov, VIII:2933-2935
    Skinner, IX:3431-3434
Behistun Inscription, I:233
Behrens, Peter, VIII:1486, 2520
Behring, Emil von, **V:182-184;** VII:1032
Béla I, II:574
Belasco, David, IX:3006, 3094
Belaúnde Terry, Fernando, VIII:1586
Belgian Antarctic Expedition, VII:66
Belgrade, III:375
Belisarius, II:554, 555
Bell, Alexander Graham, **V:185-189**
Bell, Andrew, VI:1310
Bell, Edward, VII:383
Bell, J. Franklin, VIII:2429
Bellarmino, Roberto, IV:47, 48
Bellay, Jean du, III:633, 634
Bellini, Gentile, III:58
Bellini, Giovanni, **III:58-61,** 305, 306
    Adoration of the Child, III:60
    Agony in the Garden, III:59
    Coronation of the Virgin, III:58,59
    Enthroned Madonna and Child, III:60
    Feast of the Gods, III:58, 60
    Pietà with Virgin and Saint John, III:59
    Portrait of Doge Leonardo Loredan, III:60
    Saint Francis in Ecstasy, III:60
Bellini, Jacopo, III:58
Bellow, Saul, **VII:247-250**
    Adventures of Augie March, The, VII:247, 249
    Dangling Man, VII:247
    Dean's December, The, VII:249
    Henderson and the Rain King, VII:249
    Herzog, VII:249
    Humboldt's Gift, VII:249
    Mosby's Memoirs and Others Stories, VII:249
    Mr. Sammler's Planet, VII:249
    Seize the Day, VII:247
    To Jerusalem and Back, VII:249
    Victim, The, VII:247
Bellum Judaicum, I:472
Belvedere Palace, IV:655-657
Bemis, Edward W., V:1046
Benavides, Oscar R., VIII:1585
Bence, Eli, V:283

Benchley, Robert, IX:2884
Benedict III, II:673
Benedict VIII, II:451
Benedict XII, II:211, 212, 671, 683
Benedict XV, IX:3026, 3030
Benedict, Ruth, **VII:255-258;** VIII:2468, 2470
 Chrysanthemum and the Sword, VII:257
 Patterns of Culture, VII:257, 258
 Race Science and Politics, VII:257
Benedict, Saint, **VII:255-258**
Benedictine Order, II:994
Benedictine Rule, II:136, 137
Benedict of Nursia, Saint, **II:136-139**
Benes, Edvard, **VII:259-262**
Benét, Stephen Vincent, **VII:263-266**
 Five Men and Pompey, VII:263
 John Brown's Body, VII:265, 266
 Western Star, VII:265, 266
Bengal Legislative Council, VII:185
Ben-Gurion, David, VII:244, 245, **251-254;**
 IX:3932
Benincasa, Caterina. *See* Catherine of Siena, Saint
Benito Juárez Democratic Club, VIII:2345
Benizzi, Saint Filippo, III:24
Benjamin, Walter, **VII:267-270**
 "Author as Producer, The," VII:268
 Origin of German Tragic Drama, The, VII:267
 "Theses on the Philosophy of History," VII:269
 "Work of Art in the Age of Mechanical
  Reproduction, The," VII:268
Benjamin of Tudela, **II:140-142**
 Itinerary of Benjamin of Tudela, The, II:140-142
Bennett, Floyd, VII:534, 535
Bennett, James Gordon, **V:190-194;** VI:2101
Benois, Aleksander, VII:919, 920
Benson, Edward White, VI:2062
Bentham, Jeremy, **IV:107-110**
 Burr, V:371
 Chadwick, V:457-460
 Condillac, IV:346
 Constitutional Code, V:460
 Fragment on Government, A, IV:108
 *Introduction to the Principles of Morals and
  Legislation, An,* IV:108
 Mill, James, VI:1556, 1557
 Mill, John Stuart, VI:1559, 1560
 Owen, VI:1709
 Rationale of Judicial Evidence, VI:1787
Bentinck, Lord George, V:653
Bentley, Thomas, IV:1422, 1423
Benton, Thomas Hart, **V:195-198,** 839;
 IX:3048, 3049

Bentson, Lloyd, VII:520, 521
Benz, Carl, **V:199-201**
Berardi, Giannetto, III:758
Berengar of Ivrea, II:707
Berengar of Tours, II:374
Berg, Alban, **VII:271-274,** 386, 387; IX:3359
 Five Songs with Orchestra, VII:272
 Lulu, VII:273
 Woyzeck, VII:272, 389
Bergius, Friedrich, **VII:275-277**
Bergman, Ingmar, **VII:278-282**
 After the Rehearsal, VII:280
 Autumn Sonata, VII:280
 Cries and Whispers, VII:280
 Devil's Wanton, The, VII:278
 Dream Play, A, VII:281
 Face to Face, VII:280
 Fanny and Alexander, VII:280, 281
 From the Life of the Marionettes, VII:280
 Hamlet, VII:281
 Hedda Gabler, VII:280, 281
 Hour of the Wolf, VII:280
 King Lear, VII:281
 Lesson in Love, A, VII:278
 Long Day's Journey into Night, VII:281
 Magician, The, VII:280
 Misanthrope, The, VII:281
 Naked Night, The, VII:278
 Passion of Anna, The, VII:280
 Persona, VII:280
 Scenes from a Marriage, VII:280
 Secrets of Women, VII:278
 Serpent's Egg, The, VII:280
 Seventh Seal, The, VII:278
 Shame, VII:280
 Silence, The, VII:280
 Smiles of a Summer Night, VII:278
 Three Sisters, The, VII:281
 Through a Glass Darkly, VII:280
 Torment, VII:278
 Touch, The, VII:281
 Virgin Spring, The, VII:280
 Wild Duck, The, VII:280
 Wild Strawberries, VII:278
 Winter Light, VII:280
Bergson, Henri, **VII:283-286,** 342, 343, 650, 1374;
 VIII:1920, 2425, 2426, 2755; IX:3090
 Annals of Mathematics, VII:283
 Creative Evolution, VII:283, 284
 "Evolution of German Imperialism, The,"
  VII:284
 Introduction to Metaphysics, An, VII:283

Laughter, VII:283

Matter and Memory, VII:283

"Meaning of War, The," VII:284

Time and Free Will, 1910, VII:283

Two Sources of Morality and Religion, The,
VII:284

Beria, Lavrenty, VIII:1961, 2377, 2378

Berigan, Bunny, VIII:1419, 1420

Bering, Vitus Jonassen, **IV:111-113**

Bering Strait, IV:111, 112

Berkeley, George, **IV:114-117,** 683, 685, 883, 884

Alciphron, IV:115

Analyst, The, IV:883

Defense of Free-thinking in Mathematics, A,
IV:115

De Motu, IV:114

Essay Towards a New Theory of Vision, An,
IV:114, 115

Siris, IV:115

Theory of Vision, IV:115

Three Dialogues Between Hylas and Philonous,
IV:114

*Treatise Concerning the Principles of Human
Knowledge, A,* IV:114, 344

Berkeley, Sir William, IV:80-82

Berkman, Alexander, VIII:1412, 1413, 1732

Berkshire Music Center, VII:768

Berlage, Hendrik Petrus, IX:2859

Berlin, Congress of, VI:1944

Berlin, Irving, **VII:287-290**

"Alexander's Ragtime Band," VII:287

Annie Get Your Gun, VII:289, 290; IX:3202

Call Me Madam, VII:289

Cocoanuts, The, VII:288

"Easter Parade," VII:288

"God Bless America," VII:288, 289

Holiday Inn, VII:289

Miss Liberty, VII:289

Mr. President, VII:289

"Puttin' on the Ritz," VII:288

"Supper Time," VII:289

This Is the Army, VII:289

Top Hat, VII:288

Watch Your Step, VII:288

"When I Lost You," VII:288

"White Christmas," VII:289

Yip, Yip, Yaphank, VII:288

Ziegfield Follies, VII:288

Berlin Agitation Committee, IX:4113

Berlin airlift, VII:316

Berliner Abendblätter, VI:1295

Berliner Tageblatt building, VIII:2487

Berlin Olympics of 1936, IX:2862, 2863

Berlin Party, VIII:1404

Berlin Wall, VII:428; VIII:1963; IX:3779, 3780

Berlioz, Hector, **V:202-206**

Béatrice et Bénédict, V:205

Death of Sardanapalus, The, V:203

Enfance du Christ, L', V:205

Harold in Italy, V:203, 204

Huit Scènes de Faust, V:203

Lélio, V:203, 204

Requiem, V:204, 205

Symphonie fantastique, V:203, 204; VIII:2450

Troyens, Les, V:205; VIII:2770, 2771

Bernac, Pierre, IX:3067

Bernadote, Count Folke, VII:502

Bernard, Claude, **V:207-210;** VIII:2136

*Introduction to the Study of Experimental
Medicine, An,* V:208; VI:2420; VIII:2134

Bernard, Émile, IX:3826

Bernard of Clairvaux, Saint, II:13, 14, **143-146,**
535, 860, 994-996

Treatise on Consideration, II:144

Bernardotte, Jean-Baptiste-Jules.
See Charles XIV John

Bernhardt, Sarah, VIII:2141

Bernini, Gian Lorenzo, **IV:118-121,** 167, 168

Aeneas, Anchises, and Ascanius Fleeing Troy,
IV:118

Apollo and Daphne, IV:118

David, IV:118

Ecstasy of Saint Teresa, The, III:715;
IV:119, 583

*Goat Amalthea with the Infant Jupiter and a
Faun, The,* IV:118

Pluto and Persephone, IV:118

Tomb of Pope Urban VIII, V:408

Bernoulli family, **IV:122-125,** 443; IX:4076

Ars conjectandi, IV:122

Exercitationes quaedam mathematicae, IV:122

Hydrodynamics by Daniel Bernoulli, IV:123

Théorie de la manoeuvre des vaisseaux, IV:123

Bernstein, Carl, VII:1084

Bernstein, Eduard, **VII:291-294;** VIII:2285

Evolutionary Socialism, VII:292

Bernstein, Leonard, **VII:295-299**

Age of Anxiety, The, VII:296, 298

Candide, VII:296, 298

Clarinet Sonata, VII:295

Fancy Free, VII:296

I Hate Music, VII:295

Jeremiah Symphony, VII:295, 298

Kaddish, VII:298

Mass, VII:298
On the Waterfront, VII:296
Trouble in Tahiti, VII:296
West Side Story, VII:296
Wonderful Town, VII:296
Berny, Château de, IV:898
Berry, Joan, VII:655
Berryman, John
    Homage to Mistress Bradstreet, IV:195
Berthelot, Philippe, VII:1379
Berthold, Elector of Mainz, III:491, 492
Bertholet, Alfred, VIII:2714
Berzelius, Jöns Jakob, VI:2403, 2404
Besant, Annie, **V:211-214**
Beseda, the, VIII:1835
Bessel, Friedrich Wilhelm, **V:215-217**
    Fundamenta astronomiae, V:216
    Refraction Tables, V:216
Bessemer, Sir Henry, **V:218-221**
Best, Charles H., VII:188, 189; VIII:2329, 2330
Best, Peter, VII:226
Betaille, Nicolas, VIII:1817
Bethany College, V:403
Bethe, Hans Albrecht, **VII:300-303**
    Handbuch der Physik, VII:301
Bethlehem Steel Company, IX:3619
Bettelheim, Bruno, IX:3388
Betto Bardi, Donato di Niccolò di.
    See Donatello
Betts v. Brady, VII:322
Beust, Friedrich von, **V:222-224**
Bevan, Aneurin, **VII:304-307**
    In Place of Fear, VII:306
Bevatron, VIII:2123, 2338
Beveridge, Lord, **VII:308-312**
    Full Employment in a Free Society, VII:310
    India Called Them, VII:311
    Power and Influence, VII:311
    Prices and Wages in England, VII:310
    Social Insurance and Allied Services,
        VII:310
    Unemployment, VII:308
    Voluntary Action, VII:311
Bevin, Ernest, VII:138, **313-317**, 1345
Beyle, Marie-Henri. *See* Stendhal
BGEA. *See* Billy Graham Evangelistic Association
Bible. *See* New Testament; Old Testament
Biddle, John, **IV:126-128**
    Confession of Faith Touching the Holy Trinity,
        IV:126
    Testimonies Concerning That One God, and the
        Persons of the Holy Trinity, IV:126

    Twelve Arguments Drawn Out of Scripture,
        IV:126
    Twofold Catechism, A, IV:127
Biddle, Nicholas, **V:225-229;** VI:2077
Biedermeier, V:726
Bierce, Ambrose, **V:230-232;** VIII:1603
    "Affair at Coulter's Notch, The," V:232
    "Chickamauga," V:231
    Cobwebs from an Empty Skull, V:230
    Devil's Dictionary, The, V:231, 232
    Fiend's Delight, The, V:230
    In the Midst of Life, V:231, 232
    "Man and the Snake, The," V:232
    Nuggets and Dust Panned in California, V:230
    "Occurrence at Owl Creek Bridge, An," V:231
    "Suitable Surroundings, The," V:232
Bierstadt, Albert, **V:233-235**
    Base of the Rocky Mountains, Laramie Peak,
        The, V:234
big bands, VIII:1419, 1420, 1422
big bang theory, VIII:1582, 2157-2159
Bigelow, Henry Jacob, VI:1597
Bigge, John Thomas, V:992
Bigland, Reuben, VII:385
Bildungsroman, II:1007
Billy Graham Evangelistic Association,
    VIII:1448, 1449
Bindusara, I:112
Binet, Alfred, V:869
Bingham, George Caleb, **V:236-239**
    Fur Traders Descending the Missouri, V:237, 238
    Jolly Flatboatmen, The, V:237
    Order 11, V:238
    Self-Portrait of the Artist, V:236
    Western Boatman Ashore, V:236, 237
Bingham, William, IV:1291
Bion of Borysthenes, I:303
Biraima, Damel, V:764
Birkbeck, George, VI:1787
Birney, James G., V:477
birth control
    Besant, V:211, 212
    Buck, VII:488
    Malthus, VI:1469
    Paul VI, IX:2916, 2917
    Sanger, IX:3313-3315
    Stopes, IX:3551-3553
    Supreme Court ruling, VII:322
Biruni, al-, **II:147-149,** 1014
    Beruni's India, al-, II:147
    Canon Masudicus, II:147
    Chronology of Ancient Nations, The, II:147, 148

Bishapur VI, I:781
Bismarck, Otto von, **V:240-243**
    Bancroft, V:127
    Beust, V:222-224
    Bülow, VII:494, 495
    Francis Joseph I, V:830
    Holstein, V:1130, 1131
    Kulturkampf, VI:1783
    Lassalle, VI:1324, 1325
    Scharnhorst, VI:1971
    Social Democrats, VI:1370
    Virchow, VI:2313
    William II, IX:4003, 4004
Bithynia, I:558
Bizet, Georges, **V:244-246**
    Carmen, V:244-246; VI:1685; VIII:1534, 2771
    Coupe du Roi de Thulé, La, V:245
    Djamileh, V:245
    Don Procopio, V:244
    Guzla de lémir, La, V:244
    Ivan IV, V:244
    Jolie Fille de Perth, La, V:244
    Pêcheurs de perles, Les, V:244
    Vasco de Gama, V:244
Bizone, VII:1095
Bjarni Herjolfsson, II:577, 578
Bjerknes, Vilhelm, **VII:318-320**
    Dynamic Meteorology and Hydrography,
        VII:319
    On the Dynamics of the Circular Vortex, VII:319
Black, Hugo L., **VII:321-324**
Black, Joseph, IV:1184, 1409, 1411
Black Army, III:487-489
black death
    Boccaccio, II:152
    David II, II:295
    Edward III, II:331
    Ibn Battutah, II:496
    Margaret of Denmark, Norway, and Sweden,
        II:626
    Orcagna, II:700
    Rienzo, II:791
    Venette, II:936
Black Elk, V:576
Blackfeet Indians, V:429
Blackfish, IV:164
Blackfriars, II:1011; III:689
Black Guelfs. *See* Guelfs
Black Hand, VII:1198
Black Hawk, **V:247-250;** VI:2010
    Life of Ma-ka-tai-me-she-kia-kiak, V:247
Black Hawk War, VI:1380, 2195

Black Legend, III:23, 600
Black Legion, VIII:2373
blacklisting. *See* Un-American Activities, House
        Committee on
Black Muslims. *See* Nation of Islam
black nationalism, VII:1314; VIII:2373
Black Panther Party, VII:298; VIII:2376
Black Power movement, VIII:1773, 1774,
        1974, 2627
Black September, VII:91
Blackshirts, VIII:2668
Black Star Line, VII:1312
Blackstone, William, IV:107, 108, **129-131**
    Commentaries on the Laws of England,
        IV:129-131, 1455; VI:1277
Blackwell, Elizabeth, **V:251-254**
Blackwell, Samuel, V:251
Blaiberg, Philip, VII:197
Blaine, James G., **V:255-258,** 513, 1054, 1055;
        VIII:1402, 2219
Blair, Eric Arthur. *See* Orwell, George
Blair, Robert
    Grave, The, IV:138
Blair, Tony, VIII:2371
Blair Mountain, Battle of, VIII:1881
Bland-Allison Act, VI:1454
Blane, Gilbert, IV:1180
Blaise Hamlet, IV:1013
Blake, Edward, VIII:2101
Blake, Robert, **IV:132-136,** 1342-1344
Blake, William, **IV:137-142,** 1163; VIII:2689
    Descriptive Catalogue, A, IV:140
    French Revolution, The, IV:138
    Grave, The, IV:138
    Jerusalem, V:778
    Original Stories from Real Life, IV:138
    Poetical Sketches, IV:137, 141
    Songs of Experience, IV:141
    Songs of Innocence, IV:137, 138, 141
    Wise and Foolish Virgins, The, IV:811
Blanc, Louis, **V:259-262**
Blanche, Jacques Émile, VII:594
Bland-Allison Act, V:1078
Blaue Reiter Almanac, The, VIII:2405
Blaue Reiter movement. *See* Blue Rider
        movement
Blavatsky, Helena, V:212
Bleda, I:124
Blenheim, Battle of, IV:923
Blenheim Castle, IV:635, 636, 1353; VII:691
Blenheim Park, IV:205
Blériot, Louis, **VII:325-327**

Blessed Virgin, Brotherhood of the, III:70
Bleuler, Eugen, **VII:328-331**
    Dementia Praecox, VII:329
Bligh, William, **IV:143-146**
Bliss, George, V:1143
Blitzkrieg, VIII:1949
Bloch, Ivan
    Future of War, The, VI:2177
Bloc National, VII:705
Bloc Québéc, VII:550, 551
Bloemfontein, VII:377
Blok, Aleksandr, **VII:332-334;** IX:3754
    Nechayannaya radost, VII:332
    Puppet Show, The, VII:332
    Scythians, The, VII:333
    Stikhi o prekrasnoy dame, VII:332
    Twelve, The, VII:333
    Zemlya v snegu, VII:332
blood
    anemia, IX:3957-3959
    Aretaeus of Cappadocia, I:82
    capillaries, VIII:2027-2029
    circulatory system, I:82; VIII:2027-2029;
      IX:2933
    Diocles of Carystus, I:261
    Empedocles, I:284
    Erasistratus, I:299-301
    Harvey, IV:626, 628,629
    Herophilus, I:399
    Hippocrates, I:412
    Malpighi, IV:891
    Servetus, III:675-677
    sickle-cell anemia, IX:2927
    Spallanzani, IV:1260-1262
Blood, Fanny, IV:1475
Blood, Princes of the, IV:1049
Bloody Assizes, IV:982
Bloody Marsh, Battle of, IV:1045, 1046
Bloody Mary. *See* Tudor, Mary
Bloomsbury Group, VII:1193, 1254; VIII:1955,
    2606; IX:4056
Blow, Peter, VI:1999-2001
Bloy, Léon, VIII:2425
Blücher, Gebhard Leberecht von,
    V:263-266, 942
Blücher, Heinrich, VII:98, 100
Blue Nile, IV:208-210
Blue Rider movement, VIII:1903, 2005,
    2404-2406, 2454, 2487
blues music, VII:658; IX:3442, 3444, 3445
Blum, Léon, **VII:335-338;** VIII:1699, 2491
    For All Mankind, VII:337

    Lettres sur la réforme gouvernementale, VII:335
    Stendhal et le Beyisme, VII:335
Boadicca, **I:136-139**
Boas, Franz, **VII:339-341;** VIII:2468
    Handbook of American Indian Languages,
      VII:339
    Mind of Primitive Man, VII:339, 340
Boavista Bank, VIII:2740
Bobadilla, Francisco de, III:174
Boccaccio, Giovanni, **II:150-154,** 730
    Book of Theseus, The, II:150
    Concerning Famous Women, II:262
    Decameron, The, II:152, 223, 470
    Filostrato, The, II:150
    Genealogia deorum gentilium, II:153
    Life of Dante, II:153
Boccherini, Luigi, **IV:147-150**
    Clementina, La, IV:148
    Tirana, La, IV:148
Bocchus, I:529, 833
Boccioni, Umberto, **VII:342-344**
    City Rises, The, VII:343
    Manifesto tecnico della scultura futurista,
      VII:343
    Pittura scultura futuriste (dinamismo plastico),
      VII:343
    States of Mind, VII:343
    Technical Manifesto of Futurist Painting, VII:342
    Unique forms of Continuity in Space, VII:343
Bodley, Sir Thomas, **III:62-65**
Boeotia, I:18, 290, 292
Boeotian League, I:611
Boerhaave, Hermann, IV:827
Boer War
    Allenby, VII:58-61
    Baden-Powell, V:105, 106
    Botha, VII:376
    Fawcett, V:778
    Hobhouse, VIII:1708
    Kitchener, VIII:2002-2004
    Lansdowne, VIII:2091
    Laurier, VIII:2102
    Rhodes, VI:1875
    Salisbury, VI:1945
    Seddon, VI:2019
    Smuts, IX:3455
Boethius, **II:155-158**
    Consolation of Philosophy, The, II:156, 157,
      250, 897
    On the Trinity, II:155
Boffrand, Germain, **IV:151-153**
    Livre d'architecture, IV:151-153

Bogart, Humphrey
  African Queen, The, VIII:1639
  Bad Sister, VII:843
  Petrified Forest, The, VII:843
Boggs, Lilburn W., VI:2415
Bogot, Father, IV:801
Bohemond I, **II:159-162**
Böhme, Jakob, **IV:154-156**
  Aurora, The, IV:154
  Concerning the Election of Grace, IV:155
  Concerning the Three Principles of the Divine
    Essence, IV:155
  Forty Questions of the Soul, IV:155
  High and Deep Searching Out of the Threefold
    Life of Man, The, IV:155
  Mysterium Magnun, IV:155
  Signatura Rerum, IV:155
  Theosophic Questions, IV:155
  Way to Christ, The, IV:155
Bohr, Niels, **VII:345-348**
  Bothe, VII:379
  Heisenberg, VIII:1617, 1618
  Hevesy, VIII:1654
  Landau, VIII:2073
  Meitner, VIII:2477
  Rutherford, IX:3278, 3279
  Teller, IX:3632
  Urey, IX:3787
Bohun, Henry de, II:188
Boleslaw Chrobry, II:449, 450, 871
Boleyn, Anne, **III:66-69**
  Catherine of Aragon, III:138, 139
  Cranmer, III:204
  Cromwell, III:208, 209
  Donizetti, V:685
  Henry VIII, III:351, 733
  Howard, III:367-369
  Mary I, III:479
  More, III:535
Boleyn, Mary, III:66
Bolingbroke, First Viscount, **IV:157-162,** 1400
  Dissertation upon Parties, A, IV:160, 161
  Fragments, or Minutes of Essays, IV:160
  Idea of a Patriot King, The, IV:159, 160
  Letter on the Spirit of Patriotism, IV:159
  Letter to Sir William Wyndham, A, IV:159
Bolivar, Simón, **V:267-270;** VI:2164-2166;
  VII:1295
Böll, Heinrich, **VII:349-352**
  Acquainted with the Night, VII:349
  Adam, Where Art Thou?, VII:349
  Billiards at Half-Past Nine, VII:349, 350

  Bread of Our Early Years, The, VII:349
  Clown, The, VII:350
  Group Portrait with Lady, VII:350
  Lost Honor of Katharina Blum, The, VII:350
  Safety Net, The, VII:351
  Soldier's Legacy, A, VII:351
  Train Was on Time, The, VII:349
  Women in a River Landscape, VII:351
Bologna, Concordat of, III:275
Bolshevik Revolution. *See* Russian Revolution of
  1917
Bolshoi Ballet, VIII:2448
Boltzmann, Ludwig, VIII:2476; IX:3362
Bolyai, János, VI:1403, 1404
Bombelli, Rafael, I:274
Bona of Savoy, III:682
Bonaparte, Louis Napoleon. *See* Napoleon III
Bonaparte, Lucien, IV:149
Bonaparte, Napoleon. *See* Napoleon I
Bonaventure, Saint, **II:163-166,** 978, 991
  Breviloquium, II:163
  Collations on the Six Days, II:165
  Journey of the Mind to God, The, II:165
  Sentences, II:163
Bondfield, Margaret, **VII:353-357**
Bo'ness. *See* Borrowstounness
Bonfini, Antonio, III:489
Bonham, Dr., IV:331
Bonhoeffer, Dietrich, **VII:358-361**
  Cost of Discipleship, The, VII:359
  Ethics, VII:359
  Prisoner for God, VII:360
  Sanctorum Communio, VII:358
  Schöpfung und Fall, VII:358
  Bonhomme Richard, IV:740, 741
Boniface VIII, II:79, **171-174,** 288, 738
  Clericis laicos, II:172
  Unum Sanctam, II:173
Boniface, Saint, **II:167-170**
Bonnard, Pierre, **VII:362-364;** IX:3826, 3827
Bonnat, Léon, VIII:2658
Bonnivet, Admiral, III:49, 50
Bonpland, Aimé, V:1160
Bonus Army, VIII:1730, 2296
Book of Changes. See *I Ching*
Boone, Daniel, **IV:163-166**
Boonesborough, IV:163, 164
Booth, Edwin, **V:271-274**
Booth, John Wilkes, V:271, 272
Booth, Junius Brutus, V:271, 272; VI:1261
Booth, William, **V:275-278**
  In Darkest England and the Way Out, V:275

Borah, William E., **V:279-282**
Borah-Jones Act, V:280
Borden, Lizzie, **V:283-285**
Borden, Robert Laird, **VII:365-367; VIII:**1777
Borg, Björn, **VII:368-370;** IX:2982
Borges, Jorge Luis, **VII:371-375**
 Aleph and Other Stories, The, VII:374
 "Approach to al-Mu'tasism, The," VII:373
 Discusión, VII:373
 Ficciones, VII:374
 "Library of Babel, The," VII:373
 "Pierre Menard, Author of Don Quixote,"
  VII:373
 "Poem About Gifts," VII:374
 Selected Poems, VII:371
 "Streetcorner Man," VII:373
 "Truco, El," VII:373
 Universal History of Infamy, A, VII:373
Borghese, Scipione, IV:118
Borgia, Cesare, III:14-17, 405, 450, 451
Borgia, Rodrigo, III:448
Borinquén, III:629, 630
Boris I of Bulgaria, II:**175-177,** 675
Borja y Doms, Rodrigo de. *See* Alexander VI
Bork, Robert, IX:3658
Born, Max, IX:3363
Borodin, Aleksandr, **V:286-289**
 Bogatiri, V:287
 Petite Suite, V:288
 Prince Igor, V:287
Borodino, Battle of, V:45
Borough, Edward, III:592
Boroughbridge, Battle of, II:327
Borough Road school, VI:1309, 1310
Borrell, Count, II:869
Borromeo, Charles, VIII:1858
Borromini, Francesco, **IV:167-169,** 583, 584
Borrowstounness, IV:1184
Borujerdi, Mohammad-Hussein, VIII:1957
Bosch, Carl, VII:275
Bosch, Hieronymus, **III:70-73,** 85, 86; IV:606
 Adoration Triptych, III:71
 Christ Carrying the Cross, III:70
 Crowning with Thorns, The, III:71
 Garden of Earthly Delights, The,
  III:70, 71
 Haywain, III:70
 Hell, III:70
 Landloper, III:71
 Saint John the Baptist, III:71
 Ship of Fools, The, III:70
Boso, Guntram, II:404

Bossuet, Jacques-Bénigne, **IV:170-173**
 Discourse on the History of the Whole World, A,
  IV:170, 172
 Funeral Oration for Henrietta of England, IV:170
 Sermon on Death, IV:170, 171
 Sermon on Providence, IV:170
Boston Arnold Arboretum, VII:1130
Boston Celtics, IX:3268, 3270, 3271
Boston Committee of Six, VI:1729
Boston Massacre, IV:616, 693
Boston Port Act, IV:616
Boston Red Sox, IX:3273, 3274
Boston Symphony Orchestra, VI:2232; VII:767
Boston Tea Party
 Adams, John, IV:16
 Adams, Samuel, IV:23
 Franklin, IV:494
 George III, IV:541
 North, IV:1035
 Revere, IV:1157
 Wilson, IV:1456
 Witherspoon, IV:1468
Boston Vigilance Committee, VI:1729
Boswell, James, **IV:174-178**
 Account of Corsica, An, IV:175
 Boswell on the Grand Tour, IV:175
 Boswell's London Journal, IV:174, 176, 177
 Journal of a Tour to the Hebrides, The, IV:175
 Life of Samuel Johnson, The, IV:174, 176,
  226, 730
Boswell, Percy, VIII:2146
Bosworth Field, Battle of, III:345, 651
Botha, Louis, **VII:376-378;** IX:3453
Bothe, Walther, **VII:379-381**
Botheric, I:44
Bothwell, Fourth Earl of, III:477
Bothwell Bridge, Battle of, IV:980
Botticelli, Sandro, **III:74-76**
 Adoration of the Magi, III:74, 75
 Birth of Venus, The, III:75
 Fortitude, III:74
 Judith and Her Maid, III:74
 Primavera, III:75
 Saint Augustine in His Cell, III:75
Bottomley, Horatio W., **VII:382-385**
Bouchefort, IV:152
Boucher, François, IV:414, 488, 489, 1415
Boudica. *See* Boadicca
Boudin, Eugène, VIII:2579
Boudinot, Elias, VI:1911
Bougainville, Louis-Antoine de, **IV:179-181**
Boulanger, Georges, VII:703

Boulanger, Nadia, VII:766, 767
Boulez, Pierre, **VII:386-390**
 Boulez on Music Today, VII:387
 Deux Improvisations sur Mallarmé,
  VII:388,
 Domaines for Clarinet Alone or with 21 Other
  Instruments, VII:388
 . . . explosante-fixe . . . , VII:388
 Livre pour cordes, VII:388
 Marteau sans maître, Le, VII:387, 389
 Pli selon pli, VII:388, 389
 Rug Concerts, VII:389
 Second Piano Sonata, VII:389
 Strophes, VII:388
 Third Piano Sonata, VII:388
Boulton, Matthew, **IV:182-184**
 Murdock, IV:1008, 1010
 Roebuck, IV:1184
 Trevithick, VI:2251
 Watt, IV:1411
 Wilkinson, IV:1444
Bounty, H.M.S., IV:143, 145, 146
Bourbon, Charlotte de, III:783
Bourbon, House of
 Catherine de Médicis, III:132, 133
 Charles III, IV:287
 David, V:611
 Francis I, III:275
 Orléans, IV:1048-1050
Bourbon Reforms, IV:287-289
Bourbon Restoration, VI:2187
Bourdon, Sébastien, IV:317
Bourguiba, Habib, **VII:391-394**
Bourke-White, Margaret, **VII:395-398**
 Eyes on Russia, VII:397
 North of the Danube, VII:397
 Portrait of Myself, VII:397
 Say, Is This the U.S.A.?, VII:397
 Shooting the Russian War, VII:397
 They Called It Purple Heart Valley, VII:397
 You Have Seen Their Faces, VII:397
Bourne, William, IV:850
Boutros-Ghali, Boutros, VII:50, **399-402**
Bouvines, Battle of, II:734
Bovell, William, VI:1698
Bow, Clara, VII:117
Bowen, Seabury, V:283, 284
Bowles, Samuel, V:668, 669
Boxer Rebellion, V:468, VI:1365
Boyle, Robert, **IV:185-188,** 805, 855, 858, 1059
 Experiments and Considerations Touching
  Contours, IV:186

 New Experiments and Observations Touching
  Cold, IV:186
 New Experiments Physio-Mechanicall, IV:186
 Sceptical Chymist, The, IV:186
Boy Scouts, V:105-107; VIII:2246, 2247
Boys' Life magazine, IX:3198
Boxer, Barbara, VII:1139
boxing
 Ali, VII:53-56
 Dempsey, VII:900-903
 Louis, VIII:2241-2245
 Mailer, VIII:2366
 Marciano, VIII:2411-2413
Bozeman Trail, VI:1851
Bracton, Henry de, **II:178-180**
 De legibus et consuetudinibus Angliae, II:178-180
Braddock, Edward, IV:511
Braddock, James, VIII:2243
Braden, Spruille, IX:2970
Bradford, William, **IV:189-192,** 1274, 1484, 1485
 Governor Bradford's Letter Book, IV:191
 Of Plimmoth Plantation, IV:191
Bradlaugh, Charles, V:211, 212; VII:382
Bradlee, Ben, VIII:1453
Bradley, F.H., **V:290-293;** VIII:1707, 1708
 Appearance and Reality, V:290
 Essays on Truth and Reality, V:290
 Ethical Studies, V:290
 Principles of Logic, V:290
Bradley, James, V:215
Bradley, Omar N., **VII:403-406;** IX:2913
Bradley, William, III:472
Bradman, Donald G., **VII:407-409**
Bradstreet, Anne, **IV:193-195**
 Four Monarchies, The, IV:194
 Meditations Divine and Moral, IV:194
 "Prologue, The," IV:194
 Tenth Muse Lately Sprung up in America, The,
  IV:193, 194
Brady, Matthew B., **V:294-298**
Bragadin, Senator, IV:254, 255
Bragg, Sir Lawrence, **VII:410-413**
Brahe, Tycho, II:21; **III:77-80,** 545; IV:774
 De nova et nullius aevi memoria prius visa stella,
  III:78
Brahmagupta, II:91, **181-183**
 Brahma sphuta siddhanta, II:181-183
Brahmo Sabba, VI:1848
Brahms, Johannes, **V:299-302;** VI:2156
 Choréartium, VIII:2450
 Concerto No. 1 in D Minor, Op. 15, V:300
 German Requiem, Op. 45, V:300

Piano Trio in B Major, Op. 8, V:300
Sonata in F Minor, Op. 5, V:300
Symphony No. 1 in C Minor, Op. 68, V:301
Braille, Louis, **V:303-305**
brain
 Alcmaeon, I:35, 36
 Aretaeus of Cappadocia, I:82, 83
 Asclepiades, I:102
 cerebral angiography, VII:1023-1025
 computed tomography, VIII:1751-1753
 conditioned reflexes, IX:2934
 Eccles, VII:1009, 1010
 Erasistratus, I:299-301
 Galen, I:339
 Herophilus, I:399
 Malpighi, IV:891
 prefrontal lobotomy, VII:1023-1025
 tumors, VII:824
Bramante, Donato, **III:81-84,** 407
 Christ of the Pillar, III:81
 Democritus, III:81
 Heraclitus, III:81
 Tempietto, III:83
Bramer, Leonaert, IV:1368
Brancacci Chapel, III:485
Branch Davidians, IX:3155
Brancusi, Constantin, **VII:414-418**
 Antinous of Belvedere, VII:414
 Bird in Space, VII:416
 Bust of a Boy, VII:416
 Cock, VII:417
 Endless Column, VII:417
 Gate of the Kiss, VII:417
 Portrait of G. Lupescu, VII:416
 Pride, VII:416
 Table of Silence, VII:417
Brandeis, Louis D., **VII:419-423,** 577;
 IX:3619
 "Brandeis brief," VII:421, 423
 Other People's Money, VII:421
Brandenburgischer Flugzeugwerke, VIII:1614
Brando, Marlon, **VII:424-426**
 Apocalypse Now, VII:426
 Chase, The, VII:426
 Désirée, VII:425
 Godfather, The, VII:426
 Guys and Dolls, VII:425
 Hannele's Way to Heaven, VII:424
 I Remember Mama, VII:424
 Julius Caesar, VII:425
 Last Tango in Paris, VII:426
 Men, The, VII:425

 Mutiny on the Bounty, VII:426
 One-Eyed Jacks, VII:425
 On the Waterfront, VII:425, 426
 Reflections in a Golden Eye, VII:426
 Sayonara, VII:426
 Streetcar Named Desire, A, VII:425, 426
 Wild One, The, VII:425
 Young Lions, The, VII:426
Brandon, Frances, III:318, 319
Brandt, Willy, **VII:427-430;** VIII:2009
Brandywine, Battle of, IV:367, 574
Braniff International Airlines, VII:540
Brant, Joseph, **IV:196-200**
Brant, Molly, IV:196, 198, 199
Braque, Georges, **VII:431-435;** IX:2998
 Aria de Bach, VII:432
 Bay at Antwerp, The, VII:431
 Black Fish, VII:434
 Doves, VII:434
 Estaque, Road with two Fingers, L',
  VII:431
 Fruit Dish and Glass, VII:432
 Guédridon, Le, VII:434
 Guitar and Fruit Dish, VII:432
 Harbor in Normandy, VII:431
 Homage to Bach, VII:432
 Houses at L' Estaque, VII:431
 Interior: Grey Table, The, VII:434
 Landscape at Antwerp, VII:431
 Musician, The, VII:432
 Portuguese, The, VII:432
 Ship in Harbour, Le Havre, VII:431
 Standing Nude, VII:431
 Still Life with Musical Instruments, VII:431
 Still Life with Playing Cards, VII:432
 View from the Hôtel Mistral, VII:431
 Violin and Palette, VII:432
 Violin and Pitcher, VII:432
 Weeding, The, VII:434
 Zéphere et Flore, VIII:2450
Brasilia, VIII:2740
Braudel, Fernand, **VII:436-439**
 Civilization and Capitalism, VII:437
 Mediterranean and Mediterranean World in the
  Age of Philip II, The, VII:437
Braun, Wernher von, **VII:440-443;** VIII:1615;
 IX:2778, 2779
Breadbasket, Operation, VIII:1824-1826
Breakspear, Nicholas. *See* Adrian IV
Brecht, Bertolt, VII:268, **444-447;** IX:3927, 3928
 Baal, VII:444
 Caucasian Chalk Circle, The, VII:445

Didactic Play of Baden, The, VIII:1633
Drums in the Night, VII:444
Good Woman of Setzuan, The, VII:445
In the Jungle of Cities, VII:444
Life of Galileo, VII:446
Mother, The, VII:444
Mother Courage and Her Children, VII:444, 446
Rise and Fall of the City of Mahagonny, The,
    IX:3927
St. Joan of the Stockyards, VII:445
Breckinridge, Sophonisba, IX:3604
Breda, Declaration of, IV:284, 310
Breda, Peace of, IV:285
Breitenfeld, Battle of, IV:1335-1337
Brennan, William J., Jr., VII:1214
Brentano, Franz, VII:1026
Bresdin, Rodolphe, VI:1854
Brest-Litovsk, Treaty of, VII:1103
Bretel, Jehan, II:23
Brétigny, Peace of, II:331
Breton, André, **VII:448-451,** 632, 829, 1075,
    1099, 1100; VIII:2351, 2353, 2548
    Air de l'eau, L', VII:450
    Amour fou, L', VII:450
    Arcane 17, VII:450
    Breasts of Tiresias, The, VII:448
    Champs magnétiques, Les, VII:448, 449
    Fata Morgana, VII:450
    Free Union, VII:450
    Manifesto of Surrealism, VII:449, 450
    Nadja, VII:449
    Ode to Charles Fourier, VII:450
    Second Manifesto of Surrealism, VII:450
    Vases communicants, Les, VII:450
Bretton Woods Conference, VIII:1954
Breuer, Josef, **VII:452-455,** 1224
Breuil, Henri-Édouard-Prosper, **VII:456-458**
Brewster, Mary, IX:3837
Brezhnev, Leonid Ilich, **VII:459-462,** 969, 970;
    VIII:1423, 1963, 2213
bridge construction
    Eads, V:729-731
    Freyssinet, VII:1228-1230
    Roebling, VI:1904-1906
    Stanton, VI:2106
    Telford, VI:2208-2210
    Wilkinson, IV:1443-1445
Bridges, Calvin Blackman, VIII:2651
Bridget of Sweden, Saint, II:626
Bridgewater, Duke of, IV:201
Bridgewater Foundry, VI:1624, 1626
Bridgman, Laura, V:1150, 1152

Bridgman, Percy Williams, **VII:463-465**
    Intelligent Individual and Society, The, VII:464
    Logic of Modern Physics, The, VII:464
Briggs, Henry, III:545
Bright, John, **IV:306-309;** V:527, 528
Bright v. Eynon, IV:907
Brik, Osip, VIII:2461
Brill, Paul, IV:317
Brindley, James, **IV:201-203**
Brinkley, John, V:1025
Britain, Battle of, VII:234, 236; VIII:1949
Britannicus, I:551
British and Foreign Anti-Slavery Society, VI:1600
British and Foreign School Society, VI:1787
British Broadcasting Corporation
    Collins, VII:737-740
    Orwell, IX:2849
    Reith, IX:3146-3148
British East India Company
    Burke, IV:224
    Burton, V:374, 375
    Clive, IV:325-327
    Cornwallis, IV:368, 369
    George III, IV:542, 542
    Hastings, IV:631-633
    Kidd, IV:779
    Lawrence, VI:1331
    Leeds, IV:823
    North, IV:1035
    Outram, VI:1705, 1706
    Paterson, IV:1067
British Expeditionary Force, VII:45, 46, 59
British Fourteenth Army, IX:3435-3437
British Mandate in Palestine, VIII:1791
British Medical Association building, VII:1087
British Museum, IV:85, 86
British North America Act of 1867, VI:1435,
    1437; VII:681
British Open, VIII:1876, 1877; IX:3040, 3041
British South Africa Company, VI:1874
Britten, Benjamin, **VII:466-471**
    Albert Herring, VII:469
    Ballad of Heroes, VII:468
    Billy Budd, VII:469
    Boy Was Born, A, VII:466
    Burning Fiery Furnance, The, VII:470
    Cantata Misericordium, VII:469
    Canticle II: Abraham and Issac, VII:469
    Canticle III: Still Falls the Rain, VII:469
    Canticle IV: The Journey of the Magi, VII:470
    Ceremony of Carols, VII:468
    Children's Crusade, VII:470

Curlew River, VII:469
Death in Venice, VII:470
Fairy Queen, The, VII:470
Gloriana, VII:469
Golden Vanity, The, VII:470
Hymn to St. Cecelia, A, VII:468
Midsummer Night's Dream, A, VII:469
Mont Juic, VII:468
Nocturne, VII:469
Noye's Fludde, VII:469
On This Island, VII:468
Our Hunting Fathers, VII:468
Owen Wingrave, VII:470
Paul Bunyon, VII:468
Phaedra, VII:470
Phantasy Quartet, VII:466
"Praise We Great Men," VII:470
Prince of Pogodas, The, VII:469
Prodigal Son, The, VII:470
Rape of Lucretia, The, VII:468
Rejoice in the Lamb, VII:468
Sacred and Profane, VII:470
Saint Nicolas, VII:469
Serenade, VII:468
Simple Symphony, VII:466
Sinfonietta, VII:466
Six Hölderlin Fragments, VII:469
Six Metamorphoses After Ovid, VII:469
Songs and Proverbs of William Blake, VII:470
Spring Symphony, VII:469
String Quartet in D, VII:466
Suite for Harp, VII:470
Suite on English Folk Tunes, VII:470
Turn of the Screw, The, VII:469
Variations on a Theme of Frank Bridge, VII:468
Welcome Ode, VII:470
Winter Words, VII:469
Broad Bottom cabinet, IV:1075
Broadway musicals. *See* musical theater
Brodribb, John Henry. *See* Irving, Henry
Brodsky, Joseph, VII:39
Broglie, Louis de, **VII:472-474;** IX:3363
Bronowski, Jacob, IX:3307
Bronstein, Lev Davidovich. *See* Trotsky, Leon
Brontë Anne, **V:310-313**
Agnes Grey, V:310-312
Tenant of Wildfell Hall, The, V:310
Brontë, Charlotte, **V:310-313**
Jane Eyre, V:157, 310, 312
Professor, The, V:311, 312
Shirley, V:312
Villette, V:312

Brontë, Emily, **V:310-313**
Wuthering Heights, V:310-312; VIII:1417
Brooke, Alan Francis. *See* Alanbrooke, First
   Viscount
Brook Farm, VI:1728
Brooklyn Bridge, VI:1905
Brooklyn Dodgers, IX:3193, 3194
Brooks, William Keith, VIII:2618
Brotherly Agreement, IV:1489
Brothers Club, IV:158
Brough, Louise, VII:1363
Brougham, Henry, **IV:314-317;** V:722; VI:1518
*Inquiry into the Colonial Policy of the European
   Powers, An,* V:314
Brown, George, **V:318-320**
Fame and Glory of England Vindicated, The,
   V:319
Brown, John, **V:321-326**
Benét's poem
Child, V:491
Douglass, V:697
Higginson, V:1110
Howe, V:1151
Lee, VI:1338
Parker, VI:1729
Tubman, VI:2265, 2266
Warren, IX:3894
Brown, Lancelot, **IV:204-207,** 529
Brown, Ray, VII:1159
Brown, Robert, IV:86
Browne, Sir Thomas, VIII:2690
Browning, Elizabeth Barrett, **V:327-330**
Aurora Leigh, V:329
Battle of Marathon, The, V:327
Casa Guidi Windows, V:327
"Cry of the Children, The," V:327
"Lady Geraldine's Courtship," V:327
Last Poems, V:329
Poems Before Congress, V:329
Poems, by Elizabeth Barrett Browning, V:327
"Runaway Slave at Pilgrim's Point, The,"
   V:327
Seraphim and Other Poems, The, V:327
Sonnets from the Portuguese, V:327
Browning, Robert, V:327, 329
Strafford, VI:1461
Brownlow, Kevin, VII:1275, 1276
Brown v. Board of Education
Frankfurter, VII:1214
Hughes, VIII:1769
Hurston, VIII:1789
Marshall, VIII:2434, 2435

Myrdal, VIII:2672
Robeson, IX:3187
Stevenson, IX:3525
Warren, IX:3889
White, IX:3963
Broz, Josip. *See* Tito
Bruce, David. *See* David II
Bruce, James, **IV:208-210**
   Travels to Discover the Source of the Nile, IV:209
Bruce, Robert, **II:184-189,** 294, 324, 327, 956
Bruce, Stanley M., VIII:1776
Brücke, Die, VIII:1991, 1992; IX:3354-3356
Brücke, Ernst, VII:452, 1224
Bruckner, Anton, **V:331-334;** VIII:2363
   Symphony No. 1 in C Minor, V:332
   Symphony No. 2 in C Minor, V:332
   Symphony No. 4 in E-flat Major, V:332
   Symphony No. 8, V:332
   Symphony No. 9, V:332
Bruegel, Pieter the Elder, **III:85-88**
   Battle Between Carnival and Lent, III:86
   Blue Cloak, The, III:86
   Children's Games, III:86
   Cripples, The, III:86
   Hunters in the Snow, III:88
   Massacre of the Innocents, The, III:86
   Parable of the Blind, III:86
   Peasant Dance, III:86
   Peasant Wedding, III:86
   Road to Calvary, The, III:86
   Sea Battle in the Straits of Messina, III:85
   Seven Deadly Sins, III:86
   Temptation of Saint Anthony, The, III:86
Brueys, Francis, VI:1636
Brugha, Cathal, VII:734
Brunel, Isambard Kingdom, **V:335-338,** 339, 341;
   VI:2134
Brunelleschi, Filippo, III:28, 84, **89-92,** 302,
   483, 485
Brunetti, Gaetano, IV:148
Bruni, Leonardo, **III:93-95**
   Concerning the Study of Literature, III:94
   De militia, III:94
   Dialoghi ad Petrum Paulum historum, III:93
   Historiae Florentini populi, III:93
   Laudatio Florentinae urbis, III:93
   Rerum suo tempore gestarum commentarius,
   III:94
Brunner, Emil, **VII:475-478**
   Christianity and Civilization, VII:476
   Divine Imperative: A Study of Christian Ethics,
   The, VII:476

Dogmatics, VII:477
Erlebnis, Erkenntnis und Glaube, VII:475
Man in Revolt: A Christian Anthropology,
   VII:476
Mediator: A Study of the Central Doctrine of the
   Christian Faith, The, VII:476
Mystik und das Wort, Die, VII:475
Theology of Crisis, The, VII:476
Bruno, Giordano, **III:96-100;** IV:950
   Cena de le Ceneri, III:97
   On the Infinite Universe and Worlds, III:97
Bruno of Egisheim. *See* Leo IX
Brunswick, duke of, IV:919
Brussels, Union of, III:783
Brussels Conference, VI:1508
Brutus, Lucius Junius, I:140
Brutus, Marcus Junius, **I:140-143,** 150, 159, 160
Bryan, William Jennings, V:56, 515, 1030;
   VI:1454; **VII:479-482**
Bryant, William Cullen, **V:343-345**
   "Embargo, The," V:343
   "Forest Hymn, A," V:344
   "Prairies, The," V:344
   "Thanatopsis," V:343, 345
   "To a Waterfowl," V:343, 345
Brzezinski, Zbigniew, VII:49, 50
Buber, Martin, **VII:483-485;** VIII:2408, 2409
   For the Sake of Heaven, VII:484
   Good and Evil, VII:485
   Hasidism and Modern Man, VII:484
   I and Thou, VII:476, 483, 484
   Origin and Meaning of Hasidism, The, VII:484
   Tales of the Hasidism, VII:484
bubonic plague. *See* black death
Bucareli Agreements of 1923, IX:2783
Bucer, Martin, I:883; **III:101-104,** 675
   Deregno Christi, III:103
   Institutes of the Christian Religion, III:103
Buchanan, James, V: 197, **346-348,** 794
Buck, Pearl S., **VII:486-490**
   "America's Gunpowder Women," VII:488
   "America's Medieval Women," VII:488
   Bridge for Passing, A, VII:488
   Child Who Never Grew, The, VII:488
   Command the Morning, VII:488
   Exile, The, VII:486, 489
   Fighting Angel, VII:486, 489
   Good, Earth, The, VII:486, 488, 489
   House Divided, A, VII:486
   Imperial Women, VII:488
   Of Men and Women, VII:488
   Sons, VII:486

This Proud Heart, VII:488
Townsman, The, VII:488
Buckingham, First Duke of, **IV:211-214**
    Charles I, IV:279
    Coke, IV:332, 333
    James I, IV:700, 701
    Laud, IV:797
    Leeds, IV:821
    Monck, IV:971
Buckley, William, Jr., IX:3663
Buddha, **I:144-146;** VIII:1921
Budé, Guillaume, III:274
Budge, Don, IX:2981
Buena Vista, V:615
Buen Retiro, IV:236
Buffalo Bill. *See* Cody, William Frederick
Buffon, Comte de, **IV:215-217,** 1260
    Epochs of Nature, The, IV:216, 217
    Natural History, General and Particular, IV:215
Buffoons, War of the, IV:1149
Bufford, John, V:1133
Bugeaud, Thomas Robert, V:2
Buggiano, Il, III:91
Bukharin, Nikolai Ivanovich, **VII:491-493**
    ABC of Communism, The, VII:491
    Imperialism and World Economy, VII:491
Bulan, II:550
Bulfinch, Charles, **V:349-352**
Bulganin, Nikolai, IX:4118
Bulgar Empire, II:86, 87, 175-177, 904, 952
Bulge, Battle of the, VIII:1695
Buller, Sir Redvers, VII:376
Bull Run, Battle of, V:1205; VI:2059
Bülow, Bernhard von, **VII:494-497**
    Imperial Germany, VII:496
Bülow, Hans von, IX:3555
Bultmann, Rudolf, **VII:498-500**
    Gospel of John, The, VII:499
    History of Synoptic Tradition, The, VII:498
    Jesus and the Word, VII:499
    Theology of the New Testament, VII:499
Bumppo, Natty, V:562, 564
Bunche, Ralph, VII:144, **501-504**
    American Dilemma, An, VII:501
Bunker Hill, Battle of, IV:677, 678, 1157, 1239
Bunsen, Robert, V:1010; VI:1530
Bunstead, Henry, VII:858
Buñuel, Luis, **VII:505-508**
    Adventures of Robinson Crusoe, The, VII:506
    Âge d'or, L', VII:506, 507, 829
    Andalusian Dog, An, VII:505, 507, 829
    Belle de jour, VII:506

Diary of a Chambermaid, VII:506
Discreet Charm of the Bourgeoisie, The, VII:506
Exterminating Angel, The, VII:506
Forgotten Ones, The, VII:506
Golden Age, The, VII:505
Land Without Bread, VII:505
Milky Way,The, VII:506
My Last Sigh, VII:506
Nazarin, VII:506
Phantom of Liberty, The, VII:506
That Obscure Object of Desire, VII:506
Tristana, VII:506
Viridiana, VII:506
Woman Without Love, A, VII:506
Bunyan, John, **IV:218-221**
    Grace Abounding to the Chief of Sinners, IV:219
    Holy War, The, IV:219, 220
    Life and Death of Mr. Badman, The, IV:219, 220
    Pilgrim's Progress, The, IV:218-220
Buoninsegna, Duccio di. *See* Duccio di Buoninsegna
Burbank, Luther, **V:353-357**
    Luther Burbank: His Methods and Discoveries and Their Practical Applications, V:356
    New Creations in Fruits and Flowers, V:355
Burckhardt, Jacob, III:720; **V:358-360**
    Age of Constantine the Great, The, V:359
    Cicerone, The, V:359
    Civilization of the Renaissance in Italy, The, V:359
Burger, Warren E, **VII:509-511**
Burgess, Anthony
    Cyrano, IV:387
Burgesses, House of, IV:81, 82, 647, 648
Burgh, Hubert de, **II:190-193**
Burghley, Lord. *See* Cecil, William
Burgos, III:696
Burgoyne, John, IV:677
Burgundy, Duchy of
    Charles V, III:159
    Charles the Bold, III:163-165
    Clement VII, III:166
    Henry II the Saint, II:450
    Maximillian I, III:491-493
    Philip the Good, II:740-742
    Sluter, II:832
    Warwick, III:776, 777
Buridan, Jean, **II:194-197**
    Consequentie, II:194
    Sophismata, II:194, 195
    Summula de dialectica, II:194

Burke, Edmund, II:992; IV:160, 161, **222-225,** 481, 482, 528, 555, 556, 1035
   Annual Register, The, IV:222
   Appeal from the New to the Old Whigs, IV:224
   Letter to a Noble Lord, A, IV:224
   Philosophical Inquiry into the Origin of Our Ideas of the Sublime and Beautiful, IV:222
   Reflections on the Revolution in France, IV:224, 556, 1056, 1477
   Thoughts on the Cause of the Present Discontents, IV:222
Burmese Independence Army, IX:3647
Burne-Jones, Edward, V:161; VI:1288, 1588
Burnet, Sir Macfarlane, **VII:512-515**
   Biological Aspects of Infectious Disease, VII:512
   Immunological Surveillance, VII:514
Burnett, Frances Hodgson, **V:361-364**
   Dawn of a Tomorrow, The, V:363
   Little Lord Fauntleroy, V:362, 363
   Little Princess, The, V:362
   Lost Prince, The, V:363
   My Robin, V:363
   Secret Garden, The, V:363
   Shuttle, The, V:362
   Surly Tim and Other Stories, V:361
   That Lass o' Lowrie's, V:361
Burney, Charles, **IV:226-228**
   Cunning Man, The, IV:226
   General History of Music, A, IV:226-228
   Memoirs of the Life and Letters of the Abate Metastasio, IV:228
   Present State of Music in France and Italy, The, IV:227
   Present State of Music in Germany, the Netherlands, and the United Provinces, IV:227
Burnham, Daniel Hudson, **V:365-368**
Burns, Anthony, VI:1729
Burns, Lucy, IX:2919
Burns, Robert, **IV:229-234;** VI:2374; VIII:1952
   "A Man's a Man for a' That," IV:231
   "Cotter's Saturday Night, The," IV:231
   "Holy Willie's Prayer," IV:231
   "Jolly Beggars, The," IV:231
   "O Wert Thou in the Cauld Blast," IV:232
   Poems, Chiefly in the Scottish Dialect, IV:231, 232
   "Poet's Welcome to His Love-Begotten Daughter, A," IV:231
   Scots Musical Museum, The, IV:232
   "Tam o' Shanter," IV:231
   "Twa Dogs, The," IV:231

Burr, Aaron, IV:611, 718, 719, 1096; **V:369-373,** 507, 517
Burroughs, Edgar Rice, **VII:516-519**
   Princess of Mars, A, VII:517, 519
   Tarzan of the Apes, VII:517, 519
Burroughs, William, VIII:1945, 1946
Burrus, Sextus Afranius, I:772
Burton, Dan, VII:710
Burton, James, IV:1013
Burton, Sir Richard Francis, **V:374-377;** VI:2083-2085
   City of the Saints, V:375
   First Footsteps in Africa, V:375
   Lake Regions of Central Africa, V:375
   Personal Narrative of a Pilgrimage to El-Medinah and Meccah, V:375
Busby, Richard, IV:854
Bush, George, **VII:520-523**
   Clinton, VII:708
   Dole, VII:948
   Greenspan, VIII:1472
   Persian Gulf War, VIII:1432
   Powell, IX:3071, 3072
   Thomas, IX:3658
   Walesa, IX:3847
Bushnell, Robert, V:855
Busoni, Ferruccio, IX:3794, 3926
Buss, Frances Mary, V:157, 158
Bute, Lord, IV:539, 1034
Buthos, I:912
Butler, Benjamin, V:143
Butler, Frank, VI:1677, 1678
Butler, James. *See* Ormonde, second Duke of
Butler, Nicholas Murray, **VII:524-528**
Butler, Pierce Mease, VI:1273, 1275
Butler, R.A., **VII:529-533**
Butler, Samuel
   Hudibras, IV:668
Butler Act. *See* Education Act of 1944
Butt, Isaac, VI:1740
Butts, Thomas, IV:138
Buxton, Sir Thomas Fowell, **V:378-380**
Buyids, II:678
Bye and Main Plots, III:661
Bykovsky, Valeri, IX:3639, 3640
Byng, John, IV:56, 57
Byng, Lord, VIII:1982
Byrd, Richard E., **VII:534-537**
Byrd, Richard F., VIII:1784
Byrd William, **III:105-109**
   "Alleluia, Confitemini Domino," III:105
   "Attollite portas," III:106

Cantiones Sacrae, III:106
"Christus resurgens," III:105
"Emendemus in melius," III:106
Gradualia, III:107
"Libera me, Domine, de morte aeterna," III:106
My Ladye Nevells Booke, III:107
Ne irascaris, III:106
Parthenia, III:107
Psalmes, Sonets, and Songs of Sadness and Pietie, III:107
Songs of Sundrie Natures, III:107
Byrhtnoth, II:345
Byron, Lord, **V:381-385,** 482, 483, 646, 647; VI:1261, 2053, 2054
Beppo, V:382
Bride of Abydos, The, V:381
Childe Harold's Pilgrimage, V:381, 382, 384; VI:1959, 1960
Corsair, The, V:382
Don Juan, V:382, 384
English Bards and Scotch Reviewers, V:381
Giaour, The, V:381
Hours of Idleness, V:381
Lara, V:382
Manfred, V:382
Prisoner of Chillon, The, V:382; VI:2053
Vision of Judgment, The, V:382
Byurakan Observatory, VII:63, 64

Cabala, II:648-650; III:440, 441
Cabalists, II:500
See also Safed Cabalists
Cabell, James Branch, VIII:2484
Cabeza de Vaca, Alvar Núñez, **III:110-112,** 180, 699
Naufragios, Los, III:111
Cabot, John, **III:113-116,** 347
Cabral, Pedro Alvars, III:288, 464
Cabrini, Frances Xavier, **V:386-389**
Cadet School of Mars, IV:1207
Cadore Letter, IV:888
Cædmon, **II:198-200**
Hymm, II:199
Caedwalla, II:824
Caenis, I:933
Caesar, Gaius Julius. *See* Caligula
Caesar, Julius, **I:147-151**
Agrippa, I:20
Antony, I:69
Augustus, I:132, 133
Britain, I:136
Brutus, I:141, 142

Cassius, I:159, 160
Cato the Younger, I:166-168
Catullus, I:169, 170
Cicero, I:196
Civil Wars, The, I:147
Cleopatra VII, I:218, 220, 221
Commentaries, I:830; III:581
Conquest of Gaul, The, I:922
Gallic Wars, The, I:147
Gracchi, I:347
Herod the Great, I:390
Marius, I:528
Mommsen, VI:1567, 1568
Plutarch, I:671
Pompey the Great, I:680, 681
Sallust, I:742, 743
Sosigenes, I:811-813
Tiberius, I:892
Varro, I:918
Vercingetorix, I:922, 924
Caesarion, I:218, 220
Caetani, Benedict. *See* Boniface VIII
Cage, John, VII:387, 388
Cahiers du cinéma, VIII:1391
Cairo Agreement, VII:91
Cajamarca, III:699
Cajetan, Thomas, III:443, 445
Calamity Jane, **V:390-393**
Calced Carmelites, III:402, 714, 715
calculus
Babbage, V:101-103
Bernoulli, IV:123
Copernicus, III:178
Euler, IV:444
Lagrange, IV:787
Leibniz, IV:830
Maclaurin, IV:882-884
Caldecott, Randolph, IX:3389
Calder, Alexander, **VII:538-541**
Calder Piece, VII:540
Circus, VII:538
Frisco, VII:540
Man, VII:540
Object in Five Planes (Peace), VII:540
Plastic Interludes, VII:539
Spirale, VII:539
Universe, VII:539
Whirling Ear, VII:539
Calderón de la Barca, Pedro, **IV:235-238**
Amor, honor y poder, IV:235
Constant Prince, The, IV:235
Great Theater of the World, IV:235

Judas Macabeo, IV:235
Life Is a Dream, IV:235
Love, the Greatest Enchantment, IV:236
Phantom Lady, The, IV:235
selva confusa, La, IV:235
sitio de Breda, El, IV:235
Caldor, Louis J., VIII:2633
Caldwell, Erskine, VII:397
Caleb, I:563
Caledonian Canal, VI:2208, 2209
calendars
    Brahmagupta, II:182
    Chinese dynastic calendar, IV:757
    Dionysius Exiguus, 298-300
    Eudoxus of Cnidus, I:312
    Julian calendar, I:150
    Muslim calendar, II:652
    Pelham, IV:1076
    Rabanus Maurus, II:767
    Verrius Flaccus, I:930, 931
Calhoun, John C., **V:394-397**
    Benton, V:196
    Discourse on the Constitution of the United States, A, V:396
    Disquisition on Government, A, V:396
    Gadsden Purchase, V:858, 859
    Tyler, VI:2288, 2289
Caliari, Paolo. *See* Veronese, Paolo
Calico Act of 1774, IV:60
California,
    Compromise of 1850, V:510
    Feinstein, VII:1137-1139
    Field, V:787, 789
    Fillmore, V:792, 793
    Frémont, V:840, 842
    Jackson, V:1201, 1202
    Polk, VI:1803
    Reagan, IX:3138
    Sinclair, IX:3428
    Stanford, VI:2096-2099
    Warren, IX:3888, 3889
California Welfare Reform Act of 1971, IX:3138
Caligula, **I:152-155,** 203, 632, 770
Callender, John, IV:295
Calles, Plutarco Elias, **VII:542-545**
Calley, John, IV:1022, 1023
Callias of Alopeke, I:199
calligraphy
    Mi Fei, II:639, 640
    Ogata Korin, IV:1041, 1042
    Sotatsu, IV:1257
    Wang Hsi-chi, I:946-948

Callimachus, **I:156-158**
    Aetia, I:156, 157
    Eratosthenes of Cyrene, I:303
    Hecale, I:157
    Iambi, I:156, 157
Callistus, I:417
Calloway, Cab, VII:1370
Calmette, Albert, **VII:546-548**
Caloosa Indians, III:631
Calvin, John, **III:117-121**
    Institutes of the Christian Religion, III:103, 117, 118, 120, 362, 468, 676; IV:428
    On Clemency, III:117
    Servetus, III:676, 677
Calvinism
    Catherine de Medicis, III:132, 133, 135
    Gomarists, III:575
    Hotman, III:362-365
    Jansen, IV:707
    Napier, III:544
    Pym, IV:1141
    Winthrop, IV:1463
    See also Calvin, John; Protestant Reformation
Calzabigi, Raniero, IV:549, 550
Camacho, Manuel Ávila, VII:544
Cambacérès, Jean-Jacques-Régis de, **V:398-400**
Cambio, Arnolfo di. *See* Arnolfo di Cambio
Cambria, Treaty of, III:326
Cambridge Camden Society, VI:1822
Cambridge University
    Acton, V:12, 13
    Babbage, V:101, 102
    Baskerville, IV:96
    Cranmer, III:204
    Fisher, III:265
    Marlowe, III:471
    Nashe, III:548
    Parker, III:589
    Ridley, III:654
    Rothschild, VI:1918
    Spenser, III:703
Cambyses II, I:236
Camden, William, IV:744
Camera Work, IX:3503, 3534
Cameron, Richard, **IV:239-241**
    "Cameron's Covenant, The," IV:240
    Sanquhar Declaration, IV:240
Camillus, Marcus Furius, I:505
Camões, Luís de, **III:122-124**
    Filodemo, III:122,123
    Lusiads, The, III: 123, 124
    Lyrides, The, III:123

Campañón, Francisco, III:699
Campbell, Alan, IX:2886
Campbell, Alexander, **V:401-404**
Campbell, Kim, **VII:549-552; VIII:**2656
Campbell-Bannerman, Sir Henry, VII:121, 122
Campbell v. Hall, IV:907
Camp David Accords, VII:245, 399, 591, 592;
    VIII:1794; IX:3290
Campe, Joachim Heinrich, IV:93
Camperdown, Battle of, IV:145
Campin, Robert, III:778, 779
Campra, André, IV:1149, 1150
Camulodunum, I:136, 137
Camus, Albert, **VII:553-556;** IX:3327, 3328
    Caligula, VII:553
    Fall, The, VII:555
    Just Assassins, The, VII:555
    Myth of Sisyphus and Other Stories, The,
        VII:553, 554
    Nuptials, VII:553
    Plague, The, VII:554
    Rebel, The, VII:553, 555
    State of Siege, The, VII:555
    Stranger, The, VII:553
    Wrong Side and Right Side, The, VII:553
    Canadian Freeman, VI:1449
Canadian Pacific Railroad. *See* Northern Pacific
    Railway Company
Canal, Giovanni Antonio. *See* Canaletto
Canaletto, **IV:242-245**
    Bucentoro at the Molo on Ascension Day, The,
        IV:243
    Entrance to the Grand Canal: Looking East,
        IV:243
    Old Walton Bridge, IV:244
    Ponti della Pescaria and Buildings on the Quay,
        The, IV:243
    Portico of a Palace, IV:244
    Regatta on the Grand Canal, A, IV:243
    Stonemason's Yard, The, IV:243
    Thames and the City of London from Richmond
        House, The, IV:243, 244
    Whitehall and the Privy Gardens, IV:243
Canaris, Wilhelm, VIII:1616
cancer
    actinomycin D, IX:3834
    Burnet, VII:514
    Domagk, VII:952, 953
    Ehrlich, VII:1033, 1034
    Guy de Chauliac, II:415
    Hevesy, VIII:1656
    Lawrence, VIII:2121, 2122

Razi, II:780
    vitamin C, IX:2928
    Watson, IX:3898, 3899
Candela, Felix, **VII:557-559**
Candolle, Alphonse de, V:868
Cannae, Battle of, I:760
Canning, George, **V:405-407,** 440, 904, 905;
    VI:1396, 1517, 2351
Cannizzaro, Stanislao, V:100
canon law
    Alexander III, II:48-50
    Boniface VIII, II:172
    Dionysius Exiguus, 298-300
    Gregory IX, II:399-401
    Raymond of Peñafort, II:776, 777
    Sergius I, II:824
Canova, Antonio, **V:408-412**
    Cupid and Psyche, V:410
    Hebe, V:410
    Pauline Borghese as Venus Victorious, V:410
    Theseus and the Minotaur, V:408
    Tomb of Archduchess Maria Christina, V:410
    Tomb of Pope Clement XIV, V:408
    Venus Italica, V:411
Cantor, Georg, V:639
Canudo, Ricciotto, VII:1274
Canute VI, II:733, 932
Canute the Great, **II:201-205,** 315, 346, 426
Canutt, Yakima, IX:3901
Cão, Diego, III:215
Capek, Josef, VII:560, 561
Capek, Karel, **VII:560-562**
    Insect Play, The, VII:560
    Krakatit, VII:561
    Makropulos Secret, The, VII:561
    Musaion, VII:560
    Pragmatismus, VII:560
    President Masaryk Tells His Story, VII:560
    Veci kolemnás, VII:560
    War with the Newts, The, VII:561
Capel, Arthur "Boy," VII:648, 650
capitalism
    Beard, VII:222
    Bernstein, VII:292
    Blanc, V:259-262
    Brandeis, VII:419
    Engels, V:760-762
    Goldman, VIII:1411-1413
    Greenspan, VIII:1471
    Keynes, VIII:1954
    Kollwitz, VIII:2016
    Laski, VIII:2093, 2094

Lenin, VIII:2161
Luxemburg, VIII:2285-2287
Malthus, VI:1468
Marx, VI:1492-1494
Morgan, VI:1579, 1581, 1582
Niebuhr, VIII:2737
Peru, VIII:1585
Randolph, IX:3113, 3114
Sinclair, IX:3428, 3429
Smith, IV:1249-1251
Veblen, IX:3805, 3806
Weber, IX:3910, 3911
Zetkin, IX:4112, 4113
capital punishment. *See* death penalty
Capodistrias, John, VI:2417, 2418
Capone, Alphonse, **VII:563-566**
Capote, Truman, **VII:567-570;** IX:3303
    Answered Prayers, VII:568, 569
    Beat the Devil, VII:567
    Breakfast at Tiffany's, VII:567
    Dogs Bark, The, VII:568
    Glass House, The, VII:568
    Grass Harp, The, VII:567
    House of Flowers, VII:567
    In Cold Blood, VII:568, 569
    Innocents, The, VII:567
    "Miriam" VII:567
    Muses are Heard, The, VII:567
    Music for Chameleons, VII:569
    Other Voices, Other Rooms, VII:567
    Tree of Night and Other Stories, A, VII:567
Cappadocia, I:353, 558, 896
Caprini, Palazzo. *See* Raphael, House of
Caprivi, Leo von, V:1131
Caraffa, Gian Petro, III:597
Caratacus, I:136
Caravaggio, V:610
Carbo, Gaius Papirius, I:758
Carbonari, the, VI:1514
Carcophorus, I:417
Carden, John, V:635, 636
Cárdenas, Lázaro, VII:543, **571-574**
Cárdenas, López de, III:181, 182
Cardinals, College of
    Gregory VII, II:397
    Innocent IV, II:516
    John XXIII, VIII:1859, 1860
    Paul VI, IX:2916
    Urban II, II:929, 930
cardiology. *See* heart
Cardozo, Benjamin Nathan, **VII:575-578**
    Growth of the Law, The, VII:576

    Nature of the Judicial Process, The, VII:576
    Paradoxes of Legal Science, The, VII:576
Care of Dependent Children, Conference on the,
    IX:3838
Carey, George Saville, VI:1259
Carey, Harry, Sr., IX:3902
Carey, Nance, VI:1259
Carib Indians, III:631
Carignano, IV:584
Carleton, Guy, **IV:246-249**
Carlevaris, Luca, IV:242
Carlism, V:414, 415
Carlos II, IV:1448
Carlos, Don, **V:413-415**
Carlson, Chester F., **VII:579-581**
Carlyle, Thomas, V:59, **416-419,** 755;
    VI:2370, 2371
    Chartism, V:417
    French Revolution, The, V:417; IX:2871
    History of Friedrich II of Prussia, The, V:417
    Latter-Day Pamphlets, V:417
    Past and Present, V:417
    Reminiscences, V:418
    Sartor Resartus, V:416, 757; VI:2370
Carmelites
    Cruz, IV:382
    John of the Cross, III:401-403
    Lorenzettis, II:595
    Stein, IX:3508, 3509
    Teresa of Ávila, III:714
    Venette, II:935, 937
Carnap, Rudolf, **VII:582-584**
    Formalization of Logic, VII:583
    Introduction to Semantics, VII:583
    Introduction to Symbolic Logic and Its
        Applications, VII:582
    Logical Foundations of Probability, VII:583
    Logical Syntax of Language, The, VII:583
    Logische Aufblau der Welt, Der, VII:582
    Meaning and Necessity, VII:583
Carnarvon, Fifth Earl of, I:905, 906
Carneades, I:725
Carnegie, Andrew, **V:420-424,** 662; VI:1898
Carnegie Corporation of New York, V:423
Carnegie Corporation Survey of the Negro,
    VII:501
Carnegie Endowment for International Peace,
    VII:525
Carnegie Foundation, V:749; VII:1169
Carnegie Steel Company, V:421; VIII:2480
Carnot, Sadi, VI:1343-1345; VIII:2714
Caroline, Fort, III:508

Caroline, Queen, IV:535; V:315, 406
Caroline Affair, VI:2011
Carolingian Empire
    Charlemagne, II:228-230
    Charles Martel, II:242-244
    Louis II the German, II:599-602
    Philip the Good, II:740
    Rabanus Maurus, II:766-768
Carolus-Duran, Charles Jurand, VI:1961
Carpenter Center for Visual Arts, VIII:2139
Carpentier, Georges, VII:902
Carpini, Giovanni da Pian del, **II:206-209**
    Historia Mongalorum quos nos Tartaros
      appellamus, II:208
Carr, Thomas, VI:1480
Carracci family, **III:125-128**
    Bean Eater, The, (Annibale) III:126
    History of Jason, III:125
    Last Communion of Saint Jerome, The,
      (Agostino) III:126
    Madonna of the Bargellini Family, (Ludovico)
      III:126
    Madonna with Saint John Evangelist and Saint
      Catherine, (Annibale) III:126
Carranza, Venustiano, VII:542; IX:2782, 3813,
    4106
Carrel, Alexis, VIII:2196
Carrera, José, VI:1688
Carrillo, Alfonso, III:260
Carroll, Charles, **IV:250-253**
Carroll, James, VI:1858, 1859
Carroll, Lewis, **V:425-428**
    Alice's Adventures in Wonderland, V:427, 428;
      VIII:2143
    Hunting of the Snark, The, V:427
    Silvie and Bruno, V:427
    Through the Looking-Glass, V:427
Carron ironworks, IV:1183-1185
Carson, Kit, **V:429-433**
Carson, Rachel, **VII:585-588**
    Edge of the Sea, The, VII:586
    Sea Around Us, The, VII:586
    Silent Spring, VII:585-588
    "Undersea," VII:585
    Under the Sea-Wind, VII:585
Cartegena, Juan de, III:454
Carter, Howard, I:905, 906
Carter, Jimmy, **VII:589-593**
    Blood of Abraham, The, VII:591
    Bush, VII:521
    Clinton, Bill, VII:707
    Clinton, Hillary Rodham, VII:714

    Dole, VII:948
    Ford, VII:1182
    Jordan, VIII:1889
    Keeping Faith, VII:591
    Khomeini, VIII:1958, 1959
    Kirkpatrick, VIII:1995
    Presley, IX:3079
    Reagan, IX:3138
    Sadat, IX:3290
    Why Not the Best?, VII:590
Carteret, Phillip, IV:180
Cartesianism. *See* Descartes, René
Carthage
    Archimedes, I:79
    Cato the Censor, I:164
    Flaubert, V:798
    Hanno, I:368-370
    Second Punic War, I:336, 364-366, 535-537,
      739-741, 761
    Third Punic War, I:757-759
Carthaginian Peace, I:366
Cartier, George Étienne, VI:1436-1438;
    VIII:2100
Cartier, Jacques, **III:129-131**
Cartier-Bresson, Henri, **VII:594-597**
    Decisive Moment, The, VII:595
    retour, Le, VII:595
    Victoire, VII:595
cartoons
    Geisel, VII:1329-1331
    Disney, VII:940, 941
    Nast, VI:1627-1629
    Orozco, IX:2837
    Thurber, IX:3677, 3678
Carus, I:263
Caruso, Enrico, **VII:598-601**
Carver, George Washington, **VII:602-605**
Casablanca Conference, VIII:1737, 2643
Casals, Pablo, **VII:606-609**
    Hymn to the United Nations, VII:608
Casals Festival, VII:608
Casanova, Giovanni Giacomo, **IV:254-256**
    Memoirs of Jacques Casanova de Seingalt,
      IV:256
Casella, Mario, II:286
Casimir the Great, **II:210-214**
Cassady, Neal, VIII:1945, 1946
Cassander, I:516
Cassatt, Mary, **V:434-437**
Cassian, John, II:137, 138
Cassin, René, **VII:610-613**
Cassini, Giovanni, IV:600

Cassino, Monte, II:137
Cassiodorus, **II:215-217**
  Commentary on the Psalms, II:216
  Deorthographia, II:216
  Historia ecclesiastica triparita, II:216
  History of the Goths, II:215, 897
Cassirer, Ernst, **VII:614-616**
  Essay on Man, An, VII:615
  Kant's Life and Thought, VII:614
  Language and Myth, VIII:2088
  Myth of the State, The, VII:615
  Philosophy of Symbolic Forms, The, VII:615
  Philosophy of the Enlightenment, The, VII:615
  Substance and Function, VII:614
Cassirer, Paul, VIII:2013
Cassius, I:141, 142, **159-161**
Cassius, Avidius, I:525
Castelli, Benedetto, IV:1331
Castelli, Francesco. *See* Borromini, Francesco
Castiglione, Baldassare, III:645
Castillo, Ramón S., IX:2970
Castle Howard, IV:635, 1352, 1353
Castlereagh, Viscount, V:406, **438-442;**
    VI:1396
Castro, Fidel, VII:**617-620;** VIII:1494-1496
Catalonia, II:79, 529
Cat and Mouse Act of 1913, IX:2873
Catesby, Robert, III:258, 259
Catharist movement, II:49, 301, 302, 511
Cathay, II:988
Cather, Willa, V:1228-1230; **VII:621-626**
  Alexander's Bridge, VII:624
  April Twilights, VII:623
  Death Comes for the Archbishop, VII:625
  My Antonia, VII:621, 624
  Old Beauty and Others, The, VII:625
  One of Ours, VII:621, 624
  O Pioneers!, VII:624; V:1230
  Professor's House, The, VII:625
  Song of the Lark, VII:621, 624
  Troll Garden, The, VII:623
Catherine II. *See* Catherine the Great
Catherine de Médicis, **III:132-135**
  Henry IV, III:333
  Mary, Queen of Scots, III:475
  Medici, Lorenzo de', III:498
  Mornay, III:537
  Nostradamus, III:568
Catherine of Aragon, **III:136-139**
  Boleyn, III:68
  Clement VII, III:167
  Cranmer, III:204-206

Fisher, III:264, 265
  Henry VIII, III:349, 351, 732, 733
  Mary I, III:479
  Wolsey, III:786
Catherine of Siena, Saint, **II:218-222**
  Dialogue, The, II:220
  Life of Catherine of Siena, The, II:220, 221
Catherine the Great, **IV:257-260**
  Alexander I, V:44
  Brown, IV:206
  Dickinson, IV:414
  Frederick the Great, IV:505
  Jones, IV:741
  Joseph II, IV:752
  Peter III, IV:1087, 1089
  Suvorov, IV:1298, 1299
Catholic Association, VI:1681, 1683, 1753
Catholic Center Party, VII:1102-1104
Catholic Committee, VI:1680
Catholic Emancipation, V:995; VI:1680-1683
Catholic League, IV:451, 452
Catholic Liberalism, VIII:2100
Catholicon, III:330
Catholic Reformation. *See* Counter-Reformation
Catholic Revival. *See* Counter-Reformation
Catholic Worker movement, VII:850-852
Catilina, Lucius Sergius, I:196, 743
Catlin, George, V:234, **443-445**
Cato the Censor, **I:162-165**
  Ad filium, I:164
  De re militari, I:164
  Ennius, I:287
  On Agriculture, I:164
  Origines, I:164
  Pompey the Great, I:680, 681
  Verrius Flaccus, I:930
Cato the Elder, I:759
Cato the Younger, I:140, **166-168,** 743
Cato Uticensis. *See* Cato the Younger
Catt, Carrie Chapman, VII:23, **627-630**
Cattle Problem, I:79
Catullus, **I:169-172,** 704
Cauchon, Pierre, III:398
Cauldron, Battle of the, IX:3214
Cavalcanti, Guido, **II:223-225,** 286
  New Life, The, II:223
Cavalier Parliament, IV:1230
Cavalier Poets, VIII:2530
Cavelier, René-Robert. *See* La Salle, Sieur de
Cavendish, Henry, **IV:261-264,** 976
Cavendish, Thomas, **III:140-142,** 213
Cavendish, William, IV:662

Cavendish Laboratory, VII:412, 635-637, 797; IX:3277, 3279, 3897

Cavour, Count, **V:446-449;** VI:1783

Caxton, William, I:180; **III:143-146,** 457
    Arte and Crafte to Know Well to Die, The, III:143
    Canterbury Tales, The, III:144
    Dicteis or Sayenges of the Phylosophers, III:144
    Game and Playe of the Chesse, The, III:143
    Myrrour of the Worlde, The, III:144
    Recuyell of the Historyes of Troye, III:143

Cayley, Sir George, **V:450-452**

Cayor, kingdom of, V:764

Cazes, Pierre-Jacques, IV:275

CBS, VII:177; VIII:2662, 2664, 2665

CCAR. *See* Central Conference of American Rabbis

CDU. *See* Christian Democratic Union

Cecchetti, Enrico, IX:2937, 2939

Cecil, Robert. *See* Salisbury, Third Marquess of

Cecil, William, **III:147-150,** 241, 660, 661; IV:330

Celestine I, I:937

Celestine V, II:171, 173

Cellini, Benvenuto, **III:151-154,** 168
    Life Benvenuto Cellini, The, III:153,154
    Perseus, III:153

Celsus, Aulus Cornelius, **I:173-175**
    De artibus, I:173
    Eight Books of Medicine, The, I:173-175

Celtiberians, I:758

Cem, III:51, 53

Cendrars, Blaise, VII:83

censorship
    Catherine the Great, IV:260
    Cato the Censor, I:162-165
    Claudius I, I:203
    Dreiser, VII:954, 955, 958; VIII:2484
    Forster, VII:1195
    Galileo, IV:521, 522
    Joyce, VIII:1892
    Kurosawa, VIII:2043, 2044
    Lawrence, VIII:2118, 2119
    Lessing, IV:844
    Mencken, VIII:2484
    Nazi Germany, VIII:1405
    Scipio Africanus, I:761, 762
    Wang Yang-ming, III:771
    West, IX:3949, 3950

Central African Federation, VII:531

Central Conference of American Rabbis, VI:2400, 2402

Central Intelligence Agency
    Bush, VII:521
    Cuba, VII:618; VIII:1930
    Eisenhower, VII:1044
    Guatemala, VIII:1494
    Mohammad Reza Shah Pahlavi, VIII:2567
    Sihanouk, IX:3417

Central Pacific Railroad, VI:2096-2099

Central Park, V:344; VI:1691, 1692

Ceolfrid, II:132

Ceraunus, I:716

Cerchi family, II:288

Cerealis, Petillius, I:137

Ceres, V:893, 894

CERN, VIII:2338; IX:3103

Cervantes, Miguel de, **IV:265-270**
    Commerce of Algiers, The, IV:266
    Don Quixote de la Mancha, IV:265-269, 1312
    Exemplary Novels, IV:268
    Galatea, IV:265, 266
    Numantia, IV:266
    Travels of Persiles and Sigismunda, The, IV:268
    Voyage to Parnassus, The, IV:268, 269

Césaire, Aimé, **VII:631-634;** IX:3391
    Discourse on Colonialism, VII:633
    Letter to Maurice Thorez, VII:632, 633
    My Native Land, VII:631-633
    Season in the Congo, A, VII:633
    Tempest, The, VII:633
    Toussaint Louverture, VII:633
    Trajedy of King Christopher, The, VII:633

Ceuta, III:354

Cézanne, Paul, **V:453-456**
    Braque, VII:431
    Delaunay, VII:888, 889
    Denis, VII:910
    Léger, VIII:2154
    Milhaud, VIII:2528
    Monet, VIII:2581
    Picasso, IX:2998
    Poussin, IV:1120
    Renoir, VI:1870
    Self-Portrait, V:454
    Zola, VI:2420

Chacabuco, Chile, VI:1689

Chacón, Gonzalo, III:260

Chadwick, Edwin, **V:457-461**
    Internment Report, V:459
    Report on the Sanitary Condition of the Labouring Population, The, V:459

Chadwick, James, **VII:635-638;** VIII:1871, 1873
    Radiations from Radioactive Substances, VII:635

Chagall, Marc, **VII:639-642**
    Birthday, VII:639
    Double Portrait with a Glass of Wine, VII:639

Fiddler, The, VII:639
Firebird, VII:641
I and the Village, VII:639
Over the Town, VII:639
Praying Jew, The, VII:639
Rabbi of Vitebsk, VII:639
Self Portrait with Seven Fingers, VII:639
White Crucifixion, VII:641
Chaghatay tribes, II:884, 885
Chaghrï Beg, II:67, 677
Chaikin, Joseph, IX:3643
Chain, Ernst, VII:1167, 1173, 1174
Chait Singh, IV:632
Chalcedon, Council of, I:862, 863, 865, 866;
    II:820, 824
Chalcidian League, I:629
Chaldaean Oracles, I:684
Challenger space shuttle, VII:112, 113; IX:3179
Chalukya, II:430
Chamberlain, Austen, VII:169
Chamberlain, Joseph, **V:462-465,** 804; VII:643
Chamberlain, Neville, **VII:643-647**
    Attlett, VII:138
    Baldwin, VII:170
    Beaverbrook, VII:236
    Bevan, VII:304
    Chamberlain, Joseph, V:464
    Eden, VII:1016
    Lyons, VIII:2294
    Macmillan, VIII:2341
    Reith of Stonehaven, IX:3148
Chamberlain, Wilt, IX:3271
Chamberlain of London v. Allen Evans, IV:906
chamber music
    Bach, IV:78
    Boccherini, IV:149
    Borodin, V:286-288
    Franck, V:832-834
    Zwilich, IX:4121-4123
Chambers, Whittaker, VIII:1683-1685
Chambers, William, IV:206
Chambers v. Florida, VII:322
Champier, Symphorien, III:676
Champlain, Samuel de, **IV:271-274**
Champlain Canal, V:520
Chanca, III:577, 578
Chandasoka, I:112
Chanel, Coco, **VII:648-652;** VIII:2182
Chanel No. 5, VII:650, 651
Chang Chih-tung, **V:466-469**
Chang Chiu-ling, II:965, 966
Chang Lei, II:588

Chang-sun Wu-chi, II:877
Channing, William Ellery, **V:470-473;** VI:1336
    Remarks on American Literature, V:472
    Slavery, VI:1275
Chantelou, Paul Fréart de, IV:1119
Chanute, Octave, IX:4064
Chao Kao, I:178
Chao K'uang-yin. *See* T'ai Tsu
Chao Ming-ch'eng, II:588, 589
Chaplin, Charles, **VII:653-656,** 789; IX:3008, 3159
    Circus, The, VII:654
    Gold Rush, The, VII:654
    Great Dictator, The, VII:654
    Immigrant, The, VII:656
    Jimmy the Fearless, VII:653
    Kid, The, VII:653
    King in New York, A, VII:655
    Limelight, VII:655
    Mabel's Strange Predicament, VII:653
    Modern Times, VII:654
    Monsieur Verdoux, VII:655
    Tramp, The, VII:655, 656
    Twenty Minutes of Love, VII:653
    Woman of Paris, A, VII:654
Chapman, George, **III:155-158**
    All Fools, III:155
    Blind Beggar of Alexandria, The, III:155
    Bussy D'Ambois, III:156, 157
    Caesar and Pompey, III:157
    *Conspiracy and the Tragedy of Charles, Duke of
        Byron, The,* III:157
    Eastward Ho!, III:156
    Gentleman Usher, The, III:155
    Humorous Day's Mirth, An, III:155
    Revenge of Bussy D' Ambois, The, III:156
    Tragedy of Chabot, Admiral of France, The,
        III:157
    Widow's Tears, The, III:156
Chapman, John. *See* Appleseed, Johnny
Chapman, J. Wilbur, IX:3583
Chapman, Leo, VII:627
Chapultepec, Battle of, VI:2011, 2012
Char, René, VII:387
Charaxus, I:750
Charbonneau, Toussaint, VI:1933
Charcot, Jean-Martin, VII:448, 1224
Chardin, Jean Siméon, **IV:275-278,** 488, 489
Chardin, Teilhard de, II:313
Charest, Jean, VII:550
Charity, Confraternity of, IV:1380, 1381
Charity, Daughters of, IV:1381
Charity, Missionaries of, IX:3636, 3637

Charity of St. Joseph, Sisters of, VI:2030, 2031
Charlemagne, **II:226-231**
 Alcuin, II:44, 46
 Augustine, I:129
 Charles the Bald, II:239, 240
 Louis II the German, II:601
 Rabanus Maurus, II:766
 Widukind, II:973-975
Charles I (of England), **IV:279-282**
 Buckingham, IV:212
 Charles II, IV:283
 Clarendon, IV:308, 309
 Coke, IV:333, 334
 Cotton, IV:372
 Cromwell, IV:378, 380
 English Civil War, IV:99, 132, 501
 Hale, IV:596
 James I, IV:700
 James II, IV:703
 Jones, IV:735-737
 Jonson, IV:748
 Lambert, IV:789, 790
 Laud, IV:797, 799
 Milton, IV:960
 Pride, IV:1126-1128
 Pym, IV:1141, 1142
 Shaftesbury, IV:1228
 Strafford, IV:1285-1288
 Winthrop, IV:1463
Charles I (of Portugal), III:453
Charles II (of England), **IV:283-286**
 Boyle, IV:187
 Clarendon, IV:309-311
 Cromwell, IV:380
 Dryden, IV:424, 425
 Godolphin, IV:552
 Hale, IV:597
 Hobbes, IV:665
 James II, IV:703, 704
 Lambert, IV:791
 Leeds, IV:821-823
 Locke, IV:855-857
 Mather, Increase, IV:938, 939
 Monck, IV:973
 Monmouth, IV:980-982
 Oates, IV:1038, 1039
 Parliament, IV:99, 219
 Pride, IV:1127
 Purcell, IV:1137, 1138
 Scotland, IV:239
 Shaftesbury, IV:1228
 Vanbrugh, IV:1351

 Virginia land grants, IV:80
 Wren, IV:1480-1482
Charles II (of France), II:24
Charles III (of Spain), IV:147, 148, **287-289,** 569, 570, 1325
Charles IV (Holy Roman Emperor), **II:235-238,** 729, 730, 791, 792, 969
Charles IV (of Spain), V:413
Charles V (Holy Roman Emperor), **III:159-162**
 Alva, III:18-20
 Alvarado, III:23
 Bucer, III:103
 Christine de Pizan, II:260, 261
 Clement VII, III:166, 167
 Coronado, III:180
 Cortés, III:190
 Edward VI, III:239
 Francis I, III:274, 275, 277
 Marguerite of Navarre, III:468
 Mary I, III:479, 480
 Paul III, III:597, 598
 Süleyman the Magnificent, III:707
 Titian, III:721
 Vesalius, III:755
 Vitoria, III:768
 Wolsey, III:786
Charles VI (of France), III:338-340
Charles VI (Holy Roman Emperor), IV:914; 1384
Charles VII (of France), III:396, 398, 399, 434
Charles VII (Holy Roman Emperor), IV:915
Charles VIII (of France), III:14, 16, 48, 405, 668, 682
Charles IX (of France), III:132, 133
Charles X (of France), VI:2226, 2238
Charles X (of Sweden), IV:304, 838
Charles XII (of Sweden), **IV:290-292,** 924, 1082, 1084
Charles XIV John (of Sweden), **V:474-476**
Charles, Prince (of England), VII:923-925, 1062, 1064; VIII:2644, 2645
Charles, Ray, **VII:657-659**
 "America the Beautiful," VII:658
 "Born to Lose," VII:658
 "Busted," VII:658
 "Crying Time," VII:658
 "Georgia on My Mind," VII:657
 "Greenbacks," VII:657
 "Hit The Road, Jack," VII:657
 "I Can't Stop Loving You," VII:658
 "I Got A Woman," VII:657
 "It Should Have Been Me," VII:657
 Message to the People, VII:658

Modern Sounds in Country and Western Music,
    VII:657
    "One Mint Julep," VII:657
    "Song for You, A," VII:658
    "Unchain My Heart," VII:657
    "What'd I Say?," VII:657
Charles d'Orléans, **II:232-234**
Charles Martel, II:226, **242-244**
Charles of Anjou, II:606
Charles of Austria, III:241; IV:1279
Charles River Bridge v. Warren Bridge, VI:2191
Charles the Bald, **II:239-241,** 599-601, 773
Charles the Bold, **III:163-165,** 491
Charles the Fat, II:794
Charles the Simple, II:794
Charles the Wise. *See* Charles V
Charleston, South Carolina, V:859
Charlestown Neck, Battle of. *See* Bunker Hill,
    Battle of
Charlier, Jean. *See* Gerson, Jean de
Charlottetown Accord, VIII:2656
Charmides, I:795
Chartier, Alain, **II:245-247**
    "Belle Dame sans merci, La," II:246
    Epistola de Puella, II:245
    Invective Quadrilogue, The, II:246, 247
Chartreuse of Champmol, II:832
Chase, Salmon P., **V:477-480,** 551, 552
Chase, Samuel, **IV:293-296**
Chastaigner, Louis de, III:671, 672
Chateaubriand, **V:481-484**
    Atala, V:482
    Genius of Christianity, The, V:482, 483
    *Historical, Political, Moral Essay on
        Revolutions, An,* V:482
    Martyrs, The, V:482
    Natchez, The, V:483
    On Buonaparte and the Bourbons, V:483
    René, V:482, 483
Chatham, First Earl of. *See* Pitt the Elder, William
Chaucer, Geoffrey, **II:248-252**
    Boece, II:250
    Book of the Duchess, II:248, 250, 251
    Canterbury Tales, The, II:130, 150, 250, 251,
        776; III:144; IV:138
    Consolation of Philosophy, The, II:250
    House of Fame, The, II:250, 251
    Legend of Good Women, The, II:250
    Parliament of Fowls, The, II:250
    Troilus and Criseyde, II:250
Chauliac, Guy de. *See* Guy de Chauliac
Chautemps, Camille, VII:336

Chavez, César, VIII:1762-1764
Chekhov, Anton, **V:485-488;** VIII:1442, 1444
    Cherry Orchard, The, V:486; IX:3403
    Ostrov Sakhalin, V:486
    Pystrye rasskazy, V:485
    Seagull, The, V:486; IX:3487
    Tales of Melpomene, V:485
    Three Sisters, The, V:486; VIII:2143
    Uncle Vanya, V:486
    V synerkakh, V:485
    Wood Demon, The, V:485
Cheltenham Ladies' College, V:157-159
Cheng Ch'eng-kung, **IV:297-299**
Cheng Chih-lung, IV:297
Cheng Ho, **II:253-256,** 1023
Cheng-shih dynasty, I:949
Ch'en-hao, III:772
Ch'en Hui, II:482
Ch'en Tu-hsiu, **VII:660-663**
Chermoye, Philip, III:763
Chernyshevsky, Nikolay, V:1100, 1101; VIII:2675
    What Is to Be Done?, V:689; VI:1612; VIII:1411
Cherokee Indians
    Boone, IV:163
    Houston, V:1137
    Lockwood, VI:1407
    Mankiller, VIII:2389, 2390
    Rogers, IX:3204
    Ross, VI:1910-1912
    Scott, VI:2011
    Sequoyah, VI:2025, 2027, 2028
Cherokee Nation v. Georgia, VI:2149
Chersonese, I:254, 553, 554
Chesapeake Bay, battle in, IV:180
Chesterfield Act, IV:1076
Cheves, Langdon, V:225
Cheyenne Indians, V:575, 576
Chiang Ch'ing, VII:689; VIII:2214
Chiang Kai-shek, **VII:664-667**
    Ch'en Tu-hsiu, VII:662
    Chou En-lai, VII:676, 677
    Chu Teh, VII:688
    Ho Chi Minh, VIII:1700
    Kuo Mo-jo, VIII:2034
    Liu Shao-ch'i, VIII:2212
    Luce, VIII:2262
    P'eng Te-huai, IX:2954
    Tseng Kuo-fan, VI:2262
    Wang Ching-wei, IX:3878, 3879
Chicago
    Addams, VII:22, 23
    Altgeld, V:54-56

Burnham, V:365, 367, 368
Capone, VII:563-565
Darrow, VII:839
Field, V:783-786
meat inspection, IX:3428
Mies van der Rohe, VIII:2522, 2533
Perkins, IX:2961
Pullman Strike of 1894, VII:881
Sandburg, IX:3308, 3309
Ward, VI:2331-2334
Wells-Barnett, IX:3943, 3944
Wright, IX:4060
Chicago, University of
    Eliade, VII:1056
    Fermi, VII:1147
    Field, V:785
    Harper, V:1044-1047
    Hutchins, VIII:1800-1802
    Lathrop, VIII:2097
    Millikan, VIII:2539
    Palmer, VI:1717
    Rockefeller, VI:1898
    Talbot, IX:3603-3605
    Veblen, IX:3806
    Wach, IX:3829-3831
Chicago Lyric Opera, IX:3608
Chicago Opera Festival, VI:2167, 2168
Chicago Orchestra. *See* Chicago Symphony
    Orchestra
Chicago Plan of 1909, V:367
Chicago Sun-Times, V:786
Chicago Symphony Orchestra, VI:2230, 2232
Chicago White Sox, IX:3274
Chicago World's Fair of 1893. *See* World's
    Columbian Exposition
Chicherin, Georgi Vasilievich, VIII:2209
Chickamauga, Battle of, V:876
Chickasaw Indians, IV:1045
Ch'ien-lung, **IV:300-303**
Chien-wen, II:1022
Child, Lydia Maria, **V:489-492**
    Appeal for the Indians, An, V:491
    *Appeal in Favor of That Class of Americans
        Called Africans, An,* V:490, 491
    Autumnal Leaves, V:491
    Fact and Fiction: A Collection of Stories,
        V:491
    First Settlers of New England, The, V:489
    Freedmen's Book, The, V:491
    Frugal Housewife, The, V:489
    Hobomok, V:489
    Juvenile Miscellany, V:489

Letters from New York, V:490, 491
Children's Bureau, United States, VIII:2096,
    2097, 2099
Children's Houses, VIII:2598
children's literature
    Alger, V:51-53
    Andersen, V:58-60
    Baum, V:154-156
    Burnett, V:361-364
    Calder, VII:539
    Carroll, V:425, 427, 428
    Geisel, VII:1329-1331
    Lewis, VIII:2167-2169
    Milne, VIII:2543-2545
    Newbery, IV:1019-1021
    Potter, IX:3063-3065
    Sandburg, IX:3310
    Sendak, IX:3387-3389
    Stevenson, VI:2139, 2141, 2142
    Tolkien, IX:3696-3698
    Wilder, IX:3992-3994
Chimalpopoca, III:378
Ch'in Dynasty, I:176-179; II:1018, 1019
    See also Eastern Chin Dynasty; Later
        Chin Dynasty
Chinese Civil War, VIII:2189, 2213
Chinese Communist Party
    Ch'en Tu-hsiu, VII:660-662
    Chiang Kai-shek, VII:664-667
    Chou En-lai, VII:676-678
    Chu Teh, VII:687-689
    Deng Xiaoping, VII:905-907
    Kuo Mo-jo, VIII:2033-2035
    Lin Piao, VIII:2189-2191
    Li Peng, VIII:2178-2180
    Liu Shao-ch'i, VIII:2212-2214
    Lu Hsün, VIII:2252-2254
    Mao Tse-tung, VIII:2400-2402
    P'eng Te-huai, IX:2954
    Sun Yat-sen, IX:3579
    Wang Ching-wei, IX:3879, 3879
Chinese Nationalist Party. *See* Kuomintang
Ch'ing Dynasty
    Abahai, IV:1-3
    Chang Chih-tung, V:466-469
    Cheng Ch'eng-kung, IV:297
    Ch'ien-lung, IV:300, 302
    Dorgon, IV:421-423
    Hung Hsiu-Ch'üan, V:1165, 1166
    Li Hung-chang, VI:1362, 1354, 1365
    Lin Tse-hsü, VI:1376-1379
    Sun Yat-sen, IX:3578-3580

Tseng Kuo-fan, VI:2260-2262
Wang Ching-wei, IX:3879
Ching Hsiang, I:188
Ch'ing-liu, V:466
Ch'in Kuei, II:1019
Ch'in Shih Huang-ti, **I:176-179**
Chionites, I:779, 780
Chios, I:420
Chiplunkar, Vishnu Krishna, IX:3682
Chippewa, Battle of, VI:2010
Chippewa Indians, VII:1092, 1093
Chirac, Jacques, VIII:2560
Chiricahua, V:917
Chisholm, Shirley, **VII:668-672**
Chisholm v. Georgia, IV:713, 1458
chivalry
    Balboa, III:45-47
    Cervantes, IV:268, 269
    Charles the Bold, III:163
    Froissart, II:368
    Henry the Navigator, III:354
    Sidney, III:693
Chlorus, Constantius, I:375
Chlotsuinda, II:41
Choctaw Indians, III:700
Choeikai, IX:3337
Chogaku temple, II:924
Chomsky, Noam, **VII:673-675**
    Aspects of the Theory of Syntax, VII:673
    Counter-Revolutionary Violence, VII:674
    Language and Mind, VII:674
    Sound Pattern of English, The, VII:674
Chopin, Frédéric, **V:493-496; VI:1392**
Chopin, Kate, **V:497-500**
    At Fault, V:497, 498
    Awakening, The, V:497-499
    Bayou Folk, V:498
    Night in Acadie, A, V:498
    "Story of an Hour, The," V:498
Choshu, VI:1937
Chotek, Sophie, VII:1197-1199
Chou, Duke of, I:224
Chou Dynasty, I:222-224, 544
Chou En-lai, **VII:676-679**
    Chu Teh, VII:688
    Deng Xiaoping, VII:906
    Khrushchev, VIII:1963
    Nixon, VIII:2759
Chou Shu-jên. *See* Lu Hsün
Chou Wen-chung, IX:3796
Chremonidean War, I:717
Chrétien, Jean, **VII:680-682**

Chrétien de Troyes, **II:257-259,** 1005
    Cligés, II:257, 258
    Erec and Enide, II:257, 258
    Lancelot, II:257, 258
    Perceval, II:257, 258, 1005
    Yvain, II:257, 258
Christ, Church of, V:351, 401, 403
Christ, Disciples of, V:401, 403
Christ, Jesus. *See* Jesus Christ
Christian IV, III:79
Christian, Charlie, VIII:1420
Christian, Fletcher, IV:143, 145
Christian Association of Washington, V:401
Christian Baptist, V:402
Christian Connexion, IV:895
Christian Democratic Party of Italy, VII:864, 865
Christian Democratic Union, VII:27;
    VIII:2009, 2010
Christian Science. *See* Christ, Scientist, Church of
Christian Science Monitor, The, V:741
Christian Trade Union Movement, VII:1102
Christian Union, V:175
Christie, Agatha, **VII:683-686**
    Curtain; Poirot's Last Case, VII:685
    Mousetrap, The, VII:685
    Murder at the Vicarage, VII:685
    Murder of Roger Ackroyd, The, VII:683, 685
    Murder on the Orient Express, VII:685
    Mysterious Affair at Styles, The, VII:683
    Mystery of the Blue Train, The, VII:683
    Secret Adversary, The, VII:683
    Sleeping Murder, VII:685
    Ten Little Indians, VII:685
    Witness for the Prosecution, VII:685
Christina, **IV:304-307,** 360, 1052, 1053, 1213;
    V:708
Christine de Pizan, **II:260-264**
    Book of the City of Ladies, The, II:261-263
    Dit de la rose, Le, II:261
    "Dittié sur Jeanne d'Arc," II:263
    Épistre du dieu d'amours, L', II:261
    Livre de la mutacion de fortune, Le, II:261
    Livre de la paix, Le, II:263
    Livre des trois vertus, Le, II:262
    Livre du chemin de long éstude, Le, II:261
Christophe, Henri, **V:501, 502; VII:633**
Christopher, Saint, **I:180-183**
Christy Minstrels, V:811
Chrysler Corporation, VII:112
Chrysogonus, I:195
Chrysoloras, III:93

Chrysostom, Saint John, **I:184-186,** 861
    On the Priesthood, I:184
Chuang-tzu, **I:190-193**
Chu Hsi, **II:265-267,** 841
    Four Books, II:266, 267
    Reflections on Things at Hand, II:266
Church, Benjamin, IV:955
church and state
    Acton, V:11
    Ambrose, I:45
    Canada, V:320
    Frankfurter, VII:1214
    Gibbons, V:921
    Herriot, VIII:1644
    O'Connell, V:1680-1683
    Peter the Great, IV:1032
    Pufendorf, IV:1135
    Williams, IV:1451-1453
Church Council of 1666, IV:1032
Churchill, John. *See* Marlborough, First Duke of
Churchill, Lord Randolph, VI:1945; VII:691, 819
Churchill, Sarah. *See* Marlborough, Duchess of
Churchill, Sir Winston, **VII:691-694**
    Alanbrooke, VII:46, 47
    Asquith, VII:122, 123
    Atlantic Charter, VIII:2257
    Attlee, VII:138
    Baldwin, VII:169, 170
    Beaverbrook, VII:236
    Bevan, VII:304, 306
    Beveridge, VII:308
    Butler, VII:530, 531
    Canada, VII:365; VIII:1984
    Chamberlain, VII:646
    Chanel, VII:651
    de Gaulle, VII:866, 867
    Eden, VII:1016, 1017
    George VI, VII:1344-1346
    Heath, VIII:1607
    History of the English Speaking Peoples, A,
      VII:694
    Hopkins, VIII:1737, 1739
    Inönü, VIII:1813
    Macmillan, VIII:2341
    Marshall, VIII:2431
    Monnet, VIII:2583
    Mountbatten, VIII:2643, 2644
    Reith, IX:3147, 3148
    Roosevelt, IX:3225
    Second War, The, VII:694
    Sutherland's portrait, IX:3588
Chu Teh, **VII:687-690**

Chu Ti. *See* Yung-lo
Ch'ü Yüan, **I:187-189**
    "Great Summons," I:188
    "In Praise of the Orange Tree," I:187
    Li Sao, The, I:188
    Nine Songs, The, I:187
    "Princess of the Hsiang, The," I:187
CIA. *See* Central Intelligence Agency
Cibber, Colley, IV:1352, 1353
Cibber v. Sloper, IV:904
Cicero, **I:194-197**
    Cassius, I:159
    De oratore, I:787, 788
    gladiators, I:814
    Isocrates, I:456, 458
    On Friendship, I:758
    On Old Age, I:194
    Philippics, I:69
    Plutarch, I:671
    Posidonius, I:687
    Pro Archia, II:728
    Pro Quinctio, I:194
    Pro Roscio Amerino, I:194
    Regulus, I:741
    Sallust, I:743
    Varro, I:918-921
Cicero, Illinois, VII:563, 564
Cid, El, **II:268-271**
Cigar-makers' Union, V:956
Cilicia, I:196
Cimabue, **II:272, 273,** 306, 388
    Madonna Enthroned, II:273
    Rucellai *Madonna,* II:273
Cimbri, I:529
Cimon, **I:198-202**
    Aspasia, I:115
    Miltiades the Younger, I:553
    Pericles, I:609
    Polygnotus, I:676, 677
Cinadon, I:17
Cincinnati Reds, IX:3239, 3240
Cincinnati Penny Post, VI:2015
Cinématograph, VIII:2278
Cinna, Lucius Cornelius, I:159, 160, 530, 834
CIO. *See* Congress of Industrial Organizations
Cione, Andrea di. *See* Orcagna, Andrea
Cisco Kid, V:1098
Cistercian Order, II:143-145, 534, 995
Cité Industrielle, VII:1308-1310
Citroën, André-Gustave, **VII:695-698**
City Dionysia. *See* Greater Dionysia
Civil Engineering, Institution for, VI:2209, 2210

Civilian Conservation Corps, VIII:2297
Civil Rights Act of 1866, V:1235
Civil Rights Act of 1875, V:697
Civil Rights Act of 1964
  Abernathy, VII:9, 10, 12
  Dole, VII:948
  Humphrey, VIII:1784
  Johnson, VIII:1867, 1868
  King, VIII:1971, 1973, 1974
  sexual harassment, VIII:2325
Civil Rights Commission, U.S., IX:3858
Civil Rights Memorial, VIII:2185-2187
Civil War, United States. *See* United States
  Civil War
Clagny, Château de, IV:901
Clairmont, Claire, VI:2048, 2053, 2054
Clairvaux, II:143-145
Clan-na-Gael, V:1123, 1124
Clanton family, V:736
Clapham Sect, IV:1435, 1436
Clare, Gilbert de. *See* Gloucester, Earl of
Clarence, Duke of, III:647, 649, 650
Clarendon, Constitutions of, II:49, 128-130, 446
Clarendon Code, IV:284, 310, 598
Clarendon, First Earl of, **IV:308-311,** 821
  Autobiography, IV:308, 310, 311
  *History of the Rebellion and Civil Wars in
    England,* IV:308, 310, 311
Clari, Robert de, II:943
Clark, George Rogers, IV:164, 198, **312-316**
Clark, Joe, VIII:2655; IX:3345, 3733
Clark, Ramsey, VIII:2435
Clark, William, V:443; **VI:1358-1361,** 1933-1935
Clarke, Arthur C., VI:2304
Clarke, Charles Cowden, VI:1264, 1266
Clarke, Samuel, IV:831
Clarksville, Indiana, IV:312, 314, 315
classical music
  Beethoven, V:178-181
  Bernstein, VII:295, 296, 298
  Gluck, IV:549-551
  Mozart, IV:1003, 1005, 1006
  Segovia, IX:3383-3386
  Telemann, IV:1319
  See also conducting, orchestral; opera;
    symphonies
Claude, Georges, **VII:699-701**
  Liquid Air, Oxygen, Nitrogen, VII:699
Claudel, Paul, VIII:2525, 2526
Claude Lorrain, **IV:317-320**
  Ascanius and the Stag, IV:318
  Harbor Scene, IV:318

  Liber veritatis, IV:317
  Marriage of Isaac and Rebecca, The, IV:318
  Mill, The, IV:317
Claude Neon Company, VII:700
Claudian, I:825, 826
Claudius I, **I:203-206,** 550, 551, 577, 770, 772
Claus, Daniel, IV:199
Clausewitz, Carl von, **V:503-506,** 940, 942;
    VI:1969, 1971; VIII:2267
  On War, V:503-505, 942
Clausius, Rudolf, VIII:2713
Clay, Cassius Marcellus, Jr.. *See* Ali, Muhammad
Clay, Henry, **V:507-511**
  Adams, John Quincy, V:22
  Cushing, V:582
  Fillmore, V:792, 793
  Jackson, V:1197
  Monroe, VI:1573
  Polk, VI:1802, 1803
  Tyler, VI:2289, 2290
Claypoole, John, IV:1193
Clazomenae, I:47
Cleanthes of Assos, I:970; IV:684
Cleisthenes of Athens, **I:207-209,** 554
Clemenceau, Georges, **VII:702-705;** IX:3045
  Grandeur and Misery of Victory, The, VII:705
Clemens, Flavius, I:210, 211
Clemens, Samuel Langhorne. *See* Twain, Mark
Clement I, **I:210-213**
  First Epistle of Clement to the Corinthians,
    I:211, 212
  Recognitions, I:210
  Second Epistle of Clement to the Corinthians,
    I:212
Clement III, II:396
Clement IV, II:112, 985
Clement V, II:790
Clement VI, II:235, 236, 790, 792
Clement VII, **III:166-168**
  Boleyn, III:66, 68
  Catherine de Médicis, III:132
  Catherine of Aragon, III:138
  Cellini, III:151, 152
  Franco-Turkish War, III:160
  Guicciardini, III:325, 326
  Machiavelli, III:450, 451
  Medici, Lorenzo de', III:498
  Michelangelo, III:519
  Paul III, III:595
  Wolsey, III:786
Clement VIII, III:334
Clement IX, IV:709

Clement XIV, V:408
Clement of Rome. *See* Clement I
Cleomenes I, **I:214-215**
Cleomenes II, **I:215**
Cleomenes III, **I:215-216**
Cleon, I:88
Cleopatra VII, **I:218-221**
    Antony, I:70, 71
    Augustus, I:133
    Caesar, I:149, 150
    Propertius, I:703, 704
Clephane, James O., VI:1541
Clerici, Palazzo, IV:1324
Clérisseau, Charles-Louis, IV:8
Clermont, Council of, II:930
Clerville, Chevalier de, IV:1358
Cleveland, Grover, **V:512-516**
    Altgeld, V:55
    Blaine, V:256
    Bryan, VII:479
    Godkin, VIII:1402
    Harrison, V:1054, 1055
    Liliuokalani, VI:1374
    Lockwood, VI:1408
    Lodge, VIII:2221
    Morgan, VI:1582
    Nast, VI:1628
    Pullman Strike of 1894, VII:881
Cleveland, Reverend James, VII:1216
Cleveland Orchestra, VII:389
Cleveland Penny Post, VI:2015
Clifford, Sir Thomas, IV:285
Cline, Patsy, VIII:2080, 2081
Clinton, Bill, **VII:707-712**
    Albright, VII:50, 51
    Boutros-Ghali, VII:400
    Bush, VII:522
    Clinton, Hillary Rodham, VII:713-715
    Dole, VII:949
    Gore, VIII:1432, 1433
    Greenspan, VIII:1472, 1473
    Hobby, VIII:1705
    Latino cabinet appointments, IX:2842
    Perot, IX:2974, 2975
    Reno, IX:3154, 3155
    speed limit, VIII:2681
Clinton, DeWitt, **V:517-521**
Clinton, George, IV:321; V:369, 370, 517
Clinton, Sir Henry, IV:66, **321-324,** 367, 368, 677, 678
Clinton, Hillary Rodham, VII:50, 707, **713-716**
Clinton, James, IV:818

Clive, Robert, **IV:325-328,** 631, 632
Clodia, I:170
Clough, Arthur Hugh, V:69, 70
Clovis, II:226, **274-277**
Cluniacs, II:144, 994
Clurman, Harold, VII:794, 795
Clyfton, Richard, IV:189
Cnemon, I:539
Cnidian Lesche, I:676, 677
Cnidus, I:310, 412, 691
coal
    Brindley, IV:201, 202
    hydrogenation, VII:275-277
    Lewis, VIII:2170-2172
    mining, V:622, VI:2251
    Stephens, VI:2130
Coalbrookdale, IV:396-398
Coal Smoke Abatement Society, V:1115
Cobb, Ty, **VII:717-720**
Cobbett, William, **V:522-524**
    Advice to Young Men, V:523
    Farmer's Friend, The, V:523
    Parliamentary History of England, V:523
    Political Register, The, V:522-524
    Poor Man's Friend, The, V:523
    Rural Rides, V:524
    Soldier's Friend, The, V:522
Cobden, Richard, V:306, 307, **525-529**
    England, Ireland, and America, V:526
    Russia and the Eastern Question, V:526
Cobden-Chevalier Treaty, V:528
Cobham, Viscount, IV:1098
Cochise, V:915, 917
Cochlaeus, Johannes, III:736
Cock, Hieronymus, III:85
Cockerill, John A., VI:1825
Cocteau, Jean, **VII:721-724;** IX:3066, 3068, 3069, 3333
    Beauty and the Beast, VII:723, 724
    Blood of a Poet, The, VII:723, 724
    Cap de Bonne-Espérance, Le, VII:721
    Children of the Game, VII:723
    Difficulty of Being, The, VII:723
    Infernal Machine, The, VII:723, 724
    Orpheus, VII:721, 723, 724
    Parade, VII:721; VIII:2449
    Thomas the Imposter, VII:721
Codex Argenteus, I:909, 910
Codex Justinianus, II:555
Cody, William Frederick, **V:530-533**
    Calamity Jane, V:392

Hickok, V:1109
Oakley, VI:1677, 1678
Sitting Bull, VI:2072
Whitney, IX:3970
Coe, Sebastian, **VII:725-728**
Coele-Syria, I:63, 64
Cognac, League of, III:166, 326
Cogswell, Joseph, V:125
Cohen, Hermann, VII:614
Cohn, Ferdinand Julius, **V:534-536;** VI:1298
Cohn, Harry, VIII:1597
coinage
    Altgeld, V:55, 56
    Boulton, IV:182, 183
    David I, II:292
    Diocletian, I:265
    Kanishka, I:496
    Menander, I:541
    Newton, IV:1027
COINTELPRO, VIII:1733
Coke, Sir Edward, **IV:329-335,** 700
    Institutes, IV:333, 334
    Reports, IV:333, 334
Colbert, Claudette, VII:119
Colbert, Jean-Baptiste, **IV:336-340**
    Huygens, IV:695
    Louis XIV, IV:866, 868, 869
    Louvois, IV:871-873
    Mansart, IV:899
    Mazarin, IV:946, 947
Colborne, Sir John, VI:1449
Colburn, Zerah, V:1025
Coldstream Guards, IV:973
Cold War
    Attlee, VII:139
    Bevin, VII:313
    Bradley, VII:405
    Bush, VII:522
    Gorbachev, IX:4086
    Hammarskjöld, VIII:1530
    Harriman, VIII:1562, 1563
    Hiss, VIII:1683-1685
    Hitler, VIII:1696
    Hoover, VIII:1733
    Japan, VIII:1810
    Kapitsa, VIII:1908
    Lippmann, VIII:2205
    Molotov, VIII:2572
    Neumann, VIII:2726
    Oppenheimer, IX:2834
    space exploration, VII:1272
    Truman, IX:3742, 3743

Colebrooke, Henry, VI:1846
Colenso, John, VI:1505
Coleridge, Samuel Taylor, IV:156; V:381, **537-539,**
    1012; VI:2406, 2407
    Biographia Literaria, V:538
    Christabel, V:537, 538
    "Dejection: An Ode," V:538
    "Frost at Midnight," V:538
    "Kubla Khan," V:537
    Lyrical Ballads, IV:114
    "Pains of Sleep, The" V:538
    Rime of the Ancient Mariner, The, IV:391;
        V:537, 538
    "To William Wordsworth," V:538
Coleridge, Stephen, IX:3495
Colet, John, **III:169-171**
Colette, **VII:729-732**
    Chéri, VII:730, 731
    Claudine at School, VII:729
    Claudine in Paris, VII:729
    Claudine Married, VII:729
    Creatures Great and Small, VII:729
    Gigi, VII:731
    Innocent Wife, The, VII:729
    Last of Chéri, The, VII:730, 731
    Mitsou: Or, How Girls Grow Wise, VII:730
    Vagabond, The, VII:730
Coligny, Gaspard de, III:537
College Entrance Examination Board, VII:524
Colleoni, Bartolommeo, III:751, 752
Collier, Jeremy, IV:1352
Collins, Michael (Irish leader), **VII:733-736**
Collins, Michael (U.S. astronaut), VII:112
Collins, Norman, **VII:737-740**
    Bat That Flits, The, VII:738
    Bond Street Story, The, VII:738
    Children of the Archbishop, VII:738
    Dulcimer Street, VII:738
    Facts of Fiction, The, VII:737, 738
    Flames Coming Out of the Top, VII:737
    Governor's Lady, The, VII:738
    Husband's Story, The, VII:738
    I Shall Not Want, VII:737
    Love in Our Time, VII:737
    Penang Appointment, VII:737
    Quiet Lady, VII:738
    Three Friends, The, VII:737
    Trinity Town, VII:737
Collip, James Bertram, VII:189
Colombo, Mattero Realdo, III:676
Colonial Advocate, VI:1449, 1450
Colonna, Pompeo, III:167

Colorado
    Hayden, V:1072-1074
    mining industry, VIII:1881
    Pike, IV:1094, 1096, 1097
    women's suffrage, VII:627
Colorado River, VI:1810, 1812, 1813
Colosimo, Big Jim, BII:563
Colt, Samuel, **V:540-542**
Coltrane, John, **VII:741-744**
    Ascension, VII:742
    Ballads, VII:742
    Blue Train, VII:741
    Coltrane, VII:741
    Crescent, VII:742
    Giant Steps, VII:741
    John Coltrane and Johnny Hartman,
        VII:742
    Live at the Village Vanguard, VII:742
    Love Supreme, A, VII:742
    "My Favorite Things," VII:742
Columbia Broadcasting System. *See* CBS
Columbia Players, VIII:1533
Columbia Records, VII:1217
Columbia University
    Boas, VII:339
    Butler, VII:524-527
    Research in Contemporary Cultures, VII:257,
        258; VIII:2470
    School of Journalism, VI:1826
Columbus, Bartolomeo, III:217
Columbus, Christopher, **III:172-175**
    Cabot, III:113, 115, 116
    Cortés, III:188
    Dias, III:218
    Ferdinand and Isabella, III:262
    Iceland, II:579
    Ponce de Léon, III:629
    Ptolemy, I:713
    Vespucci, III:758, 759, 761
Comanche Indians, V:432
Combination Laws, VI:1787
Comenius, John Amos, IV:92
Comintern, VII:661, 662, 688; IX:3779, 4114
Commodus, I:340, 417
Commoner, The, VI:2396
common law, English. *See* English common law
Common Prayer, Book of, III:204-206, 238, 655;
    IV:199
Commons, House of
    abolitionism, IV:1236; V:379
    Asquith, VII:122, 123
    Astor, VII:129-131

Attlee, VII:138
Baldwin, VII:168, 169
Balfour, VII:173, 174
Bevan, VII:304
Beveridge, VII:310
Bright, V:306-308
Brougham, V:314-316
Burke, IV:223
Butler, VII:529, 530
Canning, V:406
Castlereagh, V:438, 440, 441
Catholic emancipation, VI:1681
Chamberlain, V:462-464
Charles I, IV:280, 281
Clarendon, IV:308, 309
Coke, IV:329-334
Curzon, VII:819, 820
Derby, V:652-654
Disraeli, V:675, 677, 678
Durham, V:721
Eden, VII:1015, 1016
Edward III, II:329, 331
Fox, IV:479, 481, 482
George I, IV:532
George II, IV:535-537
George III, IV:542
Grey, Second Earl, V:995, 996
Grey, Sir Edward, VIII:1475
Henry IV, II:458
Ireland, IV:369
Law, VIII:2112, 2113
Lloyd George, VIII:2216
MacDonald, VIII:2312
Macmillan, VIII:2340, 2343
Mansfield, IV:904, 906
Melbourne, VI:1517
North, IV:1034-1036
O'Connor, IX:2793-2795
Palmerston, VI:1719
Parnell, VI:1740-1742
Pelham, IV:1074-1076
Pitt the Elder, IV:1098-1100
Pitt the Younger, IV:1102-1105
Pride, IV:1126, 1127
Reith, IX:3148
Ricardo, VI:1879
Russell, VI:1930
Salisbury, VI:1943
Scott, VI:2003
Stanley, VI:2104
Strafford, IV:1287
Thatcher, IX:3649, 3651

Walpole, IV:1400-1403
Wilkes, IV:1440, 1441
William IV, VI:2392-2395
See also Parliament (English)
Commonwealth Electoral Act of 1902, VIII:2291
Commonwealth Protectorate, IV:310, 790
communism
    Acheson, VII:17-19
    Bukharin, VII:491-493
    Castro, VII:617-619
    Césaire, VII:632
    Czechoslovakia, VII:261
    Engels, V:760-762
    Gramsci, VIII:1459-1461
    Guevara, VIII:1494-1496
    Harriman, VIII:1560-1563
    Haya de la Torre, VIII:1584
    Hiss, VIII:1683-1685
    Hoover, VIII:1732, 1733
    Hutchins, VIII:1801, 1802
    John Paul II, VIII:1863, 1864
    Khrushchev, VIII:1961-1963
    Lenin, VIII:2160-2162
    Liebknecht, VI:1369
    Lukács, VIII:2272-2274
    McCarthyism, VIII:2300-2302
    Machel, VIII:2317-2319
    Malthusian economics, VI:1468
    Marx, VI:1492-1494
    Merleau-Ponty, VIII:2501
    Mill, VI:1562
    Orwell, IX:2849
    Randolph, IX:3114
    Reagan administration, VIII:1995
    Stalin, IX:3482-3484
    Truman, IX:3742
    See also socialism
Communist International, VIII:2315
Communist League, V:761
Communist Party of Australia, VIII:2497
Communist Party of Chile, VIII:2717, 2718
Communist Party of China. *See* Chinese
    Communist Party
Communist Party of France, VII:335; VIII:1698,
    1755, 1872, 2559, 2560
Communist Party of Germany, IX:379
Communist Party of Indonesia, IX:3572
Communist Party of Italy, VIII:1459, 2670
Communist Party of Slovakia, VII:968
Communist Party of the Philippines, VIII:2421
Communist Party of the Soviet Union
    Akhmatova, VII:38

    Brezhnev, VII:459-461
    Bukharin, VII:491-493
    Gorbachev, VIII:1423, 1424; IX:4086, 4087
    Malenkov, VIII:2377, 2378
    Molotov, VIII:2571-2573
    Shostakovich, IX:3410
    Yeltsin, IX:4086, 4087
    Zhukov, IX:4116-4119
Communists, Union of, VI:1369
Comnenus, Isaac, II:759, 760
Comnenus, Manuel, II:28, 336, 337
Compagnia dello Scalzo, III:24, 26
Comparative Zoology, Museum of, V:30, 31
Comprehensive Test Ban Treaty, VII:51; IX:3633
Compromise of 1850. *See* 1850, Compromise of
Compton, Arthur Holly, **VII:745-747**
Compton, Sir Spencer, IV:536, 1075
Comstock, Anthony, IX:3314
Comte, Auguste, **V:543-546,** 1057, 1058; VII:988;
    VIII:2135
    Considerations sur le pouvoir spirituel, V:545
    Cours de philosophie positive, V:543, 544
    System of Positive Polity, V:544
Comunero Revolt, III:159
CONAKAT, IX:3745
Conant, James Bryant, **VII:748-752**
    American High School Today, The, VII:751
    Slums and Suburbs, VII:751
concentration camps
    Baeck, VII:149
    Frank, VII:1205, 1206
    Himmler, VIII:1666-1668
    Hitler, VIII:1694, 1695
    Niemöller, VIII:2743
    South African War, VIII:2003
    Wiesel, IX:3980
concertos
    Boccherini, IV:147-149
    Corelli, IV:360-362
    Schumann, VI:1993
    Tchaikovsky, VI:2198, 2200, 2201
    Vivaldi, IV:1383-1385
Concini, Concino, IV:863, 864
Cone Crater, IX:3407
Condé, the Great, **IV:341-343,** 872, 873, 946
Condillac, Étienne Bonnot de, **IV:344-347**
    *Commerce et le gouvernement considérés
        relativement l'un à l'autre,* IV:346
    Condillac's Treatise on the Sensationes, IV:345
    *Cours d'études pour l'instruction du prince de
        Parme,* IV:346
    Dissertation sur la liberté, IV:346

Essai sur l'origine des connaissances humaines,
    IV:344, 345
Traité de animaux, IV:346
Traité des systémes, IV:344
Condorcet, Marquis de, **IV:348-350;** VI:1468
    Life of M. Turgot, The, IV:348
    Life of Voltaire, The, IV:348
    *Sketch for a Historical Picture of the Progress of
        the Human Mind,* IV:349, 350
conducting, orchestral
    Bernstein, VII:295, 296, 298
    Boulez, VII:386-389
    Casals, VII:606-609
    Karajan, VIII:1910-1912
    Mahler, VIII:2360, 2361
    Sibelius, IX:3414
    Thomas, VI:2230-2233
    Toscanini, IX:3094, 3096, 3707, 3709
    Varèse, IX:3795
    Villa-Lobos, IX:3817
    Weber, VI:2341
    Webern, IX:3915, 3916
Confederate States of America
    Davis, V:614-619
    Gorgas, VIII:1434
    Houston, V:1138
    Jackson, V:1204-1206
    Johnson, V:1235
    Lee, VI:1338-1341
    Maury, VI:1509
    Ross, VI:1911
    Stephens, VI:2129-2131
Confederation, Articles of
    Dickinson, IV:410
    Madison, IV:886
    Monroe, VI:1570
    Morris, IV:999-1001
    Shays, IV:1240, 1241
    Sherman, IV:1243
Confédération Générale de Travail, IX:3711
Confessing Church, VII:359, 360, 499;
    VIII:2742, 2743
Confucianism, I:222-224
    Chang Chih-tung, V:466
    Ch'ien-lung, IV:301
    Chu His, II:265-267
    Ch'ü Yüan, I:187-189
    Hsün-tzu, I:433-435
    Hung Hsiu-Ch'üan, V:1166
    Legalists, I:176
    Mencius, I:543-546
    Ou-yang Hsui, II:709

Shih Huang-ti, I:177
    Shotoku Taishi, II:826
    Wang An-shih, II:963
    Wang Ch'ung, I:943-945
    Wang Pi, I:949-951
    See also Neo-Confucianism
Confucius, **I:222-225**
    Analects, I:222-224, 543, 546, 949
    Book of Documents, I:224, 543
    Book of Odes, I:543
    Book of Songs, I:224
    Lao-Tzu, I:498, 499
    Spring and Autumn Annals, I:224, 819
    Ssu-ma Ch'ien, I:818-820
Congo Crisis, VIII:1530
Congregationalism, IV:371, 372, 935, 938, 939;
    V:470-472
Congress, U.S.
    antilynching laws, IX:3692
    Electoral Commission, V:1076
    federal election laws, V:1078
    Jackson, V:1201
    Luce, VIII:2256, 2257
    Madison, IV:888
    Mason, IV:927
    Pierce, VI:1775
    pocket veto, V:1198
    Sherman, IV:1244
    slavery, VI:2192
    Smith, IX:3446-3448
    Walesa, IX:3847
    Washington, IV:1407
    Wilson, IV:1457
    See also Representatives, House of; Senate, U.S.
Congress of Industrial Organizations
    Gompers, V:958
    Lewis, VIII:2170-2172
    Reuther, IX:3163
Congress of Racial Equality (CORE), VIII:1824
Congress Party of India, VII:1278, 1280;
    VIII:2709; IX:2869, 2903, 2904
Congreve, Richard, V:1057
Conkling, Roscoe, V:78, 80, 256, 1078
Conn, Billy, VIII:2243, 2244
Connecticut
    Allen, IV:35
    Barnard, V:130, 131
    Barnum, V:133
    Board of Education, VII:1356
    Sherman, IV:1243, 1244
    Stuyvesant, IV:1296
Connecticut Compromise, IV:1244

Conner, David, VI:1761
Connors, Jimmy, VII:1113
Conon, II:823
Conrad II, II:464
Conrad III, II:357, 358
Conrad, Joseph, **VII:753-758**
    Almayer's Folly, VII:755, 756
    Chance, VII:756,
    Heart of Darkness, VII:757
    Inheritors, The, VII:756
    Lord Jim, VII:756, 757
    Mirrors of the Sea, The, VII:756
    Nature of a Crime, The, VII:756
    Nigger of the "Narcissus," The, VII:755-757
    Nostromo, VII:756, 757
    One Day More, VII:756
    Outcast of the Islands, An, VII:755, 756
    Personal Record, A, VII:756
    Romance, VII:756
    Secret Agent, The, VII:756
    Set of Six, A, VII:756
    Suspense, VII:756
    Tales of Unrest, VII:756
    'Twixt Land and Sea, VII:756
    Under Western Eyes, VII:756, 757
    Victory, VII:756
Conrad of Marburg, II:340, 342
conscription
    Canada, VII:367; VIII:1984, 2103
    England, VII:124
    Selective Service Act, VII:882
Conservative Party (Canada)
    Borden, VII:365, 366
    Chrétien, VII:681, 682
    King, VIII:1982, 1983
    Laurier, VIII:2101-2103
    Mulroney, VIII:2656
Conservative Party (England)
    Asquith, VII:122, 123
    Baldwin, VII:168, 169
    Balfour, VII:172, 173
    Beaverbrook, VII:235
    Bevan, VII:304
    Butler, VII:529-531
    Chamberlain, Joseph, V:462, 464
    Chamberlain, Neville, VII:643, 644
    Disraeli, V:675, 677, 678
    Eden, VII:1016, 1017
    George V, VII:1340, 1341
    Gladstone, V:935, 936, 938
    Heath, VIII:1606-1608
    Home Rule Bill, VI:1741
    Lansdowne, VIII:2091
    Law, VIII:2112-2114
    Lloyd George, VIII:2217
    Macdonald, VI:1436
    Major, VIII:2369, 2370
    Pankhurst, IX:2874
    Salisbury, VI:1944, 1945
    Thatcher, IX:3649, 3651, 3652
    See also Tory Party (England)
Constable, John, **V:547-550,** 646; VIII:2579, 2733
    Hadleigh Castle, V:549
    Hay Wain, The, V:549
    Mouth of the Thames--morning after a stormy night, The, V:549
    Salisbury: Morning, V:548
    Trees Near Hampstead Church, V:549
    View on Hampstead Heath, V:549
    View on the Stour near Dedham, V:549
    Watermeadows at Salisbury, V:549
    White Horse, The, V:548
Constance, Council of, II:489, 971
Constance, Treaty of, II:358
Constantine V, II:903, 904
Constantine VI, II:437
Constantine IX, II:758, 759
Constantine, Baron, **VII:759-761**
Constantine, Donation of, II:583; III:740
Constantine the Great, **I:226-230**
    Anthony of Egypt, I:58
    Athanasius, I:119, 121
    Eusebius of Caesarea, I:322, 324
    Helena, I:375-377
    Shapur II, I:779
Constantinople
    Attila, I:126
    Constantine the Great, I:228, 229
    Fourth Crusade, II:284
    Gregory of Nazianzus, I:349
    Heraclius, II:470-472
    Justinian I, II:554-557
    Leo IX, II:582
    Mehmed II, III:500
    Sergius I, II:820, 821
    Theoleptus of Philadelphia, II:899-901
    Trullan Synod, II:824
    Villehardouin, II:942
Constantinople, Council of, I:352-354, 869, 909; II:675
Constantius, I:266
Constitution, U.S.
    Acton, V:12
    Adams, John, IV:18, 19

Adams, Samuel, IV:24
Anthony, V:62
Bancroft, V:127
Beard, VII:222
centralization, VIII:1766
contract clause, VI:1490
Dickinson, IV:408, 410
Hamilton, IV:609, 610
Hancock, IV:617
Henry, IV:649
Jefferson, IV:718, 719
Kent, VI:1277-1280
Madison, IV:886-889
Mason, IV:926-928
Mexican Constitution, V:95
Montesquieu, IV:986-988
Revere, IV:1158
Rush, IV:1202, 1203
Shays, IV:1239-1241
Sherman, IV:1242-1244
slavery, VI:2192
Stevens, VI:2137
treason, VI:1490
Webster, Daniel, VI:2344-2346
Webster, Noah, IV:1419
Wilson, IV:1455, 1457, 1458
women's suffrage, VI:2112
Constitutional Convention, U.S.
    Adams, IV:18
    Dickinson, IV:410, 411
    Madison, IV:889
    Marshall, VI:1488
    Mason, IV:927
    Morris, IV:1001
    Shays, IV:1239, 1240
    Washington, IV:1405, 1406
consumer advocacy, VIII:2679-2681
Continental Association, IV:617
Continental Congress
    Adams, John, IV:16, 18
    Adams, Samuel, IV:24
    Carroll, IV:251
    Chase, IV:293
    Franklin, IV:494
    Hamilton, IV:608-610
    Hancock, IV:613, 617
    Henry, IV:648
    Jay, IV:711
    Madison, IV:886
    Morris, IV:999
    Sherman, IV:1243
    Witherspoon, IV:1467-1470

Continuation War, VIII:2398
contraceptives. See birth control
Conventicle Act of 1664, IV:100, 239
Convention Parliament, IV:597
Convention People's Party, VIII:2763
Conyers, John, IX:2890
Cook, Frederick, IX:2941, 2942, 2945
Cook, Captain James, **IV:351-355**
    Banks, IV:83, 85, 86
    Bligh, IV:143
    Dampier, IV:391
    Kamehameha I, VI:1255
    Vancouver, IV:1355, 1356
Cooke, Jay, **V:551-554**
Cooke, William Fothergill, **V:555-559**
Coolidge, Calvin, **VII:762-765**; VIII:1542, 1880,
    2556; IX:3547
Cooper, Anthony Ashley. See Shaftesbury, Earl of
Cooper, Henry, VII:54
Cooper, James Fenimore, **V:560-564**; VIII:2465
    American Democrat, The, V:563
    Crater, The, V:563
    Deerslayer, The, V:562, 563
    History of the Navy of the United States, The,
        V:564
    Home as Found, V:563
    Homeward Bound, V:563
    Last of the Mohicans, The, V:562
    Leatherstocking Tales, V:562, 563
    Letter to His Countrymen, A, V:563
    Monikins, The, V:563
    Notions of the Americans, V:563
    Pilot, The, V:562
    Pioneers, The, V:560
    Precaution, V:560
    Redskins, The, V:563
    Spy, The, V:560, 562
    Virgin Land, V:564
Coowescoowe. See Ross, John
Copenhagen, Battle of, IV:145
Copernicus, Nicolaus, **III:176-179**
    Apollonius of Perga, I:74
    Brahe, III:78, 79
    Commentariolus, III:176
    First Account, The, III:178
    Galileo, IV:519, 521, 522
    Kepler, IV:772, 775
    Lobachevsky, VI:1404
    Mersenne, IV:950, 951
    On the Revolutions of the Celestial Spheres,
        III:176, 179, 755; IV:521
    Pythagoras, I:729

Copland, Aaron, **VII:766-769;** VIII:1821, 2363
   Appalachian Spring, VII:769
   Concerto for Piano and Orchestra,
    VII:767
   Duo for Flute and Piano, VII:768
   Music for the Theater, VII:767
   Passacaglia, VII:767
   Salón México, El, VII:768
   Second Hurricane, The, VII:768
   What to Listen for in Music, VII:769
Copley, John Singleton, **IV:356-359**
   Boy with a Squirrel, IV:357
   Death of the Earl of Chatham, The, IV:358
   Siege of Gibraltar, The, IV:358
   Three Youngest Daughters of King George III,
    The, IV:358
   Watson and the Shark, IV:358
Copperhead Democrats, VI:2401
Coquelin, Constant, IV:387
Coquillards, III:763
Coral Sea, Battle of, VIII:1525
Corazzo monastery, II:534
Corbie, abbey of, II:773
Córdoba, Treaty of, VI:1955
Cordovero, Moses, III:440
CORE. *See* Congress of Racial Equality (CORE)
Corelli, Arcangelo, **IV:360-362**
Corey, Robert B., IX:2927
Corinna of Tanagra, I:644
Corinth, League of, I:630
Corinthian Church, I:210-212, 605
Corinthians, Letters to the, I:605, 606
Corinthian War, I:18, 290
Cormack, Allan, VIII:1752
Cornaro, Alvise, III:58
Cornaro Chapel, IV:119
Corneille, Pierre, **IV:363-366,** 1120, 1145, 1146
   Cid, The, IV:363, 364
   Cinna, IV:364
   Horace, IV:364
   Illusion comique, L', IV:363, 365
   Nicomède, IV:364
   Pertharite, roi des Lombards, IV:364
   Polyeucte, IV:364
   Suréna, IV:365
Cornell University, VII:301, 395;
   VIII:2637, 2676
Cornet, Nicolas, IV:170
Cornish Engine, VI:2253
Corn Laws, V:306, 307, 526-528, 653, 677;
   VI:1396, 1879
   See also Anti-Corn Law League

Cornwallis, Charles. *See* Cornwallis, First
   Marquess
Cornwallis, First Marquess, **IV:367-370**
   Clinton, IV:323
   Greene, IV:575-577
   Rochambeau, IV:1175, 1176
   Washington, IV:1406
Coronado, Francisco Vásquez de, **III:180-183**
Corot, Camille, VI:1779
Coroticus, I:602
Corpus Christi College, III:589, 590; VIII:1707
Corpus Juris Civilis, II:555, 557
Correggio, **III:184-187;** V:434
   Adoration of the Magi, III:184
   Assumption of the Virgin, III:186
   Christ Taking Leave of His Mother, III:184
   Danae, III:186
   Deposition, The, III:186
   Ganymede, III:186
   Io, III:186
   Leda, III:186
   Loves of Jupiter, III:186
   Madonna and Child with Saint Francis,
    III:184
   Marriage of Saint Catherine, III:184
   Martyrdom of Four Saints, The, III:186
   Nativity, III:184
   School of Love, III:186
   Venus, Cupid, and Satyr, III:186
Corrèze Plateau, VII:1228
Corrigan, Michael, V:388
Cortés, Hernán, III:21-23, **188-192,** 529, 531;
   VI:1815
Cos, I:412
Cosby, William, IV:1484, 1485
Cosgrave, William T., **VII:770-773**
Cosmas, II:544
cosmology
   Anaximander, I:51
   Empedocles, I:282, 284, 285
   Eudoxus of Cnidus, I:310-312
   Guericke, IV:588
   Heraclitus of Ephesus, I:383-385
   Peregrinus de Maricourt, II:719-721
Cossacks, IV:725, 726, 1084
Costa, Lucio, VIII:2739, 2740
Coster, Dirk, VIII:1655
Costruzioni Cementizie, Societa per, VIII:2720
Coteau-Cambreis, Treaty of, III:19
Cotton, John, **IV:371-373,** 687, 938
   True Constitution of a Particular Visible Church,
    The, IV:372

Way of the Churches of Christ in New England, The, IV:372
Way of the Congregational Churches Cleared, The, IV:372
cotton gin, IV:1431, 1433, 1434; VI:2075
cotton industry
    Arkwright, IV:59-62
    Hargreaves, IV:623-625
    Whitney, IV:1431, 1433, 1434
Coubertin, Pierre de, **VII:774-777**
Counter-Reformation
    Bernini, IV:118-120
    Borromini, IV:169
    Ferdinand II, IV:452
    Greco, El, III:311, 313
    Ignatius of Loyola, III:438
    John of the Cross, III:401-403
    Joseph II, IV:750, 751
    Leopold I, IV:838
    Neri, III:551
    Paul III, III:595, 597, 598
    Spanish Netherlands, IV:707-709
    Tasso, III:711, 712
    Teresa of Ávila, III:714, 715
    Wenceslaus, II:970
country music, VII:658; VIII:2080, 2081;
    IX:2896-2898
Couperin, François, **IV:374-377**
    Art de toucher le clavecin, L', IV:375
    Concert instrumental sous le titre d'apothéose composé à la mémoire immortelle de l'incomparable Monsieur de Lully, IV:375
    Concerts royaux, IV:375
    Goûts-réunis, Les, IV:375
    Nations, Les, IV:374, 375
    Parnasse, Le, IV:375
    Pièces de violes avec la basse chifrée, IV:375
    Pièces d'orgues constitantes en deux messes, IV:374
Courbet, Gustave, V:434, **565-568**; VI:1473, 1869
    After Dinner at Ornans, V:565
    Bathers, The, V:566
    Burial at Ornans, The, V:565-567
    Cliffs at Étretat After the Storm, V:567
    Fighting Stags, V:566
    Painter's Studio, The, V:566
    Stonebreakers, The, V:565, 566
    Stormy Sea, The, V:567
    Woman with a Parrot, V:566
    Young Ladies of the Village, V:566
Cournot, Augustin, IX:3865

courtly literature
    Chrétien de Troyes, II:257-259
    Christine de Pizan, II:260-264
    Eleanor of Aquitaine, II:338
    Gottfried von Strassburg, II:392-394
    Hartmann von Aue, II:433-435
    Walther von der Vogelweide, II:959-961
    Wolfram von Eschenbach, II:1005-1007
Cousteau, Jacques-Yves, **VII:778-782**
    Living Sea, The, VII:779
    Silent World, The, VII:779
    World of Jacques Cousteau, The, VII:781
    World Without Sun, VII:779
Couture, Thomas, VI:1471
Covenanters, IV:239, 240, 283
Covent Garden, IV:226; VI:1273, 1460, 1461
Coverdale, Miles, **III:193-196**
Covey, Edward, V:695
Covilhã, Pêro da, **III:197-199**
Coward, Noël, **VII:783-788**; VIII:1588, 2142
    Ace of Clubs, VII:787
    Astonished Heart, The, VII:787
    Bitter Sweet, VII:785
    Blithe Spirit, VII:786, 787
    Brief Encounter, VII:787
    Cavelcade, VII:786
    Design for Living, VII:786
    Easy Virtue, VII:785
    Fallen Angels, VII:785
    Hay Fever, VII:785, 787
    High Spirits, VII:787
    Home Chat, VII:785
    I'll Leave It to You, VII:783
    In Which We Serve, VII:787; VIII:2643
    London Calling!, VII:785
    "Mad Dogs and Englishmen," VII:786
    Marquise, The, VII:785
    Nude with Violin, VII:787
    On with the Dance, VII:785
    Operette, VII:786
    Pacific, VII:787
    Peace in Our Time, VII:787
    Point Valaine, VII:786
    Present Laughter, VII:786, 787
    Private Lives, VII:786; IX:2808
    Queen Was in the Parlour, The, VII:785
    Rat Trap, The, VII:783
    Relative Values, VII:787
    Scoundrel, The, VII:786
    Second Man, The, VII:785
    Sigh No More, VII:787
    Sirocco, VII:785

Suite in Three Keys, VII:787
This Happy Breed, VII:786, 787
This Was a Man, VII:785
This Year of Grace!, VII:785
Tonight at Eight-thirty, VII:786
To Step Aside, VII:786
Vortex, The, VII:785
Young Idea, The, VII:785
Cowper, Lord, VI:1719
Crabbe, George, VII:468
Crab nebula, IX:2828, 2829
Craft, Ellen and William, VI:1729
Craig, Gordon, VI:2216, 2217
Cram, Steve, VII:727, 728
Cramm, Gottfried von, IX:2981
Cranach, Hans, III:200
Cranach, Lucas, the Elder, **III:200-203**
    Agony in the Garden, III:200
    Allegory of Redemption, III:202
    Allegory of the Law and the Gospel, III:202
    Crucifixion, III:200
    Dr. Johannes Scheyring, III:200
    Holy Kinship Altarpiece, III:200
    Judgment of Paris, The, III:200, 202
    Reclining River Nymph at the Fountain,
        III:202
    Saint Jerome in Penitence, III:200
    Venus and Cupid, III:200
    Venus with Cupid at the Honey-Thief, III:202
Cranach, Lucas, the Younger, III:200, 202
Cranch, Richard, IV:12
Crane, Hart, **VII:789-792**
    Bridge, The, VII:791
    "Chaplinesque," VII:789
    "For the Marriage of Faustus and Helen,"
        VII:789
    "Voyages," VII:789
    White Buildings, VII:789
Crane, Stephen, **V:569-572**
    Black Riders, The, V:572
    George's Mother, V:571, 572
    *Little Regiment and Other Episodes of the
        American Civil War, The,* V:571
    Maggie, V:569, 571, 572
    Open Boat and Other Tales of Adventure, The,
        V:571
    Red Badge of Courage, The, V:569, 571, 572
    Third Violet, The, V:569, 571
    Whilomville Stories, V:569
Cranmer, Thomas, **III:204-207**
    Coverdale, III:193
    Edward VI, III:238

Gardiner, III:292
    Henry VIII, III:167
    Howard, III:368, 369
    Ridley, III:654-656
Crassus, Marcus Licinius, I:149, 159, 166, 168,
        680, 681, 816
Crates of Thebes, I:68, 967
Crawford, Cheryl, **VII:793-796**
Crawford, Jack, IX:2981
Crawford, Joan, VII:119, 125
Crayford, battle of, I:380
Crazy Horse, **V:573-577**
Creation Society, VIII:2033, 2034
Crécy, Battle of, II:331
Credi, Lorenzo di, III:751
Credit Molilier, VI:1919
Creek Indians
    Crockett, V:578
    Key, VI:1283
    McGillivray, IV:875-877
    Osceola, VI:1695, 1697
    Racine, IV:1044, 1045
    Ross, VI:1910
    Soto, III:700
Crelle, August Leopold, V:8, 9
Creoles, VI:2164
Crepy, Peace of, III:18
Crete, IX:3808, 3809
Crewe, John, IV:243
Crick, Francis, **VII:797-800;** IX:2927, 2928, 3897,
        3898, 3996, 3997
    Life Itself, VII:799
    Of Molecules and Men, VII:799
    "On Protein Synthesis," VII:798
cricket, V:971-973; VII:407-409, 759-761
Crimean War
    Bessemer, V:219
    Bright, V:307
    Godkin, VIII:1400
    Napoleon III, VI:1621
    Nicholas I, VI:1651
    Nightingale, VI:1668, 1670
    Palmerston, VI:1721
Crippen, Robert L., IX:3179
Cripps, Sir Richard Stafford, VII:304, 314;
        VIII:2710
Crisis, The, VII:964, 965; VIII:1771
Crispus, I:376
Cristero War, VII:543
Cristobal of La Gardia, San, III:727
Critias, I:795
Crixus, I:816

Croce, Benedetto, **VII:801-803,** 1336-1338;
  IX:3464
  Filosofia come sciensa dello spirito, VII:801
  *Historical Materialism and the Economics of
    Karl Marx,* VII:801
  History as the Story of Liberty, VII:802
  History of Europe in the Nineteenth Century,
    VII:802
  History of Italy, A, VII:802
  "Manifesto of Anti-Fascist Intellectuals,"
    VII:802
Crockett, David, **V:578-580**
  *Account of Colonel Crockett's Tour to the North
    and Down East, An,* V:579
  Life of Martin Van Buren, The, V:579
  *Narrative of the Life of David Crockett of the
    State of Tennessee,* V:579
  *Sketches and Eccentricities of Colonel David
    Crockett of West Tennessee,* V:580
Crocus Plain, Battle of the, I:629
Croesus, I:13, 396, 652
Croker, Richard, IX:3439
Cromeck, Robert, IV:138
Cromwell, Oliver, **IV:378-381**
  Baxter, IV:99
  Biddle, IV:126, 127
  Charles I, IV:281
  Charles II, IV:283
  Clarendon, IV:310
  Dryden, IV:424
  Fairfax, IV:446-449
  Lambert, IV:789-791
  Monck, IV:972, 973
  Pride, IV:1126, 1128
  Scotland, IV:239
  Shaftesbury, IV:1228
Cromwell, Thomas, **III:208-211**
  Boleyn, III:68
  Cranmer, III:204-206
  Gardiner, III:292
  Henry VIII, III:351
  Howard, III:367, 368
  Tyndale, III:736
  Wolsey, III:786
Crook, George, V:575, 576, 917
Crook Factory, VIII:1626
Crosby, Bing, VII:1159
Cross Keys, battle of, V:842
Crow Indians, VI:2077
Crucifixion
  Ballou, V:472
  Chagall, VII:641

Giotto, II:388, 390
Grünewald, III:323
Jesus Christ, I:469
John the Apostle, I:475
Rubens, IV:1198
Sluter, II:833
Virgin Mary, I:939
Cruickshank, Bobby, VIII:1876
Crusades
  Afonso I, II:31
  Bohemond I, II:159-161
  Dandolo, II:282, 284
  Duns Scotus, II:311
  Eleanor of Aquitaine, II:336
  France, II:124-126
  Germany, II:359, 360
  Gregory IX, II:399, 400
  Hartmann von Aue, II:434
  Henry the Lion, II:466
  Innocent III, II:511
  Louis IX, II:605, 606
  Raymond of Peñafort, II:776, 777
  Richard I, II:782
  Saladin, II:810, 811
  Tancred, II:887, 888
  Theoleptus of Philadelphia, II:899
  Urban II, II:930
  Villehardouin, II:942-945
Cruz, Joaquim, VII:727
Cruz, Sor Juana Inés de la, **IV:382-384**
  Carta atenagórica, IV:383
  divino Narciso, El, IV:383
  Neptuno alegórico, El, IV:383
  "Primero sueño," IV:383
  Reply to Sor Filotea de la Cruz, IV:383
Crystal Palace Exposition, VI:2069
CSO. *See* Community Service Organization
Ctesibius of Alexandria, **I:231, 232**
Ctesiphon, I:255
Cuban Missile Crisis, VIII:1930, 1933, 1963;
  IX:3525
Cubism
  Appolinaire, VII:82, 83
  Boccioni, VII:343
  Brancusi, VII:416
  Braque, VII:431, 432, 434
  Delaunay, VII:889
  Duchamp, VII:972, 973
  Gris, VIII:1483-1485
  Klee, VIII:2005
  Krasner, VIII:2023
  Kupka, VIII:2037

Léger, VIII:2154
Lipchitz, VIII:2199-2201
Magritte, VIII:2349
Marc, VIII:2405
Miró, VIII:2546
Nevelson, VIII:2729
Picasso, IX:2997, 2998, 3000
Rivera, IX:3185
Stieglitz, IX:3534
Cujas, Jacques, III:672
Cukor, George, VIII:2232
Culpeper, Thomas, III:368, 369
Cultural Revolution
    Chou En-lai, VII:678
    Chu Teh, VII:689
    Deng Xiaoping, VII:905, 906
    Kuo Mo-jo, VIII:2033-2035
    Lin Piao, VIII:2189, 2190
    Li Peng, VIII:2178-2180
    Liu Shao-ch'i, VIII:2212-2214
    Lu Hsün, VIII:2252
    Mao Tse-tung, VIII:2401, 2402
    P'eng Te-huai, IX:2954, 2955
Cumans, II:574, 575
Cumberland, Duke of, IV:37, 1474
Cumberland, Earl of, III:140
cummings, e.e., **VII:804-807**
    1 x 1, VII:806
    XLI Poems, VII:806
    50 Poems, VII:806
    73 Poems, VII:806
    95 Poems, VII:806
    Collected Poems, VII:806
    Eimi, VII:806
    Enormous Room, The, VII:804
    i: six nonlectures, VII:806
    Is 5, VII:806
    No Thanks, VII:806
    Tulips and Chimneys, VII:806
    Xaipe, VII:806
Cummings v. Missouri, V:788
Cunha, Tristao da, III:12
Cunimund, II:41
Cunningham, Imogen, **VII:808-810**
    After Ninety, VII:809
    Magnolia Blossom (Tower of Jewels),
        VII:809
Curchold, Suzanne, IV:1016
Curia, the, VIII:1860
Curie, Marie, V:167; VII:410, **811-815;**
    VIII:1870-1872
Curie, Pierre, **VII:811-815;** VIII:1870-1872

Curtin, John, **VII:816-818**
Curtis Institute of Music, VII:191, 295
Curtiss, Glenn H., IX:4066, 4067
Curzon, Lord, **VII:819-822**
Cushing, Caleb, **V:581-584**
Cushing, Harvey Williams, **VII:823-826**
    Life of Sir William Osler, VII:825
Cushite dynasty, I:709, 711
Cust, Henry, V:777
Custer, George A., V:390, 574, 575, **585-588**;
    VI:1585, 2072
Cuvier, Georges, **V:589-591**
Cuvilliés, François, IV:152
Cuyen, IV:1
Cuzcatlán, kingdom of, III:23
Cuzco, III:577, 578, 699
Cylon, I:280
Cynaxares, I:570
Cynicism
    Antisthenes, I:66-68
    Aristippus, I:86
    Diogenes, I:268-271
    Eratosthenes of Cyrene, I:303
    Menippius, I:507
    Socrates, I:795
    Zeno of Citium, I:967, 969
Cynosarges gymnasium, I:66, 67
Cynthia, I:702-704
Cyrano de Bergerac, **IV:385-388**
    Lettres, IV:385, 386
    Mort d' Agrippine, La, IV:385, 386
    Other World, The, IV:385
    Pédant joué, Le, IV:385-387
    States and Empires of the Sun, The,
        IV:385
Cyrene, I:156, 303, 304
Cyril (bishop), I:437, 438
Cyril, Saint, **II:278-281**
Cyrrhus, I:865, 866
Cyrus Cylinder, I:234
Cyrus the Great, **I:233-235,** 330
Czech National Opera, V:726
Czechoslovak Communist Party, VII:968-970
Czechoslovak National Council, VII:259, 260
Czolgosz, Leon, VIII:1412, 1413

Dacian wars, I:901
Dada movement
    Appolinaire, VII:83
    Breton, VII:448-450
    Duchamp, VII:973
    Ernst, VII:1098-1100

Magritte, VIII:2351
Miró, VIII:2548
Satie, IX:3334
Daedalus Hyperboreus, IV:1302
Dagnus, I:182
Daguerre, Jacques, **V:592-596;** VI:1594, 1659, 1660
Dahl, Nikolai, IX:3105
Daily Express, VII:235
Daily Mail, VIII:1554, 1555; VII:235, 325
Daimler, Gottlieb, V:200, 201, **597-599**
Daimler Motor Company, V:599; VIII:2071; IX:3881
daimyo lords, IV:1329
Dalai Lama, VII:821; VIII:2711
Dale, Thomas, IV:1107, 1108
Dalhousie, First Marquess of, **V:600-601;** VI:1706
Dali, Salvador, VII:505, 506, **827-831,** 1075
 Age of Gold, The, VII:829
 Andalusian Dog, An, VII:829
 Aphrodisiac Jacket, VII:829
 Dream of Christopher Columbus, The, VII:829
 Exploding Raphaelesque Head, VII:829
 Hidden Faces, VII:829
 Honey Sweeter than Blood, VII:827
 Secret Life of Salvador Dali, The, VII:829
Dalton, John, V:99, **602-605**
 New System of Chemical Philosophy, V:604
Damasus, I:465
Damietta, II:605
Damon, I:609
Dampier, William, **IV:389-392**
 Captain Dampier's Vindication of His Voyage to the South Seas in the Ship St. George, IV:390
 New Voyage 'Round the World, A, IV:389
 Voyages and Descriptions, IV:389
Dana, Charles, V:984, 985
Dana, Richard Henry, Jr., VI:1522, 1601
 "Discourses on Women," VI:1602
Danckelmann, Eberhard von, IV:497
Dandolo, Enrico, **II:282-285**
Danegeld, II:345
Danforth, John, IX:3657
Daniel, Book of, I:685
Daniell, John Frederic, V:1010
Danilova, Alexandra, **VII:832-836**
 Apollo Musagète, VII:833
 Beau Danube, Le, VII:833
 Boutique fantasque, La, VII:833
 Coppélia, VII:833
 Firebird, The, VII:832
 Gods Go A-Begging, The, VII:833

Paquita, VII:835
Prodigal Son, The, VII:833
Raymonda, VII:833
Triumph of Neptune, The, VII:833
Waltzes from Vienna, VII:833
Danis, Ida, VII:1274
Danish War of 1864, V:1130
Danjon, André-Louis, **VII:837, 838**
Danjon astrolabe, VII:837
Danley, Earl of, III:476, 477
Dannebrog, II:933
Dante, II:103, 153, **286-290,** 730; III:272
 Banquet, The, II:288
 Divine Comedy, The, I:440, II:223, 286, 288, 289, 768, IV:349; V:122, 646; VI:1416, 1485
 Inferno, II:286, 288, 699
 New Life, The, II:286, 288
 Purgatorio, II:286, 288, 289
D'Anthès, Georges-Charles, VI:1833, 1834
Danton, Georges, **IV:393-395,** 1206
Dara Shukoh, IV:69, 70
Darby, Abraham, **IV:396-398,** 1443, 1444
Darcet, Jean, IV:813, 814
Dardanelles, Battle of the, VII:123, 134, 691
Dardanus, Treaty of, I:558
Dare, Virginia, III:638
Darien scheme, IV:1066-1068
Darius the Great, **I:236-240**
 Alexander the Great, I:40
 Behistun Inscription, I:233
 Clazomenae, I:47
 Herodotus, I:394
 Leonidas, I:501
 Miltiades the Younger, I:553, 554
 Xerxes I, I:962, 964, 965
Darmstadt, Germany, VIII:1633
Darrow, Clarence, VII:481, **839-842**
Dartmouth College v. Woodward, VI:2148, 2344
Daru, Pierre, VI:2125, 2126
Darvall, Denise, VII:197
Darwin, Charles, **V:606-609**
 Baer, V:110
 Descent of Man and Selection in Relation to Sex, The, V:608
 Le Bon, VIII:2136
 London, VIII:2226
 Lyell, VI:1420-1422
 On the Origin of Species, V:32, 606, 608, 609, 868, 980, 1018, 1172, 1173; VI:1421, 2348; VII:283
 Spencer, VI:2087
 Wedgwood, IV:1422

Darwin, Erasmus
  Botanic Garden, The, IV:138
Datis, I:238
Daudet, Alphonse, V:245
Davaine, Casimir-Joseph, VI;1298
David, **I:241-245,** 748, 749, 798; IV:118
David I, **II:291-293**
David II, **II:294-297**
David, Jacques-Louis, IV:490; **V:610-613,** 1183
  Battle of the Romans and Sabines, The,
    V:611, 612
  Belisarius, V:610
  Brutus Receiving the Bodies of His Sons, V:611
  Cupid and Psyche, V:612
  Death of Socrates, The, V:611
  Oath of Horatii, The, V:610
  Oath of the Tennis Court, The, V:611
  Telemachus and Eucharis, V:612
Davies, John, IV:174
Davies, Marion, VIII:1604
Davis, Bette, **VII:843-846**
  All About Eve, VII:845
  All This and Heaven Too, VII:845
  Bad Sister, VII:843
  Dangerous, VII:843
  Dark Victory, VII:845
  Great Lie, The, VII:845
  Hush Hush Sweet Charlotte, VII:844
  Jezebel, VII:845
  Letter, The, VII:845
  Little Foxes, The, VII:845
  Night of the Iguana, The, VII:845
  Now, Voyager, VII:845
  Of Human Bondage, VII:843
  Old Maid, The, VII:845
  Petrified Forest, The, VII:843
  Whales of August, The, VII:845
  What Ever Happened to Baby Jane?, VII:845
Davis, Clive, VII:1218
Davis, Jefferson, **V:614-620**
  Black Hawk, V:249
  Greeley, V:985
  Lee, VI:1338, 1340, 1341
  Stephens, VI:2130
Davis, John, **III:212-214**
  Seaman's Secrets, III:213
  World's Hydrographical Description, III:213
Davis, Miles, VII:741, 742, 744; IX:2882
Davis, Theodore, I:905
Davis Cup, VII:368, 369; VIII:2109, 2110;
    IX:2979, 2981, 2982
Davy, Sir Humphry, **V:621-624,** 767, 768, 899

Dawidowicz, Lucy S., **VII:847-849**
  Golden Tradition, The, VII:848
  Holocaust and the Historians, The, VII:849
  Holocaust Reader, A, VII:848
  Jewish Presence, The, VII:848, 849
  War Against the Jews, The, VII:848
Dawlat al-atrak, II:125
Dawlat Khan Lodi, III:38
Dawson, John William, VI:1420
Day, Dorothy, **VII:850-853**
  Eleventh Virgin, The, VII:850
Day, John, VII:489
Dayan, Moshe, VII:253, **854-857**
Dayr el-Bahri, temple at, I:373
Deák, Ferenc, **V:625-629**
Deakin, Alfred, **V:630-633**
Deane, Richard, IV:132, 134, 972
Death, Union of, VII:1198
death penalty, V:379; VII:840; VIII:1574, 1864,
    2099, 2435; IX:3283
DeBakey, Michael E., VII:197
De Beers Mining Company, VI:1874, 1785
Deborah, **I:246-248**
Debs, Eugene V., **VII:880-883,** 940;
    IX:3660, 3661
Debussy, Claude, VI:2366; **VII:884-887;** IX:3129,
    3332, 3333
  Afternoon of a Faun, VIII:2748
  Chansons de Bilitis, VII:885
  Children's Corner Suite, VII:886
  Douze Préludes, VII:886
  Etudes, VII:886
  Fetes galantes, VII:884, 885
  Images, VII:885
  Jeux, VII:886
  Mer, La, VII:885
  Noctures, VII:885
  Pelléas et Mélisande, VII:884, 885; VIII:2503
  Pour le piano, VII:886
  Prélude à l'aprés-midi d'un faune,
    VII:884, 885
  Suite bergamasque, VII:886
decathlon, IX:3674
Decatur, Stephen, **V:634-637;** VI:1765
Deccan, IV:71, 1247
Deccan Education Society, IX:3682
Deceased Wife's Sister's Marriage Act, V:1170
Decebalus, I:901
Decembrist Revolt, VI:1650, 1651, 1833, 2090
De Chirico, Giorgio, VII:1098
Decianus, Catus, I:137
Decius, I:182

Declaration of Independence. *See* Independence, Declaration of

Declaratory Act, IV:367

Decretalists, II:179, 776

Dedekind, Richard, **V:638-640**

Dee, John, III:212

Defense, U.S. Department of, VIII:2752

Defense Mobilization, Office of, IX:3103

Defiance Campaign, VIII:2281, 2386

Defoe, Daniel, **IV:399-402**
   Captain Singleton, IV:401
   Colonel Jacque, IV:401
   Consolidator, The, IV:401
   Essay on Projects, An, IV:399
   Family Instructor, The, IV:401
   History of the Union, The, IV:401
   Journal of the Plague Year, A, IV:401
   Jure Divino, IV:401
   Memoirs of a Cavalier, IV:401
   Moll Flanders, IV:401
   Robinson Crusoe, IV:390, 391, 401
   Roxana, IV:401
   Shortest Way with Dissenters, The, IV:399
   True-Born Englishman, The, IV:399
   True Relation of the Apparition of One Mrs. Veal, the Next Day After Her Death, to One Mrs. Bargrave, IV:401

de Forest, Lee, VII:102, **858-861**

Degas, Edgar, V:435, 436, **641-644,** 890, 891; VI:2247, 2249
   Bellelli Family, The, V:641
   Dance Class, The, V:643
   Mlle. Fiocre in the Ballet "La Source," V:641
   Orchestra of the Opera, The, V:643
   Scene of War in the Middle Ages, V:641
   Self-Portrait, V:641, 642
   Steeplechase, The, V:641
   Woman Bathing in a Shallow Tub, V:643

de Gasperi, Alcide, **VII:862-865**

de Gaulle, Charles, **VII:866-869**
   Algeria, VII:7
   Ben-Gurion, VII:254
   Blum, VII:338
   Cassin, VII:610, 611
   French Equatorial Africa, VII:1006
   Macmillan, VIII:2341
   Malraux, VIII:2380, 2381
   Mendès-France, VIII:2491-2493
   Mitterrand, VIII:2558-2560
   Pétain, IX:2988, 2989
   Pompidou, IX:3052-3054
   United Nations, VIII:1530

Degen, Ferdinand, V:7

degenerate art
   Ernst, VII:1099
   Kirchner, VIII:1993
   Klee, VIII:2006
   Kokoschka, VIII:2014
   Kollwitz, VIII:2017
   Marc, VIII:2406
   Munch, VIII:2660
   Webern, IX:3916

Degeorge, Frédéric, V:259

Deism, IV:412, 428, 430, 844, 1055-1057

Dekker, Thomas
   Satiromastix: Or, The Untrussing of the Humorous Poet, IV:746

de Klerk, F.W., **VII:870-873;** VIII:2387

De Kruif, Paul, VIII:2175

Delacroix, Eugène, **V:645-648**
   Algerian Women in Their Quarters, V:647
   Arabs Skirmishing in the Mountains, V:647
   Barque of Dante, The, VI:1472
   Dante and Virgil Crossing the Styx, V:646
   Death of Sardanapolus, The, V:646, 647
   Liberty Leading the People, V:647
   Lion Hunt, The, V:647
   Massacre at Chios, The, V:646

Delahaye, Ernest, VI:1886

Delane, John Thaddeus, VI:2326

Delano Grape Strike, VIII:1763

Delaunay, Robert, **VII:888-891,** 1098; VIII:2405
   Breton Woman, VII:888
   Cities, VII:889
   City of Paris, The, VII:889
   Eiffel Tower, VII:889
   Haystacks of Berry, VII:888
   Landscape of La Ronchère, VII:888
   Landscape with Disc, VII:888
   Seaweed Gatherer, VII:888
   Vases and Objects, VII:888
   Views of Saint-Séverin, VII:889
   Windows, VII:889

Delaware and Hudson Canal, VI:1904

De la Warr Pavilion, VIII:2488

Delcassé, Théophile, VII:704

Delian League, I:47, 198-200, 609, 611, 858

Delian Problem, I:305, 311

Delibes, Léo, **V:649-651**
   Coppélia: Ou, La Fille aux yeux d'émail, V:649-651
   Cour du roi Pétaud, La, V:649
   Deux Vielles Gardes, V:649
   Jean de Nivelle, V:650

Kassya, V:650, 651
Lakmé, V:650
Roi l'a dit, Le, V:650
Roi s'amuse, six airs de danse dans le style ancien, Le, V:650
Source: Ou, Naila, La, V:649
Sylvia: Ou, La Nymphe de Diane, V:650, 651
Delius, Frederick, **VII:892-895**
  Appalachia, VII:893
  Brigg Fair, VII:893
  Eventyr, VII:893
  Fennimore and Gerda, VII:893
  Leute von Seldwyla, Die, VII:893
  Margot la rouge, VII:892
  Mass of Life, A, VII:893
  North Country Sketches, VII:893
  On Hearing the First Cuckoo in Spring, VII:893
  Paris: The Song of a Great City, VII:893
  Sea Drift, VII:893
  Song of the High Hills, A, VII:893
  Songs of Sunset, VII:893
  String Quartet No. 2, VII:894
  Summer Night on the River, VII:893
  Village Romeo and Juliet, A, VII:893
della Rovere, Giuliano. *See* Julius II
Delphi, Oracle at
  Cleomenes, I:501
  Cylon, I:280
  Demosthenes, I:254
  Diogenes, I:268
  Eudoxus of Cnidus, I:311
  Leonidas, I:502
  Pisistratid family, I:649, 650
  Socrates, I:793
  Xenophon, I:958
Demaratus, I:214, 215
Demarcation, Line of, III:16, 262
Demea, IV:684
Demeter, cult of, I:9
Demetrius of Phalerum, I:873
Demetrius Poliocretes, I:60
de Mille, Agnes, **VII:874-876**
  Black Ritual (Obeah), VII:875
  Brigadoon, VII:875
  Kwamina, VII:875
  Oklahoma!, VII:875, 876
  Rodeo, VII:875
  Texas Fourth, VII:876
DeMille, Cecil B., **VII:896-899;** VIII:14154
  Cheat, The, VII:896
  Cleopatra, VII:897
  Crusades, The, VII:897

  Greatest Show on Earth, The, VII:898
  King of Kings, The, VII:897
  Sign of the Cross, The, VII:897
  Squaw Man, The, VII:896
  Ten Commandments, The, VII:897, 898
DeMille Foundation for Political Freedom, VII:898
Demiurges, I:633, 912, 913
Democedes, I:34
democracy
  Acton, V:12
  Adams, IV:16
  Antisthenes, I:67
  Bolívar, V:268, 269
  Calhoun, V:396
  Carlyle, V:417
  Indonesia, VIII:1578; IX:3571, 3572
  Kerensky, VIII:1941-1944
  Lippmann, VIII:2203-2206
  Mosca, VIII:2632
  Nasser, VIII:2693
  Poland, IX:3847
  Tocqueville, VI:2238-2240
  Wallace, IX:3861
Democratic Farm-Labor Alliance, VIII:1783
Democratic Party, U.S.
  Albright, VII:50, 51
  Altgeld, V:55, 56
  Bancroft, V:125, 126
  Benton, V:197
  Bryan, VII:479-481
  Buchanan, V:346-348
  Carter, VII:589-592
  Chisholm, VII:670, 671
  Cleveland, V:512, 513, 515
  Clinton, VII:707-710
  Cushing, V:582
  Feinstein, VII:1137-1139
  Ferraro, VII:1153-1155
  Gore, VIII:1431-1433
  Harriman, VIII:1562, 1563
  Hayes, V:1078
  Hearst, VIII:1603
  Hobby, VIII:1704, 1705
  Houston, V:1138
  Humphrey, VIII:1783-1786
  Jackson, V:1197
  Johnson, Andrew, V:1232
  Johnson, Lyndon B., VIII:1866-1868
  Kansas-Nebraska Act, V:693
  Kennedy, John F., VIII:1928-1931
  Kennedy, Robert F., VIII:1932-1935

Kirkpatrick, VIII:1994, 1995
Kissinger, VIII:1999
Madison, IV:888
O'Neill, IX:2824-2826
organized labor, VIII:2171, 2172
Pierce, VI:1775-1777
Polk, VI:1801-1803
Reagan, IX:3138
Richards, IX:3169-3171
Roosevelt, IX:3222-3226
Ross, IX:3243, 3244
Sinclair, IX:3428
Spock, IX:3479
Stephens, VI:2129, 2131
Stevenson, IX:3523-3526
Taney, VI:2190, 2191
Truman, IX:3740, 3742, 3743
Tweed, VI:2284
Tyler, VI:2288, 2289
Wallace, George C., IX:3858, 3859
Wallace, Henry A., IX:3860-3863
Whitman, VI:2368
Wilson, IX:4020
Democratic Union of the Algerian Manifesto,
    VII:6, 7
Democritus, I:101, **249-252,** 511, 705
demography, II:940; VI:1467-1469, 1562, 1879;
    VIII:2671
Demoiselle, IX:3322
Demosthemenes, **I:253-256,** 671
    "First Philippic," I:253
    "Olynthiacs," I:253
    "On the Chersonese," I:254
    "Third Philippic," I:254
Dempsey, Jack, **VII:900-904**
Deneuve, Catherine, VII:506
Denger, Adam, VIII:2735
Deng Xiaoping, **VII:905-908**
    Lee Kuan Yew, VIII:2152
    Li Peng, VIII:2178, 2179
Denis, Maurice, VI:1473; **VII:909-911;** IX:3826,
    3828
    April, VII:909
    Ascent to Calvary, The, VII:910
    Battle of Jacob and the Angel, The, VII:910
    Hommage à Cézanne, VII:910
Denis, Saint, **I:257-259**
Dennis v. United States, VII:322
dentistry, VI:1596-1598
deoxyribonucleic acid. *See* DNA
Deprez-d'Arsonval mirror galvanometer, VII:1040
Derain, André, VIII:2454

Derby, Fourteenth Earl of, **V:652-655,** 677, 678
Dereham, Francis, III:367-369
Derrida, Jacques, **VII:912-915**
    Dissemination, VII:914
    Glas, VII:914
    Margins of Philosophy, VII:914
    Of Grammatology, VII:912, 913
    *Post Card: From Socrates to Freud and Beyond,
        The,* VII:914
    Speech and Phenomena, VII:913
    Truth in Painting, VII:914
    Writing and Difference, VII:913
Descartes, René, IV:345, **403-407,** 978
    Discourse on Method, IV:405
    Fermat, IV:458-460
    Geometry of Descartes, The, I:594
    Gilson, VII:1374, 1376
    Huygens, IV:695, 696
    Leibniz, IV:830
    Marcel, VIII:2407, 2408
    mechanics, IV:787
    Meditations on First Philosophy, IV:405
    Mersenne, IV:949-952
    nature of space, IV:586
    Pascal, IV:1062
    Passions of the Soul, The, IV:405
    Rules for the Direction of the Mind, IV:403
    Spinoza, IV:1264-1266
    Steiner, VI:2119
Deschamps, Eustache, II:617
Deschevaux-Dumésnil, Suzanne, VII:239
desegregation, VIII:1769, 1789. *See also*
    segregation
Desert Shield, Operation, IX:3071
Desert Storm, Operation, VII:522, 1116;
    IX:3071
Desilu Productions, VII:176-178
de Sitter, Willem, VIII:2158, 2159
Desmichels, Louis Alexander, V:1, 2
Despenser, Hugh le, II:326, 327
Despenser the Younger, Hugh, II:326, 327
Dessalines, Jean-Jacques, V:501
Destour Party, VII:391
detective stories
    Christie, VII:683, 685, 686
    Doyle, V:700-702
    Gardner, VII:1297-1299
    Poe, VI:1796
Detroit Automobile Company, VII:1186
Detroit Evening News, VI:2014
Detroit Tigers, VII:717, 719
Detroit Tribune, VI:2014

Dettingen, Battle of, IV:537, 1471
Deuchar, David, VI:1836
Deuteronomy, Book of, I:563
Deutsche Gotteserkenntnis, VIII:2266
Deutsche Oper Berlin, VIII:2769, 2770
de Valera, Eamon, VI:1481; VII:734, 735, 770-
    772, **877-879**; IX:2805, 2806
Devereux, Robert. *See* Essex, Second Earl of
Devereux, Walter. *See* Essex, First Earl of
Devolution, War of, IV:343
De Wette, W.M.L., VI:1727, 1728
Dewey, George, **V:656-659**
    Experience and Nature, VII:917
    Human Nature and Conduct, VII:917
    Individualism, Old and New, VII:917
    Psychology, VII:916
    Quest for Certainty, The, VII:917
    Reconstruction in Philosophy, VII:917
    School and Society, The, VII:917
    Studies in Logical Theory, VII:917
Dewey, John, VI:1769; **VII:916-918**
Dewey, Melvil, **V:660-662**
Dewey, Thomas, VIII:1704; IX:3889
Dewey decimal classification system, V:660-662
diabetes, I:83
    Banting, VII:187-190
    Houssay, VIII:1759, 1760
    Macleod, VIII:2329-2331
Diaconus, Paulus, II:41
Diaghilev, Sergei, **VII:919-922**
    Afternoon of a Faun, VII:920
    Apollo, VII:921
    Balanchine, VII:156
    Carnival, Le, VII:920
    Cleopatra, VII:919
    Cocteau, VII:721
    Coq d'Or, Le, VII:920
    Danilova, VII:833
    Duncan, VII:981
    Festin, Le, VII:919
    Firebird, The, VII:920
    Gris, VIII:1484
    Legend of Joseph, The, VII:920
    Lifar, VIII:2182-2184
    Massine, VIII:2448, 2449
    Narcisse, VII:920
    Nijinsky, VIII:2746, 2748, 2749
    Noces, Les, VII:921
    Pavilion d'Armide, Le, VII:919
    Pavlova, IX:2937
    Petrushka, VII:920
    Prodigal Son, The, VII:921

Prokofiev, IX:3085
    Spectre de la Rose, Le, VII:920
    Stravinsky, IX:3559
    Swan Lake, VII:920
    Sylphides, Les, VII:919
Dial, The, V:757, 849; VI:2234; VIII:2614, 2616
diamond industry, VI:1873, 1874
Diana, Princess of Wales, **VII:923-926,** 1064
Dias, Bartolomeu, **III:215-219**
Diaspora, II:549
Diaz, Porfirio, V:1253; VIII:2345, 2347;
    IX:3811, 4104
Díaz de Vivar, Rodrigo. *See* Cid, El
Dibbs, Sir George Richard, V:148
Dickens, Charles, V:59, **663-666**; VIII:2174, 2465
    American Notes, V:663, 1150
    Barnaby Rudge: A Tale of the Riots of '80, V:663
    Bleak House, V:663, 665
    Christmas Carol, A, V:663, 666
    David Copperfield, V:663
    Dombey and Son, V:663
    Great Expectations, V:665
    Hard Times, V:663, 665
    Household Words, V:663
    Little Dorrit, V:663, 665
    Martin Chuzzlewit, V:663, 665
    Mystery of Edwin Drood, The, V:665
    Nicholas Nickleby, V:663, 666; VI:1461
    Old Curiosity Shop, The, V:663
    Oliver Twist, V:663, 666
    Our Mutual Friend, V:665
    Pickwick Papers, V:663
    Sketches by Boz, V:663
    Tale of Two Cities, A, V:665; VIII:2724
Dickinson, Charles, V:1196
Dickinson, Emily, **V:667-671,** 1110-1112, 1200
    "Letter to the World," V:671; VIII:1458
    "Master Letters," V:669
    "Narrow Fellow in the Grass, A" V:668
Dickinson, John, **IV:408-411,** 1455, 1456
    *Late Regulations Respecting the British Colonies
        on the Continent of America Considered, The,*
        IV:408
Diderot, Denis, **IV:412-415**
    Alembert, IV:30-33
    Condillac, IV:344, 345
    Dorval, IV:413
    Encyclopédie, IV:31-33, 226, 348, 413, 414
    Essay on Blindness, An, IV:412
    Est-il bon? Est-il méchant?, IV:414
    Father of the Family, The, IV:413
    Indiscreet Toys, The, IV:412

Jacques the Fatalist and His Master, IV:414
Letter on the Deaf and Dumb, IV:413
Paradox of Acting, The, IV:413
Penseés philosophiques, IV:412
Promenade du sceptique, La, IV:412
Rameau, IV:1149
Rameau's Nephew, IV:413, 414
Rousseau, IV:1194
Supplement to Bougainville's "Voyage,", IV:414
Didrikson, "Babe". *See* Zaharias, "Babe" Didrikson
Diego of Acebo, II:301, 302
Diels, Otto Paul Hermann, **VII:927-929**
Dientzenhofer, Johann, IV:656
Diepkloof, IX:2907
Dieppe raid, VIII:2602, 2643
Diesel, Rudolf, **V:672-674**
   *Theory and Construction of a Rational Heat
      Motor,* V:673
Dietrich, Marlene, **VII:930-933**
   Angel, VII:932
   Blue Angel, The, VII:930, 932
   Destry Rides Again, VII:932; IX: 3528, 3529
   Dishonored, VII:932
   Foreign Affair, A, VII:932
   Garden of Allah, The, VII:932
   Knight Without Armor, VII:932
   Martin Roumaganic, VII:932
   Morocco, VII:932
   Scarlet Empress, The, VII:932
   Seven Sinners, VII:932
   Tragedy of Love, VII:930
Dieudonné, Albert, IX:3157
differential calculus
   Alembert, IV:30
   Dedekind, V:638
   Fermat, IV:458-460
   Maclaurin, IV:883
   Newton, IV:1025, 1027, 1028
   Torricelli, IV:1331-1333
Digambara, I:915
Dikaiopolis, I:88, 90
Dilke, Charles, V:462
Dilke, Lady Emilia, VII:353
Dill, Sir John, VII:46
DiMaggio, Joe, **VII:934-937,** 1323; VIII:2589
Dimmesdale, Arthur, V:1054, 1066
Dingiswayo, VI:2041
Dingley Act, VI:1454
Dio Cassius, I:136, 141, 142
Diocles of Carystus, **I:260-262**
   Anatomy, I:261
   Arkhidamos, I:260

Diokles epistole prophulakike, I:261
Directions on Health for Pleistarchos, I:261
Rhizotomika, I:261
Diocletian, I:226, **263-267**
Diodore, I:861
Diodorus of Sicily, I:547, 732
Diogenes, I:66, 68; **268-271;** 795
Dionysian festival. *See* Greater Dionysia
Dionysius, I:257, 690, 787; VI:1664
Dionysius Exiguus, **II:298-300**
   "First letter written in the year of Christ 525,"
      II:299
   Paschal Tables, II:299
Dionysius the Aeropagite, Saint, I:258
Diophantus, **I:272-275;** II:20
   Arithmetica, I:272-274, 437
   Moriastica, I:274
   Porismata, I:274
Dioscorides, Pedanius, **I:276-279**
   De materia medica, I:276
Dioscuri, I:676
Dirichlet, Peter Gustav Lejeune, V:638, 639
Dirksen, Everett, VIII:2258
Discalced Carmelites, III:401, 402, 714, 715;
   IV:382
Discovery, IV:1355, 1356
discrimination, racial
   Bunche, VII:501, 502
   Constantine, VII:760
   Dunham, VII:985
   Garvey, VII:1311
   Hernandez, VIII:1641
   Myrdal, VIII:2671-2673
   Parks, IX:2888-2891
   Randolph, IX:3114
   Walker, IX:3855
   Washington, VI:2337
   See also apartheid; racism; segregation
Disney, Walt, **VII:938-943**
   Adventures of Ichabod and Mr. Toad, The,
      VII:941
   Alice in Cartoonland, VII:940
   Bambi, VII:941
   Cinderella, VII:941
   Dumbo, VII:941
   Fantasia, VII:940; IX:3560
   Make Mine Music, VII:941
   Mary Poppins, VII:941
   Mickey Mouse Club, VII:941
   Old Mill, The, VII:940
   Oswald the Rabbit, VII:940
   Reluctant Dragon, The, VII:940

Saludos Amigos, VII:941
Snow White and the Seven Dwarfs, VII:940
So Dear to My Heart, VII:941
Song of the South, VII:941
Steamboat Willie, VII:940
Three Caballeros, VII:941
Three Little Pigs, VII:940
Tortoise and the Hare, The, VII:940
True-Life Adventure series, VII:941
Ugly Duckling, The, VII:940
Disneyland, VII:941, 942
Disraeli, Benjamin, **V:675-679**
   Bright, V:307, 308
   Coningsby: Or, The New Generation, V:677
   Derby, V:653, 654
   Forster, V:805
   Gladstone, V:936, 938
   O'Connor, IX:2789
   Peel, VI:1754
   Rothschild, VI:1918
   Salisbury, VI:1944
   Sybil, V:677
   Victoria, VI:2308
   Vivian Grey, V:675
   Young Duke, The, V:675
Dissenters. *See* Radical Dissenters
di Stefano, Giuseppe, IX:2930
Divinsky, Nathan, VII:549
Dix, Dorothea, **V:680-683**
Dizé, J.J., IV:814
Djilas, Milovan, **VII:944-946**
   Anatomy of a Moral, VII:944
   Conversations with Stalin, VII:945
   Land Without Justice, VII:945
   Leper and Other Stories, The, VII:945
   Montenegro, VII:945
   New Class, The, VII:945
   Njegos, VII:945
   Stone and the Violets, The, VII:945
   Under the Colors, VII:945
   Unperfect Society, The, VII:945
DNA
   Crick, VII:797-799
   Bragg, VII:412
   Jacob, VIII:1827
   Pauling, IX:2927
   Watson, IX:3897-3899
   Wilkins, IX:3995-3997
Dnieper River, II:804
Döbereiner, Johann, VI:1532
Dobrynia, II:953
Dockers' Union, VII:313

Dodge City, V:735, 736
Doering, William, IX:4053
Dohnányi, Ernó, VII:210
Dole, Robert J., VII:400, 710, **947-950,** 1182;
   IX:2975
Döllinger, Johann Joseph Ignaz von, V:10, 11
Domagk, Gerhard, **VII:951-953**
Domaine Musical series, VII:387
Domesday Book, II:1000
Dominic, Saint, **II:301-304**
Dominican Order
   Albertus Magnus, II:37
   Angelico, III:28, 29
   Bonaventure, II:163
   Bruno, III:96
   Bucer, III:101
   Catherine of Siena, II:218, 220
   Dominic, II:301-303
   Inquisition, II:401
   Luther, III:443
   Pecham, II:717
   Raymond of Peñafort, II:776, 777
   Thomas Aquinas, II:911, 913, 914
   Torquemada, III:725
   Vincent of Beauvais, II:946
   William of Moerbeke, II:985, 986
   William of Saint-Amour, II:990, 991
Domitian, I:356, 488, 489, 533, 838, 839, 933
Donald III, II:291
Donatello, **III:220-223,** 303, 460, 461, 483
   David (bronze), III:222
   David (marble), III:220
   Equestrian Monument of General Gattamelata,
     III:220
   Feast of Herod, The, III:220
   Mary Magdalene, III:220
   Saint George and the Dragon, III:220
   Saint John the Evangelist, III:220
   Zuccone, III:220
Donati, Corso, II:286
Donatists, I:228, 344
Donatus, I:463, II:757
   Ars grammatica, II:756
Donauschingen Festival, VIII:1670
Donders, Franciscus Cornelius, VII:1039
Donelson, Fort, V:976
Donizetti, Gaetano, **V:684-686**
   Anna Bolena, V:685
   Daughter of the Regiment, The, V:685
   Don Pasquale, V:685
   Elixer of Love, The, V:685; VII:599
   favorite, La, V:685

Lucia di Lammermoor, V:685
Lucrezia Borgia, V:685
Marino Faliero, V:685
Roberto Devereux, V:685
zingara, La, V:684
Donnacona, III:129, 130
Donne, John, IV:48 **416-420**
   Anatomy of the World, IV:418
   "Canonization, The," IV:418
   Devotions upon Emergent Occasions, IV:419
   "Ecstasy, The," IV:416
   "Flea, The," IV:416
   "Good Friday, 1613, Riding Westward," IV:418
   "Hymn to God My God, in My Sickness," IV:419
   Of the Progress of the Soule, IV:418
   Songs and Sonnets, IV:416
   "Valediction, A," IV:418
Doolittle, Hilda. *See* H.D.
Doolittle, James H., VIII:1525
Doppler, Johann, IX:3490
Dorat, Jean, III:657, 671
Dorchester, Lord. *See* Carleton, Guy
Dorgon, IV:1, 2, **421-423**
Dorieus, I:214, 501
Dorris, Michael, VII:1091
Doson, I:216
Dostoevski, Fyodor, **V:687-691;** VI:2269; VII:153
   Brothers Karamazov, The, V:670; VIII:2533
   Crime and Punishment, V:689
   Double, The, V:687
   Idiot, The, V:689; VIII:2746
   Notes from the Underground, V:689
   Poor Folk, V:687
   Possessed, The, V:689
Doubleday, Frank, VII:955
Douglas, Lord Alfred, VI:2379
Douglas, Sir Archibald, II:294
Douglas, Stephen A., V:347, 510, **692-694,** 793; VI:1382, 1383
Douglass, Frederick, **V:695-699;** VI:2257
   Life and Times of Frederick Douglass, V:697
   My Bondage and My Freedom, V:697
   Narrative of the Life of Frederick Douglass, V:697
Douhet, Giulio, VIII:2556
Dover, Treaty of, IV:285, 1039
Dow, Arthur, IX:2800
Dow Jones Industrial Average, VIII:1472, 1473
Downs, Battle of the, IV:501
Doyen, Gabriel-François, IV:488
Doyle, Sir Arthur Conan, **V:700-703**
   Adventures of Sherlock Holmes, The, V:700, 701

Case-Book of Sherlock Holmes, The, V:701
His Last Bow, V:701
History of Spiritualism, The, V:702
Hound of the Baskervilles, The, V:701
Lost World, The, V:700, 702
Return of Sherlock Holmes, The, V:701
Sign of Four, The, V:700
Study in Scarlet, A, V:700
Valley of Fear, The, V:701
War in South Africa, The, V:701
Draco, **I:280, 281**
Dragon Boat Festival, I:188
Drake, Sir Francis, **III:224-226,** 279, 315, 316, 693
Drake, H.M.S., IV:740
Draper, John William, V:294, 296
Dred Scott decision. *See* Scott, Dred
Dreisch, Hans, VIII:2619, 2620
Dreiser, Theodore, **VII:954-958**
   American Tragedy, An, VII:957, 958
   Bulwark, The, VII:957
   Dreiser Looks at Russia, VII:957
   Financier, The, VII:955
   "Genius" The, VII:955; VIII:2484
   Jennie Gerhardt, VII:955
   Sister Carrie, VII:954, 955, 957, 958; IX:2812
   Stoic, The, VII:955
   Titan, The, VII:955
Drexel, Morgan, and Company, VI:1581
Dreyer, Carl Theodore, **VII:959-962**
   Bride of Glomdal, The, VII:959
   Day of Wrath, VII:959-961
   Gertrud, VII:960
   Good Mothers, VII:960
   Jesus fra Nasaret, VII:960
   Leaves from Satan's Book, VII:959
   Love One Another, VII:959
   Master of the House, VII:959
   Michael, VII:959, 960
   Once Upon a Time, VII:959
   Ordet, VII:959-961
   Parson's Widow, The, VII:959
   Passion of Joan of Arc, The, VII:959, 960
   President, The, VII:959
   "They Caught the Ferry," VII:961
   Two People, VII:960
   Vampyr, VII:960
Dreyfus affair
   Clemenceau, VII:703, 704
   Fowler, V:825, 827
   Herriot, VIII:1644
   Herzl, V:1102, 1104

Jaurès, V:1222
   Maritain, VIII:2425
   Poincaré, IX:3044, 3045
   Sorel, IX:3463
   Zola, VI:2420, 2421, 2423
Drosophila, VIII:2618-2620
Drusus, I:152
Druyan, Ann, IX:3293
Dryden, John, **IV:424-427,** 1116, 1130
   Absalom and Achitophel, IV:425
   All for Love, IV:425, 426
   Annus Mirabilis, IV:425
   Astraea Redux, IV:424
   Conquest of Granada by the Spaniards, The,
     IV:425
   Essay of Dramatic Poesy, An, IV:425
   Hind and the Panther, The, IV:425
   Indian Emperor, The, IV:424
   Indian Queen, The, IV:424
   MacFlecknoe, IV:425
   Religio Laici, IV:425
   Wild Gallant, The, IV:424
Duarte, Eva. *See* Perón, Eva
Dubcek, Alexander, VII:460, **968-971**
Du Bois, W.E.B., VI:2258, 2338; **VII:963-967,**
   1312; IX:3113, 3943
   Black Reconstruction, VII:965
   Philadelphia Negro, The, VII:964
   Souls of Black Folk, The, VII:964, 965
   Suppression of the African Slave Trade to the
     United States, The, VII:963
Dubos, René J., IX:3834, 3835
Du Camp, Maxime, V:796
Duccio di Buoninsegna, **II:305-308,** 632
   Madonna (Crevole), II:305
   Madonna (Rucellai), II:305, 306
   Maestà, II:305-307
   Duchamp, Marcel, **VII:972-975**
   Bride Stripped Bare by Her Bachelors, Even,
     VII:973
   Fountain, VII:973
   In Advance of the Broken Arm, VII:973
   Kupka, VIII:2037
   Nude Descending a Staircase No. 1, VII:972
   Nude Descending a Staircase No. 2, VII:973
   Sad Eyed Man in a Train, VII:972
Dudley, John. *See* Northumberland, Duke of
Dudley, Robert. *See* Leicester, Earl of
Dudley, Thomas, IV:193
Duggan, Stephen Pierce, VIII:2662
Duhig, James, VI:1482
Dühring, Eugen, V:761

Duke, James Buchanan, **V:704-707**
Dulany, Daniel, IV:250
Dulles, John Foster, **VII:976-979;** IX:3663
Dumas, Alexandre, *père,* **V:708-710;** VI:2303, 2304
   Black Tulip, The, V:709
   Camille, VIII:2143
   Catherine of Cleves, V:708
   Chevalier d'Harmental, Le, V:709
   Christine, V:708
   Count of Monte Cristo, The, V:709; VIII:2227;
     IX:2819
   Ladies of Saint-Cyr, The, V:1163
   Marriage of Convenience, A, V:709
   My Memoirs, V:710
   Three Musketeers, The, IV:387; V:709
   Tour de Nesle, La, V:709
   Twenty Years After, V:709
   Vicomte de Bragelonne, Le, V:709
Dumbarton Oaks, VII:1130, 1131
Dunant, Jean-Henri, **V:711-713**
   Memory of Solferino, A, V:711
Dunbar, Battle of, IV:1127
Dunbar, Paul Laurence, **V:714-717**
   Fanatics, The, V:715
   Folks from Dixie, V:715
   Love of Landry, The, V:715
   Lyrics of Lowly Life, V:715
   Lyrics of the Hearthside, V:715
   Majors and Minors, V:715
   Oak and Ivy, V:714, 715
   "Ode to Ethiopia," V:714
   Sport of Gods, The, V:717
   Strength of Gideon and Other Stories, The,
     V:715
   "Sympathy," V:714
   Uncalled, The, V:715
Dunbar, Samuel, IV:1242
Duncan II, II:291
Duncan, Isadora, VII:919, **980-983,** 1263, 1264;
   VIII:2746
Dundee, Angelo, VII:54
Dunes, Battle of the, IV:380, 703
Dungeness, Battle off, II:134
Dunham, Katherine, **VII:984-987**
   Bamboche, VII:986
   Cabin in the Sky, VII:985
   Carnival of Rhythm, VII:985
   Green Mansions, VII:986
   Journey to Accompong, VII:985, 986
   Ode to Taylor Jones, VII:986
   Pins and Needles, VII:985
   Star Spangled Rhythm, VII:985

Stormy Weather, VII:985
Touch of Innocence, VII:986
Dunkirk, Battle of, VII:45, 46
Dunkirk House, IV:310
Dunn School of Pathology, VII:1173
Duns Scotus, John, **II:309-314;** VIII:1610
Opus Oxiniese, II:310, 313
Quaestiones quodlibetales, II:310, 313
Dunstable, John, **III:227-229**
Quam pulcra es, III:228
Rex seculorum, III:228
Veni Sancti Spiritus, III:228
Duperron, Jacques Davy, III:334
Dupes, Day of the, IV:865
Dupin, Amandine-Aurore-Lucile, Baronne
Dudevant. *See* Sand, George
Duplessis, Maurice, IX:3730
Du Pont, Eleuthère Irénée, **V:718-720**
Du Pont Company. *See* E.I. Du Pont de Nemours
and Company
Durbar, the, VII:820
Dürer, Albrecht, III:61, 200, 201, **230-233;** IV:975;
VIII:1991
Adam and Eve, III:231
Adoration of the Magi, The, III:231
Apocalypse, III:230
Erasmus of Rotterdam, III:231, 248
Feast of the Rose Garlands, The, III:231
Four Apostles, III:231
Four Horsemen of the Apocalypse, The,
III:231
Holy Family with the Butterfly, III:231
Madonna and Child, III:231
Melencolia I, III:231
Saint Jerome Curing the Lion, III:230
Self-Portrait, III:230
*This Present Boke Named Shyp of Folys of the
Worlde,* III:230
Durham, First Earl of, V:117, **721-724;** VI:2322
Report on the Affairs of British North America,
V:721-723
Durham Bull Company, V:704-706
Durkheim, Émile, **VII:988-991**
Division of Labor in Society, The, VII:988, 990
Elementary Forms of the Religious Life, The,
VII:988
Montesquieu and Rousseau, VII:988
Suicide, VII:988
Dusan, Stefan. *See* Stefan Dusan
Duse, Eleonora, VIII:2141, 2142
Dutch East India Company, IV:502, 680, 681,
1313, 1314

Dutch West India Company, IV:644, 645, 1294,
1296
Dvořák, Antonín, **V:725-728;** VIII:1835-1837
Alfred, V:726
Armida, V:727
Bells of Zlonice, V:726
From the Bohemian Forest, V:726
From the New World, V:727
Hussite Overture, V:726
King and Collier, V:726
Moravian Duets, V:726
Requiem Mass, Op. 89, V:727
Rukopis kralovedvorsky, V:726
Rukopis zelenohorsky, V:726
Second Symphony in B flat major, V:726
Slavonic Dances, V:726
Spectre's Bride, The, V:726
Stabat mater, V:726
String Quartet in F minor, Op. 9, V:726
Symphonic Variations for Orchestra, V:726
Symphony in D minor, Op. 13, V:726
Symphony in F, Op. 24, V:726
Symphony in G, Op. 88, V:727
Wanda, V:726
Dworkin, Andrea, VIII:2326
Dwyer, Ada, VIII:2249
Dyrrhachium, Battle of, I:167
Dzhugashvili, Joseph Vissarionovich. *See* Stalin,
Joseph

Eads, James Buchanan, **V:729-731**
Eads Bridge, V:729-731
Eakins, Thomas, **V:732-734**
John Biglin in a Single Scull, V:732
Max Schmitt in a Single Scull, V:732
Ealhmund, II:333
Earhart, Amelia, **VII:992-995**
Fun of It, The, VII:994
Twenty Hours Forty Minutes, VII:992, 994
Early Closing Act of 1904, VII:353
Earp, Wyatt, **V:735-737**
Earth
age of, IV:217
Anaximander, I:50, 51
Anaximenes of Miletus, I:54
Aryabhata, II:89-91
black holes, IX:3367
Brahe, III:78
circumference of, I:304; II:182
density of, IV:263
Empedocles, I:282, 284
Galileo, IV:519, 521, 522

Heraclitus of Ephesus, I:382-385
Kepler, IV:775
magnetic field, V:167, 897
motion of, VII:837; VIII:2236
nuclear winter, IX:3294
origins of life, VII:799; IX:2830, 2831
Peregrinus de Maricourt, II:719-721
Ptolemy, I:712
Pythagoras, I:729
East and West Association, VII:488
Eastern Chin Dynasty, II:640
Eastern Grove Monastery, I:429, 430
Eastern Han Dynasty, I:590
Eastern Orthodoxy, I:119, 121
    Chrysostom, I:185
    Easter, 298-300
    Iconoclastic Controversy, II:544-546
    Leo IX, II:583
    Stefan Dusan, II:845
    Theoleptus of Philadelphia, II:899-901
    Trullan Synod, II:824
    Vladimir I, II:952-954
Easter Uprising, VII:733, 770, 877; IX:2794, 2804,
    4083
East India Act, IV:1102, 1103
Eastman, George, **VII:996-999;** VIII:1457
Eastman School of Music, VIII:1457
East Meets West Foundation, VIII:1593-1595
Eban, Abba, **VII:1000-1003**
Ebenezer Baptist Church, VIII:1971, 1973
Eberhard of Franconia, II:706
Ebers Papyrus, I:445
Eberst, Jacob. *See* Offenbach, Jacques
Ebissa, I:380
Ebner, Ferdinand, VII:476
Éboué, Felix, **VII:1004-1007**
Eccles, Sir John Crew, **VII:1008-1010**
    Facing Reality, VII:1010
    Neurophysicological Basis of the Mind, The,
        VII:1009
    Physiology of Nerve Cells, The, VII:1009
    Physiology of Synapses, The, VII:1009
    Self and Its Brain, The, VII:1010
Ecclesiastes, I:297, 801
Ecevit, Bülent, VIII:1814
Eck, Johann, III:443, 445, 504
Eckener, Hugo, **VII:1011-1014**
Eckstine, Billy, IX:2882
École Polytechnique, IV:975, 977
ecology
    Cousteau, VII:781
    Geiger, VII:1327

Linnaeus, IV:848
    Theophrastus, I:874, 875
Economic Journal, VIII:1953, 1954
Economic Recovery Tax Act of 1981, VII:949
Economist, The, VI:2086
Eddington, Sir Arthur Stanley, VIII:2157,
    2158
Eddy, Mary Baker, **V:738-742**
    Christian Healing, V:739
    Science and Health, V:740, 741
Eddy, Richard M., VI:1597
Edecon, I:126; II:685
Edelman, Marian Wright, VII:713, 714
Eden, Anthony, VII:531, **1015-1019,** 1063;
    VIII:2342
Eden, Garden of, II:500; III:72
Eden, Robert, IV:250
Edessa, II:560
Edinburgh, Treaty of, II:184, 185, 187, 188
Edinburgh, University of, IV:9, 882
Edinburgh Review, The
    Brougham, V:314
    Carlyle, V:416
    Jeffrey, V:1224-1226
    Macauley, VI:1427-1429
    Mill, James, VI:1556
    Mill, John Stuart, VI:1560
Edison, Thomas Alva, **V:743-747;** VI:2180, 2219,
    2360; VII:1186; VIII:2278
Edison Central Electric Station, IX:3020
Edmeston, James, VI:2002
Edo, V:1117, 1118
Education Act of 1870, V:804
Education Act of 1902, VII:173
Education Act of 1944, VII:529-532
Edward I, **II:322-325**
    Boniface VIII, II:172
    Bruce, II:185, 187
    Circumspecte agatis, II:322
    De viris religiosis, II:322
    Edward II, II:326
    Nisi prius, II:322
    Pecham, II:715, 716
    Statute of Wales, II:323
    Wallace, II:955-957
    Westminster II, II:322
    Westminster III, II:322
Edward II, II:187, 188, **326-328,** 329
Edward III, II:294-296, **329-332,** 786
Edward IV, **III:234-236**
    Fortescue, III:268
    Henry VI, III:342, 343

Henry VII, III:345
Louis XI, III:434
Richard III, III:647, 649-652
Warwick, III:775, 776
Edward V, III:650
Edward VI, **III:237-240**
Coverdale, III:194
Cranmer, III:204, 205
Gardiner, III:292, 293
Grey, III:318-320
Mary I, III:479
Tudor family, III:733
Edward VII, VI:2307, 2309; **VII:1020-1022,** 1339, 1340
Edward VIII, VII:170, 1062, 1345; VIII:2641; **IX:4025-407**
Edwards, Jonathan, **IV:428-431**
Faithful Narrative of the Surprising Work of God, A, IV:429
Freedom of Will, IV:430, 431
"Nature of True Virtue, The," IV:430
"Sinners in the Hands of an Angry God," IV:429
Treatise Concerning Religious Affections, A, IV:429-431
Edward the Confessor, **II:315-318,** 426, 997
Edward the Elder, **II:319-321**
EEOC. *See* Equal Employment Opportunity Commission
Efros, Israel, II:549
Égalité, Philippe, IV:814, 815, 1050
Egas Moniz, António, **VII:1023-1025**
Egbert, **II:333-335**
Egerton, Sir Thomas, IV:418
Egyptian National Revolution, VIII:2355
Ehrenfels, Christian von, **VII:1026-1030**
Comogony, VII:1026
Kampf des Prometheus, Der, VII:1027
Mutter des Legionärs, Die, VII:1027
Sängerweihe, VII:1027
Sternenbraut, Die, VII:1027
System der Werttheorie, VII:1027
Ehrlich, Eugen, **VII:1029-1031**
Fundamental Principles of the Sociology of Law, VII:1030
Ehrlich, Paul, V:183; **VII:1032-1034**
Eichmann, Adolf, VII:99, 100; IX:3984, 3985
Eickemeyer, Rudolf, VI:2121, 2122
E.I. Du Pont de Nemours and Company, V:718-720
Eielson, Carl Ben, IX:4000
Eiffel Tower, VIII:1693
1807, Embargo of, IV:719

1809, Plan of, VI:2090
1812, War of
Benton, V:195
Biddle, V:225
Burr, V:372
Calhoun, V:394
Clay, V:507
Decatur, V:634-636
Gallatin, V:861, 862
gunpowder, V:719
Harrison, V:1062
Houston, V:1137
Jackson, V:1196
Key, VI:1281
Madison, IV:888, 889
naval weapons, V:856
Perry, VI:1764
Pike, IV:1096
Scott, VI:2009
Tecumseh, VI:2204
Thayer, VI:2223, 2225
Van Buren, VI:2292
White House attack, VI:1465
Webster, VI:2345
1830, Revolution of, VI:1817, 1917
1832, Convention of, V:96
1833, Convention of, V:96
1837, Panic of, V:226; VI:2294
1848, Revolutions of
Bakunin, V:112
Beust, V:222-224
Blanc, V:260, 261
Courbet, V:565
Lassalle, VI:1324
Michelet, VI:1549
Proudhon, VI:1818
Stein, VI:2117
Tocqueville, VI:2239
1850, Compromise of
Brown, V:322
Clay, V:510
Davis, V:615
Douglas, V:692, 693
Houston, V:1138
Seward, VI:2037
Stephens, VI:2129
Tubman, VI:2265
Webster, VI:2345
1857, Mutiny of, V:34
1868, Treaty of, VI:2070
1870, Revolution of, V:113
1873, Panic of, V:1076; VIII:2480

1893, Panic of, V:513, 515; VI:1582
1898, Generation of, IX:3784
Eighteenth Amendment, VI:1633
Eightfold Path, I:145
Eighty Years' War, IV:500-502
Einhorn, David, VI:2401
Einstein, Albert, **VII:1035-1038**
    Bohr, VII:347
    Broglie, VII:473
    Compton, VII:746
    Hawking, VIII:1580, 1582, 1583
    Lagrange, IV:785
    lasers, VII:215
    Lemaître, VIII:2157, 2159
    Lorentz, VIII:2236
    Stark, IX:3491
Einstein Tower, VIII:2487
Einthoven, Willem, **VII:1039-1042**
Eire Constitution of 1937, IX:2805
Eisenhower, Dwight D., **VII:1043-1046**
    atomic energy, IX:3103
    Bradley, VII:403, 404
    Burger, VII:509
    Conant, VII:750
    Crusade in Europe, VII:1043
    Dulles, VII:977
    Graham, VIII:1448
    Hobby, VIII:1704, 1705
    Johnson, VIII:1867
    Khrushchev, VIII:1963
    Lippmann, VIII:2205
    McCarthy, VIII:2301, 2302
    Macmillan, VIII:2341
    Marshall, VIII:2431
    Montgomery, VIII:2603
    Moses, VIII:2635
    Nehru, VIII:2711
    Nixon, VIII:2758
    Owens, IX:2863
    Rundstedt, IX:3262
    Smith, IX:3447
    Stevenson, IX:3524, 3525
    Taft, IX:3592, 3593
    Truman, IX:3743
    Warren, IX:3889
    Zhukov, IX:4117
Eisenstein, Sergei, **VII:1047-1050**
    Alexander Nevsky, VII:1048, 1049
    Behzin Meadow, VII:1048
    Die Walküre, VII:1048
    Enough Stupidity in Every Wise Man, VII:1047
    Film Sense, The, VII:1048

    General Line, The, VII:1048
    Ivan the Terrible, VII:1048, 1049; IX:3087
    October: Or Ten Days That Shook the World,
        VII:1048
    Potemkin, VII:1048, 1049
    Protivogazy, VII:1047
    Que viva Mexico!, VII:1048
    Romance Sentimentale, VII:1048
    Strike, VII:1047-1049
    Thunder Over Mexico, VII:1048
Elchingen, Battle of, VI:1646
Elder, Louisine, V:435
Elea, I:596, 597, 955
Eleanor of Aquitaine, **II:336-339,** 782
Eleatics, I:249-251, 955
Eleazar, I:3, 4
Eleazar ben Arariah, I:27, 28
Electrical and Musical Instruments Limited. *See*
    EMI
Electric Boat Company, V:1125
electric lighting
    Edison, V:743, 745, 746
    Swan, VI:2179-2181
    Westinghouse, VI:2358, 2360, 2361
electricity
    Becquerel, V:166-168
    Faraday, V:767, 768, 770
    Franklin, IV:493, 494
    Galvani, IV:523-525
    Guericke, IV:586-588
    Helmholtz, V:1091
    Henry, V:1095
    Kelvin, VI:1270
    Maxwell, VI:1512
    Picard, IX:2995
    Popov, VI:1806-1808
    Siemens family, VI:2066-2069
    Steinmetz, VI:2121, 2122, 2124
    Tesla, VI:2219, 2220, 2222
    Volta, IV:1387, 1389, 1390
Electric Telegraph Company, V:557, 558
electromagnetism
    absorption spectra, VII:214
    Becquerel, V:166-168
    Broglie, VII:472
    Faraday, V:767, 768, 770
    Hawking, VIII:1582
    Henry, V:1094
    Kelvin, VI:1271
    Lorentz, VIII:2235-2237
    Maxwell, VI:1512, 1513
    Popov, VI:1807

electron
 Bohr's atomic model, VIII:1617
 cyclotron development, VII:379, 380; VIII:2121
 diffraction, VIII:2698
 dissociation hypothesis, VI:1412
 exclusion principle, IX:2923-2925
 K-capture, IX:4091
 phase stability, VIII:2337
 photoelectric effect, VIII:2539
 Sommerfeld, VII:300
 theory of, VIII:2235-2237
 Urey, IX:3788
 wave-matter composition of, VII:472-474;
  IX:3363
Electronic Data Systems, IX:2973, 2974
electronic music, IX:3542, 3794-3796
Elementary Education Act of 1870, V:988
elementary-particle physics, IX:4090-4092
Eleutherius, I:257, 258, 448
Elgar, Sir Edward, **VII:1051-1054**
 Black Knight, The, VII:1052
 Caractacus, VII:1052
 Cockaigne Overture, VII:1053
 Dream Gerontius, The, VII:1052
 Falstaff, VII:1053
 Froissart, VII:1051
 In the South, VII:1053
 Light of Life, The, VII:1052
 Pomp and Circumstance, VII:1053
 Scenes from the Saga of King Olaf, VII:1052
 Symphony No. 1 in A-flat Major, Op. 55,
  VII:1053
 Symphony No. 2 in E-flat Major, Op. 63, VII:1053
 Variations on an Original Theme ("Enigma"),
  VII:1052
 Violin Concerto in B Minor, Op. 61, VII:1053
Eli, I:746
Eliade, Mircea, **VII:1055-1057; IX:3831**
 Forbidden Forest, The, VII:1056
 History of Religious Ideas, A, VII:1057
 Huliganii, VII:1055
 Isabel si apele diavolului, VII:1056
 Sacred and the Profane, The, VII:1055
 Salazar si revolutia în Portugalia, VII:1056
Elijah ben Solomon, **IV:432-434**
 Be'ur ha-Gra, IV:433
Eliodoro, Stanza d', III:643
Eliot, Charles William, **V:748-750**
Eliot, George, **V:751-754**
 Adam Bede, V:752, 753
 Daniel Deronda, V:753
 Felix Holt, Radical, V:752

Life of Jesus, The, V:751
Middlemarch, V:753
Mill on the Floss, The, V:752
Romola, V:752
Scenes of Clerical Life, V:752
Silas Marner, V:752
Spanish Gypsy, The, V:752
Eliot, John, **IV:435-438**
 Bay Psalm Book, IV:435
 Indian Grammar, The, IV:437
Eliot, T.S., **VII:1058-1061**
 Andrewes, IV:48
 Ash Wednesday, VII:1059
 Barnes, VII:201
 "Burnt Norton," VII:1059
 Cocktail Party, The, VII:1058, 1060
 Confidential Clerk, The, VII:1060
 "Dry Salvages, The," VII:1059
 "East Coker," VII:1059
 Elder Statesman, The, VII:1060
 Ezra Pound, VII:1058
 Family Reunion, The, VII:1059
 Fitzgerald, VII:1163
 Four Quartets, VII:1059; VIII:1506
 H.D., VIII:1506
 "Little Gidding," VII:1059
 "Love Song of J. Alfred Prufrock, The,"
  VII:1058
 Murder in the Cathedral, VII:1058, 1059
 Old Possum's Book of Practical Cats, VII:1060
 Pirandello, IX:3015
 Prufrock and Other Observations, VII:1058
 Rock, The, VII:1058
 Sacred Wood, The, VII:1058
 Sweeney Agonistes, VII:1058
 Villon, III:766
 Waste Land, The, IV:637; VII:791, 1058-1060
Elis, I:625, 626
Elisha ben Abuyah, I:28
Elizabeth I, **III:241-245**
 Bacon, III:41
 Catholic persecution, III:257
 Cecil, III:147-149
 Cranmer, III:204, 206
 Cromwell, III:209
 Frobisher, III:278
 James I, IV:699
 Mary I, III:480, 482
 Mary, Queen of Scots, III:475-477
 Parker, III:588-590
 Raleigh, III:638, 639
 Salisbury, III:660, 661

Sidney, III:691-693
Tudor family, III:733, 734
Elizabeth II, **VII:1062-1065**
Britten, VII:469
Graham, VIII:1449
Macmillan, VIII:2343
Walton, IX:3874
Elizabethan Settlement, III:148, 149
Elizabeth of Hungary, Saint, **II:340-343**
Eliezer, Israel ben. *See* Ba'al Shem Tov
Ellicott, Andrew, IV:88, 90
Ellicott, George, IV:88, 90
Ellington, Duke, **VII:1066-1069**
Black, Brown, and Beige, VII:1068
"Mood Indigo," VII:1068
"Portraits," VII:1066
"Take the A Train," VII:1068
Elliot, Charles, VI:1377, 1378
Elliot, Jesse Duncan, VI:1764, 1765
Ellis, Charles D., VII:635
Ellis, Havelock, **VII:1070-1073**
Dance of Life, The, VII:1071
My Life, VII:1070
Sexual Inversion, VII:1071
Studies in the Psychology of Sex, VII:1071
Ellis, John McTaggert, VIII:2605, 2606
Ellison, Ralph, VIII:1868
Ellsworth, Lincoln, VII:534; IX:4001
Elpinice, I:198, 676
Elsheimer, Adam, IV:317, 318
Éluard, Paul, **VII:1074-1077;** IX:3067-3069
Capital of Pain, VII:1075
Dessous d'une vie, Les, VII:1075
Devoir et l'inquiétude, Le, VII:1074
Dialogues des inutiles, VII:1074
Livre ouvert I, 1938-1940, Le, VII:1076
Mourir de ne pas mourir, VII:1075, 1076
Nécessités de la vie et les conséquences des rêves, VII:1075
Phénix, Le, VII:1076
Poèmes pour la paix, VII:1074
Poésie ininterrompue, VII:1076
Poetry and Truth, VII:1076
Premiers poèmes, VII:1074
Répétitions, VII:1075
Temps déborde, Le, VII:1076
Emancipation Proclamation, V:479, 886; VI:1383, 1773, 2172
Embargo Act, IV:888; V:343; VI:2147
Embargo of 1807. *See* 1807, Embargo of
embryology
Baer, V:109-111

Diocles of Carystus, I:261
Empedocles, I:284
Harvey, IV:629
Herophilus, I:400
Lankester, VI:1316, 1317
Malpighi, IV:892
Morgan, VIII:2618
Spallanzani, IV:1261
Emergency Society for German Science, VIII:1511
Emeric, II:575
Emerson, John, VI:1999, 2000
Emerson, Ralph Waldo, **V:755-759**
Agassiz, V:31, 32
"American Scholar, The," V:757, 758
Bancroft, V:126
Boston Unitarianism, V:472
"Brahma," V:758
"Character of Socrates, The," V:755
Conduct of Life, The, V:755, 758
"Days," V:758
"Divinity School Address," V:757, 758
English Traits, V:758
Essays, V:757
Essays: Second Series, V:757
Frost, VII:1252
Fuller, V:849, 850
Lazarus, VI:1334, 1336
Letters and Social Aims, V:758
Nature, V:755, 757
Parker, VI:1730
Poems, V:758
"Poet, The," V:758
"Present State of Ethical Philosophy, The," V:758
Representative Men, V:755, 758
"Self-Reliance," V:757
"Snow Storm, The," V:758
Society and Solitude, V:758
"Sphinx, The," V:758
"Terminus," V:758
Thoreau, VI:2234
Whitman, VI:2370, 2371
Emerson, Roy Stanley, VIII:2109-2111
EMI, VIII:1751-1753
EMIDEC 1100, VIII:1751
Emin Pasha, VI:2103
Emmanuel College, IV:371
Empedocles, I:260, 261, **282-286,** 512
On Nature, I:282, 284
Purifications, I:282, 284
Empire, VI:1731, 1732

Empiricism
    Aretaeus of Cappadocia, I:81
    Berkeley, IV:114-116
    Boyle, IV:185
    Bradley, V:291
    Celsus, I:173
    Comte, V:543
    Condillac, IV:345, 346
    Duns Scotus, II:312
    Green, V:987
    Leibniz, IV:829
    Locke, IV:854-858
    Pyrrhon of Elis, I:724, 725
Empiricus, Sextus, I:725
Enabling Act of 1956, VIII:1755
Enciso, Martín Fernández de, III:45
Encyclopaedia Britannica, V:767; VII:49, 301;
        VII:1220; VIII:1801
Enders, John F., IX:3305
Endoradiosonde, IX:4127
Endymion, V:636
energy, conservation of
    Gay-Lussac, V:898
    Grove, V:1011-1013
    Heimholtz, V:1089-1091
    Kelvin, VI:1270
    Bothe, VII:379
    Planck, IX:3033
Enfantin, Prosper, VI:1355
Engelhardt, Moritz von, VIII:1557
Engels, Friedrich, **V:760-762;** VI:1324,
        1325, 1492
    Condition of the Working Class in England, The,
        V:760; VI:1369
    Herr Eugen Dühring's Revolution in Science,
        V:761; VII:291
    *Origin of the Family, Private Property, and the
        State, The,* V:761
    Socialism: Utopian and Scientific, V:761
Engel v. Vitale, VII:322
England, Bank of, IV:1066-1068; VI:1396
England, Church of
    Andrewes, IV:46-49
    Anne, IV:50, 52, 53
    Anselm, II:72-74
    Baxter, IV:98, 99
    Becket, II:128-130
    Boleyn, III:66, 68, 69
    Bolingbroke, IV:157-161
    Bunyan, IV:218, 219
    Charles I, IV:280
    Clarendon, IV:308, 310

    Cranmer, III:204-206
    Cromwell, III:208, 209
    Education Act of 1870, V:804
    Ferrar, IV:462-464
    Gardiner, III:291-293
    George I, IV:533
    Gladstone, V:935, 936
    Henry II, II:446-448
    Henry VIII, III:349, 351
    James II, IV:703-705
    Lancaster, VI:1310
    Laud, IV:797-799
    Madison, IV:886
    Manning, VI:1476-1478
    More, III:533-536
    Newman, VI:1641, 1643, 1644
    Parker, III:588-590
    Pusey, VI:1828-1831
    Pym, IV:1141
    Ridley, III:654-656
    Swift, IV:1305, 1307
    Tyndale, III:736, 737
    Williams, IV:1451
English Bible, III:193-195, 204-206
English Bill of Rights, IV:940
English Civil Wars
    Baxter, IV:98, 99
    Blake, IV:132, 134, 135
    Charles I, IV:279-281
    Charles II, IV:283
    Cromwell, IV:380
    Fairfax, IV:446-449
    Frederick Henry, IV:501
    Hobbes, IV:664, 665
    James II, IV:703
    Lambert, IV:789-792
    Monck, IV:971-973
    Pride, IV:1126-1128
    Scotland, IV:239
    Sydenham, IV:1310
    Winthrop, IV:1464
English common law
    Bentham, IV:107-109
    Blackstone, IV:129-131
    Bracton, II:178-180
    Coke, IV:329-334
    Hale, IV:596-598
    Kent, VI:1278, 1279
    Mansfield, IV:907
English Commonwealth Navy, II:132-135
English Historical Review, V:12
English Opera Group, VII:470

English Reform Bill of 1832. *See* Reform Bill of 1832
English Revolution, IV:308-311
Ennius, Quintus, **I:287-289**
   Ambracia, I:288
   Annals, I:288, 289
   Miscellanies, I:288
   Sabinae, I:288
Enrile, Juan Ponce, VIII:2421
Enryakuji, III:571
Entente Cordiale of 1904, V:1131; IX:3691
Enver Pasha, **VII:1078-1082**
Environmental Protection Agency, VII:586
Enzo, II:363, 364
EPA. *See* Environmental Protection Agency
Epaminondas, **I:290-294**
Ephesus, I:626, 941
Ephesus, Council of, I:866
Ephetae, I:281
Ephialtes, I:609
Ephraimites, I:246
Ephron, Nora, **VII:1083-1086**
   All the President's Men, VII:1084
   Cookie, VII:1084
   Crazy Salad, VII:1084
   Heartburn, VII:1084
   My Blue Heaven, VII:1085
   Perfect Gentlemen, VII:1084
   Scribble Scribble, VII:1084
   Sleepless in Seattle, VII:1085
   This Is My Life, VII:1085
   Wallflower at the Orgy, The, VII:1083
   When Harry Met Sally, VII:1084
Epicurus, I:87, 251, **295-298,** 511, 512
   On Nature, I:296
Epidus, I:926
Epinician ode, I:787
Epstein, Brian, VII:226, 228
Epstein, Sir Jacob, **VII:1087-1090**
   Adam, VII:1089
   Christ, VII:1088
   Christ in Majesty, VII:1089
   Consummatum Est, VII:1089
   Ecce Homo, VII:1089
   Genesis, VII:1089
   Head of an Infant, VII:1087
   Lazarus, VII:1089
   Lucifer, VII:1089
   Madonna and Child, VII:1089
   Memorial to W.H. Hudson, VII:1088
   Rock Drill, VII:1088
   Social Consciousness, VII:1089
   "Strand" statues, VII:1087, 1088
   Sun God, VII:1089
   T.U.C. War Memorial, VII:1089
   Venus, VII:1088
Equal Employment Opportunity Commission, IX:3657, 3658
Equal Rights Amendment, VIII:2537; IX:2919, 2920, 2922, 3447; IX:3521
Erasistratus, **I:299-302**
Erasmus, Desiderius, **III:246-249**
   Bucer, III:101
   Colet, III:169
   Colloquies of Erasmus, The, III:248
   De Copia, III:247
   Education of a Christian Prince, The, III:247
   Holbein the Younger, III:358
   Lucian, I:509
   Luther, III:445, 446
   Manual of the Christian Knight, The, III:246
   Marguerite of Navarre, III:467
   Melanchthon, III:503
   More, III:533, 535
   Praise of Folly, The, III:247, 248
   Proverbs or Adages, III:246, 247
   Scaliger, III:671
   Valla, III:741
   Vitoria, III:768
   Zwingli, III:791
Eratosthenes of Cyrene, **I:303-306**
   Ancient Comedy, I:305
   Ariston, I:303
   Biography of Arsinoe III, I:305
   Chronological Tables, I:305
   Erigone, I:303
   Euclid, I:308
   Geographica, I:304
   Hermes, I:303
   Hipparchus, I:409
   On Means, I:305
   On the Measurement of the Earth, I:304
   Platonicus, I:303
Ercker, Lazarus, III:3
Erdrich, Louise, **VII:1091-1093**
   Baptism of Desire, VII:1093
   Beet Queen, The, VII:1091, 1092
   Bingo Palace, The, VII:1092
   Broken Cord, The, VII:1091, 1093
   Crown of Columbus, The, VII:1093
   Jacklight, VII:1091
   Love Medicine, VII:1091, 1092
   Tracks, VII:1092
   Yellow Raft in Blue Water, A, VII:1093

Erfurt Program, VII:292

Ergriffenheit, VII:1244

Erhard, Ludwig, **VII:1094-1097**

Erie, Lake, VI:1764

Erie Canal, V:517, 519, 520

Eriksson. *See* Leif Eriksson

Erik the Red, II:577

Erkenntnis, VII:583

Ernst, Max, VII:1075, **1098-1101;** VIII:2548

    After Me, Sleep, VII:1100

    Coloradeau of Medusa, VII:1100

    Elephant Célèbes, The, VII:1099

    Eye of Silence, The, VII:1100

    Flowers and Fish, VII:1098

    King Playing with the Queen, The, VII:1100

    Landscape with Sun, VII:1098

    Lunar Asparagus, VII:1100

    Marriage of Heaven and Earth, The, VII:1100

    Oedipus Rex, VII:1099, 1100

    Pietà, VII:1099

    Two Children Are Menaced by a Nightingale,
      VII:1099

    Two Sisters, VII:1099

    Ubu Imperator, VII:1099

    Vox Angelica, VII:1100

Ernst, Wilhelm. *See* Saxe-Weimar, Duke of

Ernst Heinkel Flugzeugwerke, VIII:1614, 1615

Errors, Syllabus of, VI:1784

Erskine, First Baron, **IV:439-442**

Erzberger, Matthias, **VII:1102-1106**

Esarhaddon, I:105, 111

Eschenbach, Wolfram von. *See* Wolfram von
    Eschenbach

Esenin, Sergei Aleksandrovich, VII:982

Eshkol, Levi, VIII:2473, 2474

Eshnunna, I:362

Eskimos. *See* Inuits

Esma'il I, III:38, 39, 52

Esperanto, IV:385; VII:583

Esquiline Hill, I:520, 521

Esquire magazine, VII:1083, 1084

Essenes, I:467

Essex, First Earl of, III:41, 148, 149, 639, 691

Essex, Second Earl of, III:660, 661

Este, House of, III:32-34, 60, 710

Esterházy, Miklós József, IV:639

Étampes, Madame d', III:153

Etelköz, II:86, 87

Ethelflaed, II:320

Ethelred II, the Unready, II:201, 202, 315,
    344-346, 688

Ethelweard, Chronicle of, II:319

Ethelwold, II:319

Ethelwulf, II:334

Ethical Culture Society, V:26, 27, 29

Étudiant noir, L', VII:631

Euchidas, I:622

Eucken, Rudolf Christoph, **VII:1106-1108;**
    IX:3347

    *Geschichte und Kritik der Grundbegriffe der
      Gegenwart,* VII:1106

    Knowledge and Life, VII:1107

    Meaning and Value of Life, The, VII:1107

    Mensch und Welt, VII:1107

    Problem of Human Life, The, VII:1106

    Truth of Religion, The, VII:1106

Euclid, **I:307-309**

    Abu Wefa, II:20

    Apollonius of Perga, I:73

    Data, I:307

    Elements, I:307, 308, 310, 311, 729; II:63

    Hypatia, I:437

    Lobachevsky, VI:1403-1405

    Optics, I:308

    Phaenomena, I:308

    Sectio canonis, I:308

Euclidian geometry, VI:1403-1405

Eudemos, I:339

Eudoxus of Cnidus, **I:310-313**

    Enoptron, I:312

    Phainomena, I:312

Eugene IV, III:559

Eugene of Savoy, IV:655-657

Eugenius, I:871

Eugenius III, II:357, 358, 474

Eukles, I:622

Euler, Leonhard, **IV:443-445,** 884

    Institutiones calculi differentialis, IV:445

    Institutiones calculi integralis, IV:445

    Introductio in analysis in infinitorum,
      IV:445

    *Letters of Euler to a German Princess, on
      Different Subjects in Physics and Philosophy,*
      VII:318

    *Mechanica sive motus scientia analytice
      exposita,* IV:445

    *Theoria motus corporum solidorum seu
      rigidorum,* IV:445

Eumenes, I:60, 767

Eunomia, rule of, I:646

Eunomius, I:353

Eupalinus of Megara, **I:314-316**

Eupatrids, I:9

Euratom, VIII:2585

Euripides, **I:317-321**
  Alcestis, I:317, 807
  Andromache, I:318
  Aristophanes, I:91
  Bacchae, The, I:319
  Children of Herakles, The, I:318
  Electra, I:318, 808
  Hecuba, I:318
  Helen, I:319
  Hippolytus, I:318
  Ion, I:319
  Iphigenia in Aulis, I:319
  Iphigenia in Tauris, I:319
  Medea, I:317, 318, 807
  Orestes, I:319
  Peliades, I:317
  Suppliants, The, I:318
  Trojan Women, The, I:318
Europe, Council of, VIII:1645
European Atomic Energy Community, IX:3477
European Center of Nuclear Research. *See* CERN
European Coal and Steel Community, VIII:2584,
  2585; IX:3477
European Common Market, VIII:2585; IX:3053,
  3054
European Court of Human Rights, VII:611
European Defense Community, VIII:2585
European Economic Commission, VIII:2672
European Economic Community
  Attlee, VII:139
  Heath, VIII:1606-1608
  Israel, VII:1002
  Major, VIII:2369-2371
  Spaak, IX:3477
  Wilson, IX:4017, 4018
European Economic Cooperation, Organization of,
  VIII:1529
European Monetary System, VIII:2585
European Nuclear Research, Center for. *See* CERN
European Recovery Program. *See* Marshall Plan
Eurydice, VI:1685
Euryphon, I:412
Eusebius of Caesarea, **I:322-325**
  Chronicle, I:322; III:672, 673
  Ecclesiastical History, I:322-324, 447, 448
  Helena, I:375
  Hippolytus of Rome, I:417, 418
  Life of Constantine, I:227, 323, 375
Eustace, II:849
Eutaw Springs, Battle of, IV:576
Euthymenes, I:370
Euterpe, V:1003

evangelism
  Graham, VIII:1447-1449
  Moody, VI:1575-1577
  Pusey, VI:1828, 1830
  Sunday, IX:3582-3584
  Wesley, IV:1426-1429
  Wilberforce, IV:1435-1438
Evangelical Synod, VIII:2735
Evans, Mary Ann. *See* Eliot, George
Evatt, Herbert Vere, **VII:1109-1111**
  Conveyancing Precedents and Forms, VII:1109
  King and His Dominion Governors, The,
    VII:1110
Eve. *See* Adam and Eve
Everest, Mount, VIII:1662-1664, 2507
Everett, Edward, V:126; VI:1772
Evert, Chris, **VII:1112-1114;** VIII:2703
Evesham, Battle of, II:646
Evian Conference, VIII:2472
evolution, theory of
  Agassiz, V:32
  Baer, V:110
  Beecher, V:175
  Bergson, VII:283, 284
  Buffon, IV:215-217
  Cuvier, V:589-591
  Darwin, V:606, 608, 609
  Empedocles, I:284
  Gray, V:979, 980
  Haeckel, V:1018, 1020, 1021
  Huxley, V:1172-1174
  Leakey, VIII:2145-2148
  Linnaeus, IV:848
  Monkey Trial, VII:481, 840
  Oparin, IX:2830, 2831
  Spencer, VI:2087, 2088
  Teilhard de Chardin, IX:3628
  Tennyson, VI:2211
  Weismann, VI:2350
evolutionary socialism, VI:1323, 2122
Ewing, Thomas, VI:2059
Exchequer, II:444; IV:309; VII:121, 122, 168, 532
Exclusion Crisis of 1679-1681, IV:1230
Execestides, I:803
Execration Texts, I:774
existentialism
  Beauvoir, VII:230-232
  Bellow, VII:247
  Camus, VII:553-555
  Hardy, V:1043
  Heidegger, VIII:1610-1612
  Hesse, VIII:1650-1653

Ibsen, V:1178
Jaspers, VIII:1843-1845
Kafka, VIII:1902
Kierkegaard, VI:1284, 1286, 1287
Kleist, VI:1294, 1295
Marcel, VIII:2407-2409
Merleau-Ponty, VIII:2500-2507
Montaigne, III:526
Ortega y Gasset, IX:2844
Parmenides, I:597, 598
psychiatry, VII:330
Rouault, IX:3251
Sartre, IX:3327, 3329, 3330
Schelling, VI:1972-1974
Teilhard de Chardin, IX:3629
Unamuno y Jugo, IX:3783-3785
Exner, Sigmund, VII:1235
Exodus, I:1, 3, 4
Expiatory Church of the Sagrada Familia,
    VII:1316, 1317
Explorer I, VII:111
Expressionism
Frankenthaler, VII:1208
Kandinsky, VII:1903-1905
Kirchner, VIII:1991-1993
Kokoschka, VIII:2012-2015
Krasner, VIII:2023-2025
Martin, VIII:2437-2439
Mondrian, VIII:2577
Pollock, IX:3048-3050
See also Blue Rider movement
Expressive Dance Movement, VIII:2058-2060
Extraordinary Arab Summit, VIII:1794
Eyck, Hubert van, **III:250-253**
Ghent Altarpiece, III:251, 252
Heures de Turin, III:250, 251
Three Marys at the Sepulcher, The, III:251
Eyck, Jan van, II:834; **III:250-253,** 778, 779
Arnolfini Wedding, The, III:252
Ghent Altarpiece, III:251, 252
Heures de Turin, III:250, 251
Madonna with Chancellor Rolin, III:252
Man with the Red Turban, III:250
Eylau, Battle of, VI:1646
Eymard, Pierre-Julien, VI:1900
Ezekiel, **I:326-329,** 570; II:10
Ezhov, Nikolai, VIII:2377
Ezra, **I:330-333**

Fabian, John, IX:3179
Fabian Society, V:212; VIII:1707, 1708; IX:2871,
    3399, 3400, 3402, 3905-3907, 3939, 3940

Fabius, **I:334-337,** 365
fables
Aesop, I:13-15
Callimachus, I:156
Hyginus, I:398
La Fontaine, IV:781-783
Phaedrus, I:618-620
Fabricius, IV:626, 628
Fabrizi, Aldo, VII:1141
Factory Acts, V:458, 678, 996; VI:1709
Fahd, **VII:1115-1117;** IX:4080, 4081
Fahd Plan, VII:1115
Faidherbe, Louis, **V:763-766**
Fairbanks, Douglas, Jr., VIII:1638
Fair Deal, IX:3740, 3743
Fairfax, Third Baron, **IV:446-449;** 789, 790,
    1126
Fairfax Resolves, IV:926
Fairhair, Harald, II:688
Fair Labor Standards Act, IX:2963
fairy tales, V:58-60, 1006-1008, 1162-1164
Faisal, **VII:1118-1121**
Faisal I, **VII:1122-1126**
Faisal II, VIII:1793, 2695
Fakhr al-Din al-Razi, **II:347-349**
Kitab al-tafsir al-kabir, II:348
Muhassal, II:348
Fa Koli, II:863, 864
Falkland, Lord, IV:308
Falkland Islands, III:213; IX:2959, 3651
Falköping, Battle of, II:627
Fall, Albert B., VIII:1551, 1552
Falla, Manuel de, **VII:1127-1129**
amor brujo, El, VII:1127, 1128
Atlántida, L', VII:1128, 1129
Four Spanish Pieces, VII:1127
Noches en los jardines de Espana, VII:1127,
    1128
Three Cornered Hat, The, VII:1127
vida breve, La, VII:1127, 1128
Fallen Timbers, Battle of, VI:2204
Fallingwater, IX:4061
Fallopio, Gabriello, III:756
Fallot, VI:1817
Falloux Law, VI:2227
Falstaff, I:659, 660
FAMOUS, Project, VII:180
Famous Players-Lasky Company, VII:897;
    VIII:1415; IX:3006, 3008
Fan Chung-yen, II:709, 710
Fang Hsuan-ling, II:877, 879
Fan Li, II:918

Faraday, Michael, **V:767-771**
  Chemical History of a Candle, The, V:768
  Edison, V:743
  Kelvin, VI:1269-1271
  Maxwell, VI:1512, 1513
  Nernst, VIII:2713
  Various Forces of Nature, The, V:768
Farington, Joseph, V:547
Farinier, William, II:683
Farm Security Administration, VIII:2084, 2085;
    IX:3861
Farm Workers Association, VIII:1762-1764
Farnese, Alessandro, **III:254-256**
Farnese Gallery, III:126, 127
Farnsworth House, VIII:2523
Farragut, David G., V:656, **772-775**
Farrand, Beatrix Jones, **VII:1130-1132**
Farrell, Edelmiro J., IX:2970
Fars Province, II:806, 807
Fascism
  Croce, VII:801, 802
  De Gasperi, VII:863
  Franco, VII:1201
  Futurism, VII:342
  Gentile, VII:1336-1338
  Hellman's plays, VIII:1622
  Hopkins, VIII:1736
  Lukács, VIII:2274
  Mann, VIII:2393
  Montale, VIII:2592
  Mosca, VIII:2630-2632
  Mussolini, VIII:2667-2670
  Pirelli, IX:3021
  Sorel, IX:3464
  Tunisia, VII:391
  Visconti's films, IX:3818
Fatah, al-, VII:90-92, 1120
Fatamids, II:7, 68, 69
Fatimah of Cordova, II:491
Faulkner, William, VII:283, **1133-1136;** VIII:2626
  Absalom, Absalom!, VII:1134
  As I Lay Dying, VII:1134
  Fable, A, VII:1135
  Flags in the Dust, VII:1133, 1134
  Go Down, Moses, VII:1135
  Hamlet, The, VII:1135
  Intruder in the Dust, VII:1135
  Light in August, VII:1134
  Mansion, The, VII:1135
  Marble Faun, The, VII:1133
  Mosquitoes, VII:1133
  Pylon, VII:1134

  Reivers, The, VII:1135
  Sanctuary, VII:1134, 1135
  Sartoris, VII:1134
  Soldiers' Pay, VII:1133
  Sound and the Fury, The, VII:1133, 1134
  Town, The, VII:1135
  Unvanquished, The, VII:1135
  Wild Palms, The, VII:1135
Faure, Abbé Jean-Baptiste, VI:2249
Fausta, I:376
Faustus, I:159
Fauvism
  Braque, VII:431
  Delaunay, VII:888
  Matisse, VIII:2452, 2454, 2455
  Mondrian, VIII:2576
  Rivera, IX:3185
Fawcett, Dame Millicent Garrett, **V:776-779**
  Janet Doncaster, V:776
  Political Economy for Beginners, V:776
Fawkes, Guy, **III:257-259,** 662
Faye, Antoine de la, III:96
Faysal ibn al-Husayn, VIII:2126, 2127
FBI. *See* Federal Bureau of Investigation
FDIC. *See* Federal Deposit Insurance Corporation
February House, VIII:2308
February Revolution. *See* Russian Revolution of
  1917
Fechner, Gustav Theodor, **V:780-782**
  Elements of Psychophysics, V:781
  Nanna, V:780
  Vorschule der Aesthetik, V:781
  Zend-Avesta, V:780
Federal Art Project, U.S., IX:3048
Federal Bureau of Investigation, U.S.,
    VIII:1732-1734
Federal Bureau of Prisons, U.S., VII:510
Federal Children's Bureau, U.S., IX:3838
Federal Deposit Insurance Corporation, U.S.,
    IX:3224
Federal Emergency Relief Adminstration, U.S.,
    VIII:1736; IX:2963
Federalist Party, U.S.
  Adams, John, IV:18, 19
  Adams, John Quincy, V:20
  Buchanan, V:346
  Burr, V:370
  Chase, IV:295
  Clinton, V:518
  Constitution, IV:1457, 1458
  Garrison, V:883
  Hamilton, IV:611

Jay, IV:713, 714
Jefferson, IV:718, 719
Madison, IV:888, 889
Monroe, VI:1571, 1573
Morris, IV:1000, 1001
Federalists, Mexican, V:95
Federal Reserve System, U.S., VI:2295; VII:421;
    VIII:1471-1473
Federal Security Agency, U.S., VIII:1704
Federal Trade Commission, U.S., VII:421;
    VIII:2680
Federal Union, VII:610
Federal Works Theater Project, U.S., VII:985
Federation League, V:148
Feinstein, Diane, **VII:1137-1140,** 1154
Felician controversy, I:696, 791
Felix V, III:559, 560
Felix of Trier, I:791
Fell, Margaret, IV:485
Fellini, Federico, **VII:1141-1144**
    Amarcord, VII:1142
    And the Ship Sails On, VII:1143
    Casanova, VII:1142
    City of Women, VII:1142
    dolce vita, La, VII:1142
    8 1/2, VII:1142
    Fellini Roma, VII:1142
    Fellini Satyricon, VII:1142
    Juliet of the Spirits, VII:1142
    Nights of Cabiria, The, VII:1141
    Strada, La, VII:1141
    Variety Lights, VII:1141
    White Sheik, The, VII:1141
feminism
    Adams, John Quincy, V:24
    Anthony, V:61-64
    Arzner, VII:119
    Barton, V:143
    Burr, V:371
    Christine de Pizan, II:262
    Friedan, VII:1231, 1233
    Fuller, V:849, 850, 852
    Grass, VIII:1464
    Horney, VIII:1746
    Hutchinson, IV:689
    MacKinnon, VIII:2325-2327
    Millay, VIII:2529, 2530, 2532
    Millett, VIII:2536-2538
    Montagu, IV:984
    Morrison, VIII:2628
    Plato, I:657
    Ross, IV:1192

Rukeyser, IX:3259
Sexton, IX:3395-3397
Spock, IX:3479
Stanton, VI:2111
Steinem, IX:3519, 3521, 3522
Terry, IX:3642-3644
Theodora, II:892
Virgin Mary, I:941
Willard, VI:2390
Wollstonecraft, IV:1475-1478
Workman, VI:2412
Zetkin, IX:4112
Feng, Marshal, VII:905
Feng Sacrifice, I:818
Feng Yün-shan, V:1165, 1166
Fenian Model, V:1124
Fenian Order, V:1123, 1124
Fenian Ram, V:1124
Fenstanton, IV:205
Fenway Court, VII:1301, 1302
Ferdinand II (Holy Roman Empire), **IV:450-453,**
    1397; V:625, 626
Ferdinand II (Spain), **III:260-263**
    Cabot, III:113
    Catherine of Aragon, III:136
    Columbus, III:172-174
    Jiménez de Cisneros, III:393, 394
    Manuel I, III:465
    Ponce de Léon, III:630, 631
    Prescott, VI:1814
    Vespucci, III:759
Ferdinand III (Spain), II:56
Ferdinand V (Spain), III:45, 46, 725, 726
Ferdinand VII (Spain), V:413, 414
Fergana, III:36
Ferguson, Adam, **IV:454-457**
    Essay on the History of Civil Society, An, IV:454
    *History of the Progress and Termination of the
        Roman Republic,* IV:454
    Institutes of Moral Philosophy, IV:454
    Principles of Moral and Political Science,
        IV:454
Fergusson, Robert, IV:229
Fermat, Pierre de, **IV:458-461**
Fermi, Enrico, **VII:1145-1149**
    Bethe, VII:300
    Chadwick, VII:636
    Compton, VII:747
    Hahn, VIII:1514
    Hevesy, VIII:1655
    Meitner, VIII:2477
Fernando VII, VI:1958

Fernando Po, IX:3757
Ferrante of Naples, III:496
Ferrar, Nicholas, **IV:462-464**
Ferrara, Duchy of, III:32-34, 48, 117, 710; IV:990, 991
Ferrari, Enzo, **VII:1150-1152**
Ferraro, Geraldine, **VII:1153-1156**
Fersen, Hans Axel von, IV:919
Festus, Sextus Pompeius, I:931
Fetterman Massacre, VI:1851
Fetti, Domenico
    Ecce Homo, IV:1488
feudalism
    Alexander I, V:44
    Alexander II, V:48, 49
    Bohemia, IV:750, 751
    Edward I, II:322
    Fronde, IV:866
    Germany, II:357-360, 392, 1005
    Godunov, III:308
    Heine, V:1085-1087
    Henry II, II:447, 448
    Henry III, II:454, 646
    Henry the Lion, II:467
    Hungary, V:625-628
    Ivan the Great, III:383
    Louis IX, II:603, 605
    Louis XI, III:434, 435
    Matthias I Corvinus, III:488, 489
    Oda Nobunaga, III:570-572
    Peasants' Revolt, II:921-923
    Philip IV the Fair, II:736
    Prussia, IV:506; VI:2116
    Richard II, II:786
    Rollo, II:795
    Rudolf I, II:798
    Russia, IV:259, 1087-1089
    Saigo Takamori, VI:1936-1939
    Scandinavia, II:626
    Scharnhorst, VI:1970
    Scotland, II:184, 185, 291, 292
    Stephen, II:848
    Tokugawa Ieyasu, IV:1327-1329
    Toyotomi Hideyoshi, III:729, 730
    Turgot, IV:1350
    William the Conqueror, II:997, 998
Feuerbach, Ludwig, VI:1492
Few, William P., V:706
Fez Plan. *See* Fahd Plan
Fiammetta, II:150, 152
Fianna Fáil, VII:878; IX:2804-2806
Fibonacci, Leonardo. *See* Leonardo of Pisa

Fichte, Johann Gottlieb, **IV:465-468;** VI:1972, 1974
    Addresses to the German Nation, IV:467
    Attempt at a Critique of All Revelation, IV:465
    Beitrag zur Berichtigung der Urteile des Publikums über die französische Revolution, IV:465
    Science of Ethics as Based on the Science of Knowledge, The, IV:467
    Science of Knowledge, The, IV:465, 466
    Science of Rights, The, IV:467
    Vocation of Man, The, IV:467
    Way Towards the Blessed Life, The, IV:467
    Zurückforderung der Denkfreiheit von der Fürsten Europens, IV:465
Field, Marshall, **V:783-786**
Field, Stephen J., **V:787-791**
Fielding, Henry, **IV:469-472**
    Amelia, IV:471
    Apology for the Life of Mrs. Shamela Andrews, IV:470
    History of the Adventures of Joseph Andrews, and of His Friend Mr. Abraham Adams, IV:470
    History of the Life of the Late Mr. Jonathan Wild the Great, The, IV:470
    History of Tom Jones, A Foundling, The, IV:470, 471
    Journal of a Voyage to Lisbon, The, IV:471
    "Masquerade, The," IV:469
    Tragedy of Tragedies, The, IV:469
Fields, Annie, V:1228
Fields, Lew, VIII:1588
Fields, W.C., IX:3950
Fieschi, Sinibaldo. *See* Innocent IV
Fifth Extermination Campaign, VII:688
Fifth Republic of France, VII:866
Fifth Street Gym, VII:54
Fifth Syrian War, I:64
Filioque doctrine, II:583, 899, 900
Fillmore, Millard, **V:792-795**
Finch, Anne, IV:195
Fine Gael, VII:772
Finisterre, first battle of, IV:56, 57
Finlay, Carlos Juan, VI:1858, 1859
Finnish War for Independence, VIII:2396
Fiore, Order of, II:535
Firdusi, **II:350-353**
    Shahnamah, II:350-352
Firpo, Luis Angel, VII:903
First Aero Squadron, VIII:2554
First Amendment
    Black, VII:323
    Cardozo, VII:577

Frankfurter, VII:1214
MacKinnon, VIII:2326
Zenger, IV:1484-1486
See also freedom of speech
First Bourbon Restoration, V:611
First Carlist War, V:414
First Church of Christ, Scientist, V:740
First Five-Year Plan of the Soviet Union, IX:3483
First International, V:113
First International Women's Conference, IX:4113
First Jewish Revolt, I:880
First Manassas, Battle of, V:1205
First Mover, II:829
First National Woman's Rights Convention,
    VI:2143
First-Quarter Storm, VIII:2421
First Reform Bill, V:935
First Seminole War. *See* Seminole Wars
First Sikh War, VI:1331
First Syrian War, I:717
First Triumvirate, I:149, 166-168, 196, 680, 681
Fischer, Emil, VII:927; VIII:2476
Fischer von Erlach, Johann Bernhard, **IV:473-475**
Fischer von Erlach, Joseph Emanuel, IV:655, 657
Fisher, Andrew, VIII:1775
Fisher, George, V:1141
Fisher, John, V:548, 549
Fisher, Saint John, **III:264-266**
Fisk, Diamond Jim, VI:1581, 2285
Fitch, John, **IV:476-478**
Fitzgerald, Ella, **VII:1157-1160**
    "Cole Porter Songbook, The," VII:1159
    "Tisket, a Tasket, A," VII:1157
    "You Showed Me the Way," VII:1157
Fitzgerald, F. Scott, **VII:1161-1165; IX:4012**
    Beautiful and Damned, The, VII:1163
    Crack-Up, The, VII:1164
    Great Gatsby, The, VII:1163, 1164
    Last Tycoon, The, VII:1163
    Tender is the Night, VII:1162-1164
    This Side of Paradise, VII:1161-1163
    Three Comrades, VII:1163
    Vegetable, The, VII:1163
Fitzgerald, Zelda, VII:1161-1164
Five Hundred, Council of, V:398
Flaminius, Gaius, I:334, 365
Flamsteed, John, IV:600, 601
Flaubert, Gustave, **V:796-799**
    Bouvard et Pécuchet, V:798
    Madame Bovary, V:796, 798; VII:569, 756;
        IX:3158
    Over Strand and Field, V:796

Salammbô, V:798; VI:1611
Sentimental Education, A, V:798
Temptation of Saint Anthony, The, V:796
Three Tales, V:798; VIII:1816
Flaxman, John, IV:1423; V:411
Fleet, Biddy, IX:2880
Fleetwood, Charles, IV:527
Flémalle, Master of, III:779
Fleming, Sir Alexander, **VII:1166-1168,**
    1172, 1174
Fletcher, Frank Jack, VIII:2751
Fletcher, John, **III:54-57,** 689
    Captain, The, III:56
    Cardenio, III:56
    Coxcomb, The, III:56
    Cupid's Revenge, III:56
    Faithful Shepherdess, The, III:54
    Henry VIII, III:56
    King and No King, A, III:55, 689
    Maid's Tragedy, The, III:55
    Philaster, III:55, 689
    Scornful Lady, The, III:56
    *Tragedy of Thierry, King of France and His
        Brother Theodoret,* III:55
    Two Noble Kinsmen, The, III:56
    Fletcher v. Peck, VI:2147
Flexner, Abraham, **VII:1169-1171**
    American College, The, VII:1169
    Medical Education in Europe, VII:1169
    *Medical Education in the United States and
        Canada,* VII:1169
    Universities, VII:1170
Fliess, Wilhelm, VII:1225
Florence, Italy
    Arnolfo di Cambio, II:82-84
    cathedral at, III:302
    Dante, II:286, 288
    Giotto, II:388
    Martini, II:632
    Pisano, II:744
    Villani, II:938, 940
Florentius, II;136, 137
Florey, Baron, VII:1167, **1172-1174**
Florida
    Adams, John Quincy, V:22
    Cabeza de Vaca, III:110
    Gadsden, V:858-860
    Menéndez de Avilés, III:507-509
    Ponce de Léon, III:629-631
    Soto, III:699, 700
    Tyler, VI:2291
Florinus, I:448

Flowers, Gennifer, VII:714
Foch, Ferdinand, VII:705
Fokine, Michel, VII:920; VIII:2746, 2749;
    IX:2937, 2939
folk literature. *See* fable
folk music, IV:229; VIII:1835-1837; IX:3798,
    3799, 3815-3817
Folsom, James "Big Jim," IX:3858
Fontainebleau, Edict of, IV:873
Fontana, Prospero, III:125
Fontanne, Lynn, VII:786
Fonteyn, Dame Margot, **VII:1175-1179**
    Moor's Pavane, The, VII:1178
    Ondine, VII:1177
    Paradise Lost, VII:1177
    Pelléas and Mélisande, VII:1177
    Poème d'extase, VII:1178
Foraker, Joseph B., V:1029, 1031
Ford, Gerald R., **VII:1180-1183**
    Bush, VII:521
    Carter, VII:590
    Dole, VII:948
    Greenspan, VIII:1471
    Nixon, VIII:2760
    Reagan, IX:3138
Ford, Henry, IV:1023; VI:1345; **VII:1184-1188**
Ford, John, IX:3902
Ford, Philip, IV:1080
Ford, Richard, IV:397
Ford Foundation, VII:158, 165, 1184, 1187;
    VIII:802
Ford Motor Company
    Ferrari, VII:1151
    Ford, VII:1184, 1186, 1187
    Fuller, VII:1268
    Lenoir, VI:1345
    Niebuhr, VIII:2735
    Reuther, IX:3162
    Toyota Motor Company, IX:3720
Fordney-McCumber Tariff, VIII:1551
Forel, Auguste, VIII:2012
Foreman, George, VII:56
Forest, Charter of the, II:329
Forester, C.S., **VII:1189-1192**
    African Queen, The, VII:1190
    Beat to Quarters, VII:1190
    Brown on Resolution, VII:1189
    Commodore Hornblower, VII:1191
    Flying Colours, VII:1191
    General, The, VII:1190
    Good Shepherd, The, VII:1191
    Gun, The, VII:1190

Hornblower and the Crisis, VII:1191
    Lieutenant Hornblower, VII:1191
    Long Before Forty, VII:1189
    Lord Hornblower, VII:1191
    Mr. Midshipman Hornblower, VII:1191
    Paid Piper, The, VII:1190
    Pawn Among Kings, A, VII:1190
    Payment Deferred, VII:1190
    Rifleman Dodd, VII:1190
    Ship of the Line, A, VII:1191
    Ship, The, VII:1191
Forkbeard, Sven, II:688
Former Han Dynasty, I:224, 590
Forrest, Edwin, V:272, **800-803;** VI:1461
Forster, E.M., **VII:1193-1196**
    Alexandria, VII:1194
    Aspects of the Novel, VII:1195
    Maurice, VII:1194
    Passage to India, A, VII:1194, 1195
    Pharos and Pharillon, VII:1194
    Room with a View, A, VII:1193
Forster, William Edward, **V:804-806**
Forten, Charlotte, **V:807-809**
Fortescue, Sir John, **III:267-269**
    De laudibus legum Angliæ, III:268, 269
    De natura legis naturæ, III:268
    Governance of England, The, III:268
Fortunatus, Venantius, II:405
Fortune magazine, VII:395, 397
Fortune, Reo, VIII:2469
Fort Wayne, Treaty of, VI:2204
Fort William, College of, VI:1846
Fossey, Dian, VIII:2148
Foster, Stephen Collins, **V:810-813**
    "Beautiful Dreamer," V:812
    "Oh! Susanna," V:810, 811
    "Old Black Joe," V:812
    "Swanee River," V:811
Fothergill, John, IV:182, 183
Foucault, Jean-Bernard-Léon, VI:1551
Fouquet, Nicolas, IV:336, 337, 781, 782, 834, 835
Fourier, Charles, **V:814-818;** VI:1817; VII:450
    Social Destiny of Man, V:814
    Social Science, V:814
Fourier, Joseph, **V:819-821**
    Analytical Theory of Heat, The, V:820
Fourteenth Amendment
    Anthony, V:62
    Cushing, V:583
    Dred Scott decision, VI:2001
    Field, V:788, 790
    Frankfurter, VII:1214

Hayes, V:1078
Holmes, VIII:1721
Hughes, VIII:1769
Johnson, V:1235-1237
MacKinnon, VIII:2326
Marshall, VIII:2434
Stevens, VI:2137
Fourteenth Army. *See* British Fourteenth Army
Fourth Amendment, VII:422
Fourth Party, VII:172
Fourth Republic of France
    Blum, VII:337
    de Gaulle, VII:867
    Herriot, VIII:1646
    Mendès-France, VIII:2491-2493
    Mitterrand, VIII:2558-2560
Four Winds, III:85, 86
Fowler, Lydia Folger, **V:822-824**
Fox, Charles James, IV:224, **479-483,** 542, 1036, 1102, 1103
Fox, George, **IV:484-486**
Foxe, John, III:655
Fox Libel Act, IV:440, 1486
Fracastoro, Girolamo, **III:270-273**
    De causis criticorum dierum libellus, III:271
    De contagione et contagiosis morbis et eorum curatione, III:271
    De sympathia et antipathia rerum, III:271
    "Fracastorius sive de anima dialogus," III:272
    Homocentricorum sive de stellis, III:271
    Naugerius sive de poetica dialogus, III:272
    Syphilis, III:270, 271
    "Turrius sive de intellectione dialogus," III:272
Fragonard, Jean-Honoré, IV:414, **488-491**
    Corésus Sacrificing Himself to Save Callirhoé, IV:488
    Fête at Saint-Cloud, The, IV:490
    Good Mother, The, IV:489
    Progress of Love, IV:489
    Swing, The, IV:488, 489
    Fram, VIII:2686
France, Anatole, **V:825-828**
    Balthasar, V:825
    Crime of Sylvestre Bonnard, The, V:825
    Gods Are Athirst, The, V:828
    Jocasta and the Famished Cat, V:825
    Merrie Tales of Jacques Tournebroche, The, V:827
    Monsieur Bergeret in Paris, V:827
    Noces corinthiennes, Les, V:825
    Penguin Island, V:827
    Red Lily, The, V:827
    Revolt of the Angels, The, V:827, 828
    Seven Wives of Bluebeard and Other Marvellous Tales, The, V:827
    Tales from a Mother of Pearl Casket, V:827
    Thaïs, V:825
    Well of Santa Clara, The, V:827
    White Stone, The, V:827
Francesca, Piero della, III:59
Franciabigio, III:24
Francis I, **III:274-277**
    Andrea del Sarto, III:24
    Bayard, III:49
    Cartier, III:129, 130
    Cellini, III:152, 153
    Clement VII, III:166
Francis II, III:243, 333, 475
Francis, Convers, VI:1727
Franciscan Order
    Anthony of Padua, II:76, 77
    Bacon, II:110, 112
    Bonaventure, II:163-165
    Carpini, II:206-208
    Duns Scotus, II:309, 311
    Francis of Assisi, II:354-356
    Gregory IX, II:399, 401
    Ockham, II:682
    Pecham, II:715-717
    Rienzo, II:791
    Salimbene, II:812, 813
    William of Saint-Amour, II:990, 991
Francis Ferdinand, **VII:1197-1199;** IX:4005
Francis Joseph I, V:626, 627, **829-831;** VI:2158
Francis of Assisi, Saint, **II:354-356,** 812; III:60
    "Canticle of Creatures," II:354
    Gregory IX, II:399
    See also Franciscan Order
Franck, César, **V:832-835**
    Béatitudes, Les, V:833
    Djinns, Les, V:833
    Éolides, Les, V:833
    Quintet in F Minor for Piano and Strings, V:833
    Rédemption, V:833
    Ruth, V:832, 833
    Sonata in A Major for Violin and Piano, V:834
    String Quartet in D Major, V:834
    Symphony in D Minor, V:834
    Variations symphoniques, V:833
Franck, James, VIII:1647, 1648
Franckert, Hans, III:86
Franco, Francisco, **VII:1200-1203**
    Blum, VII:336, 337
    Buñuel, VII:506

Candela, VII:557
  Garcia Lorca, VII:1291
  Perón, IV:2969
François I, III:467, 468, 470
Franco-Prussian Wars
  Bismarck, V:241
  Bizet, V:245
  Faidherbe, V:763-765
  Hindenburg, VIII:1674
  Kutuzov, VI:1306, 1307
  Liebknecht, VI:1369, 1370
  Pius IX, VI:1783
  Poincaré, IX:3044
  Redon, VI:1855
  Thiers, VI:2228
Franco-Russian Alliance of 1893-1894, V:1131
Franco-Turkish War, III:159, 160
Frank, Anne, **VII:1204-1207**
  Diary of Anne Frank, The, VII:1204-1206
Frankenthaler, Helen, **VII:1208-1211**
  Mountains and Sea, VII:1208
Frankfurter, Felix, VII:17, 323, **1212-1215**
  Case of Sacco and Vanzetti, The, VII:1212
Frank Leslie's Illustrated Newspaper, VI:1627
Franklin, Aretha, **VII:1216-1219**
  Amazing Grace, VII:1217
  Aretha Live at Fillmore West, VII:1217
  Aretha Now, VII:1217
  I Never Loved a Man (the Way I Loved You),
    VII:1217
  Lady Soul, VII:1217
  "Respect," VII:1217
  Young, Gifted, and Black, VII:1217
Franklin, Benjamin, **IV:492-496**
  Adams, IV:18, 19
  André, IV:42
  Edwards, IV:430
  electricity, IV:523
  Fitch, IV:476, 477
  Hutchinson, IV:693
  Poor Richard's Almanack, IV:493
  Volta, IV:1387
Franklin, John, VI:1908
Franklin, Rosalind, VII:797; IX:3996, 3997
Franz Joseph, VII:1197, 1198
Fraser, John, VIII:2110
Fraser, Neale Andrew, VIII:2109
Frateschi, III:669
Frazer, Sir James George, **VII:1220-1223**
  Anthologia Anthropologica, VII:1221
  *Belief in Immortality and the Worship of the
    Dead, The,* VII:1221

Fear of the Dead in Primitive Religion, The,
    VII:1221
  Folk-Lore of the Old Testament, VII:1221
  Golden Bough, The, VII:1220-1223
  Lectures on the Early History of the Kingship,
    VII:1221
  Totemica, VII:1221
  Totemism and Exogamy, VII:1221
  Worship of Nature, The, VII:1222
Frazier, Joe, VII:56
Frazier-Lemke Act, IX:3548
Frederick I, **IV:497-499**
Frederick I Barbarossa, **II:357-361**
  Adrian IV, II:28, 48
  Alexander III, II:49, 50
  Henry the Lion, II:467, 468
  Rudolf I, II:797
  Treaty of Constance, II:358
Frederick II of Saxony, III:443, 445
Frederick II of Sicily, **II:362-365,** 399-401, 510,
    514, 605
Frederick III (Holy Roman Emperor), III:164, 375,
    487, 488, 491
Frederick V (Holy Roman Emperor), IV:451
Frederick Henry, **IV:500-503**
Fredericksburg, Battle of, V:1205
Frederick the Great, IV:32, 444, **504-507,** 1394
Frederick William II, IV:148
Frederick William III, V:940-942, 1033; VI:1969,
    1970, 2115, 2116
Frederick William IV, VI:1840
Frederick William, The Great Elector, **IV:508-510**
Fredericq, Paul, IX:3023
Free Cultivator's Law, V:44
Free Democratic Party, VII:428; VIII:2009
Freedmen's Bureau, V:1151, 1235; VI:2108, 2137
Freedom Charter, VIII:2281
Freedom League, VIII:2253
freedom of speech
  Adams, IV:19
  Black, VII:322
  Brandeis, VII:422
  Bryant, V:344
  Erskine, IV:440
  Fichte, IV:465
  Goldman, VIII:1414
  Holmes, VIII:1721
  Mill, VI:1562
  Nazi Germany, VIII:1405
  Phillips, VI:1772
  pornography, VIII:2326
  See also censorship; First Amendment

freedom of the press, IV:440, 1484-1486
    See also censorship; First Amendment
Free French movement, IX:3924
free jazz, VII:741, 742, 744
Freemasonry, IV:844, 1005, 1048; VI:2208;
    VIII:1941
Free Officers Revolution, VIII:2356
Free Officers Society, VIII:2693; IX:3098,
    3289
Free Parliament, IV:284
Freer, Charles, VI:2364, 2366
Free Silver movement, VII:479
Free Society of Artists, IV:1187
Free-Soil Party, IV:895; V:322, 477, 478, 1138;
    VI:2294
Free Synagogue, IX:4034
free trade
    Chamberlain, V:463
    Cobden, V:526-528
    Derby, V:653
    Germany, VII:1094, 1095
    Heath, VIII:1607
    Kohl, VIII:2010
    Liverpool, VI:1397
    NAFTA, VII:522, 682, 709, VIII:2656, 2681
    Peel, VI:1754
    Smith, IV:1249-1251
Free Traders, V:631, 632
Free Unionist Officers, IX:3098, 3099
free will
    Ahmad ibn Hanbal, II:34
    Alberti, III:9
    Ash'ari, II:94
    Boethius, II:156
    Buridan, II:195
    Duns Scotus, II:312
    Edwards, IV:429
    Hartmann, VIII:1571
    Jansen, IV:708
    Kant, IV:762
    Nishida, VIII:2755
    Schopenhauer, VI:1984-1986
    Taine, VI:2182
    Theodore of Mopsuestia, I:862
    Valla, III:739
Frege, Gottlob, **V:836-838**; VII:582
    Begriffsschrift, V:836, 838
    Foundations of Arithmetic, The, V:836
    Grundgesetze der Arithmetik, V:837
Freikorps, IX:3381
FRELIMO. *See* Mozambique Liberation Front
Frémont, John C., V:77, 197, 429-432, **839-844**

French-American Mid-Ocean Undersea Study.
    See FAMOUS, Project
French and Indian War. *See* Seven Years' War
French Indochina War, VIII:2493
French National Liberation Committee, VIII:2491
French Open, VII:368, 369
French Revolution
    Acton, V:12
    Adams, John Quincy, V:20
    Blake, IV:138
    Burke, IV:224
    Castlereagh, V:438, 439
    Catherine the Great, IV:260
    Chateaubriand, V:482
    Condorcet, IV:348-350
    Danton, IV:393-395
    David, V:611
    Du Pont, V:718, 719
    Fichte, IV:467
    Fourier, V:819
    Fox, IV:482
    Gay-Lussac, V:897
    George III, IV:542
    Herder, IV:652
    Joséphine, V:1246
    Lagrange, IV:787
    Lavoisier, IV:807
    Leblanc, IV:815
    Marat, IV:910-912
    Marie-Antoinette, IV:920
    Michelet, VI:1549
    Monge, IV:975, 977
    Napoleon I, VI:1616-1618
    Necker, IV:1018
    Orléans, IV:1048-1050
    Paine, IV:1055-1057
    Pitt the Younger, IV:1104
    Priestley, IV:1130
    Robespierre, IV:1170-1173
    Saint-Just, IV:1205-1207
    Staël, VI:2093, 2094
    Taine, VI:2183
    Thiers, VI:2226
    Turgot, IV:1348, 1349
    Wollstonecraft, IV:1475, 1477
    Wordsworth, VI:2406
French Royal Gardens, IV:215
Freud, Sigmund, **VII:1224-1227**
    Adler, VII:30, 31
    Benjamin, VII:269
    Bleuler, VII:329, 330
    Breuer, VII:452-454

Fourier, V:817

Fromm, VII:1246, 1247

H.D., VIII:1506

Hesse, VIII:1652

Horney, VIII:1744-1746

Interpretation of Dreams, The, I:400; VII:829, 1225; VIII:2062

Jung, VIII:1896, 1898, 1899

Lacan, VIII:2061-2063

Le Bon, VIII:2136

Leonardo da Vinci, VII:1226

Mahler, VIII:2363

penis envy, VIII:2537

Psychopathology of Everyday Life, VII:1226

schizophrenia, IX:3576

Schopenhauer, VI:1986

sex research, VIII:1987

Studies in Hysteria, VII:1224

Three Essays on the Theory of Sexuality, VII:1225

Totem and Taboo, VII:1226

Wit and Its Relation to the Unconscious, VII:1226

Freyssinet, Eugène, **VII:1228-1230**

Friars Preachers, Order of. *See* Dominican Order

Frick, Henry Clay, V:421; VIII:1412, 2480

Fried, Alfred Hermann, VI:2177

Friedan, Betty, **VII:1231-1234**; VIII:1642

Feminine Mystique, The, VI:2154; VII:1231; VIII:1642

Fountain of Age, The, VII:1233

It Changed My Life, VII:1233

Second Stage, The, VII:1233

Friedjung, Heinrich, VIII:2441

Friedland, Battle of, VI:1646

Friedland, duchy of, IV:1397

Friendly, Fred, VIII:2664

Friends, Religious Society of. *See* Quakers

Friendship, Mutual Assistance, and Postwar Cooperation, Treaty of, VII:261

Friends of the People, Society of the, V:994, 995

Fries, John, IV:295

Frigidus River, Battle of the, I:825

Frisch, Karl von, **VII:1235-1237**

Frisch, Max, **VII:1238-1241**

Andorra, VII:1239

Biography: A Game, VII:1239

Bluebeard, VII:1239

Chinese Wall, The, VII:1239

Don Juan, VII:1238

Fire Raisers, The, VII:1238

Homo Faber, VII:1239

I'm Not Stiller, VII:1238

Man in the Holocene, VII:1239

Montauk, VII:1239

Sketchbook 1946-1949, VII:1238

Sketchbook 1966-1971, VII:1239

Wilderness of Mirrors, A, VII:1239

Frisch, Otto, VIII:2478

Frisians, I:378; II:167, 243

Fritigern, I:908

Frizer, Ingram, III:472

Froben, Johann, III:358

Frobenius, Leo, **VII:1242-1245**

Atlantis, VII:1243

Black Decameron, The, VII:1243

Erlebte Erdteile, VII:1243

Origin of African Civilization, The, VII:1242

Frobisher, Sir Martin, III:212, **278-280**

Froebel, Friedrich, **V:845-848**; VIII:2596

Education of Man, The, V:846

Pedagogics of the Kindergarten, V:847

Mother-Play and Nursery Songs, V:847

Froissart, Jean, **II:366-369**

Chronicles, II:366-369

Fromm, Erich, **VII:1246-1249**

Art of Loving, The, VII:1248

Beyond the Chains of Illusion, VII:1248

Dogma of Christ, VII:1246

Escape from Freedom, VII:1247

Man for Himself, VII:1247

Marx's Concept of Man, VII:1248

Psychoanalysis and Religion, VII:1248

Sigmund Freud's Mission, VII:1248

You Shall Be Gods, VII:1248

Zen Buddhism and Psychoanalysis, VII:1248

Fronde, IV:336, 341-343, 386, 866, 946, 1358

Fronde of the Princes, IV:342

Frontenac, Louis de Baude, VI:1736, 1737

Frost, Elihu B., V:1124, 1125

Frost, Robert, **VII:1250-1252**

Boy's Will, A, VII:1250

Further Range, A, VII:1251

"Gift Outright, The," VII:1252

In the Clearing, VII:1252

Masque of Mercy, A, VII:1252

Masque of Reason, A, VII:1252

Mountain Interval, VII:1251

New Hampshire, VII:1251

North of Boston, VII:1250

"Oven Bird," VII:1251

"Road Not Taken, The," VII:1251

Steeple Bush, VII:1252

"Trial by Existence, The," VII:1250

"Tuft of Flowers, A," VII:1250
West-Running Brook, VII:1251
Witness Tree, A, VII:1251
Fry, Roger, **VII:1253-1256**
  Cézanne, VII:1255
  Transformations, VII:1254
  Vision and Design, VII:1254; VIII:2609
Fry, Shirley, VII:1364
Fry, W.H., V:984
Frye, Northrop, I:509
Fryxell, Eva, VIII:2065
FSA. *See* Farm Security Administration
FTC. *See* Federal Trade Commission
Fuchs, Arved, VIII:2508
Fuchs, Vivian, VIII:1663, 1664
Fugard, Athol, **VII:1257-1260**
  Blood Knot, The, VII:1258
  Boesman and Lena, VII:1258
  Cell, The, VII:1257
  Hello and Goodbye, VII:1258
  Island, The, VII:1258, 1259
  Klass and the Devil, VII:1257
  Lesson from Aloes, A, VII:1259
  "MASTER HAROLD". . . and the boys,
    VII:1257, 1259
  My Children, My Africa, VII:1260
  No-Good Friday, VII:1257
  Orestes, VII:1258
  Place for the Pigs, A, VII:1257
  Road to Mecca, The, VII:1259
  Sizwe Bansi Is Dead, VII:1257, 1259
  *Statements After an Arrest Under the Immorality
    Act,* VII:1259
  Tsotsi, VII:1258
Fugitive Slave Act
  Brown, V:322
  Chase, V:478
  Fillmore, V:793
  Forten, V:807
  Garrison, V:886
  Parker, VI:1729
  Pierce, VI:1777
  Story, VI:2148
  Taney, VI:2191
  Tubman, VI:2265
Fujisawa, Takeo, VIII:1724-1726
Fujiwara Michinaga, **II:370-372,** 537, 538
Fujiwara no Tametoki, II:657
Fukien, IV:297, 298
Fulbert of Chartres, Saint, **II:373-375**
Fulda, II:767
Full Employment Act of 1946, IX:3862

Fuller, Loie, **VII:1261-1264**
  Fifteen Years of a Dancer's Life, VII:1263
  "Fire Dance," VII:1263
  "Serpentine Dance," VII:1261
  "Shadow Ballets," VII:1263
Fuller, Margaret, **V:849-853,** 984
  Papers on Literature and Art, V:850
  Summer on the Lake, V:850
  Women in the Nineteenth Century, V:850, 852
Fuller, R. Buckminster, **VII:1265-1269**
Fulton, Robert, IV:478; **V:854-857**
  Torpedo War and Submarine Explosions, V:856
  *Treatise on the Improvement of Canal
    Navigation,* V:854
Furneaux, Tobias, IV:353
Furness, Frank, VI:2167
fur trade
  Astor, V:82, 84
  La Salle, IV:793, 794
  Lewis and Clark, VI:1359
  Mackenzie, IV:879-881
  Smith, VI:2077, 2078
Fuseli, Henry, IV:1477
Fusion Ministry, V:631
Fust, Johann, III:328, 329
Futa-Toro, V:763
Futurama exhibit, VII:1321
Futurism
  Blok, VII:332, 333
  Boccioni, VII:342-344
  Duchamp, VII:972
  Magritte, VIII:2349
  Mayakovsky, VIII:2461, 2462
  Pasternak, IX:2899
FWA. *See* Farm Workers Association

Gabbard, Battle off the, II:135
Gabbard Shoal, Battle of the, IV:1343
Gabin, Jean, VII:932
Gable, Clark, VIII:2232
Gabriel, archangel, III:28
Gabrieli, Andrea, **III:281-283**
  Concerti, III:282
  Psalmi Davidici, III:282
Gabrieli, Giovanni, **III:284-286;** IV:1221, 1222
  Canzoni e sonate, III:285
  Sacrae symphoniae, III:285
Gaddi, Palazzo, III:664
Gadsden, James, **V:858-860**
Gadsden Purchase, V:583, 615, 858-860; VI:1956
Gaelic League, VII:877
Gaelic Nationalist Revival, IX:2804-2806

Gagarin, Yuri Alekseyevich, VII:111, **1270-1273;**
    IX:3407, 3639, 3640
Gage, Thomas, **IV:511-514**
    Adams, Samuel, IV:23, 24
    Carleton, IV:247
    Clinton, IV:321, 322
    Hancock, IV:616, 617
    Howe, IV:677, 678
Gagnan, Émile, VII:779
Gaia, I:403
Gaillardet, Frédéric, V:709
Gaillieni, Joseph, VIII:1851, 1852
Gainsborough, Thomas, **IV:515-518,** 529,
    1163, 1164
Gaitskill, Hugh, VII:305, 306; IX:4106
Gaius Octavius. *See* Augustus
Gale, Leonard Dunnell, VI:1593
Galen, **I:338-341**
    Asclepiades, I:103
    bloodletting, I:301
    Celsus, I:174
    Diocles of Carystus, I:262
    Harvey, IV:628
    Nostradamus, III:567
    On the Usefulness of the Parts of the Body, I:339
    Vesalius, III:754-756
Galerius, I:226, 227, 267
Galigai, Leonora, IV:863, 864
Galilee, I:472, 642, 880
Galileo, **IV:519-522**
    Archimedes, I:80
    Boyle, IV:185
    Brecht, VII:446
    Descartes, IV:403
    *Dialogue Concerning the Two Chief World
      Systems,* IV:521, 951, 1331
    Kepler, IV:774
    Mersenne, IV:951
    Milton, IV:958
    parabola, IV:695
    pulsilogium, IV:1209
    Saggiatore, IV:521
    Santorio, IV:1209, 1210
    Sidereal Messenger, The, IV:521
    telescope, IV:852
Gallatin, Albert, **V:861-863**
Gallaudet, Thomas, V:130
Gallic Wars, I:149
Gallienus, I:667
Gallman, Rolando, VII:86
Galloway, Joseph, IV:678
Gallus, Didius, I:136

Galois, Èvariste, **V:864-866**
Galton, Francis, **V:867-870**
    Art of Travel, V:868
    English Men of Science, V:868
    Finger-Prints, V:869
    Hereditary Genius, V:868
    *Inquiries into the Human Faculty and Its
      Development,* V:869
    Memories of My Life, V:867
    Natural Inheritance, V:869
    Record of Family Faculties, V:869
    Tropical South Africa, V:868
Galvani, Luigi, **IV:523-526,** 1389
    *Commentary on the Effect of Electricity on
      Muscular Motion,* IV:524, 525
Gama, Vasco da, III:117, 118, 120, 218,
    287-290, 464
Gamaliel II, I:27, 28, 473
Gambetta, Leon, **V:871-874;** VI:2103
Gance, Abel, **VII:1274-1277**
    Digue, La, VII:1274
    Folie du Docteur Tube, La, VII:1274, 1275
    J'Accuse!, VII:1274, 1275
    Life and Loves of Beethoven, The, VII:1275
    Mater Dolorosa, VII:1274
    Napoléon, VII:1274-1276
    Roue, La, VII:1274, 1275
Gandhara, I:779
Gandhi, Indira, **VII:1278-1281;** VIII:2712;
    IX:2867, 2869
Gandhi, Mahatma, I:916; VII:397, 1278, **1282-
    1285;** VIII:1847, 2683, 2709-2711; IX:2867
Gandhi, Mohandas, VI:2235; VIII:1971
Gang of Four, VII:906; VIII:2214
Ganjojuin temple, II:924, 925
Gao, III:522
Garber, Paul, IX:3973
Garbett, Samuel, IV:1182-1184
Garbo, Greta, **VII:1286-1289**
    Anna Christie, VII:1287
    Anna Karenina, VII:1288
    Camille, VII:1288
    Conquest, VII:1288
    Flesh and the Devil, VII:1286
    Grand Hotel, VII:1287
    Joyless Street, The, VII:1286
    Ninotchka, VII:1288
    Painted Veil, The, VII:1288
    Queen Christina, VII:1288; IX:2808
    Temptress, The, VII:1286
    Torrent, The, VII:1286
    Two-Faced Woman, VII:1288

Garcia, Manuel, Jr., VI:1385
Garcia Lorca, Federico, **VII:1290-1292;**
    VIII:2716, 2717; IX:3067
    Blood Wedding, VII:1291
    Gypsy Ballads of Garcia Lorca, The, VII:1290
    House of Bernarda Alba, The, VII:1291
    Lament for the Death of a Bullfighter, VII:1291
    Poet in New York, VII:1291
    Songs, VII:1290
    Yerma, VII:1291
Garcia Márquez, Gabriel, **VII:1293-1296**
    Clandestine in Chile, VII:1295
    funerales de la Mamá Grande, Los, VII:1294
    general en su laberinto, El, VII:1295
    In Evil Hour, VII:1293
    Leaf Storm and Other Stories, VII:1293
    Love in the Time of Cholera, VII:1295
    *Monologue of Isabel Watching It Rain in
        Macondo,* VII:1293
    No One Writes to the Colonel and Other Stories,
        VII:1293
    One Hundred Years of Solitude, VII:1294, 1295
Gardiner, Stephen, **III:291-294**
    Episcopi de vera obedientia oratio, III:292
    King's Book, III:292
Gardner, Alexander, V:296, 297
Gardner, Erle Stanley, **VII:1297-1299**
    Bigger They Come, The, VII:1298
    Case of the Velvet Claws, The, VII:1298
Gardner, Isabella Stewart, **VII:1300-1303**
Gardner, John
    Wreckage of Agathon, The, I:952
Gardoqui, Diego, IV:713
Garfield, James, V:77, 78, 80, 81, 256, **875-878;**
    VI:2389
Garibaldi, Giuseppe, V:447, 447, 709, **879-882;**
    VI:1782, 1783
Garland, Judy, **VII:1304-1307**
    Babes in Arms, VII:1305
    Broadway Melody of 1938, VII:1304
    Child Is Waiting, A, VII:1306
    Easter Parade, VII:1305
    For Me and My Girl, VII:1305
    I Could Go on Singing, VII:1306
    Judgment at Nuremberg, VII:1306
    Star is Born, A, VII:1305, 1306, 1354
    Wizard of Oz, The, VII:1305
Garnier, Tony, **VII:1308-1310**
Garrick, David, IV:226, **527-530,** 567
    Lethe, IV:527
    Lying Valet, The, IV:527
    Ode, IV:529

Garrison, William Lloyd, V:489, 697, **883-887;**
    VI:1772, 1773, 2143, 2374
Garter, Order of the, II:329
Garvey, Marcus, VII: 668, **1311-1314;** VIII:2373;
    IX:3114
Gasherbrum I, VIII:2507, 2508
Gaskell, Elizabeth
    Mary Barton, V:361
Gasmotorenfabrik Deutz, VI:1703
Gates, Horatio, IV:66, 1406
Gattoni, Giulio, IV:1387
Gaudi, Antonio, **VII:1315-1318**
Gauge War, V:336
Gauguin, Paul, V:946, **888-892;** VI:1922; VII:362,
    363, 910; IX:2836
    Breton Village Covered by Snow, V:890
    Ia Orana Maria, V:890
    Noa Noa, V:890
    Talisman, The, VII:909
    Vision After the Sermon, The, V:888
    *Where Do We Come From? What Are We?
        Where Are We Going?,* V:890
Gaulle, Charles de. *See* de Gaulle, Charles
Gaunt, John of. *See* Lancaster, Duke of
Gauss, Carl Friedrich, **V:893-896;** VI:1403, 1404
    Arithmetical Inquisitions, V:893-895
    General Investigations of Curved Surfaces,
        V:895
Gauss, Christian, IX:4012
Gautama. *See* Buddha
Gauthier-Villars, Henri, VII:729
Gaveston, Piers, II:326
Gay, John, IV:27, 158, 668
Gay-Lussac, Joseph-Louis, V:98, **897-901**
Gdansk Lenin Shiyards, IX:3844, 3845
Gedaliah, I:461
Geddes, Norman Bel, **VII:1319-1321**
    Magic Motorways, VII:1321
Gehrig, Lou, **VII:1322-1325**
Geiger, Hans, VII:379
Geiger, Rudolf Oskar Robert Williams,
    VII:1326-1328
    Climate Near the Ground, The, VII:1326, 1327
Geisel, Theodor Seuss, **VII:1329-1332**
    And to Think That I Saw It on Mulberry Street,
        VII:1329
    Butter Battle Book, The, VII:1331
    Cat in the Hat, The, VII:1330
    5,000 Fingers of Dr. T, The, VII:1329
    How the Grinch Stole Christmas!, VII:1330
    Lorax, The, VII:1330, 1331
    Oh, the Places You'll Go!, VII:1331

Sneetches, The, VII:1330
You're Only Old Once, VII:1331
Gembloux, Battle of, III:254
Gemeinschaft, IX:3703-3705
Gemellus, Tiberius, I:153, 154
Gemini space program, VII:111, 112; VIII:2021;
    IX:3405
General Education Board, VI:1898
General Electric Company, V:743; VI:2122, 2124;
    IX:3138
General German Workers' Association, VI:1324,
    1325, 1369
General Motors, VII:1321; VIII:2679, 2680;
    IX:2974, 3162, 3881
General Overseas Service, VII:737
Genesis, Book of, I:5, 6; III:72; IV:215, 1303;
    VII:481
Genet, Edmond Charles, IV:718
Genet, Jean, **VII:1333-1335;** VIII:2537;
    IX:3329
    Balcony, The, VII:35, 1334
    Blacks, The, VII:79, 1334
    Deathwatch, VII:1334
    Funeral Rites, VII:1333
    Maids, The, VII:1334
    Miracle of the Rose, VII:1333
    Our Lady of the Flowers, VII:1333
    Querelle of Brest, VII:1333
    Screams, The, VII:35
    Screens, The, VII:1334
    Thief's Journal, The, VII:1333
Geneva, Treaty of, V:143
Geneva, University of, III:118
Geneva Accords, VII:977; VIII:1701
Geneva Conventions, V:712
Genghis Khan, **II:376-380,** 381, 566; IV:2, 3
Gennadius of Marseilles, I:938
Genseric, **I:342-344**
Gensfleisch zur Laden, Johannes. *See* Gutenberg,
    Johann
Genshin sect, II:537
Gentile, Giovanni, **VII:1336-1338**
Gentili, Alberico, **III:295-297**
    De iuris interpretibus dialogi sex, III:295
    Three Books on Embassies, III:295, 296
    Three Books on the Law of War, The, III:295,
    296
    Two Books of the Pleas of a Spanish Advocate,
    The, III:296
Geoffrey Martel, II:997
Geoffrey of Monmouth
    History of the Kings of Britain, I:378, 380

Geoffroi de Villehardouin. *See* Villehardouin,
    Geoffroi de
Geological Society of London, VI:1418, 1421
Geological Survey of Territories, U.S.,
    V:1072-1074; VI:1812, 1813, 2328
geometry
    Aristoxenus, I:99
    Euclid, I:308
    Gauss, V:893-895
    Hero of Alexandria, I:388
    Leonardo of Pisa, II:586
    Lobachevsky, VI:1403-1405
    Maclaurin, IV:884
    Monge, IV:975-978
    Steiner, VI:2118-2120
George I, **IV:531-534**
    Addison, IV:27
    Bolingbroke, IV:159
    George II, IV:535, 536
    Stanhope, IV:1277-1279
    Vanbrugh, IV:1352
    Walpole, IV:1402, 1403
George II, **IV:535-538**
    Amherst, IV:37
    Cosby, IV:1485
    George I, IV:532, 533
    George III, IV:539
    Handel, IV:621
    Pelham, IV:1074
    Walpole, IV:1403
George III, **IV:539-544**
    Adams, Samuel, IV:24
    Amherst, IV:39, 40
    Anson, IV:57
    Banks, IV:85
    Brown, IV:206
    Burke, IV:222-224
    Castlereagh, V:440
    Ch'ien-lung, IV:300
    Copley, IV:358
    Fox, IV:481, 482
    George IV, V:902-904
    Howe, IV:676, 677
    Lawrence, IV:810
    New Hampshire, IV:34
    North, IV:1034-1036
    Paine, IV:1057
    Palmerston, VI:1719
    Pennsylvania, IV:408
    Pitt the Younger, IV:1102, 1104
    Union, Act of, IV:369
    Victoria, VI:2307, 2308

Virginia tobacco, IV:647
Wilkes, IV:1439
William IV, VI:2392
George IV, **V:902-905**
  Brougham, V:315
  Canning, V:406
  Grey, V:995
  Nash, IV:1013, 1014
  Raeburn, VI:1837
  Victoria, VI:2307, 2308
  William IV, VI:2392
George V, VII:170, 1020, 1062; **1339-1342,** 1343,
  1344; IX:4025, 4026
George VI, VII:170, 315, 595, 1062, **1343-1346;**
  IX:4026, 4027
George, Henry, **V:906-909**
  Our Land and Land Policy, V:907
  Progess and Poverty, V:907, 908
George of Transylvania, IV:838
Georgia
  Carter, VII:589, 592
  lynching, IX:3961
  Massachusetts speculators, VI:2147
  Native American removal, VI:1910, 1911
  Oglethorpe, IV:1043-1046
  Stephens, VI:2129-2131
Gepids, II:41, 42
Gerann of Reims, II:869
Gerard of Cremona, II:985
Gerbert of Aurillac. *See* Sylvester II
Géricault, Théodore, V:645, 646, **910-914**
  African Slave Trade, V:913
  Charging Chasseur, V:912
  Liberation of the Prisoners of the Spanish
    Inquisition, V:913
  Raft of the Medusa, The, V:646, 912, 913
  Wounded Cuirassier, V:912
Gerlach, Adrian de, VII:66
Germain, Lord George, IV:248, 677
German Association of Engineers, IX:4109
German Evangelical Church, VIII:2742-2744
Germanic Diet, III:159
German High Seas Fleet, IX:3688-3690
Germanicus, I:152
German Inland Ice Expedition of 1930, IX:3920
German Inner-African Exploration Expedition,
  VII:1242
German People's Party, IX:3564
Germany, reunification of, VIII:2009-2011
Gerome, Jean-Leon, V:732; VI:1854
Geronimo, **V:915-918**
Gerousia, I:216

Gershwin, George, **VII:1347-1351,** 1352,
  1354, 1355
  American in Paris, An, VII:1349
  Blue Monday, VII:1347
  Concerto in F, VII:1349, 1350
  Lady Be Good, VII:125, 1349, 1352
  Of Thee I Sing, VII:1349, 1352, 1354
  Porgy and Bess, VII:1347, 1349, 1354;
    IX:3081, 3083
  Rhapsody in Blue, VII:1347, 1350
  Shocking Miss Pilgrim, The, VII:1355
  Strike Up the Band, VII:1349, 1354
  "Swanee," VII:1347
Gershwin, Ira, VII:1347, 1349, 1350, **1352-1355**
  Cover Girl, VII:1354
  Girl Crazy, VII:1354
  Goldwyn Follies, The, VII:1354
  Lady Be Good, VII:125, 1349, 1352
  Lady in the Dark, VII:1354; IX:3928
  Lyrics on Several Occasions, VII:1355
  "Man That Got Away, The," VII:1354
  Of Thee I Sing, VII:1349, 1352, 1354
  Porgy and Bess, VII:1347, 1349, 1354
  Shall We Dance, VII:1354
  Star is Born, A, VII:1354
  Strike Up the Band, VII:1349, 1354
  Sweetheart Shop, The, VII:1352
Gerson, Jean de, II:907
Gesell, Arnold, **VII:1356-1358**
  Biographies of Child Development, VII:1357
  Child from Five to Ten, The, VII:1357, 1358
  Infant and Child in the Culture of Today,
    VII:1357, 1358
  Infant Behavior, VII:1357
  Youth, VII:1357
Gesner, Conrad, III:3, **298-301**
  Bibliotheca universalis, III:298
  De rerum fossilium, lapidum, et gemmarum
    maximé, figuris et similitudinibus liber, III:299
  De tulipa Turcarum, III:299
  Historia plantarum et vires, III:298
  Historiae animalium, III:299
  Opera botanica, III:299
Gessho, VI:1936
Gestapo
  Adenauer, VII:27
  Göring, VIII:1439
  Niemöller, VIII:2743
Gettysburg Address, VI:1383, 2346
Géza, II:574
Ghana Shifimo, VIII:2763, 2764
Ghazan, Mahmud, **II:381-384**

Ghaznavid dynasty, II:70, 147, 677
Ghazzali, al-, **II:385-387**
   Incoherence of the Philosophers, II:385
   Revival of Religious Sciences, The, II:385,386
Ghent, Pacification of, III:783
Ghent, Treaty of, IV:889; V:21, 507, 862
Ghent, University of, IX:3023
Ghibellines, II:286, 288, 515
Ghiberti, Lorenzo, II:272, 745, 746; III:91, 220, **302-304**
Ghirlandaio, Domenico, III:517
Ghose, Sri Aurobindo. *See* Aurobindo, Sri
Ghost Dance, VI:1851, 2072
Giacometti, Alberto, **VII:1359-1362**
   Busts of Diego, VII:1361
   Composition, VII:1359
   Couple (Man and Woman), The, VII:1359
   Palace at 4 A.M., The, VII:1359
   Spoon-Woman, The, VII:1359
   Suspended Ball, VII:1359
   Three Figures Outdoors, VII:1359
Giap, Vo Nguyen. *See* Vo Nguyen Giap
Gibbon, Edward, **IV:545-548,** 564
   *History of the Decline and Fall of the Roman
     Empire, The,* IV:545-547; V:75; VI:1873
Gibbons, James, **V:919-922**
   Faith of Our Fathers, The, V:919
Gibbons, Thomas, VI:2296
Gibbons v. Ogden, VI:1490
Gibbs, Josiah Willard, **V:923-926**
   Elementary Principles in Statistical Mechanics,
     V:925
Gibbs, Oliver Wolcott, VI:1367
Gibson, Althea, **VII:1363-1366**
Gide, André, VII:910, **1367-1369**
   Corydon, VII:1368
   Counterfeiters, The, VII:1368
   Fruits of the Earth, VII:1368
   If It Die . . . , VII:1368
   Immoralist, The, VII:1368
   Lafcadio's Adventures, VII:1368
   Madeleine, VII:1369
   Marshlands, VII:1367
   Notebooks of Andre Walter, The, VII:1367
   Pastoral Symphony, VII:1368
   Return from the U.S.S.R., VII:1369
   Return of the Prodigal Son, The, VII:1367
   Strait Is the Gate, VII:1368
   Theseus, VII:1369
   Urien's Voyage, VII:1367
Gideon v. Wainwright, VII:322
Gielgud, John, IX:2808, 2810, 2812

Gierek, Edward, IX:3844
Gifford, John, IV:218
Gilbert, Adrian, III:212
Gilbert, Sir Humphrey, III:315, 316, 639
Gilbert, Olive, VI:2257
Gilbert, Susan, V:668
Gilbert, William, IV:588
Gilbert, W.S., **V:927-931**
   Bab Ballads, The, V:927, 930
   Dulcamara, V:927
   Grand Duke, The, V:929
   H.M.S. Pinafore, V:929
   Patience, V:929
   Pirates of Penzance, The, V:927, 929
   Pygmalion and Galatea, V:928
   Thespis, V:928
   Trial by Jury, V:929
   Utopia, Limited, V:929
Gilchrist, Alexander, IV:141
Gillespie, Dizzy, **VII:1370-1373;** IX:2882
   Greatest Jazz Concert Ever, The, VII:1371
Gillot, Claude, IV:1413
Gilson, Étienne, **VII:1374-1378**
   Arts of the Beautiful, The, VII:1376
   Being and Some Philosophers, VII:1376
   Dantesques, VII:1377
   Forms and Substances in the Arts, VII:1376
   *History of Christian Philosophy in the Middle
     Ages,* VII:1376
   Painting and Reality, VII:1376
   Spirit of Medieval Philosophy, The, VII:1375
   Thomis Realism and the Critique of Knowledge,
     VII:1376
   Unity of Philosophical Experience, The,
     VII:1376
Gingrich, Newt, VII:709, 710
Ginsberg, Allen, VII:792; VIII:1945
Gioberti, Vincenzo, **V:932-934**
   Del primato morale e civile degli italiani, V:932,
     933; VI:1782
   rinnovamento civile d'Italia, Il, V:933
Giorgione, **III:305-307**
   Bellini, III:60
   Concert Champêtre, III:306
   Tempest, The, III:306
   Three Philosophers, The, III:306, 307
   Titian, III:721
   Toilet of Venus, III:305
Giotto, II:272, 305, **388-391,** 632, 633, 698, 700,
   745; III:483; VII:1359
   Last Judgment, The, II:390
   Life of Saint Francis, II:390

Raising of Drusiana, The, II:390
Saint John the Baptist, II:390
Giovanni di Simone Guidi, Tommaso di. *See*
    Masaccio
Girardon, François, IV:151
Giraudoux, Jean, **VII:1379-1382**
    Amphitryon, VII:1380
    Bella, VII:1379
    Choix des élues, VII:1380
    Combat avec l'ange, VII:1380
    Eglantine, VII:1380
    Electra, VII:1380
    Enchanted, The, VII:1380
    Madwoman of Chaillot, The, VII:1380
    My Friend from Limousin, VII:1379, 1380
    Ondine, VII:1380
    Sigfried, VII:1380
    Tiger at the Gates, VII:1379
Girl Guides. *See* Girl Scouts
Girl Scouts, V:105-107; VIII:2246-2248
Girodet, Louis, V:411
Girondins
    Condorcet, IV:348-350
    Danton, IV:394
    Marat, IV:911, 912
    Orléans, IV:1050
    Robespierre, IV:1171, 1172
    Saint-Just, IV:1205
Gish, Dorothy, VII:1383, 1385, 1386
Gish, Lillian, **VII:1383-1386**
    Birth of a Nation, The, VII:1383
    Broken Blossoms, VII:1385
    Camille, VII:1385
    Hamlet, VII:1385
    Intolerance, VII:1383
    Life With Father, VII:1385
    Mothering Heart, The, VII:1383
    Uncle Vanya, VII:1385
    Unseen Enemy, An, VII:1383
    Way down East, VII:1385
    Whales of August, The, VII:845
Giza, temples at, VI:1412
Gladstone, William Ewart, **V:935-939**
    Acton, V:12
    Asquith, VII:121
    Balfour, VII:172
    Bradley, V:290
    Bright, V:307, 308
    Disraeli, V:677, 678
    Forster, V:804, 805
    Lansdowne, VIII:2090, 2091
    Irish home rule, VI:1741

Khartoum, V:965
Liberal Party, V:1036
Peel, VI:1753, 1754
State in Its Relations with the Church, The,
    V:935
Glanville, Ranulf de, II:179, 447
glasnost, VIII:1424, 1426, 1963; IX:3299
Glass, Philip, VII:34, 35
Glaucia, Gaius, I:529
Gleichheit, Die, IX:4113, 4114
Glendower, Owen, II:459
Glen Grey Act of 1894, VI:1876
Glenn, John H., Jr., **VII:1387-1390**
Glorious Revolution of 1688
    Addison, IV:26
    Blackstone, IV:130
    Kidd, IV:777
    Locke, IV:857
    Marlborough, IV:922
    Mather, Cotton, IV:934
    Mather, Increase, IV:939
    Monmouth, IV:982
    Shays, IV:1040
    William III, IV:1447
Gloster Meteor, IX:3974
Gloucester, Duke of, III:341
Gloucester, Earl of, II:645, 646
Gloucester, Statute of, II:322
Gluck, Cristoph, **IV:549-551**
    Alceste, IV:549, 550
    Artaserse, IV:549
    Don Juan, IV:549
    Fausse Esclave, La, IV:549
    Iphigénie en Aulide, IV:550
    Orfeo ed Euridice, IV:549, 550
    Paride ed Elena, IV:550
    Semiramide riconosciuta, IV:549
Glyn, Elinor, V:290
G.M. *See* General Motors
Gneisenau, August von, V:264, 265, **9
    40-943**
Gnosticism
    Irenaeus, I:447-450
    John the Apostle, I:477
    Origen, I:581, 582
    Rumi, II:800
    Valentinus, I:911-914
Goa, III:12, 788, 799
Go Daigo, II:97
Godard, Jean-Luc, **VIII:1391-1395**
    All the Boys Are Called Patrick, VIII:1391
    Alphaville, VIII:1393

Band of Outsiders, VIII:1393

Breathless, VIII:1391, 1392

Carabiniers, Les, VII:1049

Contempt, VIII:1392

Detective, VIII:1393

Every Man for Himself, VIII:1393

First Name: Carmen, VIII:1392

Hail Mary, VIII:1393

Joy of Learning, The, VIII:1393

King Lear, VIII:1393

Little Soldier, The, VIII:1392

Married Woman, The, VIII:1393

Masculin-féminin, VIII:1393

My Life to Live, VIII:1392

Pierrot le fou, VIII:1393

Riflemen, The, VIII:1392

Sympathy for the Devil, VIII:1393

Weekend, VIII:1393

Woman is a Woman, A, VIII:1392

Goddard, Robert H., **VIII:1396-1399,** 1500;
   IX:2777

   Method of Reaching Extreme Altitudes, A,
   VIII:1397

   Rocket Development, VIII:1397

Gödel, Kurt, VIII:2725

Godey, Alexis, V:430

Godey, Louis, V:1022-1024

Godey's Lady's Book, V: 361, 1022-1024

Godkin, Edwin Lawrence, **VIII:1400-1403**

Godolphin, First Earl of, **IV:552-554**

Godse, Nathuram, VII:1284

Godunov, Boris Fyodorovich, **III:308-310**

Godwin, Edward William, VI:2215, 2216

Godwin, Mary. *See* Shelley, Mary Wollstonecraft

Godwin, William, **IV:555-559,** 1477; VI:1468,
   2048, 2049, 2051, 2054

   Caleb Williams, VI:2048

   *Cursory Strictures on the Charge Delivered by
   Lord Chief Justice Eyre to the Grand Jury,*
   IV:557

   Enquiry Concerning Political Justice, An,
   IV:555, 556, 558; VI:1787, 2053

   *Historical and Moral View of the Origin and
   Progress of the French Revolution, An,* IV:57

   Memoirs, IV:57

   St. Leon, IV:57

   Things as They Are, IV:557, 558

   Vindication of the Rights of Woman, A, IV:57

Goebbels, Joseph, VII:1013; **VIII:1404-1407,**
   2078

Goethals, George Washington, **VIII:1408-1410,**
   1436

Goethe, Johann Wolfgang von, **IV:560-563,**
   651-653, 1217, 1219; V:1020, 1159, 1160;
   VI:1989; VIII:2274

   Autobiography of Goethe, The, IV:562

   Elective Affinities, IV:562, 563; VII:267

   Erlebnislyrik, IV:562, 564

   Gotz von Berlichingen with the Iron Hand,
   IV:560

   Iphigenia in Taurus, IV:560

   Roman Elegies, IV:562

   Sorrows of Young Werther, IV:560; VII:208

   Theory of Colors, IV:562

   Tragedy of Faust, The, IV:562; V:203; VI:1988,
   1993

   West-Eastern Divan, IV:562

   Wilhelm Meister's Apprenticeship, IV:562, 563

Gogh, Vincent van, V:889, 891, **944-948;**
   VIII:1992, 2404; IX:3354, 3355

   Potato Eaters, The, V:945

   Self-Portrait, V:944, 946

   Starry Night, The, V:946, 947

Gogol, Nikolai, V:687, **949-952;** VI:2268

   Arabesques, V:949

   Dead Souls, V:950, 951;VII:641

   "Diary of a Madman," V:949; VIII:2252

   Evenings on a Farm Near Dakota, V:949

   Inspector General, The, V:950; VIII:2511

   "Nose, The," V:950

   "Overcoat, The," V:950

   Petersburg Cycle, V:949

   "St. John's Eve," VI:1612

Gokhale, Gopal Krishna, IX:3681-3684

Golan Heights, VII:856

Golden Bull of 1356, II:236, 237

Golden Fleece, Order of the, II:741, 742

Golden Horde, II:53, 54, 378, 382, 884, 987;
   III:382

Goldfisch, Samuel. *See* Goldwyn, Samuel

Goldie, Sir George, **V:953-955;** VIII:2269

Goldman, Emma, **VIII:1411-1414,** 1732

   Mother Earth, VIII:1413

Goldmark, Rubin, VII:766

Goldoni, Carlo

   Mistress of the Inn, The, VIII:2143

Gold Rush of 1849, VI:2060

Goldsmith, Oliver, **IV:564-568**

   Citizen of the World, The, IV:565, 1020

   Deserted Village, The, IV:566, 567

   *Enquiry into the Present State of Polite Learning
   in Europe, An,* IV:565

   Good-Natured Man, The, IV:566, 567

   Goody Two-Shoes, IV:565

Grecian History, IV:564, 566
History of England, The, IV:566
History of England in a Series of Letters from a Nobleman to His Son, IV:566
History of the Earth, An, IV:564, 566, 567
Life of Richard Nash, Esq., The, IV:564, 566
Retaliation, IV:567
Roman History, The, IV:566
She Stoops to Conquer, IV:564, 567
Traveller, The, IV:564-566
Vicar of Wakefield, The, IV:564, 566, 1020; VI:2216
gold standard
    Bevin, VII:314
    Bryan, VII:479
    Keynes, VIII:1952
    MacDonald, VIII:2315
    McKinley, VI:1454
    Rhodes, VI:1874
    Ricardo, VI:1878
Goldstein, Eugen, IX:3491
Goldwater, Barry, VII:713
Goldwyn, Samuel, VII:119, 176, 896; **VIII:1415-1418;** IX:3205
    Best Years of Our Lives, The, VIII:1417
    Little Foxes, The, VIII:1417
    Porgy and Bess, VIII:1417
    Squaw Man, The, VIII:1415
    These Three, VIII:1417
    Wuthering Heights, VIII:1417
Goldwyn Pictures Corporation, VIII:1417
golf
    Didrikson, IX:4096-4098
    Jones, VIII:1874-1877
    Nicklaus, IX:3041, 4050
    Palmer, IX:3041
    Player, IX:3040-3042
    Woods, IX:4049-4051
Goliath, I:241
Gomarists, III:575
Gompers, Samuel, V:26, **956-959;** VIII:2170
Gonatas, Antigonus, I:970
Goncharov, Ivan, VI:2269
Goncourt brothers, IV:1414
Gondi family, IV:1380
Gondomar, Count of, IV:700
Gonne, Maud, IX:4082, 4083, 4085
Gonzaga, Ludovico, III:9
Gonzaga dynasty, IV:990, 991
Gonzaga Palace, III:462
González, José Victoriano. *See* Gris, Juan
González, Pablo, IX:4106

González Prada, Manuel, VIII:1584
Goodall, Jane, VIII:2148
Good King Canute. *See* Canute the Great
Goodman, Benny, **VIII:1419-1422**
    "Honeysuckle Rose," VIII:1420
    "King Porter Stomp," VIII:1419
    Let's Dance, VIII:1419
    "Scarecrow," VIII:1420
    "Sing, Sing, Sing," VIII:1420
    "Stealin' Apples," VIII:1420
Good Neighbor Policy, VII:573; VIII:1729, 1768, 1780
Goodyear, Charles, **V:960-963**
G.O.P. *See* Republican Party
Gorbachev, Mikhail, **VIII:1423-1426**
    Bukharin, VII:492, 493
    Bush, VII:522
    Dubcek, VII:970
    Khrushchev, VIII:1963
    Li Peng, VIII:2179
    Sakharov, IX:3299
    Yeltsin, IX:4086-4088
Gordimer, Nadine, **VIII:1427-1430**
    Burger's Daughter, VIII:1429
    Guest of Honor, A, VIII:1429
    July's People, VIII:1429
    Late Bourgeois World, The, VIII:1429
    Lying Days, The, VIII:1427, 1429
    Occasion for Loving, VIII:1429
    World of Strangers, A, VIII:1429
Gordon, Anna A., VI:2388, 2389
Gordon, Charles George, V:936, **964-966**
Gordon, George. *See* Byron, Lord
Gordon Riots of 1780, IV:1237
Gore, Albert, VII:708; **VIII:1431-1433;** IX:3155
Gorenko, Anna Andreyevna. *See* Akhmatova, Anna
Gorgas, William Crawford, **VIII:1434-1437**
Gorgeous George, VII:54
Gorham, Maurice, VII:737, 738
Göring, Hermann, VII:1013; **VIII:1438-1441,** 1615, 1910, 1949, 1950
Gorky, Maxim, **VIII:1442-1446;** IX:2899
    Life of Klim Samgin, The, VIII:1444
    Lower Depths, The, VIII:1444, 1445
    Mother, The, VIII:1444, 1445
Gorky Institute, VII:153
gospel music, VII:657, 1216
Gospel of Wealth, The, V:423
Gospels, I:56, I:450, 467-470
    See also John, Gospel of; Luke, Gospel of; Matthew, Gospel of; Mark, Gospel of

Gosse, Sir Edmund, VIII:2683
Gosson, Stephen, III:692, 693
Gostling, John, IV:1138
Gotha Canal, VI:2208
Gotha Program, VI:1370
Gothardt, Matthias. *See* Grünewald, Matthias
Goths. *See* Visigoths
Gottfried von Strassberg, **II:392-394,** 435
  Tristan and Isolde, II:392-394
Göttingen, University of, VIII:1797
Göttingen Observatory, V:894
Gottsched, Johann Christoph, IV:842, 843
Gough, John, V:602
Gould, Jay, V:731; VI:1581, 2285
Gould, Stephen Jay, V:609
Goulue, La, VI:2248
Gounod, Charles, **V:967-970**
  Colombe, La, V:968, 969
  Faust, V:968
  Médecin malgré lui, Le, V:969
  Messe solennelle de Sainte Cécile, V:968
  Nonne sanglante, La, V:968
  Philèmon et Baucis, V:969
  Polyeucte, V:968, 969
  Rédemption, La, V:969
  Sapho, V:968
Government of India Act, VIII:1849
Goya, Francisco de, **IV:569-573;** VI:1854
  Black Paintings, The, IV:571
  Caprices, The, IV:571, 572
  Clothed Maja, The, IV:571
  Disasters of War, The, IV:571, 572; VI:1960
  Duke and Duchess of Osuna, The, IV:570
  Executions of May Second, The, IV:571
  Executions of May Third, The, IV:571, 572
  Milkmaid of Bordeaux, The, IV:571
  Naked Maja, The, IV:571
  Parasol, The, IV:570
  Portrait of Don Manuel Orsorio, IV:570
  Portrait of the Count of Floridablanca, The, IV:570
  Portrait of the Family of King Charles IV, IV:571
  Proverbs, The, IV:571, 572
  Qué Valor, VI:1960
  Washerwoman, The, IV:570
Goyathlay. *See* Geronimo
Gracchi, The, **I:345-348**
Grace, Covenant of, IV:1464
Grace, Pilgrimage of, III:205, 209
Grace, William Gilbert, **V:971-974**
Graf Zeppelin, VII:1012, 1013; IX:4111

Graham, Billy, **VIII:1447-1450**
  Personal History, VIII:1452
Graham, John, VIII:2023, 2024
  System and Dialectics of Art, VIII:2023
Graham, Katharine, **VIII:1451-1454**
  Lower Depths, The, VIII:1444
Graham, Martha, VII:1178; **VIII:1455-1458**
  Appalachian Spring, VIII:1458
  Heretic, VIII:1457
  Horizons, VII:539
  Letter to the World, VIII:1458
  Panorama, VII:539
  Primitive Mysteries, VIII:1458
  Revolt, VIII:1457
  Vision of the Apocalypse, VIII:1457
  Xochital, VIII:1455
Graham, Philip L., VIII:1451
Graham, Sheilah, VII:1163
Graham's Magazine, VI:1796
Grahn, Judy, VIII:1508
Gramsci, Antonio, **VIII:1459-1462**
  Quaderni del carcere, VIII:1459, 1461
  Selections from the Prison Notebooks, VIII:1459
Granada, Cathedral of, III:696, 697
Grand Alliance, War of the, IV:873, 923, 924
Grand Alliance of European powers, IV:1447, 1448
Grand Council of French Western Africa, VIII:1755
Grandfathers, War of the, V:126
Grand Prix racing, VII:1150
Grand Remonstrance, IV:309, 1142
Grands Rhétoriqueurs, II:245
Grand Trunk Railway, VIII:1981, 2102
Grant, James Augustus, VI:2084, 2085
Grant, Ulysses S., **V:975-978**
  Arthur, V:78
  Barnard, V:131
  Blaine, V:256
  Greeley, V:985
  Hayes, V:1075
  Johnson, V:1235
  Joseph, V:1242
  Michelson, VI:1551
  Nast, VI:1628
  Powell, VI:1810
  Sherman, VI:2059, 2060
  Stanton, VI:2108
  Sumner, VI:2172, 2173
Granvelle, Antoine Perrenot de, III:599, 781
Granville, Earl of, IV:1074
Granz, Norman, VII:1159

Grass, Günter, **VIII:1463-1466**
  Cat and Mouse, VIII:1464
  Dog Years, VIII:1464
  Flounder, The, VIII:1464
  From the Diary of a Snail, VIII:1464
  Headbirths, VIII:1464
  Local Anaesthetic, VIII:1464
  Meeting at Telgte, The, VIII:1464
  Only Ten Minutes to Buffalo, VIII:1463
  Plebeians Rehearse the Uprising, The,
    VIII:1464
  Rat, The, VIII:1465
  Show Your Tongue, VIII:1465
  Tin Drum, The, VIII:1463, 1464
Grasse, François-Joseph-Paul, Comte de, IV:1175
Grassman, Hermann Günther, IX:3966
Gratian, I:44, 695, 868, 870; II:179
Gratus, Valerius, I:640
Graves, Robert
  I, Claudius, I:551
gravity, I:79; IV:263
  Guericke, IV:588
  Hawking, VIII:1582
  Huygens, IV:697
  Kepler, IV:775, 775
  Lagrange, IV:786
  Laplace, VI:1319-1322
  Maclaurin, IV:882-884
  Newton, IV:601, 1025, 1027, 1028
Gray, Asa, V:32, **979-981**
Gray, Thomas
  Elegy in a Country Churchyard, IV:1473
Great Awakening, IV:429, 1202; V:470; VI:1425
Great Books of the Western World, VIII:1801, 1802
Great Bouwerie, IV:1294
Great Camp of Kiangnan, VI:2261
Great Compromise. *See* Connecticut Compromise
Great Contract of 1610, III:662
Great Depression
  Alger, V:52
  Baldwin, VII:170
  Broadway musicals, VIII:1567
  Canada, VIII:1982, 1983
  Catholic Worker movement, VII:851
  Hoover, VIII:1727, 1729, 1730
  Humphrey, VIII:1785
  Japan, VIII:2458
  Keynes, VIII:1954
  London School of Economics, VII:309
  Miller's plays, VIII:2533
  Nazi Party, VIII:1405, 1676, 1694
  photography, VII:397; VIII:2083, 2084

  Rogers, IX:3206
  Roosevelt, IX:3224, 3225
  Sandburg, IX:3310
  Steinbeck, IX:3515
Greater Dionysia
  Aeschylus, I:10
  Aristophanes, I:91
  Demosthenes, I:255
  Euripides, I:317
  Pisistratus, I:649
  Sophocles, I:10, 11, 807
  Thespis, I:877-879
Great Leap Forward
  Chou En-lai, VII:678
  Deng Xiaoping, VII:905
  Khrushchev, VIII:1962
  Lin Piao, VIII:2190
  Liu Shao-ch'i, VIII:2213, 2214
  Mao Tse-tung, VIII:2401, 2402
  P'eng Te-huai, IX:2955
Great Northern Expedition, IV:111, 112
Great Northern Railroad, IV:660, 661;
    VII:881
Great Northern War, IV:290-292, 533
Great Ordinance, II:606
Great Parliament, II:645
Great Persecution, I:266
Great Persian Wars. *See* Persian Wars
Great Proletarian Cultural Revolution. *See* Cultural
  Revolution
Great Purge, VIII:2571
Great Reform Bill. *See* Reform Bill of 1832
Great Renunciation, I:915
Great Saltash Bridge, V:337
Great Schism, II:220, 237, 760, 899, 969-971,
    1009-1011
Great Service, III:107, 108
Great Sioux Reservation, VI:2070
Great Society, VII:948; VIII:1868
Great Swamp Battle, IV:955
Great Trek, V:380
Great Wall of China, I:177
Greco, El, **III:311-314**
  Assumption of the Virgin, V:436
  Burial of the Count of Orgaz, The, III:312
  Martyrdom of Saint Maurice, The, III:311
  Trinity, The, III:313
  View of Toledo, V:436
Greco-Persian Wars. *See* Persian Wars
Greek mythology
  Aesop, I:13-15
  Antisthenes, I:67

Aristophanes, I:91
Bernini, IV:118-120
Callimachus, I:157
Dionysius, I:878
Empedocles, I:282
Epicurus, I:295
Hesiod, I:402-405
Homer, I:420-422
Ingres, V:1184, 1185
Offenbach, VI:1685, 1686
Phidias, I:624-626
Philo of Alexandria, I:632
Pindar, I:644-646
Racine, IV:1146
Ronsard, III:657-659
Scopas, I:765
Xenophanes, I:955-957
Greek Orthodox Church, I:121
Greeley, Horace, V:192, 850, **982-986;**
    VIII:1533
Green, Thomas Hill, **V:987-989;** VIII:1707
Greene, Ann Terry, VI:1771
Greene, Catherine, IV:1431
Greene, Graham, VII:731; **VIII:1467-1470**
    Brighton Rock, VIII:1468
    Dr. Fischer of Geneva, VIII:1469
    Heart of the Matter, The, VIII:1468
    Human Factor, The, VIII:1468
    It's a Battlefield, VIII:1468
    Journey without Maps, VIII:1468
    Labyrinthine Ways, The, VIII:1468
    Man Within, The, VIII:1467
    Monsignor Quixote, IV:269; VIII:1469
    Quiet American, The, VIII:1469
    Shipwrecked, The, VIII:1468
    Sort of Life, A, VIII:1467
    Stamboul Train, VIII:1467
Greene, Nathanael, **IV:574-578,** 1406, 1431
Greene, Robert, III:548, 686, 687
Greenland
    Davis, III:212, 213
    Eriksson, II:577-579
    Peary, IX:2941
    Wegener, IX:3918-3920
Green Mountain Boys, IV:34-36
Green River, VI:1810, 1812
Greenspan, Alan, **VIII:1471-1474**
Green Spring Faction, IV:80
Greenville, Treaty of, VI:2204
Greenway, Francis, **V:990-993**
Greenwich Village Follies, VIII:1457
Gregory II, II:167, 900

Gregory III, II:243
Gregory VI, II:395
Gregory VII, **II:395-398,** 461, 462, 575, 583,
    928, 929
    Dictatus papae, II:396
Gregory IX, **II:399-402**
    Anthony of Padua, II:77
    Elizabeth of Hungary, II:342
    Frederick II, II:362, 363
    Innocent IV, II:514
    Raymond of Peñafort, II:776, 777
    William of Auvergne, II:977
    William of Auxerre, II:982
Gregory X, II:165, 796, 797, 985
Gregory XI, II:220, 1010
Gregory XIII, I:813; III:552, 715
Gregory XVI, VI:1782
Gregory, William
    Lectures on Experimental Philosophy,
        Astronomy and Chemistry, V:1093
Gregory, MacLeod, and Company, IV:879
Gregory of Nazianzus, **I:349-351,** 352, 869
    On His Life, I:349
    On St. Basil the Great, I:350
    Theological Orations, I:349
Gregory of Nyssa, **I:352-355**
    Contra Eunomium, I:353, 354
Gregory of Tours, II:274-276, **403-406**
    History of the Franks, The, II:274, 403-405
    Life of the Fathers, II:404
    Miracles of St. Martin, The, II:403,404
Gregory the Great, II:405, **407-410**
    Dialogues of Saint Gregory the Great,
        II:136-138
    Moralia, II:407
    Pastoral Care, II:408
Gregory v. Ashcroft, IX:2791
Grenadier Guards, VIII:2340
Grenville, Sir Richard, **III:315-317**
    Cavendish, III:140
    Raleigh, III:639
    Wilkes, IV:1439
Greuze, Jean-Baptiste, IV:414
Grey, Charles. *See* Grey, Second Earl
Grey, Lady Jane, III:237, 239, **318-321,** 479, 480
Grey, Second Earl, IV:42; **V:994-997;** VI:2393
Grey, Sir Edward, **VIII:1475-1477**
Grey, Sir George Edward, **V:998-1001;** VIII:1475
Grieg, Edvard, **V:1002-1005;** VII:892-894
    Peer Gynt, V:1003
    Piano Concerto in A Minor, V:1003
    Sörgemarsch over Rikard Nordraak, V:1003

Griffith, D.W., VII:1274; **VIII:1478-1482,** 1690, 2231, 2232, 2234; IX:3006, 3008
  Birth of a Nation, The, VII:1383; VIII:1480, 1481
  Broken Blossoms, VII:1385; VIII:1481
  Hearts of the World, VII:783
  Intolerance, VII:959, 1383; VIII:1480, 1481, 2232, 2234
  Mothering Heart, The, VII:1383
  One Million B.C., VIII:1481
  Orphans of the Storm, VIII:1480, 1481
  Struggle, The, VIII:1481
  Unseen Enemy, An, VII:1383
  Way Down East, VII:1385
Griffith, John, VII:798
Griffith, Richard R, III:458
Griffith, Sir Samuel, V:149
Griffiths, Ralph, IV:565
Grijalva, Juan de, III:21
Grimes, Peter, VII:471
Grimké, Angelina, V:885
Grimké, Francis, V:808
Grimké, Sarah, V:808
Grimm, Jacob and Wilhelm, **V:1006-1009;** VIII:1712
  Grimm's Fairy Tales, V:1006-1008
Grindal, Edmund, III:590
Gris, Juan, VII:432; **VIII:1483-1485**
  Harlequin, VIII:1484
  Portrait of Picasso, VIII:1483
  "Possibilités de la Peinture, Les," VIII:1484
  Siphon and Bottles, VIII:1483
Griswold v. Conneticut, VII:322
Grolman, Karl, V:940-942
Gromyko, Andrei, VII:461; VIII:1424; IX:3102
Groote, Gerhard, II:906, 907
Gropius, Walter, **VIII:1486-1489**
  Klee, VIII:2006
  Kokoschka, VIII:2013
  Mahler, VIII:2363
Grosseteste, Robert, II:110, 985
Grotius, Hugo, **IV:579-582**
  Adamus Exul, The, IV:579
  Christ's Passion, IV:579
  Commentary on the Law of Prize and Booty, IV:579
  Freedom of the Seas, The, IV:579
  Gentili, III:296
  international law, III:769
  Introduction to Dutch Jurisprudence, IV:580
  Oldenbarnevelt, III:575

  On the Law of War and Peace, IV:579-581
  Pufendorf, IV:1134
Group 47, VII:349
Group 64, VII:809
Group Theatre, VII:795; IX:4009, 4010
Grove, Sir William Robert, **V:1010-1014**
  On the Correlation of Physical Forces, V:1012
Groves, Leslie, VII:637
Gruen, David. *See* Ben-Gurion, David
Grundy, Felix, VI:1801
Grünewald, Matthias, **III:322-324**
  Isenheim altarpiece, III:322-324
Guadalcanal, VIII:1527
Guadalupe Hidalgo, Treaty of, V:859; VI:2416
Guajardo, Jesús M., IX:4106
Gualterotti, Raffaelo, IV:850
Guarini, Battista
  Faithful Shepherd, The, IV:990, 991
Guarini, Guarino, **IV:583-585**
  Architecttura civile, IV:584, 585
  Desegni d'architettura civile e ecclesiastica, IV:584
Guderian, Heinz, **VIII:1490-1493**
Guelfs (Guelphs), II:286, 288, 515, 961; V:934
Guericke, Otto von, **IV:586-588**
Guerin, Camille, VII:547
Guerin, Pierre-Narcisse, V:645, 910
guerrilla warfare
  Arafat, VII:90
  Collins, VII:733, 734
  Guevara, VIII:1494-1496
  Lawrence, VIII:2128
  Mozambique, VIII:2317
  South African War, VIII:2003
  Utah miners, VIII:1499
  Viet Cong, VIII:1701
  Vo Nguyen Giap, IX:3824
  Zapata, IX:4104, 4106
  Zimbabwe, VIII:2647-2649
Guesde, Jules, V:1222
Guettard, Jean-Étienne, IV:805
Guevara, Che, VII:617; **VIII:1494-1497,** 1634
  Che Guevara on Guerrilla Warfare, VIII:1495, 1496
Guggenheim, Daniel, **VIII:1498-1501**
Guggenheim, Meyer, VIII:1498
Guggenheim, Peggy, IX:3048, 3049
Guggenheim Foundation, VIII:2733
Guggenheim Museum, IX:4062
Guicciardini, Francesco, **III:325-327,** 498
  Accusatoria, III:326

*Considerations on the Discourses of
Machiavelli,* III:325
Consolatoria, III:326
Cose fiorentine, III:326
Defensoria, III:326
Dialogo del reggimento di Firenze, III:325
History of Italy, The, III:326, 327
Ricordi, III:326, 327
Guido d'Arezzo, **II:411-413**
   Aliae regulae, II:412
   Epistola de ignoto cantu, II:412, 413
   Micrologus, II:411, 412
   *Regulae rhythmicae in antiphonarii prologum
prolate,* II:412, 413
Guilbert, Yvette, VI:2248, 2249
Guillaume, Charles-Édouard, **VIII:1502-1504**
   Traité pratique de la thermométrie de précision,
VIII:1495
Guinizelli, Guido, II:224
Guiscard, Marquis de, IV:158
Guiscard, Robert, II:159
Guise, House of
   Catherine de Médicis, III:132, 133
   Henry IV, III:333
   Hotman, III:363-365
   Mary, Queen of Scots, III:475
   Mornay, III:538
Guizot, François, VI:2226, 2227
Gulf Oil, VIII:2481
Gulf Stream, III:629, 631
Gulf War. *See* Persian Gulf War
Gullichsen, Harry and Maire, VII:2
Gumilyov, Nikolai, VII:37, 38
Gumm, Frances. *See* Garland, Judy
Gundobad, II:276
gunpowder, II:988, 989; IV:1335; V:718-720;
   VI:1674
Gunpowder Plot, III:257-259, 662; IV:47, 700, 747
Gunpowder Women, VII:488
guns
   Colt, V:540-542
   Oakley, VI:1677-1679
   Rehnquist, IX:3144
Gupta Dynasty, I:491
Gustavus II Adolphus, IV:304, 452, **589-592,**
   1052, 1335, 1336
Gutenberg, Johann, **III:328-332**
Gutenberg Bible, III:328, 330, 331
Guthrum, II:60
Guy de Chauliac, **II:414-416**
   Chirurgia magna, II:414, 415
Guyuk. *See* Kuyuk

Gyges, I:106
Gypsies, VII:210, 1128; VIII:1854-1856
Gzhantsk, VII:1272

Haakon Sigurdsson, II:688, 689
Ha'am, Ahad, IX:3930
Habeler, Peter, VIII:2507, 2508
Haber, Fritz, **VIII:1509-1512,** 1654
Habsburg, House of
   Alva, III:18-20
   Charles V, III:159-161
   Czechoslovakia, VII:259
   Ferdinand II, IV:450, 451
   Ferdinand and Isabella, III:262
   Fischer von Erlach, IV:473-475
   Francis I, III:274, 275, 277
   Francis Ferdinand, VII:1197
   Frederick Henry, IV:500
   Frederick the Great, IV:504
   German Protestantism, IV:590
   Guicciardini, III:326
   Henry IV, III:335
   Imperial Style, IV:655
   Joseph II, IV:750-752
   Leopold I, IV:838-840
   Louis XIV, IV:868
   Maria Theresa, IV:914-916
   Marie-Antoinette, IV:918
   Maximillian I, III:491, 492
   Philip II, III:599, 600, 602
   Richelieu, IV:1166, 1167
   Rudolf I, II:796, 797
   Strauss, VI:2158
   Süleyman the Magnificent, III:707, 708
   Titian, III:721
   Wallenstein, IV:1396
Hadden, Briton, VIII:2260, 2262
Hadfield, James, IV:441
Hadfield, Sir Robert Abbott, **V:1015-1017**
Hadi, al-, II:437
Hadrian, I:28, **356-359,** 901, 902
Hadrian's Temple, I:358
Hadrian's Wall, I:358
Haeckel, Ernst, **V:1018-1021**
   Evolution of Man, The, V:1021
   Generelle Morphologie der Organismen,
V:1020, 1021
   History of Creation, The, V:1021
   Report on the Deep-Sea Medusae, V:1020
   Report on the Radiolara, V:1018, 1020
   Riddle of the Universe, The, V:1021
   Wonders of Life, The, V:1021

Hafiz, **II:417-420**
  Divan, The, II:417, 418
Haganah, VII:243, 245, 251, 252, 854
Hagar, I:6
Hageladas. *See* Ageladas
Hagenau, Reinmar von, II:960
Haghia Sophia, II:556
Hague, The, III:574; IX:2860
Hague Peace Conferences, VI:2177; VIII:2051
Hahl, August, VI:1541
Hahn, Otto, **VIII:1513-1516,** 1618, 1648,
  2476, 2477
  Applied Radiochemistry, VIII:1516
Hahnemann, Samuel, **IV:593-595**
  Organon of the Healing Art, IV:594
Haig, Douglas, VII:58, 59
Haile Selassie, **VIII:1517-1521**
Haitian Revolution, V:501, 502
Hakodate, VI:1762
Haldimand, Frederick, IV:198
Hale, Matthew, **IV:596-599**
  History of the Common Law, IV:598
  History of the Pleas of the Crown, IV:598
Hale, Sarah Josepha, **V:1022-1024**
  Northwood, V:1022, 1023
  Poems for Our Children, V:1023
  Sketches of American Character, V:1022
  Traits of American Life, V:1022
  Woman's Record, V:1024
Haley, Sir William, VII:737, 738
Halffter, Ernesto, VII:1129
Half World's Convention, V:1110
Halicarnassus, Mausoleum of, I:764
Halide Edib Adivar, **VIII:1522-1524**
  Clown and His Daughter, The, VIII:1524
  Memoirs of Halide Edib, VIII:1524
  Seviye Talip, VIII:1523
  Shirt of Flame, The, VIII:1523
  Turkish Ordeal, The, VIII:1524
  Yeni Turan, VIII:1523
Halidon, Battle of, II:294
Halifax, Lord, VII:530
Halil, Candarli, III:499, 500
Hall, James, VI:1420
Hallaj, al-, **II:421-425**
  Kitab al-tawasin, II:422
  Riwayat, II:422
Hallam, Arthur Henry, VI:2211, 2213
Haller, Albrecht von, IV:523
Halley, Edmond, **IV:600-603,** 785, 883, 1027; V:215
  Astronomie cometicae synopsis, IV:602
  Catalogus Stellarum Australium, IV:600

Halley's Comet, IV:602; V:215
Haloid Corporation. *See* Xerox
Hals, Frans, **IV:604-607**
  Laughing Cavalier, The, IV:605
  Lute Player, The, IV:606
  Seated Man Holding a Branch, IV:606
Halsey, William F., **VIII:1525-1528,** 2751
Halske, Johann Georg, VI:2067
Halsted, William, VII:823
Hamaguchi Yuko, VIII:1574
Hamann, Johann Georg, IV:651
Hamburg Opera, IV:1320, 1321
Hamilcar, I:740
Hamilton, Alexander, **IV:608-612**
  Burr, V:369, 370
  Federalist, The, IV:610
  Federalist Party, IV:19
  Jay, IV:714
  Jefferson, IV:718, 719
  Madison, IV:886, 888
  Parrington, IX:2893, 2894
  *Report Relative to a Provision for the Support of
    Public Credit,* IV:610
Hamilton, Andrew, IV:1486
Hamilton, Gavin, V:408
Hamilton, Henry, IV:314
Hamilton, Lady, IV:1188
Hamilton, Sir William Rowan, **V:1025-1028**
Hammadid kingdom, II:4
Hammarskjöld, Dag, VII:502; **VIII:1529-1532;**
  IX:3103, 3647, 3746, 3747
Hammerstein, Oscar, II, **VIII:1533-1536;**
  IX:3201, 3202
  Allegro, VIII:1534
  Always You, VIII:1533
  Annie Get Your Gun, VII:289, 290
  Carmen Jones, VIII:1534
  Carousel, VIII:1534, 1536
  Desert Song, VIII:1533
  Flower Drum Song, VIII:1536
  King and I, The, VIII:1534, 1536
  Me and Juliet, VIII:1534
  Music in the Air, VIII:1534
  New Moon, The, VIII:1534
  Oklahoma, VIII:1534, 1536
  Pipe Dream, VIII:1536
  Rose Marie, VIII:1533
  Show Boat, VIII:1533, 1536
  Sound of Music, The, VIII:1536
  South Pacific, VIII:1534, 1536
  State Fair, VIII:1534, 1536
  Sunny, VIII:1533

Sweet Adeline, VIII:1534
Tickle Me, VIII:1533
Very Warm for May, VIII:1534
Hammett, Dashiell, VIII:1620, 1623
Hammond, John, VII:1217; VIII:1717
Hammurabi, **I:360-363,** 569
Hampton Court Conference, III:661
Hamsun, Knut, **VIII:1537-1540**
   August, VIII:1538
   Bjoerger, VIII:1537
   Children of the Age, VIII:1538
   Dreamers, VIII:1538
   gaadefulde, Den, VIII:1537
   Growth of the Soil, VIII:1538
   Mysteries, VIII:1537
   On Overgrown Paths, VIII:1538
   Pan, VIII:1538
   Segelfoss Town, VIII:1538
   Victoria, VIII:1538
Hancock, John, IV:357, **613-618**
Hancock, Thomas, V:962
Hand, Learned, **VIII:1541-1544**
   "Spirit of Liberty, The," VIII:1542
Handel, George Friederic, IV:228, **619-622**
   Almira, IV:619
   Deborah, VIII:2770
   Fireworks Music, IV:621
   Messiah, IV:621, 622, 641
   Nero, IV:619
   Resurrezione, La, IV:620
   Rinaldo, IV:620
   Rodrigo, IV:620
   St. John Passion, IV:619
Han dynasty, I:178, 590, 944, 949
Han-fei-tzu, I:433
Hangchow, II:479, 612, 856
Hanging Gardens, I:569, 570
Hanks, John, VI:1380
Hanna, Marcus A., **V:1029-1032**
Hannah, I:746
Hannibal, I:334-336, **364-367,** 535, 536, 761
Hanno, **I:368-370**
Hanoverian Dynasty, IV:53, 531-538,
   1277-1279
Hansberry, Lorraine, **VIII:1545-1549**
   Blancs, Les, VIII:1547, 1548
   Drinking Gourd, The, VIII:1547, 1548
   "Negro Writer and His Roots, The,"
     VIII:1547, 1548
   Raisin in the Sun, A, VIII:1545, 1547
   Sign in Sidney Brustein's Window, The,
     VIII:1547, 1548

   To Be Young, Gifted, and Black, VIII:1548
   What Use Are Flowers?, VIII:1547, 1548
Hanseatic League, II:933
Han Yu, II:709
Haoge, IV:421
Hapsburg, House of. *See* Habsburg, House of
Harbach, Otto, VIII:1533
Hard, Darlene, VII:1364
Hardenberg, Karl von, **V:1033-1035;** VI:2116
Hardie, James Keir, **V:1036-1039**
Harding, Warren G., **VII:1550-1553**
   Butler, VII:525
   Coolidge, VII:762, 763
   Debs, VII:882
   Hughes, VIII:1767
   Mellon, VIII:2481
Hardinge, Lord, VI:1331
Hardouin-Mansart, Jules. *See* Mansart, Jules
   Hardouin-
Hardy, Thomas, **V:1040-1043;** VI:1786
   Desperate Remedies, V:1040
   Dynasts, The, V:1042
   Far from the Madding Crowd, V:1040, 1042
   Jude the Obscure, V:1042
   Mayor of Casterbridge, The, V:1040, 1042
   "Poor Man and the Lady, The," V:1040
   Return of the Native, The, V:1040, 1042
   Tess of the D'Urbervilles, V:1042
   Under the Greenwood Tree, V:1040
   Winter Words, V:1042
   Woodlanders, The, V:1042
Hare, David
   Judas Kiss, The, VI:2380
Hare, Julius Charles, VI:1457, 1458
Harewood House, V:138
Hargreaves, James, **IV:623-625,** 770
Harlem Railroad, VI:2297
Harlem Renaissance, VIII:1771-1774, 1787-1789
Harley, Robert, IV:52, 53, 157, 158, 401, 1400
Harmonists, I:99
Harmsworth, Alfred, **VIII:1554-1556**
Harmsworth, Harold, **VIII:1554-1556**
Harnack, Adolf von, **VIII:1557-1559**
   Grundriss der Dogmengeschichte, VIII:1558
   History of Dogma, VIII:1558
   Luke the Physician, VIII:1558
   What Is Christianity?, VIII:1558
Harold II, **II:426-429**
Harold Godwinson. *See* Harold II
Harper, Henry Alpert, VIII:1981
Harper, William Rainey, **V:1044-1048**
Harper's Bazaar, VIII:2310

Harper's Ferry
    Brown, V:322, 324, 491, 1151
    Lee, VI:1338
    Parker, VI:1729
    Thoreau, VI:2235
    Tubman, VI:2266
Harper's Weekly
    Homer, V:1133, 1134
    Nast, VI:1627, 1628
    Remington, VI:1861, 1862
    Schurz, VI:1997
    Tweed, VI:2285, 2286
Harries, Carl, IX:3497
Harriman, William Averell, **VIII:1560-1565**
Harringay Crusade, VIII:1448
Harris, Joel Chandler, **V:1049-1052**
    Balaam and His Master, V:1051
    Free Joe and Other Georgian Sketches, V:1050
    "Free Joe and the Rest of the World," V:1051
    Mingo, V:1049
    Nights with Uncle Remus, V:1049
    Uncle Remus, V:1049
    "Where's Duncan?," V:1051
Harris, Middleton
    Black Book, The, VIII:2628
Harris, Theodore, VII:489
Harris, Townshend, V:1181, 1182
Harrison, Benjamin, V:257, 513, **1053-1056**
Harrison, Francis, IV:1485
Harrison, Frederic, **V:1057-1060**
Harrison, George, VII:226-229
Harrison, John, IV:185
Harrison, Thomas, IV:789, 790
Harrison, William Henry, **V:1061-1063**
    Clay, V:509
    Cushing, V:582
    Perry, VI:1764, 1765
    Tecumseh, VI:2204
    Tyler, VI:2288-2290
    Webster, VI:2345
Harris Treaty, V:1182
Harris v. Forklift Systems, VIII:2326
Harsha, **II:430-432,** 484
    Nágánanda, II:431
    Retnavali, II:431
Hart, Lorenz, **VIII:1566-1570; IX:3201, 3202**
    Babes in Arms, VIII:1568
    "Bewitched, Bothered and Bewildered,"
        VIII:1568
    "Blue Room, The," VIII:1567
    Boys from Syracuse, The, VIII:1568
    Connecticut Yankee, The, VIII:1567, 1569

Dearest Enemy, VIII:1567
Garrick Gaieties, The, VIII:1566, 1567
Girl Friend, The, VIII:1567
"I Could Write a Book," VIII:1568
I'd Rather Be Right, VIII:1568
I Married an Angel, VIII:1568
Jumbo, VIII:1568
On Your Toes, VIII:1568
Pal Joey, VIII:1568
Peggy-Ann, VIII:1567
Hartford, Treaty of, IV:1296
Hartford Female Seminary, V:170
Harthacnut, II:315
Hart House, VI:1496
Hartmann, Nicolai, **VIII:1577-1579**
    Aufbau der realen Welt, Der, VIII:1572
    Ethics, VIII:1571
    Grundzuge einer Metaphysik der Erkenntis,
        VIII:1572
    Möglichkeit und Wirklichkeit, VIII:1572
    New Ways of Ontology, VIII:1572
    Zur Grundlegung der Ontologie, VIII:1572
Hartmann von Aue, **II:433-436**
    De arme Heinrich, II:433, 434
    Erec, II:433
    Gregorius, II:433, 434
    Iwein, II:433, 434
    Klage, Die, II:433
Harty, Sir Hamilton, IX:3874
Harun al-Rashid, **II:437-439**
Harvard Botanic Garden, V:980
Harvard Law School
    Frankfurter, VII:1212
    Hand, VIII:1541
    Holmes, VIII:1720, 1721
    Marshall, VIII:2433
    Richardson, VI:1883
Harvard Observatory, VI:1756
Harvard University
    Adams, V:15
    Agassiz, V:30, 31
    Bancroft, V:124, 125
    Bernstein, VII:295
    Carpenter Center for Visual Arts, VIII:2139
    Conant, VII:749
    Du Bois, VII:963
    Dumbarton Oaks, VII:1131
    Eliot, V:748, 749
    Emerson, V:757, 758
    Fuller, VII:1265
    Gray, V:979, 980
    Higginson, V:1110

Kissinger, VIII:1998, 1999
Krogh, VIII:2029
Laski, VIII:2093
Lippmann, VIII:2203
Mather, Cotton, IV:935, 936
Mather, Increase, IV:941
Royce, IX:3254
Santayana, IX:3317
Whitehead, IX:3967
See also Harvard Law School; Harvard
  Observatory
Harvey, Gabriel, III:549
Harvey, William, **IV:626-630,** 891, 1210
  Anatomical Exercises of Dr. William Harvey,
    The, IV:628
  Anatomical Exercitations, IV:629
  Circulation of the Blood, The, IV:629
  De venarum ostiolis, IV:626
Hasan al-Basre, al-, **II:440-442**
Hashemite Kingdom of Transjordan, VIII:1791;
    IX:4079
Hasidic Judaism, IV:73-75, 432, 433; VII:484, 485
Haskalah, IV:432, 433
Hasmonaean dynasty, I:390-392
Hastings, Battle of, II:998
Hastings, Warren, IV:224, **631-634**
Hastings, William Lord, III:650
Hatoyama Ichiro, **VIII:1574-1576**
Hatshepsut, **I:371-374,** 889
Hatta, Mohammad, **VIII:1577-1579;** IX:3571
Hauptmann, Bruno Richard, VIII:2194
Haushofer, Karl, VIII:2322
Haüy, Valentin, V:303, 304
Havel, Václav, VII:970
Havelock, Sir Henry, VI:1706
Havemeyer, H.O., V:435, 436
Hawaii
  Cook, IV:353, 354
  Heyerdahl, VIII:1660
  Kamehameha I, VI:1255, 1257
  Liliuokalani, VI:1372, 1374
  McKinley, VI:1455
  New Zealand, VI:2019
  Vancouver, IV:1355, 1356
Hawke, Sir Edward, IV:57
Hawking, Stephen W., **VIII:1580-1583**
Hawkins, John, Sir, III:224, 225
Hawksmoor, Nicholas, **IV:635-638,** 1352, 1353
Hawley-Smoot Tariff, VIII:1729, 1779, 1780
Hawthorne, Nathaniel, **V:1064-1067;** VI:1524,
    1776, 1777, 1796
  Blithedale Romance, The, V:1066

Fanshawe, V:1064
House of the Seven Gables, The, V:1066
Life of Franklin Pierce, The, V:1066
Marble Faun, The, I:691; V:1066
"Minister's Black Veil, The," IV:430
Mosses from an Old Manse, V:1064
Scarlet Letter, The, V:715, 1064, 1066
Twice-Told Tales, V:1064; VI:1794
Hawtrey, Charles, VII:783
Hay, John, **V:1068-1071**
  Abraham Lincoln, V:1066
  Bread-Winners, The, V:1066, 1070
  Castilian Days, V:1068
  Pike County Ballads and Other Pieces,
    V:1068, 1070
Haya de la Torre, Víctor Raúl, **VIII:1584-1587**
Hayden, Ferdinand Vandeveer, **V:1072-1074**
Hayden, Scott, V:1240
Haydn, Franz Joseph, **IV:639-643**
  Beethoven, V:178, 179
  Boccherini, IV:149
  Brahms, V:301
  Creation, The, IV:641
  "Glorius Things of Thee Are Spoken," IV:642
  Seasons, The, IV:641
  Surprise Symphony, IV:639
Haydon, Benjamin Robert, VI:1266
Hayes, Helen, **VIII:1588-1592**
  Airport, VIII:1591
  Anastasia, VIII:1591
  Bab, VIII:1588
  Coquette, VIII:1588
  Dear Brutus, VIII:1588
  Harriet, VIII:1589
  Mary of Scotland, VIII:1589
  Sin of Madelon Claudet, The, VIII:1589
  Victoria Regina, VIII:1589
  What Every Woman Knows, VIII:1588
Hayes, Rutherford B., V:78, 80, 256, **1075-1079**
Hay-Herbert Treaty, V:1070
Hay-Herrán Treaty, V:1090
Hayley, William, IV:138, 1188
Hayman, Francis, IV:515
Haymarket Square Riot, V:54; VIII:1411
Haymes, Dick, VIII:1598
Hay-Pauncefote Treaty, V:1069
Hayslip, Le Ly, **VIII:1593-1595**
  Child of War, Woman of Peace, VIII:1593
  When Heaven and Earth Changed Places,
    VIII:1593, 1594
Hayward, Nathaniel, V:961
Haywood, William D., V:280

Hayworth, Rita, **VIII:1596-1600**
  Affair in Trinidad, VIII:1598
  Blood and Sand, VIII:1597
  Cover Girl, VIII:1597
  Gilda, VIII:1597-1599
  Lady from Shanghai, The, VIII:1597
  Miss Sadie Thompson, VIII:1598
  Only Angels Have Wings, VIII:1597
  Pal Joey, VIII:1598
  Strawberry Blonde, The, VIII:1597
  You'll Never Get Rich, VIII:1597
Hazlitt, William, VI:1266, 1267
H.D. (Hilda Doolittle), **VIII:1505-1508**
  Choruses from the Iphigenia in Aulis, VIII:1506
  Hedylus, VIII:1506
  "Hermes of the Ways," VIII:1505-1508
  Palimpsest, VIII:1506
  Sea Garden, VIII:1506
  Tribute to Freud, VIII:1506
  Tribute to the Angels, VIII:1508
  Trilogy, VIII:1506
  Walls Do Not Fall, The, VIII:1506
Head, Sir Francis Bond, VI:1450
Health, Education, and Welfare, Department of,
  VIII:1704, 1705
Hearst, William Randolph, **VIII:1601-1605**
  Eckener's zeppelin, VII:1012
  Graham, VIII:1447
  Oakley's libel suit, VI:1678
heart
  Aretaeus of Cappadocia, I:82
  Diocles of Carystus, I:261
  electrocardiograms, VII:217, 1039-1041
  Empedocles, I:284
  Erasistratus, I:300
  Galen, I:339
  Harvey, IV:628
  Starling, IX:3494-3496
  transplants, VII:195, 197
Heartland Theory, VIII:2321-2323
Heath, Edward, VIII:**1606-1609;** IX:3649,
  3650, 4017
Heath, John, VI:1765
Hebard, Grace Raymond, VI:1934
Hebra, Ferdinand von, VI:2021, 2023
Hegel, Georg Wilhelm Friedrich, **V:1080-1084**
  Böhme, IV:155
  Croce, VII:801
  Dewey, VII:916, 917
  Difference Between Fichte's and Schelling's
    Philosophy, The, V:1080
  Encyclopedia of Philosophy, V:1082

Fichte, IV:468
Herzen, V:1099
Kierkegaard, VI:1284, 1286
Lassalle, VI:1323
Lectures on the Philosophy of History, V:1082
Marx, VI:1492
Moore, VIII:2605, 2606
Phenomenology of Spirit, The, V:1080, 1082,
  1083; VIII:2061
Philosophy of Right, V:1083
Philosophy of the Unconscious, VI:1986
Ritschl, VI:1892
Schelling, VI:1972-1974
Schopenhauer, VI:1985
Science of Logic, V:1082
Tönnies, IX:3703
Veblen, IX:3806
Hegesias, I:87
Heidegger, Martin, II:313; VII:499, 615;
  VIII:1610-1613, 1798
  Being and Time, VIII:1610-1612; VII:615
  Letter on Humanism, VIII:1612
  Selbstbehauptung der deutschen Universität,
    VIII:1611
  Was ist Metaphysik?, VIII:1611
Heiler, Friedrich, IX:3829, 3830
Hein, Piet, IV:502, **644-646**
Heine, Heinrich, V:204, **1085-1088;** VI:1336
  Atta Troll, V:1086
  Book of Songs, V:1086
  Germany: A Winter's Tale, V:1086
  Pictures of Travel, V:1086
  Salon, The, V:1086
Heinkel, Ernst Heinrich, **VIII:1614-1616**
Heinkel Corporation, IX:3974
Heinmot Tooyalakekt. *See* Joseph, Chief
Heisenberg, Werner, **VIII:1617-1619,** 2705
Helena, Saint, **I:375-377**
Helen of Troy, VI:1686
Helenopolis, I:228
Helfferich, Karl, VII:1104
Hellespont, I:963
Hellman, Lillian, **VIII:1620-1623;** IX:2886
  Another Part of the Forest, VIII:1622
  Autumn Garden, The, VIII:1622
  Children's Hour, The, VIII:1620, 1622
  Little Foxes, The, VII:845; VIII:1417, 1610,
    1622, 1638
  Toys in the Attic, VIII:1622
  Watch on the Rhine, VIII:1622
Helmechis, II:42
Helots, I:17, 18

Helmasperger Instrument, III:328
Helmholtz, Hermann von, **V:1089-1092;**
    VIII:2713, 2714; IX:4069
    *On the Sensations of Tone as a Physiological
        Basis for the Theory of Music,* V:1090
    Treatise on Physiological Optics, V:1090
Hélöise, II:11, 13, 14
Helpmann, Robert, VII:1175, 1178
Helsinki Accord, VII:460, 612
hematology. *See* blood
Hemerken, Thomas. *See* Thomas à Kempis
Hemingway, Ernest, VII:1163; **VIII:1624-1628;**
    IX:3512, 4043
    Across the River and into the Trees, VIII:1626
    Death in the Afternoon, VIII:1626
    Farewell to Arms, A, VIII:1589, 1626
    Fifth Column, The, VIII:1626
    For Whom the Bell Tolls, VIII:1626
    Garden of Eden, The, VIII:1626
    Green Hills of Africa, VIII:1626
    In Our Time, VIII:1624, 1626
    "Killers, The," VIII:1742
    Moveable Feast, A, VIII:1626
    Old Man and the Sea, The, VII:937; VIII:1626,
        1627
    Sun Also Rises, The, VIII:1626
    To Have and Have Not, VIII:1626
Henderson, Arthur, VIII:2313
Henderson, Fletcher, VII:105
Henderson, Richard, IV:163, 164
Hengist, **I:378-381**
Hengstenberg, Ernst Wilhelm, VI:1828
Henie, Sonja, **VIII:1629-1632**
    Sun Valley Serenade, VIII:1630
Hennebique, François, IX:2976
Henri, Robert, VIII:1740
Henrietta Anne, Princess, IV:171
Henry (of Anjou), II:292, 849
Henry (of Blois), II:847, 848
Henry (of Burgundy), II:30
Henry (of Condé), IV:863
Henry (of Navarre). *See* Henry IV (of France)
Henry (of Schwerin), II:933
Henry I (of England), **II:443-445**
    Anselm, II:74
    David I, II:291
    Henry II, II:446
    Stephen, II:847
Henry I (of France), II:997
Henry II (of England), **II:446-448**
    Adrian IV, II:29
    Alexander III, II:49

Becket, II:128
Eleanor of Aquitaine, II:338
John, King, II:540
Philip II, II:732
Richard I, II:782, 783
Stephen, II:850
Henry II (of France), III:756
Henry II the Saint, **II:449-452**
Henry III (of England), II:190-192, **453-456,**
    581-583, 642-646
Henry III (of France), III:133, 333, 365, 538
Henry IV (of England), **II:457-460;** III:337
Henry IV (of France), III:255, **333-336**
    Catherine de Médicis, III:133, 135
    Champlain, IV:271, 273
    Hotman, III:364, 365
    Louis XIII, IV:863
    Mansart, IV:898
    Montaigne, III:525, 526
    Mornay, III:537-539
    Philip II, III:600
    Richelieu, IV:1165
Henry IV (of Germany), **II:461-465**
Henry IV (of Spain), III:260
Henry V (of England), **III:337-340,** 341
Henry VI (of England), **III:341-344**
    Fortescue, III:267, 268
    Innocent III, II:510
    Richard III, III:647
    Warwick, III:774, 776
Henry VII (of England), **III:345-348**
    Cabot, III:113, 115
    Catherine of Aragon, III:136
    Henry VIII, III:349
    More, III:533
    Richard III, III:651
    Tudor family, III:732, 734
    Warwick, III:776
Henry VIII (of England), **III:349-353**
    *Assertio septem sacramentorum adversus
        Martinum Lutherum,* III:351
    Boleyn, III:66, 68, 69
    Catherine of Aragon, III:136, 138, 139
    Clement VII, III:167, 168
    Colet, III:170
    Coverdale, III:193-195
    Cranmer, III:204-206
    Cromwell, III:208-210
    Edward VI, III:237-239
    Elizabeth I, III:241
    Fisher, III:264, 265
    Gardiner, III:291, 292

Grey, III:318
Holbein the Younger, III:358-360
Howard, III:367-369
Mary I, III:479
Mary, Queen of Scots, III:475
More, III:533-536
Parr, III:592-594
Ridley, III:654-656
Tudor family, III:732-734
Tyndale, III:736
Wolsey, III:785, 786
Henry, Charles, VI:2035
Henry, Fort, V:976
Henry, Joseph, V:103, **1093-1095; VI:1593**
Henry, O., **V:1096-1098**
    Cabbages and Kings, V:1097
    "Gift of the Magi, The," V:1098
    "Miracle of Lava Canyon, The," V:1097
    "Whistling Dick's Christmas Stocking," V:1097
Henry, Patrick, IV:312, **647-650**
Henry Street Settlement, IX:3837-3839
Henry the Lion, **II:466-469**
    Lucidaris, II:468
Henry the Navigator, Prince, III:215, **354-357**
Henry the Proud, II:466
Henson, Matthew, IX:2942, 2944
Henze, Hans Werner, **VIII:1633-1636**
    Bassarids, The, VIII:1634
    Cimarrón, El, VIII:1634
    Elegy for Young Lovers, VIII:1634
    Essay on Pigs, VIII:1634
    King of Harlem, The, VIII:1635
    König Hirsch, VIII:1633, 1634
    Novae de infinito laudes, VIII:1634
    Oven, The, VIII:1635
    Raft of the Medusa, The, VIII:1634
Hepburn, Katharine, VII:794; **VIII:1637-1640**
    African Queen, The, VIII:1639
    Bill of Divorcement, A, VIII:1638
    Bringing Up Baby, VIII:1638
    Christopher Strong, VII:119; VIII:1638
    Guess Who's Coming to Dinner, VIII:1639
    Lake, The, VIII:1638
    Lion in Winter, The, VIII:1639
    Little Women, VIII:1638
    Long Day's Journey into Night, VIII:1639
    Morning Glory, VIII:1638
    On Golden Pond, VIII:1639
    Philadelphia Story, The, VIII:1638; IX:3529
    Stage Door, VIII:1638
    Warrior's Husband, The, VIII:1637
    Woman of the Year, VIII:1638

Hepburn Act, IX:3229
Hepburn v. Griswald, V:789
Hephthalite Huns, II:559, 560
Heracleopolis, I:637
Heracles, I:67, 317, 318
Heraclitus of Ephesus, I:157, **382-386,** 972
    On Nature, I:382
Heraclius, **II:470-473,** 819-821
Herbert, George. *See* Carnarvon, Fifth Earl of
Herbst, Josephine, IX:3061
Hercules, I:69
Herder, Johann Gottfried, **IV:651-654**
    Adrastea, IV:652
    God: Some Conversations, IV:652
    Kritische Wälder, IV:651
    Letters for the Advancement of Humanity,
        IV:652
    Outlines of a Philosophy of the History of Man,
        IV:652
    Treatise upon the Origin of Language, IV:651
    Über die neuere deutsche Literatur, IV:651
heresy
    Abelard, II:14, 144
    Ambrose, I:44
    Andrewes, IV:47
    Bayle, IV:103
    Catharist movement, II:49
    Dominic, II:301, 302
    Galileo, IV:521
    Gardiner, III:293
    Gregory the Great, II:408
    Hippolytus of Rome, I:415
    Irenaeus, I:448-450
    Mary I, III:480
    Ockham, II:682, 683
    Philip II, III:599
    Priscillian, I:695, 696
    Siger of Brabant, II:830
    Spinoza, IV:1264
    Stephen, I:823
    Tertullian, I:849
    Vincent of Lérins, I:936-938
    Wyclif, II:1011
Hering, Ewald, VII:452
Hering-Breuer reflex, VII:452
Hermann I, II:340
Hermann, Wilhelm, VII:498
Hermarchus, I:295
Hermeias, I:95
Hermes, I:690-692
Hermeticism, IV:949-951
Hermias, I:63

Hermippus, I:115
Hermitage, the, IV:801
Hermite, Charles, IX:2994, 2995
Hermopolis, I:637
Hernandez, Aileen Clarke, **VIII:1641-1643**
Herod Antipus, I:480
Herodotus, **I:394-397**
    Aesop, I:14
    African exploration, I:370
    Eupalinus of Megara, I:314
    Hesiod, I:405
    History of Herodotus, The, I:233, 394, 396, 397,
        621, 622, 706
    Pheidippides, I:621, 622
    Pisistratus, I:650
    Thucydides, I:886, 887
Herod the Great, **I:390-393**
Heron of Alexandria. *See* Hero of Alexandria
Hero of Alexandria, **I:387-389;** IV:787
    Automata, I:387
    Belopoeica, I:387
    Catoptrica, I:387
    Cheiroballistra, I:387
    Dioptra, I:387
    Mechanica, I:387
    On Measures, I:387, 388
    Pneumatics of Hero of Alexandria, The, I:387, 388
    Stereometrica, I:387, 388
Herophilus, **I:398-401**
    Against Common Opinions, I:400
    Erasistratus, I:299-301
    On Anatomy, I:398, 399
    On Delivery, I:399
    On Pulses, I:399
Herring, Constantine, IV:594
Herriot, Édouard, **VIII:1644-1646;** IX:3046
Herrmann, Bernard, VIII:1821
Herrnhut, IV:1488-1490
Herschel, William, IX:3701
Hertz, Gustav, **VIII:1647-1649**
Hertz, Heinrich, VI:1513, 1806, 1807; VII:318,
    319; VIII:1647, 2415
Hertz, Rudolph, V:1090
Hertzog, Jan, VII:377
Herzen, Aleksandr, **V:1099-1101**
    Diletantizm v nauke, V:1099
    From the Other Shore, V:1100
    My Past and Thoughts, V:1100
    Pisma iz Frantsii i Italii, V:1099
    Pisma ob izuchenii prirody, V:1099
    Who Is to Blame?, V:1099
    Zapski odnogo molodogo cheloveka, V:1099

Herzl, Theodor, **V:1102-1106;** VIII:2767;
    IX:3930, 3931
    Jewish State, A, V:1104
    Old-new Land, V:1105
Heseltine, Philip, IX:3873
Hesiod, **I:402-406**
    Shield of Herakles, I:403
    Thales of Miletus, I:852, 855
    Theogony, I:402-404
    Works and Days, I:15, 402-404
Hesse, Hermann, **VIII:1650-1653**
    Peter Camenzind, VIII:1650, 1651
    Demian, VIII:1650, 1651
    Glass Bead Game, The, VIII:1650-1652
    Klingsor's Last Summer, VIII:1650, 1651
    Steppenwolf, VIII:1651, 1652
    Prodigy, The, VIII:1651
    Siddhartha, VIII:1651
    Death and the Lover, VIII:1652
    Journey to the East, The, VIII:1652
Hesychasm, II:899-901
Heth, Joice, V:135
Hetzel, P.J., VI:2303
Heuga, Jimmy, VIII:1965
Hevelius, Johannes, IV:600
Hevesy, Georg von, **VIII:1654-1657**
HEW. *See* Health, Education, and Welfare,
    Department of
Heyerdahl, Thor, **VIII:1658-1661**
    Aku-Aku, VIII:1659
    American Indians in the Pacific, VIII:1659
    Archaeology of Easter Island, VIII:1659
    Fatu-Hiva, VIII:1658
    Kon-Tiki, VIII:1658
    Ra Expeditions, The, VIII:1660
Hezekiah, I:454
Hicesias, I:268
Hickok, James Butler. *See* Hickok, Wild Bill
Hickok, Wild Bill, V:390, 391, **1107-1109**
Hicks, Amelia, VII:353
Hierapolis, I:784
Hiero, I:788, 789
Hieron, I:10
Hieron II, I:76, 78, 79
Hieronymus, I:79
Higginson, Thomas Wentworth, V:670,
    1110-1112, 1201
Highjump, Operation, VII:535
Highs, Thomas, IV:61, 624
Hijaz Railway, VIII:2126, 2127
Hilalians, II:5
Hilbert, David, VIII:2725

Hildebrandt, Johann Lucas von, **IV:655-658**
Hildegard von Bingen, **II:474-478**
  Ordo virtutum, II:476
  Scivias, II:474,476
  Symphonia harmonia caelestium revelationum,
    II:476
Hilderic, I:344
Hill, Anita F., IX:3657, 3658
Hill, James Jerome, **IV:659-661**
Hill, Octavia, **V:1113-1116**
Hillary, Sir Edmund, **VIII:1662-1665**
Himmler, Heinrich, VII:440; VIII:1492,
  1666-1669
Hincmar of Reims, II:673
Hindemith, Paul, **VIII:1670-1673;** IX:3873
  Cardillac, VII:471
  Craft of Musical Composition, The, VIII:1671
  Harmonie der Welt, Die, VIII:1672
  Kammermusik, VIII:1671
  Ludus Tonalis, VIII:1672
  Mathis der Maler, VII:471; VIII:1671
  Sancta Susanna, VIII:1671
  Symphonic Metamorphosis of Themes by Carl
    Maria von Weber, VIII:1672
  Wirbauen eine Stadt, VIII:1672
Hindenburg, IX:4111
Hindenburg, Paul von, **VIII:1674-1677,**
  2265-2267; IX:2877
Hindustan Seva Dal, VIII:2709
Hines, Earl, VII:106, 107; IX:2882
Hinton, James, VII:1070
Hipparchus, **I:407-410,** 649, 712, 787, 813
  Commentary on the Phaenomena of Eudoxus
    and Aratus, I:407
  On Bodies Carried Down by Their Weight,
    I:407
Hipparete, I:31
Hippasus of Metapontum, I:728
Hippias, I:214, 649, 650, 857
Hippocrates, I:174, 175, 260, 262, 400, **411-414;**
  II:713, 779, 780
  Ancient Medicine, I:35, 412
  Corpus Hippocraticum, I:411
  "Life Is short, Art long," I:413
  Regimen, I:412
Hippodrome, II:890-892
Hippolytus of Rome, **I:415-419**
  Apostolic Tradition of Hippolytus, The, I:417
Hiram of Tyre, I:800
Hiraoka, Kimitake. *See* Mishima, Yukio
Hirohito, **VIII:1678-1682**
  Akihito, VII:41, 42

Hiroshige, **V:1117-1119,** 1121
  Meisho Edo Hyakkei, V:1118
  Tokaido Gojusantsugi, V:1118
Hiss, Alger, VII:18; **VIII:1683-1686,** 1733, 2758
  In the Court of Public Opinion, VIII:1684
  Recollections of a Life, VIII:1684
Histadrut, VII:252
Hitchcock, Alfred, **VIII:1687-1691;**
  IX:3736, 3738
  Alfred Hitchcock Presents, VIII:1688
  Blackmail, VIII:1687
  Dial M for Murder, VIII:1690
  Family Plot, VIII:1690
  Frenzy, VIII:1690
  Lifeboat, VIII:1688; VII:397
  Lodger, The, VIII:1687
  Man Who Knew Too Much, The, VIII:1688;
    IX:3530
  North by Northwest, VIII:1690
  Notorious, VIII:1688
  Psycho, VIII:1690
  Rear Window, VIII:1690; IX:3530
  Rebecca, VIII:1688; IX:2810
  Rope, IX:3530
  Sabotage, VIII:1688
  Shadow of a Doubt, VIII:1688
  39 Steps, The, VIII:1688
  To Catch a Thief, VIII:1690
  Topaz, VIII:1690
  Torn Curtain, VIII:1690
  Vertigo, VIII:1690; IX:3530
Hitler, Adolf, **VIII:1692-1697**
  Astor, VII:130
  atom bomb, VII:380
  Baldwin, VII:170
  Berlin Olympics of 1936, IX:2862
  Capek, VII:561
  Chamberlain, VII:644-646
  Chaplin, VII:654
  evangelical church, VIII:2742
  Finland, VIII:2398
  Franco, VII:1201, 1202
  Goebbels, VIII:1404-1406
  Göring, VIII:1438-1441
  Guderian, VIII:1490, 1492
  Heinkel, VIII:1616
  Henie, VIII:1631
  Himmler, VIII:1666-1668
  Hindenburg, VIII:1674-1676
  Kesselring, VIII:1949, 1950
  Lang, VIII:2078
  Laval, VIII:2106, 2107

Lewis, VIII:2176
Lloyd George, VIII:2218
Luce, VIII:2262
Ludendorff, VIII:2266
Lyons, VIII:2294
Mackinder, VIII:2322
Mann, VIII:2393
Mein Kampf, VII:645; VIII:1694, 1695, 2135
Napoleon I, VI:1617, 1618
Nobel Prize policy, VII:952
Papen, VII:2876, 2877
Perón, IV:2969
Rommel, IX:3215
Rundstedt, IX:3260-3262
Wagner, VI:2319
Williams's music, IX:3799
zeppelins, VII:1013
Hittite empire, I:736, 904; VIII:2125
Hoad, Lewis A., VIII:2110
Hoare, Sir Samuel, VII:1016
Hoare-Laval Agreement, VIII:2105, 2107
Hobbes, Thomas, IV:160, **662-667,** 855, 857,
    951, 1134
    Behemoth, IV:665
    De Sive, IV:664
    Elements of Law, Natural and Politic, The,
      IV:662, 664
    Leviathan, IV:664, 665, 855
Hobby, Oveta Culp, **VIII:1703-1706**
Hobhouse, Leonard T., **VIII:1707-1710**
    Labour Movement, The, VIII:1707
    Metaphysical Theory of the State, The, VIII:1709
    Mind in Evolution, VIII:1709
    Morals in Evolution, VIII:1709
    Theory of Knowledge, The, VIII:1708
Hobomok, IV:1274
Hochhuth, Rolf
    Deputy, The, IV:1219
Ho Chi Minh, **VIII:1698-1702;** IX:3821, 3823
Hockney, David, **VIII:1711-1714**
    American Collectors, VIII:1712
    Bigger Splash, A, VIII:1712
    Boy About to Take a Shower, VIII:1712
    Christopher Isherwood and Don Bachardy,
      VIII:1712
    Doll Boy, VIII:1711
    Mr. and Mrs. Clark with Percy, VIII:1712
    Myself and My Heroes, VIII:1711
    Rake's Progress, A, VIII:1711, 1712
    Shell Garage, VIII:1712
    We 2 Boys Together Clinging, VIII:1711
Hoffa, Jimmy, VIII:1933

Hoffman, Friedrich, IV:1268, 1269, 1271
Hoffmann, August Wilhelm von, VI:1367
Hoffmann, Roald, IX:4054
Hofmann, Hans, VIII:2023, 2728; IX:3049
Hofmann, Hugo von, IX:3556
Hofmeyr, Jan Hendrik, IX:2907
Hofstadter, Robert, IX:4090
Hogarth, William, **IV:668-671,** 1163; V:237
    Analysis of Beauty, The, IV:669
    Artist Painting the Comic Muse, The, IV:670
    Bathos, The, IV:670
    Harlot's Progress, A, IV:668, 669
    Industry and Idleness, IV:669
    Marriage à la Mode, IV:669, 670
    Painter and His Pug, The, IV:669
    Rake's Progress, The, IV:669; VIII:1711
Hogarth Press, IX:4056
Hogben, Lancelot, VII:309
Hogg, Thomas Jefferson, VI:2052
Högskola, VII:114, 115
Hohenheim, Philippus Aureolus Theophrastus
    Bombast von. *See* Paracelsus
Hohenstaufen Dynasty, II:466, 468, 531, 643, 796,
    932, 961
Hohenzollern family, IV:508-510
Hojoji Muryojuin, II:537, 538
Hojo Ujimasa, IV:1327
Hokke, II:667
Hokusai, V:1118, **1120-1122**
    Fugaku hyakkei, V:1121
    Fugaku sanjurokkei, V:1121
    Fuji Under the Wave at Kanagawa, V:1121
    Mount Fuji at Dawn, V:1121
    Mount Fuji in Storm, V:1121
Holbein, Hans the Younger, **III:358-361**
    Body of the Dead Christ in His Tomb, The,
      III:360
    Christiana of Denmark, Duchess of Milan,
      III:359
    Erasmus, III:248
    Fisher, III:264
    Portrait of His Wife and Two Elder Children,
      III:359
Holbrooke, Richard, VII:51
Holder, Wesley, VII:670
Holiday, Billie, VII:1157; **VIII:1715-1719,** 1885
    "Billie's Blues," VIII:1717
    "God Bless the Child," VIII:1718
    Lady in Satin, VIII:1718
    Lady Sings the Blues, VIII:1715
    "Strange Fruit," VIII:1717
Holland, John Philip, **V:1123-1125**

Holliday, Doc, V:735
Hollywood League Against Nazism, VIII:1534
Holmes, Oliver Wendell, **V:1126-1129; VI:2022;**
    VIII:1720
    Autocrat of the Breakfast-Table, The, V:1127
    Elsie Venner, V:1129
    Guardian Angel, The, V:1129
    "Last Leaf, The," V:1127
    Medical Essays, 1842-1882, V:1126
    Mortal Antipathy, A, V:1129
    "Old Ironsides," V:1127
Holmes, Oliver Wendell, Jr., VII:576, 882;
    VIII:1720-1723
    Common Law, The, VIII:1721
Holmes, Sherlock, V:700-702
Holocaust
    Baeck, VII:149, 150
    Bourke-White, VII:397
    Dawidowicz, VII:847-849
    Diary of Anne Frank, The, VII:1204-1206
    Göring, VIII:1438-1441
    Himmler, VIII:1666-1668
    Hitler, VIII:1692, 1694, 1695
    Niemöller, VIII:2743
    Sachs, IX:3285-3287
    Stein, IX:3508-3510
    Wiesel, IX:3980, 3982
    Wiesenthal, IX:3984-3987
Holstein, Friedrich von, **V:1130-1132**
Holy Alliance, V:46, 407, 414; V:1034
Holy Apostles, Church of the, II:556
Holy Brotherhood, III:261, 262
Holy Cross, Cathedral of the, V:351
Holy Cross, Mountain of the, V:1073, 1074
Holy League, III:407, 450, 493, 669
Holy Sepulchre, Church of the, I:375
Holy Shroud, Chapel of the, IV:584, 585
Holy Spirit
    Filioque doctrine, II:583
    Gregory of Nazianzus, I:349
    Irenaeus, I:449
    Theoleptus of Philadelphia, II:899, 900
    Ulfilas, I:909
    Valentinus, I:912
Holy Synod, VI:1790-1792
Holy Trinity, I:849, 869, 909, 910; III:485, 675
    Biddle, IV:126, 127
    Boethius, II:155
    Channing, V:471
    Clovis, II:275
    Joachim of Fiore, II:534, 535
    Russian Orthodox Church, IV:1031

    Schleiermacher, VI:1978
    Swedenborg, IV:1303
    William of Saint-Thierry, II:995
Holzschuh, Dietrich, II:797
Home, John
    Douglas, V:800
Home Monthly, VII:623
Homer, **I:420-423,** 624, 649, 852, 855, 955-957
    Iliad, I:420-422, 758, 830; III:155; IV:1115;
        V:344, 1184; VI:1982
    Odyssey, I:304, 420-422, 598, 685; III:155;
        IV:1116; V:344, 1184; VIII:1921, 2128
Homer, Winslow, **V:1133-1136**
    Adolescence, V:1133
    Carnival, The, V:1135
    Driftwood, V:1135
    Gulf Stream, The, V:1135
    Herring Net, The, V:1134
    Lookout—All's Well, V:1135
    Prisoners from the Front, V:1134
    Punishment for Intoxication, V:1134
    Sharpshooter, The, V:1134
    Skirmish in the Wilderness, A, V:1134
    Wreck, The, V:1135
Home Rule Confederation of Great Britain,
    VI:1740
Homestead Strike of 1892, V:421, 423; VII:419
Honami Koetsu, IV:1041, 1257, 1258
Honda, Soichiro, **VIII:1724-1726**
Honda Motor Company, VIII:1724-1726
Hong Kong, VI:1378; VII:906; VIII:2270
Honnoji Incident, III:571
Honoria, I:126
Honorius, I:342, 871
Hood, John Bell, VI:2060
Hooke, Robert, IV:186, 600, 601, 825, 826, 1025
    Micrographia, IV:825
Hooker, Joseph, V:608
Hooker, Richard, IV:46, 47
Hook of Holland project, IX:2860
Hoopes, Darlington, IX:3662
Hoover, Herbert, VIII:1552, **1727-1731;** IX:3224
    Principles of Mining, VIII:1727
Hoover, J. Edgar, **VIII:1732-1735;** IX:3547
Hoover Moratorium, VIII:1729
Hopkey, Sophia, IV:1426, 1427
Hopkins, Gerard Manley, II:313
Hopkins, Harry, **VIII:1736-1739**
Hopkins, Samuel, V:470
Hopper, Edward, **VIII:1740-1743**
    Cape Cod Evening, VIII:1742
    Hotel Room, VIII:1742

House by the Railroad, VIII:1742
Mansard Roof, The, VIII:1740
Nighthawks, VIII:1742, 1743
Night on the El Train, VIII:1742
Night Windows, VIII:1742
Office at Night, VIII:1742
Summer Evening, VIII:1742
Two Comedians, VIII:1742
Horace, **I:424-428**
    Art of Poetry, The, I:426; IV:1115
    Carmen Saeculare, I:426
    Epistles, I:425, 426
    Epodes, I:425
    Maecenas, I:521
    Odes, I:425, 426, 520
    Ovid, I:585, 587
    Ronsard, III:657
    Satires, I:424, 425, 926
Horemheb, I:25
Hormuz, Strait of, III:12
Hornblower, Horatio, VII:1189-1191
Horney, Karen, VII:1247; **VIII:1744-1746**
    Neurosis and Human Growth, VIII:1745
    Neurotic Personality of Our Time, The,
      VIII:1745
    New Ways in Psychoanalysis, VIII:1745
    Our Inner Conflicts, VIII:1745
    Self-Analysis, VIII:1745
Horos, I:912, 913
Horowitz, Vladimir, **VIII:1747-1750**
Horseshoe Bend, Battle of, V:1196
Horti Sallustianai, I:743
Ho-shen, IV:302
Hotman, François, **III:362-366**
    De statu primitivae ecclesiae, III:363
    Franco-Gallia, III:364
Hotta Masayoshi, V:1181
Hou Hsien, II:1023
Hounsfield, Godfrey Newbold, **VIII:1751-1753**
Houphouët-Boigny, Félix, **VIII:1754-1758**
Hours, Book of, II:307
House Committee on Un-American Activities. *See*
    Un-American Activities, House Committee on
House of Representatives. *See* Representatives,
    House of
Houssay, Bernardo Alberto, **VIII:1759-1761**
    Human Physiology, VIII:1760
Houston, Charles H, VIII:2433
Houston, Sam, **V:1137-1140**
Houston *Post,* VIII:1703-1705
Hoveve Zion, V:1104
Hoveyda, Amir Abbas, VIII:2568

Howard, Catherine, III:205, 209, **367-370**
Howard, Otis, V:1242, 1244
Howard, Sir Robert, IV:424
Howard, Thomas. *See* Norfolk, Duke of
Howe, Elias, **V:1141-1144**
Howe, Julia Ward, **V:1145-1149,** 1151
    "Battle Hymn of the Republic, The," V:1145,
      1146
    Passion Flowers, V:1146
Howe, Admiral Richard, **IV:672-675**
Howe, Samuel Gridley, V:680, 681, 1145, 1146,
    1150-1153
Howe, General William, IV:322, 367, **676-679**
Howells, William Dean, V:715; IX:3806
Ho Yen, I:949
Hoyle, Fred, VIII:1580, 1582
Hsia Kuei, **II:479-481,** 613
Hsiang Hsiu, I:192
Hsiao Yi, I:948
Hsieh Hun, I:429
Hsieh Ling-yün, **I:429-432**
    "On Distinguishing What Is Essential," I:430
Hsien-yang, I:177
Hsin ch'ing-nien, VII:661
Hsin Dynasty, I:590
Hsüan-tsang, **II:482-486**
    Ta T'ang Hsi-yü-chi, II:484
Hsüan Tsung, II:592, 918, 965-967
Hsün-tzu, **I:433-435**
    Shih chi, I:433
Hua Guofeng, VII:906
Huai Army, VI:1362
Huai Wang, I:187
Huáscar, **III:371-373**
Huayna Capac, III:371, 373
Hubble, Edwin Powell, VIII:2157, 2158
Hubertsburg, Treaty of, IV:505
Hudson, Henry, **IV:680-682**
Hudson River Railroad, VI:2297
Hudson's Bay Company, VI:1437
Huerta, Dolores, **VIII:1762-1765**
Huerta, Victoriano, VIII:2347; IX:3811, 3813,
    4021, 4016
Huggins, Miller, VII:1322, 1323
Hughes, Charles Evans, VIII:1552, **1766-1770**
Hughes, Langston, **VIII:1771-1774**
    Ask Your Mama, VIII:1773
    Barrier, The, VIII:1773
    Big Sea, The, VIII:1773
    Esther, VIII:1773
    Fine Clothes to the Jew, VIII:1771
    I Wonder as I Wander, VIII:1773

Little Ham, VIII:1773
Montage of a Dream Deferred, VIII:1773
Mulatto, VIII:1773
Not Without Laughter, VIII:1773
Panther and the Lash, The, VIII:1773
Simple Speaks His Mind, VIII:1773
Simple's Uncle Sam, VIII:1773
Simple Takes a Wife, VIII:1773
Simply Heaven, VIII:1773
Tambourines of Glory, VIII:1773
Ways of White Folks, The, VIII:1773
Weary Blues, The, VIII:1771
Hughes, Ted, IX:3036, 3037
Hughes, Thomas
    Tom Brown's School Days, V:75
Hughes, William Morris, **VIII:1775-1778,**
    2292-2294
Hugh of Lusignan, II:540, 541
Hugo, Victor, **V:1154-1158;** VI:1901
    Art d'être grand-père, L', V:1157
    Burgraves, The, V:1155
    Châtiments, Les, V:1155
    Contemplations, Les, V:1155
    Feuilles d'automne, Les, V:1155
    Hans of Iceland, V:1154
    Hernani, V:1154, 1155
    Hunchback of Notre-Dame, The, V:1155, 1157
    King Amuses Himself, The, V:1155
    Last Day of a Condemned, The, V:1158
    Legend of the Centuries, The, V:1155
    Lucrezia Borgia, V:685
    Misérables, Les, V:1155, 1157, 1158; VII:880
    Ninety-three, V:1157
    Odes et ballades, V:1154
    Orientales, Les, V:1154
    Préface de Cromwell, La, V:1154
    Ruy Blas, V:1155
Huguccio of Pisa, II:509
Huguenots
    Buckingham, IV:212, 213
    Calvin, III:118
    Henry IV, III:333, 334
    Hotman, III:362-365
    Louis XIII, IV:864
    Louis XIV, IV:868
    Mornay, III:537-539
    Philip II, III:600
    Richelieu, IV:1165, 1167
Hu Han-min, IX:3878
Hu Hao, I:178
Huitzilopochtli, cult of, III:378, 379, 528,
    529, 531

Hui-yüan, I:429, 430
Hülagü, II:381
Hull, Cordell, **VIII:1779-1782**
Hull House, VII:21, 23; VIII:2096; IX:2961
human behavior. *See* behavior, human
human rights
    Carter, VII:590
    Evatt, VII:1110, 1111
    Gorbachev, VIII:1426
    Malcolm X, VIII:2375
    Robeson, IX:3190
    Sakharov, IX:3296, 3298, 3299
    Universal Declaration of Human Rights,
        VII:610-612, 1110
human sexuality. *See* sexuality, human
human species, origin of. *See* evolution, theory of
Humayun, III:5
Humble Petition and Advice, IV:380, 790
Humboldt, Alexander von, V:267, 862, 898,
    1159-1161; VI:1366
    *Voyage aux régions équinoctales du Nouveau
        Continent,* V:1160
Humboldt, Wilhelm von, VI:2118
Hume, David, **IV:683-686**
    Berkeley, IV:114-116
    Dialogues Concerning Natural Religion,
        IV:684, 685
    Enquiries Concerning Human Understanding,
        IV:684
    *Enquiry Concerning the Principals of Morals,
        An,* IV:684
    Ferguson, IV:454
    Gibbon, IV:547
    Green, V:987
    History of England, IV:684
    Nicholas of Autrecourt, II:671
    Treatise of Human Nature, A, IV:683, 684
Hume, Joseph, VI:1787, 1880
humors
    Aretaeus of Cappadocia, I:82
    Bradstreet, IV:194
    Diocles of Carystus, I:261
    Galen, I:339
    Herophilus, I:399
Humperdinck, Engelbert, **V:1162-1164**
    Bubschens Weihnachtstraum, V:1163
    Dornröschen, V:1163, 1164
    Hänsel and Gretel, V:1163, 1164
    Heirat wider Willen, Die, V:1163
    Königskinder, V:1163, 1164
    Mirakel, Das, V:1164
    sieben Geisslein, Die, V:1163

Humphrey, Hubert H., VII:670; **VIII:1783-1786,** 2758
Hunan Army, VI:2260, 2261
Hundred Flowers Campaign, VII:905
Hundred Slain, Battle of a, VI:1851
Hundred Years' War
    Charles IV, II:235, 237
    Chartier, II:245, 246
    Chaucer, II:248
    Edward III, II:329, 331
    Edward IV, III:234
    Froissart's *Chronicles,* II:366, 368
    Henry VI, III:341
    Joan of Arc, III:396
    Louis XI, III:434
    Venette, II:936
Huneric, I:344
Hungarian Revolution, VIII:1963
Hung Hsui ch'üan, **V:1165-1167**
Hung-li. *See* Ch'ien-lung
Hunkpapa tribe, VI:2070, 2072, 2073
Huns
    Attila, I:124-127
    Chionites, I:779, 780
    Khosrow I, II:559, 560
    Odoacer, II:685
    See also Avars
Hun Sen, IX:3419, 3420
Hunt, John, VIII:1663
Hunt, Leigh, VI:1266
Hunt, Walter, V:1143
Hunt, William Holman, **V:1165-1167**
    Finding of the Saviour in the Temple, The, V:1169
    Flight of Madeline and Prophyro, V:1168
    Light of the World, The, V:1169
    Scapegoat, The, V:1169
    Shadow of Death, The, V:1169, 1170
    Valentine Rescuing Sylvia from Proteus, V:1169
Hunter, John, IV:721
Hunyadi, János, **III:374-376,** 487
Hunyadi, Mátyás. *See* Matthias I Corvinus
Hur, I:1
Hurok, Solomon, VII:70
Hurons, IV:273
Hurst, Fannie, VIII:1787
Hurston, Zora Neale, **VIII:1787-1790;**
    IX:3849-3851
    Color Struck, VIII:1787
    "Drenched in Light," VIII:1787
    Dust Tracks on a Road, VIII:1787, 1788
    In Search of Our Mothers' Gardens, VIII:1789

Jonah's Gourd Wine, VIII:1787, 1788
    Moses, Man of the Mountain, VIII:1788
    Mules and Men, VIII:1788
    Seraph on the Suwanee, VIII:1788, 1789
    "Spunk," VIII:1787
    Their Eyes Were Watching God, VIII:1788
Hus, Jan, **II:487-490,** 971, 1009-1011, 1030, 1031
    On the Church, II:489
Husayn ibn 'Ali, al-, VII:1122, 1124; VIII:2126
Hussein I, VII:92; **VIII:1791-1796**
Hussein, Saddam, VII:50, 1116; IX:3071
Husserl, Edmund, **VIII:1797-1799**
    Derrida, VII:913
    Heidegger, VIII:1610, 1611
    Merleau-Ponty, VIII:2501
    Scheler, IX:3347
    Stein, IX:3506-3508
Hussey, Obed, VI:1431
Hussite movement. *See* Hus, Jan
Hutchins, Robert M., **VIII:1800-1803**
    Freedom, Education, and the Fund, VIII:1800
Hutchinson, Anne, IV:371, **687-690,** 1464
Hutchinson, Thomas, IV:23, 24, 494, 617, **691-694**
    History of the Colony and Province of Massachusetts Bay, The, IV:23, 693
Huxley, Aldous, **VIII:1804-1808**
    Antic Hay, VIII:1804
    Brave New World, VII:1187; VIII:1804
    Doors of Perception, The, VIII:1807
    Ends and Means, VIII:1804
    Eyeless in Gaza, VIII:1804
    Point Counter Point, VIII:1804
    Those Barren Leaves, VIII:1804
    What Are You Going To Do About It?, VIII:1804
Huxley, Thomas Henry, V:277, 608, **1172-1174;** IX:3938
    Evidence as to Man's Place in Nature, V:1173
    Evolution and Ethics, V:1173
    Workingman Lectures, V:1173
Hu Yaobang, VIII:2178, 2179
Huygens, Christiaan, **IV:695-698,** 826, 830, 1059, 1060; VI:1343
    Discours de la cause de la pesanteur, IV:697
    Horologium, IV:695
    Horologium oscillatorium, IV:695
Hydatius of Emerita, I:694-696
Hyde, Edward. *See* Clarendon, First Earl of
Hyde Park Declaration, VIII:1983
hydrodynamics
    Bjerknes, VII:318, 319
    Prandtl, IX:3073

Torricelli, IV:1333
Landau, VIII:2074
hydrogen
    Avogadro, V:99
    Cavendish, IV:262
    Gay-Lussac, V:898, 899
    liquefaction of, VIII:1907
    Lockyer, VI:1411, 1412
    Urey, IX:3788
hydrogen bomb
    Bethe, VII:302
    Fermi, VII:1148
    Kurchatov, VIII:2040
    Lawrence, VIII:2123
    Neumann, VIII:2726
    Oppenheimer, IX:2834
    Rabi, IX:3102
    Sakharov, IX:3299
    Teller, IX:3631, 3633
    Urey, IX:3789
    See also nuclear weapons
Hyginus, I:398
Hyksos, I:636
hymnody, I:157; II:409; III:658; IX:3798
Hypatia, I:74, **436-439**
    On the Astronomical Canon of Diophantus, I:437
    On the Conics of Apollonius, I:437
Hyrcanus, I:390, 391

IBM, IX:2973
Ibn al-'Arabi, **II:491-494**
    Fusus al-hikam, II:492
    Futuhat al-Makkiyah, al-, II:491, 492
Ibn Battutah, **II:495-497**
    Rihlah, II:495
Ibn Gabirol, **II:498-501**
    Improvement of Moral Qualities, The,
        II:498-500
    Kingly Crown, The, II:499
Ibn Khaldun, **II:502-505,** 637
    Muqaddimah, The, II:503, 504
Ibn Nagrella. *See* Samuel ha-Nagid
Ibn Rushd. *See* Averroës
Ibn Tufayl, II:100
Ibn Tumart, II:4-6
Ibo, VII:13, 145, 146
Ibsen, Henrik, V:1003, **1175-1179;** VIII:1891;
        IX:3400
    Brand, V:1175
    Burial Mound, V:1175
    Catiline, V:1175
    Doll's House, A, V:1176; IX:3400

Emperor and Galilean, V:1176
Ghosts, V:1176
Hedda Gabler, V:1176; VII:280, 281; VIII:2143
League of Youth, The, V:1176
Master Builder, The, V:1176; VIII:2142
Peer Gynt, V:1003, 1175
Rosmersholm, V:1176
Wild Duck, The, VII:280; IX:2821
Ibuka, Masaru, VIII:2622, 2623
ICBMs. *See* intercontinental ballistic missiles
Icelandic sagas
    Greenlanders' Saga, II:577, 578
    Laxness, VIII:2131, 2132
    Saga of Erik the Red, II:577, 578
    Snorri Sturluson, II:836-839
Iceni, I:136-138
I Ching, I:190, 224, 949-951
Iconoclastic Controversy, II:544-546, 903
Idealism, German
    Baer, V:111
    Eucken, VII:1107
    Fichte, IV:465-468
    Hegel, V:1082, 1083
    Hobhouse, VIII:1707, 1709
    Schelling, VI:1972-1974
    Schiller, IV:1217, 1219, 1220
Idrisi, al-, **II:506-508**
    Kitab nuzhat al-mushtaq fi ikhiraq al-afaq,
        II:506, 508
Idrisi tribe, VII:1118
Idumaea, I:390
Ifriqiya, II:5
Ignatius of Antioch, **I:440-442**
Ignatius of Loyola, Saint. *See* Loyola, Saint
        Ignatius of
Ii Naosuke, **V:1180-1182;** VI:1936
Ikeda, Hayato, **VIII:1809-1811**
Ikhnaton. *See* Akehnaton
Ikko. *See* Shinshu Buddhism
Ilceo, myth of, III:270
ILGWU. *See* International Ladies' Garment
        Workers Union
Illinois
    Altgeld, V:54-56
    Black Hawk, V:249
    Lathrop, VIII:2096, 2097, 2099
    Mormonism, VI:2081
    Stevenson, IX:3524
Illinois Indians, IV:733
Illyria, I:263, 628, 629
ILP. *See* Independent Labour Party
Iltani, I:362

Ilu-bi'di, I:754

Imagist movement, VIII:1505, 1506, 1508, 2249-2251

Imhotep, **I:443-446,** 978

Imlay, Gilbert, IV:1477

immunology
  Burnet, VII:512-514
  Ehrlich, VII:1032, 1033
  Fleming, VII:1166
  Jenner, IV:723
  Pasteur, VI:1744, 1747
  Salk, IX:3305-3307
  Smith, IX:3451, 3452

impeachment
  Chase, IV:293-296
  Clinton, VII:710, 715
  Johnson, IV:296, 479, 1233; VII:710
  Nixon, VIII:1888, 2760
  Sherman, IV:1244
  Strafford, IV:1287
  Tyler, VI:2291

Imperial Ballet Company, VIII:2748, 2749

Imperial East Africa Company, VIII:2269

Imperial Hotel of Tokyo, IX:4061

Imperial Russian Musical Academy, VI:1891

Imphal and Kohima, battles of, IX:3437

Impressionism
  Bonnard, VII:362, 363
  Cassatt, V:434-436
  Cézanne, V:453, 455
  Debussy, VII:884, 885
  Degas, V:641-643
  Delaunay, VII:888
  Duchamp, VII:972
  fauves, VIII:1991
  Gauguin, V:888-891
  Goya, IV:571, 572
  Hopper, VIII:1740, 1742
  Léger, VIII:2154
  Magritte, VIII:2349, 2352
  Manet, VI:1473
  Matisse, VIII:2452, 2454
  Monet, VIII:2579-2581
  Pissarro, VI:1779-1781
  Renoir, VI:1869-1871
  Sargent, VI:1961, 1963, 1964
  Seurat, VI:2033-2035
  Toulouse-Lautrec, VI:2247-2250
  Whistler, VI:2363, 2364

immunization. *See* vaccination

Inca Empire
  Heyerdahl, VIII:1660
  Huáscar, III:371-373
  Pachacuti, III:577-579
  Prescott, VI:1815
  Soto, III:699

Indemnity, Act of, IV:310

Independence, Declaration of
  Adams, IV:16
  Carroll, IV:250-252
  Chase, IV:293
  Dickinson, IV:411
  Franklin, IV:494
  George III, IV:541
  Hancock, IV:613, 617, 618
  Jefferson, IV:716
  North, IV:1035
  Rush, IV:1202, 1203
  Sherman, IV:1243
  Wilson, IV:1457
  Witherspoon, IV:1467, 1469

Independent Labour Party, V:1036, 1037; VII:354;
    VIII:2312, 2314; IX:2849

Independent Treasury, VI:1803

Index Librorum Prohibitorum. See Prohibited
    Books, Index of

India Act of 1784, IV:633

India Act of 1935, VII:529

India Bill, IV:481

India Independence Act of 1947, VIII:1849

Indian Affairs, Bureau of, IX:3011

Indian Association, VII:183

Indian Mutiny of 1857, VI:1331-1333

Indian National Congress, VII:184, 1283;
    VIII:2683

Indian National Fund, VII:183

Indian Ocean, II:636

Indian Removal Bill, VI:1910

Indian Wars, V:374

Indochinese Communist Party, VIII:1698-1701;
    IX:3821

Indo-European languages, IX:3340, 3341

Indulgence, Declaration of, IV:704

Industrial Charter, VII:530

Industrial Revolution
  Boulton, IV:182-184
  Brindley, IV:201-203
  Brunel, V:339-342
  communism, V:761
  cotton industry, IV:59-62
  Darby, IV:396-398
  Hargreaves, IV:623-625
  Kay, IV:769, 770
  Murdock, IV:1008-1010

Nasmyth, VI:1624-1626
Newcomen, IV:1022-1024
Owen, VI:1708-1710
Papin, IV:1059-1061
Scotland, IV:1182-1185
sewing machine, V:1141-1143
Siemens family, VI:2066-2069
telegraphy, V:555-558
textiles, VI:2074-2076
Watt, IV:1409, 1411, 1412
Wedgwood, IV:1421-1424
Western conception of history, VIII:2165
Whitney, IV:1431-1434
women, V:64
Infante, John, III:217
inflation, economic
    Carter, VII:591
    Ford, VII:1181
    Greenspan, VIII:1471-1473
    Japan, VIII:1809
    Nixon, VIII:2759
    Trudeau, IX:3733
Ingeborg, II:511
Ingres, Jean-Auguste-Dominique, V:411,
    1183-1186; VI:2033
    Antiochus and Stratonice, V:1185
    Apotheosis of Homer, The, V:1184
    Baronne de Rothschild, V:1185
    Bathing Woman, The, V:1185
    *Death of Leonardo da Vinci in the Arms of
        Francis, The,* V:1183
    Grand Odalisque, The, V:1185
    Odalisque with the Slave, V:1185
    Oedipus Solving the Riddle of the Sphinx,
        V:1184
    Princess de Broglie, V:1185
    Roger Freeing Angelica, V:1183
    Turkish Bath, The, V:1185
    Valpincon Bather, The, V:1185
    Vicomtesse d'Haussonville, V:1185
    Vow of Louis XIII, The, V:1183, 1184
Inner Mission of Westphalia, VIII:2742
Innocent III, II:29, 144, 301, 303, 354, 360, 399,
    509-513, 541
    On the Misery of the Human Condition, II:509
    Sacred Mystery of the Altar, The, II:509
Innocent IV, II:207, 363, **514-516,** 991
Innocent V, III:405
Inoocent VI, II:792
Innocent VIII, III:462, 496, 667, 668, 725
Innocent X, IV:168, 1062, 1366
Inönü, Ismet, **VIII:1812-1815**

Inquisition. *See* Roman Inquisition; Spanish
    Inquisition
Instantius, I:695
Institute de France, IV:338
insulin
    Banting, VII:189, 190
    Houssay, VIII:1759, 1760
    Krogh, VIII:2029
    Macleod, VIII:2329-2331
integration, racial. *See* desegregation; segregation
Intellectual Cooperation, Institute of, VIII:2052
Intercolonial Union, VIII:1699
intercontinental ballistic missiles, VIII:2020, 2021
International Association of Co-Workers of
    Mother Teresa, IX:3635, 3636
International Associations, Union of, VIII:2051
International Bureau of Weights and Measures,
    VIII:1502-1504
International Business Machines, IX:2973
International Congress of Women, VII:161
International Council of Women, VI:2045
International Encyclopedia of Unified Science,
    VII:583
International Geophysical Year, VIII:2020;
    IX:4001
International Labor Organization, VIII:1781
International Ladies' Garment Workers Union,
    VIII:1641
international law
    Butler, VII:525
    Gentili, III:295-297
    Grotius, IV:579-581
    Universal Declaration of Human Rights,
        VII:610-612, 1110, 1111
    Vitoria, III:768, 769
    See also United Nations
International Monetary Fund, VIII:1954, 2492
International Olympic Committee, VII:774-776;
    IX:3675
International Peace Bureau, VIII:2051
International Psychoanalytic Association,
    VII:329, 330, 1225, 1226
International Red Cross, V:143, 711, 712;
    VIII:1624
International Rehovot Conferences, VII:1001
International Style of architecture, VII:1-3;
    VIII:2487-2489, 2575; IX:2859, 2860
Interparliamentary Union, VIII:2051
Interstate Commerce Act, VI:1898
Intifada, VII:92, 93
Intolerable Acts, IV:16, 616, 617, 716
Intrepid, V:634

Inuits
    Davis, III:212, 213
    Frobisher, III:278, 279
    Peary, IX:2942, 2944
    Rasmussen, IX:3121-3123
    Ross, VI:1907
Invalides, Dome des, IV:903
Investiture Controversy, II:357, 464
Investment Canada, VIII:2655
Ionesco, Eugène, **VIII:1816-1819**
    Bald Soprano, The, VIII:1817
    Chairs, The, VIII:1818
    Exit the King, VIII:1818
    Lesson, The, VIII:1817
    Rhinoceros, VIII:1818
Ionia, I:238, 554
Ionian school of philosophy, I:855
Iophon, I:809
Iov, III:309
Ipsus, Battle of, I:60, 768
IRA. *See* Irish Republican Army
Iranian hostage crisis, VII:591; IX:3139
Iran-Iraq War, VIII:1958
IRB. *See* Irish Republican Brotherhood
Irenaeus, Saint, **I:447-451**
    Against Heresies, I:449
Irgun Z'vai Leumi, VII:243, 244, 253; IX:3932
Irish Church Reform Act of 1833, V:996
Irish Coercion Bill of 1881, V:805
Irish Free State, VII:770-772, 878; VIII:2217;
        IX:2805, 4085
Irish Home Rule Movement
    Asquith, VII:121
    George V, VII:1340
    Joyce, VIII:1891
    Law, VIII:2112
    Parnell, VI:1740, 1741
    Rhodes, VI:1875
    Salisbury, VI:1944, 1945
Irish Independence, War for, IX:2805
Irish Land Acts, V:308
Irish Literary Renaissance, VIII:1891
Irish Nationalist Party, VI:1740-1742
Irish National Land League, VI:1740-1742
Irish National Theatre, IX:4082
Irish potato famine, VI:1754, 1930, 1931
Irish Question, IV:1105; VI:2394; VIII:1475
Irish Rebellion, IV:1142
Irish Republican Army, VII:771, 877; VIII:2644
Irish Republican Brotherhood, VII:733, 877
Irish Volunteers, VII:770, 877; IX:2804
Iron Curtain, VII:693; VIII:1696

ironmaking, IV:396-398, 1182-1185; V:218-221
Iron Ore Company of Canada, VIII:2655
Ironsides, the, IV:378
Iroquois Indians
    Brant, IV:196, 198, 199
    Cartier, III:129-131
    Champlain, IV:273
    Jolliet, IV:733
    Laval, IV:801
    Pontiac, IV:1110
    Tekakwitha, IV:1316, 1317
Irrigation Act, V:632
Irving, Henry, **V:1187-1191;** VI:2216, 2217
    Bells, The, V:1187, 1189
Irving, Washington, **V:1192-1195**
    Astoria, V:84
    Bracebridge Hall, V:1193
    History of New York, A, V:84
    "Legend of Sleepy Hollow, The,"
        V:1192, 1194
    "Rip Van Winkle," V:1192-1194
    Sketch Book of Geoffrey Crayon, Gent, The,
        V:1193
    Tales of a Traveller, V:1193
    Tour of the Prairies, A, V:1193
Irwin, Noel, IX:3437
Isaac, I:6
Isaaco, VI:1724, 1725
Isabella I, **III:260-263**
    Cabot, III:113
    Catherine of Aragon, III:136
    Columbus, III:172-174
    Jiménez de Cisneros, III:392-394
    Manuel I, III:465
    Prescott, VI:1814
    Torquemada, III:725
Isabella of Aragon. *See* Isabella I
Isabella of France, II:327, 329
Isabella of Portugal, III:163, 260, 599
Isabelle of Angoulême, II:540
Isagoras, I:214
Isaiah, **I:452-455**
Isham, Colonel Ralph, IV:177
Ishiyama Hongan-ji War, III:571
Ishmael, I:6
Ishmael ben Elisha, I:28, 29
Ishme-Dagan, I:360
Isidore of Seville, Saint, **II:518-521**
    Etymologiae, II:519
Isin, I:361
Isis, I:13
Islam, Nation of. *See* Nation of Islam

Islamic law
    Ash'ari, II:93-95
    Ghazzali, II:385
    Hanbalite school, II:33-35
    Hanifite school, II:16-18
    Tabari, II:874
Islamic Revolution of 1979, VIII:2566-2569
Islets of Langerhans, VII:187, 188
Isma'ili sect, II:522
Ismay, Sir Hastings, VII:47
Isocrates, **I:456-458**
    Against the Sophists, I:457, 458
    Antidosis, I:457
    Aristotle, I:95, 96
    Evagoras, I:457
    Panegyricus, I:456, 457
    Plataeicus, I:456
    To Philip, I:457
Isodice, I:199
isotopes
    cyclotron development, VIII:2122
    Hevesy, VIII:1654-1656
    uranium, VIII:1647-1649
    Urey, IX:3787, 3788
Ispahan, IV:5, 6
Israel, ancient
    Abraham, I:5, 7
    Deborah, I:246, 247
    Isaiah, I:453
    Moses, I:561-564
    Samuel, I:746, 748, 749
    Solomon, I:798, 800, 801
Israeli Defense Forces, VII:854-856
Israel Philharmonic, VII:296
Istanbul. *See* Constantinople
Istanbul, Treaty of, IV:4
Italian Catholic University Students, Federation of,
    IX:2915
Italian Wars, III:18; VI:1919
Italus, John, II:760
Ithacius, I:696
Itzcóatl, **III:377-380**
Ivan the Great, II:54; **III:381-384**
Ivan the Terrible, III:308, **385-388**
Iveragh, Ireland, VI:1680
Ives, Charles, **VIII:1820-1823**
    "I. A Contemplation of a Serious Matter,"
        VIII:1821
    All the Way Around and Back, VIII:1821
    "Bells of Yale," VIII:1820
    "Camp Meeting, The" VIII:1820
    Celestial Country, The, VIII:1820

Concord Sonata, VIII:1821
Fourth of July, VIII:1821, 1822
Fourth Symphony, VIII:1821
"Slow March," VIII:1820
Third Symphony, VIII:1821
Three Places in New England, VIII:1821
Ives, George Edward, VIII:1820
Ivinskaya, Olga Vsevolodovna, IX:2900
Iwakura Tomoni, VI:1937, 1938
Iwerks, Ub, VII:938, 940
Izambard, Georges, VI:1886

Jabin, I:247
Jabir ibn Hayyan, **II:522-525**
Jabotinksy, Vladimir, VII:243
Jackson, Andrew, **V:1196-1199**
    Adams, John Quincy, V:23, 24
    Benton, V:195-198
    Biddle, V:226
    Calhoun, V:395
    Clay, V:508, 509
    Crockett, V:578, 579
    Gadsden Purchase, V:858, 859
    Harrison, V:1062
    Houston, V:1137
    Key, VI:1283
    Mackenzie, VI:1449
    Perry, VI:1760
    Polk, VI:1801, 1802
    Ross, VI:1910, 1911
    Scott, VI:2009, 2010
    Seminole Wars, VI:1695
    Taney, VI:2190
    Tyler, VI:2288, 2289
    Van Buren, VI:2293, 2294
    Webster, VI:2345
Jackson, Charles T., VI:1596-1598
Jackson, Helen Hunt, **V:1200-1203**
    Century of Dishonor, V:1201, 1202
    Ramona, V:1200-1202
Jackson, Jesse L., **VIII:1824-1826,** 2245
Jackson, Joe, VII:718
Jackson, Stonewall, **V:1204-1206**
Jacob, François, **VIII:1827-1830**
Jacobi, Carl Gustav Jacob, V:8, 9
Jacobins
    Danton, IV:394, 395
    Du Pont, V:718
    Marat, IV:911
    Marlborough, IV:922
    Mirabeau, IV:964
    Oglethorpe, IV:1043

Orléans, IV:1049
Pelham, IV:1075
Robespierre, IV:1171, 1172
Saint-Just, IV:1205-1207
Stanhope, IV:1278
Jacobs, Mike, VIII:2241, 2243, 2244
Jacopo della Quercia, **III:389-391**
  Madonna and Child, III:390
  Silvestri Madonna, III:389
Jadwiga, **II:1001-1004**
Jael, I:247
Ja'far al-Sadiq, II:522
Jahangir, IV:1232
Jahiz, al-, **II:526-528**
  Characters of Theophrastus, II:527
  Kitab al-bukhala', II:527
  Kitab alhayawan, II:526
Jai Singh, IV:1247
Jakobson, Roman, **VIII:1831-1834**
  *Child Language, Aphasia and Phonological
    Universals,* VIII:1832
  Noveshaya russaya poeziya, VIII:1831
  Preliminaries to Speech Analysis,
    VIII:1832
Jamahiriyah, IX:3099
Jamaica, III:173
Jamal al-Din al-Afghani, V:4, 5, **1207-1210**
James (Apostle), I:475, 616
James I (of England), **IV:699-702**
  Andrewes, IV:46-48
  Basilikon Doron, IV:699
  Buckingham, IV:211
  Coke, IV:331-334
  Daemonologie, IV:699
  Raleigh, III:639-641
  Salisbury, III:660-662
  Shakespeare, III:687
  True Law of Free Monarchies, The, IV:699
James I the Conqueror, **II:529-533**
  Furs, II:531
James II (of England), **IV:703-706**
  Anne, IV:50, 52
  Dryden, IV:425
  Eliot, IV:437
  Godolphin, IV:553
  Kidd, IV:777
  Leeds, IV:823
  Locke, IV:857
  Marlborough, IV:922
  Mather, IV:939
  Monmouth, IV:980-982
  Oates, IV:1038-1040

  Penn, IV:1079
  Purcell, IV:1138
  Roman Catholicism, IV:100
James IV (of Scotland), III:346
James VI (of Scotland), III:243, 244, 661;
    IV:279, 330
James, Harry, IX:3422
James, Henry, **V:1211-1215,** 1216; VI:1589;
    VII:625; IX:3953
  Ambassadors, The, V:1213
  American, The, V:1211, 1212
  "Art of Fiction, The," V:1212
  Bostonians, The, V:1212
  Daisy Miller, V:1211, 1212
  Golden Bowl, The, V:1213
  Portrait of a Lady, The, V:1211, 1212
  Princess Casamassima, The, V:1212
  Roderick Hudson, V:1211
  Tragic Muse, The, V:1212
  Turn of the Screw, VII:568
  Wings of the Dove, The, V:1213
James, Thomas, III:63
James, William, V:781, **1216-1220;** VI:1757;
    VII:560; VIII:1708
  Principles of Psychology, The, V:1218, 1219;
    IX:3669
  Varieties of Religious Experience, The, V:1218
  Will to Believe, The, V:1218
Jameson, Leander Starr, VI:1875
Jameson Raid, V:463; VI:1875
Jamestown, Virginia, IV:1122-1124, 1253
Jammes, Francis, VIII:2525
Janácek, Leos, **VIII:1835-1838**
  Beginning of a Romance, The, VIII:1836
  From the House of the Dead, VIII:1837
  Glagolitic Mass, VIII:1837
  Janufa, VIII:1836
  *Mr. Broucek's Excursion to the Fifteenth
    Century,* VIII:1837
  Sárka, VIII:1836
  Taras Bulba, VIII:1837
Jan Ch'iu, I:223
Janet, Pierre, **VIII:1839-1842**
  Automatisme psychologique, L', VIII:1840
  Mental State of Hystericals, The, VIII:1840
Janissaries, III:708
Jankow, Battle of, IV:1336, 1337
Jannings, Emil, VII:930
Jansen, Cornelius Otto, **IV:707-710,** 1062, 1064,
    1144-1146, 1381, 1382
  Augustinus, IV:707, 708
  Delectatio coelestis, IV:707

Delectatio terrena, IV:707
Mars gallicus, IV:707
Jansenism. *See* Jansen, Cornelius Otto
Janssen, Pierre Jules César, VI:1411
Janssen, Zacharias, IV:850
Jardine, Douglas, VII:408
Jarring, Gunnar, VII:1001
Jarry, Alfred
Ubu Roi, VIII:1712
Jaruzelski, Wojciech, IX:3846, 3847
Jason the Argonaut, I:318
Jaspers, Karl, **VIII:1843-1846**
Future of Germany, The, VIII:1845
Future of Mankind, The, VIII:1844
General Psychopathology, VIII:1843, 1844
Great Philosophers, The, VIII:1845
Idea of the University, The, VIII:1844
Origin and Goal of History, The, VIII:1845
Philosophical Faith and Revelation, VIII:1844
Philosophy, VIII:1844
Philosophy of Existence, VIII:1844
Psychologie der Weltanschauungen, VIII:1843
Question of German Guilt, The, VIII:1844
Reason and Existenz, VIII:1844
Játiva, battle at, II:270
Jaurès, Jean, **V:1211-1215; VII:335**
Democracy and Military Service, V:1222
Jay, John, IV:315, **711-715,** 1291; VI:1277, 1278
Federalist, The, IV:610, 713
Jay Treaty, IV:713, 1407
jazz
Armstrong, VII:105-108
Charles, VII:658
Coltrane, VII:741, 742, 744
Copland, VII:767
Davis, VII:741, 742, 744; IX:2882
Ellington, VII:1066-1068
Fitzgerald, VII:1157-1160
Gershwin, VII:1347, 1349
Gillespie, VII:1370, 1371, 1373; IX:2882
Goodman, VIII:1419, 1420, 1422
Holiday, VIII:1715-1718
Hughes, VIII:1773
Milhaud, VIII:2526
Mondrian, VIII:2576
Monk, VII:741
Morrison, VIII:2628
Parker, IX:2880-2883
Shaw, VIII:1420, 1718
Jean II, II:949
Jean de Venette. *See* Venette, Jean de
Jeanneret, Charles-Édouard. *See* Le Corbusier

Jefferson, Thomas, **IV:716-720**
Adams, IV:18
Banneker, IV:91
Bayle, IV:105
Brown, IV:206
Bulfinch, V:349
Burr, V:369, 370
Chase, IV:295
Gallatin, V:861, 862
Hamilton, IV:611
Lewis, VI:1358
Madison, IV:886, 888; VI:1464
Monroe, VI:1571
Parrington, IX:2894
Summary View of the Rights of British America, A, IV:716
Jeffersonian, V:984
Jeffrey, Lord, **V:1224-1227**
Jehoiachin, I:326
Jehoiakim, I:326, 459
Jekyll, Gertrude, VII:1130, 1132
Jena, Battle of, V:940, 1033, 1080
Jena, University of, VI:1972
Jenkin, Fleeming, V:609
Jenkins' Ear, War of, IV:55, 1045, 1471
Jenkinson, Robert Banks. *See* Liverpool, Second Earl of
Jenner, Edward, **IV:721-724**
Cursory Observations on Emetic Tartar, IV:722
Inquiry into Cause and Effects of the Variolæ Vaccinæ, IV:723
Observations on the Natural History of the Cuckoo, IV:722
Jeremiah, I:328, **459-462,** 468, 569
Jeremiah II, III:308
Jerome, Saint, **I:463-466,** 511, 513
Jerome Clock Company, V:135
Jerusalem
architecture, VIII:2488
Augustine, I:129
Ezekiel, I:326, 328
Ezra, I:330-333
Hadrian, I:358
Herod the Great, I:391
Hussein I, VIII:1794
Jeremiah, I:459, 460
Nebuchadnezzar II, I:570
Pilate, I:640, 642
Tancred, II:888
tunnel, I:315
Jerusalem, Temple of
Eusebius of Caesarea, I:325

Ezekiel, I:328
Ezra, I:330
Herod the Great, I:391
Johanan ben Zakkai, I:471-473
Solomon, I:798, 800
Jervis, John, VI:1635
Jessup Wagon, VII:604
Jesuit Order
Alembert, IV:32
Bossuet, IV:170
Charles III, IV:288, 289
Counter-Reformation, III:160, 161
Ferdinand II, IV:450
Ignatius of Loyola, III:437-439
Jansen, IV:707-709
Joyce, VIII:1891
K'ang-hsi, IV:757
Laval, IV:801, 802
Pascal, IV:1062, 1064
Paul III, III:597
Teilhard de Chardin, IX:3626, 3627
Tekakwitha, IV:1316, 1317
Voltaire, IV:1392
Xavier, III:788-790
Jesup, Thomas S., VI:2195
Jesus, Society of. *See* Jesuit Order
Jesus Christ, **I:467-470**
Abraham, I:7
Anabaptists, III:510, 511
Angelico, III:29
Anthony of Egypt, I:56
Arianism, I:353
Christopher, Saint, I:180, 182
David, I:241, 243
divine grace, IV:708
divine nature, I:849, 862, 863; II:819, 820
Epstein's art, VII:1088
Eucharistic controversy, II:773
Giotto, II:388
Gospel of, VIII:1558, 1559
governmental authority, VII:360
Holbein the Younger, III:360
Islamic recognition, II:422
John the Apostle, I:475, 477
John the Baptist, I:478-481
Josephus, I:485
kerygma, VII:498, 499
Last Temptation of Christ, The, VIII:1922
Moses, I:4, 564
Nietzsche, VI:1662
Origen, I:581
Paul, I:605

Peter, I:614-616
Pilate, I:640, 642
rabbinical scholarship, VII:148
Renan's biography, VI:1865-1867
Ritschl, VI:1892-1894
Teilhard de Chardin, IX:3629
Theodoret of Cyrrhus, I:865, 866
Thomas, I:880, 882, 883
Unitarian doctrine, III:675-677
Valentinus, I:912, 913
Vergil, I:928
Virgin Mary, I:939, 941
Jesus Christ of Latter-day Saints, Church of. *See* Mormonism
Jet Scientific Research Institute, VIII:2019
Jewett, Sarah Orne, **V:1228-1231**
Country Doctor, The, V:1228
Country of the Pointed Furs, The, V:1229, 1230
Deephaven, V:1228, 1229
"Jenny Garrow's Ghost," V:1228
"Mr. Bruce," V:1228
Queen's Twin and Other Stories, The, V:1229
Tory Lover, The, V:1229
White Heron and Other Stories, A, V:1229
Jewish Colonial Trust, V:1005
Jewish Disabilities, Removal of, V:677
Jewish Documentation Center, IX:3984, 3985
Jewish National Committee, VII:484
Jewish Nationalization Act, IV:1076
Jewish Revolt, I:483-486, 880
Jiang Qing, VII:906
Jim Crow laws. *See* segregation
Jiménez de Cisneros, Francisco, III:262, **392-395**
Jinnah, Mohammed Ali, VII:1283; **VIII:1847-1850,** 2684, 2710, 2711
Jirgalang, IV:421
Joab, I:798
Joachim of Fiore, **II:534-536,** 812, 813
Liber figurarum, II:535
Psalterium decem chordarum, II:534
Joan of Arc, **III:396-400**
Joan the Mad, III:393
Job, Book of, II:407
Jocho, **II:537-539**
Jocho style, II:924
Jodenburt, IV:1264
Joffre, Joseph-Jacques-Césaire, **VIII:1851-1853**
Johanan ben Zakkai, **I:471-474**
Johann Georg I, Elector of Saxony, IV:1221-1223
Johansen, Hjalmer, VIII:2687
John (Apostle), **I:475-478**
Jesus Christ, I:467-469

Logos, I:634
Peter, I:615
Thomas, I:882
Virgin Mary, I:939
John (King of England), II:190, 510, 511, **540-543,** 643, 644
John I (of Portugal), III:354
John II (of Portugal), III:172, 173, 197, 215, 287, 464
John III Sobieski, **IV:725-727**
John VI Cantacuzenus, II:844
John XIII (Pope), II:707, 869
John XXII (Pope), II:682, 683, 950
    Mater et magistra, VIII:1860
    Pacem in terris, VIII:1860
John XXIII (Pope), **VIII:1854-1857;** IX:2916, 2917
John, Augustus, **VIII:1858-1861**
    Chiaroscuro, VIII:1856
    Finishing Touches, VIII:1856
    In Memoriam Amedeo Modigliani, VIII:1855
    Joseph Hone, VIII:1855
    Merekli, VIII:1854
    Moses and the Brazen Serpent, VIII:1854
    Saints-Maries de la Mer with Sainte Sara l'Egyptienne, Les, VIII:1856
    Sir Matthew Smith, VIII:1855
John, Gospel of, VII:499
John Bull, VII:382-385
John Frederick the Magnanimous, III:200, 201
John of Cappadocia, II:553, 892
John of Damascus, **II:544-547**
    Exposition of the Orthodox Faith, II:546
    On Holy Images, II:546
John of Lisbon, III:453
John of Luxembourg, II:211, 235, 615
John of Parma, II:163, 164
John of Ravenna, II:673, 674
John of the Cross, Saint, **III:401-404,** 714, 715; IX:3509
    Ascent of Mount Carmel, The, III:403
    Living Flame of Love, III:403
    Spiritual Canticle of the Soul, A, III:403
John Paul II, **VIII:1862-1865**
    Canadian visit, IX:3346
    Tekakwitha, IV:1317
    Waldheim, IX:3843
    Walesa, IX:3844
John P. Holland Torpedo Boat Company, V:1124, 1125
Johnson, Andrew, **V:1232-1238**
    Cushing, V:583

Grant, V:977
    impeachment, IV:296; V:479, 1233
    Stanton, VI:2108, 2109
    Stephens, VI:2130
    Stevens, VI:2137
    Sumner, VI:2172
Johnson, Ben. *See* Jonson, Ben
Johnson, Charles S., VIII:1787
Johnson, Esther, IV:1307
Johnson, Guy, IV:198
Johnson, Jack, VIII:2241
Johnson, James, IV:232
Johnson, James Weldon, IX:3961
Johnson, Joseph, IV:138, 1475
Johnson, Lyndon B., **VIII:1866-1869**
    Civil Rights Act, VIII:1974
    Ford, VII:1181, 1182
    Graham, VIII:1449
    Harriman, VIII:1562, 1563
    Hernandez, VIII:1641
    Humphrey, VIII:1784, 1785
    Kennedy, John F., VIII:1930
    Kennedy, Robert F., VIII:1934
    Kissinger, VIII:1999
    Lippmann, VIII:2205
    Marshall, VIII:2434, 2435
    O'Neill, IX:2825
    Stevenson, IX:3525
    Wallace, IX:3863
    Washington Post, VIII:1451, 1453
Johnson, Samuel, **IV:728-731**
    Account of the Life of Mr. Richard Savage, An, IV:728
    Addison, IV:28
    Berkeley, IV:114
    Boswell, IV:174-176
    Bruce, IV:209
    Burney, IV:226, 227
    Canaletto, IV:243
    Chase, IV:295
    Goldsmith, IV:567
    Journey to the Western Islands of Scotland, IV:175, 227
    London, IV:728
    Newbery, IV:1019, 1020
    Plan of a Dictionary of the English Language, The, IV:728, 729
    Plays of William Shakespeare, The, IV:728, 729
    Pope, IV:1116
    Rasselas, Prince of Abyssinia, IV:728
    Reynolds, IV:1162
    Swift, IV:1308

Vanity of Human Wishes, The, IV:728
    Walpole, IV:1402, 1403
Johnson, W.A., VI:1698
Johnson, William, IV:198, 199
Johnson v. Transportation Agency of Santa Clara
    County, IX:2790
Johnson Wax Company, IX:4062
Johnston, Joseph E., V:617; VI:1340, 2060
Johnstown flood, V:143
John the Baptist, **I:479-482,** 880
Joinville, Treaty of, III:600
Joliot, Frédéric, VII:636, 815; **VIII:1870-1873,**
    2039-2041
Joliot-Curie, Irène, VII:636, 812, 815;
    VIII:1870-1873
Jolliet, Louis, **IV:732-734**
Jomini, Antoine-Henri, V:504
Jonah, VI:1829
Jones, Anson, V:1138
Jones, Bobby, **VIII:1874-1878**
Jones, Don, VII:713
Jones, K.C., IX:3268, 3270, 3271
Jones, Inigo, **IV:735-737,** 747, 748
    Masque of Blackness, The, IV:735, 747
Jones, John Paul, **IV:738-743**
Jones, Mary Harris "Mother," **VIII:1879-1882**
Jones, Quincy, VII:657
Jones, Wharton, VI:1388
Jones, William, V:1007; VI:1846
Jong Sumatranen Bond, VIII:1577
Jonson, Ben, **IV:744-749**
    Alchemist, The, IV:747, 749
    Bartholomew Fair, IV:747, 749
    Beaumont and Fletcher, III:54, 56
    Bunyan, IV:220
    Case Is Altered, The, IV:746
    Catiline, IV:747
    Chapman, III:156
    Devil Is an Ass, The, IV:747
    Eastward Ho!, IV:747
    Epicoene: Or, The Silent Woman, IV:747
    Every Man in His Humour, IV:746
    Isle of Dogs, The, IV:746
    Jones, IV:735, 736
    Masque of Blackness, The, IV:747
    Nashe, III:548-550
    Part of King James, IV:747
    Sejanus, IV:747
    Shakespeare, III:689, 690
    Staple of News, The, IV:747
    Tale of a Tub, A, IV:747
    Volpone: Or, The Fox, III:54; IV:747, 749; V:162

Joplin, Janis, **VIII:1883-1886;** IX:3444
    Cheap Thrills, VIII:1883
    "Me and Bobby McGee," VIII:1884
    Pearl, VIII:1884
Joplin, Scott, **V:1239-1241**
    "Breeze From Alabama, A," V:1240
    "Cascades, The," V:1240
    "Easy Winner, The," V:1240
    "Entertainer, The," V:1240
    Guest of Honor, A, V:1240
    "Harlem Rag," V:1240
    "Maple Leaf Rag," V:1239, 1240
    "Original Rag," V:1240
    "Peacherine Rag," V:1240
    "Picture of Her Face, A," V:1240
    "Please Say You Will," V:1240
    Ragtime Dance, V:1240
    Treemonisha, V:1241
Jordan, Barbara, **VIII:1887-1890**
Jordan, Dorothea, VI:2392
Joseph II (of Habsburg), **IV:750-753,** 914,
    916, 918
Joseph, Chief, **V:1242-1245**
Joséphine, V:**1246-1249;** VI:1617
Joseph of Lamego, III:198
Josephus, Flavius, I:247, 392, 480, **483-487,** 548
    Against Apion, I:485
    Antiquities of the Jews, The, I:484, 485
    Jewish Revolt, The, I:484
Joshua, I:563
Joshua ben Hananiah, I:27, 28
Jotapata, I:484
Joule, James Prescott, VI:1269, 1270
journalism. *See* freedom of the press; newspapers;
    yellow journalism
Jouvet, Louis, VII:1380, 1381
Jovinian, I:792
Joyce, James, IV:1374; VII:238, 239; VIII:1537,
    1891-1895
    Dubliners, VIII:1892
    Finnegans Wake, VII:1223; VIII:1892, 1894
    Portrait of the Artist as a Young Man, A,
        VIII:1892, 1894
    Ulysses, VII:199, 1223; VIII:1891, 1892, 1894;
        IX:4014
Juan Carlos I, V:415
Juárez, Benito, **V:1250-1254**
Juchen, II:867, 1018; IV:3
Judah, Theodore Dehone, VI:2097
Judah ben Solomon Harizi, II:551
Judah ha-Levi, **II:548-552**
    Book of the Kuzari, II:550, 551

Judd, Charlex, IX:4070
Jude, Der, VII:484
Judea, kingdom of, I:390-393; II, I:569
Judges, Book of, I:246, 247
Judson, Edward, VIII:1596, 1597
Jugendstil movement, VIII:2036
Jugurtha, I:743
Julia, I:528
Julian, I:121, 229, 509, 780
Julian calendar, I:150, 811-813; II:300
Julius II, III:16, 17, 83, 84, **405-408,** 450, 519
July Days crisis, VIII:1942
July manifesto, IV:919
July Monarchy, V:260; VI:2226-2229
July Revolution, V:865
July 26th Movement, VII:617, 618; VIII:1494
July 28, 1838, Ordinance of, V:722
Jumbo the Elephant, V:136
Junayd, al-, II:422
Jung, Carl, **VIII:1896-1899**
    Answer to Job, VIII:1898
    Bleuler, VII:329
    Breton, VII:448, 451
    collective unconscious, VIII:2134
    Freud, VII:1226
    Hesse, VIII:1652
    Psychology of the Unconscious, VIII:1898
Junian Law, I:163
Junius Letters, IV:908
Jupiter-C missile, VII:441
Jurgurthine War, I:528, 529, 833
Jurieu, Pierre, IV:103, 104
Jussieu, Bernard de, IV:805
Justin I, II:553, 559
Justin II, II:560, 561
Justinia, I:44
Justinian I, I:656; II:118 **553-558,** 560, 890-892
Justinian II, II:824
Justus of Tiberias, I:485
Jutta of Spanheim, II:474
Juvenal, **I:488-490**
    "On an Education in Avarice," I:490
    Satires, I:488, 489
    "Vanity of Human Wishes, The," I:489
juvenile literature. *See* children's literature

Kadaulatan rakyat, VIII:1578
Kadesh, Battle of, I:736
Kaffraria tribe, V:999
Kafka, Franz, VII:240, 241, 1027; VIII:1463, **1900-1902**
    Castle, The, VII:240; VIII:1901

"In the Penal Colony," VIII:1901
Judgment, The, VIII:1900
Letter to His Father, VIII:1901
Metamorphosis, The, V:950; VIII:1900; VII:373
Trial, The, VIII:1901
Kahlenburg, Battle of, IV:726
Kahn, Otto, VIII:2142
Kahnweiler, Daniel-Henry, VIII:1483, 1484
Kaiho Yusho, IV:1257
Kaikei, II:926
Kaiser, Georg, IX:3927
Kaiserstil, IV:475, 655
Kaiser Wilhelm Institute, VIII:1510, 1511, 1514, 1618, 2476; IX:2857
Kakulima, Mount, I:369
Kalanikupule, V:1255
Kalhu, I:110
Kalidasa, **I:491-493**
    Birth of the War-God, The, I:492
    Cloud Messenger, The, I:491
    Dynasty of Raghu, The, I:492
    Rtusamhara, I:491
    Sakuntala, I:492
    Vikrama and Urvasi, I:492
Kalingas, I:112
Kalisz, Treaty of, II:212
Kallir, Otto, VIII:2633, 2635
Kalmar Union, II:626, 627
Kamakura shogunate, II:97, 882, 924-926
Kamchatka Expeditions, IV:112
Kamehameha I, **VI:1255-1258**
Kamehameha II, V:1257
Kamehameha IV, VI:1372
Kamehameha V, VI:1372
Kämpfer, Engelbert, **IV:754-756**
    Amoenitatum exoticarum, IV:755
    History of Japan, The, IV:755, 756
KAN. *See* Kenyan African Union
Kandalanu, I:106
Kandinsky, Wassily, **VIII:1903-1905,** 2005, 2006, 2038, 2404, 2405
    Black Arc, VIII:1903
    Composition VIII, VIII:1904
    Composition X, VIII:1904
    Concerning the Spiritual in Art, VIII:1903, 2037
    Fugue, VIII:1903
    Point and Line to Plane, VIII:1904
    Several Circles, VIII:1904
    Tempered Elan, VIII:1904
K'ang-hsi, **IV:757-760**
Kanishka, **I:494-497**

Kansas
 Coronado, III:180
 Dred Scott decision, VI:2000
 Earp, V:735-737
 Hickok, V:1108, 1109
 temperance movement, VI:1630, 1631
Kansas-Nebraska Act
 Benton, V:197
 Brown, V:322
 Buchanan, V:347
 Chase, V:478
 Douglas, V:692, 693
 Greeley, V:985
 Houston, V:1138
 Lincoln, VI:1382
 Pierce, VI:1777
 Stephens, VI:2129
 Sumner, VI:2171
Kant, Immanuel, **IV:761-764**
 Barth, VII:203
 Bayle, IV:105
 Cassirer, VII:614
 Critique of Judgment, The, IV:763
 Critique of Practical Reason, The, IV:762
 Critique of Pure Reason, The, IV:761; VII:449;
  IX:3965
 Dreams of a Spirit-Seer, IV:1303
 Duns Scotus, II:313
 Durkheim, VII:988
 Fichte, IV:465-468
 Foundations of the Metaphysics of Morals,
  IV:762
 Gilson, VII:1376
 Hartmann, VIII:1571
 Hegel, V:1082
 Herder, IV:651-653
 Hume, IV:685
 Kleist, VI:1294
 Leibniz, IV:832
 Moore, VIII:2606
 Nishida, VIII:2755
 Perpetual Peace, IV:763
 Religion Within the Boundaries of Pure Reason,
  IV:763
 Ritschl, VI:1893, 1894
 Schelling, VI:1973
 Schiller, IV:1219
 Schopenhauer, VI:1985
 Transcendentalists, V:757
KANU. *See* Kenyan African National Union
Kanze Motomasa, II:1026
Kanze Saburo, II:1026

Kao Tsung, II:1019
Kao Tzu, I:944
Kapitsa, Pyotr Leonidovich, **VIII:1906-1909,**
 2074
Kapteyn, Jacobus, IX:2827
Karaite movement, II:550
Karajan, Herbert von, **VIII:1910-1912;** IX:3083
Karaji, al-
 Fakhri, I:273
Karakoram Mountains, VI:2411
Karakorum, II:987-989
Karameh, Battle of, VII:91
Karlsbad Decrees, V:1034
Karlskirche, IV:474, 475, 657
Kármán, Theodore von, IX:3074, 3075
Karnak, I:24, 547, 890, 891; VI:1412
Karno, Fred, VII:653
Kasavubu, Joseph, VIII:2562, 2563; IX:3745-3747
Kaskaskia, IV:312
Katsukawa Shunsho, V:1120
Katsushika Hokusai. *See* Hokusai
Katusky, Karl, VII:291, 292
Kauai, V:1255
Kauffmann, Angelica, **IV:765-768**
 *Artist Hesitating Between the Arts of Music and
  Painting, The,* IV:765
 Parting of Hector and Andromache, The, IV:767
Kaufmann House, IX:4061
Kaumualii, V:1257
Kautsky, Karl, VIII:2285, 2286
Kavadh, II:559
Kawabata, Yasunari, **VIII:1913-1916,** 2551
 *House of Sleeping Beauties and Other Stories,
  The,* VIII:1913
 Izu Dancer, The, VIII:1913
 Jurukosai no nikki, VIII:1913
 Master of Go, The, VIII:1914
 Shokonsai ikkei, VIII:1913
 Snow Country, VIII:1914
 Thousand Cranes, VIII:1914
 Tokyo no hito, VIII:1915
Kay, James Phillips. *See* Kay-Shuttleworth, First
 Baronet
Kay, John, IV:59, 61, **769-771**
Kay-Shuttleworth, First Baronet, **VIII:1917-1919**
Kazan, Battle of, III:387
Kazantzakis, Nikos, **VIII:1920-1923**
 Last Temptation of Christ, The, VIII:1922
 Odyssey: A Modern Sequel, The, VIII:1921
 Saint Francis, VIII:1922
 Saviors of God, The, VIII:1921
 Zorba the Greek, VIII:1920-1922

Kazin, Alfred, VIII:2273
Kchessinskaya, Mathilde, VIII:2746
Kean, Edmund, **VI:1259-1263,** 1460, 2215
Kearns, Jack, VII:900, 902, 903
Kearny, Stephen Watts, V:431, 840
Keating-Owen Act, VIII:2097
Keats, John, **VI:1264-1268,** 2055; VIII:2251
    Endymion, VI:1266
    Eve of St. Agnes, The, V:1168
    Fall of Hyperion: A Dream, The, VI:1266, 1267
    "Lamia," VI:1267
    "Ode on a Grecian urn," VII:1196
    "On First Looking into Chapman's Homer," VI:1266
    "Sleep and Poetry," VI:1266
    "To Autumn," VI:1267
    "To Solitude," VI:1266
Keble, John, V:75; VI:1641, 1829, 1830
Kedleston House, IV:9
Keita dynasty, II:623, 624
Keller, Hellen, **VIII:1924-1927**
    My Religion, VIII:1926
    Out of the Dark, VIII:1924
    Song of the Stone Wall, The, VIII:1924
    Story of My Life, The, VIII:1924
    Teacher, VIII:1926
    World I Live In, The, VIII:1924
Kelley, Florence, IX:3838, 3839
Kellogg-Briand Pact, V:281; VII:525; VIII:2209
Kelly, Gene, VII:1305
Kelly, William, V:220
Kelvin, Lord, V:609, 768; **VI:1269-1272**
Kemble, Charles, VI:1273
Kemble, John Philip, IV:810; VI:1260, 1261
Kemble, Fanny, **VI:1273-1276**
    Francis I, VI:1273
    Journal of a Residence on a Georgian Plantation in 1838-1839, VI:1273, 1275, 1276
Kemmu Formulary of 1336, II:98
Kemmu Restoration, II:97
Kempis, Thomas à. *See* Thomas à Kempis
Kennedy, Jacqueline. *See* Onassis, Jacqueline Kennedy
Kennedy, John F., **VIII:1928-1931**
    Civil Rights Act, VIII:1973
    Harriman, VIII:1562
    Humphrey, VIII:1784
    Johnson, VIII:1867, 1868
    Jordan, VIII:1887
    Kennedy, Robert F., VIII:1930
    Khrushchev, VIII:1963
    Malcolm X, VIII:2375

Monroe, VIII:2590
    Nixon, VIII:2758
    Onassis, IX:2815-2817
    Profiles in Courage, VIII:1928, 1933; IX:2815
    space exploration, VII:1272
    Stevenson, IX:3525
    Thomas, IX:3663
    Wallace, IX:3863
    Warren Commission, IX:3890
    Why England Slept, VIII:1928
Kennedy, Robert F., VIII:1764, 1785, 1930, **1932-1935**
Kenner, Hugh, VIII:2334
Kent, Edward, Duke of, VI:2307
Kent, James, V:562; **VI:1277-1280**
    Commentaries on American Law, VI:1277-1280
Kent, William, IV:204
Kentucky Resolutions, IV:718
Kentucky v. Dennison, V:478
Kenya African National Union, VIII:1938
Kenya African Union, VIII:1936
Kenyatta, Jomo, **VIII:1936-1940,** 2147
    Facing Mount Kenya, VIII:1936
Kenzan, IV:1041
Keokuk, V:249
Kephisodotos
    Hermes Carrying the Infant, I:690
    Peace and Wealth, I:690
Kepler, Johannes, **IV:772-776**
    Ad Vitellionem paralipomena, quibus astronomiae pars optica traditur, IV:774
    Alhazen, II:66
    Apollonius of Perga, I:74
    Astronomia nova, IV:774, 775
    Brahe, III:78, 79
    De fundamentis astrologiae certioribus, IV:774
    De stella nova in pede serpentarii, IV:774
    Dioptrice, IV:774
    Epitome of Copernican Astronomy, IV:775
    Galileo, IV:519, 521
    Harmonies of the World, IV:775
    Kepler's Conversation with Galileo's Sidereal Messenger, IV:774
    Napier, III:545
    Prodromus dissertationum mathematicarum continens mysterium cosmographicum, IV:774
    Tabulae Rudolphinae, IV:775
Keppel, Augustus, IV:1160, 1161
Keppler, Wilhelm, IX:3881, 3882
Keraunos, Ptolemy, I:768, 769
Kerensky, Aleksandr Fyodorovich, **VIII:1941-1944**

Kern, Jerome, VIII:1533, 1534; IX:3201
Kerouac, Jack, **VIII:1945-1948**
   Book of Dreams, VIII:1946
   Desolation Angels, VIII:1947
   Dharma Bums, The, VIII:1945, 1947
   Doctor Sax, VIII:1945, 1946
   Maggie Cassidy, VIII:1946
   Mexico City Blues, VIII:1947
   On the Road, VIII:1945-1947
   Subterraneans, The, VIII:1946
   Town and the City, The VIII:1946
   Tristessa, VIII:1947
   Visions of Cody, VIII:1946
   Visions of Gerard, VIII:1945, 1947
Kesserling, Albert, **VIII:1949-1951**
Kestrel engine, IX:3211
Kew Observatory, V:868
Key, Francis Scott, **VI:1281-1283,** 2189, 2618
   "Star Spangled Banner, The," VI:1281-1283
Key, Philip B., VI:2107
Keyes, Lawrence, IX:2880
Keynes, John Maynard, **VIII:1952-1956**
   Economic Consequences of the Peace, The,
     VIII:1952
   General Theory of Employment, Interest, and
     Money, VIII:1952, 1954, 1955
   How to Pay for the War, VIII:1954
   Indian Currency and Finance, VIII:1952
   Treatise on Money, A, VIII:1954
Khadijah bint Khuwaylid, II:651, 652
Khanate, Il-, II:381
Kharijites, II:1013
Khayyám, Omar. *See* Omar Khayyám
Khazars, I:127; II:952, 953
Khedive Isma'il, V:1208
Khitans, II:866, 867
Khmer Rouge, IX:3419, 3420
Khomeini, Ruhollah, **VIII:1957-1960,** 2568
   'Abbas the Great, IV:6
   Islamic Government, VIII:1958
Khosrow I, **II:559-562**
Khrushchev, Nikita S., **VIII:1961-1964**
   Brezhnev, VII:459, 460
   Eisenhower, VII:1044
   Hammarskjöld, VIII:1530, 1531
   Joliot, VIII:1872
   Kennedy, VIII:1930
   Malenkov, VIII:2378
   Molotov, VIII:2572, 2573
   Pasternak, IX:2901
   Sakharov, IX:3296, 3297
   "Secret Speech," VIII:1962

   space exploration, VIII:2020, 2021;
     IX:3639, 3640
   Tupolev, IX:3765, 3766
   Zhukov, IX:4116, 4118, 4119
Khwarizmi, al-, **II:563-569**
   Algoritmi de numero indorum, II:564
   Kitab al-jabr wa almuquabalah, II:563
   Kitab surat al-ard, II:565
   Liber ysagogarum Alchorismi in artem
     astronomicam a magistro A. compositus, II:564
Kiakhta, Treaty of, IV:1084
Kiangsi, III:772
Kiangsi Soviet, VIII:2189
Kidd, Billy, VIII:1965
Kidd, Thomas I., VII:839
Kidd, William, **IV:777-780**
Kierkegaard, Soren, **VI:1284-1287**
   Concluding Unscientific Postscript, VI:1286,
     1287
   For Self-Examination, VI:1286
   Philosophical Fragments, VI:1286
   What Christ's Judgment Is About Official
     Christianity, VI:1286
Kiev Rus, Confederation of, II:803-805, 952-954
Kikuyu, VIII:1936-1939, 2145, 2147
Kikuyu Central Association, VIII:1936-1939
Killy, Jean-Claude, **VIII:1965-1967**
Kilmainham Treaty, V:805
Kilwardby, Robert, II:715-717
Kimball, William W., V:1124
Kimberly Division, VI:1873, 1874, 1876
Kim Chi-Ha, IX:3258
Kimmel, Husband E., VIII:2750
King, Billie Jean, VII:1112, 1113; **VIII:1968-1970**
King, Charles, V:562
King, Ernest J., VIII:2750-2752
King, Martin Luther, Jr., **VIII:1971-1976**
   Abernathy, VII:9, 10, 12
   Angelou, VII:80
   Bunche, VII:503
   Charles, VII:658
   Civil Rights Memorial, VIII:2186
   Hoover, VIII:1733
   Jackson, VIII:1824-1826
   Malcolm X, VIII:2375
   Parker, IX:2886
King, Stephen, **VIII:1977-1980**
   Carrie, VIII:1977, 1978
   Danse Macabre, VIII:1978
   Dead Zone, The, VIII:1978
   Green Mile, The, VIII:1978
   Insomnia, VIII:1978

Misery, VIII:1978
Shining, The, VIII:1978
Tommyknockers, The, VIII:1978
King, Tabitha, VIII:1977, 1979
King, William Lyon Mackenzie, **VIII:1981-1985**
    Canada and the Fight for Freedom, VIII:1983
    Canada at Britain's Side, VIII:1983
    Industry and Humanity, VIII:1982
    Secret of Heroism, The, VIII:1981
King David Hotel, bombing of, VII:244
Kingdom, Brotherhood of the, IX:3126
King Features, VIII:1604
King James Bible, III:661; IV:47, 229, 622;
    VI:1829
King Manuel, Ordinances of, III:464
King Philip's War, IV:437, 932, 933, 955, 956
Kings, Valley of the, I:23, 904, 905
King's Bench, Court of the, III:267; IV:332, 904,
    906-908, 1440
Kingsbury, Mary, VII:160
King George's War. *See* Austrian Succession, War
    of
Kingsley, Charles, VI:1504, 1643
    Two Years Ago, VI:1458
    Westward Ho!, VI:1458
Kinney, Abbot, V:1201
Kingston, Council of, II:334
Kinsey, Alfred Charles, VII:1072; **VIII:1986-1990**
    Human Sexual Response, VIII:1988
    Introduction to Biology, An, VIII:1986
    Sexual Behavior in the Human Female,
        VIII:1988, 1989
    Sexual Behavior in the Human Male, VIII:1988,
        1989
Kiowa Indians, V:432
Kipchak, Khanate of. *See* Golden Horde
Kipling, Rudyard, **VI:1288-1293;** VII:168, 554
    Barrack-Room Ballads, VI:1290
    Captains Courageous, VI:1290
    Courting of Dinah Shadd, The, VI:1290
    "Danny Deever," VI:1290
    Departmental Ditties, VI:1288
    "Gunga Din," VI:1292
    Irish Guards in the Great War, VI:1290
    Jungle Book, The, VI:1290; VII:517
    Just So Stories, VI:1290
    Kim, VI:1290, 1292
    Light That Failed, The, VI:1290
    "Mandalay," VI:1292
    "Mary Postgate," VI:1291
    Puck of Pook's Hill, VI:1290
    "Recessional," VI:1290

Second Jungle Book, The, VI:1290
Soldiers Three, VI:1288
Stalky & Co., VI:1288, 1291
"Strange Ride of Morrowbie Jukes, The,"
    VI:1288
"White Man's Burden, The," VI:1291
Kirchhoff, Robert, VI:1411
Kirchner, Ernst Ludwig, **VIII:1991-1993**
    Emmy Frisch with Red Flowers, VIII:1992
    Self-Portrait as a Soldier, VIII:1992
    Street, Berlin, VIII:1992
    View of Basel and the Rhine, VIII:1992
Kirill, Metropolitan, II:53
Kirkpatrick, Jeane, **VIII:1994-1997**
    New Presidential Elite, The, VIII:1995
    Political Woman, VIII:1995
    Strategy of Deception, The, VIII:1994
Kirstein, Lincoln, VII:156
Kishi, Nobusuke, VIII:1575, 1809, 1810
Kissinger, Henry, **VIII:1998-2001**
    Chinese relations, VIII:2191
    Faisal, VIII:1120
    Ford, VII:1181
    Nixon, VIII:2759
    Nuclear Weapons and Foreign Policy, VIII:1999
    Perot, IX:2973
    Walters, IX:3870
    White House Years, VIII:2000
    World Restored, 1812-1822, A, VIII:1998
    Years of Upheaval, VIII:2000
Kitaj, Ron, VIII:1711
Kitchen Cabinet, V:196
Kitchener, Lord, VII:123, 376, 821;
    VIII:2002-2004
Kitty Hawk, IX:4066
Kiwalao, V:1255
Klangfarbenmelodie, IX:3914, 3915
Kleberg, Richard M., VIII:1866
Klee, Paul, **VIII:2005-2008,** 2406
    Ad Parnassum, VIII:2007
    Before the Gates of Kairouan, VIII:2006
    Creative Credo, VIII:2006
    Death and Fire, VIII:2006
    Inventions, VIII:2005
    Once Emerged from the Gray of Night,
        VIII:2006
    Pedagogical Sketchbook, VIII:2006
    Twittering Machine, VIII:2006
Klein, Johann, VI:2021-2023
Kleist, Heinrich von, **VI:1294-1296**
    Amphitryon, VI:1294, 1295
    Broken Jug, The, VI:1294, 1295

Cathy of Heilbronn, VI:1295
Marquise of O, The, VI:1295
Penthesilea, VI:1295
Prince of Homburg, The, VI:1295
Robert Guiskard, VI:1294, 1295
Kleisthenes, I:214
Klinger, Max, VIII:2016, 2017
Leben, Ein, VIII:2016
Knäred, Peace of, IV:589
Knidos. *See* Cnidus
Knight, Richard Payne, IV:1012
Knights' Academy, IV:76
Knights Hospitallers, II:311
Knights of Labor, V:919, 921
Knights Templars, II:144, 311, 609
Knopf, Alfred A., VII:624
Knopf, Edwin H., VIII:1637
Know-Nothing Party, V:794, 1138
Knox, Frank, IX:3524
Knox, John, **III:409-412**
    Appelation of John Knox, The, III:411
    *First Blast of the Trumpet against the Monstrous
        Regiment of Women, The,* III:411
    First Book of Discipline, The, III:411
    *History of the Reformation of Religion Within the
        Realm of Scotland, The,* III:411
    Letter to the Commonalty of Scotland, III:411
Knut, II:692, 693
Kober, Arthur, VIII:1620
Kober, Tobias, IV:154
Koch, Christoph Wilhelm, VI:1544
Koch, Robert, V:535; **VI:1297-1300,** 1747;
    VII:1032; IX:3450, 3451
Kodály, Zoltán, VII:210
Kofi, Francis Nwia. *See* Nkrumah, Kwame
Kohl, Helmut, **VIII:2009-2011**
Kohler, Elmer Peter, VII:748
Köhler, Wolfgang, VII:1027
Kojève, Alexandre, VIII:2061, 2063
Kojo, II:537
Kokoschka, Oskar, **VIII:2012-2015**
    irrende Ritter, Der, VIII:2013
    Morder Hoffnung der Frauen, VIII:2012
    Red Egg, VIII:2014
    Self-portrait of a Degenerate Artist, VIII:2014
    traeumenden Knaben, Die, VIII:2012
    What We Are Fighting For, VIII:2014
Kollwitz, Käthe, **VIII:2016-2018**
    Death, VIII:2017
    Mourning Parents, VIII:2017
    Peasant War, The, VIII:2017
    Proletariat, VIII:2017

War, VIII:2017
Weavers' Revolt, A, VIII:2017
Kölreuter, Gottlieb, VI:1528
Komarov, Vladimir, VII:1271
Komitet Gosudarstvennoi Bezopasnosti.
    See KGB
Komyo, II:97
König, Franz Niklaus, V:592
Königgrätz, Battle of, V:830; VIII:1674
Konigsberg v. State Bar of California, VII:322
Ko no Moronao, II:97, 98
Kon-Tiki, VIII:1658-1660
Korah, I:3
Koran
    Ash'ari, II:94, 348
    Hanbalite school, II:34
    Hanifite school, II:16-18
    Mahfouz, VIII:2357
    Muhammad, II:651-655
    Tabari, II:873
Korean Provisional Government, IX:3165, 3166
Korean War
    Bradley, VII:405
    Chiang Kai-shek, VII:666
    Glenn, VII:1387
    Lin Piao, VIII:2189, 2190
    Luce, VIII:2263
    MacArthur, VIII:2298
    Marshall, VIII:2431
    Rhee, IX:3165-3167
    Truman, IX:3742, 3743
    Wallace, IX:3862
Korechika, II:370
Korematsu v. United States, VII:322
Kornei, Otto, VII:579, 580
Kornilov Revolt, VIII:1943
Korolev, Sergei, **VIII:2019-2022;** IX:3751
Kosovo, Battle of, II:845; III:499
Kossuth, Lajos, V:626, 627
Kostrowitzky, Guillaume Albert Wladimir
    Alexandre Apollinaire de. *See* Apollinaire,
    Guillaume
Koussevitsky, Serge, VII:212, 295, 296, 767
Krasner, Lee, **VIII:2023-2026;** IX:3048, 3049
    Blue and Black, VIII:2024
    Imperfect Indicative, VIII:2025
    "Little Image" paintings, VIII:2024
    Past Conditional, VIII:2025
    Rising Green, VIII:2025
Kraus, Gregor, VII:1327
Kraus, Karl, VIII:2012
Kreisky, Bruno, IX:3986

Kremer, Gerhard. *See* Mercator, Gerardus
Krewo, Treaty of, II:1001
Krio, I:215
Krishnamurti, Jiddu, V:213
Kristallnacht, VIII:1406
Krogh, August, **VIII:2027-2029**
   Anatomy and Physiology of Capillaries, The,
     VIII:2028
   Comparative Physiology of Respiratory
     Mechanisms, The, VIII:2028
Kruger, Paul, VII:376
Krupa, Gene, VIII:1419, 1420
Krupp, Alfred, **VI:1301-1304**
Kubitschek, Juscelino, VIII:2740
Kublai Khan, II:378, **566-569,** 750, 868
Kübler-Ross, Elisabeth, **VIII:2030-2032**
   On Death and Dying, VIII:2031
Kubrick, Stanley, VII:96
   2001: A Space Odyssey, IX:3292
Kugler, Franz, V:358, 359
Kuhnau, Johann, IV:1320
Ku Klux Klan
   Black, VII:321
   Borah, V:281
   Grant, V:977
   Griffith, VIII:1480
   Johnson, VIII:1866
   Lin, VIII:2187
   Stephens, VI:2131
Kumara, II:484
Kumin, Maxine, IX:3395-3397
Kuná Hora decree, II:971
Kunckel von Löwenstjern, Johann, IV:1269
Kundu, II:86
Kunersdorf, Battle of, IV:1298
Kung, Prince, VI:1362, 1364
K'ung Ch'iu. *See* Confucius
Kunstschau, VIII:2012
Kuo Hsiang, I:192
Kuomintang
   Chiang Kai-shek, VII:664-666
   Chou En-lai, VII:676, 677
   Chu Teh, VII:687, 688
   Lu Hsün, VIII:2253, 2254
   Mao Tse-tung, VIII:2400, 2401
   Sun Yat-sen, IX:3578-3580
   Wang Ching-wei, IX:3877-3879
Kuo Mo-jo, **VIII:2033-2035**
   Ch'u Yüan, VIII:2034
   Li Pai yü Tu Fu, VIII:2034
   Mo-jo wên-chi, VIII:2034
Kuo Wei, II:866

Kupka, Frantisek, **VIII:2036-2038**
   Amorpha, Fugue in Two Colors, VIII:2034
   Animated Lines, VIII:2034
   "Girl with a Ball," VIII:2036
   Newton's Discs, VIII:2034
Kurchatov, Igor Vasilyevich, **VIII:2039-2042**
Kurds, VII:134
Kurosawa, Akira, **VIII:2043-2046**
   "Akira Kurosawa's Dreams," VIII:2045
   Dersu Uzala, VIII:2045
   Dodesukaden, VIII:2045
   Drunken Angel, VIII:2044
   High and Low, VIII:2045
   Horses, VIII:2043
   Idiot, The, VIII:2044
   Ikiru, VIII:2044
   I Live in Fear, VIII:2044
   Kagemusha: The Shadow Warrior, VIII:2045
   Most Beautiful, The, VIII:2044
   Ran, VIII:2045
   Rashomon, VIII:2044; VII:280
   Red Beard, VIII:2045
   Sanshiro Sugata, VIII:2044
   Scandal, VIII:2044
   Seven Samurai, The, VIII:2044
   Stray Dog, VIII:2044
   Throne of Blood, VIII:2045
   Tora! Tora! Tora!, VIII:2045
   Yojimbo, VIII:2045
Kurth, Godefroid, IX:3023
Kushan Empire, I:494-496, 636-638
Kutter, Hermann, VII:475
Kutuzov, Arseny Golenishchev, VI:1613
Kutuzov, Mikhail Illarionovich, **VI:1305-1308**
Kuyuk, II:207
Kyd, Thomas, III:471, 472
Kyrle, John, V:1114
Kyrle Society, V:1114, 1115

Laban, Rudolf, **VIII:2058-2060**
   Choreutics, VIII:2059
   Effort, VIII:2059
   Mastery of Movement on the Stage, The,
     VIII:2059
   Modern Educational Dance, VIII:2059
   Titan, VIII:2059
   Welt des Tänzers, Die, VIII:2059
La Boétie, Etienne de, III:524
Labor Action, Alliance for, IX:3163
Labor Party (Australia), VII:816-818, 1109-1111;
   VIII:2289-2292, 2498
Labor Party (England). *See* Labour Party

Labor Party (Israel), VIII:2474, 2475
labor unions. *See* unionism, trade
Labour and Socialist International, VIII:2313
Labour Party (England)
    Angell, VII:76, 77
    Attlee, VII:137-139
    Baldwin, VII:169
    Bevan, VII:304-306
    Bevin, VII:313-316
    Churchill, VII:693
    Fawcett, V:778
    George V, VII:1341
    George VI, VII:1345
    Hardie, V:1036-1038
    Heath, VIII:1607, 1608
    Hughes, VIII:1775, 1776
    Laski, VIII:2093-2095
    MacDonald, VIII:2312-2314
    Major, VIII:2370, 2371
    Soviet relations, VIII:1645
    Thatcher, IX:3651, 3652
    Webb, Beatrice and Sidney, IX:3907, 3908
    Wilson, IX:4016-4018
Labour Representation Committee, V:1037, 1038
Lacaille, Abbé Nicolas-Louis de, IV:805
Lacan, Jacques, **VIII:2061-2064**
    Ecrits, VIII:2062, 2063
Laclos, Choderlos de, IV:1049
Lacordaire, Père, V:967
La Cosa, Juan de, III:116
Lacy, James, IV:528
Ladies Home Journal, VII:623
Ladies Professional Golfer's Association, IX:4098
Laelius, I:758
Laertius, Diogenes, I:653, 967
La Fayette, Madame de
    Princess of Clèves, The, IV:172
Lafayette, Marquis de, IV:1175, 1176; V:562, 563
La Follette, Robert M., **VIII:2047-2050;** IX:3661
    La Follette's Weekly Magazine, VIII:2048
La Fontaine, Henri-Marie, **VIII:2051-2053**
    Great Solution: Magnissima Charter, The,
      VIII:2052
    International Judicature, VIII:2052
La Fontaine, Jean de, **IV:781-784**
    Adonis, IV:781, 783
    Discours à Mne de La Sablière, IV:782
    Épitre à Huet, IV:783
    Eunuque, L', IV:781
    Fables Written in Verse, IV:782
    Loves of Cupid and Psyche, The, IV:782
    Relation d'un voyage en Limousin, IV:782

    Songe de Vaux, Le, IV:781
    Tales and Short Stories in Verse, IV:782, 783
La Fontaine, Louis Hippolyte, V:118
La Gardia Trial, III:726
Lagerlöf, Selma, **VIII:2065-2068;** IX:3285, 3286
    Christ Legends, VIII:2066
    Diary of Selma Lagerlöf, The, VIII:2066
    Emperor of Portugallia, The, VIII:2066
    Further Adventures of Nils, The, VIII:2066, 2077
    Gösta Berlings Saga, VIII:2065
    Holy City: Jerusalem II, The, VIII:2066
    Jerusalem, VIII:2066
    Liliecrona's Home, VIII:2066
    Marbacka, VIII:2066
    Memories of My Childhood, VIII:2066
    Miracles of the Antichrist, The, VIII:2065
    Ring of the Löwenskölds: A Trilogy, The,
      VIII:2066, 2077
    Wonderful Adventures of Nils, The, VIII:2066,
      2077
Lagrange, Joseph-Louis, **IV:785-788,** 885;
    IX:4039
    Mécanique analytique, IV:785-787
La Guardia, Fiorello Henry, **VIII:2054-2057**
La Guardia Trial. *See* La Gardia Trial
Laika, VIII:2021
laissez-faire economics
    Biddle, V:228
    Blanc, V:260
    Erhard, VII:1096
    Greenspan, VIII:1471
    Macmillan, VIII:2341
    Mill, VI:1562
    Smith, IV:1251
    Spencer, VI:2087
    Turgot, IV:1348
Lake Placid Club, V:661
Lamachos, I:90
Lamar, Mirabeau B., V:1138
Lamarckism, VI:2349
Lamb, William. *See* Melbourne, Second Viscount
Lambert, Constant, IX:3873, 3874
Lambert, John, **IV:789-792,** 972, 973
Lambton, John George. *See* Durham, First Earl of
Lamé, Series of. *See* Fibonacci sequence
Lamm, Richard, IX:2974
Lamoureaux, Charles, VII:606
Lamprocles, I:952, 953
Lancaster, Duke of, II:457, 458, 786, 1010
Lancaster, House of
    Edward II, II:326
    Edward IV, III:234, 235

Fortescue, III:267-269
Henry IV, II:457-460
Henry VI, III:341-343
Henry VII, III:345, 346
Richard III, III:647, 649-652
Warwick, III:774-777
Lancaster, Joseph, **VI:1309-1312**
Lancaster, Thomas, Earl of, II:326
Lanchester, Frederick William, **VIII:2069-2072;**
   IX:3074
   Aerial Flight, VIII:2071
Landais, Pierre, IV:740
Landau, Lev Davidovich, **VIII:2073-2076**
   Physics for Everyone, VIII:2075
Landauer, Gustav, VII:483
Landed Qualifications Act, IV:158
Landfriede, III:492, 493
Landini, Francesco, **II:570-573**
Lang, Fritz, **VIII:2077-2079**
   Destiny, VII:505; VIII:2077
   Dr. Mabuse the Gambler, VIII:2077
   Fury, VIII:2078
   Halbblut, VIII:2077
   Liliom, VIII:2078
   M, VIII:2077
   Man Hunt, VIII:2078
   Metropolis, VIII:2077, 2078
   Niebelungen, Die, VIII:2077, 2078
   Rancho Notorious, VIII:2078
   Return of Frank James, The, VIII:2078
   Scarlet Street, VIII:2078
   Western Union, VIII:2078
   While the City Sleeps, VIII:2078
   Woman in the Window, The, VIII:2078; IX:2777
   You Only Live Once, VIII:2078
Lang, K.D., **VIII:2080-2082**
   Absolute Torch and Twang, VIII:2081
   Angel with a Lariat, VIII:2080, 2081
   "Constant Craving," VIII:2082
   Ingenue, VIII:2081
   Shadowland, VIII:2080, 2081
   Truly Western Experience, A, VIII:2080
Lange, Dorothea, **VIII:2083-2086**
   "Migrant Mother," VIII:2085
   Notes from the Field, VIII:2084
   "White Angel Bread Line," VIII:2084
Langen, Eugen, V:597; VI:1702, 1703
Langer, Susanne K., **VIII:2087-2089**
   *Cruise of the Little Dipper, and Other Fairy
      Tales, The,* VIII:2087
   Feeling and Form, VIII:2088
   Introduction to Symbolic Logic, An, VIII:2087
   Mind, VIII:2088
   Philosophy in a New Key, VIII:2088
   Practice of Philosophy, The, VIII:2087
   Problems of Art, VIII:2088
Langland, William, II:114
Langley, Samuel Pierpont, **VI:1313-1315;** IX:4067
Langley's Law, VI:1314
Langton, Stephen, II:510, 511, 541, 542
Languet, Hubert, III:691
Lankester, Sir Edwin Ray, **VI:1316-1318**
La Noue, François, III:537
Lansbury, George, VII:314
Lansdowne, Fifth Marquess of, **VIII:2090-2092**
Lansing, Robert, IV:609
Lansing Declaration, VIII:2442
Lanuvinus, Luscius, I:845
Lanzmann, Claude, VII:231
Lao Ai, I:176
Lao-tzu, **I:498-500**
   Tao-te Ching, I:190, 191, 498-500, 949, 951
Lapidoth, I:246
Laplace, Pierre-Simon, V:819, 820; **VI:1319-1322**
   Philosophical Essay on Probabilities, A,
      VI:1320
   Théorie analytique des probabilitiés, VI:1320
   Treatise of Celestial Mechanics, A, V:1025
Laporte, Pierre, IX:3732
la Pouplinière, Le Riche de, IV:1148, 1149
Largus, Scribonius, I:277
Larichus, I:750
Larsa, I:361, 362
La Salle, Sieur de, **IV:793-796;** VI:1736, 1737
Las Casas, Bartolomé de, **III:413-415**
   Apologética historia de las Indias, III:415
   Del único modo, III:415
   History of the Indies, III:413, 414
   *Relation of the First Voyages and Discoveries
      Made by the Spainiards in America, A,* III:413
Lascaux cave paintings, VII:457
Lascelles, John, III:368
Laski, Harold J., **VIII:2093-2095**
   American Democracy, The, VIII:2094
   Authority in the Modern State, VIII:2093
   *Foundations of Sovereignty and Other Essays,
      The,* VIII:2093
   Grammar of Politics, A, VIII:2093
   Studies in the Problem of Sovereignty, VIII:2093
Lasky, Jesse L., VII:896, 897; VIII:1415, 1417
Las Navas de Tolosa, Battle of, II:103
Lassalle, Ferdinand, **VI:1323-1326**
   *Lassalle's Open Letter to the National Labor
      Association of Germany,* VI:1324

Lasso, Orlando di, III:107, 108, 284
LaStarza, Roland, VIII:2413
Lasus, I:787
László I, Saint, **II:574-576**
Lateran Councils, II:50, 396, 488, 511, 512, 716;
    III:407
Lateran Pacts, VII:1337
Lateran Palace, II:823
Later Chin Dynasty, IV:1
Later Chou Dynasty, II:866
Later Han Dynasty, I:590
Lathrop, Julia C., **VIII:2096-2099**
    Hull-House Maps and Papers, VIII:2096
Lathrop, William, VIII:2096
Latimer, Hugh, **III:416-418,** 656
Latini, Brunetto, II:286
Latin language
    Alcuin, II:44, 46, 47
    Boniface, II:167
    Cicero, I:196
    Greek manuscripts, II:985, 986
    Lucretius, I:511-513
    Phaedrus, I:619, 620
    Priscian, II:755-757
    Psellus, II:759
    Scaliger, III:671-673
    Valla, III:740
    Verrius Flaccus, I:930
Latin literature, Golden Age of, I:519-521
Latin poetry
    Catullus, I:171
    Cicero, I:194
    Ennius, I:287-289
Latrobe, Benjamin Henry, **VI:1327-1330**
Laud, William, IV:280, **797-800,** 1142
Laue, Max von, VII:410
Laurel, Salvador, VII:88
Laurence, Saint, IV:118
Laurier, Sir Wilfrid, VIII:1981, 1982, **2100-2104**
Lausanne, Academy of, III:363
Lausanne, Treaty of, VIII:1812
Lautaro Lodge, VI:1947
Laval, François, **IV:801-804**
Laval, Pierre, **VIII:2105-2108;** IX:2988
Laver, Rod, **VIII:2109-2111**
Lavoisier, Antoine-Laurent, IV:262, **805-807;**
    V:718
    *Elements of Chemistry, in a New Systematic
        Order,* IV:263, 806
    Essays, Physical and Chemical, IV:806
    Methods of Chemical Nomenclature, IV:263, 806
Lavon, Pinhas, VII:253

Law, Bonar, VII:168, 234, 235; **VIII:2112-2114**
Lawrence, D.H., V:1066; VI:1523; VII:625;
    VIII:1805, **2115-2120,** 2537
    Aaron's Rod, VIII:2118
    Birds, Beasts, and Flowers, VIII:2118
    Fantasia of the Unconscious, VIII:2118
    Kangaroo, VIII:2118
    Lady Chatterley's Lover, VIII:2118; VII:322
    Lost Girl, The, VIII:2118
    Man Who Died, The, VIII:2119
    Movements in European History, VIII:2118
    Plumed Serpent, The, VIII:2118
    Psychoanalysis and the Unconscious, VIII:2118
    Rainbow, The, VIII:2117
    St. Mawr: Together with the Princess, VIII:2118
    Sea and Sardinia, VIII:2118
    Sons and Lovers, VIII:2117
    Studies in Classic American Literature,
        VIII:2118
    Trespasser, The, VIII:2117
    Twilight in Italy, VIII:2117
    White Peacock, The, VIII:2115
    Women in Love, VIII:2117
Lawrence, Ernest Orlando, **VIII:2121-2124,** 2336,
    2338; IX:2833, 3376
Lawrence, First Baron, **VI:1331-1333**
Lawrence, Gertrude, VII:786
Lawrence, John Laird Mair. *See* Lawrence, First
    Baron
Lawrence, T.E., VII:1124, 1125; **VIII:2125-2130**
    Crusader Castles, VIII:2125
    Mint, The, VIII:2128
    Seven Pillars of Wisdom: A Triumph,
        VIII:2127, 2128
Lawrence, Sir Thomas, **IV:808-812**
    Portrait of an Actress, IV:809
    Princess of Wales and Princess Charlotte, The,
        IV:810
    Satan Summoning up His Legions, IV:810
Lawrence Berkeley Laboratory, VIII:2123
Lawrence Livermore Laboratory, IX:3633
Lawson, Nigel, VIII:2369, 2370
Laxness, Halldór, **VIII:2131-2133**
    Atom Station, The, VIII:2132
    Happy Warriors, The, VIII:2132
    Independent People, VIII:2131
    Islandsklukkan, VIII:2131
    Salka Valka: A Novel of Iceland, VIII:2131
    Vefarinn mikli frá Kasmir, VIII:2131
    World Light, VIII:2131, 2132
Lazarists. *See* Mission, Congregation of the
Lazarus, IV:170

Lazarus, Emma, **VI:1334-1337;** VII:289
   Admetus and Other Poems, VI:1334
   Alide, VI:1334
   "By the Waters of Babylon," VI:1336
   Dance to Death, The, VI:1336
   "Epistle to the Hebrews, An," VI:1336
   "In the Jewish Synagogue at Newport," VI:1334
   "New Colossus," VI:1334, 1336, 1337
   Poems and Ballads of Heinrich Heine, VI:1336
   Poems and Translations by Emma Lazarus, VI:1334
   Songs of a Semite, VI:1336
Lazear, Jesse, VI:1858, 1859
LDP. *See* Liberal Democratic Party of Japan
Leach v. Three King's Messengers, IV:906
Leadership Conference on Civil Rights, IX:3115
League of Augsburg, War of the, IV:840
Leakey, L.S.B., **VIII:2145-2149**
Leander, II:518
Leary, Timothy, VIII:1807
Léaud, Jean-Pierre, IX:3737, 3738
Lebanon Civil War, VII:91
Lebed, II:86
Lebedia, II:86
Lebedev Physics Institute, VII:214, 215
Leblanc, Nicolas, **IV:813-816**
Le Bon, Gustave, **VIII:2134-2136**
   Crowd, The, VIII:2134, 2135
   Psychology of Peoples, The, VIII:2134, 2135
   Psychology of the Great War, The, VIII:2135
Lech, Battle of, IV:1336
Leclerc, Charles-Victor-Emmanuel, IV:1340
Leclerc, Georges-Louis. *See* Buffon, Comte de
Le Corbusier, VII:1309, 1310; **VIII:2137-2140,** 2739, 2740; IX:4075-4077
   Towards a New Architecture, VIII:2138
Lee, Ann, **IV:817-820**
Lee, Robert E., V:977, 1205, 1206; **VI:1338-1342**
Lee, William, IV:817-819
Leeds, First Duke of, **IV:821-824**
Lee Kuan Yew, **VIII:2150-2153**
Leeuwenhoek, Antoni van, **IV:825-828;** VI:1746
Lefèvre d'Etaples, Jacques, III:467
Le Gallienne, Eva, **VIII:2141-2144**
Legal Tender Act, IV:251
Legate, Bartholomew, IV:47
Legendre, Adrien-Marie, V:8
Léger, Fernand, **VIII:2154-2156**
   Ballet mécanique, Le, VIII:2155
   Constructeurs, Les, VIII:2155
   Contrasts of Forms, VIII:2154
   Disques, Les, VIII:2155

   Eléments mécaniques, VIII:2155
   Grand Déjeuner, Le, VIII:2155
   Nus dans la forêt, Les, VIII:2154
Le Goulet, Treaty of, II:540
Leguia, Augusto, VIII:1584, 1585
Leibniz, Gottfried Wilhelm, **IV:829-833**
   Condillac, IV:345
   Duns Scotus, II:313
   Frederick I, IV:498
   New Essays Concerning Human Understanding, IV:831
   Principles of Nature and Grace, The, IV:831
   Theodicy, IV:105, 831
Leicester, Earl of, III:147, 243, 295, 693
Leicester House, IV:536
Leiden, University of, III:673; VII:1039; VIII:2235; IX:2827
Leif Eriksson, **II:577-580,** 689
Leigh, Vivian, IX:2811, 2812
Leipzig, Battle of, V:264, 475, 942
Leipzig, University of, IX:2855, 4069
Leipzig Opera, IV:1319, 1320
Leiter, Levi Z., V:783
Leith Hill Music Festival, IX:3798
Lemaître, Georges, **VIII:2157-2159**
   Discussion sur l'evolution de l'univers, VIII:2158
   Primeval Atom, The, VIII:2158
Lemercier, Jacques, IV:899
Lemon v. Kurtzman, VII:510
Lenaia, I:88, 91
Lend-Lease Act, VIII:1560, 1562, 1737, 1984
Lenin, Vladimir Ilich, VI:1494; **VIII:2160-2163**
   Bukharin, VII:491
   Gorky, VIII:1444, 1445
   Gramsci, VIII:1461
   Kazantzakis, VIII:1921
   Kerensky, VIII:1942
   Litvinov, VIII:2208, 2209
   Lukács, VIII:2273
   Molotov, VIII:2571
   Sorel, IX:3464
   Trotsky, IX:3726-3728
   What Is to Be Done?, VIII:2161; IX:3726
   Wilson, IX:4014
Leningrad affair, VIII:2378
Lennon, John, VII:226-229
Lenoir, Étienne, V:597; **VI:1343-1346,** 1702
Le Nôtre, André, **IV:834-83**
Lenya, Lotte, IX:3927, 3928
Leo I, I:785; II:894
Leo III, II:229, 544, 545, 903, 904

Leo IV, II:59
Leo V, II:904
Leo VI, II:86, 87, 117-119
Leo VIII, **V:1347-1350**
Leo IX, Pope, **II:581-584**
Leo X, **III:419-422**
    Andrea del Sarto, III:24
    Catherine de Médicis, III:132
    Clement VII, III:166
    Erasmus, III:247
    Guicciardini, III:325
    Luther, III:443
    Medici, Lorenzo de', III:498
    Michelangelo, III:519
Leo XIII, V:386, 919, 921; **VI:1347-1350,** 1644;
    VIII:2100
    *Concerning Modern Errors, Socialism,
        Communism, Nihilism,* VI:1348
    Condition of Labor, The, VI:1348
    Grande munus, VI:1349
    Human Liberty, VI:1348
    On Christian Marriage, VI:1349
    On Civil Government, VI:1348
    On the Christian Constitution of States, VI:1348
    On the Study of Scriptures, VI:1348
    Scholastic Philosophy, VI:1349
Leonardo da Vinci, **III:423-427**
    Adoration of the Magi, III:424
    Andrea del Sarto, III:24, 26
    Annunciation, The, III:423
    Battle of Anghiari, III:642
    Bramante, III:81
    Dürer, III:232
    Head of a Woman, III:424
    Last Supper, The, III:26, 81, 424, 684, IV:604
    Madonna Benois, III:424
    Madonna of the Rocks, III:424
    Mona Lisa, III:275, 425, IV:605
    Portrait of Ginevra dei Benci, III:751
    Raphael, III:642, 645
    Saint John the Baptist, III:425
    Treatise on Painting, IV:1187
    Valéry, IX:3791
    Vasari, III:745
    Verrocchio, III:750-752
    *Virgin and Child with Saint Anne and the Infant
        Saint John,* III:425
Leonardo of Pisa, **II:585-587**
    Flos, II:586
    Liber abaci, II:585, 586
    Liber quadratorum, II:586
    Practica geometriae, II:586

Leonico, III:45
Leonidas, **I:501-503,** 964
Leonidas II, I:215, 216
Leopold I, IV:498, **838-841**
Leopold II, VI:2103, 2398
Leopold, Nathan F., Jr., VII:840
Leopold of Anhalt-Dessau, IV:93
Leopold of Saxe-Coburg-Saalfeld, VI:1720
Leo the Great, I:126; II:823
Leotychides, I:16
Lepanto, Battle of, III:254; IV:265
Lepidus, Marcus Aemilius, I:132, 133, 140, 154
Lermontov, Mikhail, **VI:1351-1354**
    "Angel," VI:1352
    "Cossack Lullaby," VI:1353
    "Death of a Poet, The," VI:1352
    "Demon," VI:1352
    Hero of Our Time, A, VI:1351-1353
    "I Walk Out Alone onto the Road," VI:1353
    Masquerade, VI:1352
    "Novice, The," VI:1353
    "Parus," VI:1352
    Princess Ligovskaya, VI:1352
    Vadim, VI:1352
Leroux, Pierre, VI:1952
Lesage, Jean, IX:3730
Lesbia. *See* Clodia
Lesbos, I:651-653, 750-752
Lescot, Pierre, **III:428-430**
Leslie, Frank, VI:1627, 1629; VII:628
Lesseps, Ferdinand de, **VI:1355-1357;** VIII:1408
Lessing, Gotthold Ephraim, IV:465, **842-845;**
    VI:1287
    Briefe, die neueste Literatur betreffend, IV:842
    Education of the Human Race, The, IV:844
    Emilia Galotti, IV:843
    Free-thinker, The, IV:842
    Hamburg Dramaturgy, IV:843
    Jews, The, IV:842
    Laocoön, IV:843
    Masonic Dialogues, IV:844
    Minna von Barnhelm, IV:842, 843
    Miss Sara Sampson, IV:842
    Nathan the Wise, IV:842, 844
Lesslie, James, VI:1451
Le Tellier, François-Michel. *See* Louvois,
    Marquis de
Lethion, VI:1597, 1598
Leucippus, I:249
Leuckart, Rudolf, VI:2348
Leuctra, Battle of, I:215, 292
Leuven, Adolphe de, V:708

Levanevsky, Sigesmund, IX:4001
Levant, Oscar, VIII:1749
Levellers, IV:380
Le Vendre Bridge, VII:1229
Levesque, René, IX:3732
Lévi-Strauss, Claude, **VIII:2164-2166**
Levy, Lucien, VII:103
Lewaro, Villa, IX:3855
Lewes, Battle of, II:454, 645
Lewes, George Henry, V:751-753
Lewinsky, Monica, VII:710, 715
Lewis, C.S., **VIII:2167-2169; IX:3696**
   Allegory of Love, The, VIII:2167
   Chronicles of Narnia, VIII:2168
   Discarded Image, The, VIII:2168
   English Literature in the Sixteenth Century,
     VIII:2168
   Four Loves, The, VIII:2168
   Grief Observed, A, VIII:2168
   Mere Christianity, VIII:2168
   Perelandra, VIII:2168
   Problem of Pain, The, VIII:2168
   Screwtape Letters, The, VIII:2168
   Surprised by Joy, VIII:2168
   Till We Have Faces, VIII:2168
Lewis, Carl, IX:2865
Lewis, Edith, VII:624
Lewis, Eleanor Francis, IX:2884
Lewis, Gilbert N., IX:3375, 3787
Lewis, John L., **VIII:2170-2173**
Lewis, Meriwether, **VI:1358-1361**, 1933-1935
Lewis, Sinclair, **VIII:2174-2177**
   Ann Vickers, VIII:2175, 2176
   Arrowsmith, VIII:2174-2176
   Babbitt, VIII:2175, 2176, 2484
   Cass Timberlane, VIII:2176
   Dodsworth, VIII:2175
   Elmer Gantry, VIII:2175
   Free Air, VIII:2174
   Innocents, The, VIII:2174
   It Can't Happen Here, VIII:2174, 2176
   Job, The, VIII:2174
   Kingsblood Royal, VIII:2176
   Main Street, VIII:2174, 2175, 2484
   Mantrap, VIII:2175
   Our Mr. Wrenn, VIII:2174
   Prodigal Parents, The, VIII:2175
   The Man Who Knew Coolidge, VIII:2174,
     2175
   Work of Art, VIII:2175
Lewis and Clark Expedition, VI:1358-1361,
   1933-1935, 2077

Lex Regia, II:791
Ley Lerdo, V:1252
Leyte Gulf, Battle of, VIII:1527, 1528, 2752
Lhote, André, VII:594
Libanius, I:184
Liberal-Conservative Party (Canada), VI:1436
Liberal Democratic Party (Japan), VIII:1574,
   1575, 1809-1811; IX:3336, 3337
Liberal Party (Australia), V:631; VIII:2498
Liberal Party (Canada), VII:680-682;
   VIII:1981-1983, 2100-2103; IX:3345
   Trudeau, IX:3731, 3733, 3734
Liberal Party (England)
   Asquith, VII:121, 122
   Beveridge, VII:310
   Brougham, V:316
   Chamberlain, Joseph, V:462, 464
   Chamberlain, Neville, VII:644
   Churchill, VII:691
   Fawcett, V:778
   Forster, V:804, 805
   George V, VII:1339, 1340
   Gladstone, V:936
   Grey, VIII:1475, 1476
   Hardie, V:1036, 1037
   Hobhouse, VIII:1709
   Home Rule Bill, VI:1741
   Lansdowne, VIII:2090, 2091
   Lloyd George, VIII:2217
   McDonald, VIII:2312, 2315
   Pankhurst, IX:2871, 2874
   Pusey, VI:1829
Liberal-Protectionist Party, V:631
Liberal Triennium, V:413
Libération du Québec, Front de, IX:3732
Liberation of Palestine, Front for the, VII:91
Liberation Rally, VIII:2693
Liberator, The, V:884, 885; VI:2143
Liberty, IV:617, 618
Liberty, Statue of, VI:1334, 1336, 1337; IX:2841
libraries
   ancient Rome, I:918, 919
   Carnegie, V:423, 662
   Córdoba, II:8
   York, II:46
Library, The, VII:623
Li Ch'ing-chao, **II:588-590**
   Chin shih lu, II:589, 590
   "Wu-his chung-hsing sung shi," II:588
Licinius, I:226-228, 346
Lie, Trygve, VIII:1529, 1530
Liebermann, Carl, VIII:1509

Liebig, Justus von, **VI:1366-1368,** 2403, 2404
  Animal Chemistry, VI:1367
  Organic Chemistry in Its Applications to Agriculture and Physiology, VI:1367
Liebknecht, Karl, VIII:2287
Liebknecht, Wilhelm, **VI:1369-1371**
Liège, battle of, III:163
Liège, Jacques de, II:661
Liehmann, Antonin, V:725
Li Fan Yuan, IV:2
Lifar, Serge, **VIII:2182-2184**
  Bacchus et Ariadne, VIII:2183
  Icare, VIII:2184
  Manifeste du choregraphe, Le, VIII:2183
Life magazine, VII:397, 398; VIII:2256, 2262, 2263
Life of Aesop, The, I:13-15
Life of Saint Boniface, The, II:167, 168
Li-Fournier Agreement, V:466
Ligny, Battle of, V:942
Ligonier, John, IV:37, 38
Li Hung-chang, **VI:1362-1365**
Li Lin-fu, II:918, 966
Li Ling, I:820
Liliuokalani, **VI:1372-1375**
Lily, William, III:170
Limited Nuclear Test Ban Treaty, IX:3377, 3448
Limoges, IV:1348
Limousin, Claude, VII:1229
Lin, Maya Ying, **VIII:2185-2188**
  Civil Rights Memorial, VIII:2185-2187
  "Groundswell," VIII:2187
  "TOPO," VIII:2187
  Vietnam Veterans Memorial, VIII:2185-2187
  "Women's Table," VIII:2187
Lincoln, Abraham, **VI:1380-1384**
  assassination, V:272; VI:1383
  Bennett, V:193
  Brady, V:296
  Chase, V:478-480
  Douglas, V:693
  Douglass, V:697
  Frémont, V:842, 843
  Garibaldi, V:881
  Garrison, V:886
  Gettysburg Address, VI:1383, 2346
  Grant, V:976, 977
  Greeley, V:985
  Hay, V:1068, 1069
  Holmes, V:1127
  House Divided Speech, VI:1382

  Johnson, V:1233
  Parrington, IX:2894
  Phillips, VI:1772, 1773
  Pierce, VI:1778
  Sandburg's biography, IX:3310, 3311
  Saint-Gaudens, VI:1940
  Schurz, VI:1996, 1997
  Seward, VI:2038, 2039, 2172
  Stanton, Edwin M., VI:2107-2109
  Stanton, Elizabeth Cady, VI:2112
  Stowe, VI:2151
  Taney, VI:2192
  Tarbell's biography, IX:3614
  Truth, VI:2256, 2257
  Whitman, VI:2371
  Wilson's *Patriotic Gore,* IX:4014
Lincoln, Battle of, II:848
Lincoln, Benjamin, IV:1240, 1406
Lind, Jenny, V:59, 135; **VI:1385-1387**
Lindbergh, Charles A., VII:326; VIII:1397, 1500, **2193-2198**
  Autobiography of Values, VIII:2196
  Boyhood on the Upper Mississippi, VIII:2196
  Culture of Organs, The, VIII:2196
  Wartime Journals, VIII:2196
  We, VIII:2196
Linde, Carl von, VII:699, 700
Lindsay, Vachel, VIII:1771; IX:3622, 3624, 3625
Linnaeus, IV:216, **846-849;** 589
  General System of Nature, A, IV:846, 847
  Species plantarum, IV:847
Linné, Carl von. *See* Linnaeus
Linnean Society, V:608; VI:1418
Lin Piao, **VIII:2189-2192,** 2401, 2402
Lin Tse-hsü, **VI:1376-1379**
Lionne, Hugues de, IV:947
Lipchitz, Jacques, **VIII:2199-2202**
  Bellerophon Taming Pegasus, VIII:2201
  Chimene, VIII:2201
  Dancer, VIII:2199, 2200
  Encounter, VIII:2199
  Government of the People, VIII:2201
  Half-Standing Figure, VIII:2201
  Head, VIII:2201
  Joy of Life, VIII:2201
  Man with Guitar, VIII:2200
  Mother and Children, VIII:2200
  Our Tree of Life, VIII:2201
  Pilgrim, VIII:2201
  Sailor with Guitar, VIII:2200
  Sculpture, VIII:2200
  Standing Personage, VIII:2200

Woman and Gazelles, VIII:2199
Woman with Serpent, VIII:2199
Li Peng, **VIII:2178-2180**
Li Po, II:**591-594,** 918
   Song of Pure Happiness, A, II:592
Lippershey, Hans, **IV:850-853**
Lippi, Fra Filippo, III:74, 460
Lippmann, Gabriel, VIII:2277
Lippmann, Walter, **VIII:2203-2207**
   Cold War, VIII:2205
   Drift and Mastery, VIII:2203
   Essays in the Public Philosophy, VIII:2205
   Good Society, The, VIII:2204
   Phantom Public, The, VIII:2204
   Preface to Morals, A, VIII:2204
   Preface to Politics, A, VIII:2203, 2205
   Public Opinion, VIII:2204, 2205
   U.S. Foreign Policy, VIII:2205
   U.S. War Aims, VIII:2205
Lisette Model, VII:95
Li Shih-min. *See* T'ai Tsung
Li Ssu, I:177, 433, 946
Lister, Joseph, **VI:1388-1390**
Liston, Sonny, VII:54
Liszt, Franz, V:833, 1003; **VI:1391-1394;** VII:210
   Années de pèlerinage, VI:1391, 1393
   Apparitions, VI:1391
   Faust Symphony, A, VI:1392
   "Fountains of the Villa d'Este, The," VI:1393
   Mountain Symphony, VI:1392
   "Nuages gris," VI:1393
   Préludes, Les, VI:1392
   Réminiscences de Don Juan, VI:1391
   Sonata in B Minor, VI:1392
   Symphony to Dante's "Divina Commedia," A, VI:1392
   "Unstern," VI:1393
   Via Crucis, VI:1393
literary criticism
   Barthes, VII:207-209
   Eliot, VII:1058
   Fuller, V:852
   Lessing, IV:842-844
   Lukács, VIII:2272-2274
   Millet, VIII:2537, 2538
   Poe, VI:1794, 1796
   Proust, IX:3089-3091
   Wilson, IX:4012-4015
Li Tsung-jen, VII:666
Little, Malcolm. *See* Malcolm X
Little Big Horn, Battle of the, V:575, 585, 587; VI:2072

Little Galleries of the Photo-Secession, IX:3534
Little Gidding, IV:462-464
Little Steel strike, VIII:2171
Littleton, Sir Thomas, **III:431-433**
   Tenures, III:432, 433
Litvinov, Maksim Maksimovich, **VIII:2208-2211,** 2571, 2572
Litvinov Protocol, VIII:2210
Li Tzu-ch'eng, IV:421, 422
Liu Chin, III:771
Liu Hsiang-shan, II:963
Liu Hsiu, I:590
Liu Pang, I:178
Liu Shao-ch'i, **VIII:2212-2215**
Liu Tzu-cheng, I:944
Liu Yï, I:429, 430
Liu Yü, I:429, 430
liver, I:82
   Bernard, V:208
   Erasistratus, I:300
   Galen, I:339
   Herophilus, I:398
   Malpighi, IV:891
Livermore Radiation laboratories, VIII:2123
Liverpool, VI:2133, 2134
Liverpool, Second Earl of, **VI:1395-1398**
Livingston, Robert, V:369, 370, 855, 856
Livingstone, David, **VI:1399-1402,** 2101, 2102
   Missionary Travels and Researches in South Africa, VI:1399
   Narrative of an Expedition to the Zambezi and Its Tributaries, VI:1400
Livius, Peter, IV:248
Livonian War, III:387
Livy, **I:504-506**
   History of Rome, The, I:504, II:728
Li Yuan, II:1015
Llewelyn ap Gruffyd, II:323
Lloyd George, David, V:778; **VIII:2216-2218**
   Allenby, VII:61
   Asquith, VII:122, 123
   Baldwin, VII:168
   Balfour, VII:174
   Beaverbrook, VII:234, 235
   Bevan, VII:304, 305
   Chamberlain, VII:643
   Cosgrave, VII:770
   Curzon, VII:821
   Harmsworths, VIII:1555
   Hughes, VIII:1777
   Imperial War Cabinet, VII:366
   John, VIII:1855

Keynes, VIII:1952
Law, VIII:2112-2114
Sinn Féin, VII:877
Lobachevsky, Nikolay Ivanovich, **VI:1403-1405**
   Geometriya, VI:1404
   Pangéométrie, VI:1404, 1405
Lobengula, VI:1874
Local Government Act of 1888, VI:1945
Locarno, Treaty of, VII:169
Lochner v. New York, VII:421
Locke, John, **IV:854-859**
   Berkeley, IV:114-116
   Blackstone, IV:130
   Bolingbroke, IV:160
   Bradley, V:291
   Condillac, IV:345
   Essay Concerning Human Understanding, An,
      IV:344, 430, 856-858
   Hume, IV:683, 685
   Letter Concerning Toleration, A, IV:856, 857
   Second Treatise of Government, IV:665
   Shaftesbury, IV:1231
   Some Thoughts Concerning Education, IV:92,
      93, 1021
   Third Letter for Toleration, A, IV:103
   Transcendentalists, V:757
   Two Treaties of Government, IV:857
Lockwood, Belva A., **VI:1406-1409**
Lockwood Bill, VI:1407
Lockyer, Sir Joseph Norman, **VI:1410-1413**
   Chemistry of the Sun, The, VI:1412
   Dawn of Astronomy, The, VI:1413
   Inorganic Evolution as Studied by Spectrum
      Analysis, VI:1412
   Meteoritic Hypothesis, The, VI:1412
   Stonehenge and Other British Monuments
      Astronomically Considered, VI:1413
   Sun's Place in Nature, The, VI:1412
Lodge, Henry Cabot, **VIII:2219-2222;** IX:3234
   Life and Letters of George Cabot, The,
      VIII:2219
   Senate and the League Nations, The, VIII:2221
   Short History of the English Colonies in
      America, A, VIII:2219
Lodi, Ibrahim, III:38
Loeb, Jacques, VIII:2619, 2620
Loeb, Richard, VII:840
Log Cabin, V:984
Lok, John, III:278
Lombard, Peter, II:983
   Sentences, II:163, 913; III:768
Lombard League, II:363, 364, 400

Lombardy
   Alboin, II:41-43
   Alexander III, II:50
   Frederick I Barbarossa, II:358, 359
   Gregory the Great, II:407-409
   Henry II the Saint, II:450, 451
Lomonosov, Mikhail Vasilyevich, **IV:860-862**
   Kratkoy rossiyskoy letopisets, IV:861
   Rossiyskaya grammatika, IV:860
London, Jack, **VIII:2223-2226**
   Call of the Wild, The, VIII:2223, 2225
   Cruise of the Snark, The, VIII:2225
   Iron Heel, The, VIII:2225
   John Barleycorn, VIII:2225
   Martin Eden, VIII:2223, 2225
   People of the Abyss, The, VIII:2225
   Sea-Wolf, The, VIII:2225
   Smoke Bellew Tales, VIII:2225
   Valley of the Moon, The, VIII:2225
   War of the Classes, The, VIII:2225
   White Fang, VIII:2225
Long, Huey, **VIII:2227-2230;** IX:3894
Longfellow, Henry Wadsworth, V:1145;
   VI:1414-1417, 1796
   Ballads and Other Poems, VI:1416
   Courtship of Miles Standish, The, IV:1274;
      VI:1416
   "Cross of Snow, The," VI:1416
   Evangeline, VI:1416; VIII:2229
   Hyperion, VI:1416
   Kavanagh, VI:1416
   Outre-Mer, VI:1414
   "Paul Revere's Ride," IV:1157; VI:1416
   Poems on Slavery, VI:1416
   Song of Hiawatha, The, VI:1416, 1862, 1863,
      2370
   Tales of a Wayside Inn, VI:1416
   Voices of the Night, VI:1416
Longinus, Cassius, I:140, 150
Long Island, Battle of, IV:367
Long March, VII:688, 905; IX:2954, 2955
Longnon, Auguste, III:765
Long Parliament
   Charles II, IV:284
   Clarendon, IV:308
   Lambert, IV:790
   Laud, IV:799
   Monck, IV:972
   Pym, IV:1141-1143
   Shaftesbury, IV:1228
Longus, Tiberius Sempronius, I:364
Lon Nol, IX:3419

Lono, VI:1255

Loos, Adolph, VIII:2012

Loos, Anita, **VIII:2231-2234**
    Gentlemen Prefer Blondes, VIII:2232, 2234
    His Picture in the Papers, VIII:2232
    Intolerance, VIII:2232, 2234
    Mystery of the Leaping Fish, The, VIII:2232
    New York Hat, The, VIII:2231
    Reaching for the Moon, VIII:2232
    Red-Headed Woman, VIII:2232
    Road to Plaindale, The, VIII:2231
    San Francisco, VIII:2232
    Wild and Woolly, VIII:2232

Lord, Otis Phillips, V:670

Lord Dunmore's War, IV:163, 312

Lords, House of
    Asquith, VII:122
    Beaverbrook, VII:234
    Beveridge, VII:308-311
    Brougham, V:316
    Butler, VII:531
    Byron, V:381
    Charles I, IV:281
    Constantine, VII:759, 760
    Dalhousie, V:600
    Derby, V:654
    George V, VII:1339, 1340
    Grey, V:994-996
    Lansdowne, VIII:2091
    Lawrence, VI:1332
    Lloyd George, VIII:2216
    Melbourne, VI:1517
    Pitt the Elder, IV:1099
    Pitt the Younger, IV:1102
    Pride, IV:1127
    Reith, IX:3148
    Salisbury, VI:1944, 1945
    Strafford, IV:1287
    Walpole, IV:1403
    William IV, VI:2393-2395

Lorentz, Hendrik Antoon, **VIII:2235-2237**

Lorenz, Konrad, **VIII:2238-2240**
    On Agression, VIII:2240

Lorenzetti, Ambrogio, **II:595-598**
    Good and Bad Government, II:596, 597
    Maestà, II:596
    Presentation in the Temple, II:597
    Vico l'Abate Madonna, II:595

Lorenzetti, Pietro, **II:595-598**
    Birth of the Virgin, II:596, 597
    Descent from the Cross, II:596

Lorenzo, Nicola di. *See* Rienzo, Cola di

Lorrain, Claude. *See* Claude Lorrain

Lorris, Guillaume de
    Romance of the Rose, The, II:261, 947

Los Alamos Laboratories, VII:1147, 1148;
    VIII:2122; IX:2833, 2834, 3632, 3633

Lot, I:5, 6

Lothar, II:239, 599-601

Lothar II, II:601, 674

Lothar III, II:466

Lotharingia, III:164, 165

Lothario of Segni. *See* Innocent III

Lotus Society, I:841

Louis II de Bourbon, Prince de Condé. *See* Condé,
    the Great

Louis II the German, II:239, **599-602**

Louis IV, II:235, 359

Louis VI, II:336

Louis VII, II:336-338, 732, 860, 861

Louis VIII, II:190, 603

Louis IX, **II:603-607**
    Carpini, II:208
    Crusades, II:124
    Mise of Amiens, II:454
    Montfort, II:644, 645
    Vincent of Beauvais, II:946
    William of Rubrouck, II:987, 988

Louis X, II:738

Louis XI, III:163, 164, **434-436,** 775, 776

Louis XII, III:16, 48, 49, 274, 406, 407, 683

Louis XIII, III:539; IV:273, **863-865,** 1165-1167

Louis XIV, **IV:866-870**
    Bernini, IV:119
    Boffrand, IV:151
    Bossuet, IV:171, 172
    Charles II, IV:285
    Colbert, IV:336-339
    Condé, IV:342, 343
    Couperin, IV:374
    Dover Treaty, IV:1039
    Frederick William, The Great Elector, IV:509
    George I, IV:531
    John III Sobieski, IV:726
    La Fontaine, IV:782
    Laval, IV:801, 803
    Leeds, IV:822
    Louis XIII, IV:865
    Louvois, IV:871-874
    Marie-Antoinette, IV:918-920
    Marlborough, IV:922-924
    Mazarin, IV:945-947
    Molière, IV:966, 968
    Vauban, IV:1358

Versailles Palace, IV:834-836, 901-903
Voltaire, IV:1392, 1394
William III, IV:1447, 1448
Louis XV
    Marie-Antoinette, IV:919
    Necker, IV:1016, 1017
    Orléans, IV:1048
    Rochambeau, IV:1174
    Turgot, IV:1348, 1349
Louis XVI
    Cambacérès, V:398
    Danton, IV:393
    Marat, IV:911
    Marie-Antoinette, IV:919, 920
    Monge, IV:977
    Orléans, IV:1049, 1050
    Robespierre, IV:1170, 1171
    Saint-Just, IV:1205
    Turgot, IV:1349
Louis XVIII, V:483; VI:1647
Louis, Joe, **VIII:2241-2245,** 2413
Louis, Morris, VII:1209
Louisiana
    La Salle, IV:794, 795
    Lewis and Clark, VI:1359
    Long, VIII:2227-2229; IX:3894
    Warren, IX:3894
    See also Louisiana Purchase
Louisiana Purchase
    Douglas, V:693
    Jefferson, IV:719
    Lewis, VI:1360
    Madison, IV:888
    Monroe, VI:1571
    Sacagawea, VI:1933, 1934
Louis of Blois, II:943
Louis-Philippe, V:708; VI:1818, 1917, 2227
Louis the Great, II:1001
Louis the Lion. *See* Louis VIII
Louis the Pious, II:599, 600, 602, 767
Louis the Younger, II:601
Loutherbourg, Philippe Jacques de, IV:528
Louvois, Marquis de, IV:336, 338, 343, 868, 869,
    871-874, 947
Louvre, the
    Apollinaire, VII:82
    Cartier-Bresson, VII:595
    Chagall, VII:641
    Francis I, III:275
    John XXIII, VIII:1854
    Pei, IX:2947
    Renoir, VI:1869

Lovejoy, Elijah P., V:885; VI:1772
Lovelace, Countess Ada, V:102
Low, Juliette Gordon, **VIII:2246-2248**
Low, Seth, VII:524
Low, William Mackay, VIII:2246
Lowe, George, VIII:1662-1664
Lowell, Amy, **VIII:2249-2251**
    Critical Fable, A, VIII:2251
    Dome of Many-Colored Glass, A, VIII:2250
    Fir-Flower Tablets, VIII:2251
    John Keats, VIII:2251
    Legends, VIII:2251
    Sword Blades and Poppy Seeds, VIII:2250
    Tendencies in Modern American Poetry,
        VIII:2250
Lowell, James Russell, V:516, 1127
Lowell, Percival, IX:3700, 3701
Lower Creek Indians, IV:1044, 1045
Lowery, Samuel R., VI:1407
Lowie, Robert H.
    Primitive Society, VIII:2164
Loyola, Saint Ignatius of, **III:437-439,** 788
    Constitutions, III:438
    Spiritual Exercises, The, III:437, 438
LPGA. *See* Ladies Professional Golfer's
    Association
LRC. *See* Labour Representation Committee
Luce, Clare Boothe, **VIII:2256-2259,** 2262
    Europe in Spring, VIII:2256
    Women, The, VIII:2232, 2256, 2258
Luce, Henry R., VII:395, 397; VIII:2256,
    2260-2264
Lu Chiu-yüan, II:266
Lucian, **I:507-510,** 622
    Carousal, The, I:507
    Dialogues of the Dead, I:507
    Dialogues of the Gods, I:507, 509
    Philosophies for Sale, I:508
    True Story, A, I:508
Lucius, I:762
Lucius III, II:359
Lucknow Pact, VIII:1847, 1848; IX:3683, 3684
Lucretius, **I:511-514**
    Democritus, I:251
    On the Nature of Things, I:296, 511-513
Lucullus, Lucius, I:559
Ludendorff, Erich, **VIII:2265-2268**
Ludlow, Daniel, IV:721
Ludlow, J.M., VI:1504
Ludlow Massacre, VIII:1881
Ludwig II, VI:2317, 2319
Ludwig IV, II:682

Ludwig, Nikolaus. *See* Zinzendorf, Graf von
Luft, Sidney, VII:1305
Lufthansa, VIII:1615
Luftwaffe, VIII:1439-1441, 1949, 1950, 2262
Lugard, Lord, **VIII:2269-2271**
    Dual Mandate in British Tropical Africa, The,
      VIII:2270
Lugdunum, I:447
Lu Hsün, **VIII:2252-2255**
    "Diary of a Madman, The," VIII:2252
    "True Story of Ah Q, The," VIII:2252
Luis, Don, IV:148
Lukács, György, **VIII:2272-2275**
    Goethe and His Age, VIII:2273
    History and Class Consciousness, VII:268;
      VIII:2272, 2274
    Lenin, VIII:2273
    Soul and Form, VIII:2272, 2274
    Studies in European Realism, VIII:2273
Luke, Gospel of, I:467-469
    Bossuet, IV:170
    Harnack, VIII:1558
    John the Baptist, I:478
    Origen, I:583
    Ritschl, VI:1892
    Stephen, I:822-824
    Virgin Mary, I:939
Lull, Raymond, **II:608-611**
    Ars generalis ultima, II:609
    Blanquerna, II:609, 610
    Book of Contemplation, II:608
Lumière, Auguste, **VIII:2276-2280**
Lumière, Louis, **VIII:2276-2280**
    Arrivée du train en gare, L', VIII:2278
    Workers Leaving the Lumiére Factory,
      VIII:2278
Lumumba, Patrice, VII:633; VIII:2562, 2563;
    IX:3745-3747
Luna 2, VIII:2021
Lunar Society, IV:183
Lundula, Victor, VIII:2562
Lundy's Lane, Battle of, VI:2010, 2011
Lunéville, Château, IV:151, 152
Lunt, Alfred, VII:786, 794
Lu Pu-wei, I:176, 177
Luria, Issac ben Solomon, **III:440-442**
Luscombe Castle, IV:1013
Lutetia, I:257
Luther, Martin, **III:443-447**
    Aristippus, I:87
    Bucer, III:101, 103
    Calvin, III:117, 118, 120

Charles V, III:159
Commentary on St. Paul's Epistle to the
    Galations, IV:218
Cranach, Lucas, the Elder, III:202
Erasmus, III:248
Fisher, III:264, 265
Henry VIII, III:68, 351
Marguerite of Navarre, III:467
Melanchthon, III:503-505
Zwingli, III:791-794
See also Protestant Reformation
Lutheranism. *See* Luther, Martin; Protestant
    Reformation
Lutuli, Albert, **VIII:2272-2275**
Lützen, Battle of, IV:591, 1052, 1397
Luxembourg, Palace of, IV:898
Luxembourg Commission, V:261
Luxemburg, Rosa, VII:292; **VIII:2285-2288;**
    IX:4113, 4114
    Accumulation of Capital, The, VIII:2286
    Crisis in the German Social Democracy, The,
      VIII:2287
    Mass Strike, The, VIII:2286
    Reform or Revolution?, VIII:2285
    Russian Revolution, The, VIII:2286
Luxemburger family, II:969, 970
Luzon, Battle of, VIII:2297
Lwoff, André, VIII:1827-1829
Lyceum, I:94-96, 98, 260, 873
Lyceum Theatre, V:1190; VI:2216
Lycurgus, I:14
Lyell, Sir Charles, V:608; **VI:1418-1422**
    Elements of Geology, VI:1420
    Geological Evidences of the Antiquity of Man,
      The, VI:1421
    Principles of Geology, VI:1419-1421
    Second Visit to the United States of North
      America, VI:1420
    Travels in North America, VI:1420
Lyly, John, III:693
Lynceus, I:703
Lyne, Sir William, V:149
Lyon, Mary, **VI:1423-1426**
Lyons, Council of, II:165, 514-516, 531, 899,
    900, 985
Lyons, Dame Enid Muriel, VIII:1777, **2289-2291,**
    2292, 2293
Lyons, Israel, IV:83
Lyons, Joseph Aloysius, VIII:2289-2291,
    2292-2294, 2497
Lysander, I:16, 32
Lysandrus, I:716

Lysenko, Trofim Denisovitch, VIII:2652;
    IX:3802, 3803
Lysimachus, I:716
Lysippus, **I:515-518**
    Apoxyomenos, I:516

Maastricht summit, VIII:2370
Ma'at, I:734
Mabou Mines, VII:34, 35
Macapagal, Diosadado, VIII:2421
Macaulay, Thomas Babington, **VI:1427-1430,**
    1558
    Critical and Historical Essays, VI:1429
    History of England, The, VI:1427, 1429
    Lays of Ancient Rome, VI:1429
McCall, Jack, V:391
MacArthur, Charles, VIII:1588, 1589, 1591
MacArthur, Douglas, **VIII:2295-2299**
    Acheson, VII:18
    Akihito, VII:41
    Bradley, VII:405
    Curtin, VII:817
    Eisenhower, VII:1043
    Halsey, VIII:1527
    Hirohito, VIII:1680, 1681
    Hoover, VIII:1730
    Nimitz, VIII:2750-2752
    Rhee, IX:3165
    Truman, IX:3742, 3743
Macarthur, James, VI:2356
MacArthur, Mary, VII:353, 354, 357
MacCallum, William, IX:3248
McCarthy, Eugene, VIII:1784, 1785, 1934;
    IX:2825
McCarthy, Joseph R., **VIII:2300-2303**
    Acheson, VII:18
    Eisenhower, VII:1045
    Hiss, VIII:1685
    Kennedy, John F., VIII:1928
    Kennedy, Robert F., VIII:1933
    Lippmann, VIII:2205
    Luce, VIII:2263
    Murrow, VIII:2664, 2665
    Smith's "Declaration of Conscience" speech,
        IX:3447
    Stevenson, IX:3524
    Taft, IX:3592
    Truman, IX:3742
McCarthy, Justin Huntly, III:765, 766
McCarthy, Mary, **VIII:2304-2307**
    Birds of America, VIII:2306
    Cannibals and Missionaries, VIII:2306

Charmed Life, A, VIII:2304
Company She Keeps, The, VIII:2304
Group, The, VIII:2304, 2306
Groves of Academe, The, VIII:2304
Ideas and the Novel, VIII:2306
Mary McCarthy's Theatre Chronicles,
    VIII:2306
Memories of a Catholic Girlhood, VIII:2304,
    2306
Oasis, The, VIII:2304
Sights and Spectacles, VIII:2306
Stones of Florence, The, VIII:2306
Venice Observed, VIII:2306
McCartney, Paul, VII:226-229
McClellan, George, V:1205; VI:1340, 2107
McClure's, VII:623, 624; IX:3614, 3616
McCormick, Cyrus Hall, **VI:1431-1434**
McCormick Seminary, VI:1432
McCullers, Carson, **VIII:2308-2311;** IX:3061
    "Ballad of the Sad Café," VIII:2310
    Clock Without Hands, VIII:2310
    Heart is a Lonely Hunter, The, VIII:2308, 2310
    Member of the Wedding, The, VIII:2310, 2311
    Mortgaged Heart, The, VIII:2310
    Reflections in a Golden Eye, VIII:2308, 2310
    Sights and Spectacles, VIII:2308
    Square Root of Wonderful, The, VIII:2310
    "Sucker," VIII:2308
Macdonald, Sir John Alexander, **VI:1435-1439**
MacDonald, Ramsay, **VIII:2312-2316**
    Angell, VII:75, 76
    Attlee, VII:137
    Baldwin, VII:170
    Bevin, VII:314
    Bondfield, VII:356
    Bottomley, VII:384
    Chamberlain, VII:644
    George V, VII:1340, 1341
McDowell, Irvin, V:1205
Macedonia
    Alexander the Great, I:38, 40
    Antigonus I Monophthalmos, I:60, 61
    Basil the Macedonian, II:117-119
    Bulgarian Empire, II:175
    Cato the Censor, I:164
    Demosthenes, I:253-255
    Philip II of Macedonia, I:628-630
    Ptolemy Philadelphus, I:716
    Ptolemy Soter, I:720-722
    Scipio Aemilianus, I:757
    Stefan Dusan, II:844
    Theophrastus, I:873

Macedonian, V:636
McGillivray, Alexander, **IV:875-878**
McGovern, George, VIII:1995, 2759
McGuffey, William Holmes, **VI:1440-1443**
 Eclectic Readers, VI:1440-1442
Machado de Assis, Joachim Maria, **VI:1444-1446**
 Counselor Ayres' Memorial, VI:1445
 Dom Casmurro, VI:1445
 Epitaph of a Small Winner, VI:1445
 Esau and Jacob, VI:1445
 Iaia Garcia, VI:1445
 Philosopher or Dog?, VI:1445
Machaut, Guillaume de, **II:615-618**
 Bone pastor Guillerme, II:615
 Dit dou Vergier, Le, II:617
 Fonteinne amoureuse, La, II:616
 Messe de Nostre Dame, La, II:616
 Remède de Fortune, II:615, 617
 Voir-Dit, Le, II:616, 617
Machel, Samora Moisès, **VIII:2317-2320**
McHenry, Fort, VI:1282
Machiavelli, Niccolò, III:208, 325, 326, **448-452**
 Art of War, The, III:450
 *Discourses on the First Ten Books of Titus
  Livius,* III:450
 Florentine History, The, III:450
 Mandrake, The, III:450
 Prince, The, III:208, 296, 347, 450, 451
Machu Picchu, III:578
Mackenzie, Sir Alexander, **IV:879-881**
 Voyages, IV:880, 881
Mackenzie, Henry, IV:231
Mackenzie, William Lyon, V:116, 117;
 VI:1447-1452, 1496-1498; VIII:1981
Mackenzie Rebellion, V:117
Mackenzie River, IV:879, 881
Mackinder, Sir Halford John, **VIII:2321-2324**
 Britain and the British Seas, VIII:2321
 Democratic Ideals and Reality, VIII:2321,
  2322
McKinley, William, **VI:1453-1456**
 Bryan, VII:480, 481
 Goldman, VIII:1412
 Hanna, V:1029-1031
 Hay, V:1069
 Hearst, VIII:1603
 Roosevelt, IX:3229
 Root, IX:3232
McKinley Tariff Act, VI:1374, 1453;
 VIII:1498, 2047
MacKinnon, Catharine A., **VIII:2325-2328**
 Only Words, VIII:2326

 Sexual Harassment of Working Women,
  VIII:2325
Macklin, Charles, IV:527
McLaughlin, James, VI:2072
Maclaurin, Colin, **IV:882-885**
 Geometria Organica, IV:882
 Treatise of Fluxions, IV:883, 884
McLaury family, V:736
McLean, Louis, VI:2191-2193
MacLeish, Archibald, VIII:2662
Macleod, John J.R., VII:188, 189; **VIII:2329-2331**
McLuhan, Marshall, **VIII:2332-2335**
 Gutenberg Galaxy, The, VIII:2332
 Mechanical Bride, The, VIII:2332
 Understanding Media, VIII:2333
Macmillan, Alexander and Daniel, **VI:1457-1459**
McMillan, Edwin M., VIII:2122, 2123
Macmillan, Harold, VII:1063; VIII:1607,
 2340-2344; IX:3649
 Industry and the State, VIII:2341
 Middle Way, The, VIII:2341
 Reconstruction, VIII:2341
Macmillan and Company, VI:1457-1459
Macmillan's Magazine, VI:1459
McNamara, James B. and John J., VII:839
MacPherson v. Buick Motor Company, VII:576
Macquarie, Luchlan, V:991, 992
McRae, Milton, VI:2015
Macready, William Charles, V:801, 802;
 VI:1460-1463
Macro, Naevius Cordus Sutorius, I:153, 154
McShann, Jay, IX:2882
Macy, John, VIII:1924, 1926
Madama, Villa, III:645
Mademoiselle magazine, IX:3036
Maderno, Carlo, IV:167, 168
Madero, Francisco, VII:571; **VIII:2345-2348;**
 IX:2836, 3811, 4104, 4106
 *partido nacional Antireeleccionista y la proxima
  lucha, El,* VIII:2347
 Presidential Succession in 1910, The, VIII:2345,
  2347
Madinat al-Zahra', II:8
Madison, Dolley, **VI:1464-1466,** 1570
Madison, James, **IV:886-890**
 Federalist Papers, The, IV:610, 666, 886
 Jefferson, IV:718, 719
 Jeffrey, V:1226
 Madison, Dolley, IV:1464-1466
 Marbury v. Madison, IV:296; VI:1488
 Morris, IX:1000
 pocket veto, V:1198

Madot, Jean, II:25
Madrid Riots, IV:287, 288
Maeandrius, I:705
Maecenas, Gaius, I:21, **519-522,** 702, 926, 928
Maenad, I:765
Mafeking, V:106
Maffia, VII:259
Magas, I:304
Magellan, Ferdinand, **III:453-456**
Magellan, Strait of, III:453-456
Magendie, François, V:207, 208
Maghrib, II:4, 5
Magna Carta, II:329, 453, 455, 540-542, 716
magnetism
    Becquerel, V:166-168
    Gay-Lussac, V:897
    Kelvin, VI:1270
    Néel, VIII:2705-2707
    Peregrinus de Maricourt, II:719-721
    von Guericke, IV:586-588
Magnum Concilium. *See* Great Council
Magnum Photos, VII:595
Magnus, Pompeius, I:551
Magritte, René, **VIII:2349-2354**
    Condition humaine I, La, VIII:2352
    jockey perdu, Le, VIII:2351
    Song of Love, The, VIII:2351
    Valeurs personelles, VIII:2352
Magyars, II:86, 706-708
Mahan, Alfred Thayer, IX:3688
Mahayana Buddhism, I:494-496, 949; II:483, 484
Mahfouz, Naguib, **VIII:2355-2358**
    'Abath al-aqdar, VIII:2355
    Children of Gebelawi, VIII:2356, 2357
    Fountain and Tomb, VIII:2356
    Kifah Tiba, VIII:2355
    Midaq Alley, VIII:2356
    Radubis, VIII:2355
    That al-mazalla, VIII:2357
    Thief in Search of His Identity, A, VIII:2357
    Thulathiyya, Al-, VIII:2356, 2257
Mahler, Alma, VIII:2013
Mahler, Gustav, **VIII:2359-2364;** IX:3357
    Kindertotenlieder, VIII:2362
    klagende Lied, Das, VIII:2359, 2361
    Lied von der Erde, Die, VIII:2362, 2363
    Songs of a Wayfarer, VIII:2361
Mahmud, II:350, 351
Mahmud II, VI:1604, 1606
Maiden, Stewart, VIII:1874

Mailer, Norman, **VIII:2365-2368,** 2537, 2589
    Advertisements for Myself, VIII:2365
    American Dream, An, VIII:2365, 2366
    Ancient Evenings, VIII:2367
    Armies of the Night, The, VIII:2366
    Barbary Shore, VIII:2365
    Cannibals and Christians, VIII:2366
    Deer Park, The, VIII:2365
    Executioner's Song, The, VIII:2367
    Faith of Graffiti, The, VIII:2366
    Gospel According to the Son, The, VIII:2367
    Harlot's Ghost, VIII:2367
    Marilyn, VIII:2366
    Naked and the Dead, The, VIII:2365
    Oswald's Tale: An American Mystery, VIII:2367
    Portrait of Picasso as a Young Man, VIII:2367
    Presidential Papers, The, VIII:2365, 2366
    Prisoner of Sex, The, VIII:2366
    Time of Our Time, The, VIII:2367
    Tough Guys Don't Dance, VIII:2367
    White Negro, The, VIII:2365
    Why Are We in Vietnam, VIII:2366
Maimonides, Moses, **II:619-622,** 648, 781
    Code of Maimonides, The, II:620
    Guide of the Perplexed, II:620
    Illumination, The, II:620
    Letter Concerning Apostasy, II:619
Maitland, William, II:130
Majd al-Din al-Jili, II:347
Majestas Carolina, II:236, 237
Major, John, **VIII:2369-2372**
Ma-ka-tai-me-she-kia-kiak. *See* Black Hawk
Makhpiya-Lúta. *See* Red Cloud
Malacca, III:12
Malachus. *See* Porphyry
Malatestano, Tempio, III:9
Malcolm III, II:291
Malcolmson, Alex, VII:1186
Malcolm X, **VIII:2373-2376**
    Autobiography of Malcolm X, The, VIII:2373, 2376
Malenkov, Georgi M., VIII:1961, 1962, **2377-2379;** IX:4118, 4119
Malevich, Kasimir, VII:639
Malgrange I, IV:152
Malgrange II, IV:152
Malian Empire, II:863-865
Malik ibn Anas, II:33
Malik Shah, II:677-679, 695
Malinowski, Bronislaw, VIII:2164, 2165
Mallarmé, Stéphane, V:890; VII:1367; IX:3791
Malmesbury Abbey, II:824

Malory, Sir Thomas, **III:457-459**
  Morte d' Arthur, Le, III:457, 458; V:161;
    VI:2213; IX:3515
Malouine Islands, IV:179
Malpighi, Marcello, IV:826, **891-893**
  Anatome plantarum, IV:891
  De bombyce, IV:891, 893
  De cerebro, IV:891
  De ovo incubato, IV:891
  De pulmonibus observationes anatomicae,
    IV:891
  De viscerum structura exercitatio anatomica,
    IV:891
  Dissertatio epistolica de formatione pulli in ovo,
    IV:891
Malplaquet, Battle of, IV:924
Malraux, André, **VIII:2380-2383**
  Anti-Memoirs, VIII:2382
  Conquerors, The, VIII:2380, 2381
  Lunes en papier, VIII:2380
  Man's Fate, VIII:2380-2382
  Man's Hope, VIII:2380, 2381
Malthus, Thomas Robert, V:458; **VI:1467-1470,**
    1562, 1879
  Essay on the Principle of Population, An, V:606;
    VI:1467, 1468, 1787
Malves, Gua de, IV:31
Mamluk Dynasty, II:124-126, 382, 383
Manchester Guardian, VIII:1708, 1709
Manchester Literary and Philosophical Society,
    V:603
Manchukuo, IX:3879
Manchu Dynasty. *See* Ch'ing Dynasty
Mandate of Heaven, I:544; IV:422
Mandela, Nelson, VII:871, 872; VIII:2281-2283,
    2384-2388
Mandelstam, Osip, IX:2900
Mandeville, Bernard de
  Fable of the Bees, VI:1458
Mandigo peoples, II:863-865
Manet, Édouard, III:313; V:453; **VI:1471-1475;**
    VIII:2579
  Absinthe Drinker, The, VI:1472
  Bar at the Folies-Bergère, A, VI:1473
  Déjeuner sur l'herbe, VI:1472, 1473
  Execution of Maximilian, IV:572
  Good Glass of Beer, The, VI:1473
  Luncheon on the Grass, VI:1780
  Olympia, VI:1472, 1473
  Rue Mosnier with Powers, The,
    VI:1473
  Spanish Singer, The, VI:1472

Manetho
  Aegyptica, I:547, 548
Mangu, II:566, 988
Manhattan Company, Bank of the, V:370, 372
Manhattan Project
  Bridgman, VII:464
  Compton, VII:747
  Kurchatov, VIII:2040
  McMillan, VIII:2337
  Neumann, VIII:2725
  Seaborg, IX:3376
  Stimson, IX:3539
  Teller, IX:3632
  Wilkins, IX:3995
Manichaeanism, I:694-696; II:511
Manifest Destiny
  Adler, V:27
  Cooper, V:564
  Gray, V:979
  Polk, VI:1802
  Taylor, VI:2196
Manila Bay, Battle of, V:656-658
Manilius, III:672
Manitoba, VI:1437
Mankiller, Wilma P., **VIII:2389-2391**
  Mankiller: A Chief and Her People, VIII:2390
Manly, Charles, VI:1314
Mann, Horace, **IV:894-897**
Mann, Thomas, VIII:2274, **2392-2395**
  Beloved Returns, The, VIII:2393
  Betrachtungen eines Unpolitischen, VIII:2393
  Buddenbrooks, VIII:2392, 2393
  Confessions of Felix Krull, VIII:2394
  Death in Venice, VIII:2392
  Disorder and Early Sorrow, VIII:2393
  Doctor Faustus, VIII:2393
  "Fallen," VIII:2392
  Joseph and His Brothers, VIII:2393
  Magic Mountain, The, VIII:2393
  Royal Highness, VIII:2392
  Tonio Kröger, VIII:2392
  Transposed Heads, The, VIII:2393
Mannerheim, Carl Gustaf, **VIII:2396-2399**
mannerism
  Andrea del Sarto, III:24, 26
  Carracci Family, III:125-127
  Correggio, III:186
  Greco, El, III:311-313
  Tintoretto, III:717, 719, 720
  Veronese, III:747
Mannheim National Theater, IV:1217
Manning, Henry Edward, **VI:1476-1479**

Mannix, Danile, **VI:1480-1482**
Manox, Henry, III:367
Mansa Musa, **II:623-625**
Mansart, François, **IV:898-900,** 901
Mansart, Jules Hardouin-, IV:151, 900, **901-903**
Mansa Uli, II:864
Mansfield, First Earl of, **IV:904-909**
Mansfield-Fondi Palace, IV:656
Manson, Sir Patrick, IX:3248, 3249
Manstein, Erich von, IX:3261
Mantegna, Andrea, III:58-60, **460-463**
    Madonna Enthroned with Saints, III:461
    Madonna of the Victory, III:462
    Martyrdom of Saint James, III:461
    Saint James Baptizing Hermogenes, III:461
    Saint James Before Herod Agrippa, III:461
    Saint James Led to Execution, III:461
    Triumph of Caesar, III:462
Mantinea, I:293
Manuel I, III:11-13, **464-466,** 759
Manutius, Aldus, III:246
Manzikert, Battle of, II:69, 70
Manzoni, Alessandro, **VI:1483-1486**
    Adelchi, VI:1484
    Betrothed, The, VI:1483-1485
Maori people, VI:2322
Maori Wars, V:380, 998-1000
Mao Tse-tung, **VIII:2400-2403**
    Ch'en Tu-hsiu, VII:662
    Chiang Kai-shek, VII:666
    Ch'in Shih Huang-ti, I:178
    Chou En-lai, VII:677
    Chu Teh, VII:688, 689
    Deng Xiaoping, VII:905, 906
    Hung Hsiu-ch'üan, V:1165, 1167
    Kuo Mo-jo, VIII:2034
    "Let a Hundred Flowers Bloom," VIII:2401
    Lin Piao, VIII:2189-2191
    Liu Shao-ch'i, VIII:2212-2214
    Marx, VI:1494
    Nixon, VIII:2760
    P'eng Te-huai, IX:2954-2956
Mapai Party, VII:252, 253
Marat, Jean-Paul, **IV:910-913**
    Ami du Peuple, L', IV:911
    Chains of Slavery, IV:910
    Plan of Criminal Legislation, IV:910
Maratha kingdom, IV:1246-1248
Maratha wars, IV:632, 633
Marathon, Battle of
    Aeschylus, I:10
    Darius the Great, I:238

    Herodotus, I:396
    Leonidas, I:501
    Miltiades the Younger, I:553-555
    Pheidippides, I:621-623
    Phidias, I:624
    Polygnotus, I:676
    Simonides, I:788
    Themistocles, I:857
Marble, Alice, VII:1363
Marburg, Colloquy of, III:102, 793
Marburg, University of, VII:614; IX:3918
Marbury v. Madison, IV:296; VI:1488
Marc, Franz, VII:1098; **VIII:2404-2406**
    "Brücke, Die,"VIII:2405
    Dead Sparrow, The, VIII:2404
    Deer in the Woods, VIII:2405
    Fate of Animals, VIII:2405, 2406
    Fighting Forms, VIII:2405
    Horse in Landscape, VIII:2405
    Improvisation No. 30, VIII:2405
    Tiger, The, VIII:2405
    Tower of Blue Horses, VIII:2405
    Yellow Corn, VIII:2405
Marcel, Gabriel, **VIII:2407-2410**
    Existential Background of Human Dignity, The,
        VIII:2408
    Homo Viator, VIII:2407
    Men Against Humanity, VIII:2409
    Metaphysical Journal, VIII:2407, 2409
    Mystery of Being, The, VIII:2408
    "On the Ontological Mystery," VIII:2407
Marcellina, I:43
Marcellinus, Ammianus, I:780
Marcellus, Claudius, I:335, 336
Marcet, Jane
    Conversations on Chemistry, V:767
March, Fredric, VII:117, 119
Marchand, Jean-Baptiste, VIII:2002;
    IX:3730, 3731
Märchenoper, V:1163, 1164
March to the Sea, VI:2060; VIII:2710
Marciano, Rocky, VIII:2244, **2411-2414**
Marcion, I:582
Marconi, Guglielmo, VI:1807, 1808;
    VIII:2415-2419
Marconi Company, VIII:2217
Marco Polo. *See* Polo, Marco
Marcos, Ferdinand E., VII:86-88; **VIII:2420-2424**
    "First-Quarter Storm," VIII:2421
Marcus Aurelius, **I:523-526**
    Meditations, I:523, 525, 526
Marduk, I:234, 328

Marenzio, Luca, IV:990
Marfan's law, VII:547
Margaret of Anjou, III:341, 647, 774, 775
Margaret of Denmark, Norway, and Sweden,
    II:626-628
Margaret of Scotland, Saint, II:291
Marguerite of Navarre, **III:467-470,** 634
    Heptameron, III:468, 469
    Mirror of the Sinful Soul, The, III:594
    Prisons, III:470
Mari, I:360, 362
Mariamne, I:391
Mariano Filipepi, Alessandro di. *See* Botticelli,
    Sandro
Maria Theresa, IV:504, 750, 751, **914-917,** 918
Marie-Antoinette, IV:915, **918-921,** 1376, 1378
Marie de France, **II:629-631**
    Espurgatoire Seint Patriz, L', II:630
    Fables, II:629-631
    Lays, The, II:629-631
Marie Louise, IV:725, 726
Marignano, Battle of, III:274
Marine Band, IX:3466, 3467
Marine Corps. *See* United States Marine Corps
Marinetti, Emilio Filippo, VII:342, 343
Marinus of Tyre, I:713
Marion Daily Star, VIII:1550, 1552
Maritain, Jacques, VII:1377; **VIII:2425-2428**
    Antimoderne, VIII:2426
    Art and Scholasticism, VIII:2426
    Bergsonian Philosophy and Thomism,
        VIII:2426
    Christianity and Democracy, VIII:2427
    Existence and the Existent, VIII:2426
    Man and the State, VIII:2427
    Peasant of the Garonne, The, VIII:2427
    Person and the Common Good, The, VIII:2427
    Scholasticism and Politics, VIII:2426
    Things That Are Not Caesar's, The, VIII:2427
    Three Reformers: Luther, Descartes, Rousseau,
        VIII:2426
Marius, Gaius, I:147, 347, **528-531,** 686, 743,
    833, 834
Mark, Gospel of, I:467-469; VIII:1558
Marlborough, Duchess of, IV:50, 52, 53
Marlborough, First Duke of, IV:50, 52, 157, 158,
    533, **922-925,** 1277
Marlowe, Christopher, **III:471-474**
    Amores, III:471, 473
    Dido Queen of Carthage, III:471, 473
    Doctor Faustus, III:472, 473; IV:562
    Edward II, III:472

Hero and Leander, III:473
Jew of Malta, The, III:472
Massacre at Paris, The, III:472, 473
Tamburlaine the Great, III:471, 472
Tamburlaine the Great, Part 2, III:472
Marly-le-Roi, Château de, IV:902
Marne, Battle of the, VIII:1851-1853
Maroto, Rafael, V:414
Marquette, Father Jacques, IV:732-734
marriage
    Akiba, I:29
    Anthony, V:62
    Blackwell, V:251
    canon law, II:50
    Catullus, I:170
    Chopin, V:499
    Christine de Pizan, II:262
    Epicurus, I:296
    Fourier, V:816
    Goldman, VIII:1412
    Greene, VIII:1468
    Henry II the Saint, II:451
    Innocent III, II:510
    Kinsey, VIII:1986
    Lockwood, VI:1408
    Millett, VIII:2536
    polygamy, VI:2081, 2415, 2416
    Pythagoreans, I:728
    Sand, VI:1954
    Stone, VI:2145
    Theoleptus of Philadelphia, II:899, 900
    Vanbrugh, IV:1351
    Wollstonecraft, IV:1478
Marshall, Alfred, IX:3867
Marshall, Arthur, V:1240
Marshall, George C., **VIII:2429-2432**
    Bradley, VII:404
    Chiang Kai-shek, VII:666
    Chu Teh, VII:689
    Eisenhower, VII:1043, 1045
    Hopkins, VIII:1737, 1739
    Marshall Plan, VII:315; VIII:1529, 1562, 1696,
        2205, 2258, 2431; IX:3862
    Patton, IX:2913
    Pershing, IX:2985
Marshall, John, **VI:1487-1491,** 2147-2149,
    2191, 2192
Marshall, Thurgood, **VIII:2433-2436**
Marshall Field and Company, V:783, 785, 786;
    VI:1883, 1884, 2331; VII:1266
Marshall Plan
    Bevin, VII:315

Hammarskjöld, VIII:1529
Harriman, VIII:1562
Hitler, VIII:1696
Lippmann, VIII:2205
Luce, VIII:2258
Marshall, VIII:2431
Wallace, IX:3862
Marsilius of Padua, II:683
Marston, John, III:156
Martial, **I:532-534**
On the Spectacles, I:532
Martin, Agnes, **VIII:2437-2439**
Martin, David, VI:1836
Martin, George, VII:226
Martin, Joe Elsby, VII:53
Martin, Pierre-Émile, VI:2067
Martinelli, Caterina, IV:992
Martinez Sierra, Gregorio
Cradle Song, The, VIII:2143
Martini, Simone, II:307, **632-635**
Annunciation, II:634
Guidoriccio da Fogliano, II:634
Madonna, II:633
Maestà, II:632, 633
Saint Louis of Toulouse, II:633
Martin of Tours, I:695; II:403-405
Martinsberg monastery, II:851
Martin v. Hunter's Lessee, VI:2147
martyrs
Anthony of Padua, II:76
Becket, II:128-130
bishops of Rome, I:257, 258
Christopher, I:180, 182
Hallaj, al-, II:423
Hus, II:487
Ignatius of Antioch, I:440-442
Joan of Arc, III:396, 398, 399
Montfort, II:646
Origen, I:581, 582
Pamphilus, I:322
Paul, I:605
Peter, I:616
Ridley, III:655, 656
Stephen, I:822-824
Tertullian, I:848
Maru-aton, I:24
Marville, Jean de, II:832
Mary (Virgin). *See* Virgin Mary
Mary I (of England), III:238, 239, 318, 319,
479-482
Mary II (of England), IV:922, 923
Mary of Modena, IV:50, 52, 553

Mary, Queen of Scots, **III:475-478**
Catherine de Médicis, III:132
Cecil, III:147, 148
Elizabeth I, III:243
Tudor family, III:733
Marx, Karl, **VI:1492-1495**
Bakunin, V:112-114
Blanc, V:261
Brecht, VII:444, 445
Communist Manifesto, The, V:761, 1057;
VI:1324, 1493
*Contribution to a Critique of Political Economy,
A,* VI:1370; VIII:2034
Critique of the Gotha Program, VI:1370
Economic and Philosophic Manuscripts of 1844,
VI:1493
Engels, V:760-762
George, V:908
German Ideology, The, VI:1370; VIII:2034
Kapital, Das, V:762; VI:1493, 2322; VII:160, 291
Lassalle, VI:1324, 1325
London, VIII:2226
Morgan, VI:1584
Proudhon, VI:1818, 1819
Stalin, IX:3482-3484
Veblen, IX:3806
Wilson, IX:4014
Marx Brothers, VII:288
Marxism. *See* communism; Marx, Karl
Masaccio, **III:483-486,** 517
Expulsion from Paradise, The, III:484
Holy Trinity with the Virgin and Saint John,
III:485
Madonna and Child, III:483, 484, 744, 745
Madonna and Child with Saint Anne and Angels,
III:483
Tribute Money, The, III:484, 485
Masada, I:483-486
Ma San-po. *See* Cheng Ho
Masaryk, Tomás, VII:259, 260; **VIII:2440-2443**
Ceská otázka, VIII:2440
*philosophischen und sociologischen Grundlagen
des Marxismus, Die,* VIII:2440
Spirit of Russia, The, VIII:2440
Suicide and the Meaning of Civilization,
VIII:2440
Masina, Giulietta, VII:1141-1143
Masinissa, **I:535-537,** 761
Masmuda tribes, II:5
Mason, Charlotte Osgood, VIII:1788
Mason, George, **IV:926-929**
Extracts from the Virginia Charters, IV:926

*Scheme for Replevying Goods and Distress for
    Rent,* IV:926
Mason, James, VII:1305
Mason, Perry, VII:1297-1299
Mason, William, VI:2230
Massachusetts
    Adams, John, IV:16, 18, 19
    Adams, Samuel, IV:21-24
    Arnold, IV:64
    Bancroft, V:124, 125
    Bradstreet, IV:193
    Cotton, IV:371
    Eliot, IV:435, 437, 438
    Hancock, IV:613, 615-618
    Hutchinson, Anne, IV:687-689
    Hutchinson, Thomas, IV:691-693
    Mather, Cotton, IV:934-937
    Mather, Increase, IV:938-941
    O'Neill, IX:2824
    Plymouth Colony, IV:191
    Richardson's architecture, VI:1882-1884
    Sacco and Vanzetti, IX:3283
    Shays, IV:1239
    Winthrop, IV:1463-1465
Massachusetts Anti-Slavery Society, VI:1771,
    2143, 2265
Massachusetts Bay Government Act, IV:616
Massachusetts General Court, IV:617
Massachusetts Institute of Technology
    Aalto, VII:3
    Candela, VII:557
    Chomsky, VII:673
    Eliot, V:748
    Jakobson, VIII:1832, 1833
    Ravi, IX:3102
    Wiener, IX:3976, 3977
    Woodward, IX:4052
Massachusetts Quarterly Review, The, VI:1728
Massachusetts Suffrage Association, VI:2044
Massagetae, I:234
Massalia, I:731
Massasoit, **IV:930-933,** 954, 955, 1274
Massera, Giuseppe, VII:835
Massey, Vincent, **VI:1496-1499**
Massey, William Ferguson, **VIII:2444-2447**
Massine, Léonide, VII:833, 1177; **VIII:2448-2451**
    Boutique fantasque, La, VIII:2449
    Choréartium, VIII:2450
    Femmes de bonne humeur, Les, VIII:2449
    Matelots, Les, VIII:2450
    Parade, VIII:2449
    Pas d'acier, Les, VIII:2450

    Présages, Les, VIII:2450
    Rite of Spring, The, VIII:2449, 2450
    Russian and Ludmilla, VIII:2448
    Soleil de nuit, VIII:2449
    Symphonie fantastique, VIII:2450
    Tricorne, Le, VIII:2449
    Zéphere et Flore, VIII:2449, 2450
Massinger, Philip, III:56
Masson, André, VII:1359
Mastai-Ferretti, Giovanni Maria. *See* Pius IX
Masterman, C.F.G., VII:383
Masters, Edgar Lee, VII:954
Masterson, Bat, V:736
Masters Tournament, VIII:1877; IX:3041,
    3042, 4050
Mästlin, Michael, IV:772
Mas'udi, al-, **II:636-638**
    Kitab al-Tanbih w'al-Ishraf, II:636
    Muruj al-Dhahab wa-Ma'adin al-Jawhar, II:636
Masurian Lakes, Battle of the, VIII:1675
Matabele rebellion, VI:1875
Matchmaker's Union, V:212
Mather, Cotton, IV:372, **934-937;** IX:2893, 2894
    Bonifacious, IV:936
    Christian Philosopher, IV:936
    Magnalia Christi Americana, IV:935
Mather, Increase, IV:934, 936, **938-941**
    Cases of Conscience Concerning Evil Spirits,
        IV:940
    *Essay for the Recording of Illustrious
        Providences, An,* IV:940
Mather, Richard, IV:938
Mathiapoulos, Margarita, VII:429
Matignon Agreements, VII:336
Matisse, Henri, VII:431; **VIII:2452-2456;**
    IX:3333
    Dance and Music, VIII:2454
    Decorative Figure, VIII:2454
    Desserte, La, VIII:2452
    Harmony in Red, VIII:2454
    Luxe, Calm et Volupté, VIII:2452
    Red Studio, The, VIII:2454
    Woman with the Hat, VIII:2454
Matsudaira Takechiyo. *See* Tokugawa Ieyasu
Matsuo Basho, **IV:942-944**
    Manuscript in My Knapsack, IV:943
    Monkey's Raincoat, IV:943
    Narrow Road to the Deep North, The, IV:943
    Records of a Weather-Exposed Skeleton, The,
        IV:942
    Saga nikki, IV:943
    Visit to the Kashima Shrine, A, IV:943

Matsushita, Konosuke, **VIII:2457-2460**
Matsushita Electric Company, VIII:2457-2459
Matthew, Gospel of
  Harnack, VIII:1558
  Herod the Great, I:392
  Jesus Christ, I:467-469
  John the Apostle, I:475
  Origen, I:583
  Peter, I:616
  Virgin Mary, I:939
Matthews, James Newton, V:714
Matthews, William, III:457
Matthias I, Corvinus, III:376, **487-490**
Maud, II:847-849
Maudslay, Henry, VI:1624
Maugham, W. Somerset
  Catalina, IV:269
Maulawiyah Sufism, II:800, 801
Mau Mau Rebellion, VIII:1937, 1938, 2146,
  2147, 2774
Maupassant, Guy de, V:798; **VI:1500-1502**
  "Boule de Suif," VI:1500, 1501
  "Hand, The," VI:1500
  "Horla, The," VI:1501
  "Madame Tellier's Establishment," VI:1500
  "Maison Tellier, La," VI:1501
  "Necklace, The," VI:1501
  Pierre and Jean, VI:1501
  Woman's Life, A, VI:1500
Maurice, Frederick Denison, VI:1457, 1458,
  1503-1506
  Kingdom of Christ, The, VI:1504
  Prophets and Kings of the Old Testament,
    VI:1458
  Subscription No Bondage, VI:1504
  Theological Essays, VI:1505
Maurice of Nassau, III:575; IV:590, 1335
Maurier, George du, VI:2366
Maurras, Charles, VIII:2425-2427
Maury, James, IV:647
Maury, Matthew Fontaine, **VI:1507-1510**
  *New Theoretical and Practical Treatise on
    Navigation, A,* VI:1507
  Physical Geography of the Sea, VI:1509
  Wind and Current Chart of the North Atlantic,
    VI:1508
Mauryan dynasty, I:112
Mauss, Marcel, VIII:2164
Maxentius, Marcus Aurelius Valerius, I:226, 227,
  339, 340
Maximian, I:226
Maximianus, I:265, 266

Maximilian I, III:159, 406, 407, **491-494,** 682, 683
Maximilian, Ferdinand, V:1252, 1253
Maximinus, I:266
Maximus, Magnus, I:791, 870
Maximus, Quintus Fabius. *See* Fabius
Max Planck Institute for Fluid Mechanics,
  IX:3073, 3074
Max Planck Society for the Advancement of
  Science, VIII:1515, 1618, 2238; IX:3034
Maxwell, James Clerk, **VI:1511-1513**
  Faraday, V:770
  Gibbs, V:923, 924
  Kelvin, VI:1271
  Lorentz, VIII:2235
  Lumiére, VIII:2276
Mayakovsky, Vladimir, **VIII:2461-2464**
  150,000,000, VIII:2461
  About That, VIII:2462
  At the Top of My Voice, VIII:2462
  Bathhouse, The, VIII:2462
  Bedbug, The, VIII:2462
  Cloud in Paris, A, VIII:2461
  Mystery-Bouffe, VIII:2461
  Vladimir Illich Lenin, VIII:2462
  Vladimir Mayakovsky, VIII:2461
Maybach, Wilhelm, V:597-599
Mayflower, IV:1273
Mayflower Compact, IV:189
May Fourth Movement
  Ch'en Tu-hsiu, VII:660-662
  Kuo Mo-jo, VIII:2033-2035
  Lu Hsün, VIII:2252
  Mao Tse-tung, VIII:2400
Maynooth Seminary, VI:1480, 1481
Mayo, Charles H. and William J., **VIII:2465-2467**
Mayo Clinic, VIII:2465-2467; IX:2928, 3479
Ma Yüan, II:479, 480, **612-614**
Mazarin, Jules, **IV:945-948**
  Christina, IV:306
  Colbert, IV:336, 337
  Cyrano de Bergerac, IV:386
  Jansen, IV:709
  Louis XIV, IV:866
  Oxenstierna, IV:1053
  Vincent de Paul, IV:1381
Mazdakites, II:559, 561
Mazepa, Ivan Stepanovich, IV:1084
Mazzini, Giuseppe, V:447, 879, 932;
  VI:1514-1516, 1782, 1783
Mead, Margaret, VII:257; **VIII:2468-2471**
  And Keep Your Powder Dry, VIII:2470
  Coming of Age in Samoa, VIII:2468

In Male and Female, VIII:2469
Sex and Temperament in Three Primitive
    Societies, VIII:2469
Meany, George, IX:3163, 3164
Mecca, II:495, 496, 564, 623, 652, 654; III:521, 541
Meckel, Johann, V:110
Mecklenburg-Strelitz, Charlotte of, IV:539
Medawar, Peter, VII:512, 513
Medicaid, VII:709; VIII:1868
Medicare, VII:709; VIII:1868; IX:2973
Medici, Cosimo de', III:8, 29, 153
Medici, Ferdinando de', IV:619, 1214
Medici, Giovanni de'. *See* Leo X
Medici, Guilio de'. *See* Clement VII
Medici, Lorenzo de', III:9, 325, 450, **495-498,** 517,
    667, 668
Medici, Piero de', III:496, 668
Médicis, Catherine de. *See* Catherine de Médicis
Médicis, Marie de, IV:863, 865, 1165, 1166
Medina, II:652, 654
Medvedev, Pavel Nikolayevich, VII:152, 153
Meech Lake Accord, VIII:2655, 2656
Meerssen, Treaty of, II:601
Megacles, I:648
Megara, I:314
Megarics, I:796
Megiddo, Battle of, I:890
Mehemet, VI:2227
Mehmed II, **III:499-502**
Meighen, Arthur, VIII:1982
Meiji Restoration, VIII:1680
Meir, Golda, VII:251, 253, 856; **VIII:2472-2475**
Meir, Rabbi, I:28
Meitner, Lise, VIII:1514-1516, 1648, **2476-2479**
Melanchthon, Philipp, III:446, **503-506**
    Apology, III:505
    Loci Communes, The, III:504
    Unterricht der Visitatorn, III:505
Melbourne, Second Viscount, VI:**1517-1519,** 2394
Melbye, Fritz, VI:1779
Melchizadek, I:6
Melfi, Council of, II:930
Mellon, Andrew, VII:763; **VIII:2480-2482**
Mellon Plan, VIII:2481
Melville, Herman, **VI:1520-1525**
    Battle-Pieces and Aspects of War, VI:1523
    Billy Budd, Foretopman, VI:1524
    Clarel, VI:1523
    Confidence Man, The, VI:1523
    Israel Potter, VI:1523
    Mardi and a Voyage Thriller, VI:1522
    Moby Dick, IV:430; V:1066; VI:1521, 1524

    Omoo, VI:1522, 1524
    Pierre, VI:1523
    Redburn, VI:1520, 1521
    Typee, VI:1521, 1522, 1524
    White-Jacket, VI:1522
Memmius, Gaius, I:511
Menai Bridge, VI:2209
Menander (Greek writer), I:295, **538-540,**
    845, 846
    Arbitration, The, I:539
    Bad-Tempered Man, The, I:539
    Girl from Samos, The, I:539
    Girl Who Was Shorn, The, I:539
    Shield, The, I:539
Menander (Greek king), **I:541-542**
Mencius, I:433, 434, **543-546,** 944
    Meng-tzu, I:543
Mencken, H.L., **VIII:2483-2486**
    American Language, The, VIII:2484
    George Bernard Shaw, VIII:2483
    Philosophy of Friedrich Nietzsche, The,
    VIII:2484
Mendel, Gregor Johann, V:609; **VI:1526-1528;**
    VIII:2619, 2620
Mendeleyev, Dmitry Ivanovich, **VI:1529-1533**
    Principles of Chemistry, The, VI:1530
Mendelsohn, Erich, **VIII:2487-2490**
Mendelssohn, Arnold, VIII:1670
Mendelssohn, Felix, **VI:1534-1536,** 1993
    Hebrides, The, VI:1535
    Hymns of Praise, VI:1535
    Italian Symphony, VI:1535
    Meeresstille und glückliche Fahrt, VI:1535
    Midsummer Night's Dream, A, VI:1534, 1535
    Scotch Symphony, VI:1535
Mendelssohn, Moses, IV:842
Mendès-France, Pierre, **VIII:2491-2496**
Mendicant Orders, II:163, 715, 717
Mendoza, Antonio de, III:180, 181
Mendoza, Pedro de, III:392
Menelaus of Alexandria, I:410
Menelik I, VIII:1517
Menelik II, **VI:1537-1540;** VIII:1517
Menemencioglu, Numan, VIII:1813, 1814
Menéndez de Avilés, Pedro, **III:507-509**
Menes, **I:547-549,** 979
Meng Hao-jan, I:841
Mengs, Anton Raphael, IV:569
Menippius, I:507, 509
Menninger, Karl
    Man Against Himself, VII:1247
    Sexual Behavior in the Human Male, VIII:1989

Menno, Simons, **III:510-512**
    Christian Baptism, III:511
    Foundation of Plain Instruction, A, III:511
    True Christian Faith, The, III:511
Menotti, Gian Carlo, VII:191-193; **VIII:2494-2496**
Menzies, Robert Gordon, VIII:2293, 2294,
    2497-2499
Mercator, Gerardus, **III:513-516**
    Chronologia, III:515
    Geography, III:515
    Mercator's Atlas, III:515
Mercedarians, II:776, 777
Mercer, Johnny, IX:3424
Mercer, Lucy, IX:3218
Mercers' Guild, III:169
Merchant Shipping Act of 1876, V:678
Mercia, kingdom of, II:59, 60, 62, 320, 333
Mercier, François, VII:1229
Merciless Parliament, II:787
Mercury space program, VII:111, 1387, 1388;
    IX:3405
Mercury Theater, IX:3934
Meretaton, I:25
Mergenthaler, Ottmar, **VI:1541-1543**
Mergenthaler Linotype Company, VI:1542
Mergenthaler Printing Company, VI:1542
Meritor Savings Bank v. Vinson, VIII:2326
Merleau-Ponty, Maurice, V:1083; **VIII:2500-2502**
Merman, Ethel, VII:289
Merodach-Baladan, I:754, 755
Merovingian dynasty, II:242-244, 274, 403-405
Merriam, Charles and George, IV:1420
Mersenne, Marin, **IV:949-953**
    Harmonie universelle, IV:951
    *Impiété des deistes, athées, et libertins de ce
        temps, L',* IV:950
    Quaestiones celeberrimae in Genesim, IV:950
    *Vérité des sciences, contre les sceptiques ou
        Pyrrhoniens, La,* IV:950
Merton, Thomas, II:313, 314
Meru, VIII:2773
Mesabi Range, VI:1898
Messallina, Valeria, **I:550-552**
Messenia, I:18, 292
Messerschmitt, Willy, VIII:1615, 1616
Messiaen, Olivier, VII:386; **VIII:2503-2505;**
    IX:3542, 4075
    Banquet céleste, Le, VIII:2503, 2504
    Chronochromie, VIII:2504
    Couleurs de la cité céleste, VIII:2504
    Et exspecto resurrectionem, VIII:2504
    Mode de valeurs et d'intensités, VIII:2504

Pelléas et Mélisande, VIII:2503
Quantor pour la fin du temps, VIII:2504
Saint François d'Assie, VIII:2504
*Transfiguration de Notre Seigneur Jesus-Christ,
    La,* VIII:2504
Trois Petites Liturgies, VIII:2504
Turangalîla, VIII:2504
Messina, Antonello da, III:59
Messner, Reinhold, **VIII:2506-2509**
    Seventh Grade, The, VIII:2506
Metacomet, IV:931, **954-957**
Metacom's War. *See* King Philip's War
Metaphysical Club, VI:1757
metaphysics
    Bergson, VII:283
    Böhme, IV:154, 155
    Carnap, VII:583
    Duns Scotus, II:313
    Fichte, IV:466-468
    Green, V:988
    Heidegger, VIII:1610-1612
    Hume, IV:685
    Kant, IV:761-763
    Leibniz, IV:829-832
    Parmenides, I:596
    Posidonius, I:688
    Pythagoras, I:728
    Scheler, IX:3347-3349
    Whitehead, IX:3965-3968
Metcalfe, Sir Charles, V:118
Metellus, Quintus Caecilius, I:528
Methodism, IV:1426-1429
Methodius, Saint, II:176, **278-281**
Metilius, I:335
Metius, Jacob, IV:850
metric system
    Guillaume, VIII:1502-1504
    Lagrange, IV:787
    Laplace, VI:1321
    Michelson, VI:1554
    Monge, IV:975, 977
Metro-Goldwyn-Mayer
    Demille, VII:897
    Fitzgerald, VII:1163
    Garbo, VII:1286-1288
    Garland, VII:1305-1306
    Gish, VII:1385
    Goldwyn, VIII:1417
    Loos, VIII:2232
Metropolitan Museum of New York
    Calder, VII:539
    Fry, VII:1254

Morgan, VI:1582
  Nevelson, VIII:2730
  Whitney, IX:3969
Metropolitan Opera Company
  Apollinaire, VII:82
  Balanchine, VII:156
  Barber, VII:193
  Caruso, VII:599
  Danilova, VII:835
  Geddes, VII:1320
  Karajan, VIII:1911
  Menotti, VIII:2495
  Norman, VIII:2771
  Pavarotti, IX:2930
  Price, IX:3081, 3083, 3084
  Toscanini, IX:3709
Metternich, V:222, 441, 1034; **VI:1544-1547,** 1917
Meung, Jean de
  Romance of the Rose, The, II:261, 992
Mexica, III:377-379, 528, 529, 556, 557
Mexican Confederation of Workers, VII:572
Mexican Constitution of 1824, V:95
Mexican Revolution
  Bierce, V:231
  Calles, VII:542-544
  Madero, VIII:2345-2348
  Obregón, IX:2781-2784
  Orozco, IX:2838
  Rivera, IX:3184
  Villa, IX:3811-3814
  Zapata, IX:4104, 4106, 4107
Mexican War
  Bancroft, V:126
  Calhoun, V:395
  Colt, V:541
  Davis, V:615
  Douglas, V:692
  Grant, V:975
  Lincoln, VI:1382
  Perry, VI:1761
  Pierce, VI:1777
  Pike, IV:1097
  Polk, VI:1803
  Scott, VI:2010, 2011
  Sherman, VI:2057
  Sumner, VI:2170
  Taylor, VI:2194-2196
Mey, Lev, VI:1890
Meyer, Lothar, V:100; VI:1532
Meyer-Eppler, Werner, IX:3542
Meyergold, Vsevolod Yemilyevich. *See*
  Meyerhold, Vsevolod Yemilyevich

Meyerhold, Vsevolod Yemilyevich,
  VIII:2461-2463, **2510-2513**
  Bathhouse, The, VIII:2511
  Bed-bug, The, VIII:2511
  Columbine's Scarf, VIII:2510
  Inspector General, The, VIII:2511
  Klop, VIII:2511
Miassin, Leonid Fyodorovich. *See* Massine,
  Léonide
Micah, I:468
Michal, I:241
Michael III (Byzantine emperor), II:117, 176, 279,
  674, 675
Michael V (Byzantine emperor), II:758
Michael VIII Palaeologus, II:899
Michael of Cesena, II:682, 683
Michelangelo, **III:517-520**
  Bramante, III:84
  Correggio, III:186
  Greco, El, III:311
  Jacopo della Quercia, III:391
  Julius II, III:407
  Last Judgment, III:168
  Pietà, III:16
  Raphael, III:643, 645
  Titian, III:723
  Vasari, III:743
Michele Cione, Andrea di. *See* Verrocchio,
  Andrea del
Michelet, Jules, **VI:1548-1550**
  History of France, The, VI:1548, 1549
  History of the French Revolution, The, VI:1548,
  1549
  Introduction à l'histoire universelle, VI:1548
  People, The, VI:1549
Michelin, André and Édouard, VII:696;
  VIII:2514-2516
Michelson, Albert A., VI:**1551-1555;** VIII:2539
Michener, James A., **VIII:2517-2519**
  Bridges at Toko-Ri, The, VIII:2517
  Caribbean, VIII:2519
  Hawaii, VIII:2517, 2518
  Poland, VIII:2518
  Return to Paradise, VIII:2517
  Sayonara, VIII:2517
  Source, The, VIII:2518
  Space, VIII:2519
  Tales of the South Pacific, VIII:2517
Michinaga. *See* Fujiwara Michinaga
microscopy
  Holmes, V:1126
  Koch, VI:1298

Leeuwenhoek, IV:825-827
Malpighi, IV:892
Zworykin, IX:4127
Middle Stoa, I:686
Midway Island, Battle of, VIII:1525, 1527, 2750-2752
Mies van der Rohe, Ludwig, **VIII:2520-2524**
    "Brick Countryhouse," VIII:2520
    "Concrete Countryhouse," VIII:2520
    "Concrete Office Building," VIII:2520
    "Glass Skyscrapers," VIII:2520
Mi Fei, **II:639-641**
    Pao-chang tai-fang lu, II:639
    Shu-su t'ieh, II:639
Mighty Five, the, VI:1611, 1612, 1889, 2200
Mighty Handful, the. *See* Mighty Five, the
Mihajlovic, Draza, IX:3692
Milan, Duchy of
    Alboin, II:42
    Alexander VI:III:16
    Ambrose, I:43, 44
    Bayard, III:48, 49
    Boccherini, IV:147
    Clement VII:III:166
    Francis I, III:274
    Medici, Lorenzo de', III:496
    Sforza, III:682-684
Miles, Nelson, V:575, 1244
Miletus, I:115, 852
Milhaud, Darius, **VIII:2525-2528**
    Agamemnon, VIII:2525
    Bœuf sur le toit, Le, VIII:2526
    Brebis égarée, La, VIII:2525, 2526
    Carnaval d'Aix, La, VIII:2526
    Choëphores, Les, VIII:2525
    Christophe Colomb, VIII:2526
    Création du monde, La, VIII:2526
    David, VIII:2527
    Esther de Carprentras, VIII:2526
    Euménides, Les, VIII:2525
    Homme et son désir, L', VIII:2525
    Machines agricoles, VIII:2526
    Malheurs d'Orphée, VIII:2526
    Maximilien, VIII:2526
    Protée, VIII:2525
Milindapanha, I:541
Military Government of the United States, Office of, VII:848
Military Reconstruction Act, VI:2108
Military Reorganization Commission, V:940-942
Militia Act of 1792, IV:1407
Miliukov, P.N., VIII:1942

Mill, James, **VI:1556-1558**, 1559, 1560
    History of British India, VI:1557, 1559, 1787
Mill, John Stuart, IV:108, 109; V:417, 460, 539, 776; VI:1556, 1557, **1559-1565**, 2211; VIII:2773
    Autobiography, VI:1556, 1559, 1560
    Essay on Liberty, IV:685
    On Liberty, VI:1562, 1563, 2062
    On the Subjection of Women, IV:1478; V:1059; VI:1563, 2064, 2213
    Principles of Political Economy, VI:1559, 1562
    System of Logic, A, VI:1560, 1562
    Utilitarianism, VI:1563
Millais, John Everett, V:1168
Millay, Edna St. Vincent, VIII:2251, **2529-2532**
    Aria da Capo, VIII:2530
    Conversation at Midnight, VIII:2530
    Flowers of Evil, VIII:2530
Miller, Arthur, **VIII:2533-2535**, 2589
    After the Fall, VIII:2534
    All My Sons, VIII:2533
    American Clock, The, VIII:2534
    Archbishop's Ceiling, The, VIII:2534
    Broken Glass, VIII:2534
    Creation of the World and Other Business, The, VIII:2534
    Crucible, The, VIII:2534
    Danger: Memory!, VIII:2534
    Death of a Salesman, VIII:2533
    Incident at Vichy, VIII:2534
    Last Yankee, The, VIII:2534
    Man Who Had All the Luck, The, VIII:2533
    Memory of Two Mondays, A, VIII:2533, 2534
    Mr. Peter's Connections, VIII:2534
    Price, The, VIII:2534
    Ride Down Mt. Morgan, The, VIII:2534
    Story of G. I. Joe, The, VIII:2533
    View from the Bridge, A, VIII:2534
Miller, Henry, VIII:2537
Millet, Kate, **VIII:2536-2538**
    Basement, The, VIII:2537
    Flying, VIII:2537
    Loony-Bin Trip, The, VIII:2537
    Sexual Politics, VIII:2536-2538
    Three Lives, VIII:2537
Millikan, Robert Andrews, **VIII:2539-2542**
Mills, Earle, IX:3174
Milne, A.A., **VIII:2543-2545**
    Days Play, The, VIII:2543
    Holiday Round, The, VIII:2543
    House at Pooh Corner, The, VIII:2544

It's Too Late Now, VIII:2544
Miss Elizabeth Bennett, VIII:2544
Mr. Pim Passes By, VIII:2543
Now We Are Six, VIII:2544
Once a Week, VIII:2543
Once on a Time, VIII:2543
Peace with Honour, VIII:2544
Red House Mystery, The, VIII:2543
Three Lives, VIII:2543
Toad of Toad Hall, VIII:2544
When We Were Very Young, VIII:2543
Winnie-the-Pooh, VIII:2543
Wurzel-Flummery, VIII:2543
Milner, Sir Alfred, VII:376; IX:4094
Milon, I:34
Miloslavskys, IV:1082
Miltiades the Younger, **I:553-556**
Milton, John, III:705; **IV:958-962;** IX:3258
    Areopagitica, IV:961; IX:3258
    Comus, IV:958, 961
    De doctrina Christiana, IV:961
    Of Education, IV:960
    Paradise Lost, IV:641, 960-962; VII:945;
        IX:3258
    *Ready and Easy Way to Establish a Free
        Commonwealth, The,* IV:960
    Samson Agonistes, IV:961
    Tenure of Kings and Magistrates, The, IV:960
Milvian Bridge, battle of the, I:227
Minamoto clan, II:882, 883, 924, 1025
Minangkabaus, VIII:1577
Ming Dynasty
    Abahai, IV:1, 2
    Cheng Ch'eng-kung, IV:297, 298
    Cheng Ho, II:253-255
    Ch'ien-lung, IV:300
    Dorgon, IV:421, 422
    K'ang-hsi, IV:758, 759
    Yung-lo, II:1022-1024
Minims, IV:949
Minin, Nikita. *See* Nikon
mining industry
    Agricola, III:1-3
    Baldwin, VII:169
    Boulton, IV:183
    Brindley, IV:201, 202
    Carmaux strike, V:1221, 1222
    Darrow, VII:839
    Davy lamp, V:622
    Guggenheim, VIII:1498-1500
    Hadfield, V:1016
    Hearst, VIII:1601

    Hoover, VIII:1727
    methane detection, VIII:1510
    Newcomen, IV:1023
    Republic labor policies of 1892, V:1055
    Rockefeller, VIII:1981
    Roebuck, IV:1184
    Rhodes, V:463
    Sesostris III, I:774
    Supreme Court decisions, VII:1212
    Trevithick, VI:2251
    United Mine Workers of America,
        VIII:1879-1881, 2170-2172
Mink, Ben, VIII:2081
Minkus, Ludwig, V:649
Minnedienst, II:959
Minnelli, Vincente, VII:1305, 1306
Minnesang, II:959
Minnesota
    Humphrey, VIII:1783
    Pike, IV:1094
Minorca, IV:56, 57
Minot, George Richards, IX:3959
Mint, U.S., IX:3243-3245
Minto Reforms, VII:184
Minucius, Lucius, I:335
Mirabeau, Comte de, **IV:963-965**
Miramar, II:608
Miranda, Francisco de, V:267
Miranda v. Arizona, IX:3890
Miriam, I:3
Mir Jafar, IV:326
Miró, Joan, VII:1099; **VIII:2546-2550,**
        2732, 2733
    Carbide, The, VIII:2548
    Catalan Landscape (The Hunter), VIII:2548
    Composition, VIII:2548
    Constellations, VIII:2548
    Dog Barking at the Moon, VIII:2548
    Dutch Interiors, VIII:2548
    Farm, The, VIII:2546
    Farmer's Wife, The, VIII:2548
    Harlequin Carnival, The, VIII:2548
    Little Girl in Front of the Sun, VIII:2549
    Montroig Landscaping, VIII:2546
    Nocturne, VIII:2548
    Object poétique, VIII:2548
    Olive Grove, The, VIII:2546
    Reaper, The, VIII:2548
    Romeo and Juliet, VIII:2548
    Spanish Dancer, VIII:2548
    Still Life with an Old Shoe, VIII:2548
    Still Life with Toy Horse, VIII:2546

Table with Rabbit, VIII:2546
Tilled Field, The, VIII:2548
Woman, VIII:2549
Mirza Reza Kermani, V:1209
Mishima, Yukio, **VIII:2551-2553**
   Confessions of a Mark, VIII:2551
   Death in Midsummer and Other Stories,
     VIII:2551
   Madame de Sade, VIII:2551
   "Patriotism," VIII:2551, 2552
   Sea of Fertility, The, VIII:2551
   Sun and Steel, VIII:2551
Mishnah, I:27-29
Mission, Congregation of the, IV:1380
Missionary Sisters of the Sacred Heart, V:386, 388
Mississippi River
   Eads Bridge, V:729-731
   Jolliet, IV:732-734
   La Salle, IV:793-795
   Louisiana Purchase, IV:719
   Soto, III:699-701
Missouri
   Benton, V:195, 197, 198
   Bingham, V:236-238
   Dred Scott decision, VI:2000
   Frémont, V:842
   Lewis and Clark, VI:1340
   Mormonism, VI:2081, 2415
   Schurz, VI:1997
Missouri Compromise, V:508, 693; VI:2191,
   2192, 2288
MIT. *See* Massachusetts Institute of Technology
Mitanni, I:890
Mitchell, John, VIII:2759
Mitchell, Maria, V:822
Mitchell, William, **VIII:2554-2557**
Mithradates the Great, **I:557-560,** 680, 828, 834,
   896, 897
Mitterand, François, **VIII:2558-2561**
Mobile Bay, Battle of, V:772, 774
Mobilier National Building, IX:2977
Möbius, Karl August, VI:2119
Mobutu Sese Seko, **VIII:2562-2565; IX:3745**
Mocenigo, Zuane, III:97
Mochihito, Prince, II:882
Model A automobile, VII:1186
Model T automobile, VII:1184, 1186, 1187
Modern Art, Museum of (New York)
   Aalto, VII:2, 3
   Arbus, VII:95-97
   Brancusi, VII:417
   Buñuel, VII:506

   Ernst, VII:1100
   Frankenthaler, VII:1209
   Giacometti, VII:1361
   Kupka, VIII:2037
   Moses, VIII:2633
   Nevelson, VIII:2729, 2730
   Nicholson, VIII:2733
   Orozco, IX:2838
   Oud, IX:2860
   Pollock, IX:3049, 3050
   Rouault, IX:3253
   Steichen, IX:3503
Modern Language Association, IX:4015
Modigliani, Amadeo, VII:37
Moffat, Robert, VI:1399
Moffat, W.B., VI:2002
Mohács, Battle of, III:376
Mohammad Reza Shah Pahlavi, VIII:1957-1959,
   2566-2570
Mohammed. *See* Muhammad
Mohammed I Askia, **III:521-523**
Mohawk Indians
   Brant, IV:196, 198, 199
   Champlain, IV:273
   Metacomet, IV:955
   Tekakwitha, IV:1316, 1317
Mokae, Zakes, VII:1257, 1258
Moland, John, IV:408
molecular biology
   Crick, VII:797
   Jacob, VIII:1827-1829
   Pauling, IX:2928
   Schrödinger, IX:3362
   Staudinger, IX:3499
   Watson, IX:3897-3899
Molière, IV:782, 783, **966-970,** 1145
   Affected Young Ladies, The, IV:968
   Blunderer, The, IV:968
   Don Juan, IV:968
   Fourberies de Scapin, Les, IV:387
   Imaginary Invalid, The, IV:969
   Love-Tiff, The, IV:968
   Misanthrope, The, IV:968; VII:281
   School for Husbands, The, IV:968
   School for Wives, The, IV:968
   Sganarelle, IV:968
   Tartuffe, IV:968, 969
Moller, Martin, IV:154
Molnár, Ferenc
   Liliom, VIII:2141, 2142
   Swan, The, VIII:2142
Moloch, I:801

Molon, I:63

Molotov, Vyacheslav Mikhailovich, VII:316; VIII:1961, 1962, **2571-2574**

Molotov-Ribbentrop Pact, VIII:2572

Mommsen, Theodor, **VI:1566-1569**

Corpus inscriptionum Latinarum, VI:1567, 1568

History of Rome, The, VI:1566-1568

Inscriptions regni Neapolitani Latinae, VI:1566

Provinces of the Roman Empire from Caesar to Diocletian, The, VI:1567

Römisches Staatsrecht, VI:1567

Römisches Strafrecht, VI:1567

Monadnock Building, V:365

Monaldeschi, Gian Rinaldo, IV:306

Monck, George, IV:284, 791, **971-974,** 1229, 1343

Mondale, Walter, VII:949, 1153-1155

Mondino dei Liucci, II:414

Mondrian, Piet, VII:538; VIII:1904, **2575-2578,** 2732-2734; IX:2859

Broadway Boogie Woogie, VIII:2576

Composition in Red, Yellow and Blue, VIII:2576

Oval Composition with Bright Colors, VIII:2576

Victory Boogie Woogie, VIII:2576, 2577

Monet, Claude, VI:1869, 1870, 1963, 1964; VIII:1903, **2579-2582**

Impression, Sunrise, VIII:2579

Women in the Garden, VIII:2579

Monge, Gaspard, **IV:975-979**

Elementary Treatise on Descriptive Geometry, An, IV:977

Mongols

Baybars I, II:124-126

Carpini, II:207

K'ang-hsi, IV:758

Khan, Genghis, II:376-378

Khan, Kublai, II:566-568

Nevsky, II:53

Polo, II:750

Sa'di, II:806, 807

Sung Dynasty, II:868

Tamerlane, II:884

William of Rubrouck, II:987, 988

Yaqut, II:1013

Yung-lo, II:1021, 1022

Monk, Thelonious, VII:741

Monmouth, Battle of, IV:322, 368, 575, 1405

Monmouth, Duke of, IV:704, **980-982,** 1039

Monmouth, Henry of, II:459

Monmouth, Humphrey, III:736

Monnet, Jean, **VIII:2583-2586**

Monod, Jacques, VIII:1827-1829

Mononobe clan, II:826

monopolies

Astor, V:82, 84

British Broadcasting Corporation, VII:739; IX:3147

German industrial cartels, VII:1094

Goldie, V:953

Morgan, VI:1582

Rockefeller, VI:1896-1898

Sherman Anti-Trust Act, IX:3229

United Shoe Manufacturing Company, VII:419

Vanderbilt, VI:2296

Monroe, James, **VI:1570-1574**

Calhoun, V:395

Clay, V:508

Clinton, V:519

Gadsden Purchase, V:858, 859

Jeffrey, V:1226

Paine, IV:1056

Monroe, Marilyn, VII:936; VIII:2534, **2587-2591**

Bus Stop, VIII:2589

Don't Bother to Knock, VIII:2589

Gentlemen Prefer Blondes, VIII:2589

How to Marry a Millionaire, VIII:2589

Let's Make Love, VIII:2589

Love Happy, VIII:2587, 2589

Misfits, The, VIII:2589

Prince and the Showgirl, The, VIII:2589

Some Like It Hot, VIII:2589

Something's Got to Give, VIII:2589

Monroe Doctrine

Adams, V:22

Canning, V:406

Lodge, VIII:2221

Monroe, IX:1570, 1573

Polk, VI:1803

Monroe-Pinkey Treaty, VI:1571

Montagnais, IV:273

Montagnards, IV:394, 395

Montagu, Charles, IV:26, 1066-1068

Montagu, Edward Wortley, IV:135, 983

Montagu, Mary Wortley, **IV:983-985**

Nonsense of Common Sense, The, IV:984

Turkish Embassy Letters, IV:983

Verses Addressed to the Imitator of Horace, IV:984

Montagu, Ralph, IV:822

Montaigne, Michel de, **III:524-527;** VII:723

Montale, Eugenio, **VIII:2592-2595**

Bones of the Cuttlefish, VIII:2592

Eugenio Montale: The Storm and Other Poems, VIII:2593

occasioni, Le, VIII:2593
Satura, VIII:2594
Montand, Yves, VIII:2588
Montauk Building, V:365
Montcalm, Louis de, IV:179
Monteagle, Lord, III:258
Monte Cassino, monastery of, II:911
Monterey Pop Festival, VIII:1883
Montespan, Madame de, IV:901
Montesquieu, **IV:986-989**
 Considérations sur les causes de la grandeur des
  Romains et de leur décadence, IV:986
 Persian Letters, IV:986
 Spirit of the Laws, The, IV:986-988
Montessori, Maria, **VIII:2596-2600**
 Advanced Montessori Method, The,
  VIII:2599
 Dr. Montessori's Own Handbook, VIII:2599
 Montessori Method, The, VIII:2598
Monteverdi, Claudio, **IV:990-994**
 Arianna, L', IV:992
 favola d'Orfeo, La, IV:991-993
 finta pazza Licori, La, IV:992
 incoronazione di Poppea, L', IV:992, 993
 Vespers of 1610, IV:992, 993
 vittoria d'amore, La, IV:992
Montezuma I, III:379, 556, 557
Montezuma II, III:22, 189, 190, **528-532**
Montfort, Simon V de, II:454, 455, **642-647**
Montgolfier, Jacques-Étienne, **IV:995-998**
Montgolfier, Joseph-Michel, **IV:995-998**
Montgomery, Bernard Law, **VIII:2601-2604;**
 IX:4117
Montgomery bus boycott, VII:9, 10; IX:2889,
 2890, 3941
Montgomery Improvement Association, IX:2890
Montgomery Ward and Company, VI:2331-2334
Montini, Giovanni Battista. *See* Paul VI
Montojo, Patricio, V:657
Montrose, Marquess of, IV:283
Moody, Dwight, L., **VI:1575-1578,** 2388
Moody, William H., V:284
Moon
 Braun, VII:440, 441
 eclipse, II:121
 Galileo, IV:521
 Hipparchus, I:409
 lunar calendars, I:811, 812
 Nabu-Rimanni, I:567, 568
 Posidonius, I:688
 space exploration, VII:110-113; VIII:2021,
  2022; IX:3405-3407

third inequality, II:21
three-body problem, IV:786
Mooney, Tom, VII:1212
Moore, Fred H., IX:3283
Moore, G.E., **VIII:2605-2608**
 Commonplace Book, VIII:2607
 "Ideal Utilitarianism," VIII:2606
 "Nature of Judgment, The," VIII:2606
 Philosophical Papers, VIII:2607
 Philosophical Studies, VIII:2607
 Principia Ethica, VIII:2606, 2607
 "Refutation of Idealism, The," VIII:2606
 Some Main Problems of Philosophy, VIII:2607
Moore, Henry, **VIII:2609-2613**
 Double Oval Bronze, VIII:2612
 Draped Reclining Mother and Baby, VIII:2612
 Madonna and Child, VIII:2612
 Mother and Child, VIII:2611
 North Wind, VIII:2611
 Reclining Figure, VIII:2612
 Vision and Design, VIII:2609
Moore, Marianne, **VIII:2614-2617**
 Nevertheless, VIII:2616
 Observations, VIII:2614, 2616
 Pangolin and Other Verse, The, VIII:2616
 "Past is the Present, The," VIII:2616
 What are Years?, VIII:2616
Moore, Thomas
 Epistles, Odes, and Other Poems, V:1225
Moran, Bugsy, VII:564, 565
Moran, Thomas, V:234
Moravian Church, IV:1488-1490
Moray, Sir Andrew, II:294, 956
Mordaunt, Charles. *See* Peterborough, Third Earl of
More, Anne, IV:418
More, Sir Thomas, **III:533-536**
 Erasmus, III:247
 Fisher, III:264-266
 Henry VIII, III:349, 351
 History of King Richard the Third, The, III:234,
  652
 Holbein the Younger, III:358, 359
 "Steelyard portraits," III:359
 Tyndale, III:736
 Utopia, I:509
Moreau, Gustave, VIII:2452; IX:3251
Morelli, Felice, V:388
Morgan, George, V:450
Morgan, J.P., IV:661; **VI:1579-1583,** 2220;
 IX:3501
Morgan, Lewis Henry, **VI:1584-1587**
 American Beaver and His Works, The, VI:1586

Ancient Society, VI:1586
*Houses and House-Life of the American
    Aborigines,* VI:1586
League of the Ho-de-no-sau-nee, or Iroquois,
    VI:1584
*Systems of Consanguinity and Affinity of the
    Human Family,* VI:1585
Morgan, Thomas Hunt, **VIII:2618-2621,** 2651
Drosophila, VIII:2620
Mechanism of Mendelian Heredity, The,
    VIII:2619
Morgenthau, Henry, V:26
Morgenthau Plan, VIII:1780
Mori clan, III:571, 728, 729
Morita, Akio, **VIII:2622-2625**
Moritz, Langrave, IV:1221
Morley, Edward Williams, VI:1552
Morley, Thomas, III:105, 108
Mormonism, V:840; VI:2080-2082, 2414-2416
Mornay, Philippe de, **III:537-539**
Morning Chronicle, V:1192
Morning Courier, V:191
Morones, Luis, VII:542, 543
Morris, Charles A., V:1124, 1125
Morris, Robert, **IV:999-1002**
Morris, William, **VI:1588-1591; IX:2892**
Defence of Guenevere, The, VI:1588
Dream of John Ball, A, VI:1590
Earthly Paradise, The, VI:1589
Life and Death of Jason, The, VI:1589
News from Nowhere, VI:1590
Sigurd the Volsung, VI:1589
Story of the Glittering Plain, The, VI:1590
Morrison, Herbert, VII:304
Morrison, Toni, **VIII:2626-2629**
Beloved, VIII:2627; IX:4031
Black Book, The, VIII:2628
Bluest Eye, The, VIII:2627
Jazz, VIII:2627
Song of Solomon, VIII:2627
Sula, VIII:2627
Tar Baby, VIII:2627
Morrow, Dwight M., VII:543
Morse, John Vinnicum, V:283
Morse, Samuel, F.B., V:294, 541, 1094;
    VI:1592-1595
Congress Hall, VI:1593
Louvre, The, VI:1592, 1593
Old House of Representatives, The, VI:1592
Morse code, VI:1593, 1807
Mortimer, Lord Roger, II:327, 329
Mortimer's Cross, Battle of, III:345

Morton, John, III:650-652
Morton, Thomas, III:533; IV:418
Morton, William Thomas Green, **VI:1596-1599**
Mosaddeq, Mohammad, VIII:2567
Mosca, Gaetano, **VIII:2630-2632**
Elementi di scienza politica, VIII:2630, 2631
Storia delle dottrine politiche, VIII:2632
Moscow Art Theatre, VIII:2510; IX:3486-3488
Moscow Communist Party, VIII:1961
Moscow Group for the Study of Reactive
    Propulsion, VIII:2019
Moscow Human Rights Committee, IX:3298
Moscow Linguistic Circle, VIII:1831
Moseley, Henry, VI:1533
Moses, **I:561-565**
Aaron, I:1, 3, 4
Jesus Christ, I:939
Joshua, I:246
Philo of Alexandria, I:632
Pilate, I:642
Yahweh, I:7
Moses, Grandma, **VIII:2633-2636**
Eisenhower Farm, VIII:2635
Fireboard, VIII:2633
First Automobile, The, VIII:2633
Home, In the Maple Sugar, VIII:2633
July Fourth, VIII:2635, 2636
Old Oaken Bucket, The, VIII:2635
Sugaring Off, VIII:2635
Turkey Hunt, VIII:2635
Moses, Law of, I:331-333
Moses de León, **II:648-650**
Book of Herman, The, II:648
Rose of the Testimony, II:648
Zohar, II:648-650
Moses ibn Ezra, II:548
Moslem League. *See* Muslim League
Most, Johann, VIII:1412
Motley, John Lothrop, III:602
Mott, John R., **VIII:2637-2640**
Mott, Lucretia, V:822; **VI:1600-1603; IX:2919**
Moulin Rouge, VI:2248
mountain climbing, VI:2410-2412;
    VIII:2506-2508
Mountbatten, Louis, VII:1344, 1345; VIII:1848,
    2641-2646
In Which We Serve, VIII:2643
Mouvement National Congolais, VIII:2562
Moynier, Gustave, V:712
Mozambique Liberation Front, VIII:2317-2319,
    2774
Mozambique National Resistance, VIII:2318, 2319

Mozart, Wolfgang Amadeus, IV:149, 639,
    1003-1007; V:178, 179; VI:1686
    Abduction from the Seraglio, The, IV:1003
    Artaserse, IV:550
    Clemency of Titus, The, IV:1006
    Cosi fan tutte, IV:1352
    Don Giovanni, IV:1005; V:493; VI:1391;
        VIII:2746
    Haffner, IV:1005
    Idomeno, King of Crete, IV:1003
    Magic Flute, The, IV:1005; VIII:2014
    Marriage of Figaro, The, IV:1005
    musikalischer Spass, Ein, IV:1006
    Requiem, IV:1005; VI:2155
Ms. magazine, IX:3521, 3522
muckraking
    Godkin, VIII:1402
    McClure's magazine, VII:624
    Rockefeller, VI:1898
    Sinclair, IX:3426
    Tarbell, IX:3616, 3617
Mugabe, Robert, VIII:2319, **2647-2650**
Mughal Dynasty
    Ahmad Khan, V:35, 36
    Akbar, III:5-7
    Aurangzeb, IV:69-71
    Babur, III:38
    Shah Jahan, IV:1232-1234
    Sivaji, IV:1247
Mugwumps, VI:1997; VIII:1402
Muhammad, **II:651-656**
    Abraham, I:7, 564
    Faisal I, VII:1122
    Hasan al-Basri, II:440
    Hussein I, VIII:1791
    Ibn Khaldun, II:503, 504
    Islamic law, II:17, 33
    Moses, I:564
Muhammad XI, III:261
Muhammad, Elijah, VIII:2373, 2375, 2376
Muhammad 'Ali Pasha, **VI:1604-1607**
Muhammad ibn Tughluq, II:496
Muhlberg, Battle of, III:18
Muir, John, **VI:1608-1610**
Mukhtar, Omar, IX:3098
Muller, Hermann Joseph, **VIII:2651-2654;**
    IX:3033
Müller, Johannes, V:1018, 1089
Müller, Lucas. *See* Cranach, Lucas, the Elder
Müller, William, VI:1989
Muller v. Oregon, VII:421
Mulligan Letters, V:256, 257

Mulroney, Brian, VII:550, 681, 682;
    VIII:2655-2657; IX:3345, 3346
Munch, Edvard, **VIII:2658-2661**
    Frieze of Life, The, VIII:2659
    Morning After, The, VIII:2658
    Puberty, VIII:2658
    Scream, The, VIII:2658
    Sick Child, The, VIII:2658
Muncke, Georg Wilhelm, V:555
Mundir I, II:498
Munemori, II:882
Munich Conference, VIII:2210
Municipal Corporation Act, VI:1788
Municipal Franchise Act, V:777
Munitions War Act of 1915, VII:309
Munro, Ed, VIII:1593
Murad II, III:499
Murasaki Shikibu, **II:657-659**
    Tale of Genji, The, II:657, 658; IV:1258
Murchinson, Roderick, VI:1418
Murcia, II:56
Murdock, William, **IV:1008-1011**
Murena, Lucinius, I:166
Muret, Battle of, II:529
Muret, Marc-Antoine, III:671
Murillo, Gerardo, IX:2836
Muris, Johannes de, **II:660-662**
    Ars novae musicae, II:660, 661
    Musica speculativa secundum Boetium,
        II:660, 661
    Opus quadripartitum numerorum, II:660
Murji'ism, II:18
Murphy, William P., IX:3959
Murray, William. *See* Mansfield, First Earl of
Murrow, Edward R., **VIII:2662-2666**
    Hear It Now, VIII:2664
    Person to Person, VIII:2664
    See It Now, VIII:2635, 2664
Musa. *See* Mansa Musa
Muscle Shoals Canal, VIII:1408
Mushet, Robert Forester, V:220
musical theater
    Gershwins, VII:1347, 1349, 1350
    Gilbert and Sullivan, V:930
    Hart, VIII:1566-1569
    Porter, IX:3055, 3056
    Rodgers, IX:3201, 3202
    Weill, IX:3926-3929
Muskie, Edmund, VII:49, 50
Muslim Brotherhood, VII:90; VIII:2693
Muslim League, VII:1283; VIII:1847, 1848,
    2710, 2711

Muspratt, James, VI:1367
Mussolini, Benito, **VIII:2667-2670**
    Baldwin, VII:170
    Croce, VII:801, 802
    De Gasperi, VII:863
    Franco, VII:1201
    Gentile, VII:1336-1338
    Gramsci, VIII:1459
    Haile Selassie I, VIII:1519
    Hoare-Laval Agreement, VIII:2105
    Kesselring, VIII:1950
    Luce, VIII:2262
    Lyons, VIII:2294
    Mosca, VIII:2631, 2632
    Perón, IV:2970
    Pirelli, IX:3021
    Sorel, IX:3464
    Tunisia, VII:391
Mussorgsky, Modest, V:288; **VI:1611-1615;**
    VIII:1837
    Boris Gudunov, VI:1611-1614
    Destruction of Sennacherib, The, VI:1612, 1613
    From Memories of Childhood, VI:1612
    Intermezzo in modo classico, VI:1611
    Khovanshchina, VI:1613
    Night on Bare Mountain, VI:1612, 1614
    Nursery, The, VI:1613
    Pictures from an Exhibition, VI:1613
    Porte-Enseigne Polka, VI:1611
    Rêverie, VI:1612
    Songs of Dances of Death, VI:1613
    Sunless, VI:1613
Mu'tazilites, II:34, 93-95, 526, 636
Mutual Assistance, Pact of, VIII:2150
Mutual Assured Destruction doctrine, IX:3633
Mutual Assured Survival doctrine, IX:3633
Mutual Welfare League, IX:2852-2854
Muybridge, Eadweard, VIII:2277, 2278
Muzorewa, Abel, VIII:2647, 2648
Mycenaean Greek kingdoms, I:422; VI:1982
Myrdal, Gunnar, **VIII:2671-2674**
    American Dilemma, An, VIII:2671-2673
    Asian Drama, VIII:2672, 2673
    Challenge to World Poverty, The, VIII:2673
    Rich Lands and Poor, VIII:2672
Myrick, Julian, VIII:1820
Myrsilus, I:651, 652
mysticism
    Catherine of Siena, II:218, 220, 221
    Francis of Assisi, II:354-356
    Ghazzali, II:385, 386
    Hesychasm, II:899-901

    Hildegard von Bingen, II:474-477
    Ibn al-'Arabi, II:491-493
    John of the Cross, III:401-403
    Luria, III:440, 441
    Moses de León, II:648-650
    Ritschl, VI:1893
mythology
    Botticelli, III:75
    Cassirer, VII:615
    Ch'ü Yüan, I:187
    Cocteau, VII:723
    Cranach, III:202
    Egypt, I:573
    Fortescue, III:267-269
    Herodotus, I:396
    Lévi-Strauss, VIII:2164, 2165
    Lewis, VIII:2167, 2168
Montezuma II, III:529
    Ovid, I:585-587
    Schelling, VI:1974
    Thales of Miletus, I:852, 854, 855
    Tolkien, IX:3697
    Vico, IV:1373
    See also Greek mythology
Mytilene, I:651
Mzali, Muhammad, VII:393

NAACP. *See* National Association for the
    Advancement of Colored People
Nabokov, Vladimir, **VIII:2675-2678**
    Bend Sinister, VIII:2676
    Defense, The, VIII:2675
    Eugene Onegin, VIII:2676
    Gift, The, VIII:2675, 2676
    Invitation to a Beheading, VIII:2675
    King, Queen, Knave, VIII:2675
    Lolita, VIII:2676, 2677
    Mary, VIII:2675
    Pale Fire, VIII:2677; VII:374
    Pnin, VIII:2677
    Real Life of Sebastian Knight, The, VIII:2676
    Speak, Memory, VIII:2676
Nabonidus, I:234
Nabulsi, Suleyman an-, VIII:1793
Nabu-rimanni, **I:566-569**
Nachmonides, Moses, II:649
Nacionalista Party, VIII:2421
Nader, Ralph, **VIII:2679-2682**
    Unsafe at Any Speed, VIII:2679
NAFTA. *See* North American Free Trade
    Agreement
Nagashima, Shigeo, IX:2796, 2797

Nagashino, Battle of, III:571
Nägeli, Carl von, VI:1527
Naha, Treaty of, VI:1762
Nahrain, I:890
Naidu, Sarojini, **VIII:2683-2685**
    Bird of Time, The, VIII:2683
    Broken Wing, The, VIII:2683
    Feather of Dawn, The, VIII:2683
    Golden Threshold, VIII:2683
Najm al-Din Ayyub, II:809
Nalanda, II:483
Nalundasan, Julio, VIII:2420
Nãnak, **III:540-543**
Nandakumar, IV:632
Nanga Parbat expedition, VIII:2506, 2508
Nanking, Treaty of, VI:1376, 1378, 1379
Nanking Incident, VII:486
Nansen, Fridtjof, VII:66; **VIII:2686-2688**
    First Crossing of Greenland, VIII:2686
    Norwegian North Polar Expedition, The,
      VIII:2687
Nantes, Edict of
    Catherine de Médicis, III:135
    Colbert, IV:338
    Frederick William, The Great Elector, IV:509
    Henry IV, III:334
    Hotman, III:365
    Louis XIII, IV:864
    Louis XIV, IV:868
    Mornay, III:539
Napata, I:636-638
Napier, Sir Charles, V:374
Napier, John, **III:544-547**
    Construction of a Marvelous Canon of
      Logarithms, III:545
    Description of a Marvelous Canon of
      Logarithms, III:545
    Plaine Discovery of the Whole Revelation of St.
      John, A, III:544
    Study of Divining Rods, or Two Books of
      Numbering by Means of Rods, III:545
Naples, Kingdom of
    Alexander VI, III:16
    Boccaccio, II:150, 152
    Claude Lorrain, IV:317
    Ferdinand and Isabella, III:262
    Louis XII, III:48
    Scarlatti, IV:1213, 1214
    Sforza, III:682, 683
    Torquemada, III:726
Napoleon I, **VI:1616-1619**
    Alexander I, V:44-46

Baybars I, II:126
Blücher, V:263-265
Cambacérès, V:398-400
Canova, V:410
Castlereagh, V:440, 441
Cavour, V:447, 448
Charles XIV John, V:474, 475
Chateaubriand, V:482-484
Code Napoleon, VI:1966
David, V:611
Du Pont, V:718
Fourier, V:819, 820
Fragonard, IV:490
Gance's film, VII:1274, 1275
Géricault, V:910, 912
Gneisenau, V:940-942
Hardenberg, V:1033-1035
Haydn, IV:641, 642
Joséphine, V:1246-1248
Kutuzov, VI:1305-1307
Louisiana Purchase, IV:719; VI:1571
Metternich, VI:1544-1546
Monge, IV:977, 978
Napoleon III, VI:1620
Ney, VI:1646-1648
Nonintercourse Act of 1809, IV:888
Pitt the Younger, IV:1104
Pyréolophore, VI:1657
San Martín, VI:1947
Saragossa, VI:1958, 1959
Staël, VI:2093, 2094
Stein, VI:2115, 2116
Stendhal, VI:2126
Talleyrand, VI:2186, 2187
Toussaint-Louverture, IV:1340
Volta, IV:1390
Vo Nguyen Giap, IX:3821
Wellington, VI:2351-2353
See also Napoleonic Wars
Napoleon III, **VI:1620-1623**
    Alexander II, V:49
    Bismarck, V:240, 241
    Clemenceau, VII:702
    Dunant, V:711
    Gambetta, V:871-873
    Juárez, V:1252
    Lesseps, VI:1355
    Palmerston, VI:1721
    Proudhon, VI:1818
    Rothschild family, VI:1918, 1919
    Thiers, VI:2227, 2228
    Tocqueville, VI:2239

Napoleonic Wars
  Alexander I, V:44-46
  Clausewitz, V:503-505
  Napoleon I, VI:1616-1618
  Niebuhr, VI:1654, 1655
  Perry, VI:1760
  Wellington, VI:2351-2353
Narbonne Lara, Louis, Vicomte de, VI:2092, 2093
Narkomindel, VIII:2209, 2210
Narmer, I:548
Narragansett Indians, IV:932, 955
Narses, I:778
Narváez, Pánfilo de, III:110
Naryshkins, IV:1082
NASA
  Armstrong, VII:111-113
  Braun, VII:441
  Eisenhower, VII:1045
  Glenn, VII:1387-1389
  Prandtl, IX:3074
  Ride, IX:3178, 3179
  Sagan, IX:3293
  Shepard, IX:3405-3407
Nascimento, Edson Arantes do. See Pelé
Naser od-Din, V:1209
Nash, John, IV:1012-1015
Nash, Paul, VIII:2689-2692
  Battle of Britain, The, VIII:2691
  Dawn: Sanctuary Wood, VIII:2690
  Forest, VIII:2690
  Landscape: Year of Our Lord 1917, VIII:2690
  Landscape of the Brown Fungus, VIII:2691
  Landscape of the Puff Ball, VIII:2691
  Landscape of the Red Fungus, VIII:2691
  Pyramids in the Sea, VIII:2689
  Strange Coast, VIII:2690
  Sunrise: Inverness Copse, VIII:2689, 2690
  Totes Meer, VIII:2691
  Vision at Evening, VIII:2689
  Wood Sea, VIII:2690
Nash, Richard, IV:566
Nashe, Thomas, III:548-550
  Almond for a Parrot, An, III:548
  Anatomie of Absurditie, The, III:548
  Christie's Tears over Jerusalem, III:549
  Isle of Dogs, The, III:549
  Nashe's Lenten Stuffe, III:549
  Pierce Penilesse, His Supplication to the Devil, III:548
  Strange Newes of the Intercepting of Certain Letters, III:549
  Summers Last Will and Testament, III:549

  Terrors of the Night, The, III:549
  Unfortunate Traveller: Or, The Life of Jack Wilton, The, III:549
Nasi, I:27-29
Nasmyth, James, VI:1624-1626
Naso, Publius Ovidius. See Ovid
Nasser, Gamal Abdel, VIII:2693-2697
  Dayan, VII:855, 856
  Eden, VII:1017
  Faisal, VIII:1119
  Hussein I, VIII:1793
  Qaddafi, IX:3098
  Sadat, IX:3289, 3290
Nast, Thomas, VI:1627-1629, 2284-2286
Nathan, I:243, 798
Nation, Carry, VI:1630-1633
National Advocate, V:191
National Aeronautics and Space Administration. See NASA
National African Company, V:954
National American Woman Suffrage Association, VI:2045, 2046; VII:627-629; IX:2919, 2920, 3118
National Anti-Slavery Standard, V:490
National Assembly (France)
  Gambetta, V:871, 872
  Herriot, VIII:1645
  Hugo, V:1157
  Marat, IV:910, 911
  Mendès-France, VIII:2491, 2492
  Mirabeau, IV:963-965
  Necker, IV:1017
  Robespierre, IV:1170, 1171
  Saint-Just, IV:1205, 1206
National Association for the Advancement of Colored People
  Carver, VII:604
  Disney, VII:941
  Du Bois VII:963-965
  Marshall, VI:2433, 2434
  Parker, IX:2886
  Price, IX:3083, 3084
  Randolph, IX:3113
  Robinson, IX:3196
  Washington, VI:2338
  Wells-Barnett, IX:3943
  White, IX:3961-3963
National Australasian Convention, V:148
National Broadcasting Corporation, IX:3709
National Catholic War Council, V:922
National Center for Atmospheric Research, IX:2946, 2947

National Child Labor Committee, VIII:2096, 2097
National Collegiate Athletic Association,
    IX:3270, 4049
National Constituent Assembly. *See* National
    Assembly (France)
National Consumers' League, IX:3118, 3838
National Convention of Nigeria and the
    Cameroons, VII:144-146
National Defense Education Act, VII:1045
National Economic Development Council,
    VIII:2343
National Education Association, VII:524
National Endowment for the Arts, VII:875
National Equal Rights Party, VI:1408
National Federation of Women Workers,
    VII:353, 354
National Gallery of Art, IX:2947
National Geographic Society, V:188;
    IX:2944, 2945
National Grange, VI:2332, 2333
National Guard, U.S., VIII:2295
National Indian Hall of Fame, IX:3675
National Industrial Recovery Act, VII:422;
    IX:3548
National Insurance Act of 1911, VII:308;
    VIII:2217
nationalism
    Acton, V:12
    Algeria, VII:6, 7
    Arab states, VIII:1795
    Argentina, IX:2971
    Austria, III:491-493; IX:3842
    Canada, V:118; VI:1496-1498; VII:365, 366
    China, VII:677
    Czechoslovakia, VII:969; VIII:2440
    Egypt, V:4-6; VIII:2355, 2356, 2695; IX:3290
    Germany, III:491-493; VII:494; VIII:1476,
        1612, 1692, 2266, 2742, 2743
    India, V:211-213; VII:183-185, 308;
        VIII:1847-1849; IX:2869
    Indochina, VIII:1699
    Indonesia, VIII:1577-1579
    Ireland, VI:1740-1742; VII:172, 733, 877-879
    Italy, V:932-934
    Japan, II:667, 668
    Jaspers, VIII:1844
    Libya, IX:3099
    Native Americans, VI:2206
    Nigeria, VII:144-146
    Russia, IV:860, 861
    Scotland, II:184; IV:241
    Singapore, VIII:2152
    Spanish music, VII:1128
    Tunisia, VII:391, 392
    Turkey, VIII:1522-1524, 1812
    United States, V:126-128, 279-281, 395, 507,
        694; VI:2038, 2039, 2346
    Zimbabwe, VIII:2647
Nationalist Party of Indonesia, IX:3570, 3571
National Labor Relations Act, IX:3224
National Liberal Federation, V:462; VI:1497
National Liberation Front of Algeria, VII:5-7
National Museum at Nairobi, VIII:2147
National Negro Business League, VI:2338
National Organization for Women, VII:1231;
    VIII:1641-1643
National Pact of Turkey, VII:134
National Park System, United States,
    VI:1608-1610
National Recovery Act, VIII:1768
National Reformer, VII:382
National Register of Historic Places Program,
    VI:1884
National Research Council, VII:745; VIII:2540
National Socialist Party. *See* Nazi Party
National Society for Penal Information, IX:2853
National Society for the Promotion of Industrial
    Education, VII:23
National Student Federation of America,
    VIII:2662
National Union of General and Municipal
    Workers, VII:354, 355
National Union of Women's Suffrage Societies,
    V:776, 778
National Woman's Party, VII:628; IX:2920
National Woman Suffrage Association, V:62, 64;
    VI:1407, 2045, 2112
National Youth Administration, VIII:1866
Nation of Islam, VII:54, VIII:2373-2376
Nations, Battle of the. *See* Leipzig, Battle of
Nations, League of
    Angell, VII:76, 77
    Balfour, VII:174
    Beaverbrook, VII:236
    Benes, VII:260
    Bergson, VII:284
    Butler, VII:525
    de Valera, VII:878
    Eden, VII:1016
    female participation, IX:2920
    Germany, VIII:1694, 2743; IX:3564, 3565
    Grey, VIII:1477
    Haile Selassie I, VIII:1519
    Hammarskjöld, VIII:1529

Harding, VIII:1550, 1551
Herriot, VIII:1645
Hughes, VIII:1777
Iraq, VII:1125
La Fontaine, VIII:2052
Liberia, IX:3757
Lorentz, VIII:2237
Lugard, VIII:2270
Monnet, VIII:2583
Nansen International Office for Refugees,
    VIII:2687
Nehru, VIII:2710
New Zealand, VIII:2445
palace construction, VIII:2138
Root, IX:3234
Smuts, IX:3453, 3454
Soviet Union, VIII:2210
Stimson, IX:3538
Taft, IX:3596
Turkey, VII:134
Wilson, IX:4022
Women's International League of Peace and
    Freedom, VII:162
Native Americans
    Amherst, IV:39
    ballet, IX:3607-3609
    Berkeley, IV:114
    Bible translation, IV:435, 437, 438
    Black Hawk, V:247-250
    Boas, VII:339
    Boone, IV:163-165
    Bougainville, IV:179
    Brant, IV:196-199
    Cabeza de Vaca, III:110, 111
    Catlin, V:443, 444
    Cartier, III:129-131
    Carson, V:429-432
    Charles V, III:161
    Cherokees. See Cherokee Indians
    Child, V:489
    Cody's Wild West Show, VI:1677
    Colt, V:541
    Columbus, III:173-175
    Cooper, V:562, 564
    Crazy Horse, V:573-577
    Crockett, V:578, 579
    Custer, V:585-587
    Davis, III:213
    Edwards, IV:430
    Erdrich, VII:1091-1093
    fur trade, VI:2077, 2078
    Gadsden Purchase, V:859

Georgia, IV:1044, 1045
Geronimo, V:915-918
Harrison, V:1061
Houston, V:1137
Iroquois. See Iroquois Indians
Jackson, V:1200-1202
Jolliet, IV:732, 733
Joseph, V:1242-1245
La Salle, IV:793-795
Laval, IV:801-803
Lewis and Clark, VI:1360
Lockwood, VI:1407
McGillivray, IV:875-877
Mankiller, VIII:2389-2391
Massasoit, IV:930-933
Metacomet, IV:954-956
Mohawks, IV:196, 198, 199
Ojibwe, VI:1585
Osceola, VI:1695-1697
Parkman, VI:1735-1739
Picotte, IX:3010-3012
Pike, IV:1094, 1096, 1097
Pilgrims, IV:190, 1273-1275
Pocahontas, IV:1106-1108, 1253-1255
Ponce de León, III:629-631
Pontiac's War, IV:513, 1110-1113
Powhatan, IV:1122-1125, 1253
Red Cloud, VI:1850-1853
Remington, VI:1862
Ross, VI:1910-1912
Sacagawea, VI:1933-1935
Saint Lawrence basin, IV:273, 274
Scott, VI:2010, 2011
Seneca, VI:1584
Sequoyah, VI:2025-2028
Shawnee, IV:164
Sioux. See Sioux Indians
Sitting Bull, VI:2070-2073
Soto, III:699-701
Stuyvesant, IV:1296
Tecumseh, VI:2203-2206
Tekakwitha, IV:1316, 1317
Thorpe, IX:3675
Virginia, IV:81
Vitoria, III:768, 769
Wesley, IV:1426, 1427
Nativity, Church of the, I:375, 376
NATO. See North Atlantic Treaty Organization
Natta, Giulio, **VIII:2698-2701**
natural selection
    Burnet, VII:514
    Darwin, V:606, 608, 609

Galton, V:870
Lucretius, I:512
Lyell, VI:1421
Teilhard de Chardin, IX:3628
Weismann, VI:2348-2350
Nautical Almanac Office, VI:1639
Nautilus, V:855, 856
Nautilus Submarine Boat Company, V:1124
Nauvoo, VI:2081
Navajo Indians, V:432
Navarino, Battle of, V:407
Navidad, III:173
Navratilova, Martina, VII:1112, 1113;
    VIII:2702-2704
Nawruz, II:381, 382
NAWSA. *See* National American Woman Suffrage
    Association
Nazarenes, VIII:2036
Nazi Party
    Adenauer, VII:27, 28
    Arendt, VII:98-100
    Astor, VII:130, 131
    Baeck, VII:149, 150
    Barmen Confession, VII:204
    Berg, VII:272
    Bergius, VII:277
    Bergman, VII:278
    Boas, VII:340
    Böll, VII:349-351
    Bonhoeffer, VII:358-360
    boxing, VIII:2243
    Braun, VII:440
    Bultmann, VII:499
    Camus, VII:553, 554
    Canada, IX:3986
    Czechoslovakia, VII:261
    Dreyer's *Day of Wrath,* VII:960
    Ehrlich, VII:1030
    Erhard, VII:1094
    eugenics, V:870
    Evangelical Church, VIII:2742-2743
    French collaboration, IX:2988, 2989
    Goebbels, VIII:1404-1406, 2078
    Göring, VIII:1438-1441, 1910
    Grass, VIII:1463, 1464
    Guderian, VIII:1490-1492
    Hamsun, VIII:1539
    Harriman, VIII:1560, 1561
    Heidegger, VIII:1611, 1612
    Heisenberg, VIII:1618
    Henze, VIII:1633
    Himmler, VIII:1666-1668

    Hindemith's operas, VIII:1671
    Hindenburg, VIII:1674-1676
    Hitler, VIII:1692-1696
    Hollywood League Against Nazism, VIII:1534
    Jaspers, VIII:1844
    Joliot, VIII:1872
    Joyce, VIII:1894
    Kesselring, VIII:1949-1951
    Le Bon, VIII:2135
    Ludendorff, VIII:2265, 2266
    Lukács, VIII:2273
    Molotov, VIII:2572
    Mussolini, VIII:2669
    Olympic Games, VII:776
    Papen, VII:2876-2878
    Paris Opéra, VIII:2184
    Pius XI, IX:3027
    Pius XII, IX:3031
    Rundstedt, IX:3260-3262
    Stark, IX:3491, 3492
    Strauss, IX:3557
    Visconti's films, IX:3820
    Waldheim, IX:3841-3843
    Weill, IX:3927, 3928
    Wiesenthal, IX:3984-3987
    Windsor, IX:4026
    zeppelins, VII:1013
    See also degenerate art
NBC, IX:3709
NCAA, IX:3270, 4049
Nearchus of Elea, I:973
Nebraska
    Bryan, VII:479, 480
    Dred Scott decision, VI:2000
    Omaha tribe, IX:3010, 3011
    statehood, V:1236
    See also Kansas-Nebraska Act
Nebraska, University of, VII:621, 623, 624
Nebuchadnezzar II, I:326, 328, 460, **569-572**
Necharsulm Strickmachinene Union, IX:3882
Necho I, I:709
Necker, Anne-Louise-Germaine. *See* Staël,
    Madame de
Necker, Jacques, **IV:1016-1018**
Neckham, Alexander, **II:663-665**
    Commentary on Ecclesiastes, II:664, 665
    Commentary on Martianus Capellus, II:663
    Corrogationes Promethei, II:664
    De naturis rerum, II:664, 665
    De nominibus utensilium, II:663, 664
    Laus sapiente divine, II:664
    Novus Avianus, II:663

Novus Esopus, II:663
Sacredos ad altare, II:663
Solatium fidelis anime, II:664
Suppletio defectum, II:664
Needham, John Turberville, IV:1260, 1261
Néel, Louis-Eugène-Félix, **VIII:2705-2708**
Nefertiti, I:24, 25, **573-576**
Neferure, I:371, 373
Nefretari, I:736
Negev, the, IX:3932
Negro Factories Corporation, VII:1312
Negro Leagues, IX:3193, 3196
Negro Silent Protest parade, IX:3855
Neguib, Muhammad, VIII:2693
Nehemiah, I:330, 332
Nehru, Jawaharlal, VIII:2642, 2644, **2709-2712;**
    IX:2867, 2869, 2904, 2905
    Discovery of India, The, VIII:2711
    Glimpses of World History, VIII:2710
    Jawaharial Nehru: An Autobiography,
        VIII:2710
Nelson, Judy, VIII:2703
Nelson, Lord, **VI:1634-1637**
Nemiroff, Robert, VIII:1546-1548
Nemirovich-Danchenko, Vladimir, IX:3486, 3487
Nennius, II:133
    History of the Britons, I:378, 379
Neoclassicism
    architecture, IV:10
    literature, IV:1115-1117
    music, VIII:1670-1672
    painting, IV:765, 767, 1160; V:408,
        610-612, 1185
Neo-Confucianism
    Su Tung-p'o, II:857
    Sung Dynasty, II:867
    Tseng Kuo-fan, VI:2260-2262
    Wang Yang-ming, III:771-773
Neo-Destour Party, VII:391, 392
Neo-Kantianism, VII:524, 614; VIII:1571
Neoplatonism
    Augustine, I:128
    Botticelli, III:75
    Ghazzali, II:385, 386
    Hypatia, I:437, 438
    Ibn Gabirol, II:498-500
    Lull, II:608
    Plato, I:657
    Plotinus, I:666-668
    Porphyry, I:683-685
    Posidonius, I:689
    Proclus, I:698-700

Spenser, III:703, 704
Thomas Aquinas, II:914
William of Moerbeke, II:985
neorealist film movement, IX:3818-3820
Neo-Taoism, I:945, 949-951
Nephelokokkugia, I:91
Neptune, VI:1639; IX:3701
Nerchinsk, Treaty of, IV:758
Neri, Saint Philip, **III:551-554**
Nernst, Walther Hermann, VII:275; VIII:1510,
    2713-2715
    Theoretical Chemistry, VIII:2714
Nero, **I:577-580**
    Claudius I, I:206
    Pliny the Elder, I:663
    Prasutagus, I:137
    Seneca the Younger, I:772, 773
    Vespasian, I:933
Neruda, Pablo, **VIII:2716-2719**
    Canto General, VIII:2717, 2618
    Captain's Verses, The, VIII:2718
    Crepusculario, VIII:2716
    Elemental Odes, The, VIII:2718
    Extravagaria, VIII:2718
    Memoirs, VIII:2718
    One Hundred Love Sonnets, VIII:2718
    Residence on Earth and Other Poems,
        VIII:2716, 2717
    Twenty Love Poems and a Song of Despair,
        VIII:2716
Nerva, Marcus Cocceius, I:28, 356, 899
Nervi, Pier Luigi, **VIII:2720-2723**
Nestorius, I:941
Netanyahu, Benjamin, VII:93
Netjerykhet, I:978
Neue Künstlervereingung, VIII:1903
Neue Rheinische Zeitung, V:761
Neue Zeit, VII:291
Neue Zeitschrift für Musik, VI:1992-1994
Neuf-Brisach, IV:1360
Neumann, Baltasar, IV:657
Neumann, John von, **VIII:2724-2727**
    Computer and the Brain, The, VIII:2726, 2727
    Mathematical Foundations of Quantum
        Mechanics, The, VIII:2725
    Theory of Games and Economic Behavior,
        VIII:2727
Neustria, II:242
neutrons
    Chadwick, VII:635-637
    Fermi, VII:1145, 1147
    Hahn, VIII:1514, 1515

Joliot-Curies, VIII:1871-1873
Kurchatov, VIII:2040
Lawrence, VIII:2121-2123
Teller, IX:3632
Yukawa, IX:4090
Nevelson, Louise, **VIII:2728-2731**
Atmosphere and Enviroment X, VIII:2730
Atmosphere and Enviroment XIII, VIII:2730
Canada Series I, VIII:2730
"Dawn's Wedding Feast," VIII:2729
Ice Palace I, VIII:2730
"Moon Garden + One," VIII:2729
Mrs. N's Palace, VIII:2730
Night Presense IV, VIII:2730
"Royal Tides, The," VIII:2730
"Royal Voyage, The," VIII:2729
Sky Cathedral, VIII:2729
Neville, Anne, III:649, 650
Neville, Richard. *See* Warwick, Earl of
Neville's Cross, Battle of, II:295
Nevsky, Alexander. *See* Alexander Nevsky
New Artists' Federation, VIII:2405
Newbery, John, IV:565, **1019-1021**
Little Pretty Pocket-Book, A, IV:1020
Tom Telescope, IV:1020
Newbery Award, IV:1021
Newcastle, Duke of, IV:447, 537, 539
New Christians, III:465
Newcomb, Simon, **VI:1638-1640**
New Comedy, Greek, I:88, 92, 538-540, 751, 845
Newcomen, Thomas, **IV:1022-1024,** 1061, 1409, 1411
New Deal
Altgeld, V:56
Butler, VII:525
Cardozo, VII:576, 577
Frankfurter, VII:1212
Harriman, VIII:1560
Hoover, VIII:1729, 1730
Humphrey, VIII:1783
Johnson, VIII:1866, 1868
Lippmann, VIII:2204
organized labor, VIII:2172
Reconstruction Finance Corporation, VIII:1729
Roosevelt, IX:3224, 3225
Stevenson, IX:3523
Supreme Court rulings, VII:321; IX:3548
Taft, IX:3591
Truman, IX:3740, 3742
New England Courant, The, IV:492
New England School for the Blind. *See* Perkins Institution

New England Woman's Club, V:1146
New England Woman Suffrage Association, V:1111
New Hampshire Grants, IV:34, 35
New Haven Railroad, VII:421, 422
New Industrial Cities Plan, VIII:1810
Newlands, John, VI:1532
Newman, John Henry, V:70; **VI:1641-1645,** 1829, 1830
Apologia Pro Vita Sua, VI:1643
Essay in Aid of a Grammar of Assent, An, VI:1643
Idea of a University Defined and Illustrated, The, VI:1643
New Mexico
Coronado, III:180
Fillmore, V:793
Gadsden Purchase, V:858-860
Hayden, V:1073
O'Keeffe, IX:2801
New Model Army, IV:378, 447, 1126-1128
New Orleans, Battle of, IV:889; V:1196
New Republic, The, VIII:2204; IX:4012
New South Church, V:351
newspapers
Azikiwe, VII:144
Beaverbrook, VII:234-237
Bennett, V:190-193
Bottomley, VII:382-385
Bryant, V:343-345
Dreiser, VII:954
Godkin, VIII:1400-1402
Greeley, V:982, 984-986
Harmsworths, VIII:1554-1556
Hearst, VIII:1601, 1603-1605
Herzen, V:1099, 1100
Mackenzie, VI:1447-1451
Nazi Germany, VIII:1405
O'Connor, IX:2793, 2794
political cartoons, VI:1627-1629
printing technology, VI:1541-1543
Pulitzer, VI:1825, 1826
Scripps, VI:2014-2016
Stamp Tax, VI:1788
Walter, VI:2324-2326
Newspaper Stamp Tax, VI:1788
New Statesman magazine, IX:3907
New Testament
Barth, VII:204, 205
Biddle, IV:126
Bonhoeffer, VII:360
Bultmann, VII:498-500

David, I:241
Erasmus, III:247
Harnack, VIII:1558
Hippolytus of Rome, I:416
Irenaeus, I:449, 450
John the Apostle, I:475, 477
John the Baptist, I:478-481
Luther, III:445
Paul, I:604-606
Peter, I:614-616
Pilate, I:640, 642
Renan, VI:1867
Ritschl, VI:1892-1894
Tertullian, I:849
Thomas, I:880, 882, 883
Tyndale, III:735, 737
Ulfilas, I:908
Wyclif, II:1009
Newton, Benjamin, V:668
Newton, Sir Isaac, **IV:1025-1029**
Berkeley, II:114
Boyle, IV:186, 187
Cavendish, IV:263
Dalton, V:602
De motu corporum in gyrum, IV:601
Fermat, IV:458-460
Halley, IV:600-602
Hawking, VIII:1583
Huygens, IV:697
Kepler, III:545
Kupka's painting, VIII:2037
Lagrange, IV:785, 786
law of inertia, II:195
Leibniz, IV:831
Maclaurin, IV:882-884
Mathematical Principles of Natural Philosophy,
IV:601, 602, 1027
Method of Fluxions and Infinite Series, The,
IV:215
Principia, IV:884
Smith, IV:1250
telescopes, IX:3351
New Wave cinema, VII:281; VIII:1391-1394;
IX:3159, 3736-3739
New York Age, VI:2337
New York Bureau of Municipal Research, VII:221
New York Central Railroad, VI:2298
New York City
Cabrini, V:388
Bernstein, VII:295, 296, 298
Bryant, V:344
Central Park, VI:1691, 1692

Columbia University, VII:527
engineering projects, VIII:1410
Free Synagogue, IX:4034
George, V:908
Gorky, VIII:1444
Hearst, VIII:1603
Henry Street Settlement, IX:3837-3839
Hughes, VIII:1766
Kent, VI:1278
La Guardia, VIII:2054-2056
school system, VII:524
Smith, IX:3439
Stuyvesant, IV:1296, 1297
Tammany Hall, V:513, 520; VI:2284-2287;
IX:3439, 3440
Tweed, VI:2284-2287
New York City Ballet, VII:158; IX:3607-3609,
4076, 4123
New York City Consumers' League, IX:2961
New York Committee on Safety, IX:2962
New York Customhouse, V:1076, 1078
New York Enquirer, V:191
New Yorker, The, VII:100, 567; IX:3677,
3678, 4012
New York *Evening Post,* V:343-345;
VIII:1400-1402
New York Herald, V:192, 193; VI:2101, 2102
New York Mirror, VI:1796
New York Open Theatre, IX:3642-3644
New York Philharmonic
Anderson, VII:70
Barber, VII:193
Bernstein, VII:295, 296
Boulez, VII:389
Mahler, VIII:2362
Poulenc, IX:3068
Thomas, VI:2231, 2232
Zwilich, IX:4123
New York Port Authority, VIII:1410
New York Psychoanalytic Society, VIII:1745
New York Review, V:343
New York Shakespeare Festival, VII:35
New York Society for Ethical Culture, V:26, 28, 29
New York State
Allen, IV:34-36
Arthur, V:77, 78, 80
Astor, V:82, 84
Beard, VII:222
Bennett's newspapers, V:190-193
Blaine, V:256
bridges, VI:1905
Brunel, V:339

Burr, V:369, 370
Chisholm, VII:670
Cleveland, V:512, 513
Clinton, V:517-521
Great Depression unemployment, VIII:1736
Harriman, VIII:1562
Hughes, VIII:1766
James II, IV:703
Jay, IV:711, 713, 714
Kent, VI:1277-1279
prison system, IX:2852-2854
Roosevelt, IX:3222, 3224
Root, IX:3234
Sanger, IX:3314
Stuyvesant, IV:1294, 1296, 1297
Zenger, IV:1484-1486
New York State Factory Commission, IX:2962
New York State Library School, V:661
New York State Prison Reform Commission,
    IX:2852
New York State Theater, VII:158
New York Stock Exchange, VIII:1472, 1473
New York *Sun,* V:192
New York Times, VI:2285; VII:35, 36; VIII:1400
New York Times v. Sullivan, VII:322
New York Times v. United States, VII:322, 511
New York Tribune, V:850, 852, 982, 984-986;
    VI:1542
New York v. United States, IX:3143
New York Weekly Gazette, IV:1484, 1485
New York Weekly Journal, IV:1484-1486
New York World, V:741; VI:1826; VIII:1601,
    2204
New York World's Fair of 1939-1940, VII:3, 1321
New York Woman's Temperance Society, V:62
New York Yankees, VII:934-937, 1322-1324;
    IX:3274-3276
New Zealand Company, V:722; VI:2322
Ney, Michel, **VI:1646-1649**
Nezahualcóyotl, III:378, **555-558**
Nezib, Battle of, VI:1606
Nez Perce War, V:1242, 1244, 1245
Ngengi, Kamau. *See* Kenyatta, Jomo
Ngo Dinh Diem, VIII:1701
Nguyen That Thanh. *See* Ho Chi Minh
Niagara Bridge, VI:1905
Niagara Movement, VII:964
Nicanor, I:768
Nicea, Council of
    Constantine the Great, I:376
    Easter, II:298, 299
    Eusebius of Caesarea, I:323

Gregory of Nyssa, I:352-354
Iconoclastic Controversy, II:546
Nicene Creed
    Ambrose, I:43-45
    Athanasius, I:119, 121, 122
    Constantine the Great, I:228, 376
    Gregory of Nyssa, I:353
    Theodosius the Great, I:869
    Theoleptus of Philadelphia, II:899
    Ulfilas, I:909
Nicephorus, II:437, 900
Nichiren, **II:666-668**
    *On the Establishment of the Orthodox Teaching
        and Peace of the Nation,* II:667
Nicholas I, **VI:1650-1653**
Nicholas II, VI:1790, 1791, 1842, 1844, 1845;
    VIII:1942
Nicholas III, II:682, 715, 716, 797
Nicholas V, III:9, **559-562,** 564, 741
Nicholas of Autrecourt, II:194, **669-672**
Nicholas of Cusa, III:560, **563-566**
    De coniecturis, III:564
    Of Learned Ignorance, III:564
Nicholas the Great, **II:673-676**
    Responsa Nicolai ad Consulta Bulgarorum,
        II:675
Nichols, Mike, VII:1084
Nicholson, Ben, **VIII:2732-2734**
    August 1956, VIII:2733
    1933, VIII:2732
    Vertical Seconds, VIII:2734
Nicias, I:31, 32
Nicklaus, Jack, IX:3041, 4050
Niclaes, Heinrich, IV:688
Nicolet, Jean, IV:732
Nicollet, Joseph Nicolas, V:839
Nicomedes IV, I:898, 899
Nicon, I:338
Nicopolis, battle of, II:457
Nicuesa, Diego de, III:45, 46
Niebuhr, Barthold Georg, **VI:1654-1656**
    Lectures on Ancient History, VI:1655
    Lectures on Roman History, VI:1655
    Roman History, The, VI:1655, 1839
Niebuhr, Reinhold, **VIII:2735-2738**
    Beyond Tragedy, VIII:2737
    Leaves of Notebook of Tamed Cynic, VIII:2735
    Nature and Density of Man, The, VIII:2737
Niemeyer, Oscar, **VIII:2739-2741**
Niemöller, Martin, **VIII:2742-2745**
Niépce, Isidore, V:594, 595
Niépce, Nicéphore, V:594, 595; **VI:1657-1661**

Nietzsche, Friedrich Wilhelm, **VI:1662-1666;**
    VI:1986, 2319; VIII:1611, 1650, 1651, 1920,
    2226
    Birth of Tragedy Out of the Spirit of Music, The,
        IV:1461; VI:1664
    Human, All Too Human, VI:1664
    Joyful Wisdom, The, VI:1665
    Thus Spake Zarathustra, VI:1664, 1665
    Will to Power, The, VI:1665
Nigerian Broadcasting Company, VII:13, 14
Nightingale, Florence, **VI:1667-1672,** 1732
Nijinska, Bronislawa, VII:921; VIII:2182, 2746
Nijinsky, Vaslav, VII:1178; VIII:2449, 2525,
    2746-2749
    Afternoon of a Faun, VIII:2748
    Don Giovanni, VIII:2746
    Petrushka, VIII:2748
    Rite of Spring, The, VIII:2748
    Specter of a Rose, VIII:2748
Nijmegen, Treaty of, IV:1447
Nijo Yoshimoto, II:1025
Nika Riots, II:554, 556, 892
Nikolayev, Andrian, IX:3639-3641
Nikon, **IV:1030-1033**
    Kormchaia Kniga, IV:1031
Nile, Battle of the, VI:1636
Nile River
    Bruce, IV:208-210
    Burton, V:375, 376
    Livingstone, VI:1400
    Sesostris, I:774, 776
    Speke, VI:2083-2085
Nimitz, Chester W., **VIII:2750-2753**
Nineteenth Amendment. *See* women's suffrage
Nineteenth Party Congress, VIII:2378, 2572
Nine Years' War, IV:1448, 1449
Nirmal Hriday Home for Dying Destitutes,
    IX:3636
Nisan, II:299
Nishida, Kitaro, **VIII:2754-2757**
    Art and Morality, VIII:2755
    Fundamental Problem of Philosophy,
        VIII:2755
    Hataraku-mono kara mirumono, VIII:2755
    Ippansha no jikakuteki taikei, VIII:2755
    Ishiki no mondai, VIII:2755
    Jikaku ni okeru chokkan to hansei, VIII:2755
    Mu no jikakuteki gentei, VIII:2755
    Study of Good, A, VIII:2754, 2755
    Tetsugaku rombunshu, VIII:2755
Nishida-Tanabe school of philosophy, VIII:2754
Nisibis, Peace of, I:778, 780

Nissim ben Jacob ben Nissim ibn Shahim,
    II:498, 499
Nitocris, I:709
Nixon, Edward, VII:9
Nixon, Richard M., **VIII:2758-2761**
    Armstrong, VII:112
    Burger, VII:509, 511
    Bush, VII:520, 521
    Clinton, VII:714
    Dole, VII:948
    Ellington, VII:1068
    enemy list, VII:675
    Ford, VII:1181, 1182
    Graham, VIII:1449
    Greenspan, VIII:1471
    Harriman, VIII:1563
    Hiss, VIII:1684, 1685
    Hoover, VIII:1733
    Humphrey, VIII:1785
    Israel, VII:856
    Kennedy, VIII:1930
    Kirkpatrick, VIII:1995
    Kissinger, VIII:1999, 2000
    Meir, VIII:2474
    Neruda, VIII:2718
    O'Neill, IX:2825
    Reagan, IX:3138
    Rehnquist, IX:3142
    Sato, IX:3338
    Smith, IX:3448
    Walters, IX:3870
    Watergate affair, VIII:1453, 1888
Nizam al-Mulk, II:67, 68, 70, 385, **677-680**
    Book of Government: Or, Rules for Kings, The,
        II:679
Nkomati Accord, VIII:2318
Nkomo, Joshua, VIII:2647-2649
Nkrumah, Kwame, **VIII:2762-2765**
Noah, Mordecai, V:191, 192
Nobel, Alfred, **VI:1673-1676,** 2175, 2177;
    IX:3456, 3457
Nobile, Umberto, VII:68
Nobilior, Fulvius, I:287, 288
Nobodaddy. *See* Urizen
Noche Triste, La, III:22, 190
Nodier, Charles, V:708
No drama, II:1025-1028; VIII:2552; IX:4082
Noland, Kenneth, VII:1209
non-Euclidean geometry, V:893-895
Nonintercourse Act of 1809, IV:888
Non-Proliferation Treaty of 1970, IX:3377
Non-Recognition Doctrine of 1932, IX:3538

nonviolent resistance
    Gandhi, VII:1282-1284
    King, VIII:1971, 1973, 1974
    Lutuli, VIII:2281-2283
    Luxemburg, VIII:2286
    Thoreau, VI:2235
    Tolstoy, VI:2245
    Tutu, IX:3775, 3776
Nootka Sound Crisis, IV:1103
Nordau, Max, **VIII:2766-2768**
    Conventional Lies of Our Civilization, The,
        VIII:2766, 2768
    Degeneration, VIII:2766, 2767
    Esencia de la Civilization, VIII:2768
    Interpretation of History, The, VIII:2767
    Morals and Evolution of Man, VIII:2768
    Paradoxes, VIII:2766
    Paris Sketches, VIII:2766
    Paris unter der Dritten Republik, VIII:2766
    Vom Kreml zur Alhambra, VIII:2766
Nordraak, Rikard, V:1002, 1003
Norfolk, Duke of, III:243, 316
Norgay, Tenzing. *See* Tenzing Norgay
Norge, VII:68
Noriega, Manuel, IX:3071
Norman, Jessye, **VIII:2769-2772**
    Carmen, VIII:2771
    Deborah, VIII:2770
    Diva, VIII:2771
    Troyens, Les, VIII:2770, 2771
Norman Conquest of 1066, II:201-204, 315-317,
        426, 428, 429, 997, 998, 1000
Normandy, Battle of, VIII:2603; IX:3215
North, Council of the, IV:1285, 1286
North, Lord, **IV:1034-1037**
    Burke, IV:223
    Fox, IV:479, 481
    George III, IV:541, 542
    Pitt the Younger, IV:1102, 1103
North American Free Trade Agreement
    Bush, VII:522
    Chrétien, VII:681
    Clinton, VII:709
    Mulroney, VIII:2656
    Nader, VIII:2681
North American Soccer League, IX:2952
North Atlantic Treaty Organization
    Acheson, VII:16-19
    Albright, VII:51
    Belgium, IX:3476
    Bevin, VII:316
    Boutros-Ghali, VII:400
    Eisenhower, VII:1043
    France, VII:1096
    Germany, VII:1017
    Luce, VIII:2257
    Montgomery, VIII:2603
    Nasser, VIII:2695
    Singapore, VIII:2151
    Taft, IX:3592
    Turkey, VIII:1814
Northcliffe, Lord, VII:74, 75, 235, 325
Northern Pacific Railway Company
    Hill, IV:660
    Cooke, V:552, 553
    Macdonald, VI:1438
    Morgan, VI:1581, 1582
    Sitting Bull, VI:2072
Northern Peoples Congress, VII:145
Northern Securities Company, IV:661
Northern Shoshone Indians, VI:1933-1935
Northern Sung Dynasty, II:479, 840, 867, 868,
        962, 963
Northern Virginia, Army of, VI:1340
Northern War, IV:509
North Ireland Partition, VII:878, 879
North Pole
    Amundsen, VII:66-68
    Byrd, VII:534, 535
    Davis, III:212
    Nansen, VIII:2687
    Peary, IX:2941, 2942, 2944, 2945
    Wilkins, IX:4001
North River Steamboat, The, V:856
Northumberland, Duke of, III:147, 206, 238, 239,
        318-320, 479; VI:1787
North West Company, IV:879-881; V:82, 84
Northwest Palace of Ashurbanipal II, I:110, 111
Northwest Passage
    Amundsen, VII:66-69
    Davis, III:212, 213
    Frobisher, III:278-280
    Hudson, IV:680-682
    Ross, VI:1907
    Vancouver, IV:1355, 1356
Nostradamus, **III:567-569**
    Centuries, III:567, 568
Notables, Assembly of, IV:964
Notre-Dame-du-Haut, Chapel, VIII:2138
Notre Dame organum, II:723
Nouveau, Germain, VI:1887
Nouveaux Cahiers, IX:3923
Nouvelle Vague. *See* New Wave cinema
Novak, Paul, IX:3951

Novgorod, II:52, 953; III:381, 382; IV:1030
Novotny, Antonin, VII:969
NOW. *See* National Organization for Women
No Water, V:574
Noy, William, IV:596
NSDAP. *See* Nazi Party
Nubian Dynasty, I:636-638, 774, 776
nuclear fission
    Hahn, VIII:1513-1516
    Kurchatov, VIII:2040
    McMillan, VIII:2336-2338
    Meitner, VIII:2476-2478
    Rabi, IX:3102
    Seaborg, IX:3375
nuclear physics
    Bethe, VII:300-303
    Bohr, VII:345, 347
    Broglie, VII:472-474
    Chadwick, VII:635-637
    Dali, VII:829
    Fermi, VII:1145, 1147, 1148
    Heisenberg, VIII:1617-1619
    Joliot-Curies, VIII:1870-1873
    Kapitsa, VIII:1906-1908
    Kennedy, VIII:1930
    Kurchatov, VIII:2039-2041
    Lawrence, VIII:2121-2123
    Meitner, VIII:2476-2478
    Neumann, VIII:2725, 2726
    Oppenheimer, IX:2833-2835
    Rutherford, IX:3277-3279
    Teller, IX:3631-3633
    Yukawa, IX:4090-4092
Nuclear Test Ban Treaty, VIII:2041; IX:2928
nuclear weapons
    Bethe, VII:300-303
    Bohr, VII:345, 347
    China, VIII:2190
    Comprehensive Test Ban Treaty, VII:51
    Gorbachev, VIII:1424
    Grass's novels, VIII:1464
    Hahn, VIII:1515
    Harriman, VIII:1562
    Khrushchev, VIII:1963
    Kissinger, VIII:1998-2000
    Kohl, VIII:2009
    Kurchatov, VIII:2039-2041
    Kurosawa's films, VIII:2044
    Lawrence, VIII:2121-2123
    McMillan, VIII:2336-2338
    Muller, VIII:2653
    Neumann, VIII:2725

Oppenheimer, IX:2833-2835
Pauling, IX:2928
Sakharov, IX:3296
Seaborg, IX:3377
Spock, IX:3479
Strategic Arms Limitation Treaty, VIII:2759
Teller, IX:3631-3633
    See also atom bomb; hydrogen bomb
nullification
    Adams, V:23
    Calhoun, V:395
    Scott, VI:2010
    Tyler, VI:2288, 2289
    Webster, VI:2345
Numantine Wars, I:345, 758
number theory
    Dedekind, V:639
    Fermat, IV:458-460
    Gauss, V:893-895
    Lagrange, IV:786
    Mersenne, IV:952
Numbers, Book of, I:563
Numerian, I:263
Numidia, I:529, 535, 536, 743
Nur al-Din, II:809, 810
Nuremberg Laws, IX:3491
Nurhachi, IV:1, 3, 421, 423
Nürnberg Trials, VIII:1438, 1440, 1463, 1696;
    IX:2878, 3262
Nuwar, Ali Abu, VIII:1793
NUWSS. *See* National Union of Women's
    Suffrage Societies
NWSA. *See* National Woman Suffrage Association
Nyerere, Julius, **VIII:2773-2776**
Nyssa, I:353, 354
Nystadt, Treaty of, IV:291, 1084

Oak Lane Country Day School, VII:673
Oakley, Annie, **VI:1677-1679;** VII:289
Oates, Titus, IV:285, **1038-1040**
O'Banion, Dion, VII:564
Oberth, Hermann, VII:440; VIII:1397;
    IX:2777-2780, 3751
    Menschen im Weltraum, IX:2779
    Rakete zu den Planetenräumen, Die, IX:2777
    Stoff und Leben, IX:2779
    Ways to Spaceflight, IX:2777
Oboi, IV:757
Obra de Berco, VIII:2739
Obregón, Álvaro, VII:542, 543; **IX:2780-2784**
Occasional Conformity Bill, IV:52
Occidental Literary Club, VII:880

Occitania, II:529, 530
Occoquan Workhouse Day, VII:850
Ockham, John of, II:669
Ockham, William of, II:194-196, **681-684,** 983
   Ad conditorem canonum, II:682
   Consultario de causa matrimoniali, II:683
   Cum inter nonnullos, II:682
   Dialogus, II:683
   Quia quorundam, II:682
   Quodlibeta septem, II:681
O'Connell, Daniel, V:652; **VI:1680-1683,** 1753
O'Connor, Flannery, **IX:2785-2788**
   Everything That Rises Must Converge, IX:2787
   Good Man Is Hard to Find and Other Stories, A,
     IX:2785
   Habit of Being, The, IX:2787
   Memoir of Mary Ann, A, IX:2787
   Mystery and Manners, IX:2787
   Presence of Grace, The, IX:2787
   Violent Bear It Away, The, IX:2787
   Wise Blood, IX:2785
O'Connor, Richard, V:147, 148
O'Connor, Sandra Day, **IX:2789-2792**
O'Connor, Thomas Power, **IX:2793-2795**
   Life of Lord Beaconsfield, IX:2793
Octavia, I:70
Octavian. *See* Augustus
Octavius, Marcus, I:346
October Revolution. *See* Russian Revolution of
   1917
Oda Nobuhide, IV:1327
Oda Nobunaga, **III:570-573,** 728, 1327
Oddi, II:836
Odets, Clifford, VII:795
Odoacer, **II:685-687**
Odo of Lagery. *See* Urban II
Odovacar, II:894, 895
Odria, Manuel A., VIII:1586
Odysseus, I:421, 422
Oecolampadius, Johannes, III:675
Oersted, Hans Christian, V:768
Offa, II:46
Offenbach, Jacques, **VI:1684-1687,** 2156, 2158
   Ba-ta-clan, VI:1685
   Belle Hélène, La, VI:1686
   Bonne d'enfants, La, VI:1685
   Contes d'Hoffmann, Les, V:650; VI:1686
   Deux Pêcheurs, Les, VI:1685
   Geneviève de Brabant, VI:1686
   Musiciens de l'orchèstre, Les, V:651
   Orphée aux enfers, VI:1685, 1686
   Papillon, Le, VI:1686

Offeros. *See* Christopher, Saint
Official Languages Act of 1969, IX:3732
Ogala tribe, VI:1850
Ogaryov, Nikolay, V:1099, 1100
Ogatai Khan, II:378
Ogata Korin, **IV:1041, 1042,** 1258, 1259
   Irises, IV:1041, 1042
   Red and White Plum Blossoms, IV:1041
Ogdensburg Agreement, VIII:1983
Ogé, Vincent, IV:1338
Oglala Indians, V:574-576
Oglethorpe, James Edward, **IV:1043-1047**
Oh, Sadaharu, **IX:2796-2799**
Ohain, Hans von, IX:3974
O'Hara, Maureen, IX:3903
O'Hickey, Michael, VI:1481
O'Higgins, Bernardo, **VI:1688-1691**
Ohio
   Appleseed, V:66-68
   Beecher, V:171
   Chase, V:477, 478
   Glenn, VII:1387, 1388
   Hanna, V:1030
   Harding, VIII:1550-1552
   Hayes, V:1075, 1076
   Honda Motor Company, VIII:1725
   newspapers, VI:2015
   Taft, IX:3590, 3591
   Williams, VI:2397
Ohio Company, IV:312
Ohio Indians, IV:198
oil industry
   Arab oil embargo, VII:1120
   Canada, IX:3733
   Cárdenas, VII:571-573
   Faisal, VII:1119, 1120
   Mellon, VIII:2481
   Mohammad Reza Shah Pahlavi, VIII:2566, 2567
   OPEC, VII:591, 1115, 1116, 1119;
     IX:4079-4081
   Rockefeller, VI:1896-1898
Oisc, I:380, 381
Ojeda, Alonzo de, III:45
Ojibwe Indians, VI:1585
O.K. Corral, V:736
O'Keeffe, Georgia, **IX:2800-2803,** 3534
   Barn with Snow, IX:2801
   Black Patio Door, IX:2801
   Cow's Skull: Red, White and Blue, IX:2801
   Pelvis with Moon, IX:2801
   Ram's Head with Hollyhock, IX:2801
   Ranchos Church, IX:2801

Shelton with Sunspots, The, IX:2801
Sky Above Clouds II, IX:2801
Stables, IX:2801
Okehazama, Battle of, III:570
O'Kelly, Seán T., **IX:2804-2807**
Okubo Toshimichi, VI:1936-1938
Olaf, Saint, II:201, 626, **691-694,** 837
Olaf I, **II:688-690,** 691
Olaf II. *See* Olaf, Saint
Olbers, Wilhelm, V:215
Old Age Pensions Act of 1898, VI:2018
Oldcastle, Sir John, III:338
Old Corps Whigs, IV:1074, 1075
Oldenbarnevelt, Johan van, **III:574-576**
Old Slater Mill, VI:2075
Old Testament
    Aaron, I:1-4
    Abraham, I:5-7
    Athanasius, I:12
    Cædmon, II:198, 199
    Channing, V:471
    Clement I, I:210
    Cyrus the Great, I:234
    David, I:241-244
    Deborah, I:246, 247
    Eusebius of Caesarea, I:323
    Ezekiel, I:326-329
    Ezra, I:330-333
    Irenaeus, I:449
    Isaiah, I:452-454
    Jesus Christ, I:468
    Moses, I:561-564
    Nebuchadnezzar II, I:569-571
    Origen, I:581
    Philo of Alexandria, I:632-634
    Porphyry, I:685
    Pusey, VI:1828, 1829
    Samuel, I:746, 748, 749
    Solomon, I:798, 800, 801
    Tertullian, I:849
    Tyndale, III:735, 737
Olduvai Gorge, VIII:2146, 2147
Olgierd. *See* Algirdas
O'Leary, John, VI:1740
Oliva, Treaty of, IV:508, 509
Olivares, Count-Duke of, IV:1364
Olive Branch petition, IV:617
Oliver, Andrew, IV:692, 693
Oliver, King, VII:105, 106
Olivier, Sir Laurence, **IX:2808-2814**
    Antony and Cleopatra, IX:2811
    As You Like It, IX:2810

    Carrie, IX:2811, 2812
    Hamlet, IX:2810, 2811, 3872
    Henry V, IX:2810, 2811, 3872
    Julius Caesar, IX:2808
    King Lear, IX:2811, 2813
    Macbeth, IX:2810, 2812
    Midsummer Night's Dream, A, IX:2808
    Othello, IX:2810, 2813
    Richard III, IX:2812, 3872
    Romeo and Juliet, IX:2808, 2810
    Taming of the Shrew, The, IX:2808
    Titus Andronicus, IX:2812
    Twelfth Night, IX:2808, 2810, 2812
Ollokot, V:1244
Olmstead v. United States, VII:422
Olmsted, Frederick Law, **VI:1691-1694;**
    VIII:1400, 1401
    Cotton Kingdom, The, VI:1691
Olod Mongols, IV:758
Olomouc, Peace of, III:488
Olympia, V:657
Olympian religion, I:507
Olympics
    Alcmaeon, I:34
    Ali, VII:53
    Coe, VII:725-728
    Coubertin, VII:774-776
    Didrikson, IX:4096, 4097
    Henie, VIII:1629-1631
    Killy, VIII:1965-1967
    Laban, VIII:2059
    Nero, I:579
    Nervi, VIII:2722
    Owens, IV:2862-2865
    Pheidippides, I:622, 623
    Pindar, I:644
    Russell, IX:3270
    Thorpe, IX:3672, 3674, 3675
    Tokyo, IX:3337
    Wightman, IX:3990
Olynthus, I:629
Omaha Magic Theatre, IX:3643, 3644
Omaha tribe, IX:3010, 3011
Omai, IV:353
O'Malley, Walter, IX:3196
Omar Khayyám, II:419, **695-697,** 801
Omega Point, IX:3628
Omega Workshops, VII:1254
OMGUS. *See* Military Government of the United
    States, Office of
Onassis, Aristotle, IX:2817
Onassis, Jacqueline Kennedy, **IX:2815-2818,** 3870

oncology. *See* cancer
O'Neill, Eugene, **IX:2819-2824**
    All God's Chillun Got Wings, IX:3189
    Desire Under the Elms, IX:2820
    Emperor Jones, The, IX:2819, 2820; IX:3189
    Hairy Ape, The, IX:2820
    Iceman Cometh, The, VIII:1445; IX:2821, 2822
    Long Day's Journey Into Night, VIII:1639;
       VII:281; IX:2822
    More Stately Mansions, IX:2820
    Mourning Becomes Electra, IX:2820
    Part of a Long Story, IX:2820
    Straw, The, IX:2819
    Tale of Possessors Self-Dispossessed, A,
       IX:2820
    Haunted, The, IX:2820
    Thirst, IX:2820
    Touch of the Poet, A, IX:2820
O'Neill, Thomas Philip, Jr., VII:88; **IX:2824-2826**
Oort, Jan Hendrik, **IX:2827-2828**
Oparin, Aleksandr Ivanovich, **IX:2830-2832**
    Origin of Life, The, IX:2831
OPEC. *See* Petroleum Exporting Countries,
    Organization of
Open Theatre, IX:3642-3644
opera
    Anderson, VII:70-72
    Barber, VII:191-193
    Berg, VII:272
    Berlioz, V:205
    Bizet, V:244-246
    Borodin, V:286-288
    Britten, VII:466, 468-471
    Caruso, VII:598-601
    Debussy, VII:884-886
    Delibes, V:649-651
    Delius, VII:893
    Donizetti, V:684-686
    Gluck, IV:549-551
    Henze, VIII:1633-1635
    Hindemith, VIII:1670-1672
    Humperdinck, V:1162-1164
    Janáček, VIII:1837, 1838
    Menotti, VIII:2494-2496
    Messiaen, VIII:2503-2505
    Milhaud, VIII:2526, 2527
    Monteverdi, IV:990-993
    Norman, VIII:2769-2771
    Offenbach, VI:1684-1687
    Pavarotti, IX:2930-2932
    Price, IX:3081, 3083, 3084
    Puccini, IX:3093, 3094, 3096
    Purcell, IV:1137-1139
    Rameau, IV:1149
    Ravel, IX:3129
    Rimsky-Korsakov, VI:1889-1891
    Rossini, VI:1913-1915
    Scarlatti, IV:1213-1215
    Schütz, IV:1221-1223
    Strauss, IX:3556
    Stravinsky, IX:3561
    Telemann, IV:1319, 1320
    Verdi, VI:2299-2301
    Wagner, VI:2316, 2317, 2319
    Weber, VI:2340-2342
    Weill, IX:3926-3929
Operation Breadbasket, VIII:1824-1826
Operation People United to Save Humanity,
    VIII:1825, 1826
operetta
    Gilbert and Sullivan, V:927-930
    Offenbach, VI:1684-1687
    Strauss, VI:2155, 2156, 2158
Opet Festival, I:734
Opium War, V:1166; VI:1376-1379
Oppenheimer, J. Robert, **IX:2833-2835**
    Bethe, VII:301
    Bohr, VII:347
    Conant, VII:750
    Fermi, VII:1147
    Lawrence, VIII:2122, 2123
    Neumann, VIII:2726
    Rabi, IX:3102
    Teller, IX:3632, 3633
Oppian Law, I:163
Oprichnina, III:387
Oran, Battle of, V:1
Orange, House of, IV:500-502, 1447-1449
oratorios
    Neri, III:552
    Telemann, IV:1321
    Thomas, VI:2231
    Elgar, VII:1052
    Henze, VIII:1634
    Walton, IX:3873
Oratory, Congregation of the, III:551-553
Orcagna, Andrea, **II:698-701**
    Christ Conferring Authority on Saints Peter and
       Thomas Aquinas, II:698
Ordinatio Imperii, II:599
Ordóñez, Bartholome, III:696
Ordóñez, García, II:269
Oregon Trail, V:839, 840; VI:1735, 1738, 2078
Orestes, I:437; II:685

Organic Act of 1902, IX:3233
organic chemistry
    Conant, VII:749
    Diels, VII:927-929
    Hahn, VIII:1513-1516
    Liebig, VI:1366-1368
    Mendeleyev, VI:1530
    Wöhler, VI:2403-2405
    Woodward, IX:4052-4055
Oribasius, I:261; II:712
Origen, I:416, **581-584**; II:995
    Against Celsus, I:323, 583
    Hexapla, I:582
    On First Principles, I:582
    On Prayer, I:583
    Tetrapla, I:582
Orisun Theatre group, IX:3472
Orléans, Charles d'. *See* Charles d'Orléans
Orléans, Duc d', IV:813, **1048-1051**
Orlov, Count Grigory, IV:257, 259
Ormonde, second Duke of, IV:1277, 1278
Orozco, José Clemente, **IX:2836-2839**
    Catharsis, IX:2838
    Coming of Quetzalcoatl, The, IX:2838
    Cortes and Malinche, IX:2837
    Dive Bomber, IX:2838
    House of Tears, IX:2836, 2837
    Man of Fire, IX:2838, 2839
    Omniscience, IX:2837
    Prometheus, IX:2837, 2838
    Return of Quetzalcoatl, The, IX:2838
    Social Revolution, IX:2837
    Sorrows of War, IX:2837
    Trench, The, IX:2837
    Zapatistas, IX:2838
Orphans Fund of the City of London, IV:1067
Orpheus, myth of, IV:961; VI:1685
Orphic Mysteries, I:67
Orphism, VII:889; VIII:2037
Orsini, Giordano, III:563
Ortega, Katherine Davalos, **IX:2840-2842**
Ortega y Gasset, José, **IX:2843-2845**
    Dehumanization of Art and Notes on the Novel,
      The, IX:2844
    Invertebrate Spain, IX:2843, 2844
    Meditations on Quixote, IX:2843
    Mission of the University, IX:2844
    Modern Theme, The, IX:2843
    On Love, IX:2844
    Revista de Occidente, La, IX:2843
    Revolt of the Masses, The, IX:2844
    Toward a Philosophy of History, IX:2844

Ortiz, Juan, III:700
Ortodoxo Party, VII:617
Orwell, George, **IX:2846-2851**
    Animal Farm, IX:2849, 2850
    Burmese Days, IX:2848
    Clergyman's Daughter, A, IX:2849
    Coming Up for Air, IX:2849
    Down and Out in London and Paris, IX:2848
    Homage to Catalonia, IX:2849
    "How the Poor Die," IX:2848
    Keep the Aspidistra Flying, IX:2849
    Nineteen Eighty-Four, IX:2849, 2850
    Road to Wigan Pier, The, IX:2849
Osage Nation, IX:3607, 3608
Osborne, Thomas. *See* Leeds, First Duke of
Osborne, Thomas Mott, **IX:2852-2854**
Osceola, **VI:1695-1697**
O'Shea, William Henry, VI:1740, 1742
Osiander, Andreas, III:178
Osler, Sir William, **VI:1698-1701**
    Principles and Practice of Medicine, VI:1698,
      1699
Oslo Peace Accords, VII:93
Osman, **II:702-705**
Osorio, Elena, IV:1361
Ospedale degli Innocenti, III:91
Ossining Correctional Facility, IX:2853
Ossoli, Giovanni Angelo, V:850, 852
Ostend Manifesto, V:583
Ostpolitik, VII:428; VIII:2009
Ostrogoths, II:215, 555, 755, 894-897
Ostwald, Wilhelm, V:924; VII:114; **IX:2855-2858**
    Scientific Foundations of Analytical Chemistry,
      IX:2856
Osuna, Duchess of, IV:148
Otakar II, II:797, 798
Otis, James, IV:691, 692
Otlet, Paul, VIII:2051, 2052
Otluk Beli, Battle of, III:51
Otric of Magdeburg, II:870
Öttingen, Arthur von, IX:2855
Otto I. *See* Otto the Great
Otto II, II:870
Otto III, II:449, 871
Otto IV, II:468, 510, 797
Otto, Nikolaus August, V:597; **VI:1702-1704**
Ottoboni, Cardinal Pietro, IV:360
Otto of Brunswick, II:542
Otto of Burgundy, II:798
Otto the Great, II:**706-708,** 869
Ottowa Indians, IV:513, 1110-1113
Oubangui-Chari, VII:1004, 1005

Oud, J.J.P., **IX:2859-2861**
Oudenarde, Battle of, IV:923, 924
Oudh, IV:632, 633; VI:1706
Our Lady of Mount Carmel, Order of. *See*
    Carmelites
Our Lady of Ransom, Order of. *See* Mercedarians
Outram, Sir James, **VI:1705-1707**
Ou-yang Hsui, **II:709-711**
    Hsin T'ang shu, II:710
    Hsin Wu-tai shih, II:709
Ovando, Nicolás de, III:174, 629
Overreach, Sir Giles, VI:1261
Ovetari Chapel, III:460, 461
Ovett, Steve, VII:726, 727
Ovid, **I:585-588**
    Amores, I:586; III:473
    Art of Love, I:586
    Metamorphoses, I:586, 587; IV:1118
Ovidian elegies, IV:416-419
Owen, Robert, V:402, **VI:1708-1710**
Owens, Jesse, **IX:2862-2866**
Oxenstierna, Axel, IV:304, **1052-1054**
Oxford, Provisions of, II:644, 645
Oxford Economic Society, VIII:1707
Oxford University
    Arnold, V:69-71
    Bodleian Library, III:62-64
    Burney, IV:227
    Conant, VII:749
    Green, V:988
    Heath, VIII:1606
    Hobhouse, VIII:1707, 1708
    Locke, IV:854, 855
    Mackinder, VIII:2321, 2322
    Macmillan, VIII:2340
    Neckham, II:663
    Wesley, IV:1426
    Wyclif, II:1009, 1011
Ozawa, Jisaburo, VIII:1527
Ozenfant, Amédée, VIII:2137

Pace Gallery, VIII:2730
Pacelli, Eugenio Maria Giuseppe. *See* Pius XII
Pachacuti, **III:577-579**
Pacheco, Francisco, IV:1364
Pacific Islands, VIII:1658-1660
Pacific Ocean
    Balboa, III:45-47
    Ballard, VII:181
    Dampier, IV:389
    Drake, III:225
    Mackenzie, IV:879-881
    Magellan, III:453-456
    Wegener, IX:3919
Pacific Railway Company. *See* Northern Pacific
    Railway Company
pacifism. *See* nonviolent resistance
Paderhorn, Diet of, II:973
Padua, University of
    Abano, II:2
    Fracastoro, III:270
    Harvey, IV:626
    Nicholas of Cusa, III:563
    Santorio, IV:1209, 1210
    Vesalius, III:754, 755
Páez, Jose Antonio, V:268
Paganini, Niccolò, **VI:1711-1714**
    Violin Caprice in A Minor, IX:3106
paganism
    Abraham, I:5
    Ambrose, I:44
    Assyria, I:459
    Bulgaria, II:175, 176
    Germany, II:167-169
    Gregory of Nyssa, I:352
    Helena, I:375, 376
    Lithuania, II:1001
    Siricius, I:791
    Stephen I, II:851, 853
    Tertullian, I:848
    Theodosius the Great, I:869, 871
    Widukind, II:974
    See also Neoplatonism
Page, William, V:294
Pagspa, II:566
Paine, Thomas, II:921; **IV:1055-1058;** V:523
    Age of Reason, The, IV:440, 1056
    Case of the Officers of the Excise, The, IV:1055
    Common Sense, IV:16, 1055, 1057
    Crisis papers, IV:1055, 1057
    Dissertations on Government, IV:1056
    Public Good, The, IV:1056
    Rights of Man, The, II:921; IV:440, 556, 1056;
      VI:2208
Paiva, Afonso de, III:197, 198
Palafox, José de, VI:1958, 1959
Palais Royal, IV:1048, 1049
Palatinate, IV:212
Palatine Palace, II:823
Palazzetto dello Sport, VIII:2722
Palermo Stone, I:547
Palestine
    Baeck, VII:150
    Balfour, VII:174

Begin, VII:243-245
Ben-Gurion, VII:251, 252
Bevin, VII:315
Dayan, VII:854-856
Eban, VII:1000
Faisal, VIII:1118-1120
Herzl, V:1105
Hussein I, VIII:1791, 1793-1795
Lawrence, VIII:2126, 2127
Meir, VIII:2472-2475
Mendelsohn, VIII:2488
Nasser, VIII:2695, 2696
Psamtik I, I:711
United Nations, VII:91, 502; VIII:2473
World Zionist Organization, VIII:2766-2768;
    IX:3930-3932
Palestine Liberation Organization
    Arafat, VII:90-93
    Begin, VII:245
    Dayan, VII:855
    Fahd, VII:1115
    Faisal, VIII:1120
    Hussein I, VIII:1793, 1794
    Meir, VIII:2474
    Nasser, VIII:2696
    Pérez de Cuéllar, IX:2957, 2958
Palestrina, Giovanni Pierluigi da, III:107
Palladianism, IV:8, 9, 637; V:139
Palladio, Andrea, **III:580-583;** IV:8, 152
    antichità di Roma, L', III:580
    commentari di C. Givlio Cesare, I, III:580
    quattro libri dell'architettura, I, III:580, 581
Palladius, I:602
Pallavicino, Benedetto, IV:990, 991
Palmer, Alice Freeman, **VI:1715-1718**
Palmer, A. Mitchell, VIII:1732
Palmer, Arnold, IX:3041
Palmer, Humphrey, IV:1423
Palmer, Potter S., V:783
Palmer, William, V:1012, 1013
Palmerston, Lord, V:528, 654; **VI:1719-1722,**
    1931, 2003, 2308
Palomar, Mount, IX:3352
Pamphia, I:539
Pamphili, Cardinal, IV:360
Pamphilus, I:322; IV:684
Pampulha, Lake, VIII:2739
Pan, I:539, 621
Pan Africanism
    Du Bois, VII:965
    Lutuli, VIII:2282
    Mobutu Sese Seko, VIII:2562-2564

Nkrumah, VIII:2762, 2763
Nyerere, VIII:2774
Tshombe, IX:3745
Panama Canal
    Goethals, VIII:1408-1410
    Gorgas, VIII:1435, 1436
    Hay, V:1069, 1070
    Lesseps, VI:1355-1357
    Taylor, VI:2196
Panathenaea, I:649
Pandora, I:404
Pandit, Vijaya Lakshmi, **IX:2867-2870**
Paneth, Friedrich, VIII:1654
Pangaea, IX:3919
Panhellenic League, I:501
Pan-Islamism, VII:1081; VIII:2694
Pankhurst, Emmeline, **IX:2871-2875**
Pankhurst, Richard, IX:2871
Pan Ku, **I:589-592**
    Han shu, I:589-591
Pannonia, II:41, 87
Pantheon, I:21
Pan-Turkism, VII:1081
Paoli, General, IV:175
PAP. See Partido Aprista Peruano
Papal Curia, II:930
Papal States
    Alexander VI, III:14-17
    Alva, III:19
    Canova, V:410
    Charlemagne, II:228
    Innocent III, II:510
    Italian nationalism, V:933
    Julius II, III:405-407
    Leo IX, II:582
    Mazzini, VI:1515
    Nicholas V, III:559, 560
    Paul III, III:597
    Pius IX, VI:1782, 1783
    Pius XI, IX:3026
Papen, Franz von, **IX:2876-2879**
Paperclip, Operation, VII:441
Paper Constitution of 1244, II:453
Paphlagonia, I:558
Papin, Denis, **IV:1059-1061**
Pappus, **I:593-595**
    Collection, I:73, 74, 593
Paracelsus, **III:584-587;** IV:187
    Against the Grain, III:585
    Great Astronomy, III:585
    Great Surgery Book, III:585
    Opus paramirum, III:585

Paramount Pictures, VII:117, 119, 896, 897, 932; VIII:1415; IX:3950

Paravas, III:789

Parentucelli, Tommaso. *See* Nicholas V

Pareto, Vilfredo, IX:3866

Paria, Le, VIII:1699

Paris

    Blanc, V:261

    Boffrand, IV:151

    Cambacérès, V:399

    Chanel's fashions, VII:650

    Chopin, V:493-495

    Cyrano de Bergerac, IV:385

    Hammerstein, VIII:1534

    Hardouin-Mansart, IV:901-903

    Mansart, IV:898

    Mazarin, IV:946

    Napoleon III, VI:1620-1622

    Olympic Games, VII:775, 776

    Picasso, IX:2997, 2998

    skyscrapers, VIII:2137

    Toulouse-Lautrec, VI:2247-2250

    World Exhibition of 1867, VII:268

    World's Fair of 1937, IX:3252

Paris, Peace of, II:454, 957

Paris, Treaty of:

    1259, II:605, 606

    1783, IV:39, 314, 713, 926

    1856, V:49

    1898, VI:1455; VII:480

Paris Commune, V:113; VI:1819, 2228

Parisian Geographical Society, VI:1356

Paris Observatory, VII:837, 838, 1326

Paris Opéra, VIII:2182-2184, 2504

Paris Peace Conference of 1919, VIII:2052, 2221

Park, Mungo, **VI:1723-1726**

    Travels in the Interior of Africa, VI:1724

Parker, Charlie, VII:1370, 1371; **IX:2880-2883**

    "Cherokee" IX:2882

    "Yardbird Suite" IX:2882, 2883

Parker, Dorothy, **IX:2884-2887**

    Coast of Illyria, The, IX:2886

    Ladies of the Corridor, IX:2886

    Portable Dorothy Parker, The, IX:2886

    "Soldiers of the Republic," IX:2886

    Star is Born, A, IX:2886

Parker, Matthew, **III:588-591**

Parker, Theodore, **VI:1727-1730**

Parker, Colonel Tom, IX:3076, 3078

Parkes, Sir Henry, **VI:1731-1734**

    Stolen Moments, VI:1731

Park Güell, VII:1316

Parkinson, Sydney, IV:83

Parkman, Francis, **VI:1735-1739**

    Book of Roses, The, VI:1738

    California and Oregon Trail, The, VI:1735, 1738, 1862

    Count Frontenac and New France Under Louis XIV, VI:1736

    Discovery of the Great West, The, VI:1736, 1737

    France and England in North America, VI:1735, 1736, 1739

    Half-Century of Conflict, A, VI:1736, 1738

    History of the Conspiracy of Pontiac, VI:1736

    Jesuits in North America in the Seventeenth Century, The, VI:1736

    Montcalm and Wolfe, VI:1736

    Old Regime in Canada, The, VI:1736

    Vassall Morton, VI:1736

Parks, Rosa, VII:9; VIII:1973; **IX:2888-2891**

Parliament, English

    Attlee, VII:137

    Blackstone, IV:130

    Bolingbroke, IV:158, 160

    Bottomley, VII:384

    Buckingham, IV:212, 213

    Burke, IV:222-224

    Catholic emancipation, VI:1681-1683

    Chadwick, V:457-460

    Charles I, IV:279-281

    Churchill, VII:691-693

    Clarendon, IV:308, 309

    Clive, IV:325, 327

    Cobbett, V:523, 524

    Cromwell, IV:378, 380, 381

    East India Company, IV:631, 633

    Edward I, II:322-324

    Edward II, II:326-328

    Edward III, II:329, 331

    Edward IV, III:234, 235

    English Civil War, IV:99

    Fairfax, IV:446-449

    Fortescue, III:267-269

    George III, IV:541

    George IV, V:902-905

    Gladstone, V:935, 936, 938

    Gundpowder Plot, III:257-259

    Hale, IV:597

    Henry IV, II:457-460

    James I, IV:700

    James II, IV:704, 705

    Johnson, IV:728

    Lambert, IV:789-791

    Leeds, IV:822

Liverpool, VI:1395

Macaulay, VI:1427-1430

Merciless Parliament, II:787

Monck, IV:971-973

Montfort, II:643-646

Oglethorpe, IV:1043

Paterson, IV:1066-1068

Pelham, IV:1074-1076

Place, VI:1788

Pugin, VI:1823

Pym, IV:1141-1143

Shaftesbury, IV:1228-1231

Strafford, IV:1285-1288

Walpole's architecture, V:138-140

Webb, IX:3908

Wilson, IV:1456-1459

    See also Commons, House of; Lords, House of

Parliament, French. *See* National Assembly
    (France)

Parliament Act of 1911, VII:122, 123; VIII:2112;
    IX:2804

Parma, Cathedral of, III:186

Parma, Duchess of, III:781

Parma, Duke of, III:255, 256

Parmenides, I: 249-251,**596-599**, 972

    Aletheia, I:597

    Doxa, I:597

    Peri physeos, I:596

Parmenio, I:40

Parnassus, VI:1334, 1336

Parnell, Charles Stewart, **VI:1740-1743;**
    VIII:1891; IX:2793, 2871, 2873

Parr, Catherine, III:194, 237, 241, **592-594**

    Lamentation or Complaynt of a Sinner, A,
        III:594

    Prayers and Meditations, III:594

Parrington, Vernon L., **IX:2892-2895**

    Main Currents in American Thought,
        IX:2892-2895

Parry, Caleb, IV:721, 722

Parry, William Edward, VI:1907

Parsees, I:977

Parson's Cause of 1763, IV:647

Parsua, I:236

Parsva, I:916

Parthenon, I:609, 624-626

Parthia, I:64, 70, 159, 882, 901, 902

Parti Démocratique de Guinée, IX:3711-3713

Parti Démocratique de la Côte d'Ivoire,
    VIII:1754-1756

Partido Aprista Peruano, VIII:1585, 1586

Partido Komunistang Pilipinas, VIII:2421

Partido Nacional Revolucionario, VII:543, 544

Partindo, VIII:1577

Partisan Review, The, VIII:2304

Parti Socialiste Français, V:1222

Parton, Dolly, **IX:2896-2898**

    Best Little Whorehouse in Texas, The, IX:2897

    Coat of Many Colors, IX:2897

    Dumb Blonde, IX:2896

    Here You Come Again, IX:2896

    My Tennessee Mountain Home, IX:2897

    Nine to Five, IX:2896, 2897

    Rhinestone, IX:2897

    Something Fishy, IX:2896

    Steel Magnolias, IX:2897

    Straight Talk, IX:2897

    Trio, IX:2897

    Wild Texas Wind, IX:2897

Partridge, John, IV:1307

Pascal, Blaise, IV:952, **1062-1065**

    Pensées, IV:1063

    Provincial Letters, The, IV:1062

Paschal II, II:74, 823

Paschal III, II:359

Paschasius, II:773, 774

Passerini, Silvio, III:743

Pasternak, Boris, **IX:2899-2902,** 3754, 3755

    Above the Barriers, IX:2899

    Blind Beauty, The, IX:2901

    Doctor Zhivago, IX:2900, 2901

    I Remember, IX:2901

    My Sister, Life, IX:2899

    On Early Trains, IX:2900

    Safe Conduct, IX:2900

    Second Birth, IX:2900

    Spektorsky, IX:2900

    Vastness of Earth, The, IX:2900

    When the Skies Clear, IX:2901

Pasteur, Louis, VI: 1317,**1744-1748**

Pasteur Institute, VII:546-548

Pastors, Company of, III:118

Pastors' Emergency League, VIII:2743

Patel, Vallabhbhai, Jhaverbhai, **IX:2903-2906**

Pater, Walter, **VI:1749-1751,** 2377

    Marius the Epicurean, VI:1750

    Studies in the History of the Renaissance,
        VI:1749

Paterson, William, **IV:1066-1069**

Paton, Alan, **IX:2907-2910**

    Ah, but Your Land Is Beautiful, IX:2909

    Cry the Beloved Country, IX:2908, 2909

    For You Departed, IX:2909

    Journey Continued, IX:2909

Long View, The, IX:2909
Too Late the Phalarope, IX:2908, 2909
Towards the Mountain, IX:2909
Patrick, Saint, **I:600-603**
   Confession, I:600
   Epistle to the Soldiers of Coroticus, I:600, 602
Patriotic Front, VIII:2647, 2648
Patriot King, IV:160
Patterson, Floyd, VII:54
Patton, George S., VII:403, 404; **IX:2911-2914**
Pau Casals Orchestra, VII:607
Paul, Saint, **I:604-608**
   Abraham, I:7
   Chrysostom, I:184
   Clement I, I:210
   Epicurus, I:297
   Ezekiel, I:329
   letter to the Romans, VII:204, 499
   Peter, I:615
   Renan, VI:1866
   Stephen, I:823, 824
Paul I (Russian Czar), V:44
Paul I (Pope), IV:260, 1300
Paul III (Pope), III:152, 160, 519, **595-598,** 788
Paul IV (Pope), IV:583
Paul VI (Pope), II:221; III:715; VI:2031;
   VIII:1863; **IX:2915-2918**
   Human Vitae, IX:2916
   Sacerdotalis Caelibatus, IX:2917
Paul, Alice, **IX:2919-2922**
Paulesco, Nicolas, VII:189
Paulhan, Jean, VII:1074, 1075
Pauli, Wolfgang, **IX:2923-2925**
Pauling, Linus, VII:412; **IX:2926-2929,** 3655,
   3898, 3996, 3997
   Cancer and Vitamin C, IX:2928
   *Nature of the Chemical Bond and the Sructure of
     Molecules and Crystals,* IX:2927
   Vitamin C and the Common Cold, IX:2928
Paulinus, Suetonius, I:136-138
Paul of Aegina, **II:712-714**
   Epitome, II:712, 713
Paul the Deacon, I:931
Paulus, Lucius Aemilius, I:335, 757
Pausanius, I:677, 691, 764
Pavarotti, Luciano, **IX:2930-2932**
   Bohème, La, IX:2930, 2931
   Fille du régiment, La, IX:2931
   Three Tenors in Rome, IX:2931
Pavia, Battle of, III:159, 274
Pavia, Council of, II:48
Pavlov, Ivan Petrovich, **IX:2933-2936**

Pavlova, Anna, **IX:2937-2940**
   Autumn Leaves, IX:2939
   Dumb Girl of Portici, The, IX:2939
   Giselle, IX:2939
   Immortal Swan, The, IX:2939
Pavlovich, Nikolay. *See* Nicholas I
Pawnee Indians, IV:1096
Pax Romana, I:134, 585
Payne-Aldrich Tariff Act, IX:3596
Pazzi Chapel, III:91, 92
Pazzi conspiracy, III:496
PDCI. *See* Parti Démocratique de la Côte
   d'Ivoire
Peace, University of, IX:3018
Peace River, IV:880
Peacham, Edmund, IV:332
Peachtree Creek, battle of, V:1053
Peacock Throne, IV:1233, 1234
Peale, Charles Willson, **IV:1070-1073**
Peano, Giuseppe, IX:3966
Pearl Harbor attack
   Beard, VII:224
   Halsey, VIII:1525
   Lewis, VIII:2172
   MacArthur, VIII:2297
   Roosevelt, IX:3225
Pears, Peter, VII:468, 469, 470
Pearse, Patrick, IX:2804, 2805
Pearson, Lester, VII:680; IX:3731
Peary, Robert Edwin, VII:67; **IX:2941-2945**
Peasants Revolt of 1381, II:114-116, 368, 786,
   921-923, 1011
Peasants' War, III:584
Pease, Edward, VI:2132, 2133
Pecci, Vincenzo Gioacchino. *See* Leo XIII
Pecham, John, **II:715-718**
Pechenegs, II:953
Peculiar, John, II:30
Pedersen, Knut. *See* Hamsun, Knut
Pedrarias, III:46, 47, 699
Pedrell, Felipe, VII:1127
Peel, Sir Robert, **VI:1752-1755**
   Canning, V:406
   Catholic emancipation, VI:1681, 1682
   Derby, V:653
   Disraeli, V:675, 677
   Gladstone, V:935, 936
   Hargreaves, IV:623
   Liverpool, VI:1397
   Melbourne, VI:1518, 1519
Péguy, Charles, VIII:2425
Pei, I.M., **IX:2946-2949**

Peirce, Charles Sanders, II:313; **VI:1756-1759**
Peisandros, I:17
Peisistratidae clan, I:553, 554
P'ei Ti, II:966, 967
P'ei Yao-ching, II:966
Pelagianism, I:936, 938; III:505
Pelé, **IX:2950-2953**
Pelham, Henry, IV:537, **1074-1077,** 1156
Pelham, Peter, IV:356
Pelopidas, I:290, 292
Peloponnesian League, I:611, 857
Peloponnesian War
    Alcibiades, I:31-33
    Aristophanes, I:88, 91
    Aspasia, I:115
    Cimon, I:200
    Euripides, I:318
    Pericles, I:611, 612
    Plato, I:655
    theater, I:879
    Thebes, I:290
    Thucydides, I:885-887; IV:662
    Xenophon, I:960
Pembroke, Earl of, II:326
penal system
    Australia, V:992
    Bentham, IV:108, 109
    Buxton, V:378, 379
    Cat and Mouse Act of 1913, IX:2873
    Day, VII:850
    Diepkloof, IX:2907
    Federal Bureau of Prisons, VII:510
    New York, V:369
    Oglethorpe, IV:1043
    Osborne, IX:2852-2854
    Pestalozzi, VI:1768
    Phillip, IV:1092
    Tocqueville, VI:2238
Penance, Sisters of, II:218
Pendleton Act of 1883, V:877
P'eng Hsien, I:188
P'eng Te-huai, VIII:2189-2191; **IX:2954-2956**
Peninsular War, V:406; VI:1958-1960, 2351-2353
Penn, William, IV:1046, **1078-1081**
    *Brief Account of the Province of Pennsylvania,
      A,* IV:1080
    England's Present Interest Discovered, IV:1078
    *Essay Towards the Present and Future Peace of
      Europe, An,* IV:1080
    *Further Account of the Province of Pennsylvania
      and Its Improvements, A,* IV:1080
    No Cross, No Crown, IV:1078

    Quakerism, IV:1078
    Truth Exalted, IV:1078
Pennsylvania
    Allen, IV:36
    Dickinson, IV:408, 410
    Gallatin, V:861
    Paine, IV:1056
    Penn, IV:1078-1081
    Rockefeller, VI:1896
    Wilson, IV:1458
Pennsylvania Railroad, V:420, 423; VI:1313, 1904
Penrose, Roger, VIII:1580
Pensacola, Treaty of, IV:876
Pentagon Papers. *See New York Times v. United
    States*
Pentateuch, I:561, 822; II:648; III:736, 737
Pentheus, I:319
Penthilus, I:651
People's Action Party, VIII:2150, 2151, 2400
People's Liberation Army, VII:689; VIII:2179,
    2189-2191; IX:2955
People's Will Party, V:50
People United to Save Humanity, Operation,
    VIII:1825, 1826
Pepin I, II:226, 228, 599, 600
Pepin II, II:239
Pepo, Bencivieni di. *See* Cimabue
Percy, Henry, III:66
Percy, Thomas, III:257-259
Perdiccas, I:60, 721, 767
Perdiccas III, I:628
Peregrinus de Maricourt, Petrus, **II:719-722**
Peres, Fernando, II:30
Peres, Shimon, VII:1002
Perez, Antonio, III:602
Pérez de Cuéllar, Javier, **IX:2957-2960**
Perfidious Albion, IV:158
Pergamon, I:338, 339, 346
Peri, Jacopo, IV:991, 992
Pericles, **I:609-613**
    Aeschylus, I:10
    Anaxagoras, I:47, 48
    Aspasia, I:115, 117
    Cimon, I:200
    Propylaea, I:677
Periplus, I:368, 369
Perkins, Frances, **IX:2961-2964**
Perkins, J. Maxwell, VII:1162
Perkins Institution, V:1150, 1151
Perón, Eva, **IX:2965-2967,** 2969-2971
Perón, Juan, VII:373, 374; VIII:1760, 1761;
    IX:2965-2967, **2969-2972**

Perot, H. Ross, VII:708, 710; VIII:1432;
    IX:2973-2975
Pérotin, **II:723-725**
    Magnus liber organi, II:723
Perotti, Niccolò, I:618
Perret, Auguste, **IX:2976-2978**
Perrin v. Blake, IV:907
Perry, Fred, **IX:2979-2982**
Perry, Matthew C., V:1181; **VI:1760-1763,** 1764
Perry, Oliver Hazard, **VI:1764-1766**
Persepolis, I:239
Perses, I:404
Pershing, John J., VIII:2429; IX:2911, 2913,
    2983-2986, 3813, 3814
Persian Empire
    Achaemenian empire, I:233-235
    Aeschylus, I:9, 10
    Agesilaus II, I:17, 18
    Alexander the Great, I:38, 40, 41
    Cimon, I:198-201
    Cleomenes I, I:214
    Darius the Great, I:236-239, 553, 554
    Delian League, I:47
    Miletus, I:115
    Herodotus, I:394, 396
    Jerusalem, I:330, 331
    Miltiades the Younger, I:553-555
    Sergius I, II:819-821
    Xenophon, I:958-960
    Xerxes I, I:962-965
Persian Gulf War
    Bush, VII:522
    Fahd, VII:1115, 1116
    Gore, VIII:1432
    Hussein I, VIII:1794
    Pérez de Cuéllar, IX:2958
    Powell, IX:3070-3072
Persian Wars
    Cimon, I:199
    Herodotus, I:394, 396
    Leonidas, I:501-503
    Pheidippides, I:621-623
    Phidias, I:624
    Philip II of Macedonia, I:628-630
    Themistocles, I:857-859
Perutz, Max, VII:412
Peshkov, Aleksey Maksimovich. *See* Gorky, Maxim
Pestalozzi, Johann Heinrich, V:845, 846;
    VI:1767-1770, 2118, 2119; VIII:2596
    *Christoph und Else lesen in den abendstuden das
        Buch "Lienhard und Gertrud,"* VI:1768
    Evening Hours of a Hermit, VI:1767

    How Gertrude Teaches Her Children, VI:1768
    Leonard and Gertrude: A Popular Story, VI:1768
Petacci, Clara, VIII:2669
Pétain, Phillippe, VIII:2106; IX:**2987-2989**
Peter II the Catholic, II:529
Peter III, IV:257, 259, **1087-1090,** 1298
Peter, Saint, I:211, 243, 475, 477, **614-617,** 790
Peterborough, Third Earl of, IV:1277
Peter of Castelnau, II:302
Peter the Great, **IV:1082-1086**
    Alexander Nevsky, II:54
    Charles XII, IV:290-292
    church and state, IV:1032
    Peter III, IV:1087
    Siberian exploration, IV:111
Petheneggs, II:87
Petit, Roland, VII:1177
Petit Luxembourg Palace, IV:152
Petit Pont, II:663
Petrarch, II:93, 152, 153, **726-731,** 790, 949
    Africa, II:728
    Book Without a Name, II:729
    Canzoniere, II:726, 730
    De otio religioso, II:729
    Eclogues, II:729
    Epistle to Posterity, II:730
    My Secret, II:728
    Physicke Against Fortune, II:729
    Quorundam virorum illustrium epithoma, II:728
    Rerum vulgarium fragmenta, II:730
    Triumphs, II:726
Pettazoni, Raffaele, VII:1055
Pettigrew, Richard F., V:1030, 1031
Petty, William. *See* Shelburne, Lord
Petty-Fitzmaurice, Henry Charles Keith. *See*
    Lansdowne, Fifth Marquess of
Peucestas, I:767
PGA. *See* Professional Golfers' Association
Phaedra, I:318
Phaedrus, I:15, **618-620**
    Aesopic Fables of Phaedrus, The, I:618-620
Phalanx, VIII:1903
Phalereus, Demetrius, I:538
Phanar, VI:2417
Pharisees, I:467-469, 471-473, 483, 604
Pharsalus, Battle of, I:149, 159, 167, 681, 918
Pheidias, I:76
Pheidippides, **I:621-623**
Phelps, Samuel, V:1187
phenomenology
    Barthes, VII:207
    Derrida, VII:912

Heidegger, VIII:1610
Husserl, VIII:1797, 1798
Jaspers, VIII:1843
Marcel, VIII:2408
Merleau-Ponty, VIII:2500-2507
Peirce, VI:1758
Scheler, IX:3348, 3349
Stein, IX:3506-3510
Pherecydes of Syros, I:727
Phidias, **I:624-627**
Philadelphia Convention, IV:1455, 1457, 1458;
    IV:495, 609
Philadelphia Museum, IV:1070, 1072, 1073
Philadelphia Orchestra, VII:192
Philadelphia Phillies, VII:717, 719; IX:3240
Philadelphia Research and Protection Association,
    IX:2961
Philanthropinum, IV:93, 94
Philiki Hetairia, VI:2417, 2418
Philip II (of France) II:603, **732-735,** 985
Philip II (of Macedonia), **I:628-631**
    Aristotle, I:95, 873
    Demosthenes, I:253-255
    Menéndez de Avilés, III:507-509
    Ptolemy Soter, I:720
Philip II (of Spain), **III:599-602**
    Alva, III:18-20
    Augsburg, III:161
    Braudel, VII:436, 437
    Catherine de Médicis, III:133
    Cervantes, IV:265
    Drake, III:224
    Farnese, III:254, 255
    Greco, El, III:311
    Mary I, III:479, 480
    Tudor family, III:733
    William the Silent, III:781-783
Philip III (of France), II:736
Philip III (of Macedonia), I:721
Philip IV the Fair (of France), **II:736-739**
Philip V (of Macedonia), I:64, 365
Philip V (of Spain), IV:287
Philip, King. *See* Metacomet
Philip Augustus, II:511, 782, 783
Philip of Hesse, III:102
Philippi, Battle of, I:69, 141, 142, 160
Philippines
    Cavendish, III:141
    Dewey, V:656-658
    Magellan, III:453-456
    Marcos, VIII:2420-2423
    U.S. acquisition, VI:1455

Philippine Veterans Mission, VIII:2420
Philippino-American War, V:656-658, 1069
Philips Pavilion, IX:4076
Philip the Bold, II:740, 832, 833, 834
Philip the Good, **II:740-743;** III:250
Philip the Magnanimous, **III:603-605**
Philistines, I:241, 243, 746, 748, 749
Phillip, Arthur, **IV:1091-1093**
Phillips, Henry, III:737
Phillips, Sam, IX:3076
Phillips, Wendell, **VI:1771-1774**
    Constitution a Pro-Slavery Compact, The,
        VI:1772
    Labor Question, The, VI:1773
Philo, IV:684
Philochorus, I:317, 319
Philolaus, I:729
Philo of Alexandria, **I:632-635**
    Contemplative Life, The, I:634
    Creation of the World, The, I:632
Phipps, Sir William, IV:940
Phocas, II:470, 819
Photius, II:674, 675
Photo Chemical Laboratory, VIII:2043
Photo-Secessionists, IX:3503, 3533, 3534
Phrynon, I:651
Piaget, Jean, VII:674; VIII:2599; **IX:2990-2993**
    Child's Conception of Physical Causality, The,
        IX:2991
    Child's Conception of the World, The, IX:2991
    Judgement and Reasoning in the Child, IX:2991
    Language and Thought of the Child, The, IX:2991
Piankhi, **I:636-639**
piano music
    Bartók, VII:211, 212
    Beethoven, V:178-181
    Brahms, V:299-301
    Chopin, V:493-496
    Debussy, VII:886
    Horowitz, VIII:1747-1750
    Liszt, VI:1391-1393
    Rachmaninoff, IX:3105, 3016, 3108
    Schumann, VI:1993
    Weber, VI:2340-2342
Piasts, II:210, 212
Picard, Émile, **IX:2994-2996**
    Traité d' analyse, IX:2995
Picasso, Pablo, **IX:2997-3001**
    Appolinaire, VII:82
    Braque, VII:431, 432
    Cocteau, VII:721
    Demoiselles d' Avignon, Les, VII:431; IX:2998

Diaghilev, VII:921
Duchamp, VII:974
Gris, VIII:1483-1485
Guernica, IX:2998
Hockney, VIII: 1711, 1713
Lipchitz, VIII: 2199
Ma Jolie, VII:432
Miró, VIII:2546
Nicholson, VIII:2732, 2733
Parade, VIII:2449
Rousseau, VI:1922, 1923
Piccard, Auguste and Jean-Felix, **IX:3002-3005**
Piccinni, Niccolò, IV:550
Pickford, Mary, V:363; VII:1383; **IX:3006-3009**
    Coquette, IX:3008
    Daddy Long-Legs, IX:3008
    Little Lord Fauntleroy, IX:3008
    Pollyanna, IX:3008
    Poor Little Rich Girl, IX:3006, 3008
    Rebecca of Sunnybrook Farm, IX:3008
    Rosita, IX:3008
    Secrets, IX:3008
    Sparrows, IX:3008
    Taming of the Shrew, The, IX:3008
Pickles, Samuel, IX:3497
Pico della Mirandola, Giovanni, III:667, 670
Picotte, Susan La Fresche, **IX:3010-3012**
Pierce, Franklin, V:582, 682, 693; **VI:1775-1778**
Piero della Francesca, **III:606-609**
    Baptism of Christ, III:606, 607
    Battista Sforza, III:608
    Count Federico da Montefeltro, III:608
    Flagellation of Christ, III:608
    Legend of the True Cross, III:607
    Nativity, III:608
    Resurrection, III:607
Pierre, Jean-Baptiste, IV:1376
Pietro, Guido di. *See* Angelico, Fra
Pietro d'Abano. *See* Abano, Pietro d'
Pietro della Gondola, Andrea di. *See* Palladio,
    Andrea
Pietro di Bernardone, Francesco di. *See* Francis of
    Assisi, Saint
Pigafetta, Antonio, III:455
Pike, Zebulon Montgomery, **IV:1094-1097**
Pilate, Pontius, I:469, **640-643**
Pilatus, Leontius, II:153
Pilgrims
    Bradford, IV:189-191
    Massasoit, IV:930-933
    navigational maps, IV:271, 273
    Standish, IV:1273-1275

Pillar Edicts, I:113, 114
Pinchot, Gifford, IX:3596
    Pindar, **I:644-647,** 787; III:657
        Isthmian Odes, I:644
        Nemean Odes, I:644
        Olympian Odes, I:644
        Pythian Odes, I:644
Pinkey, William, VI:1571
Pinturicchio, III:16
Pinzón Brothers, III: 172, 173, **610-612**
Pipiltin, III:528, 529, 531
Pippin II, II:242
Pi-Ramesse, I:736
Pirandello, Luigi, **IX:3013-3016**
    Henry IV, IX:3014
    Late Mattia Pascal, The, IX:3013
    Lazarus, IX:3014
    Mountain Giants, The, IX:3014
    New Colony, The, IX:3014
    One, None, and a Hundred Thousand, IX:3013
    Right You Are (If You Think So), IX:3014
    Shoot, The Notebooks of Serafino Gubbio,
        Cinematograph Operator, IX:3013
    Six Characters in Search of an Author, IX:3014
Piranesi, Giovanni Battista, IV:8
Pire, Dominique, **IX:3017-3019**
Pirelli family, **IX:3020-3022**
Pirenne, Henri, **IX:3023-3025**
    Belgian Democracy: Its Early History, IX:3024
    Histoire de Belgique, IX:3024
    Medieval Cities, IX:3024
    Mohammed and Charlemagne, IX:3024
PIRG. *See* Public Interest Research Group
Pisa, Council of, II:971
Pisano, Andrea, **II:744-746;** III:302-305
Pisano, Giovanni, II:744, **747-749,** 762
Pisano, Nicola, II:744, **747-749**
Pisistratidae, I:649
Pisistratus, **I:648-650**
Pisper, Mount, I:56, 58
Pissarro, Camille, V:453, 455, 456, 888;
    VI:1779-1781
Pisthetairos, I:91
Pithon, I:767
Pittacus of Mytilene, **I:651-654**
Pittsburgh Pact, VIII:2442
Pitt the Elder, William, **IV:1098-1101**
    George II, IV:536-538
    George III, IV:539
    Hutchinson, IV:691, 692
    Pitt the Younger, IV:1102
    Wolfe, IV:1472

Pitt the Younger, William, **IV:1102-1105**
  Bolingbroke, IV:161
  Castlereagh, V:438-440
  Erskine, IV:440, 441
  Fox, IV:481, 482
  George III, IV:542
  Liverpool, VI:1395
Pius, Antoninus, I:358, 359, 523
Pius II, III:564, **613-615**
  Chrysis, III:613
  Commentaries of Pius II, The, III:614
  Decameron, The, III:613
  Tale of Two Lovers, The, III:613
Pius III, III:405
Pius V, III:243, **616-619**
  In Coena Domini, III:617
  Regnans in Excelsis, III:618
Pius VII, V:1248; VI:1782
Pius IX, V:11, 682, 933; VI:1348, 1477, **1782-1785**
Pius X, VIII:1858, 2425; XI:3026
Pius XI, V:389; VIII:1858; **IX:3026-3028,**
    3030, 3031
  Divini Redemptoris, IX:3027
  Mit brennender Sorge, IX:3027
  Non Abbiamo Bisogno, IX:3027
  Quaragesimo Anno, IX:3027
  Ubi Arcano Dei, IX:3026
Pius XII, VIII:1858, 1859; IX:2915, 2916,
    3030-3032
  Humani Generis, IX:3031
  Mediator Dei, IX:3031
  Menti Nostrae, IX:3031
  Miranda Prosus, IX:3031
  Munificentissimus Deus, IX:3031
  Mystici Corporis Christi, IX:3031
Pixodarus Affair, I:720
Pizarro, Francisco, III:372, **620-622;** VI:1815
Pizzolo, Niccolò, III:461
Placards, Affair of the, III:468
Place, Francis, **VI:1786-1789**
  *Illustrations and Proofs of the Principle of
    Population,* VI:1787
plague. *See* black death
Plains Indian Wars, VI:1862
Planck, Max, VI:1799; VII:472; VIII:2476;
    IX:3033-3035, 3491
  Introduction to Theoretical Physics, IX:3035
  New Science, The, IX:3035
  Scientific Autobiography and Other Papers,
    IX:3035
  Universe in the Light of Modern Physics, The,
    IX:3035

*Planned Parenthood of Southeastern Pennsylvania
  v. Casey,* IX:2790
Plan of 1809. *See* 1809, Plan of
Plan Seventeen, VIII:1851-1853
Plantagenet, Geoffrey. *See* Anjou, Count of
Plantagenet, Henry, II:850
Plasgraf v. Long Island R.R., VII:576
Plassey, Battle of, IV:326
Plataea, battle of, I:788
Plath, Sylvia, **IX:3036-3039,** 3396
  Ariel, IX:3037, 3038
  Bell Jar, The, IX:3036-3038
  Colossus and Other Poems, The, IX:3036, 3038
  Crossing the Water, IX:3038
Plato, **I:655-658**
  Antisthenes, I:67, 68
  Apology, I:656
  Aristotle, I:94-96
  Banquet, The, I:507
  Euthyphro, I:656
  Galen, I:339
  Gorgias, I:656
  Jewett, V:1230
  Laws, I:656
  Menexenos, I:117
  Meno, I:656
  Parmenides, I:596, 597
  Phaedo, I:14, 94, 698
  Philebus, I:656
  Plutarch, I:670
  Posidonius, I:687
  Protagoras, I:705-707
  Razi, II:780
  Republic, I:656; II:155; VI:1458
  Socrates, I:793
  Sophist, I:973
  Symposium, I:117, 656
  Theaetetus, I:656
  Timaeus, I:698, 729
  Xenophanes, I:956
  Zeno of Citium, I:967
  See also Neoplatonism; Platonism
Platonism, I:655-658
  Abelard, II:10
  Democritus, I:251
  Eratosthenes of Cyrene, I:303
  Origen, I:582
  Philo of Alexandria, I:632
  Psellus, II:759
Plato's Academy, I:656
  Aristotle, I:94, 95
  Euclid, I:307

Eudoxus of Cnidus, I:311
Justinian I, II:557
Protagoras, I:707
Zeno of Citium, I:967
Plautius, Aulus, I:136
Plautus, I: 171, 540, **659-661**
   Amphitryon, I:659
   Braggart Warriori, The, I:659, 660
   Fabulae Varronianae, I:919
   Twin Meanaechmi, The, I:659, 660; III:687
Player, Gary, **IX:3040-3043**
Playtn, John, II:823
Plectrude, II:242
Pléiade, La, III:**623-625,** 657-659
Plekhanov, Georgy, VIII:2160
Pleroma, I:912, 913
Plessis, Armand-Jean du. *See* Richelieu,
   Cardinal de
Plessis-Marly, Seigneur du. *See* Mornay,
   Philippe de
Pleyel, Ignaz Joseph, IV:148, 149
Pliny the Elder, I:102, 368, 369, **662-665,** 764, 765
   Natural History, I:662-664, 813
   Studiosi, I:66
Pliny the Younger, I:533, 534, 837, 838, 901
PLO. *See* Palestine Liberation Organization
Plotinus, I:128, 634, **666-669,** 683, 684
   Enneads, I:667
Plowshare, Project, IX:3633
Plutarch, **I:670-672**
   Archimedes, I:76
   Brutus, I:140
   Cleopatra VII, I:220
   Democritus, I:251
   Ethica (Moralia), I:92, 541
   Lives, I:14, 670-672, 814, 816; IV:1119
   Lysippus, I:516
   Pheidippides, I:622
   Pittacus of Mytilene, I:653
   Solon, I:803
Pluto, IX:3699-3701
Plymouth colony, IV:189-191, 954, 1273-1275
Poale Zion movement, VII:251; VIII:2472
Pobedonostsev, Konstantin Petrovich,
   VI:1790-1793
   Kurs grazhdanskago prava, VI:1791
   Reflections of a Russian Statesman, VI:1791
Podestà, Palazzo del, III:81
Pocahontas, **IV:1106-1109,** 1122-1125, 1253-1255
Poe, Edgar Allan, V:150, 152, 1127; **VI:1794-1797**
   "Bells, The," IX:3106
   Eureka: A Prose Poem, VI:1796

"Fall of the House of Usher," VI:1796
   "Hans Phfall," VI:2304
   "Ligeia," VI:1796
   "Ms. Found in a Bottle," VI:1794
   "Murders in the Rue Morgue," VI:1796
   Narrative of Arthur Gordon Pym, The, VI:1796,
     2305
   "Raven, The," VI:1796
   Tales of the Grotesque and Arabesque, VI:1796
   Tamerlane and Other Poems, VI:1794
   "William Wilson," VI:1796
Poggio, **III:626-628**
   Corpus inscriptionum Latinarum, III:628
   De avarita, III:627
   De varietate fortunae, III:626, 627
   Fables of Poge the Florentyn, The, III:627
   Historiarum, Florentini populi, III:627
Poincaré, Henri, **VI:1798-1800**
   Science and Method, VI:1799
Poincaré, Raymond, VII:795; **IX:3044-3047**
Poinsett, Joel, V:839
Poisson, Siméon-Denis, V:865
Poissy, Colloquy of, III:133
Poitiers, Battle of, II:295
Pokanoket, Alexander. *See* Wamsutta
Pokanoket Indians, IV:954
Pole, Reginald Cardinal, III:480
Polignac, Jules de, V:483
Polikarpov, Nikolai, IX:3765
Polish Liberation Army, VII:243
Polish Succession, War of, IV:536, 1402
Politburo
   Brezhnev, VII:460
   Gorbachev, VIII:1423
   Khrushchev, VIII:1961, 1962
   Molotov, VIII:2571
   Yeltsin, IX:4086
   Zhukov, IX:4114
Polk, James K., **VI:1801-1805**
   Bancroft, V:126
   Barnum, V:135
   Benton, V:196
   Buchanan, V:347
   Carson, V:431
   Clay, V:509
   Tyler, VI:2290
   Van Buren, VI:2294
Pollack, Ben, VIII:1419
Pollock, Jackson, VII:1208; VIII:2024, 2025,
   2581; **IX:3048-3051**
   Autumn Rhythm, IX:3049
   Birds of Paradise, IX:3049

Covered Wagon, The, IX:3049
Easter and the Totem, IX:3049
Going West, IX:3049
Guardians of the Secret, IX:3049
Lavender Mist, IX:3049
Lucifer, IX:3049
Number 5, IX:3049
Number 8, IX:3049
Red, IX:3049
Scent, IX:3049
She-Wolf, The, IX:3049
Sleeping Effort, IX:3049
Threshers, IX:3048
Troubled Queen, The, IX:3049
White Light, IX:3049
Polo, Marco, II:567, **750-754**
   Travels of Marco Polo, The, II:753
Poltava, Battle of, IV:290
Polybius, **I:673-675,** 731, 757-759
   Histories, The, I:673, 674
Polycarp, I:447, 448
Polyclitus, I:515, 516
Polycrates, I:314, 315
Polygnotus, **I:676-678**
   Illiupersis, I:676, 677
   Nekyia, I:677
Pommersfelden, IV:656
Pompeius, Sextus, I:519, 681, 682
Pompeius Strabo, I:679
Pompey the Great, **I:679-682**
   Brutus, I:140
   Caesar, I:149
   Cassius, I:159
   Cato the Younger, I:166-168
   Crassus, I:816
   Histories, I:687
   Mithradates the Great, I:559, 897
   Posidonius, I:687
   Varro, I:918
Pompidou, Georges, **IX:3052-3054**
Ponce de Léon, Juan, **III:629-632,** 699
Pond, James B., V:715
Pond, Peter, IV:879
Pontadera, Andrea da. *See* Pisano, Andrea
Pontiac, IV:39, 40, 513, **1110-1114;** VI:1736
Pontiac's War. *See* Pontiac
Pontian, I:417
Pontus, Kingdom of, I:557-559, 828
Poona Sarvajanik Sabha, IX:3681
Poor Clares, II:401
Poor People's March on Washington, VII:10;
   VIII:1974

Pop Art, IX:3884-3886
Pope, Alexander, IV:156, 158, 159, 983, 984,
   1115-1117
   Dunciad, The, I:156; IV:984, 1116
   Eloisa to Abelard, IV:1115
   Epistle to Dr. Arbuthnot, An, IV:1116
   Essay on Criticism, An, IV:1115, 1116
   Essay on Man, An, IV:1116, 1440
   Lock of Berenice, The, I:156
   Rape of the Lock, The, I:156; IV:1115; V:162
Popham, Edward, IV:132
Popov, Aleksandr Stepanovich, **VI:1806-1809**
Poppa, II:794
Popular Front, VII:335-337; VIII:1699, 2491
Populist Party, VII:479, 480
Poquelin, Jean-Baptiste. *See* Molière
Porcia, I:140, 141
Porphyry, I:666, 667, **683-685**
   De abstinentia, I:684
   Isagoge, I:683, 685
   Kata Christanon, I:683
Porta, Giambattista della, IV:850
Porter, Cole, VII:1159; **IX:3055-3058**
   "Love For Sale," IX:3055
   "Night and Day," IX:3055
   "Old-Fashioned Garden," IX:3055
   "True Love," IX:3055
Porter, David, V:772
Porter, Edwin S., VIII:1480
Porter, Katherine Anne, **IX:3059-3062**
   "Devil and Cotton Mather, The," IX:3060
   Flowering Judas and Other Stories, IX:3060
   "Maria Concepcion," IX:3060
   Never-Ending Wrong, The, IX:3060
   "Noon Wine," IX:3059, 3060
   "Old Mortality," IX:3059, 3060
   "Pale Horse, Pale Rider," IX:3059, 3060
   Ship of Fools, IX:3060, 3061
Porter, William Sydney. *See* Henry, O.
Port Folio, The, V:225
Port of London Authority, VIII:2216
Port Royal, IV:271, 273
Posada, José Guadalupe, IX:2836
Posidonius, **I:686-689**
   On Astronomical Phenomena, I:688
   On Duty, I:688
   On Emotion, I:688
   On Heroes and Daemones, I:688
   On the Ocean, I:689
   On the Soul, I:688
   On the Sun, I:688
   On the Void, I:688

positivism
    Comte, V:543-545
    Croce, VII:801
    Gentile, VII:1336
    Harrison, V:1057-1059
    Peirce, VI:1758
Post, Wiley, IX:3206
Posthumus, Poenius, I:138
post-Impressionism
    Bonnard, VII:362, 363
    Duchamp, VII:972
    Fry, VII:1254
    Toulouse-Lautrec, VI:2247-2250
Potemkin, Grigory Aleksandrovich, IV:1299
Potter, Beatrix, **IX:3063-3065**
    Tale of Peter Rabbit, The,
        IX:3063, 3064
Poulenc, Francis, **IX:3066-3069**
    Aubade, IX:3067
    Bestiaire, Le, IX:3066
    Biches, Les, IX:3066
    Cocardes, IX:3066
    Concert champêtre, IX:3067
    Concerto in D Minor for Two Pianos and
        Orchestra, IX:3067
    Concerto in G Minor, IX:3067
    Dialogues des carmélites, IX:3068
    Figure humaine, IX:3068
    Litanies à la vierge, IX:3067
    Mamelles de Tirésias, Les, IX:3068
    Mass in G Major, IX:3067
    Mouvements perpétuels, IX:3066
    Rapsodie nègre, IX:3066
    Sept Répons des ténèbres, IX:3068
    Sonata for Violin and Piano, IX:3067
    Voix humaine, La, IX:3068
Pound, Ezra
    Eliot, VII:1058
    Frost, VII:1252
    H.D., VIII:1505, 1508
    Hemingway, VIII:1627
    Joyce, VIII:1892
    Kipling, VI:1291, 1292
    Lowell, VIII:2251
    Testament of François Villon, The, III:766
    Yeats, IX:4082
Poussin, Nicolas, IV:317-319, **1118-1121**
    Adoration of the Golden Calf, The, IV:1119
    Arcadian Shepherds, The, IV:1119
    Four Seasons, IV:1120
    Landscape with the Gathering of the Ashes of
        Phocion, IV:1119

    Martyrdom of Saint Erasmus, IV:1118
    Self-Portrait, IV:1119
Powell, Colin L., **IX:3070-3072**
Powell, John Wesley, **VI:1810-1813**
    Canyons of the Colorado, VI:1812
    Introduction to the Study of Indian Languages,
        VI:1812
    Report on the Lands of the Arid Region of the
        United States, VI:1812
Power, Tyrone, VIII:1631
Power Jets Limited, IX:3973, 3974
Powhatan, IV:1106, 1107, **1122-1125,** 1253
Poyntz, Thomas, III:737
Pozzo, Cassiano del, IV:1118, 1119
Praeconinus, Stilo, I:918-920
Praeneste, I:930, 931
Praetorian Guard, I:203, 640, 893
Prague, Peace of, IV:452, 1052
Prague National Opera, VIII:1837
Prague Spring, VII:968-970
Prandtl, Ludwig, **IX:3073-3075**
Prandtl-Glaubert rule, IX:3074
Prasutagus, I:137
Pratinas, I:878
Pravda, VII:38, 491; VIII:2571; IX:3409
Praxiteles, **I:690-693;** VIII:2611
    Aphrodite of Knidos, I:690-692
    Lizard Slayer, I:690, 692
    Satyr, I:690, 691
predestination
    Augustine, I:129, 936-938
    Calvin, III:120
    Channing, V:471
    Edwards, IV:428, 430
    Grotius, IV:579
    Laud, IV:797, 798
    Melanchthon, III:505
    Pym, IV:1141
    Racine, IV:1144
    Weber, IX:3911
Pre-emption Act, VI:2290
Pre-Raphaelite Brotherhood, III:76; V:1168-1170;
    VI:1928, 2215
Prescott, William Hickling, **VI:1814-1816**
    History of the Conquest of Mexico, VI:1815
    History of the Conquest of Peru, VI:1815
    History of the Reign of Ferdinand and Isabella
        the Catholic, VI:1814
    History of the Reign of Philip the Second, King
        of Spain, VI:1815
presidency, U.S.
    Adams, John, IV:16-20

Adams, John Quincy, V:20-24, 508
Arthur, V:77-81
Buchanan, V:346-348, 794
Bush, VII:520-522
Carter, VII:589-593
Cleveland, V:256, 512-516, 1054, 1055
Clinton, VII:707-711
Coolidge, VII:762-764
Eisenhower, VII:1043-1045
electoral college, IV:1244; V:196
Fillmore, V:792-794
Ford, VII:1180-1182
Garfield, V:77, 78, 80, 81, 256, 875-877
Grant, V:78, 131, 256, 975-978, 1075
Harding, VIII:1550-1552
Harrison, Benjamin, V:257, 582, 1053-1056
Harrison, William Henry, V:1061-1063
Hayes, V:78, 80, 256, 1075, 1076, 1078
Hoover, VIII:1727-1730
Jackson, V:195-198, 508, 1196-1199
Johnson, Andrew, V:296, 479, 583, 1232, 1233, 1235-1237
Johnson, Lyndon B., VIII:1866-1868
Jefferson, V:369, 370
Kennedy, VIII:1928-1931; IX:2815-2817
Lincoln, V:193, 272, 296, 478-480; VI:1380-1383
Madison, IV:886-890, 1000; VI:1464-1466
McKinley, V:1029-1031, 1069; VI:1453-1456
Monroe, V:395, 519; VI:1570-1573
Nixon, VIII:2758-2760
Perot, IX:2974, 2975
Pierce, V:582, 682, 693; VI:1775-1778
Polk, V:126, 135, 196, 347, 431, 509; VI:1801-1804
Reagan, IX:3136, 3138, 3139
Roosevelt, Franklin D., IX:3218, 3220, 3222-3226
Roosevelt, Theodore, V:56, 280, 1069, 1070; IX:3228, 3229, 3231
Smith, IX:3440, 3441
Spock, IX:3479
Taft, IX:3594-3597
Taylor, V:792, 793; VI:2194-2196
Truman, IX:3740-3743
Tyler, V:582; VI:2288-2291
Van Buren, V:127, 371, 372, 509; VI:2292-2295
Wallace, George C., IX:3859
Wallace, Henry A., IX:3862
Washington, IV:1405-1407
Presley, Elvis, **IX:3076-3080**
How Great Thou Art, IX:3078
Jailhouse Rock, IX:3078
King Creole, IX:3078
Love Me Tender, IX:3078
"That's All Right Mama," IX:3076
Prester John, II:567; III:197, 198, 215, 217
Prestonpans, IV:1183, 1184
Prevention Detention Act, VIII:2764
Price, Leontyne, VII:72, 193; **IX:3081-3084**
Price, Richard, IV:1475, 1477
Price, Uvedale, IV:1012
Pride, Thomas, IV:380, **1126-1128**
Pride's Purge, IV:1126-1128
Priestley, Joseph, IV:262, 805, 806, **1129-1132,** 1445
Chart of Biography, A, IV:1129
Essay on a Course of Liberal Education for Civil and Active Life, An, IV:1129
Essay on the First Principles of Government, An, IV:1130
History and Present State of Discoveries Relating to Vision, Light, and Colours, The, IV:1130
History and Present State of Electricity, The, IV:1129
Institutes of Natural and Revealed Religions, IV:1130
Letters to the Inhabitants of Northumberland, IV:1131
Political Dialogue on the General Principles of Government, A, IV:1131
Rudiments of English Grammar, The, IV:1129
Prigg v. Pennsylvania, VI:2148, 2191
Primo de Rivera, Miguel, IX:3784
Princeton, Battle of, IV:1469
Princeton University
Arendt, VII:99
campus design, VII:1131
Fitzgerald, VII:1161
Neumann, VIII:2724
Nevelson, VIII:2730
Oppenheimer, IX:2834
Turing, IX:3768
Princip, Gavrilo, VII:1198
printing press
Caxton, III:143-145
Condorcet, IV:349
Gutenberg, III:328, 330, 331
Mergenthaler, VI:1541-1543
Walter, VI:2325
Priscian, **II:755-757**
De laude imperatoris Anastasii, II:755
De siderbus, II:756

Institutiones grammaticae, II:755, 756
   Priscianus major, II:755
   Priscianus minor, II:755
Priscillian, **I:694-697,** 791
Priscus, Marius, I:838
Privilegium Ottonianum, II:707
Privy Council, IV:309
Proclus, **I:698-701;** II:985
   Elements of Theology, The, I:698
Procopius of Caesarea, II:897
   Secret History of the Court of the Emperor
      Justinian, II:890, 892
Professional Golfers' Association,
   IX:4049, 4050
Profumo, John, VIII:2343
Progressive Conservative Party of Canada,
   VIII:2655-2657
Progessives, Academy of the, III:125-127
Prohibited Books, Index of, III:16, 451, 714;
   IV:521, 522; V:933
Prohibition (of alcohol)
   Butler, VII:525
   Capone, VII:563-565
   Catt, VII:629
   Harding, VIII:1550
   Hayes, V:1078
   Nation, VI:1631, 1633
   New Zealand, VIII:2445
   Sunday, IX:3584
   Willard, VI:2389, 2390
   See also temperance movement
Prokhorov, Aleksandr, VII:214, 215
Prokofiev, Sergei, **IX:3085-3088**
   Alexander Nevsky, IX:3085, 3087
   Buffoon, The, IX:3086
   Cinderella, IX:3087
   Classical, IX:3086
   Gambler, The, IX:3086, 3087
   Ivan the Terrible, IX:3087
   Love for Three Oranges, IX:3086
   On the Dnepr, IX:3087
   Pas d'acier, Les, VIII:2450; IX:3087
   Peter and the Wolf, IX:3085, 3087, 3088
   Prodigal Son, The, VIII:2182; IX:3087
   Queen of Spades, IX:3087
   Romeo and Juliet, IX:3085, 3087
   Scythian Suite, IX:3086
   War and Peace, IX:3087
Proletkult Theater, VII:1047
Prometheus, I:404; II:664
Promised Land, I:563
Prontosil, VII:1167

Propertius, Sextus, **I:702-704**
   Elegies, I:520, 702-704
prophecy
   Deborah, I:246, 247
   Delphi oracle, I:254, 268, 280
   Ezekiel, I:326, 328, 329
   Isaiah, I:452-454
   Jeremiah, I:328, 459-461, 569
   Johanan ben Zakkai, I:472
   Nostradamus, III:567-569
   Samuel, I:748
   Savonarola, III:667-670
Propylaea, I:676, 677
Prosper of Aquitane, I:936, 937
Protagoras, I:317, 624, **705-708**
   Contrary Arguments, I:706
   On the Gods, I:706
   Truth, The, I:706
Protective Tariff of 1816, VI:2075
Protestant League, IV:591
Protestant missionary movement, IV:1488-1490
Protestant Reformation
   Aristippus, I:87
   Bucer, III:101-103
   Calvin, III:117, 118, 120
   Catherine of Aragon, III:139
   Charles V, III:159-161
   Clement VII, III:166-168
   Copernicus, III:178
   Cotton, IV:372
   Coverdale, III:193-195
   Cranach, III:200-202
   Cromwell, III:208-210
   Edward VI, III:237-239
   Erasmus, III:248
   Eucharistic controversy, II:774
   Ferdinand II, IV:450-452
   France, III:333-335; IV:104
   Gardiner, III:291-293
   Harnack, VIII:1558
   Henry IV, III:333-335
   Henry VIII, III:68
   Hotman, III:362-365
   Hus, II:487-490
   Laud, IV:797-799
   Luther, III:443, 445, 446
   Menno Simons, III:512
   Ridley, III:654-656
   Ritschl, VI:1894
   Tertullian, I:850
   Tyndale, III:735-737
   Weber, IX:3910, 3911

Wyclif, II:1011
Zwingli, III:791-794
See also Counter-Reformation
Protestant Union, IV:451
protons
    Chadwick, VII:635, 636
    cyclotron development, VII:380; VIII:2123
    McMillan, VIII:2336
    Millikan, VIII:2541
    Yukawa, IX:4090
Proudhon, Pierre-Joseph, **VI:1817-1820**
    De la capacité politique des classes ouvrières,
        VI:1819
    De la justice dans la révolution et dans l'église,
        VI:1818
    Fédération de l'unité en Italie, La, VI:1819
    *General Idea of the Revolution in the Nineteenth
        Century, The,* VI:1818
    Guerre et la paix, La, VI:1819
    *Révolution sociale démontrée par le coup d'état
        du 2 décembre, La,* VI:1818
    System of Economic Contradictions, VI:1818
    What Is Property?, VI:1817, 1818
Proust, Antonin, VI:1471
Proust, Marcel, **IX:3089-3092**
    By Way of Sainte-Beuve, IX:3089
    Jean Santeuil, IX:3090
    Pleasures and Regrets, IX:3089
    Remembrance of Things Past, IX:3090, 3091,
        4013, 4014
    Swann's Way, IX:3090
    Time Regained, IX:3090
Prouty, Olive Higgins, IX:3036
Provincetown Players, VII:794
Prudential Assurance Company, VII:384
Prussian Academy of Arts, VIII:2017
Prussian Academy of Sciences, VIII:1557
Prussian-French War. *See* Franco-Prussian War
Pruth River, battle at the, IV:290
Prynne, Hester, V:1064, 1066
Prynne, William, IV:798, 799
Przywara, Erich, IX:3508
Psalms, Book of, I:241, 243, 244, 563; III:101;
    VI:1829
Psalter, VI:1829
Psamtik I, **I:709-711**
Psellus, Michael, **II:758-761**
    Chronographia, II:759, 760
    "Dialogue on the Operation of the Daimons,"
        II:759
    "On Teaching Miscellany," II:759
    Pseudo-Dionysius, I:258, 699; II:860

Pskov, II:52
Psychical Research, Society for, VI:2063
psychoanalysis
    Bleuler, VII:329, 330
    Breuer, VII:452-454
    Freud, VII:1224-1226
    Fromm, VII:1246-1248
    Horney, VIII:1744-1746
    Jung, VIII:1896, 1898, 1899
    Lacan, VIII:2061-2063
    Piaget, IX:2990
Ptah, I:636, 637
Ptolemy, **I:712-715**
    Alhazen, II:63, 65
    Almagest, I:74, 407, 410, 567, 712-714; II:20, 63
    Battani, II:121, 122
    Copernicus, III:176, 178, 179
    geocentric theory, I:409
    Geography, I:713, 714; III:515, 676, 759
    Harmonica, I:714
    Idrisi, II:507
    Tetrabiblos, I:713, 714
Ptolemy II. *See* Ptolemy Philadelphus
Ptolemy III Euergetes, I:304
Ptolemy IV, I:63, 305
Ptolemy V, I:64
Ptolemy XII Auletes, I:218
Ptolemy XIII Philopator, I:218
Ptolemy XIV, I:218, 220
Ptolemy Philadelphus, I:231, **716-719**
Ptolemy Soter, I:307, 716, 717, **720-723,** 767-769
public health
    Chadwick, V:459, 460
    Disraeli, V:678
    Gorgas, VIII:1434-1437
    Virchow, VI:2314
Public Health Act of 1848, V:460
Public Health Act of 1875, V:678
Public Interest Research Group, VIII:2680
Public Safety, Committee of, IV:394, 395, 912,
    1172, 1206, 1207; V:398
Public Schools Act of 1866, VI:1732, 1734
Public Weal, League of the, III:434
Public Works Administration, IX:2963
Publius, IV:610
Puccini, Giacomo, **IX:3093-3097**
    Bohème, La, VII:599; IX:2930, 3707
    Edgar, IX:3093
    Fanciulla, V:1163; IX:3094
    Madame Butterfly, VII:599; IX:3094
    Manon Lescaut, IX:3094
    Mass of Glory, IX:3093

Rondine, La, IX:3094

Tosca, VII:599; IX:3094, 3158

Trittico, Il, IX:3094

Turandot, IX:3096

Villi, Le, IX:3093

Pucelle, Jean, II:307, **762-765**

    Belleville Breviary, The, II:762-764

    Breviary of Blanche of France, The, II:762

    Hours of Jeanne d'Evreux, The, II:762, 763

    Hours of Jean of Savoy, The, II:762

Pufendorf, Samuel von, **IV:1133-1136**

    Elementorum jurisprudentiae universalis libri duo, IV:1133

    On the Law of Nature and Nations, IV:1134

    Present State of Germany, The, IV:1133

    Whole Duty of Man According to the Law of Nature, The, IV:1134

Puffer Whim, VI:2252

Pugachev, Emelyan Ivanovich, VI:1833

Pugin, Augustus Welby Northmore, V:139; **VI:1821-1824,** 2002

    Contrasts, VI:1822

    True Principles of Pointed or Christian Architecture, VI:1822

Pujo Committee, VI:1582

Pulcher, Publius Clodius, I:196, 680, 681

Pulitzer, Joseph, V:741; **VI:1825-1827;** VIII:1601, 1603

Pullman Company, V:55; IX:3114

Pullman Strike of 1894, VII:881

Pulszky, Romola de, VIII:2748

Pulteney, William, IV:1074, 1075, 1403; VI:2208

Punch, VIII:2543

Punic Wars. *See* Second Punic War; Third Punic War

Punitive Expedition, IX:2984

Punt, kingdom of, I:373

Pupin, Michael, VIII:2539

Purcell, Henry, **IV:1137-1140;** VII:471

    Dido and Aeneas, IV:1139

    Dioclesian, IV:1139

    Indian Queen, The, IV:1139

    King Arthur, IV:1139

Purcell, John B., V:402

Pure Land Buddhism, II:537, 538, 666

Puritanism

    Adams, IV:12

    Andrewes, IV:46

    Beaumont and Fletcher, III:56

    Bradford, IV:190

    Bunyan, IV:219

    Cotton, IV:371, 372

    Coverdale, III:193-195

    Cromwell, IV:378, 1127

    Edwards, IV:428-431

    Eliot, IV:435

    Hale, IV:597, 598

    Hawthorne, V:1064, 1066

    James I, IV:700

    Laud, IV:798

    Massasoit, IV:930

    Mather, Cotton, IV:934-937

    Mather, Increase, IV:938-941

    Metacomet, IV:954-956

    Parker, III:589

    Parrington, IX:2893-2895

    Pym, IV:1141, 1142

    Sewall, IV:1225-1227

    Standish, IV:1273-1275

    Weber, IX:3911

    Williams, IV:1451

    Winthrop, IV:1463-1465

Pusey, E.B., **VI:1828-1831**

    Daniel the Prophet, VI:1829

    Doctrine of the Real Presence, The, VI:1829

    Eirenicon, An, VI:1829

    Historical Enquiry into the Probable Causes of the Rationalist Character, An, VI:1828

    Library of Fathers of the Holy Catholic Church, VI:1829

    Minor Prophets,, The, VI:1829

    Real Presence, The, VI:1829

    Scriptural Views of Holy Baptism, VI:1829

PUSH. *See* People United to Save Humanity, Operation

Pushkin, Alexander, VI:1352, 1353, **1832-1835**

    "André Chenier," VI:1832

    Boris Gudonov, VI:1833, 1834

    Captain's Daughter, The, VI:1833, 1834

    Count Nulin, VI:1832, 1834

    Eugene Onegin, VI:1833, 1834, 2198

    Gabriel: A Poem, VI:1833, 1834

    Gypsies, The, VI:1832

    Poltava, VI:1833

    Prisoner of the Caucasus, VI:1832

    Queen of Spades, The, VI:1833, 1834

    Ruslan I Lyudmila, VI:1832, 1834

    Tales of Belkin, The, VI:1833

Pydna, I:629

Pym, John, **IV:1141-1143,** 1287

Pyramid, Battle of the, IX:2947

Pyrenees, Treaty of the, IV:343, 947

Pyréolophore, VI:1657, 1658, 1660

Pyrgopolynices, I:660

Pyrrhon of Elis, **I:724-726**
Pyrrhonism, IV:685
Pythagoras, I:34, 35, 99, **727-730**
Pythagorean Theorem, I:729
Pytheas, **I:731-733**

Qaddafi, Muammar al-, **IX:3098-3100**
    Jamahiriyah, IX:3099
Qajar Dynasty, VIII:1957, 2566, 2567
Qandahar, III:36
Qarakhanids, II:70
Qavam, Ahmad, VIII:2566
Qavurt, II:68
Qom, VIII:1957, 1958
Quakers
    Alcott, Bronson, V:37
    Alcott, Louisa May, V:40
    Anthony, V:61
    Dalton, V:602
    Darby, IV:396, 397
    Forster, V:804, 805
    Fox, IV:484-486
    Fry, VII:1253
    Hoover, VIII:1730
    Lancaster, VI:1309
    Mott, VI:1600-1602
    Nixon, VIII:2758-2760
    Paul, IX:2919
    Penn, IV:1078-1080
    Ross, IV:1191-1193
    Truth, VI:2255
    Tubman, VI:2265
    Whittier, VI:2374
    Williams, IV:1453
quantum mechanics
    Bethe, VII:300
    Bohr, VII:345, 347
    Broglie, VII:472-474
    Einstein, VII:1035, 1036
    Hawking, VIII:1580, 1582, 1583
    Heisenberg, VIII:1617-1619
    Huygens, IV:697
    Landau, VIII:2073-2075
    Lorentz, VIII:2235-2237
    Neumann, VIII:2726
    Pauli, IX:2923-2924
    Pauling, IX:2927
    Planck, IX:3033-3035
    Poincaré, VI:1799
    Rutherford, IX:3278
    Schrödinger, IX:3362-3364
    Schwarzschild, IX:3368

    Teller, IX:3631
    Yukawa, IX:4092
Quapaw, IV:733
Quatre-Bras, Battle of, VI:1647
Quatremère de Quincy, V:411
Quayle, Dan, VII:521
Quebec
    Campbell, VII:550, 551
    Carleton, IV:246-248
    Champlain, IV:273, 274
    Chrétien, VII:680-682
    conscription, VII:367; VIII:1984
    King, VIII:1982
    Laurier, VIII:2100-2103
    Mackenzie, VI:1451
    Mulroney, VIII:2655-2657
    Official Languages Act of 1969, IX:3732
    Sauvé, IX:3344, 3345
    Trudeau, IX:3730-3732
Quebec, Battle of, IV:179, 1471-1473
Quebec Act, IV:247
Queensbury, Marquis of, VI:2379
Queenstown, Battle of, VI:2009
Quessant, battle of, IV:1048
Quetzalcóatl, III:190, 528, 529, 531
Quimby, Phineas P., V:739
Quinisext Council. *See* Second Trullan Synod
Quintana, Juan de, III:675
Quintetto Boccherini, IV:149
Quivira, III:182
Qumran, I:481
Quraysh, II:504
Qutlugh-Shah, II:383
Qutlumush ibn Arslan Israil, II:68

Rabanus, Maurus, II:756, **766-769**
    De computo, II:767
    De institution clericorum, II:766
    De laudibus sanctae crucis, II:766
    De natura rerum, II:768
    De oblatione puerorum, II:767
    De reuerentia filiorum erga patres, II:767
    De uirtuibus et uitiis, II:767
    Martyrologium, II:768
Rabelais, François, **III:633-637,** 764; VII:153
    Gargantua, III:634, 636
    Pantagruel, III:633
    Third Book, III:468
Rabi, Isidor Issac, **IX:3101-3104**
Rabin, Yitzhak, VII:93
Rachmaninoff, Sergei, **IX:3105-3108**
    Bells, The, IX:3106

Concerto No. 3 in D Minor, IX:3106
Isle of the Dead, The, IX:3105, 3108
Piano Concerto No. 2 in C Minor, IX:3105
Rhapsody on a Theme by Paganini, IX:3106
Symphonic Dances of the Op. 45, IX:3106
Symphony No. 2 in E Minor, IX:3105
Racine, Jean, IV:172, 365, **1144-1147;**
    VII:207, 208
    Alexander the Great, IV:1145
    Andromache, IV:1145
    Athaliah, IV:1146
    Bajazet, IV:1146
    Bérénice, IV:1146
    Britannicus, IV:1146
    Cantiques spirituels, IV:1146
    Esther, IV:1146
    Litigants, The, IV:1145
    Mithridates, IV:1146
    Phaedra, IV:1146
    Theban Brothers, The, IV:1145
racism
    Anderson, VII:72
    Baldwin, VII:164-166
    Benedict, VII:257
    Garvey, VII:1311-1313
    Gordimer, VIII:1429, 1430
    Hansberry, VIII:1545
    Holiday, VIII:1717
    Le Bon, VIII:2135
    Louis, VIII:2243
    Malcolm X, VIII:2373, 2375, 2376
    Morrison, VIII:2626
    Parks, IX:2888-2891
    Robinson, IX:3193, 3194, 3196
    Roosevelt, IX:3218
    Woods, IX:4050
    See also apartheid; discrimination, racial;
        segregation
Radcliffe College, V:748; VII:750
Radical Dissenters, IV:1475, 1478
Radical Republicans, VI:2137; VII:702, 703
Radical-Socialist Party, VIII:1644, 1645
Radiguet, Raymond, VII:721, 724
Radini-Tedeschi, Monsignor, VIII:1858
radio. *See* radio broadcasting; radio electronics
radioactivity
    Becquerel, V:166-168
    Bothe, VII:379
    Chadwick, VII:635
    Curies, VII:811, 812, 815
    Hahn, VIII:1513-1516
    Joliot, VIII:1870-1873

    Meitner, VIII:2476-2478
    Rutherford, IX:3278, 3279
    Whipple, IX:3959
radio broadcasting
    British Broadcasting Corporation, VII:737-740;
        IX:2849, 3146-3148
    DeMille, VII:898
    Murrow, VIII:2662, 2664
    Rogers, IX:3206
    Welles, IX:3934
Radio Corporation of America. *See* RCA
radio electronics
    Armstrong, VII:102
    Bjerknes, VII:319
    de Forest, VII:858-861
    Marconi, VIII:2415, 2417, 2418
    Popov, VI:1806-1808
    Tesla, VI:2220
Radio-Keith-Orpheum Pictures Corporation. *See*
    RKO Pictures Corporation
Raeburn, Sir Henry, **VI:1836-1838**
    George Chalmers of Pittencrieff, VI:1836
    MacNab, The, VI:1839
RAF. *See* Royal Air Force
Rafsanjani, Hashemi, VIII:1959
ragtime music, V:1239-1241; VII:287
Ragua Ocllo, III:371, 372
Rahv, Philip, VIII:2304
Rai Bhoi di Talvandi. *See* Nanak
railroads
    black labor organizations, IX:3114
    Carnegie, V:420, 423
    Chang Chih-tung, V:468
    Cooke, V:552-554
    Debs, VII:880, 881
    Field, V:789, 790
    Frémont, V:843
    Gadsden, V:859
    Hill, IV:659-661
    Krupp, VI:1301, 1303
    Langley, VI:1313
    Laurier, VIII:2101
    Macdonald, VI:1438
    Morgan, VI:1581, 1582
    New Haven monopoly, VII:421
    Rockefeller, VI:1897, 1898
    Russia, VI:1651
    Sioux Indians, VI:2070, 2072
    Stanford, VI:2096-2099
    steel production, V:220, 1016
    Stephens, VI:2130-2132
    switches, VIII:1503

telegraphy, V:558
Telford, VI:2209
Trevithick, VI:2251-2253
Tweed, VI:2285
Vanderbilt, VI:2296-2298
Westinghouse, VI:2358, 2360, 2361
Rainald of Dassel, II:358
Rainbow Coalition, VIII:1825
Rajputs, III:5
Raleigh, Sir Walter, III:140, 315, 316, **638-641,**
    704; IV:700
    Discovery of the Large, Rich, and Beautiful
      Empire of Guiana, The, III:639
    History of the World, The, II:947, III:640; IV:194
    Report of the Truth of the Fight About the Isles
      of Açores, A, III:639
Ramadan, VII:392
Raman, Sir Chandrasekhara Venkata,
    IX:3109-3111
Ramanuja, **II:770-772**
Rameau, Jean-Philippe, IV:33, **1148-1151**
    Abaris: Ou, Les Boréades, IV:1150
    Castor et Pollux, IV:1150
    Demonstration of the Principle of Harmony,
      IV:1149
    Hippolyte et Aricie, IV:1148-1150
    New System of Music Theory, IV:1148
    Nouvelles Suites de pièces de clavecin, IV:1148
    Premier Livre de pièces de clavecin, IV:1148
    Samson, IV:1149
    Treatise on Harmony, IV:1148
Ramillies, Battle of, IV:923, 924
Ramsay, James Andrew Broun. *See* Dalhousie,
    First Marquess of
Ramsay, Sir William, VIII:1513
Ramses I, I:734
Ramses II, **I:734-738**
Ramses VI, I:905
Rand, Ayn, VIII:1471, 1472
    Fountainhead, The, VII:1083
Rand, Walter Charles, IX:3683
Randall, John T., IX:3995, 3996
Randolph, A. Phillip, **IX:3112-3116**
Randolph, Edward, IV:938, 939
Random House, VIII:2626
Rangoon, Battle of, IX:3437
Ranke, Leopold von, V:358; **VI:1839-1841**
    "Great Powers, The," VI:1840
    History of England Principally in the
      Seventeenth Century, A, VI:1840
    History of the Latin and Teutonic Nations from
      1494 to 1514, VI:1839

    History of the Popes During the Last Four
      Centuries, The, VI:1840
    History of the Reformation in Germany, VI:1840
    "Political Dialogue," VI:1839
    Universal History, VI:1840
Rankin, Jeannette, VII:1153; **IX:3117-3120**
Raphael, III:24, 26, 186, **642-646**
    Adam Tempted, IV:1163
    Baldassare Castiglione, III:644
    Cardinal Virtues, III:643
    Dispute over the Sacrament, III:643
    Expulsion of Attila, III:643
    Expulsion of Heliodorus, III:643, 644
    Liberation of Saint Peter, III:643
    Madonna of the Meadows, III:642
    Marriage of the Virgin, III:642
    Mass of Bolsena, III:643
    Parnassus, V:1184
    St. George and the Dragon, III:642
    School of Athens, III:643
    Sistine Madonna, III:643
    Transfiguration of Christ, III:644; IV:808
    Triumph of Galatea, III:186
Raphael, House of, III:83
Rasmussen, Knud Johan Victor, **IX:3121-3124**
Rasputin, Grigori Yefimovich, **VI:1842-1845**
Rassemblement Démocratique Africain,
    IX:3711, 3712
Rastakhiz Party, VIII:1958
Rathbone, John, VI:1634
Rathenau, Walther, IX:3564
Ratti, Ambrogio Damiano Achille. *See* Pius XI
Ratramnus, **II:773-775**
    Concerning the Body and Blood of the Lord,
      II:773
    Contra graecorum opposita, II:774
    De nativitate Christi, II:774
    De praedestinatione, II:774
Rauschenbusch, Walter, **IX:3125-3128**
    Christianity and the Social Crisis, IX:3126
    Christianizing the Social Order, IX:3126
    For God and the People: Prayers of the Social
      Awakening, IX:3126
    Theology for the Social Gospel, A, IX:3126
Ravel, Maurice, **IX:3129-3131,** 3332, 3333, 3798
    Bolero, IX:3130, 3131
    Histoires naturelles, IX:3129
Rawdon, Lord Francis, IV:576
Ray, Rammohan, **VI:1846-1849**
    Precepts of Jesus, The, VI:1847
    Translation of an Abridgment of the "Vedant,"
      VI:1847

Ray, Satyajit, **IX:3132-3135**
    Adventures of Goopi and Bagha, The, IX:3133
    Adversary, The, IX:3133
    Big City, The, IX:3133
    Chess Players, The, IX:3134
    Company Limited, IX:3133
    Coward and the Saint, The, IX:3133
    Days and Nights in the Forest, IX:3133, 3134
    Distant Thunder, IX:3134
    Goddess, The, IX:3133
    Hero, The, IX:3133
    Home and the World, The, IX:3134
    Kanchenjungha, IX:3133
    Kingdom of Diamonds, The, IX:3133
    Lonely Wife, The, IX:3133, 3134
    Middleman, The, IX:3134
    Music Room, The, IX:3132
    Pather Panchali: Song of the Road, IX:3132
    Rabindranath Tagore, IX:3133
    Unvanquished, The, IX:3132
    World of Apu, The, IX:3132
Rayburn, Sam T., VIII:1866; IX:2824
Raymond IV, II:159, 160
Raymond of Capua, II:220, 221
Raymond of Peñafort, II:400, **776-778**
    Decretals of Gregory IX, II:400, 777
    Summa de casibus poenitentiae, II:776, 777
    Summa de matrimonio, II:776
    Summa juris canonici, II:776
Razi, al-, **II:779-781**
    Book of Secrets, The, II:781
    Book of Spiritual Physick, The, II:780
    Comprehensive Book, The, II:780
    Philosopher's Way of Life, The, II:780
    Treatise on the Smallpox and Measles, A, II:780
    Upon the Circumstances Which Turn the Head of Most Men from the Reputable Physician, II:779
RCA, VIII:2418; IX:4125, 4126
Reade, Charles, VI:2216
Reagan, Ronald, **IX:3136-3141**
    Albright, VII:50
    Bush, VII:521
    Carter, VII:591, 592
    Charles, VII:658
    Ferraro, VII:1153-1155
    Gorbachev, VIII:1424
    Greenspan, VIII:1471, 1472
    Khomeini, VIII:1958
    King's Row, IX:3136
    Kirkpatrick, VIII:1995, 1996
    Knute Rockne: All American, IX:3136

    Mulroney, VIII:2656
    nuclear deterrence, IX:3633
    O'Connor, IX:2789
    O'Neill, IX:2825
    Ortega, IX:2840, 2841
    Powell, IX:3071
    This Is the Army, VIII:2243
    Wiesenthal, IX:3986, 3987
Repeal Party, VI:1682
Reasoner, Harry, IX:3870
Rebner, Adolph, VIII:1670
Recared, II:518
Reciprocal Trade Agreements Act, VIII:1780
Reclamation Act, VI:1813
Reconciliation, Fellowship of, VIII:2735
Reconstruction era
    Beecher, V:176
    Blaine, V:256
    Chase, V:479, 480
    Godkin, VIII:1401
    Greeley, V:985
    Hayes, V:1075, 1076, 1078
    Johnson, V:1232, 1233, 1235-1237
    Stanton, VI:2108, 2109
    Stephens, VI:2131
    Stevens, VI:2136, 2137
    Sumner, VI:2172
Reconstruction Finance Corporation, VIII:1729
Rectification Movement, VIII:2212, 2213
Rectification of Names, I:223
Recusants, III:148, 257, 259; IV:700
Redbook magazine, VIII:2470
Red Cloud, V:574, 575; **VI:1850-1853**
Red Cloud's War, V:574
Red Cross. *See* American Red Cross; International Red Cross
Red Flag Act, VIII:2070
Redon, Odilon, **VI:1854-1856; VII:910**
    Eye Balloon, The, VI:1856
    Hommage à Goya, VI:1854
Redstone Rocket, IX:2779
Rée, Paul, VI:1664
Reece, Carroll, VIII:1989
Reed, Joseph, IV:1001
Reed, Walter, **VI:1857-1860; VIII:1434, 1435**
Reed Commission, VIII:1435
Reform, War of the, V:1252
Reforma, La, V:1252
Reformation, Protestant. *See* Protestant Reformation
Reform Bill of 1832
    Buxton, V:379

Disraeli, V:675, 577
Durham, V:722
Grey, V:994
Kay-Shuttleworth, VIII:1917
Macaulay, VI:1427, 1429
Mill, VI:1557, 1558
Pankhurst, IX:2874
Place, VI:1788
Russell, VI:1930
William IV, VI:2392-2394
Reform Bill of 1867, V:654, 777
Reform Bill of 1884, V:777
Reform Club, V:138; VIII:1917
Reformed Church. *See* Calvin, John; Protestant
    Reformation
Reformed Presbyterian Church, IV:239-241
Reform Judaism, VI:2400-2402; VII:148-151
Refusés, Salon de, VI:1780
Regency Crisis, IV:1103; V:902
Regensburg, Diet of, III:103
Regulating Act of 1773, IV:631
Regulus, **I:739-741**
Rehn, Frank K.M., VIII:1740
Rehnquist, William H., VII:511; **IX:3142-3145**
Reichstag
    Bülow, VII:495, 496
    Erzberger, VII:1102
    Göring, VIII:1439
    Himmler, VIII:1666-1668
    Hitler, VIII:1676
    naval building, IX:3689, 3690
    Stresemann, IX:3563, 3564
    Zetkin, IX:4114
Reichswehr, IX:3380, 3381
Reid, Sir George, V:631
Reid, Thomas, VI:2063
Reign of Terror. *See* Terror, Reign of
Reims Cathedral, II:615
Reinach, Adolf, IX:3507
Reiner, Fritz, VII:295
Reith of Stonehaven, First Baron, **IX:3146-3149**
relativity, theory of
    Broglie, VII:473
    dynamism, VII:343
    Einstein, VII:1035, 1036, 1038
    Hawking, VIII:1580, 1582, 1583
    Lemaître, VIII:2157
    Lorentz, VIII:2236
    Meitner, VIII:2476
    Michelson, VI:1554
    Pauli, IX:2923
    Planck, IX:3034

Poincaré, VI:1798-1800
    Stark, IX:3490, 3491
Reliance Building, V:365, 367
Religion, French Wars of, IV:1165
Religious Socialist Movement, VII:475
Religious Society of Friends. *See* Quakers
Remarque, Erich Maria, **IX:3150-3152**
    All Quiet on the Western Front, IX:3150-3152
    Road Back, The, IX:3150
    Three Comrades, IX:3150
    Traumbude, Die, IX:3150
Rembrandt, III:645; IV:622, **1152-1155**
    Anatomy Lesson of Dr. Tulp, The, IV:1152
    Holy Family with Angels, The, IV:1154
    Night Watch, The, IV:1152
    Old Man Seated in an Armchair, An,
      IV:1154
    Presentation of Jesus in the Temple, The,
      IV:1152
    Stoning of Saint Stephen, IV:1152
    Syndics of the Drapers' Guild, The, IV:1154
    Two Scholars Disputing, IV:1152
    Woman Bathing, IV:1154
Remington, Frederic, **VI:1861-1864**
    Bronco Buster, The, VI:1862
    John Ermine of the Yellowstone, VI:1862
Renaixença, VII:1315-1317
RENAMO. *See* Mozambique National Resistance
Renan, Ernest, **VI:1865-1868**
    Future of Science, The, VI:1865, 1866
    History of the Origins of Christianity, The,
      VI:1866
    History of the People of Israel, VI:1867
    Life of Jesus, The, VI:1866
    My Sister Henrietta, VI:1865
    Saint Paul, VI:1866
René II, III:164
Reno, Janet, **IX:3153-3156**
Renoir, Jean, VIII:2579, 2580; **IX:3157-3160**
    Boudu Saved from Drowning, IX:3158
    Chienne, La, IX:3158
    Crime of Monsieur Lange, The, IX:3158
    Day in the Country, A, VII:594; IX:3158
    French Cancan, IX:3159
    Grand Illusion, IX:3158
    Joyless Life, IX:3157
    Little Match Girl, The, IX:3157
    Little Theatre of Jean Renoir, The, IX:3159
    Lower Depths, The, IX:3158
    Madame Bovary, IX:3158
    Nana, IX:3157
    Nuit de carrefour, La, IX:3158

River, The, IX:3159
Rules of the Game, The, VII:594; IX:3158
Tosca, IX:3158
Renoir, Pierre-Auguste, **VI:1869-1872;** IX:3157
   Blacksmith (Fire), VI:1870
   Dancing at the Moulin de la Galette, Montmarte,
     VI:1869
   Diane Chassereuse, VI:1869
   Grandes Baigneuses, Les, VI:1870
   Grenouillière, La, VI:1869
   Judgment of Paris, VI:1870
   Madame Charpentier and Her Children,
     VI:1870
Representatives, House of
   Adams, V:23, 24
   Benton, V:197
   Blaine, V:255-257
   Buchanan, V:346
   Bush, VII:520
   Calhoun, V:394
   Chisholm, VII:670, 671
   Clay, V:507
   Crockett, V:578, 579
   Cushing, V:581
   Davis, V:615
   Dole, VII:948
   Ford, VII:1180, 1181
   Garfield, V:877
   Gore, VIII:1431
   Hearst, VIII:1603
   Hull, VIII:1779
   Johnson's impeachment, V:1237
   Jordan, VIII:1887-1889
   Kennedy, VIII:1928
   La Follette, VIII:2047
   La Guardia, VIII:2054
   Lincoln, VI:1382
   Lodge, VIII:2220
   McKinley, VI:1453
   O'Neill, IX:2824-2826
   Rankin, IX:3118
   Sherman, IV:1244
   Stephens, VI:2129
   Stevens, VI:2136
   Tyler, VI:2288, 2291
   Webster, VI:2344
   See also Congress, U.S.
Reprobus. *See* Christopher, Saint
Repton, Humphrey, IV:1013
Republican Party, U.S.
   Arthur, V:77, 78, 80
   Benton, V:197

Blaine, V:255-257
Borah, V:279-281
Burger, VII:509
Bush, VII:520-522
Butler, VII:524
Chase, Salmon P., V:477-479
Chase, Samuel, IV:295
Clinton, Bill, VII:709
Clinton, DeWitt, V:517-519
Coolidge, VII:762-764
Cushing, V:583
Dole, VII:947-949
Eisenhower, VII:1043-1045
elephant symbol, VI:1628
Ford, VII:1180-1182
Freedmen's Bureau, V:1235
Garfield, V:875-877
Grant, V:977
Hanna, V:1029-1031
Harding, VIII:1550, 1551
Harrison, V:513, 1053-1056
Hayes, V:1075, 1076, 1078
Hobby, VIII:1704, 1705
Hoover, VIII:1727, 1729
Hughes, VIII:1766
Kansas-Nebraska Act, V:693
Kirkpatrick, VIII:1996
Kissinger, VIII:1999
La Follette, VIII:2047-2049
La Guardia, VIII:2055
Lincoln, VI:1383
Lodge, VIII:2219-2221
Luce, VIII:2257, 2258
MacArthur, VIII:2298
McCarthy, VIII:2300
McKinley, VI:1453
Madison, IV:889
Nixon, VIII:2758-2760
O'Connor, IX:2789
Ortega, IX:2840, 2841
Perot, IX:2974
Reagan, IX:3138
Rehnquist, IX:3142
Roosevelt, IX:3229, 3231
Root, IX:3232
Schurz, VI:1996, 1997
Seward, VI:2037-2039
Smith, IX:3448
Stanford, VI:2097
Stevens, VI:2136
Sumner, VI:2171
Taft, IX:3592, 3593

Van Buren, VI:2293
Williams, VI:2396, 2397
Requiter, Bridge of the. *See* Sifting Bridge
Resaca, battle of, V:1053
Resale Prices Act, VIII:1607
Residenz, IV:657
Resistance, French. *See* French Resistance
respiration
    Aretaeus of Cappadocia, I:82
    Breuer, VII:452
    Erasistratus, I:300, 301
    Herophilus, I:399
    Krogh, VIII:2027-2029
    Malpighi, IV:891
    Spallanzani, IV:1262
Restitution, Edict of, IV:451, 452
Resurrection, Islamic concept of, II:652
Resurrection City, VII:10
retailing
    Field, V:783-786
    Mendelsohn's store designs, VIII:2488
    Ward, VI:2331-2334
    window displays, VII:1320
Reuchlin, Johannes, III:503
Reunion Association, VIII:2643
Reuther, Walter P., **IX:3161-3164**
Revelation, Book of, I:329, 338, 477; IV:1028,
    1452; VI:1867
"Revelation of St. Stephen, The," I:823
Revere, Paul, **IV:1156-1159**
Revert, Eugène, VII:631
Revista Multicolor de los Sábados, VII:373
Revolution, American. *See* American War of
    Independence
Revolutionary Command Council, VIII:2693,
    2694; IX:3289
Revolutionary Committee for Unity and Action,
    VII:6
Revue de progrès politique, social et litéraire, V:259
Reyes, Bernardo, VIII:2347
Reynolds, John Hamilton, VI:1266
Reynolds, Sir Joshua, **IV:1160-1164**
    Colonel George Coussmaker, IV:1162
    Copley, IV:357
    Discourses, IV:1160-1163
    Eliot Family, The, IV:1160
    First Lieutenant Paul Henry Ourry, IV:1160
    Gainsborough, IV:516, 517
    Kauffmann, IV:765, 767
    Lady Worsley, IV:1162
    Lawrence, IV:809, 811
    Marlborough Family, The, IV:1162

Master Crewe as Henry VIII, IV:1163
Master Hare, IV:1163
Miss Gideon and Her Brother, William, IV:1163
Mrs. Lloyd, IV:1163
Penelope Boothby, IV:1163
Raeburn, VI:1836
Rodney, IV:1179
Schoolboy, The, IV:1163
Reynolds v. Sims, IX:3890
Rex v. Almon, IV:907
Rex v. Delavel, IV:907
Rex v. Gordon, IV:907
Rex v. Webb, IV:906
RFC. *See* Reconstruction Finance Corporation
Rhee, Syngman, **IX:3165-3168**
Rheticus, Georg Joachim, III:178
rhetoric
    Bossuet, IV:170-172
    Cicero, I:194
    Isocrates, I:456-458
    Sylvester II, II:869
    Valla, III:740
Rhodes, Cecil, V:463, 1291; **VI:1873-1877;**
    IX:3453
Ribbentrop, Joachim von, VIII:2572
Ribicoff, Abraham, VIII:2679, 2680
ribonucleic acid. *See* RNA
Ribot, Théodule, VIII:1840
Ricardo, David, VI:1559, 1562, **1878-1881**
    *Essay on the Influence of a Low Price of Corn on
        the Profits of Stock, An,* VI:1879
    High Price of Bullion, The, VI:1878
    *On the Principles of Political Economy and
        Taxation,* VI:1559, 1879
    *Reply to Mr. Bosanquet's Practical Observation,
        A,* VI:1878
Ricci, Marco, IV:242
Rice, Daddy, V:810
Rich, Frank, VII:35, 36
Richard I, II:468, 732, 733, **782-785,** 810
Richard II, **II:786-789**
    Henry IV, II:457, 458
    Henry V, III:337
    Peasants' Revolt, II:114, 115, 921-923
Richard III, III:345, **647-653**
Richards, Ann, **IX:3169-3172**
Richards, Mira and Paul, VII:142
Richardson, Henry Hobson, **VI:1882-1885**
Richardson, Ralph, IX:2810, 2813, 2814
Richardson, Samuel
    Pamela, IV:470
Richard the Lion Heart. *See* Richard I

Richelieu, Cardinal de, **IV:1165-1169**
    Condé, IV:341
    Corneille, IV:363
    Frederick Henry, IV:501
    Jansen, IV:707, 709
    Louis XIII, IV:863-865
    Mazarin, IV:945
    Poussin, IV:1119
Richter, Gregorius, IV:154, 155
Ricimer, II:685
Rickard, George L. "Tex," VII:900, 902
Ricketts, Ed, IX:3516
Rickey, Branch, IX:3193, 3194
Rickover, Hyman G., **IX:3173-3177**
Riddle, Nelson, IX:3434
Ride, Sally, **IX:3178-3180**
Ridge, John, VI:1911
Ridley, Nicholas, **III:654-656**
    Book of Common Prayer, III:655
    Treatise Against the Error of
      Transubstantiation, III:655
    Treatise on the Worship of Images, A, III:655
Ridley, Robert, III:654
Riel, Louis, VI:1437, 1438; VIII:2101
Riemann, Georg Friedrich Bernhard,
    V:638, 639
Rienzo, Cola di, **II:790-792**
Riggs, Bobby, VIII:1968-1970
Righi, Augusto, VIII:2415
Right, Petition of, IV:213, 329, 333, 334, 1285
Rights, Bill of (U.S.)
    Hancock, IV:617
    Hand, VIII:1543
    Henry, IV:649
    Hughes, VIII:1769
    Madison, IV:888
    Mason, IV:927
Rijswijk, Treaty of, IV:1448
Riley, Charles, IX:2862
Rilke, Rainer Maria, **IX:3181-3184**
    Book of Hours, The, IX:3181
    Buch der Bilder, Das, IX:3182
    Duino Elegies, IX:3182
    New Poems, IX:3182, 3183
    Notebooks of Malte Laurids Brigge, The,
      IX:3182
    Sonnets to Orpheus, IX:3182
    Tale of the Love and Death of Coronet
      Christopher Rilke, The, IX:3182
Rimbaud, Arthur, **VI:1886-1888;** VII:448, 791
    "Drunken Boat," VI:1887
    Illuminations, VI:1887

    Season in Hell, A, VI:1887
    "Seer Letter," VI:1886
Rim-Sin, I:360, 361
Rimsky-Korsakov, Nikolay, V:287, 288; VI:1613,
    1614, **1889-1891**
    Christmas Eve, VI:1890
    Golden Cockerel, The, VI:1890, 1891
    Legend of the Invisible City of Kitezh and Maid
      Fevronia, The, VI:1890, 1891
    Maid of Pskov, The, VI:1889, 1890
    May Night, VI:1890
    Mlada, VI:1890
    Mozart and Salieri, VI:1890
    Pan Voyevods, VI:1890
    Sadko, VI:1890
    Servilia, VI:1890
    Snow Maiden, The, VI:1890
    Tale of Tsar Saltan, The, VI:1890
    Tsar's Bride, The, VI:1890
Rinuccini, Ottavio, IV:991, 992
Ripley, George, V:984
Riqueti, Honoré-Gabriel. *See* Mirabeau, Comte de
Risorgimento
    Browning, V:327
    Croce, VII:802
    Garibaldi, V:879, 881
    Gioberti, V:932-934
    Mazzini, VI:1514-1516
    Pius IX, VI:1782
    Visconti, IX:3818, 3819
Ritschl, Albrecht, **VI:1892-1895;** VIII:1557;
    IX:3722
    Christian Doctrine of Justification and
      Reconciliation, The, VI:1893, 1894
    Entsehung der altkatholischen Kirche, Die,
      VI:1893
    Evangelium Marcions und das Kanonische
      Evangelium des Lucas, Das, VI:1892
Ritschl, Friedrich Wilhelm, VI:1662
Rivera, Diego, **IX:3184-3186**
    Bandit Augustin Lorenzo, The, IX:3185
    Majorcan Landscape, IX:3185
    Vision of Alameda Central, IX:3185
RKO Pictures Corporation, IX:3934
RNA, VII:798; VIII:1827; IX:3997
Roanoke Island, III:638
Robbe-Grillet, Alain, VII:207
Robert I. *See* Bruce, Robert
Robert of Anjou, II:150
Robert of Normandy, II:443
Roberts, Clifford, VIII:1876, 1877
Robertson, Anna Mary. *See* Moses, Grandma

Robertson, William, IV:547
Robert the Steward, II:294, 296
Roberval, Gilles Personne de, IV:1332
Robeson, Paul, VIII:1546; IX:3081, **3187-3192**
   All God's Chillun Got Wings, IX:3189
   Emperor Jones, The, IX:3189
   Native Land, IX:3189
   "Ol' Man River," IX:3189
   Othello, IX:3189, 3191
   Proud Valley, IX:3189
Robespierre, **IV:1170-1173**
   Condorcet, IV:348
   Danton, IV:394, 395
   Fourier, V:819
   Saint-Just, IV:1205-1207
Robie House, IX:4061
Robinson, George D., V:284
Robinson, Jackie, **IX:3193-3197**
Robusti, Jacopo. *See* Tintoretto
Rochambeau, Comte de, **IV:1174-1177**
Roche, James, VIII:2679
Rochefort, Joseph J., Jr., VIII:2751
Rockefeller, John D., V:1045-1047;
   VI:1896-1900; VIII:1981
Rockefeller, Nelson, VII:1181; VIII:1999;
   IX:3196, 3633
Rockefeller Foundation
   Frisch, VII:1236, 1237
   Industrial Research Department, VIII:1981
   International Center for Genetic Epistemology,
     IX:2992
   Kinsey's sex research, VIII:1987-1989
   London School of Economics, VII:309
   National Research Council, VIII:2540
   Rockefeller, VI:1898
rocketry
   Goddard, VIII:1396-1398, 1500
   Heinkel, VIII:1614-1616
   Korolev, VIII:2019
   Oberth, IX:2777-2779
   Tsiolkovsky, IX:3749-3751
Rockingham, Lord, IV:222-224, 481, 482, 541,
   542, 1035, 1036
Rockingham, Marquess of, IV:1102
rock music
   Beatles, VII:226-229
   Charles, VII:658
   Joplin, VIII:1883-1885
   Presley, IX:3076-3079
   Terry, IX:3643
Rockwell Norman, **IX:3198-3200**
   Art Critic, The, IX:3200

Boy with Baby Carriage, IX:3198
Connoisseur, The, IX:3200
Four Freedoms, IX:3198, 3199
New Kids in the Neighborhood, IX:3199
Ruby Bridges Goes to School, IX:3199
Saying Grace, IX:3199
Southern Justice, IX:3199
Triple Self-Portrait, IX:3200
Rocky Mountain Fur Company, VI:2078
Rocroi, Battle of, IV:341, 343, 865
Rodgers, John, VI:1760, 1764
Rodgers, Richard, VIII:1533, 1534, 1536,
   1566-1569; **IX:3201-3203**
   Boys from Syracuse, The, IX:3201
   Carousel, IX:3202
   Flower Drum Song, IX:3202
   I Remember Mama, IX:3202
   King and I, The, IX:3202
   No Strings, IX:3202
   Oklahoma!, IX:3201, 3202
   On Your Toes, IX:3201
   Pal Joey, IX:3201
   Show Boat, IX:3201
   Sound of Music, The, IX:3202
   South Pacific, IX:3202
Rodin, Auguste, **VI:1900-1903;** VII:416;
   VIII:2017; IX:3181
   Age of Bronze, The, VI:1900
   Gates of Hell, The, VI:1900
   Kiss, The, VI:1901
   Saint John the Baptist Preaching, VI:1900
   Thinker, The, VI:1900
   Walking Man, VI:1901
Rodney, George, **IV:1178-1181**
Rodzevitch, Konstantin, IX:3754
Roebling, John Augustus, **VI:1904-1906**
Roebuck, John, IV:183, **1182-1186**
Roe v. Wade, VII:511; IX:3143
Roger II, II:506
Roger of Salisbury, II:848
Rogers, Buddy, IX:3008
Rogers, Ginger, VII:125, 127, 128
Rogers, Will, **IX:3204-3208**
   Laughing Bill Hyde, IX:3205
Rogers, Woodes, IV:390
Rohan, Louis-René-Édouard, prince de,
   IV:919
Rohilla War, IV:632, 633
Rohmer, Eric, VIII:1391
Roila, I:124
Rokitansky, Karl von, VI:2021
Rolfe, John, IV:1107, 1108, 1254

Rollo, **II:793-795**
Rolls, Charles Stewart, **IX:3209-3212**
Rolls-Royce Limited, IX:3209-3211
Rolph, John, V:116, 117
Roman Catholic Relief Act of 1829, V:905
Roman Inquisition
    Abano, II:2
    Bruno, III:97, 98
    Dominic, II:303
    Gregory IX, II:401
    Veronese, III:748
Romberg, Sigmund, VIII:1533, 1534
Rome, Council of, II:675
Rommel, Erwin, VIII:1950; **IX:3213-3216,** 3261
Romney, George, **IV:1187-1190**
    Death of General Wolfe, The, IV:1187
    Death of King Edmund, The, IV:1187
Roncalli, Angelo Giuseppe. *See* John XXIII
Ronsard, Pierre de, **III:657-659**
    Amours, Les, III:657
    Bocage, Le, III:657
    Derniers Vers, Les, III:659
    Discours des misères de ce temps, III:658
    Franciade, Le, III:658
    Hymnes, Les, III:658
    Nouvelle continuation de amours, III:658
    Odes, III:657
    Remonstrance au peuple de France, III:658
    Sonnets for Helen, III:658, 659
Rooney, Mickey, VII:1305
Roosevelt, Eleanor, VII:72; **IX:3217-3221,** 3222,
    3224, 3244, 3245
Roosevelt, Franklin D., **IX:3222-3227**
    Acheson, VII:17
    atom bomb development, VII:1147
    Beard, VII:223, 224
    Black, VII:321
    Butler, VII:525, 526
    Cardozo, VII:576, 577
    Churchill, VII:693
    Curtin, VII:817
    de Gaulle, VII:866, 867
    farm policy, IX:3860, 3861
    George VI, VII:1344
    Harriman, VIII:1560, 1561
    Hearst, VIII:1603
    Hindemith, VIII:1672
    Hiss, VIII:1683
    Hoover, Herbert, VIII:1729, 1730
    Hoover, J. Edgar, VIII:1733
    Hopkins, VIII:1736-1738
    Hull, VIII:1779-1781

    Johnson, VIII:1866, 1867
    King, VIII:1983, 1984
    labor legislation, VIII:2171, 2172
    La Guardia, VIII:2055, 2056
    Lippmann, VIII:2204, 2205
    Long, VIII:2228, 2229
    Luce, VIII:2256, 2257
    Lyons, VIII:2294
    Marshall, VIII:2429, 2431
    Mohammad Reza Shah Pahlavi, VIII:2567
    Nimitz, VIII:2750, 2752
    Perkins, IX:2962, 2963
    polio, IX:3307
    racial discrimination, IX:3114
    Rockwell, IX:3199
    Roosevelt, Eleanor, IX:3217, 3218, 3220
    Sinclair, IX:3428, 3429
    Smith, IX:3441
    Stimson, IX:3539
    Thomas, IX:3661
    Truman, IX:3740
    Wallace, IX:3860, 3861
    zeppelins, VII:1014
Roosevelt, Theodore, **IX:3228-3231**
    Altgeld, V:56
    Borah, V:280
    Butler, VII:525
    Canada-Alaska boundary, V:1070
    Grey, VIII:1476
    Hanna, V:1030, 1031
    Harris's books, V:1051
    Hearst, VIII:1603
    Hughes, VIII:1766-1768
    Lodge, VIII:2219-2221
    Morgan, VI:1582
    Panama, V:1069; VIII:1409, 1436
    Peary, IX:2944
    Remington, VI:1862
    Roosevelt, Franklin D., IX:3222
    Root, IX:3232, 3233
    Ross, IX:3245
    Stimson, IX:3537, 3538
    Taft, IX:3594-3596
    Washington, VI:2337
Root, Elihu, **IX:3232-3235,** 3537, 3538
Root, Elisha, V:540, 541
Root, John Wellborn, V:365
Root and Branch Bill, IV:308
Rorschach, Hermann, **IX:3236-3238**
    Psychodiagnostics, IX:3236-3238
Rosamund, II:42
Rosburg, Percy, VII:368

Roscius, I:195
Rose, Pete, **IX:3239-3242**
Rosebery, Lord, VII:121; VIII:1475, 1476
Rose Law Firm, VII:714
Rosenberg, Alfred, VIII:1405
Rosenberg, Ethel and Julius, IX:3037
Rosenwald Foundation, VII:984
Roses, Wars of the
    Edward IV, III:234, 235
    Fortescue, III:267
    Henry IV, II:457
    Henry VI, III:341, 342
    Henry VII, III:345, 346
    Richard III, III:647, 651
    Tudor family, III:732
    Warwick, III:774-777
Rosewall, Kenneth R., VIII:2110
Rosicrucian sect, IX:3331, 4082
Rosing, Boris, IX:4125
Ross, Betsy, **IV:1191-1193**
Ross, Sir James Clark, **VI:1907-1909**
Ross, John, **VI:1910-1912**
Ross, Nellie Tayloe, **IX:3243-3246**
Ross, Robert, VI:1281
Ross, Ronald, **IX:3247-3250**
Rossellini, Roberto, VII:1141, IX:3736
Rossetti, Dante Gabriel, III:765; V:1168; VI:1588;
    VIII:2689
Rossi, Persiano, III:552
Rossini, Gioacchino, VI:1686, **1913-1915**
    Barber of Seville, The, VI:1913, 1914
    cambiale di matrimonio, La, VI:1913
    Demetrio e Polibio, VI:1913
    donna del lago, La, VI:1914, 1915
    Guillaume Tell, VI:1914, 1915
    Otello, VI:1914, 1915
    Péchés de viellesse, VI:1915
    Petite messe solennelle, VI:1915
    Stabat Mater, VI:1915
    Tancredi, VI:1913, 1914
Rostand, Edmond
    Cyrano de Bergerac, IV:385-387
Rostilav, II:279
Rota, Nino, VII:1142
Roth, Hieronymus, IV:510
Rothad of Soissons, II:673
Rothermere, First Viscount. *See* Harmsworth,
    Harold
Rothmere, Lord, VII:169
Rothschild Bank, VI:1916-1919
Rothschild family, **VI:1916-1920**
Rotterdam, architecture of, IV:2859, 2860

Rouault, Georges, **IX:3251-3253**
    Miserere, IX:3252, 3253
Rouelle, Guillaume, IV:805
Rouges, Les, VIII:2100
Rough Riders, IX:3228
Round Hill School for Boys, V:125, 126
Rousseau, Henri, **VI:1921-1924;** VIII:2546
    Carnival Evening, The, VI:1932
    Dream, The, VI:1932
    Football Players, The, VI:1932
    Hungry Lion, The, VI:1932
    Sleeping Gypsy, The, VI:1932
Rousseau, Jean-Jacques, **IV:1194-1197**
    Bakunin, V:112
    Boswell, IV:175, 177
    Condillac, IV:344
    Condorcet, IV:349
    Confessions of J.-J. Rousseau, The, IV:1196
    Cunning-Man, IV:1196
    Devin du village, Le, IV:226
    Dictionary of Music, IV:227
    Discourse on the Arts and Sciences, A, IV:1194
    Discourse upon Inequality Among Mankind, A,
      IV:1196
    Emilius and Sophia, IV:1196; VI:1767, 2092
    Fragonard, IV:489
    Machiavelli, III:451
    New Héloïse, The, IV:1196
    Robespierre, IV:1171
    Saint-Just, IV:1205
    Treatise on the Social Contract, A, IV:1196,
      1205
    Voltaire, IV:1394
Royal Academy of London
    Bessemer, V:218
    Constable, V:549
    Copley, IV:358
    Gainsborough, IV:516
    Hunt, V:1169
    Kauffmann, IV:767
    Lawrence, IV:808-811
    Raeburn, VI:1837
    Reynolds, IV:1160, 1162
    Scott, VI:2003
    Stuart, IV:1290
    Turner, VI:2272, 2273
Royal Geographic Society
    Burton, V:375
    Galton, V:868
    Livingstone, VI:1399
    Mackinder, VIII:2321-2323
    Speke, VI:2084

Stanley, VI:2102
Workman, VI:2412
Royalists
　Clarendon, IV:309
　Cromwell, IV:380, 381
　Fairfax, IV:448, 449
　Hale, IV:596, 597
　Hobbes, IV:664
　James II, IV:703
　Leeds, IV:821-823
　Shaftesbury, IV:1228, 1229
Royal Marriages Act of 1772, IV:479; VII:1062
Royal Navy
　Anson, IV:55-57
　Barclay, VI:1764
　Bligh, IV:143, 145, 146
　Bonnard, VII:365
　Brunel, V:339
　Buckingham, IV:212
　Cook, IV:354
　George I, IV:533
　George VI, VII:1343
　Kidd, IV:777, 779
　Mountbatten, VIII:2641-2645
　Nelson, VI:1634-1636
　Perry, VI:1764, 1766
　Phillip, IV:1091, 1092
　Reith, IX:3148
　Rodney, IV:1178-1180
　Vancouver, IV:1355, 1356
　Windsor, IX:4025
Royal Niger Company, V:953, 954; VIII:2269, 2270
Royal Society of London
　Audubon, V:87
　Babbage, V:101, 102
　Banks, IV:83, 85, 86
　Boyle, IV:187
　Bragg, VII:410
　Cavendish, IV:261-263
　Cook, IV:351, 353
　Dalton, V:604
　Davy, V:621-623
　Dryden, IV:424
　Faraday, V:767
　Florey, VII:1174
　Grove, V:1010-1013
　Halley, IV:600-602
　Huxley, V:1172, 1173
　Jenner, IV:723
　Kämpfer, IV:755, 756
　Lanchester, VIII:2071

Lister, VI:1389, 1390
Malpighi, IV:892
Maxwell, VI:1511
Murdock, IV:1010
Newton, IV:1025, 1027
Papin, IV:1059-1061
Roebuck, IV:1185
Rutherford, IX:3279
Siemens, VI:2067
Street, VI:2162
Wedgwood, IV:1423
Wheatstone, V:558
Wren, IV:1480
Royal Supremecy, Act of, III:68, 208, 265, 351, 535, 654
Royce, Sir Frederick Henry, **IX:3209-3212**
Royce, Josiah, **IX:3254-3256**
　Outlines of Psychology, IX:3254, 3255
　Philosophy of Loyalty, The, IX:3255
　Race Questions, Provincialism and Other American Problems, IX:3255
Roye, William, III:736
Roxborough, John, VIII:2241
Rozier, Ferdinand, V:86
RSFSR. *See* Russian Soviet Federated Soviet Republic
Rubens, Peter Paul, III:88; IV:737; **1198-1201**
　Descent from the Cross, IV:1198
　Elevation of the Cross, The, IV:1198
　Landscape with a Rainbow, IV:1200
　Landscape with a Sunset, IV:1200
　Landscape with the Château De Steen, IV:1200
　Portrait of the Marchesa Brigida Spinola-Doria, IV:1198
　Three Graces, The, IV:1200
　Tigers and Lions Hunt, IV:1200
Rubenstein, Arthur, IX:3816
Rubicon, Operation, VI:1620
Rucellai, Giovanni, III:9
Rudolf I, **II:796-799**
Rudolf IV, II:729
Rudolf of Swabia, II:462
Rudolph II, III:79, 691
Rudolph III, II:450
Rufus, Publius Sulpicius, I:834
Rufus, Tineius, I:29
Rukeyser, Muriel, **IX:3257-3259**
　"Effort at Speech Between Two People," IX:3257
　"Facing Sentencing," IX:3257
　Gates, The, IX:3258
　Theory of Flight, IX:3257
Rumagan, II:560

Rumi, Jalal al-Din, **II:800-802**
  Divan-e Shams-e Tabriz, II:800
  Mathnawi, The, II:800
Rumsey, James, IV:477
Rundstedt, Gerd von, **IX:3260-3263**
Runnels, Hardin, V:1138
Rupert, Prince, IV:134
Rupert III, II:970, 971
Rural Constabulary Act, V:459
Rurik, **II:803-805**
Rusas I, I:754
Rush, Benjamin, **IV:1202-1204,** 1468
  *Medical Inquiries and Observations upon the
    Diseases of the Mind,* IV:1203
Rushdie, Salman
  Satanic Verses, The, VIII:1959
Rusk, Dean, IX:3870
Ruskin, John, V:1113, 1169, 1170; **VI:1925-1929,**
    2273, 2274, 2364, 2377; IX:3089, 3090
  Fors Clavigera, VI:1928
  Modern Painters, VI:1925, 1927
  Munera Pulveris, VI:1927
  Praeterita, VI:1928
  Seven Lamps of Architecture, The, VI:1927
  Stones of Venice, The, VI:1927
  Unto This Last, VI:1927
Ruskin Hall, VII:221
Russell, Bertrand, V:837; VII:284, 584;
    VIII:2605-2607; **IX:3264-3267,** 3432
  History of Western Philosophy, IX:3266
  Marriage and Morals, IX:3266
  Practice and Theory of Bolshevism, The,
    IX:3266
  Principles of Mathematics, The, VII:582;
    VIII:2608, 2725; IX:3264, 3966
  Principles of Social Reconstruction, IX:3266
  Problems of Philosophy, The, IX:3264
Russell, Bill, **IX:3268-3272**
Russell, Lord John, **VI:1930-1932,** 2308
Russell, Lord William, VI:1930
Russian Orthodox Church
  Alexander Nevsky, II:53, 54
  Catherine the Great, IV:257, 259
  Ivan the Great, III:383
  Ivan the Terrible, III:386
  Khrushchev, VIII:1962
  Mott, VIII:2639
  Nicholas I, VI:1650
  Nikon, IV:1030-1032
  Peter III, IV:1087-1089
  Peter the Great, IV:1085
  Pius XI, IX:3028

  Rasputin, VI:1842
  Tolstoy, VI:2243, 2245
  Ypsilanti, VI:2418
Russian Revolution of 1905
  Luxemburg, VIII:2285, 2286
  Pobedonostsev, VI:1791, 1792
  Trotsky, IX:3727
Russian Revolution of 1917
  Bernstein, VII:293
  Blok, VII:333
  Bukharin, VII:491, 492
  Gorky, VIII:1442, 1444, 1445
  Gramsci, VIII:1459, 1460
  Hoover, VIII:1732
  Horowitz, VIII:1747, 1748
  Hughes, VIII:1768
  Kandinsky, VIII:1904
  Kazantzakis, VIII:1920
  Kerensky, VIII:1941, 1942
  Lenin, VIII:2161
  Litvinov, VIII:2208
  Ludendorff, VIII:2266
  Malenkov, VIII:2377
  Masaryk, VIII:2441
  Trotsky, IX:3726-3728
  Tsvetayeva, IX:3753-3755
  Zhukov, IX:4116
Russian Social Democratic Workers' Party,
    VIII:2161, 2208; IX:3726
Russian Soviet Federated Soviet Republic,
    IX:4086, 4087
Russian Workers, Union of, VIII:1732
Russo-German War, VIII:2398
Russo-Japanese War, VIII:2091, 2396, 2429;
    IX:3233
Russo-Turkish War, IV:1299; V:143, 678
Rustichello, II:751, 753
Rusticus, I:257, 258
Ruth, Babe, VII:1323; IX:2797, 2798, **3273-3276**
Ruthenia, II:212; VII:261
Rutherford, Ernest, **IX:3277-3280**
  Bohr, VII:345
  Bragg, VII:411, 412
  Hevesy, VIII:1654-1656
  Kapitsa, VIII:1906, 1907
  Meitner, VIII:2477, 2478
  Radiations from Radioactive Substances, VII:635
Rutherglen Declaration, IV:240
Ryder, Sir Dudley, IV:906

SA. *See* Sturm Abteilung
SAA. *See* Syndicat Agricole Africain

Sabin, Albert, IX:3306

Sabina, Poppaea, I:578, 579

Sabri, Ali, IX:3290

Sacagawea, **VI:1933-1935**

Sacco, Nicola, VII:1212; IX:2885, 3060,
    3281-3284

Saccus, Ammonius, I:666

Sacheverell, Henry, IV:52, 53, 1277

Sachs, Nelly, **IX:3285-3288**
    Eli: A Mystery Play of the Sufferings of Israel,
        IX:3286
    Fahrt ins Staublose, IX:3286
    Flucht und Verwandlung, IX:3286
    In den Wohnungren des Todes, IX:3286
    O the Chimneys, IX:3287
    Sternverdunkelung, IX:3286
    Und niemand weiss weiter, IX:3286

Sachs, Sadie, IX:3313, 3314

Sac rebellion, VI:2010

Sadat, Anwar el-, **IX:3289-3291**
    Boutros-Ghali, VII:399
    Faisal, VIII:1119
    Meir, VIII:2474, 2475
    Nasser, VIII:2696
    Nixon, VIII:2760

Sadducees, I:467

Sa'di, **II:806-808**
    Orchard, The, II:806-808
    Rose Garden, The, II:806-808

Sadler Committee, V:458

Sadler's Wells Ballet, IX:3873

Safavids, IV:4-6

Safed Cabalists, III:441

Sagan, Carl, IX:2829, **3292-3295**
    Contact, IX:3294
    Cosmos, IX:3293
    Dragons of Eden, The, IX:3293

Sagarmartha National Park, VIII:1664

Sahle Mariam. *See* Menelik II

Sahle Selassie, VI:1537

Said, Mohammed, VI:1355, 1356

Saigo Takamori, **VI:1936-1939**

Sailer, Tony, VIII:1966

St. Albans, Battle of, III:647, 774, 775

St. Albans Monastery, II:663

Saint Bartholomew's Day Massacre, III:133, 333,
    364, 537, 672, 782

St. Benedict, Rule of, II:136, 137

St. Brice's Day Massacre, II:202, 345

Saint Catherine of Mount Sinai monastery,
    II:556

St.-Clair-sur-Epte, Treaty of, II:794

St. Croix Island, IV:271

Saint Cyr, Château de, IV:902

St. Denis, Ruth, VII:1263, 1264

Saint-Denis monastery, II:859-861

Saint-Domingue, IV:1338-1340

Sainte-Beuve, Charles, IX:3089

Saint Francis, Church of, II:272

Saint-Gaudens, Augustus, **VI:1940-1942**
    Diana, VI:1941
    Grief, VI:1941
    Hiawatha, VI:1940
    Silence, VI:1940

St. George, Guild of, VI:1928

St. George Civic Guard Company, IV:604, 605

St. Germain, Treaty of, VII:260

St. Gervaise, Church of, IV:374

Saint Giovanni Evangelista, church of, III:184, 186

St. Jacques-aux-Pèlerins, Confraternity of, II:762

St. James Church, VI:1448

St. James the Less, church of, VI:2161

Saint Jerome, Order of, IV:382

St. John, Henry. *See* Bolingbroke, First Viscount

Saint-Julien, Baron de, IV:488

Saint-Just, Louis de, IV:395, **1205-1208**
    *Esprit de la révolution et de la constitution de
        France,* IV:1205
    Fragmens sur les institutions républicaines,
        IV:1207

St. Lawrence River, III:129-131; IV:273, 351

St. Louis Chronicle, VI:2015

St. Louis Enquirer, V:195

St. Louis Post-Dispatch, VI:1825, 1826

St. Luke, Academy of, IV:275

Saint Luke, Guild of, III:85

St. Mark, Procurators of, III:664

St. Mark's Basilica, III:284, 285

Saint Martial organum, II:723

Saint Mary Magdalene, Order of, II:401

St. Mary Woolnoth, Church of, IV:637

St. Paul, Minneapolis, and Manitoba Railroad,
    IV:659, 660

Saint Peter, Church of, III:83, 84, 407

Saint-Simon, Claude Henri de, IV:457; V:543, 544;
    VI:1369

St. Thomas Church, IV:77

St. Valentine's Day Massacre, VII:564

Saint Vincent de Paul, Society of, IV:1382

Saint Vitalis, Church of, II:556

Saisset, Bernard, II:172

Saito Tatsuoki, III:570

Sajjan, III:541

Sakai Hoitsu, IV:1042

Sakharov, Andrei, VIII:1426; **IX:3296-3300**
Sakyamuni. *See* Buddha
Saladin, II:125, 782, **809-811**
Salah al-Din Zarkub, II:801
Salamis, Battle of, I:10, 198, 803, 857-859, 965
Salem witchcraft trials, IV:934, 935, 940, 1225-1227
Salieri, Antonio, IV:550
Salih, al-, II:810
Salim, III:6
Salimbene, **II:812-814**
    Chronicle of Salimbene de Adam, The,
      II:812-814
Salim Salim, IX:2957
Salinger, J.D., **IX:3301-3304**
    Catcher in the Rye, The, VII:350; IX:3301-3303
    "For Esmé—with Love and Squalor," IX:3301, 3302
    Franny and Zooey, IX:3302, 3303
    "Hapworth 16, 1924," IX:3303
    Nine Stories, IX:3302
    Raise High the Roof Beam Carpenters and
      Seymour: An Introduction, IX:3303
Salisbury, First Earl of, **III:660-663,** 774
Salisbury, Third Marquess of, IV:700; V:462; **VI:1943-1946**
Salk, Jonas Edward, **IX:3305-3307**
Salk Institute for Biological Studies, IX:3306, 3307
Sallust, **I:742-745**
    Histories, I:743
    War with Catiline, The, I:743
    War with Jugurtha, The, I:743
Salmon, Daniel, IX:3450, 3451
Salmone, I:475
Salomé, Lou, VI:1664
Salomon, II:574, 575
SALT I. *See* Strategic Arms Limitation Treaties
Salto de Alvarado, III:22
Saltzmann, Christian, IV:93
Salvarsan, VII:1166
Salvation Army, V:275, 277
Salvianus, I:695
Samaritan Pentateuch, I:822
Samaritans, I:642, 822-824, 868
Samarkand, II:885; III:36, 38
Sambhaji, IV:71
Samos, I:13, 314, 315
Samoset, IV:930
Samprati, I:113
Sampson, Edith, VIII:1887
Sampson, William T., V:658

Samuel, **I:746-749**
Samuel ha-Nagid, II:498, 499
San Andrea, Church of, II:748, 762
Sanarelli, Giuseppe, VI:1858
Sánchez Cerro, Luis M., VIII:1585
Sanctorius Sanctorius. *See* Santorio Santorio
Sand, George, V:70, 494, 1099; **VI:1951-1954**
    Consuelo, VI:1952
    Devil's Pool, The, VI:1952
    Francis the Waif, VI:1952
    History of My Life, VI:1952
    Indiana, VI:1951
    Jacques, VI:1951
    Lélia, VI:1951
    Letters of a Traveller, VI:1951
    Little Fadette, VI:1952
    Mauprat, VI:1951
    Miller of Angibault, The, VI:1952
    She and He, VI:1952
    Spiridion, VI:1952
    Valentine, VI:1951
Sandburg, Carl, **IX:3308-3312**
    Abraham Lincoln, IX:3310
    Always the Young Strangers, IX:3311
    American Songbag, The, IX:3310
    Chicago Poems, IX:3310
    Cornhuskers, IX:3310
    People, Yes, The, IX:3310
    Remembrance Rock, IX:3311
Sandemanians, V:767
Sander, August, VII:96
Sandwich, Earl of, IV:1440
San Francisco *Examiner,* VIII:1601
Sanger, Margaret, VII:1071; VIII:1637; **IX:3313-3316**
    Family Limitation, IX:3314
Sangha, I:145
San Giuliano, church of, III:665
San Jacinto, Battle of, V:1138
Sankey, Ira, VI:1575, 1576
San Lorenzo, church of, III:519
San Marco, Piazza, III:664-666; IV:242
San Martín, José de, V:268; VI:1688, 1689, **1947-1950**
San Mateo v. Southern Pacific, V:789
San Miniato al Monte, Church of, II:83
San Petronio, Church of, III:390
San San Juku, VIII:2754
San Sebastiano, Church of, III:747
Sansovino, Andrea, III:664
Sansovino, Jacopo, **III:664-666**
Santa Ana, III:141, 142

Santa Anna, Antonio López de, V:579, 580, 615,
1138, 1250; **VI:1955-1957**
Santa Barbara Botanic Garden, VII:1131
Santa Croce, Church of, II:83
Santa Maria del Carmine, Church of, III:484
Santa Maria del Fiore, cathedral of, II:83, 84;
III:89
Santa Maria la Antigua del Darién, III:45
Santa Maria Novella, Church of, II:83, 84;
III:9
Santayana, George, **IX:3317-3319**
Egotism in German Philosophy, IX:3317
Life of Reason, The, IX:3317
Persons and Places, IX:3318
Realms of Being, IX:3318
Santo Domingo, V:1152
Santorio Santorio, **IV:1209-1212**
Commentaria in artem medicinalem Galeni,
IV:1210
*Commentaria in primam fen primi libri canonis
Avicennae*, IV:1211
Medicina Statica, IV:1210
*Methodi vitandorum errorum omnium qui in arte
medica contingunt*, IV:1209
Santos-Dumont, Alberto, **IX:3320-3323**
San Xia project. *See* Three Gorges Dam
San Zeno, Church of, III:461, 462
Sanzio, Raffaello. *See* Raphael
Sappho, **I:750-753**
"Ode to Aphrodite," I:750, 751
"Seizure," I:750, 751
Sarabaitic monks, I:784
Saragosa, La, **VI:1958-1960**
Sarah, I:6
Sardanapalus, I:107
Sargent, Charles Sprague, VII:1130
Sargent, John Singer, **VI:1961-1965;** VII:1300
Ellen Terry as Lady Macbeth, VI:1962
Gassed, VI:1962
Jaleo, El, VI:1961
Lady Sassoon, VI:1962
Lord Ribblesdale, VI:1962
Madame Gautreau, VI:1961
Oyster Gatherers of Cancale, The, VI:1961
Triumph of Marie de' Medici, VI:1961
Woodrow Wilson, VI:1962
Wyndham Sisters, VI:1962
Sargon II, **I:754-756**
Saratoga, Second Battle of, IV:66
Sarnoff, David, IX:4125, 4127
Sarotti, Ambrose, IV:1059
Sarpi, Paolo, IV:1209

Sarraute, Nathalie, **IX:3324-3326**
Portrait of a Man Unknown, IX:3324, 3325
Tropisms, IX:3324, 3325
Sartach, Prince, II:987, 988
Sartre, Jean-Paul, **IX:3327-3330**
Age of Reason, The, IX:3327
Bariona, IX:3329
Beauvoir, VII:230-232
Being and Nothingness, IX:3329
Camus, VII:553, 555
Césaire, VII:631
Flies, The, IX:3329
Giraudoux, VII:1381
Grass, VIII:1465
Heidegger, VIII:1612
Merleau-Ponty, VIII:2501
Nausea, VII:1360; IX:3327
No Exit, IX:3329
Pirandello, IX:3015
Roads to Freedom, The, IX:3327
Saint Genet: Actor and Martyr, IX:3329
Sarraute, IX:3324
Situations, IX:3329
Wall and Other Stories, The, IX:3327
What Is Literature?, VII:207; IX:3329
Sassanid Dynasty, I:778-781
Sataspes, I:370
Satie, Erik, IX:3066, **3331-3335**
Relâche, IX:3333
Socrate, VII:539
Sports et divertissements, IX:3333
Trois Gnossiennes, IX:3331
Trois Gymnopédies, IX:3331, 3333, 3334
Trois Morceaux en forme de poire,
IX:3332, 3333
satire
Aristophanes, I:88, 90-92
Callimachus, I:156
Capek, VII:562
Catullus, I:170
Cyrano de Bergerac, IV:386
Gilbert and Sullivan, V:930
Goya, IV:572
Hogarth, IV:668-670
Juvenal, I:488, 489
Lucian, I:507-509
Plautus, I:659, 660
Rabelais, III:633, 634, 636
Rogers, IX:3204-3207
Swift, IV:1305, 1307-1309
Weill, IX:3928
Sato, Eisaku, **IX:3336-3339**

Satsuma Rebellion, VI:1936-1939
Saturday Evening Post, The, IX:3198, 3199
Saturn, IV:695
Saturninus, Lucius Appuleius, I:529
Saturn rocket, VII:440, 441
Satyrus, I:43
Sauk Indians, V:247, 249, 250
Saul, I:241, 746, 748, 749
Saunders, Charles, IV:1473
Saunders, Otis, V:1239
Saussure, Ferdinand de, VII:913; **IX:3340-3343**
    Course in General Linguistics, IX:3342
    *Mémoire sur le système primitif des voyelles
        dans les langues indo-européennes,*
        IX:3340, 3341
Sauve, Jeanne, **IX:3344-3346**
Savage, Richard, IV:728
Savannah, IV:1044
Savery, Thomas, IV:1023, 1024, 1060
Savigny, Friedrich Karl von, **VI:1966-1968**
    *History of Roman Law During the Middle Ages,
        The,* VI:1967
    *Juristische Methodenlehre, nach der
        Ausarbeitung des Jakob Grimm,* VI:1967
    Obligationenrecht, Das, VI:1967
    *Of the Vocation of Our Age for Legislation and
        Jurisprudence,* VI:1966
    System des heutigen römischen Rechts, VI:1967
    Treatise on Possession, VI:1966
    Vermischte Schriften, VI:1967
Savonarola, Girolamo, III:16, 448, 498, **667-670**
Saxe-Eisenach, Duke of, IV:1320
Saxe-Weimar, Duke of, IV:76
Saxo Grammaticus, **II:815-818**
    History of the Danes, The, II:815-817
Saxony
    Beust, V:222-224
    Carpini, II:206-208
    Charlemagne, II:228
    Charles Martel, II:243
    Henry IV, II:461
    Henry the Lion, II:466-469
Sayyid Ahmad Khan. *See* Ahmad Khan, Sir Sayyid
Scala family, II:288
Scalero, Rosario, VIII:2494
Scalia, Antonin, IX:3658
Scaliger, Julius Caesar, III:671
Scaliger, Joseph Justus, **III:671-674**
    *Coniectanea in M. Terentium Varronem de
        lingua latina,* III:671
    De emendatione temporum, III:672
    Thesaurus temporum, III:672

Scapula, Publius Ostorius, I:136
Scarlatti, Alessandro, **IV:1213-1216**
    caduta de'Decemviri, La, IV:1214
    Griselda, La, IV:1215
    honestà negli amori, L', IV:1213
    Macro Attilio Regolo, IV:1215
    Mass for S Cecilia, IV:1215
    Mitridate Eupatore, Il, IV:1214
    Pirro e Demetrio, Il, IV:1214
    Sinfonie di concerto grosso, IV:1215
    Su le sponde del Tebro, IV:1215
    Telemaco, IV:1215
    Tigrane, Il, IV:1215
    trionfo del'lonore, Il, IV:1215
Schall, Adam, IV:757
Scharnhorst, Gerhard Johann David von, V:940;
    VI:1969-1971
Scheler, Max, IX:**3347-3350,** 3507
    Genius des Krieges und der deutsche Krieg, Der,
        IX:3348
Schelling, Friedrich Wilhelm Joseph, IV:155, 467,
    468; V:1080; **VI:1972-1975**
    Ages of the World, The, VI:1973
    Introduction to Idealism, VI:1973
    Introduction to the Philosophy of Nature, VI:1973
    Of Human Freedom, VI:1973
    Philosophie der Mythologie, VI:1973
    *Über die Möglichkeit einer Form der
        Philosophie überhaupt,* VI:1972
    Vom Ich als Prinzip der Philosophie, VI:1972
    Von der Weltselle, VI:1973
Schiaparelli, Giovanni Virginio, I:311
Schiff, Jacob, IX:3837-3839
Schiller, Friedrich, IV:652, **1217-1220**
    Cabal and Love, IV:1217
    Don Carlos, Infante of Spain, IV:1217
    Fiesco, IV:1217
    Guillaume Tell, VI:1914
    *History of the Defection of the United
        Netherlands from the Spanish Empire,* IV:1217
    History of the Thirty Years' War, IV:1219
    Robbers, The, IV:1217
Schinkel, Karl Friedrich, VIII:2520
Schleicher, Kurt von, IX:2877
Schleiermacher, Friedrich, **VI:1976-1979**
    Christian Faith, The, VI:1976-1978
    On Religion, VI:1976, 1977
    Schleiermacher's Soliloquies, VI:1977
Schley, Winfield S., V:658
Schlick, Moritz, VII:582
Schlieffen, Count Alfred von, VIII:1674
Schlieffen Plan, VIII:2265

Schliemann, Heinrich, **VI:1980-1983**
  Ilios, VI:1981
  Tiryns, VI:1982
  Troja, VI:1981
  Troy and Its Remains, VI:1981
Schmalkaldic War, III:160
Schmeling, Max, VIII:2243
Schmidman, Jo Ann, IX:3643, 3644
Schmidt, Auguste, IX:4112
Schmidt, Bernhard Voldemar, **IX:3351-3353**
Schmidt, Carl, IX:2855
Schmidt, Helmut, VII:429; VIII:2009
Schmidt-Rottluff, Karl, **IX:3354-3356**
  Houses at Night, IX:3355
  Midday on the Moor, IX:3355
  Portrait of a Girl, IX:3355
Schnitzler, Arthur
  Call of Life, VIII:2142
Schoenberg, Arnold, VII:271, 272, 386, 387;
    IX:3357-3361, 3914-3916
  Erwartung, Op 17, IX:3358
  First Chamber Symphony, Op. 9, IX:3358
  Jakobsleiter, Die, IX:3359
  Pierrot Lunaire, VII:387
  String Quartet in D Minor Op. 7 No. 1, IX:3358
  Verklärte Nacht, IX:3357
Schönborn, Friedrich Carl von, IV:656, 657
Schönborn, Johann Philipp Franz von, IV:657
Schopenhaeur, Arthur, VI:1662, 1664, **1984-1987;**
    VIII:1650, 1651
  Basis of Morality, The, VI:1985
  On the Will in Nature, VI:1985
  Parerga and Paralipomena, VI:1986
  World as Will and Idea, The, VI:1984, 1986
Schott and Sons, VIII:1670
Schröder, Gerhard, VIII:2010
Schrödinger, Erwin, VII:473; **IX:3363-3365**
  What Is Life?, IX:3364
Schubert, Franz, VI:1393, **1988-1991,** 1993;
    VIII:2359
  "'Erlkonig," VI:1989
  "'Lindenbaum, Der," VI:1989
  "Schöne Müllerin, Die, VI:1989
  "'Symphony in C Major," VI:1995
  "Trout, VI:1988
  "'Unfinished" Symphony in B Minor, VI:1989
  "Winterreise, Die, VI:1989; IX:3066
  "Zwillingsbrüder, Die, VI:1988
Schumann, Clara, V:299, 300
Schumann, Robert, V:299, 300; VI:1392,
    1992-1995
  Genoveva, VI:1993

  Rhenish, VI:1994
  Spring Symphony, VI:1993
Schurz, Carl, **VI:1996-1998;** VIII:1402
Schütz, Heinrich, **IV:1221-1224**
  Becker Psalter, IV:1222, 1223
  Dafne, IV:1222
  Geistliche Chormusik, IV:1222
  Kleine geistliche Concerte, IV:1222
  Psalmen Davids, IV:1221
  Symphoniae sacrae, IV:1222, 1223
Schutzstaffel
  Baeck, VII:149
  Guderian, VIII:1491, 1492
  Himmler, VIII:1666-1668
  Rommel, IX:3213, 3215
  Wiesenthal, IX:3985, 3986
Schuyler, Philip, IV:66; V:369, 370
Schwab, Charles, V:421
Schwann, Theodor, VI:2313
Schwarzschld, Karl, **IX:3366-3369**
Schweitzer, Albert, **IX:3370-3374**
Sciama, Dennis, VIII:1580
science fiction
  Burroughs, VII:516, 517, 519
  Capek, VII:560-562
  Cyrano de Bergerac, IV:385
  Shelley, VI:2048, 2049, 2051
  Tsiolkovsky, IX:3750, 3751
  Verne, VI:2303-2305
  Wells, IX:3938-3940
Scipio, Metellus, I:167
Scipio, Publius Cornelius, I:364-366
Scipio Aemilianus, I:673, **757-759**
Scipio Africanus, I:287, 288, **760-763,** 844
Scipio the Elder. *See* Scipio Africanus
Scipio the Younger. *See* Scipio Aemilianus
SCLC. *See* Southern Christian Leadership
    Conference
Scopas, **I:764-766,** 787, 788
Scopes, John T., VII:481, 840
Scorpion, King, I:548
Scorsese, Martin, VIII:1922
Scotland Yard, IV:469, 471; VI:1752
Scots War, IV:446
Scott, Dred, **VI:1999-2001**
  Bryant, V:344
  Buchanan, V:347
  Chase, V:478
  Taney, VI:2189, 2191, 2192
Scott, Sir George Gilbert, **VI:2002-2004**
Scott, James. *See* Monmouth, Duke of
Scott, Robert Falcon, VII:67

Scott, Sir Walter, V:1225; VI:1485, 1838,
   2005-2008; VIII:2065, 2174; IX:3063
  Abbot, The, VI:2006
  Antiquary, The, VI:2006
  Black Dwarf, The, VI:2006
  Bridal of Triermain, The, VI:2006
  Castle Dangerous, VI:2007
  Count Robert of Paris, VI:2007
  Fair Maid of Perth, The, V:244
  Fortunes of Nigel, The, VI:2006
  Guy Mannering, VI:2006
  Harold the Dauntless, VI:2006
  Heart of Midlothian, The, VI:2006
  Ivanhoe, VI:2006, 2007
  Kenilworth, VI:2006
  Lady of the Lake, The, VI:1914, 2005, 2007
  Lay of the Last Minstrel, The, VI:2005, 2007
  Life of Napoleon Buonaparte, VI:2006
  Lord of the Isles, The, VI:2006
  Marmion: A Tale of Flodden Field, VI:2005
  Minstrelsy of the Scottish Border, The, VI:2005
  Monastery, The, VI:2006
  Old Mortality, VI:2006
  Peveril of the Peak, Quentin Durward,
    VI:2006
  Pirate, The, V:562; VI:2006
  Redgauntlet, VI:2006, 2007
  Rob Roy, VI:2006
  Rokeby, VI:2006
  St. Ronan's Well, VI:2006
  Tales of a Grandfather, VI:2006
  Waverly: Or, 'Tis Sixty Years Since,
    VI:2005-2007
Scott, Winfield, **VI:2009-2013**
Scottish Guardians, II:955
Scottish Labour Party, V:1037
Scottish War for Independence, II:185, 187, 188
Scottsboro boys, IX:3962
Scotus, John Duns. *See* Duns Scotus, John
Scriblerus Club, IV:1115
Scribner's Magazine, V:361
Scripps, Edward Wyllis, **VI:2014-2016**
Scripps-McRae League, VI:2015
Scrovegni, Enrico, II:388, 390
SCUBA, VII:778, 779
Scuderia Ferrari, VII:1150
Scullin, James H., VIII:2292, 2293
Scythia, I:237
Seaborg, Glenn Theodore, **IX:3375-3379**
Seaton Delaval, IV:1353
Seattle SuperSonics, IX:3271
Sebond, Raymond, III:524

secession
  Lincoln, VI:1383
  Mississippi, V:615
  Sherman, VI:2059
  Stephens, VI:2130
  Tennessee, V:1232, 1233
  Texas, V:1138; VI:1338
Sechter, Simon, V:332
Secondat, Charles-Louis de. *See* Montesquieu
Second Bourbon Restoration, V:611
Second Carlist War, V:415
Second Cataract, I:774
Second Council of Orange, I:938
Second Dutch War, IV:310
Second Great Awakening, V:470, 884; VI:1425
Second International Congress, IX:4112, 4113
Second Mithradatic War, I:558
Second Punic War, I:334-336, 364-366, 535-537,
    760-762
Second Republic of France, VI:1620-1622, 2227
Second Seminole War. *See* Seminole Wars
Second Sikh War, V:600; VI:1331
Second Syrian War, I:717
Second Triumvirate, I:69, 132, 141, 196, 220, 892
Second Trullan Synod, II:824
Second Vatican Council
  Day, VII:852
  John, VIII:1858-1860
  Maritain, VIII:2427
  Paul VI, IX:2915-2917
  Pius VII, IX:3031
  Virgin Mary, I:941
Section Française de L'internationale Ouvrière.
    See Socialist Party of France
Seddon, Richard John, V:1000; **VI:2017-2020;**
    VIII:2444, 2446
Sed Festival, I:979
Sedgmoor, Battle of, IV:982
Sedgwick, Adam, VI:1419
Sedition Act. *See* Alien and Sedition Acts
Seeckt, Hans Von, **IX:3380-3382**
Seely, Clinton Barnum, V:133
Segnatura, Stanza della, III:643
Segovia, Andrés, **IX:3383-3386**
  "Chaconne," IX:3384
segregation
  Abernathy, VII:9, 10, 12
  baseball, IX:3193
  Black, VII:322
  Brown v. Board of Education, VII:1214;
    VIII:1769, 1789, 2434, 2435, 2672; IX:3187;
    IX:3525, 3889

Frankfurter, VII:1214
Hansberry, VIII:1545
Holiday, VIII:1717, 1718
King, VIII:1973
Marshall, VIII:2434
Myrdal, VIII:2671-2673
Parks, IX:2888-2891
Stevenson, IX:3525
Wallace, IX:3857-3859
Washington, VI:2337, 2338
Wells-Barnett, IX:3941, 3943, 3944
  See also apartheid; racism
Seine River, II:793
Sejanus, Lucius Aelius, I:152, 618, 893
Sekigahara, Battle of, IV:1329
Selden Patent Case, VI:1345
Selective Service Act, VII:882
Seleucid Empire, I:896-898
Seleucus I Nicator, **I:767-769**
Seleucus III, I:63-65
self-contained underwater breathing apparatus. *See*
  SCUBA
Seligman, Joseph, V:26
Selim, III:52, 53
Selim III, VI:1604
Seljuk dynasty, II:67-70, 677-680, 695, 809
Selma, march on, VII:503; VIII:1974
Selwyn, Arch and Edgar, VIII:1415, 1417
Selznick, David, VIII:1688
Seminole Indians, V:859
  See also Seminole Wars
Seminole Wars, V:541; VI:1695, 1697, 2010,
  2011, 2057, 2195
Semmelweis, Ignaz Philipp, **VI:2021-2024**
Senate, U.S.
  Adams, V:20-24
  Benton, V:195-198
  Black, VII:321
  Blaine, V:256
  Borah, V:279-281
  Burr, V:370
  Chase, V:478
  Clay, V:507-509
  Clinton, V:518
  Dole, VII:948, 949
  Douglas, V:693
  Feinstein, VII:1137-1139
  Fillmore, V:793
  Foreign Relations Committee, VIII:2221
  Frémont, V:842
  Gallatin, V:861
  Glenn, VII:1387, 1388

Hanna, V:1029-1031
Harding, VIII:1550
Houston, V:1138, 1140
Hull, VIII:1779
Humphrey, VIII:1784, 1785
Jackson, V:1198
Johnson, Andrew, V:1232, 1233, 1235-1237
Johnson, Lyndon B., VIII:1867
Kennedy, John F., VIII:1928
Kennedy, Robert F., VIII:1933, 1934
La Follette, VIII:2047-2049
Lodge, VIII:2220
Long, VIII:2228
McCarthy, VIII:2300-2302
Mason, IV:927
Root, IX:3234
Sherman, IV:1244
Sumner, VI:2171
Taft, IX:3590-3593
Tyler, VI:2288
Van Buren, VI:2293
Washington, IV:1406
Webster, VI:2345
  See also Congress, U.S.
Sendak, Maurice, **IX:3387-3390**
  Hole Is to Dig, A, IX:3387
  In the Night Kitchen, IX:3389
  Kenny's Window, IX:3388
  Where the Wild Things Are, IX:3388, 3389
  Wonderful Farm, The, IX:3387
Seneca Falls Convention, V:697; VI:2143, 2145
Seneca Indians, VI:1584
Seneca the Younger, **I:770-773**
  Letters to Lucilius, I:772
  Three Essays on Anger, I:772
  To My Mother Helvia, I:772
Senegalese Riflemen, V:764
Senghor, Leopold, VII:631; **IX:3391-3394**
  Chants d'ombre, IX:3392
  Hosties noires, IX:3392
Senmut, I:373
Sennacherib, I:105, 454, 455
Sennett, Mack, VII:653
Sentiments, Declaration of, VI:2111
Sepoy Mutiny, VI:1706, 1707
Septennial Act, IV:532
Sequoyah, **VI:2025-2028**
Serafin, Tullio, VIII:2494
Serapion Brothers, VIII:1444
Serapis, I:722
Seres, II:988
Sergius I, II:471, **819-822**

Sergius I, Saint, **II:823-825**
Sergius Mansur, II:544
Serpent Players, VII:1258
Sert, Misia, VII:650
Sérusier, Paul, VII:909-911; IX:3826
Servetus, Michael, III:118, **675-678**
   Apologetica discetatio pro astrologia, III:676
   Christianismi restitutio, III:676, 677
   De trinitatis erroribus libri septem, III:675
   Dialogorum de trinitate libri duo, de justcia regni Christi capitual quatuor, III:675
Servile War, I:680
Servilia, I:140
Sesostris III, **I:774-777**
Sesshu, **III:679-681**; V:1120
   Amanohashidate, III:680
   Autumn and Winter Landscapes, III:680
   Haboku Landscape, III:680
   Huike Severing His Arm, III:680
   Landscapes of the Four Seasons, III:680
Seti I, I:734
Seton, Saint Elizabeth Ann Bayley, **VI:2029-2032**
Sette, Guido, II:726
Settlement of 1701, Act of, IV:50, 157, 158, 531, 1277, 1278
Seurat, Georges, VI:1780, **2033-2036**
   Bathing Place, Asnieres, A, VI:2034
   Parade, La, VI:2035
   Sunday on the Grand Jatte, A, VI:2034, 2035
Seven Cities of Cibola and Quivira, III:111, 180-183
Seven Sages of the Greeks, I:651-653, 804, 854
Seven Summits, VIII:2508
Seventeenth Amendment, V:280
Seven Wonders of the World, I:764
Seven Years' War
   Amherst, IV:37, 39, 40
   Anson, IV:56, 57
   Blücher, V:263
   Bougainville, IV:179
   Carleton, IV:246
   Carlos, V:414
   Charles III, IV:287
   Cornwallis, IV:367
   Frederick the Great, IV:506
   George II, IV:537, 538
   George III, IV:539
   Hutchinson, IV:691
   Maria Theresa, IV:915
   Peter III, IV:1088, 1089
   Pitt the Elder, IV:1098-1100
   Pontiac, IV:1111
   Rochambeau, IV:1174
   Rodney, IV:1178
   Suvorov, IV:1298
   Washington, IV:1405
   Wilkes, IV:1439
   Wolfe, IV:1471, 1472
Sever Hall, VI:1883
Severus, Septimus, I:415, 416
Sewall, Samuel, **IV:1225-1227**
   Phaenomena quondam Apolcalyptica, IV:1226
   Proposals Touching the Accomplishment of Prophecies, IV:1226
   Selling of Joseph, The, IV:1226
   Talitha Cumi, IV:1226
Seward, William H., V:792, 793, 985, 1252, 1253, **VI:2038-2041**, 2171, 2172
Sextius, I:346
Sexton, Anne, **IX:3395-3398**
   All My Pretty Ones, IX:3396
   Awful Rowing Towards God, The, IX:3397
   Bedlam and Part Way Back, IX:3396
   Book of Folly, The, IX:3397
   Death Notebooks, The, IX:3397
   "Double Image, The," IX:3396
   Live or Die, IX:3396
   Love Poems, IX:3396
   Mercy Street, IX:3396
   Transformations, IX:3396
Sextus, I:20
sexuality, human
   Ellis, VII:1070-1072
   Freud, VII:1224-1226
   Kinsey, VIII:1986-1990
   Lacan, VIII:2062, 2063
   Stopes, IX:3551-3553
Seymour, Jane, III:68, 69, 204, 209, 237, 351, 594
Seymour, Thomas, III:241, 592, 594
SFIO. *See* Socialist Party of France
Sforza, Ludovico, **III:682-685**
Shaftesbury, First Earl of, IV:285, 856, 858, **1228-1231**
   Inquiry Concerning Virtue in Two Discourses, An, IV:412
Shah Jahan, IV:69, 70, **1232-1235**
Shaka, **VI:2041-2043**
Shakers, IV:817-819
Shakespeare, William, III:56, 548-550, **686-690,** 693; IV:527-529, 728-730, 748, 749; V:203
   Anthony and Cleopatra, IX:2811
   As You Like It, IX:2810
   Comedy of Errors, The, I:659, 660; III:687; VIII:1568
   Coriolanus, I:671

Cymbeline, VII:35
Hamlet, II:816; V:272, 273, 1189; VII:281;
   IX:2809-2811
Henry IV, Part I, III:550; VII:35
Henry V, II:459; III:337-339; VI:1461;
   IX:2810-2812
Henry VI, III:653, 687
Henry VIII, III:56, 210, 687
Julius Caesar, III:689; VII:425; IX:2808
King Lear, VII:281; IX:2811
Love's Labour's Lost, III:468, 550
Macbeth, V:1189; VI:1461, 1462; VI:2299;
   VIII:2045, 2232; IX:2810, 3934, 3936
Merchant of Venice, The, V:1189; VI:1259,
   1260, 1262, 2216; IX:2813
Merry Wives of Windsor, The, VI:2300
Midsummer Night's Dream, A, IV:1139;
   VII:469; IX:2808
Much Ado About Nothing, V:205
Othello, the Moor of Venice, V:801, 1189;
   VI:2300, 2301; IX:2813, 3189, 3891, 3935
Pericles, Prince of Tyre, III:689
Rape of Lucrece, The, III:687; VI:1832
Richard II, III:687
Richard III, III:653, 687; IV:527; V:271, 1189;
   VI:1260, 1262; IX:2812
Romeo and Juliet, III:687; V:1189; VI:2198,
   2200; IX:2808, 2810
Taming of the Shrew, The, III:550, 687; IX:2808,
   2810, 3008
Tempest, The, IV:1139, 1189; VII:633
Twelfth Night, VIII:2143; IX:2808
Two Gentlemen of Verona, V:1169
Venus and Adonis, III:687
Shamash-shum-ukin, I:105, 106
Shamshi-Adad I, I:360
Shams of Tabriz, II:800
Shankar, Uday, IX:2939
Shanti Nilaya, VIII:2031
Shapur II, **I:778-782**
Sharon, Ariel, VIII:2474
Sharp, Granville, **IV:1236-1238**
   Address to the People, IV:1237
   *Declaration of the People's Natural Right to a
      Share in the Legislature, A* IV:1237
   *Defense of the Right of the People to elect
      Representatives, A* IV:1237
   On Duelling, IV:1237
   *Remarks on the Uses of the Definitive Article in
      the Greek Text of the New Testament,* IV:1237
   *Representation of the Injustice and Dangerous
      Tendency of Tolerating Society, A,* IV:1236

Sharp, James, IV:240
Sharpey, William, VI:1388
Sharp Resolution, III:575
Shaw, Anna Howard, **VI:2044-2047**
Shaw, Artie, VIII:1420, 1718
Shaw, George Bernard, I:846; **IX:3399-3403**
   Back to Methuselah, IX:3403
   Caesar and Cleopatra, IX:3400
   Candida: A Mystery, IX:3400
   Cashel Byron's Profession, IX:3399
   Common Sense About the War, IX:3402
   Heartbreak House, IX:3403
   Man and Superman, IX:3402
   Mrs. Warren's Profession, IX:3400
   Perfect Wagnerite, The, IX:3399
   Quintessence of Ibsenism, The, IX:3400
   Saint Joan, IV:1220; VIII:2142; IX:3403
   Widowers' Houses, IX:3400
Shawn, Ted, VIII:1455, 1457
Shawnee Indians, IV:164; VI:2203, 2204
Shaw v. Reno, IX:2791
Shaybani Khan, III:36
Shays, Daniel, **IV:1239-1241**
Shays's Rebellion, IV:1239-1241, 1243
Shelburne, Lord, IV:108, 481, 542, 1036, 1130
Shelley, Mary Wollstonecraft, IV:1477;
   VI:2048-2051
   Falkner, VI:2049
   Fortunes of Perkin Warbeck, The, VI:2049
   Frankenstein, VI:2048, 2049
   Last Man, The, VI:2049
   Lodore, VI:2049
   Mathilda, VI:2049
   Valperga, VI:2049
Shelley, Percy Bysshe, IV:557; V:382; VI:1264,
   1266, 2048, 2049, 2051, **2052-2056;** IX:3426
   Adonais: An Elegy on the Death of John Keats,
      VI:2055
   *Alastor: Or The Spirit of Solitude, and Other
      Poems,* VI:2053
   Cenci, The, VI:2054, 2055
   Charles the Frist, VI:2055
   Childe Harold's Pilgrimage, VI:2053
   "Defence of Poetry, A," VI:2053, 2055
   Epipsychidion, VI:2055
   Hellas: A Lyrical Drama, VI:2055
   "Hymn to Intellectual Beauty," VI:2053
   Julian and Maddalo: A Conversation, VI:2054
   Masque of Anarchy, The, VI:2055
   Mont Blanc, VI:2053
   Necessity of Atheism, The, VI:2052
   "Ode to the West Wind," VI:2055

Oedipus Tyrannus: Or, Swellfoot the Tyrant, VI:2055
Original Poetry by Victor and Cazire, VI:2052
"Ozymandias," I:737
Peter Bell the Third, VI:2055
Prisoner of Chillon, The, VI:2053
Prometheus Unbound, VI:2054, 2055
Queen Mab: A Philosophical Poem, VI:2053
Revolt of Islam, The, VI:2054
Rosalind and Helen, VI:2054
Triumph of Life, The, VI:2055
Witch of Atlas, The, VI:2055
Zastrozzi: A Romance, VI:2052
Shell Oil Company, IX:2860
Shen-tsung, II:841, 962, 963
Shen Yo, I:842
Shepard, Alan, **IX:3405-3408**
Shepard, Thomas, IV:688
Sheridan, Philip, V:586, 1236
Sheridan, Richard Brinsley
    School for Scandal, The, IV:529; VII:191
Sherman, John, V:1030; VI:1454, 1456
Sherman, Roger, **IV:1242-1245**
Sherman, William Tecumseh, V:586, 977; **VI:2057-2061,** 2108
Sherman Antitrust Act of 1890, VI:1898; IX:3229
Sherman Silver Purchase Act, V:515
Sherpas, VIII:1664
Sherrington, Sir Charles Scott, VII:1172
Shibasaburo Kitasato, V:182, 183
Shield Society, VIII:2552
Shiloh, Battle of, V:976; VI:1810, 2059
Shinshu Buddhism, III:571
Ship Money Case, IV:280
Shippen, Margaret "Peggy," IV:42, 66
Shipton, Eric, VIII:1663
Shirakawa II, II:881, 882
Shivaji Festival, IX:3683, 3684
Shklovsky, Viktor, VII:153
Shoda, Michiko, VII:42
Short Parliament, IV:1142, 1228, 1287
Shoshone Indians, VI:1933-1935
Shostakovich, Dmitri, **IX:3409-3412**
    "Babi Yar," IX:3410
    Katerina Izmailova, IX:3411
    Lady Macbeth of Mtsensk, IX:3409, 3411
Shotoku Taishi, **II:826-828**
Shrewsbury, Duke of, IV:158
Shuiskys, III:385
Shulhan Arukh, IV:433
Shunrin Shuto, III:679
Shu'ubi movement, II:527

Sian Incident, VII:665
Sibelius, Jean, VII:70; **IX:3413-3416,** 3873
    Fifth Symphony, IX:3415
    Finlandia, IX:3414
    Kullervo, IX:3413, 3414
    Seventh Symphony, IX:3415
    Sixth Symphony, IX:3415
    Symphony No. 4, IX:3414
    Tapiola, IX:3415
Sickles, Daniel E., VI:2107
Sicily
    Archimedes, I:79
    Frederick II, II:362-364
    Idrisi, II:507
    Innocent III, II:510
    Innocent IV, II:515, 516
    Mosca, VIII:2630
Siddhartha. *See* Buddha
Sidgwick, Henry, **VI:2062-2065**
    Methods of Ethics, The, VI:2063, 2064
    Outline of the History of Ethics, VI:2064
    Principles of Political Economy; Elements of Politics, VI:2064
Sidney, Sir Philip, **III:691-695,** 703
    Arcadia, III:692-694
    Astrophel and Stella, III:691-694
    Defense of Poesie, III:691-693; IV:746
    Lady of May, The, III:691
Sieff Research Institute, IX:3932
Siegfried Line, VIII:2265
Siemens family, **VI:2066-2069**
Sierra Club, VI:1609
Siete Partidas, Las, II:57
Sievers, Susanne, VII:428
Sifting Bridge, I:976
Siger of Brabant, **II:829-831,** 913
Sigismund, II:1031; III:374, 564
Signal Corps. *See* United States Signal Corps
Sigrid the Proud, II:689
Sihanouk, Norodom, **IX:3417-3421**
Sikhism, III:540-542; V:600
Sikh Wars, V:600; VI:1331
Siking, II:1015, 1016
Sikkak, Battle of, V:2
Silesia, Army of, V:264
Silings, I:342
Silliman, Benjamin, VI:1592, 1593
Siloé, Diego do, **III:696-698**
    Pietà, III:696
    Presentation, III:696
    Saint George Slaying the Dragon, III:696
    Virgin and Child, III:696

Silsbee, Joseph Lyman, IX:4060
Silvester, Saint, I:375, 376
Simango, Urias, VIII:2317
Simeon Bar Kokhba, I:29
Simeon ben Azzai, I:28
Simeon ben Zoma, I:28
Simeon Stylites, Saint, **I:783-786**
Simmel, Georg, VII:614
Simon. *See* Peter, Saint
Simon Commission on India, VII:137
Simonides, **I:787-789**
Simon of Sudbury, II:114, 115
Simpson, James, VI:1390
Simpson, Wallis Warfield, IX:4025, 4026
Sims, Thomas, VI:1729
Sin, Jaime Cardinal, VII:87, 88
Sinai Agreement, IX:3290
Sinan Bey, III:501
Sinatra, Frank, IX:3078, **3422-3425**
  From Here to Eternity, IX:3424
  "I'll Never Smile Again," IX:3422
  Nice 'n' Easy, IX:3424
  Pal Joey, VIII:1598
  Robin and the 7 Hoods, IX:3424
  Songs for Young Lovers, IX:3424
Sinclair, Upton, VII:1048; VIII:2131, 2174;
  IX:3426-3430
  Boston, IX:3428
  Journal of Arthur Stirling, The, IX:3426
  Jungle, The, IX:3426, 3428, 3429
  King Coal, IX:3428
  Manassas, IX:3428
  Oil!, IX:3428
Singer, Isaac M., V:1143
Singer, Paris, VII:981
Sinn Féin, VII:733, 770, 877, 878; IX:2794, 2805
Sino-French War, V:466; VI:1364
Sino-Japanese Wars, V:468; VI:1364, 1365;
  IX:2954
Sino-Soviet Treaty of 1950, VIII:1961
Sintra, Convention of, VI:2352
Sioux Indians
  Crazy Horse, V:573-577
  Custer, V:586
  Parkman, VI:1735
  Pike, IV:1094
  Red Cloud, VI:1850, 1851
  Remington, VI:1862
  Sitting Bull, VI:2070-2073
Siqueiros, David, IX:2837
Siricius, Saint, **I:790-792**
Sisera, I:247

Sistene Chapel, III:84, 168, 519
Sisulu, Walter, VIII:2384, 2386
Sisyphus, VII:554
Sithole, Ndabaningi, VIII:2647
Sitting Bull, V:575, 576; VI:1677, **2070-2073**
Sitwell, Edith and Osbert, IX:3872-3874
Sivaji, IV:70, 71, **1246-1248**
Six, Les, VIII:2525, 2526; IX:3066, 3333
Six-Day War
  Begin, VII:245
  Ben-Gurion, VII:253
  Dayan, VII:856
  Eban, VII:1001
  Hussein I, VIII:1794
  Meir, VIII:2474
  Nasser, VIII:2695
  Qaddafi, IX:3099
  Wiesel, IX:3982
Six Edicts, IV:1349
Sixteenth Amendment, V:280
Sixtus IV, III:496
Sixtus V, III:334
Skelton, John, III:349
skiing, VIII:1965-1967
Skinner, B.F., **IX:3431-3434**
  About Behaviorism, IX:3433
  Behavior of Organisms, The, IX:3432
  Beyond Freedom and Dignity, IX:3433
  Walden Two, IX:3433
Skinner, John S., VI:1281, 1282
Skirmishing Fund, V:1124
Skúli, Earl, II:838
skyscrapers
  Burnham, V:365, 367, 368
  Le Corbusier, VIII:2137, 2138
  Mies van der Rohe, VIII:2523
  Pei, IX:2947
  Richardson, VI:1884
  Sullivan, VI:2167, 2168
  Wright, IX:4062
Slater, Samuel, **VI:2074-2076**
Slaughterhouse cases, V:479
slavery
  Agassiz, V:32
  Bolingbroke, IV:158
  Calhoun, V:395, 396
  Campbell, V:403
  Cornwallis, IV:367
  Davis, V:614, 617
  Douglas, V:692-694
  Douglass, V:695-698
  Drake, III:224

Ethiopia, VIII:1517
folk tales, V:1049-1052
Gadsden, V:859
Grant, V:975
Jefferson, IV:718
Jerusalem, I:460
John of Damascus, II:544
Johnson, V:1233, 1235
Judaea, I:569, 570
Livingstone, VI:1399-1401
Mamluk Dynasty, II:124
Mansfield, IV:906
medieval Islam, II:1013
Monroe, VI:1571
Morrison's novels, VIII:2627
Phaedrus, I:618-620
Pierce, VI:1776-1778
Polk, VI:1801
Ponce de Léon, III:629, 630
Pufendorf, IV:1134
Roman latifundia, I:346, 347
Saudi Arabia, VII:1119
Solon, I:805
Spartacus, I:814, 816, 817
Stephens, VI:2129, 2130
Turner's revolt, VI:2276-2278
U.S. Supreme Court, VI:1490
Virginia, IV:82
Wise, VI:2401
See also abolitionism
Slavery Abolition Act, IV:1437
Slim, First Viscount, **IX:3435-3438**
Slipher, Earl and Vesto, IX:3700
Sloan, David, VIII:2121
Sloane, Sir Hans, IV:755
Sloane, William, VII:774
Slonimsky, Nicholas, VIII:1821
Sluter, Claus, **II:832-835**
    Virgin and Child, II:832
    Well of Moses, The, II:833
Sluys, battle of, II:331
Small, William, IV:1184
Small Council, II:447, 448
Smart Set, The, VII:1162
Smeaton, John, VI:1327
Smeaton, Mark, III:69
Smenkhkare, I:25
Smibert, John, IV:356
Smith, Adam, IV:454, 457, 1103, **1249-1252**
    Essays on Philosophical Subjects, IV:1251
    *Inquiry into the Nature and Causes of the Wealth
        of Nations,* VIII:2672, 2673

Theory of Moral Sentiments, IV:174, 1249, 1251
Wealth of Nations, The, IV:1249-1251; VI:1878
Smith, Alfred E., IX:2962, **3439-3441**
Smith, Bessie, VIII:1883; **IX:3442-3445**
    "Downhearted Blues," IX:3442
    "Nobody Knows You When You're Down and
        Out," IX:3442
Smith, Clyde H., IX:3446
Smith, Emma, VI:2415
Smith, Gerrit, V:321, 325
Smith, Gladys Louise. *See* Pickford, Mary
Smith, Ian, VIII:2647, 2648
Smith, Jedediah Strong, **VI:2077-2079**
Smith, John, IV:681, 1106-1108, 1123, 1124,
    1253-1256
Smith, John Thomas, V:547
Smith, Joseph (British consul), IV:242, 243
Smith, Joseph (Mormon leader),
    VI:2080-2082, 2412
Smith, Lula Carson. *See* McCullers, Carson
Smith, Margaret Chase, **IX:3446-3449**
    "Declaration of Conscience," IX:3447, 3448
Smith, Roger, IX:2974
Smith, Sydney, V:1224, 1225
Smith, Theobald, **IX:3450-3452**
Smith, William Robertson, VII:1220
Smithers, Leonard, V:162
Smithfield Bridge, VI:1904
Smith-Hughes Act, VII:23
Smithsonian Institution
    Adams, V:24
    Agassiz, V:31
    Goddard, VIII:1397
    Henry, V:1093-1095
    Langley, VI:1314; IX:4067
Smoke Abatement Exhibition, V:1115
Smoot-Hawley Tariff. *See* Hawley-Smoot Tariff
Smuts, Jan Christian, VII:376-378; **IX:3453-3455**
snake venom, VII:546, 547
Snodgrass, William DeWitt, IX:3395, 3396
Snorri Sturluson, **II:836-839**
    Egil's Saga, II:838
    Heimskringla, The, II:837, 838
    Prose Edda, The, II:837-839
Snowdon, Philip, VII:314
Soap, Charlie, VIII:2390
Soares, Lope, III:13
soccer, IX:2950-2952
Social Darwinism, VI:1469, 1738, 2086-2088;
    VIII:2484
Social Democratic Party of Germany
    Bernstein, VII:291-293

Brandt, VII:427, 428
Kohl, VIII:2009
Lassalle, VI:1323, 1325
Liebknecht, VI:1369-1371
Luxemburg, VIII:2285-2287
Paul VI, IX:2916
Steinmetz, VI:2121
Ulbricht, IX:3779
Zetkin, IX:4112, 4113
Social Democratic Party of Poland, VIII:2285
socialism
    Africa, VIII:2775
    Blanc, V:259-262
    Fourier, V:814, 816, 817
    Goldman, VIII:1411-1413
    Gompers, V:957
    Gorky's propaganda, VIII:1444
    Hardie, V:1037, 1038
    Jaurès, V:1221-1223
    Keller, VIII:1926
    Kollwitz, VIII:2016, 2017
    La Fontaine, VIII:2053
    Laski, VIII:2093, 2094
    Lassalle, VI:1323-1325
    Liebknecht, VI:1369-1371
    Luxemburg, VIII:2285
    Morris, VI:1589, 1590
    Owen, VI:1710
    Sinclair, IX:3428, 3429
    Steinmetz, VI:2121, 2124
    Zetkin, IX:4112, 4113
    See also Christian Socialism; communism
Socialist Academy, IX:3751
Socialist League, VI:1589
Socialist Party of America, VII:882; IX:3660-3663
Socialist Party of France, V:1222; VII:335, 336;
    VIII:2105, 2559, 2560
Socialist Party of Italy, VIII:2667, 2668
Socialist-Revolutionaries, Party of, VIII:1941
Socialist Unity Party, IX:3779-3781
Socialist Workers Party, VII:427
Social Labor Party of Germany, VI:1325
Social Security system, VII:577; VIII:1471, 1868;
    IX:2963, 3225
Social War, I:194, 530
Socinus, Faustus, IV:127
Socrates, **I:793-797**
    Aesop, I:14
    Alcibiades, I:31
    Anaxagoras, I:48
    Antisthenes, I:66, 67
    Aristippus, I:85, 86

    Aristophanes, I:90
    Aspasia, I:117
    Democritus, I:250
    Lysippus, I:516
    Plato, I:655, 657
    Protagoras, I:705-707
    Sorel, IX:3464
    Xanthippe, I:952-954
    Xenophon, I:958-960
    Zeno of Elea, I:972
Soddy, Frederick, IX:3278
Söderblom, Nathan, **IX:3456-3458**
Soderini, Piero, III:448, 450
Sodom and Gomorrah, I:5, 6
Soga clan, II:826, 827
Sogdiana, I:779
Soho Manufactory, IV:182, 183
Soka gakkai, II:668
Solander, Daniel Carl, IV:83, 85
solar eclipse
    Anaxagoras, I:48
    Battani, II:121
    Brahe, III:77
    Thales of Miletus, I:854
Solari, Luigi, VIII:2415, 2417
Solferino, Battle of, V:711, 830
Solidarity, IX:3844, 3846, 3847
Sol Invictus, I:226, 227
Solomon, **I:798-802**
    Book of Proverbs, I:801
    Ecclesiastes, I:297, 801
    Song of Songs, I:801
Solomon, Aubrey. *See* Eban, Abba
Solomon Islands, VIII:1527
Solon, I:281, 648, **803-806,** 877, 878
Solvay, Ernest, IV:815; VII:699
Solzhenitsyn, Aleksandr, VII:351; VIII:2273;
    IX:3459-3462
    August 1914, IX:3459, 3461
    Cancer Ward, The, IX:3460, 3461
    Experiment in Literary Investigation, An,
        IX:3460
    First Circle, The, IX:3460, 3461
    Gulag Archipelago, The, IX:3460
    One Day in the Life of Ivan Denisovich, IX:3461
    Red Wheel, The, IX:3461
    Shch-854, IX:3460, 3461
Somers, John, IV:26
Somerset, Duke of, III:237, 238, 318, 341, 342
Somerset, Earl of, IV:211
Somersett, James, IV:906, 1236
Somes, Michael, VII:1177

Sommerfeld, Arnold, VII:300, 301; IX:2923
sonatas
    Barber, VII:192
    Beethoven, V:178-181
    Bernstein, VII:296
    Brahms, V:299-301
    Corelli, IV:360-362
    Couperin, IV:374-376
    Franck, V:832-834
    Milhaud, VIII:2525
    Prokofiev, IX:3085
    Vivaldi, IV:1383
    Zwilich, IX:4121
Songhai Empire, III:521-523
"Song of Deborah," I:247
Song of Roland, II:228, 944
Sonni Ali, III:521, 522
Sonoran Dynasty, VII:542
Sony Corporation, VIII:2622-2624
Sopete, III:182
Sophia, I:912
Sophie of Bavaria, V:829, 830
Sophism
    Antisthenes, I:66
    Aristippus, I:85
    Democritus, I:250
    Euripides, I:317
    Phidias, I:624
    Plato, I:657
    Protagoras, I:705-707
Sophocles, I:10, 11, 807, **807-810,** 878
    Ajax, I:807
    Antigone, I:807, 808
    Electra, I:808
    Oedipus at Colonus, I:807, 809
    Oedipus Tyrannus, I:808, 809; III:282
    Philoctetes, I:808
    Women of Trachis, The, I:807
Sophonisba, I:535
Sophronius, II:820, 821
Sorel, Georges, **IX:3463-3465**
    Reflections on Violence, IX:3463, 3464
Sosigenes, I:150, **811-813**
Sotatsu, **IV:1257-1259**
    Bugaku Dancers, IV:1258
    Cormorants, The, IV:1258
    Flowers and Grasses of the Four Seasons,
      IV:1258
    Sekiya, IV:1258
    Wind and Thunder Gods, The, IV:1258
Soteris, I:43
Soto, Hernando de, **III:699-702**

soul music, VII:1216-1218
Sousa, John Philip, **IX:3466-3470**
    Gladiator, IX:3466
    Semper Fidelis, IX:3466
    Stars and Stripes Forever, The, IX:3467
    Washington Post, The, IX:3466
Sousa Concert Band, IX:3467-3469
South African Anglican Church, IX:3775-3777
South African Council of Churches, IX:3776
South African War. *See* Boer War
South Carolina
    Calhoun, V:394, 395
    Gadsden, V:859
    Oglethorpe, IV:1044
    Tyler, VI:2289
Southeast Asian Nations, Association of,
    VIII:2151
Southeast Asia Treaty Organization, VII:1044
Southern Africa Development Coordination
    Conference, VIII:2318, 2775
Southern Christian Leadership Conference, VII:10,
    80; VIII:1824, 1825, 1973; IX:2890
Southern Literary Messenger, VI:1794, 1796
Southern Pacific Railroad, VI:2098
Southern Poverty Law Center, VIII:2187
Southern Sung Dynasty, II:479, 480, 612, 613,
    867, 868, 1018, 1019
Southey, Robert, VI:2209
South Improvement Company, VI:1897
South Sea Company, IV:1279, 1401, 1402
South Pole, VII:66-69, 535; VIII:1662, 1664
South Sea Company, IV:158
Soviet Academy of Sciences, VIII:2020
Soviet-Chinese Friendship Meeting, VIII:2213
Soviet Writers, Union of, VIII:1445; IX:2901
Soyinka, Wole, **IX:3471-3474**
    Aké: The Years of Childhood, IX:3471, 3472
    Bacchae, The, IX:3472
    Death and the King's Horseman, IX:3472
    Interpreters, The, IX:3472
    Invention, The, IX:3471
    Jero's Metamorphosis, IX:3472
    Kongi's Harvest, IX:3472
    Lion and the Jewel, The, IX:3471
    Madmen and Specialists, IX:3472
    Myth, Literature, and the African World,
      IX:3473
    Opera Wonyosi, IX:3472
    Play of Giants, A, IX:3473
    Requiem for a Futurologist, IX:3473
    Road, The, IX:3472
    Season of Anomy, IX:3472

Strong Breed, The, IX:3472
Swamp Dwellers, The, IX:3471
Soyuz missions, VII:1271
Spaak, Paul-Henri, **IX:3475-3477**
Spallanzani, Lazzaro, **IV:1260-1263**
   Dell' azione del cuore ne' vasi sanguigni, IV:1261
   *Dissertations Relative to the Natural History of
     Animals and Vegetables,* IV:1261
   Essay on Animal Reproductions, An, IV:1260
   Experiments Upon the Circulation of the Blood?,
     IV:1261
   Letters on a Supposed New Sense in Bats,
     IV:1262
   Memoirs on Respiration, IV:1262
   *Saggio di osservazioni microsopiche
     concernenti il sistema della generazione de'
     signori di Needham e Buffon,* IV:1260
   Tracts on Animals and Vegetables, IV:1261
Spanish-American War
   American Red Cross, V:145
   Bryan, VII:480
   Dewey, V:656-658
   Goethals, VIII:1408
   Hay, V:1069
   Low, VIII:2246
   McKinley, VI:1454-1456
   Remington, VI:1862
   yellow fever, VIII:1434
   yellow journalism, VIII:1603
Spanish Armada, War of the
   Cecil, III:148
   Drake, III:225
   Elizabeth I, III:243
   Farnese, III:255
   Frobisher, III:279
   Grenville, III:315-317
   Philip II, III:600
Spanish Civil War
   Blum, VII:336
   Buñuel, VII:506
   Candela, VII:557
   Casals, VII:607
   Éluard, VII:1075
   Franco, VII:1200-1202
   Heinkel's aircraft, VIII:1615
   Malraux, VIII:2381
   Ortega y Gasset, IX:2843
   Parker, IX:2886
   Weil, IX:3923
Spanish Inquisition
   Ferdinand and Isabella, III:262
   Manuel I, III:465

   Paul III, III:597
   Raymond of Peñafort, II:777
   Servetus, III:677
   Spinoza, IV:1264
   Teresa of Ávila, III:713-715
   Torquemada, III:725-727
Spanish Succession, War of
   Anne, IV:52
   Bolingbroke, IV:157, 158
   Charles III, IV:287
   Charles XII, IV:290
   Frederick I, IV:498
   George I, IV:531
   Godolphin, IV:553
   Louis XIV, IV:868
   Marlborough, IV:922, 923
   Scarlatti, IV:1214
   Stanhope, IV:1277
   William III, IV:1448, 1449
Sparks, Chauncey, IX:3857, 3858
Sparks, Jared, V:125, 127, 471
Sparta
   Alcibiades, I:31, 32
   Alexander the Great, I:38
   Antisthenes, I:67
   Cimon, I:200, 201
   Cleomenes I, I:214, 215
   Cleomenes II, I:215
   Cleomenes III, I:215, 216
   Euripides, I:318
   Lysippus, I:515
   Macedonia, I:628
   Pericles, I:609, 611, 612
   Pheidippides, I:621, 622
   Pisistratus, I:649, 650
   Plato, I:655
   Thebes, I:290
   Themistocles, I:858, 859
   Thucydides, I:885-887
   Xenophon, I:959
Spartacus, **I:814-817**
Spartacus League, IX:4114
Speaker, Tris, VII:719
Spectator, The, V:1192
Speke, John Hanning, V:375, 376; VI:**2083-2085**
Spencer, Charles. *See* Sunderland, Third Earl of
Spencer, Herbert **VI:2086-2088,** 2330
   Principles of Psychology, The, VI:2086, 2088
   Social Statics, VI:2086
   Synthetic Philosophy, The, VI:2086, 2087
Spenser, Edmund, III:244, **703-706**
   Amoretti, III:703, 704

Colin Clout's Come Home Again, III:693
Epithalamion, III:704
Faerie Queen, The, III:703-705; VI:1264
Shepheardes Calender, The, III:692, 703, 704
Speransky, Mikhail Mikhaylovich **VI:2089-2091**
Spessivtzeva, Olga, VIII:2182, 2183
Speyer, diets of, III:160, 505
Sphaerus, I:970
Spica, I:407
Spice Islands, III:453, 455
Spielberg, Steven, IX:4030
Spinks, Leon, VII:56
Spinoza, Baruch, **IV:1264-1267;** VI:2182
Ethics, IV:1266
Political Treatise, A, IV:1266
Theologico-Political Treatise, A, IV:1265, 1266
Spirit of St. Louis, The, VIII:2193, 2196
Spitsbergen, IV:680, 682
Spock, Benjamin, **IX:3478-3481**
Commonsense Book of Baby and Child Care, The, IX:3478, 3480
Spock on Spock, IX:3479
Springfield Republican, V:668
Spruance, Raymond A., VIII:2751
Sputnik, VII:1044; VIII:2019-2021; IX:3701
Squadrille, Edward F., IX:3017
Squanto, IV:930
Squarcialupi Codex, II:570
Squarcione, Francesco, III:460
Square Deal League, VIII:2229
Sri Vaisnavas sect, II:770-772
SS. *See* Schutzstaffel
Ssu-ma Ch'ien, I:176, 177, 498, **818-821;** II:613, 963
Shih chi, I:543, 590, 591, 818-820
Ssu-ma Kuang, **II:840-842**
Tzu-chih t'ung-chien, II:840
Staehlin, Jacob von, IV:1087
Staël, Madame de, **VI:2092-2095**
Corrine: Or, Italy, VI:2094
Delphine, VI:2093, 2094
Essay on Fiction, VI:2093
Germany, VI:2094
Treatise on Ancient and Modern Literature, A, VI:2093
Treatise on the Influence of the Passions upon the Happiness of Individuals and Nations, A, VI:2093
Stahl, Georg Ernst, **IV:1268-1272**
Fundamenta chymiae dogmaticae et experimentalis, IV:1271
Tehoria medica vera, IV:1269

Stalin, Joseph, **IX:3482-3485**
Astor, VII:130
Bourke-White, VII:395
Brezhnev, VII:459
Chamberlain, VII:645
Churchill, VII:693
Czechoslovakia, VII:261
Dubcek, VII:968
Gorky, VIII:1442, 1445
Harriman, VIII:1561
Kapitsa, VIII:1908
Kenyatta, VIII:1936
Khrushchev, VIII:1962, 1963
Kurchatov, VIII:2041
Lenin, VIII:2162
Litvinov, VIII:2209, 2210
Lukács, VIII:2274
Malenkov, VIII:2377, 2378
Marx, VI:1494
Marxism and the National and Colonial Question, IX:3482
Molotov, VIII:2571, 2572
Prokofiev, IX:3087
Roosevelt, IX:3225
Shostakovich, IX:3409, 3410
Solzhenitsyn, IX:3460
Tito, IX:3694
Tupolev, IX:3765
Ulbricht, IX:3779, 3780
Zhukov, IX:4116, 4117
Stamford Bridge, battle at, II:428
Stamp Act
Adams, John, IV:16
Adams, Samuel, IV:22
Cornwallis, IV:367
Dickinson, IV:408
Gage, IV:513
Hancock, IV:617
Henry, IV:647, 648
Hutchinson, IV:692, 693
Mason, IV:926
Morris, IV:999
Pitt the Elder, IV:1099
Revere, IV:1156
Rockingham, IV:222
Wilson, IV:1456
Standard Oil Company, VI:1896-1898; VIII:2228; IX:3616, 3617
Standerin, Abraham, IV:818
Standing Rock Agency, VI:2072
Standish, Miles, IV:190, 931, **1273-1276**
Stanford, Leland, **VI:2096-2100**

Stanhope, First Earl, IV:**1277-1280,** 1401-1403
Stanislavsky, Konstantin, **IX:3486-3489**
   Actor Prepares, An, IX:3487
   Akalaitis, VII:34
   Building a Character, IX:3487
   Creating a Role, IX:3487
   Gorky, VIII:1442, 1444
   Method acting, VII:424, 3487
   My Life in Art, IX:3486, 3487
   Stanislovski's Legacy, IX:3487
Stanley, Edward George Geoffrey Smith. *See*
   Derby, Fourteenth Earl of
Stanley, Henry Morton, VI:1400, **2101-2105**
   Congo and the Founding of Its Free State, The,
     VI:2103
   How I Found Livingstone, VI:2102
   My Kalulu, VI:2102
Stanley, Thomas, Lord, III:650
Stanley, Sir William, III:257
Stanton, Edwin M., V:1236; **VI:2106-2109**
Stanton, Elizabeth Cady, I:247; V:61, 62;
   VI:1600-1602, **2110-2114**
   History of Woman Suffrage, VI:2112
   Woman's Bible, The, VI:2113
Stanton, Henry, VI:2110, 2111
Stark, Johannes, **IX:3490-3493**
Stark, John, V:1240, 1241
Starling, Ernest Henry, **IX:3494-3496**
Starr, Kenneth, VII:710; IX:3155
Starr, Ringo, VII:226-229
Star Wars program, VII:302; IX:3633
Stassen, Harold, VII:509
State Secession Convention, V:1138, 1140
Statius, Caecilius, I:844
Staudinger, Hermann, VIII:2698;
   IX:3497-3500
Staudinger's law, IX:3499
Staupitz, Johann von, III:443
Stavropol, VIII:1423
Stavrovouni Monastery, I:376
steam engine
   Boulton, IV:182-184
   Diesel, V:672
   Ford, VII:1186
   Guericke, IV:588
   Lenoir, VI:1343, 1345
   Murdock, IV:1008-1010
   Newcomen, IV:1022-1024
   Papin, IV:1059-1061
   Roebuck, IV:1184
   Siemens family, VI:2068
   Stephenson, VI:2132

   Trevithick, VI:2251-2253
   Watt, IV:1409, 1411, 1412
   Westinghouse, VI:2358, 2360
   Wilkinson, IV:1443-1445
Steber, Eleanor, VII:193
Steele, Richard, IV:26-28, 114
Steelhouse Lane, IV:1182
steel industry
   Bessemer, V:218-221
   Gibbs, V:925
   Hadfield, V:1015, 1016
   Krupp, VI:1301, 1303
   Lewis, VIII:2171
   Mellon, VIII:2480
   Morgan, VI:1581, 1582
   Siemens family, VI:2066-2069
   Taylor-White process, IX:3619
Stefan Dusan, **II:843-846**
Stefan Uros III Decanski, II:843
Steichen, Edward, **IX:3501-3505**
   "Family of Man, The," IX:3503, 3504
Stein, Edith, **IX:3406-3510**
   Science of the Cross, The, IX:3509
Stein, Freiherr vom, V:1034; VI:1654, 1655,
   2115-2117
Stein, Gertrude, VIII:1484, 1485, 1627;
   IX:3511-3514, 4014
   Autobiography of Alice B. Toklas, IX:3513
   Geography and Plays, IX:3512
   Making of Americans, The, IX:3512
   "Sacred Emily," IX:3512
   Tender Buttons, IX:3512
   Three Lives, IX:3512
Steinbeck, John, **IX:3515-3518**
   America and Americans, IX:3516
   Cannery Row, IX:3516, 3517
   Cup of Gold, IX:3515
   East of Eden, IX:3516
   Grapes of Wrath, The, VIII:2084; IX:3516, 3517
   In Dubious Battle, IX:3516, 3517
   Log from the Sea of Cortez, IX:3516
   Of Mice and Men, IX:3516, 3517
   To a God Unknown, IX:3515
   Tortilla Flat, IX:3515-3517
   Winter of Our Discontent, The, IX:3516
Steinbus, Ferdinand von, V:597
Steinem, Gloria, VII:1155; **IX:3519-3522**
   Ms. magazine, IX:3521, 3522
   Outrageous Acts and Everyday Rebellions,
     IX:3521
   Revolution from Within, IX:3521
Steiner, Jakob, **VI:2118-2120**

Steinmetz, Charles Proteus, **VI:2121-2124**
Stellaburg, III:78
Steller, Georg Wilhelm, IV:112
Stendhal, **VI:2125-2128,** 2183
    Armance, VI:2127
    Charterhouse of Parma, The, VI:2127
    Histoire de la peinture de Italie, VI:2126
    Lamiel, VI:2128
    Maxims of Love, VI:2126
    Memoirs of a Tourist, VI:2128
    Memoirs of Rossini, VI:2127
    Racine and Shakespeare, VI:2127
    Red and the Black, The, VI:2127
    Roman Journal, A, VI:2127
    Rome, Naples, and Florence in 1817, VI:2126
Stephen I (of Hungary), II:574, 575, **851-854**
Stephen II (Pope), II:226
Stephen, King (of England), **II:847-850**
Stephen, Saint, I:605, **822-824**
Stephen of Blois, II:292, 446
Stephens, Alexander H., **VI:2129-2131**
    Constitutional View of the Late War Between the States, A, VI:2130
Stephenson, George, **VI:2132-2135**
Stephenson, Robert, VI:2252
Sterling, Ernest Henry, VII:217, 218
Stern, Günther, VII:98
Stern, Otto, VIII:2336
Sternberg, Josef von, VII:930, 932
Stevens, Thaddeus, **VI:2136-2138**
Stevenson, Adlai E., VIII:1784, 1930; **IX:3523-3527,** 3743
Stevenson, Robert Louis, III:765; **VI:2139-2142**
    Black Arrow, The, VI:2141
    "Bottle Imp, The," VI:2141, 2142
    Catriona, VI:2141
    Child's Garden of Verses, A, VI:2141
    David Balfour, VI:2141
    Ebb-Tide, The, VI:2141, 2142
    Edinburgh: Picturesque Notes, VI:2139
    Inland Voyage, An, VI:2139
    Island Nights' Entertainments, VI:2141
    Kidnapped, VI:2141, 2142
    "Lodging for the Night, A," III:765
    Master of Ballantrae, The, VI:2141
    Strange Case of Dr. Jekyll and Mr. Hyde, VI:2139, 2141, 2142
    Travels with a Donkey in the Cévennes, VI:2139
    Treasure Island, VI:2139, 2141, 2142
    Weir of Hermiston, VI:2141
    Wrecker, The, VI:2141

Stewart, James, **IX:3528-3531,** 3903
    Anatomy of a Murder, IX:3530
    Destry Rides Again, IX:3528, 3529
    Harvey, IX:3530
    It's a Wonderful Life, IX:3530
    Man Who Knew Too Much, The, IX:3530
    Mr. Smith Goes to Washington, IX:3528
    Philadelphia Story, The, IX:3529
    Rear Window, IX:3530
    Rope, IX:3530
    Shenandoah, IX:3530
    Shootist, The, IX:3903
    Vertigo, IX:3530
    You Can't Take It With You, IX:3528
Stewart, Robert. *See* Castlereagh, Viscount
Stieglitz, Alfred, IX:2800, 2801, 3501, 3503, **3532-3536**
Stigand, II:426
Stijl, De, IX:2859, 2860
Stilicho, Flavius, I:342, **825-827**
Still, William, VI:2264
Stiller, Moritz, VII:1286
Stimson, Henry L., VII:1212; VIII:2431; **IX:3537-3540**
Stimson Doctrine, VIII:1729
Stirling Bridge, Battle of, II:324, 956
Stoa Poikile, I:676, 969
Stockbridge Indians, IV:430
Stockhausen, Karlheinz, **IX:3541-3545**
    Aus den sieben Tagen, IX:3544
    Carré, IX:3543
    Donnerstag aus Licht, IX:3544
    Electronishe Studien I and II, IX:3542
    Gesang der Jünglinde, IX:3543
    Gruppen, IX:3543
    Hymnen, IX:3544
    Kontakte, IX:3543
    Kontra-Punkte, IX:3542
    Licht, die sieben Tgen der Woche, IX:3544
    Mantra, IX:3544
    Momente, IX:3543
    Samstag aus Licht, IX:3544
    Stimmung, IX:3544
    Zeitmasze, IX:3543
Stockholm Conference, IX:3456, 3457
Stockholm Olympics of 1912, VII:775
Stockton, Robert F., V:840
Stockton and Darlington Railway, VI:2132, 2133
Stockton-on-Tees, VIII:2340, 2341
Stoicism
    Antisthenes, I:68
    Cato the Younger, I:166

Eratosthenes of Cyrene, I:303
Livy, I:505
Montaigne, III:524
Montesquieu, IV:986
Philo of Alexandria, I:632, 633
Posidonius, I:686-689
Poussin, IV:1120
Seneca the Younger, I:772
Zeno of Citium, I:967, 969, 970
Stölbova, Peace of, IV:589, 1052
Stone, Harlan Fiske, VII:577; **IX:3546-3550**
Stone, Lucy, **VI:2143-2146**
Stone, Oliver
    Heaven and Earth, VIII:1595
Stoner, Edmund, IX:2923
Stoner, Fed, VII:53
Stopes, Marie, **IX:3551-3554**
    Married Love, IX:3552
    Roman Catholic Methods of Birth Control,
        IX:3552
    Wise Parenthood, IX:3552
Story, Joseph, **VI:2147-2150,** 2191
    Commentaries, VI:2149
Story, William Wetmore, VI:2257
Stothart, Herbert, VIII:1533
Stowe, Harriet Beecher, V:170, 172, 174;
    VI:2151-2154, 2257
    American Woman's Home, The, V:172
    Minister's Wooing, The, VI:2152
    Oldtown Folks, VI:2152
    Pearl of Orr's Island, The, V:1228; VI:2152
    Poganuc People, VI:2152
    Uncle Tom's Cabin, VI:2151, 2152, 2177, 2268,
        2270, 2375; VIII:1589
Strabo, I:731, **828-831**
    Geography, I:407, 541, 566, 828, 830, 831
    Historical Memoirs, I:828, 830
Strachan, John, VI:1448-1450
Strachey, Lytton, VIII:2606
Stradivari, Antonio, **IV:1281-1284**
Stradonitz, Friedrich August Kekule von, VI:1367
Strafford, First Earl of, IV:308, 1142, **1285-1288**
Stralsund, IV:291
Strand, Paul, VII:594
Strand, The, V:700, 701
Strasberg, Lee, VII:794, 795; VIII:2589; IX:3488
Strasser, Gregor and Otto, VIII:1404
Strassman, Fritz, VIII:1514, 1515, 2477
Strategic Arms Limitation Treaties, VII:590, 591;
    VIII:2759
Strategic Defense Initiative. *See* Star Wars program
Stratemeyer, Edward, V:52

Strato of Lampsachus, I:873
Strauss, Johann, VI:1686, **2155-2159**
    Acceleration Waltz, VI:2156
    Blue Danube, The, VI:2156
    Fledermaus, Die, VI:2156
    Kaiserwaltzer, VI:2158
    Tales from the Vienna Woods, VI:2156
    Zigeunerbaron, Der, VI:2158
Strauss, Richard, V:1164; **IX:3555-3558,** 3794
    Ariadne auf Naxos, IX:3557
    Aus Italian, IX:3555
    Elektra, IX:3556
    Festival March, IX:3555
    Guntram, IX:3556
    Heldenleben, Ein, VII:210
    Rosenkavalier, Der, IX:3556, 3557
    Salome, IX:3556
    Serenade for Wind Instruments in Eb, IX:3555
    Thus Spake Zarathusta, VII:210
Stravinsky, Igor, **IX:3559-3562**
    Apollo Musagetes, VIII:2182; IX:3560
    Card Party, The, IX:3560
    Firebird, The, IX:3560, 3607
    Oedipus Rex, VII:721; IX:3560
    Perséphone, IX:3560
    Petrushka, VIII:2748; IX:3560
    Rake's Progress, The, VII:471; IX:3561
    Rite of Spring, The, VII:387, 389; VIII:2449,
        2748, 2749; IX:3086, 3560
    Soldier's Tale, The, IX:3560
    Symphony of Psalms, IX:3560
Straw, Jack, II:114, 116
Streep, Meryl, VII:1084
Street, George Edmund, **VI:2160-2163**
Strelow, Albert, VII:1186
Stresemann, Gustav, **IX:3563-3565**
Strindberg, August, V:890; IX:2819, **3566-3569**
    Dream Play, A, IX:3566
    Fröken Julie, VII:281
    Great Highway, The, IX:3566
    Inferno, IX:3566
    To Damascus, IX:3566
string quartet
    Bartók, VII:211
    Beethoven, V:178-181
    Boccherini, IV:147-149
    Haydn, IV:639, 641, 642
    Schumann, VI:1993
    Zwilich, IX:4121-4123
Strong, Jonathan, IV:1236
Strutt, Jedediah, VI:2074
Stryker, Ron, VIII:2084

Stuart, Alexander, IV:576
Stuart, Charles Edward, IV:884
Stuart, Gilbert, **IV:1289-1293**
    Skater, The, IV:1290
Stuart, James. *See* James I
Stuart, John Todd, VI:1382
Studd, J.E.K., VIII:2637
Student Nonviolent Coordinating Committee,
    VIII:1973
Studio, The, V:161
Sturlung Age, II:836, 838
Sturluson, Snorri. *See* Snorri Sturluson
Sturm, Der, VIII:2013
Sturm Abteilung, VIII:1438
Sturtevant, Alfred Henry, VIII:2651
Stuttgart Declaration of Guilt, VIII:2743
Stuyvesant, Peter, **IV:1294-1297**
Styron, William
    Confessions of Nat Turner, The, VI:2277, 2278
submarines
    Fulton, V:855, 856
    Holland, V:1123-1125
    Ludendorff, VIII:2266
    Rickover, IX:3173-3176
    Verne, VI:2304
    Wilkins, IX:4000, 4001
Succession, Act of, III:209, 265, 654
Succession, House of, I:105
Sucre, Antonio José de, **VI:2164-2166**
Suddhodana, I:144
Sudebnik, III:383
Suess, Dr.. *See* Geisel, Theodor Seuss
Suetonius, I:928, 930, 933
Suevi, I:342
Suez Canal, VI:1355-1357, 1537; VIII:1530, 2695
Suez Canal Company, VII:1017
Suez Crisis, VII:531, 1017, 1018; VIII:1961,
    2695
Suffolk, Earl of, II:232
suffrage, women's. *See* women's suffrage
Suffrage Act of 1918, VII:354
Sufism
    'Abbas the Great, IV:4-6
    Abdelkader, V:1
    'Abduh, V:4
    Hallaj, al-, II:421-424
    Hasan al-Basri, II:441
    Ibn al-'Arabi, II:491-493
    Nanak, III:542
    Rumi, II:800, 801
    Sa'di, II:806
Sugar Act of 1764, IV:692

Suger, **II:859-862**
    *Abbot Suger on the Abbey Church of St. Denis
        and Its Art Treasures,* II:861
Sui Dynasty, II:482, 827, 1015
Sukarno, XIII:1577, 1578; **IX:3570-3574**
Sulaiman, II:68
Süleyman the Magnificent, III:159, **707-709**
Sulla, Lucius Cornelius, **I:833-836**
    Caesar, I:147
    Cicero, I:194
    Gracchi, I:347
    Jugurthine War, I:529, 530
    Mithradates the Great, I:558
    Pompey the Great, I:679
    Tigranes the Great, I:896, 897
Sullivan, Anne, VIII:1924, 1926
Sullivan, Sir Arthur, **V:927-931**
    Contrabandistas, The, V:928
    Cox and Box, V:928
    Grand Duke, The, V:929
    H.M.S. Pinafore, V:929
    In Memoriam, V:928
    Patience, V:929
    Prodigal Son, The, V:928
    Pygmalion and Galatea, V:928
    Tempest, The, V:928
    Thespis, V:928
    Trial by Jury, V:929
    Utopia, Limited, V:929
Sullivan, Harry Stack, VII:1247; **IX:3575-3577**
Sullivan, Louis, **VI:2167-2169;** IX:4060
Sully, Duke of, III:334
Sumanguru, II:863, 864
Sumer and Akkad, I:361, 362; VIII:1660
    See also Babylonia
Sumner, Charles, V:680, 681, 1152; **VI:2170-2174**
Sumter, Fort, V:1233
Sunday, Billy, **IX:3582-3586**
Sunderland, Third Earl of, IV:1401-1403
Sundjata, **II:863-865**
Sung Dynasty, **II:866-868**
    calligraphy, II:639, 640
    Ou-yang Hsui, II:709, 710
    Ssu-ma Kuang, II:840, 841
    Su Tung-p'o, II:855-857
    See also Northern Sung Dynasty; Southern Sung
        Dynasty
Sunila Pulp Mill, VII:2
Sunni Islam, II:385, 386, 678
Sun Records, IX:3076, 3079
Sun Yat-sen, V:1165, 1167; VII:664, 665, 676,
    687; **IX:3578-3581,** 3877-3879

Supper Controversy, III:102, 103
Suppression of Vice, Society for the, IV:1436
Supreme Council of India, VI:1428
Supreme Council of the United Orders of Railroad
    Employees, VII:880
Supreme Court, U.S.
    Altgeld, V:55
    Black, VII:321-323
    Bork, IX:3658
    Brandeis, VII:419, 421-423
    Burger, VII:509-511
    Cardozo, VII:575-577
    Chase, Salmon P., V:477-479
    Chase, Samuel, IV:293-296
    Dred Scott decision, VI:2000, 2001
    Espionage Act, VII:882
    Field, V:787-789
    Frankfurter, VII:1212-1215
    Kent, VI:1280
    Holmes, VIII:1721
    Hughes, VIII:1766-1769
    Lockwood, VI:1407, 1408
    Marshall, John, VI:1487-1491
    Marshall, Thurgood, VIII:2433-2435
    O'Connor, IX:2789-2791
    Rehnquist, IX:3142-3144
    Roosevelt, IX:3225
    Scalia, IX:3658
    segregation. See Brown v. Board of Education
    sexual harassment, VIII:2326
    slavery, VI:1490
    Stone, IX:3546-3549
    Story, VI:2147-2149
    Taft, VIII:1542; IX:3594-3596
    Taney, VI:2189-2193
    Thomas, IX:3657-3658
    treason, VI:1490, 1491
    Warren, IX:3888-3891
    Wilson, IV:1458
Supremecy, Act of. See Royal Supremecy, Act of
Supreme War Council of France, VIII:1851
surgery
    anesthesia, VI:1596-1598
    Aretaeus of Cappadocia, I:82, 83
    Celsus, I:173-175
    Cushing, VII:823-825
    Guy de Chauliac, II:414-416
    heart transplants, VII:195, 197
    Lister, VI:1388-1390
    Mayo, VIII:2466
    Paul of Aegina, II:712-714
    Semmelweis, VI:2021-2023

Surrealism
    Appolinaire, VII:82-84
    Bosch, III:72
    Breton, VII:448-451
    Buñuel, VII:505-507
    Cartier-Bresson, VII:594
    Césaire, VII:631
    Dali, VII:827, 829, 830
    Éluard, VII:1074-1077
    Ernst, VII:1098-1100
    Giacometti, VII:1359-1361
    Lacan, VIII:2061
    Magritte, VIII:2349-2353
    Miró, VIII:2546, 2548, 2549
    Nash, VIII:2690
    Nevelson, VIII:2729
    Redon, VI:1855
    Rousseau, VI:1921-1923
Su Shih, II:639
Susquehannocks, IV:81
Sutcliffe, Stuart, VII:226
Sutherland, Graham Vivian, IX:3587-3589
    Bestiary, IX:3588
    Burnt-out Paper Rolls, IX:3587
    Crucufixion, IX:3588
    Thorn Heads, IX:3588
    Thorn Trees, IX:3588
Sutherland, Halliday, IX:3552
Sutherland, Joan, IX:2931
Su Tse-yu, II:855
Su-tsung, II:967
Sutter, John Augustus, V:787
Suttner, Bertha von, VI:2175-2178
    Daniela Dormes, VI:2175
    Lay Down Your Arms, VI:2175, 2177
    Maschinenzeitalter, Das, VI:2177
Su Tung-p'o, II:855-858, 968
Suvorov, Aleksandr Vasilyevich, IV:1298-1301;
    VI:1305, 1306
Suzuki, D.T., VIII:1745
Svetambara, I:915
Svevo, Italo, VIII:2592
Svoboda, Ludvik, VII:969
Swabian War, III:493
Swan, Joseph Wilson, VI:2179-2181
Swedenborg, Emanuel, IV:1302-1304; V:67, 1216;
    VIII:1926
    Heavenly Arcana, The, IV:1302, 1303
    True Christian Religion, IV:1303
Swedish Tennis Association, VII:370
Swift, Jonathan, IV:220, 984, 1305-1309
    Conduct of the Allies, The, IV:158

Drapier's Letters to the People of Ireland, The, IV:1307, 1308
Examiner, The, IV:1307
Gulliver's Travels, IV:391, 469, 1308, 1309
Journal to Stella, IV:1307
Modest Proposal, A, IV:1307, 1308
Predictions for the Ensuing Year IV:1305, 1307, 1308
Tale of a Tub, A, IV:1305, 1307, 1308; V:522
Swimmer, Chief Ross, VIII:2390
Swinburne, Algernon Charles, III:765
Poems and Ballads: First Series, V:1040
Swiss Cottage Fields, V:1114
Swiss Reformation, III:791-794
Syagrius, II:274, 275
Sydenham, Thomas, **IV:1310-1312**
Sykes-Picot Agreement, IX:3931
Sylvester II, II:373, **869-872**
Sylvius, Jacobus, III:755
Syme, James, VI:1388
Symmachus, II:756, 897
symphonies
    Barber, VII:191-193
    Bartók, VII:210
    Beethoven, V:178-181
    Berlioz, V:202-206
    Bernstein, VII:296
    Borodin, V:286-288
    Bruckner, V:331-334
    Copland, VII:768
    Dvořák, V:725-727
    Ellington, VII:1068
    Franck, V:832-834
    Henze, VIII:1634
    Liszt, VI:1391-1393
    Mahler, VIII:2359, 2361-2363
    Mendelssohn, VI:1534-1536
    Messiaen, VIII:2503-2505
    Milhaud, VIII:2527
    Prokofiev, IX:3085-3087
    Rachmaninoff, IX:3105, 3106, 3108
    Ravel, IX:3129-3131
    Rimsky-Korsakov, VI:1889-1891
    Schubert, VI:1989, 1995
    Schumann, VI:1992-1995
    Sibelius, IX:3413-3415
    Strauss, VI:2155, 2156, 2158
    Tchaikovsky, VI:2198, 2200, 2201
    Villa-Lobos, IX:3816
    Zwilich, IX:4122, 4123
Syncellus, George, II:903
Syndicat Agricole Africain, VIII:1754

Synoptic Gospels, I:477; VIII:1558
Syon House, IV:9
Syphax, I:535
Syrian Wars, I:64, 717; II:383
Szabolcs, Synod of, II:575
Szell, George, VII:389
Szilard, Leo, IX:3632

Tabari, al-, **II:873-875**
    Selections from the Annals of Tabari, II:873, 874
Tabernacles, Feast of, I:332
Tabor, Mount, I:247
Tabor Amendment, IX:3447
Taborites, II:1030, 1031
Tabriz, II:381-383
Tacitus, Cornelius, I:772, **837-840,** 894, 935; IV:304
    Agricola, I:136, 838, 839
    Annals, I:136, 550, 551, 839; II:903
    Dialogue on Orators, I:838, 839
    Germania, I:838, 839
    Histories, I:839
Tacitus, Marcus Claudius, I:839
Tafari Makonnen. *See* Haile Selassie I
Tafawa Balewa, Abubakar, VII:145, 146
Tafna, Treaty of, V:2
Taft, Robert A., VIII:2298; **IX:3590-3593**
Taft, William Howard, **IX:3594-3597**
    Borah, V:280
    Brandeis, VII:422, 481
    Hand, VIII:1541, 1542
    Hughes, VIII:1766
    La Follette, VIII:2048
    Lathrop, VIII:2097
    Roosevelt, IX:3229, 3231
    Washington, VI:2337
Taft-Hartley Act, VIII:1867, 2172; IX:3447, 3592
Tagore, Debendranath, VI:1848
Tagore, Rabindranath, IX:3132, 3133, **3598-3602**
    Flight of Swans, A, IX:3599
    Gitanjali (Song of Offerings), IX:3599, 3601
    Gora, IX:3599
    Kari O Komal, IX:3598
    Religion of Man, IX:3601
Taharqa, I:105, 106
Tahiti, IV:143, 145, 180, 351, 353, 890
Taika Reforms, II:827
Taine, Hippolyte-Adolphe, **VI:2182-2184**
    History of English Literature, VI:2182
T'ai-p'ing Heavenly Kingdom, V:1165, 1166
Taiping Rebellion, VI:2260-2262
Taira Kiyomori, **II:881-883**

Taira Tadamori, II:881
Taisho, Emperor, VIII:1678, 1680
Tait, David, IV:875
T'ai Tsu, II:866
T'ai Tsung, **II:876-880,** 1015-1017
  Chen-kuan cheng-yao, II:879
  Li Wei-kung wen-tui, II:879
Taitu, Empress, VIII:1517
Taj al-Mulk, II:679
Taj Mahal, IV:1233
Takauji. *See* Ashikaga Takauji
Takeda Katsuyori, III:571
Takigawa Yukitoki, VIII:1574
Talal, Crown Prince, VIII:1791
Talavera, Battle of, VI:2352
Talbot, Henry Fox, VI:1660
Talbot, Marion, **IX:3603-3606**
  Food as a Factor in Student Life, IX:3604
  Home Sanitation, IX:3604
  Modern Household, The, IX:3604
  More Than Lore, IX:3604
Talenti, Francesco, II:84
Tale of the Heike, The, II:882
Tallchief, Maria, **IX:3607-3610**
Talleyrand, **VI:2185-2188**
Talmud
  Akiba, I:29
  Elijah ben Solomon, IV:432, 433
  Johanan ben Zakkai, I:471-473
  Maimonides, II:620
  Wise, VI:2401
Tambo, Oliver, VIII:2281, 2384, 2386
Tamerlane, II:418, **884-886,** 1022; IV:1232, 1233
Tamm, Igor, IX:3296, 3298
Tammen, Harry, V:532
Tanaka Giichi, VIII:1574
Tananarive accords, IX:3746
Tancred, II:160, **887-889**
Taney, Roger Brooke, VI:2000, 2147-2149, **2189-2193**
Tanganyika African Association, VIII:2773
Tanganyika African National Union, VIII:2773, 2774
T'ang Chien, VI:2260
T'ang Dynasty, II:482-485, 593, 876-879, 918, 1015-1017
T'ang T'ai Tsung, II:484
Tanguy, Julien, V:946
Tanizaki, Jun'ichiro, **IX:3611-3613**
  Chijin no ai, IX:3611
  Diary of a Mad Old Man, IX:3612
  Makioka Sisters, The, IX:3612, 3613

"Portrait of Shunkin, A," IX:3612
Some Prefer Nettles, IX:3612
Tannenberg, Battle of, II:1003
Tanutamon, I:106
Tanzimat, V:1207, 1208
T'ao Ch'ien, **I:841-843**
  "Returning to the Farm to Dwell," I:842
Taoism
  Chuang-tzu, I:190-193
  Confucius, I:223
  Lao-Tzu, I:498-500
  Li Po, II:591, 592
  Shih Huang-ti, I:178
Tarbell, Ida, **IX:3614-3617**
  History of the Standard Oil Company, The, IX:3616
Tardieu, André Pierre Gabriel Amédée, VIII:2105
Tariff Reform League, V:464
Tarzan, VII:517, 519
Tashunca-uitko. *See* Crazy Horse
Tasman, Abel Janszoon, **IV:1313-1315**
Tassi, Agostino, IV:317
Tasso, Torquato, **III:710-712;** IV:990
  Aminta, III:710, 711; V:650
  Creation of the World, III:711
  Discourses on the Heroic Poem, III:711
  Jerusalem Conquered, III:711
  Jerusalem Delivered, III:711; IV:990
  Rinaldo, III:710
Tatanka Iyotake. *See* Sitting Bull
Tatars, II:52; III:382; IV:726
Tatti, Jacopo. *See* Sansovino, Jacopo
Tatum, Art, IX:2880
Tawaraya Sotatsu, IV:1041, 1042
taxation
  Akbar, III:6, 7
  Almohad empire, II:5
  Asquith, VII:122
  Cato the Younger, I:166
  Chrétien, VII:681
  clergymen, II:172
  Darius the Great, I:237
  Diocletian, I:265
  Dole, VII:949
  Edward III, II:331
  Frederick the Great, IV:506
  Frederick William, IV:509
  George, V:907, 908
  Hancock, IV:615, 616
  Harding, VIII:1551
  Henry II, II:446, 447
  Hoover, VIII:1729

Joseph II, IV:751
Lavoisier, IV:806
Louis XI, III:435
Maria Theresa, IV:915
Matthias I Corvinus, III:488
Mellon Plan, VIII:2481
Muhammad 'Ali Pasha, VI:1604
nationalization of land, IX:3866
Peasants' Revolt, II:114, 786, 921-923
Persia, II:559
Philip IV the Fair, II:737, 738
Poincaré, IX:3046
Pompey the Great, I:680
Prussia, V:1035
Robespierre, IV:1170
Shays, IV:1239
Townshend Revenue Act, IV:408, 409
Toyotomi Hideyoshi, III:729
Trajan, I:900
Tseng Kuo-fan, VI:2261
U.S. Supreme Court, V:280
Walpole, IV:1402, 1403
See also Stamp Act
Tax Equity and Fiscal Responsibility Act of 1982, VII:949
taxonomy
Agassiz, V:32
Audubon, V:88
Cohn, V:534, 535
Cuvier, V:589-591
Gesner, III:299
Gray, V:979, 980
Linnaeus, IV:846-848
Taylor, Bayard, V:984
Taylor, Frederick Winslow, **IX:3618-3621**
Principles of Scientific Management, The, IX:3619
Taylor, Graham, VIII:2096
Taylor, Jeremy, IV:46
Taylor, John, IV:95
Taylor, Tom
Our American Cousin, VI:2215
Taylor, Paul Schuster, VIII:2084, 2085
Taylor, Zachary, **V:2194-2197**
Clay, V:510
Davis, V:615
Fillmore, V:792, 793
Grant, V:975
Scott, VI:2011
Webster, VI:2345
Tchaikovsky, Peter Ilich, **VI:2198-2202;** VII:884
Manfred, VI:2200

Nutcracker, The, VI:2200; IX:3608
Pathétique, VI:2200
Présages, Les, VIII:2450
Queen of Spades, The, VI:2200
Romeo and Juliet, VI:2198, 2200
Sleeping Beauty, The, VII:155
Yevgeny Onyegin, VI:2198
Teapot Dome Scandal, VIII:1551, 1552
Teasdale, Sara, **IX:3622-2625**
Answering Voice, The, IX:3624, 3625
Dark of the Moon, IX:3624
Flame and Shadow, IX:3624
Helen of Troy and Other Poems, IX:3622
Mirror of the Heart, IX:3625
Potter's Wheel, The, IX:3622
Rainbow Gold, IX:3624
River to the Sea, IX:3624
Sonnets to Duse and Other Poems, IX:3622, 3624
Tecumseh, **VI:2203-2206**
Tefnakhte, I:637, 638
Teilhard de Chardin, Pierre, **IX:3626-3630**
Divine Milieu, The, IX:3628
Phenomenon of Man, The, IX:3628, 3629
Tekakwitha, Kateri, **IV:1316-1318**
Tekere, Edgar, VIII:2648
telegraph
Carnegie, V:420
Colt, V:541
Cooke, V:555-558
Edison, V:743
Henry, V:1094
Kelvin, VI:1269
Lenoir, VI:1343
Maury, VI:1508
Morse, VI:1592-1594
Siemens family, VI:2066
Wheatstone, V:555-558
Telemann, Georg Philipp, **IV:1319-1322**
telescopes
Galileo, IV:521
Lippershey, IV:850-852
Newton, IV:1025
Schmidt, IX:3351, 3352
Tombaugh, IX:3701
television broadcasting
Associated Television Corporation, VII:739
Ball, VII:176-178
Cousteau, VII:781
Garland, VII:1306
Gish, VII:1385
Murrow, VIII:2662, 2664

Parton, IX:2897
Reagan, IX:3138
Walters, IX:3868, 3870, 3871
West, IX:3951
Winfrey, IX:4029-4031
television electronics
   de Forest, VII:860
   Sony Corporation, VIII:2623, 2624
   Zworykin, IX:4125, 4127
Telford, Thomas, IV:203; **VI:2207-2210**
Teller, Edward, VII:301, 302; **IX:3631-3634**
Telneshae, I:784, 785
temperance movement
   Anthony, V:61-64
   Astor, VII:130
   Bright, V:308
   Fowler, V:823
   Hayes, V:1078
   Mann, IV:894
   Manning, VI:1477
   Nation, VI:1630, 1631, 1633
   Picotte, IX:3009
   Shaw, VI:2044-2046
   Stanton, VI:2111
   Stone, VI:2143
   Willard, VI:2388-2390
   See also Prohibition (of alcohol)
Tempietto, III:582
Temple, Frederick, V:1040
Temple, Henry John. *See* Palmerston, Lord
Temple, Sir William, IV:1305, 1308
Temüjin. *See* Genghis Khan
Ten Commandments, I:563
Tendai sect, II:666
Teng Hsiao-p'ing, VIII:2213, 2214
Teng T'ing-chen, VI:1377
Ten Hours' Act, V:307
Tenka fubu, III:570
Tenkai Togaro, III:679, 680
Tennant, Charles, IV:815
Tennessean, VIII:1431
Tennessee
   Benton, V:195
   Crockett, V:578
   Gore, VIII:1431
   Houston, V:1137, 1140
   Polk, VI:1802
   secession, V:1232, 1233
Tennessee, Army of, VI:2059
tennis
   Borg, VII:368-370
   Evert, VII:1112-1114

   Gibson, VII:1363, 1364
   King, VIII:1968-1970
   Laver, VIII:2109-2111
   Navratilova, VIII:2702-2704
   Perry, IX:2979-2982
   Wightman, IX:3989-3991
Tennyson, Alfred, Lord, V:966; VI:1462,
   2211-2214
   Idylls of the King, VI:2212
   In Memoriam, VI:2212, 2213
   Maud and Other Poems, VI:2212
   Poems by Two Brothers, VI:2211
   Poems, Chiefly Lyrical, VI:2211
   Princess, The, VI:2212
Tenochtitlán, III:188-191, 377-379, 557
Tensho Shubun, III:679
Ten Thousand, March of the, I:959
Tenure of Office Act, V:1236
Tenzing Norgay, VIII:1662, 1663
Terah, I:5
Terence, I:540, **844-847;** III:155
   Andria, I:845
   Brothers, The, I:845
   Eunuch, The, I:845
   Mother-in-Law, The, I:845
   Phormio, I:845
   Self-Tormentor, The, I:845
Teresa, Mother, **IX:3635-3638**
Teresa, Princess, II:30
Teresa of Ávila, Saint, III:401, 402, **713-716;**
   VII:568; IX:3507
   Interior Castle, The, III:714, 715
   Life of the Mother Teresa of Jesus, The, III:714
   Way of Perfection, The, III:714
Tereshkova, Valentina, VII:1271; IX:3180,
   3639-3641
Terkhen-Khatun, II:679
Terror, Reign of
   Danton, IV:394
   Fourier, V:819
   Joséphine, V:1246
   Lavoisier, IV:807
   Marat, IV:912
   Marie-Antoinette, IV:920
   Michelet, VI:1548
   Robespierre, IV:1172, 1176
   Saint-Just, IV:1206
   Staël, VI:2093
terrorism
   Arafat, VII:92, 93
   Begin, VII:245
   Böll, VII:350, 351

Irish Republican Army, VII:771
    Qaddafi, IX:3100
Terry, Alfred H., VI:2072
Terry, Ellen, **VI:2215-2218**
Terry, Megan, **IX:3642-3645**
    Approaching Simone, IX:3643
    Babes in the Bighouse, IX:3644
    Calm Down Mother, IX:3643
    Hot House, IX:3642, 3644
    Mollie Bailey's Traveling Family Circus,
        IX:3644
    Viet Rock, IX:3643
Tertullian, **I:848-851**
Tesla, Nikola, **VI:2219-2222,** 2360
Tessin, Carl Gustaf, IV:243
Test Acts
    Bolingbroke, IV:157
    Charles II, IV:284
    James II, IV:704, 705
    Leeds, IV:821
    Oates, IV:1039
    Peel, VI:1753
    Shaftesbury, IV:1229
    Stanhope, IV:1279
Tet Offensive, IX:3823
Teton Mountains. *See* Grand Teton Mountains
Teton Sioux Indians, VI:2070
Tetrapolitana, III:102
Tettenhall, Battle of, II:320
Tetzel, Johann, III:443
Teutonic Order
    Alexander Nevsky, II:52, 53
    Casimir the Great, II:211-213
    Copernicus, III:178
    Wladyslaw II Jagiello and Jadwiga,
        II:1001-1003
Teutons, I:529
Tewkesbury, Battle of, III:268, 343
Texas
    Adams, V:24
    Austin, V:94-96
    Benton, V:196
    Burr, V:371
    Cabeza de Vaca, III:110, 111
    Calhoun, V:395
    Clay, V:509
    Coronado, III:180
    Crockett, V:579
    Fillmore, V:793
    Hobby, VIII:1703
    Houston, V:1137, 1138, 1140
    Jackson, V:1198

    Johnson, VIII:1866, 1867
    Jordan, VIII:1887-1889
    Polk, VI:1803
    Richards, IX:3169-3171
    Santa Anna, VI:1955
    secession, V:1138; VI:1338
    Tyler, VI:2291
Texas Medley Quartette, V:1240
Texas Revolution, V:94-96, 579, 1137, 1138, 1140
Texas v. White, V:479
textile industry
    cotton spinning, IV:59-62
    flying-shuttle, IV:769, 770
    Hargreaves, IV:623-625
    Slater, VI:2074-2076
Tezozómoc, III:555, 556
Thackeray, William Makepeace, V:752
Thales of Miletus, I:50, 51, 53, **852-856,** 955, 972
Thames, Battle of the, VI:1765
Thanh Nien, VIII:1699
Thant, U, **IX:3646-3648**
Thapsus, Battle of, I:167
Thatcher, Charles A., V:715
Thatcher, Margaret, **IX:3649-3653**
    Heath, VIII:1608
    Major, VIII:2369-2371
    National Health Service, VII:306
Thayendanegea. *See* Brant, Joseph
Thayer, Sylvanus, **VI:2223-2225**
Thayer, Webster, VII:1212, 1213; IX:3283
Theagenes, I:280
Theaters, War of the, IV:746
Theatine Order, IV:583, 584
Théâtre-Français, VI:1685
Theatrical Licensing Acts, IV:470
Theatrum Pompeii, I:681
Thebes
    Agesilaus II, I:16-18
    Akhenaton, I:23
    Alexander the Great, I:38
    Cleomenes II, I:215
    Epaminondas, I:290, 292, 293
    Hatshepsut, I:371, 373, 374
    Macedonia, I:628
    Psamtik I, I:709
Thelwall, John, IV:440
Themistocles, I:199, 788, **857-860**
Thenard, Louis Jacques, V:898
Theobald, Archbishop of Canterbury, II:128, 411
Theoctistus, II:278
Theodatus, Count, II:851
Theodora, II:553-557, 758, 759, **890-893**

Theodore of Mopsuestia, **I:861-864**
   On the Incarnation, I:862
   On the Twelve Prophets, I:863
Theodoret of Cyrrhus, **I:865-867**
   Dialogues, I:866
   Reprehensio duodecim capitum seu anathema anathematismorum Cyrilli, I:866
   Treatise of Laws, A, I:865
Theodoric Fund, I:254
Theodoric the Great, II:155, 215, **894-898**
Theodosius I, I:862
Theodosius II, I:124
Theodosius the Great, **I:868-872**
   Ambrose, I:44, 45
   Gregory of Nyssa, I:354
   Stilicho, I:825
   Ulfilas, I:909
Theoleptus of Philadelphia, **II:899-902**
Theological Declaration of Barmen. *See* Barmen Confession
Theon, I:436, 437
Theophanes Continuatus, II:904
Theophanes the Confessor, **II:903-905**
   Chronographia, II:903, 904
Theophilus, I:185
Theophrastus, I:53, 597, **873-876**
   Characters, I:539, 873, 875; II:527
   De historia plantarum, I:874
   Enquiry into Plants, I:874
   Metaphysics, I:874
   On Stones, I:874
   On Winds and On Weather Signs, I:874
Theorell, Axel Hugo Teodor, **IX:3654-3656**
Theosebeia, I:352
Theosophical Society, V:211-213
Therapeutae, I:634
Thermidorians, IV:1207
Thermopylae, Battle of, I:501, 502, 964
Theseum, I:676
Theseus, I:199, 318
Thespis, **I:877-879**
Thessalonica, I:44; II:943
Thessaly, I:629
Thicknesse, Philip, IV:516
Thiers, Adolphe, **VI:2226-2229**
   History of the Consulate and the Empire of France Under Napoleon, VI:2228
   History of the French Revolution, The, VI:2226
Third Carlist War, V:415
Third International, VII:491
Third Plenary Council, V:919

Third Punic War, I:345, 757, 762
Third Reich. *See* Nazi Party
Third Republic of France
   Blum, VII:337
   Clemenceau, VII:706
   Coubertin, VII:774
   de Gaulle, VII:867
   Herriot, VIII:1645
   Laval, VIII:2106, 2107
   Poincaré, IX:3044-3046
   Thiers, VI:2226-2229
   William II, IX:4004
Third Zionist Congress, VII:484
Thirteenth Amendment, VI:1383, 2137
Thirteen Years' War, II:1002
39 Articles of Religion of the Church of England, III:206; IV:107; VI:1503, 1504, 2063
Thirty Tyrants, I:655
Thirty Years' Peace, I:611
Thirty Years' War
   Brandenburg, IV:508
   Buckingham, IV:211-213
   Condé, IV:341, 342
   Ferdinand II, IV:450-452
   Grotius, IV:581
   Guericke, IV:586
   James I, IV:700
   Laud, IV:797
   Louis XIV, IV:866, 868
   Mazarin, IV:945, 946
   Pym, IV:1141
   Richelieu, IV:1165-1167
   Schütz, IV:1222
   Sweden, IV:304, 590, 591, 1335-1337
   Wallenstein, IV:1396-1398
Thomas, Clarence, **IX:3657-3659**
Thomas, Lowell, VIII:2127
Thomas, Norman, **IX:3660-3664**
Thomas, Saint, **I:880-884**
Thomas, Theodore, **VI:2230-2233**
Thomas, William, V:1142
Thomas à Kempis, **II:906-910**
   Imitation of Christ, The, II:904-909, III:594
   Modern Devotion, The, II:907
Thomas Aquinas, Saint, **II:911-916**
   Albertus Magnus, II:37
   Averroës, II:103
   Bonaventure, II:163
   Gilson, VII:1374-1377
   Joyce, VIII:1891
   Leo XIII, VI:1349
   Maritain, VIII:2425-2427

Raymond of Peñafort, II:777
Scriptum super "Libros sententiarum," II:913
Siger of Brabant, II:830
Stein, IX:3508
Summa contra gentiles, II:913
Summa theologica, II:303, 913, 914, 947, 986;
 III:334, 768
Vitoria, III:768, 769
William of Auvergne, II:978
William of Auxerre, II:982, 983
William of Moerbeke, II:985, 986
William of Saint-Amour, II:991
Thomas Gallus, II:76
Thomism. *See* Thomas Aquinas, Saint
Thompson, Leonard, VIII:2329
Thompson, Ruth Plumly, V:156
Thompson, Wiley, VI:1695
Thomson, J.J., IX:3277
Thomson, Tom, **IX:3665-3668**
Thomson, Virgil, IX:3513
Thomson, Sir William. *See* Kelvin, Lord
Thoreau, Henry David, V:31, 32, 40;
 VI:2234-2237, 2370
 Cape Cod, VI:2235
 "Civil Disobedience," VI:2235
 Maine Woods, The, VI:2235
 "Plea for Captain John Brown, A," VI:2235
 "Slavery in Massachusetts," VI:2235
 Walden, V:758; VI:2234, 2235, 2237
 Week on the Concord and Merrimack Rivers, A,
 VI:2234, 2235
Thorkell the Tall, II:201, 203
Thorndike, Edward L., **IX:3669-3671**
 Teachers Word Book, The, IX:3669
Thorne, George R., VI:2332
Thorpe, Jim, **IX:3672-3676**
Thousand Year Reich, VIII:1695
Thrale, Henry, IV:730
Three Blue Days of 1831, VI:2276
Three Gorges Dam, VIII:2180
Three Henrys, War of, III:333, 538
Three Principles of the People, IX:3579, 3580
Throckmorton, Elizabeth, III:639
Thucydides, I:484, 744, **885-888;** IV:662
Thule, I:732, 733
Thule expedition, IX:3122, 3123
Thurber, James, **IX:3677-3680**
 Great Quillow, The, IX:3678
 Male Animal, The, IX:3678
 Many Moons, IX:3678
 "Secret Life of Walter Mitty, The," IX:3678
 Thirteen Clocks, The, IX:3678

White Deer, The, IX:3678
Wonderful O, The, IX:3678
Thurii, I:706
Thuringia, II:340, 342
Thutmose I, I:371
Thutmose II, I:371
Thutmose III, I:371, 373, **889-891**
Tiananmen Square massacre, VII:906; VIII:2179
Tiberius, I:134, 152, 153, **892-895**
Tibor de Nagy Gallery, VII:1208, 1209
Ticknor, George, VI:2224
Ticonderoga, Battle of, IV:179
Ticonderoga, Fort, IV:35, 36, 64
Tiepolo, Giovanni Battista, **IV:1323-1326**
 Adoration of the Magi, IV:1324
 Angel Appealing to Sarah, IV:1323
 *Apollo Conducting Barbarossa's Bride, Beatrice
 of Burgundy,* IV:1324
 Apotheosis of Spain, IV:1325
 Banquet of Antony and Cleopatra, IV:1324
 Consilium in Arena, IV:1324
 Death of Saint Jerome, IV:1324
 Fall of the Rebel Angels, IV:1323
 Glory of Saint Teresa, IV:1323
 Last Communion of Saint Jerome, The, IV:1324
 Madonna of Carmelo and the Souls of Purgatory,
 IV:1323
 Neptune Offering to Venice the Riches of the Sea,
 IV:1324
 *Phaethon Begging Apollo to Allow Him to Drive
 the Chariot of the Sun,* IV:1323
 Power of Eloquence, IV:1323
 Repudiation of Hagar, IV:1323
 Sacrifice of Iphigenia, IV:1324
 Sacrifice of Isaac, The, IV:1323
 Story of Scipio, IV:1323
 Triumph of the Arts, IV:1323
 *Virgin in Glory Adored by the Apostles and
 Saints, The,* IV:1324
Tiglathpileser III, I:754
Tigranes V, I:779
Tigranes the Great, **I:896-898**
Tigranocerta, I:897
Tiguex War, III:182
Tilak, Bal Gangadhar, VII:141; **IX:3681-3684**
Tilden, Samuel J., V:1076
Tillich, Paul, VII:1056; **IX:3685-3687**
Tilly, Count, IV:1396
Tilsit Alliance, V:45
Tilsit, Treaties of, V:1033; VI:2115, 2116, 2187
Time magazine, VIII:2260, 2262, 2263
Timon, I:724, 725

Timoshenko, Semyon K., IX:4116, 4117
Timurid Dynasty, II:885
Tin Pan Alley, VII:287, 1347
Tintoretto, **III:717-720;** VII:1359
    Crucifixion, III:719
    Entombment, III:719
    Finding the Body of Saint Mark, III:719
    Last Supper, III:717, 719
    Miracle of the Loaves and Fishes, III:717
    Sacre Conversazioni, III:717
    Saint Mark Rescuing a Slave, III:717
    Saint Ursula and Her Virgins, III:717
    Susanna and the Elders, III:717
    Translation of the Body of St. Mark, III:719
Tippecanoe, Battle of, V:1061-1063; VI:2204
Tippu, IV:368, 369
Tiran, Strait of, VII:855
Tirpitz, Alfred von, **IX:3688-3691**
Tisquantum. *See* Squanto
Tissaphernes, I:32
Titanic, VII:181; IX:3970
Titian, III:60, 306, 598, 717, 719, 720, **721-724**
    Assumption of the Virgin, III:721
    Bacchanal of the Andrians, The, III:721
    Bacchus and Ariadne, III:721
    Gypsy Madonna, The, III:723
    Madonna of the Pesaro Family, The, III:723
    Rape of Europa, The, III:723
    Worship of Venus, The, III:721
Titicaca, Lake, VIII:1659
Tito, **IX:3692-3695**
Titus, I:662, 933, 934
Tlascalans, III:21, 22
Tmutorakan, II:953
Toba-Fushimi, Battle of, VI:1937
Tobey, Henry A., V:715
Tocqueville, Alexis de, **VI:2238-2241**
    Democracy in America, VI:2239
    Old Regime and the Revolution, The, VI:2239
    *On the Penitentiary System in the United States
        and Its Application in France,* VI:2238
    Recollections of Alexis de Tocqueville, The,
        VI:2239
Toghrïl Beg, II:67, 68, 677
Toklas, Alice B., IX:3511, 3513
Tokugawa Bakufu, VI:1936, 1937
Tokugawa Ieyasu, III:728, 730; **IV:1327-1330**
Tokugawa shogunate, III:570-572; IV:1258;
        V:1117, 1118, 1180-1182
Tokugawa Yoshinobu, VI:1937
Tolbiacum, Battle of, II:275
Toleration, Edict of, III:133; IV:751

Toleration Act of 1689, IV:100
Tolkien, J.R.R., VIII:2168; **IX:3696-3698**
    Hobbit, The, IX:3696, 3697
    Lord of the Rings, The, IX:3697
    Silmarillion, The, IX:3697
    Tree and Leaf, IX:3696
Tolstoy, Leo, V:1101; VI:2177, **2242-2246,** 2269;
        VIII:1442; IX:2899
    Anna Karenina, VI:2243
    Childhood, VI:2242
    Confession, A, VI:2243
    Death of Ivan Ilich, The, VI:2243
    Kreutzer Sonata, The, VI:2243
    Power of Darkness, The, VI:2243
    Resurrection, VI:2243
    Sebastopol, VI:2242
    War and Peace, VI:1833, 2242, 2243; IX:3087
    What Is Art?, VI:2243
Toltecs, III:529
Tombaugh, Clyde William, **IX:3699-3702**
Tombouctou, III:521
Tomyris, Queen, I:234
tonality
    Berg, VII:271-273
    Boulez, VII:387
    Hindemith, VIII:1670-1672
Tonga, IV:1313
Tonge, Israel, IV:1038, 1040
Tönnies, Ferdinand Julius, **IX:3703-3706**
    Community and Associations, IX:3703, 3704
    Gemeinschaft, IX:3704, 3705
    Gesellschaft, IX:3704, 3705
    Kürwille, IX:3704
    Wesenwille, IX:3704
Tontine Crescent, V:350, 351
Tooke, John Horne, IV:440
Toorop, Jan, VIII:2575
Topa Inca, III:578
Torah, I:330, 471, 472; II:648
Tordesillas, Treaty of, III:262
Toronto *Globe,* V:318-320
Toronto Star, VIII:1624
Torquemada, Tomás de, **III:725-727**
Torretti, V:408
Torrey, John, V:979
Torricelli, Evangelista, IV:586, **1331-1333**
    Opera geometrica, IV:1331-1333
Torrio, Johnny, VII:563, 564
Torstenson, Lennart, **IV:1335-1337**
Tory Party, English
    Anne, IV:52, 53
    Asquith, VII:123

Bevan, VII:305
Bolingbroke, IV:157-161
Brougham, V:314-316
Catholic emancipation, VI:1681
Charles II, IV:285
Defoe, IV:399, 401
Derby, V:653, 654
Disraeli, V:675, 677, 678
George I, IV:531, 532
Heath, VIII:1607, 1608
Kidd, IV:777, 779
Law, VIII:2112
Leeds, IV:821-823
Liverpool, VI:1395
Macmillan, VIII:2340-2342
Palmerston, VI:1719, 1720
Peel, VI:1752, 1753
Shaftesbury, IV:1230
Swift, IV:1307
Walpole, IV:1400-1403
See also Conservative Party (England)
Toscanelli dal Pozzo, Paolo, III:172
Toscanini, Arturo, VII:70, 192; XIII:1747, 1749;
    IX:3094, 3096, **3707-3710**
Tou Hsien, I:591
Toulouse-Lautrec, Henri de, **VI:2247-2250;**
    VII:363
    Artist's Mother at Breakfast, The, VI:2247
    Au Moulin Rouge: La Danse, VI:2248
    Cirque Fernando: Circus Rider, Le, VI:2247
    Corner of the Moulin de la Galette, A, VI:2248
    Englishwoman at the "Star," Le Havre,
        VI:2249
    Examination Board, VI:2249
    Goulue au Moulin Rouge, La, VI:2248
    Jane Avril at Divan Japonais, VI:2248
    Jane Avril at the Jardin de Paris, VI:2248
    Jane Avril Dancing at Moulin Rouge, VI:2248
    Jane Avril Entering Moulin Rouge, VI:2248
    Jane Avril Leaving Moulin Rouge, VI:2248
    Jockey, The, VI:2249
    Loie Fuller at the Folies Bergère, VI:2249
    Portrait of the Artist's Mother Reading,
        VI:2247
    Salon des Moulins, The, VI:2249
    Woman with Black Boa, VI:2249
Touré, Ahmed Sékou, **IX:3711-3714**
Tours, Battle of, II:242, 243
Tours, Council of, II:49
Toussaint-Louverture, IV:501, **1338-1341;** VII:633
Townes, Charles, VII:215
Townesend, Stephen, V:362

Townsend, Captain Peter, VII:1062
Townshend, Lord, IV:532, 533, 535, 1278,
    1401-1403
Townshend Revenue Act of 1767, IV:408, 409,
    615, 616
Towns Improvement Company, V:459
Toynbee, Arnold, **IX:3715-3718**
    Study of History, A, IX:3716, 3717, 3762
    Survey of International Affairs, IX:3715
    Western Question in Greece and Turkey, The,
        IX:3715
Toynbee Hall, VII:21, 308
Toyoda, Eiji, **IX:3719-3721**
Toyota Motor Company, IX:3719-3721
Toyotomi Hideyoshi, III:570, 571, **728-731,**
    1327, 1328
track and field
    Coe, VII:725-728
    Didrikson, IX:4096
    Lewis, IX:2865
    Owens, IX:2862-2865
    Thorpe, IX:3672, 3674, 3675
Tractarians, VI:1829
Tracy, Spencer, VIII:1639
Trades Union Congress, V:1037; VII:313,
    353-356
trade unions. See unionism, trade
Trafalgar, Battle of, VI:1636
Trafalgar Square, V:140
Trail of Tears, VI:1911, 2011, 2027;
    VIII:2389, 2390
Trajan, I:212, 356, 358, 440, 441, **899-903**
Trans-Asiatic Expedition, VII:696
Transcendentalism
    Alcott, Bronson, V:37-39
    Alcott, Louisa May, V:40
    Channing, V:472
    cummings, VII:806
    Emerson, V:757, 758
    Fuller, V:849, 850
    Hawthorne, V:1066
    Howe, V:1152
    Parker, VI:1727-1730
    Thoreau, VI:2234-2237
Transcontinental Air Transport. See TWA
Transjordan, Hashemite Kingdom of, VIII:1791
Transkei tribe, V:999
Transport and General Workers Union,
    VII:313-316
Trans-Sahara Expedition, VII:696
Transvaal, VII:376, 377
Trarza, V:763

treason
    Burr, V:371; VI:1490
    Fries, IV:295
    Ludendorff, VIII:2266
    Lutuli, VIII:2282
    Mandela, VIII:2386
    Masaryk, VIII:2441
    medieval England, II:331
    U.S. Supreme Court, VI:1490, 1491
Treasons, Statute of, II:331
Trent, Council of
    Charles V, III:160, 161
    Dominic, II:303
    Gabrieli, III:282, 283
    Greco, El, III:311
    Neri, III:551-553
    Paul III, III:595, 597
    Philip II, III:599
    Richelieu, IV:1165
    Veronese, III:748
Treppenhaus, IV:474
Tresham, Francis, III:258, 259
Trevithick, Richard, **VI:2251-2254**
Triangle Shirtwaist Factory fire, IX:2962
Tribonian, II:553, 555
trigonometry
    Abul Wefa, II:20, 21
    Aryabhata, II:89-91
    Battani, II:121, 122
    Euler, IV:444
    Fourier, V:820, 821
    Hipparchus, I:407, 409
    Khwarizmi, II:564
    Napier, III:545
Trinitarianism. *See* Holy Trinity
Trinity. *See* Holy Trinity
Trinity Church (Boston), VI:1882, 1883
Triple Monarchy, VII:1197
Trissino, Count Gian Giorgio, III:580
Troeltsch, Ernst, **IX:3722-3725**
    *Absoluteness of Christianity and the History of
        Religions, The*, IX:3723
    Historicism and It's Problems, IX:3723
    Social Teaching of the Christian Churches, The,
        IX:3723
Trois-Frères caves, VII:457
Trojan asteroids, IX:4039
Trojan War, I:287, 394, 421, 651
Tromp, Cornelus, **IV:1342-1344**
Tromp, Maarten, IV:134, **1342-1344**
Trondheim, II:689
Tropiques, VII:632

Trotsky, Leon, **IX:3726-3729,** 3764
    History of the Russian Revolution, The, IX:3728
    My Life, IX:3728
    Revolution Betrayed, The, IX:3728
    What Is to Be Done?, IX:3726
Troy, excavation of, VI:1980-1982
Troyes, Chrétien de. *See* Chrétien de Troyes
Troyes, Treaty of, III:339
Troy Female Seminary, VI:2385, 2386
Trudeau, Pierre Elliott, VII:680; IX:3344, 3345,
    3730-3735
True Whig Party, IX:3757, 3758
Truffaut, François, IX:3159, **3736-3739**
    Bed and Board, IX:3738
    Breathless, IX:3737
    Bride Wore Black, The, IX:3738
    Day for Night, IX:3738
    Farenheit 451, IX:3737
    400 Blows, The, IX:3736, 3737
    Green Room, The, IX:3738
    Hitchcock, IX:3736
    Jules and Jim, IX:3737
    Love at Twenty, IX:3738
    Mississippi Mermaid, IX:3738
    Shoot the Piano Player, IX:3737
    Soft Skin, The, IX:3737
    Story of Adèle H., IX:3738
    Such a Gorgeous Kid Like Me, IX:3738
    Two English Girls, IX:3738
    Wild Child, The, IX:3738
Trullan Synod, II:824
Truman, Harry S, **IX:3740-3744**
    Acheson, VII:17, 18
    Attlee, VII:138
    Harriman, VIII:1562
    Hoover, VIII:1733
    Hopkins, VIII:1738
    Humphrey, VIII:1784
    Lippmann, VIII:2205
    Luce, VIII:2263
    MacArthur, VIII:2298
    Marshall, VIII:2431
    military desegregation, IX:3114
    Moses, VIII:2635
    Nimitz, VIII:2752
Truman Doctrine, VII:315; VIII:1562, 2205
Truth, Sojourner, **VI:2255-2259**
Truth and Reconciliation Commission, IX:3777
Tse Lan, I:188
Tseng Kuo-fan, VI:1362, 1364, **2260-2263**
Tserclaes, Johann. *See* Tilly, Count
Tshombe, Moïse, **IX:3745-3748**

Tsiolkovsky, Konstantin, IX:2777, 2779, **3749-3752**
Tsvetayeva, Marina, **IX:3753-3756**
   Lebediny stan, IX:3754
   Poema gory, IX:3754
   Poema konca, IX:3754
   Stikhi k Bloku, IX:3754
   Vertsty I, IX:3754
tuberculosis
   Behring, V:183
   Calmett, VII:546-548
   Domagk, VII:952
   Ehrlich, VII:1032
   Koch, VI:1297-1299
   Waksman, IX:3835
Tubman, Harriet, **VI:2264-2267**
Tubman, William V.S., **IX:3757-3759**
Tucca, Plotius, I:927, 928
Tuc d'Audoubert cave paintings, VII:457
Tuchman, Barbara, **IX:3760-3763**
   Bible and Sword, IX:3760, 3762
   Distant Mirror, A, IX:3762
   First Salute, The, IX:3760
   Guns of August, The, IX:3760
   March of Folly, The, IX:3762
   Stilwell and the American Experience in China,
     IX:3760, 3762
Tudor, Mary, III:195, 293, 655, 733
Tudor family, **III:732-734**
   Catherine of Aragon, III:136
   Charles I, IV:279
   Edward VI, III:237-239
   Elizabeth I, III:241-245
   Henry III, II:453-455
   Henry VII, III:345-347
   Henry VIII, III:349, 351
   Mary I, III:479-482
   Richard III, III:651, 652
Tu Fu, II:592, 593, **917-920**
   "Autumn Thoughts: Eight Poems," II:919
   "Ballad of the War Chariots, The," II:919
   "Brave Adventures," II:917, 918
   "500 Words to Express My Feelings when I Went
     from the Capitol to Feng-hsien," II:919
   "Frontier Duties: Nine Poems," II:919
   "Hundred Anxieties, A" II:917
   "My Thatched Roof Whirled away by an
     Autumn Gale," II:919
   "Poetry Contest after Dinner at the Tso Villa, A"
     II:918
   "Song of the Whiteheaded," II:917, 918
Tugendhat House, VIII:2522
Tuileries Gardens, IV:834

Tukhachevsky, Mikhail, IX:2900
Tull, Jethro, **IV:1345-1347**
   Horse-Hoing Husbandry, The, IV:1345, 1347
Tullus, I:703
Tung Chung-shu, I:944
Tunney, Gene, VII:903
Tunstall, Cuthbert, III:735, 736
Tupolev, Andrei Nikolayevich, **IX:3764-3767**
Turenne, Vicomte de, IV:341, 343, 871-874
Turgenev, Ivan, IV:268; VI:1334, **2268-2272**
   Fathers and Sons, V:1101; VI:2269
   Rudin, VI:2268
   Smoke, VI:2269
   Sportman's Sketches, A, VI:2268, 2270
   Torrents of Spring, The, VI:2269
   Virgin Soil, VI:2269
Turgot, Anne-Robert-Jacques, IV:1016, 1017,
   1348-1350
   Reflections on the Formation and Distribution of
     Wealth, IV:1349
Turing, Alan Mathison, **IX:3768-3770**
Turkish Grand National Assembly, VII:134
Turkish National Movement, VII:134
Turkish War of Independence, VII:61
Türkmens, II:68, 69
Turner, Addison, V:1049
Turner, Frederick Jackson, **IX:3771-3774**
Turner, John, VII:681
Turner, J.M.W., VI:1925, **2272-2275;** VIII:2579
   Battle of Trafalgar, The, VI:2273
   Calais Pier, VI:2273
   Dido Building Carthage, VI:2273
   Ducal Palace and Bridge of Sighs, IV:244
   Fifth Plague of Egypt, The, VI:2273
   Fighting Téméraire' Tugged to Her Last Berth
     to Be Broken Up, VI:2274
   Fisherman at Sea, VI:2272
   Liber Studiorum, VI:2274
   Rain, Steam, and Speed, VI:2274
   Snow Storm, VI:2273
   Sun Rising Through Vapour, VI:2273
Turner, Nat, V:885; **VI:2276-2278**
Türr Syndicate, VI:1356
Turtle Creek strike, VIII:1880
Tutankhamen, I:23, 25, **904-907**
Tutu, Desmond, **IX:3775-3778**
TWA, VIII:2194
Twain, Mark, V:741; **VI:2279-2283;** VIII:2483
   Adventures of Huckleberry Finn, The, VI:2279,
     2281, 2282; VII:247; IX:3198
   Adventures of Tom Saywer, The, VI:2281, 2282;
     IX:3198

"Celebrated Jumping Frog of Calaveras County,
The," VI:2279
Connecticut Yankee in King Arthur's Court, A,
VI:2282
Gilded Age, The, VI:2281
Innocents Abroad, The, VI:2281
Life of the Mississippi, VI:2279
Mysterious Stranger, The, VI:2281
Prince and the Pauper, The, VI:2281
Tramp Abroad, A, VI:2281
What Is Man?, VI:2281
Tweed, William Marcy, VI:1628, **2284-2287**
Twelfth Amendment, IV:719
Twelve, Council of, VI:2414, 2415
Twelver Shi'I Islam, IV:4, 6
twelve-tone composition
Berg, VII:271-273
Boulez, VII:386, 387
Henze, VIII:1633
Schoenberg, IX:3357-3359
Webern, IX:3914-3916
Twelve Years' Truce, III:575; IV:644
Twentieth Century-Fox Motion Pictures,
VIII:1630, 2589; IX:3159, 4101
Twenty-eighth Congregational Society, VI:1728
Twenty-fifth Amendment, V:80
Tyler, John, V:509, 582; **VI:2288-2291**, 2345
Tyler, Wat, II:114-116, 786, **921-923**
Tynan, Kenneth, VIII:1818
Tyndale, William, III:193, 654, **735-738**
Obedience of a Christian Man, The, III:736
Parable of the Wicked Mammon, The, III:736
Practice of Prelates, The, III:736
Tyrannio, I:828
Tyre, I:40, 800
Tyre, Synod of, I:322
Tyrkir, II:577
Tyrtamus. *See* Theophrastus
Tzu-ch'u, Prince, I:176
Tz'u-hsi, V:466, 468, 469; VI:1362, 1364, 1365

Uganda-Tanzania War, VIII:2775
Ugo of Segni. *See* Gregory IX
Uitlanders, VI:1875; VII:376
Ujiji, Sea of, V:375
Ulbricht, Walter, **IX:3779-3882**
Ulfilas, **I:908-910**
Ulster, VII:122, 771; VIII:2112
Ulster Volunteer Force, VII:877
Ulyanov, Vladimir Ilich. *See* Lenin, Vladimir Ilich
Umar, V:763, 764
Umar II, II:441

Umayyad dynasty, II:18, 441, 522
Umkonto We Sizwe, VIII:2282, 2386
U.N. *See* United Nations
Un-American Activities, House Committee on
Brecht, VII:445
Chaplin, VII:655
Hiss, VIII:1683-1685
Hughes, VIII:1773
Lang, VIII:2078
McCarthy, VIII:2300-2302
Miller, VIII:2534
Murrow, VIII:2664, 2665
Parker, IX:2886
Reagan, IX:3136
Robeson, IX:3190
Unammuno y Jugo, Miguel de, **IX:3783-3786**
Abel Sánchez, IX:3784
Agony of Chrisitianity, The, IX:3784
Christ of Veláquez, The, IX:3784
Life of Don Quixote and Sancho, The, IX:3784
Nicodemo el fariseo, IX:3784
Peace in War, IX:3784
Saint Manuel Bueno, Martyr, IX:3785
Tragic Sense of Life in Men and Peoples, The,
IX:3784
Underground Railroad, VI:1601, 2110, 2264-2267
Unger, Franz, VI:1526
Unified Arab Command, VIII:1793
Union Army
Grant, V:975-978
Hickok, V:1108
Howe, V:1146
Sherman, VI:2057, 2059-2061
Stanton, VI:2106-2109
Webster, VI:2344-2346
Zeppelin, IX:4108, 4109
Union Steel, VIII:2480
unionism, trade
Africa, VIII:1754
Argentina, IX:2969, 2970
Besant, V:212
Bevan, VII:313-316
Carnegie, V:423
China, VIII:2212
Debs, VII:880-882
Disney, VII:940
Ford Motor Company, VII:1187
George, V:907
Gibbons, V:919, 921
Gompers, V:956-958
Guggenheim, VIII:1500
guild socialism, VIII:2093

Hardie, V:1037
Harrison, V:1058
Hughes, VIII:1775
Jaurès, V:1221-1223
Krupp, VI:1303
La Follette, VIII:2048
Matignon Agreements, VII:336
Owen, VI:1710
Perkins, IX:2962
Peru, VIII:1584
Proudhon, VI:1820
Randolph, IX:3114
Solidarity, IX:3844, 3846, 3847
Sorel, IX:3463, 3464
Taft-Hartley Act, VIII:1867, 2172; IX:3447, 3592
United Automobile Workers, VIII:2172;
    IX:3161-3164
United Farm Workers Association,
    VIII:1762-1764
United Mine Workers of America, VII:839,
    1212; VIII:1879-1881, 2170-2172
Union Pacific Railroad, VIII:1560
Unitarianism
    Biddle, IV:126, 127
    Channing, V:470, 471
    Dix, V:680
    Emerson, V:755, 757
    Parker, VI:1727, 1730
    Ray, VI:1847, 1848
    Ricardo, VI:1878
    Servatus, III:675-677
    Sharp, IV:1237
Unitas Fratrum. See United Brethren Church
United African Company, V:953
United Arab Republic, VIII:2694
United Artists Corporation, VII:653, 654;
    IX:3008, 3009
United Australian Party, VIII:2289, 2290, 2497,
    2498
United Automobile Workers, VIII:2172;
    IX:3161-3164
United Brethren Church, IV:1488, 1490
United East India Company. See Dutch East India
    Company
United Farm Workers Association,
    VIII:1762-1764, 1934; IX:3163
United Gold Coast Convention, VIII:2762, 2763
Unité d'Habitation, VIII:2138
United Mine Workers of America, VII:839;
    VIII:1879-1881, 2170-2172
United Nations
    Albright, VII:50

Boutros-Ghali, VII:399-401
Bunche, VII:501-503
Bush, VII:520
Casals, VII:608
Charter of the, VII:611, 1109-1111;
    VIII:1779-1781, 1984; IX:2920, 3861
China, VII:666, 678
Congo, VIII:2562, 2563
Economic and Social Council, IX:2959
genocide, VII:488
Hammarskjöld, VIII:1529-1531
Hiss, VIII:1683
India, IX:2869, 2870
Israel, VII:1000-1002
Japan, IX:3336
Katanga reintegration, IX:3746
Kirkpatrick, VIII:1994-1996
Liberia, IX:3758
Libya, IX:3099
Luce, VIII:2257, 2258
Palestine, VII:91, 502, 854, 855; VIII:2473
Pérez de Cuéllar, IX:2957-2959
Roosevelt, IX:3225
San Francisco Conference, VIII:2572; IX:3476
Saudi Arabia, VII:1118
Smuts, IX:3453
Spain, VII:1201
Thant, IX:3646-3648
Turkey, VIII:1814
Universal Declaration of Human Rights,
    VII:610-612, 1110; IX:3220
Waldheim, IX:2957, 3841-3843
World War II refugees, IX:3017
United Nations Emergency Force, VIII:1530, 1531
United Officers, Group of, IX:2970
United Shoe Manufacturing Company, VII:419, 422
United Society of Believers in Christ's Second
    Coming. See Shakers
United States, Bank of the
    Benton, V:196, 198
    Biddle, V:225, 226, 228
    Buchanan, V:347
    Clay, V:508
    Hamilton, IV:610
    Jackson, V:1198
    Taney, VI:2189
    Tyler, VI:2288-2290
United States Air Force, VIII:2554-2557, 2752
United States Army
    Gorgas, VIII:1434-1437
    MacArthur, VIII:2295-2298
    McCarthy, VIII:2301

Marshall, VIII:2429, 2431, 2432
Mitchell, VIII:2554-2557
Patton, IX:2911-2914
Pershing, IX:2983-2985
Powell, IX:3070-3072
Presley, IX:3078
women, IX:3446
Wright brothers, IX:4067
United States Bureau of Reclamation, VI:1812
United States Children's Bureau, VIII:2096,
    2097, 2099
United States Civil War
Adams, V:15
Alcott, V:40
Arthur, V:77
Bancroft, V:126, 127
Barton, V:142, 143
Beard, VII:222
Beecher, V:175, 176
Benét's *John Brown's Body,* VII:265
Bierce, V:230
Bingham, V:238
Birth of a Nation, VIII:1480, 1481
Blackwell, V:252
Blaine, V:256
Brady, V:296, 297
Bright, V:307
Bryant, V:344
Buchanan, V:348
Calhoun, V:396
Canada, VI:1437
Carnegie, V:420
Carson, V:432
Chase, V:478
Child, V:491
Cleveland, V:512
Colt, V:542
Cooke, V:551-553
Custer, V:585, 586
Davis, V:614-619
Dewey, V:656
Dix, V:681, 682
Douglas, V:692-694
Dred Scott decision, VI:1999-2001
Eads, V:729, 730
Farragut, V:773, 774
Fillmore, V:792-794
Frémont, V:839, 840, 842, 843
Garfield, V:876
Gibbons, V:919
Godkin, VIII:1400
Grant, V:975-978

Harrison, V:1053
Hay, V:1068
Hayden, V:1072
Hayes, V:1075
Hickok, V:1108
Higginson, V:1110-1112
Holmes, VIII:1720
Homer's art, V:1133
Houston, V:1140
Howe, Elias, V:1143
Howe, Julia Ward, V:1146
Jackson, V:1204-1206
Johnson, V:1232, 1233, 1235-1237
Kemble, VI:1275
Lee, VI:1338-1341
Lincoln, VI:1383
McCormick, VI:1432
McKinley, VI:1453
Morgan, VI:1579
Morse, VI:1594
Morton, VI:1598
Olmsted, VI:1691, 1692
Phillips, VI:1773
Rockefeller, VI:1896
Ross, VI:1911
Saint-Gaudens, VI:1940
Schurz, VI:1996, 1997
Seward, VI:2038
Sherman, VI:2057, 2059-2061
Stanley, VI:2101
Stanton, VI:2106-2109
Stephens, VI:2129-2131
Stevens, VI:2136, 2137
Stowe, VI:2151
Sumner, VI:2172, 2173
Truth, VI:2257
Tubman, VI:2266
Van Buren, VI:2294
Ward, VI:2328
Webster, VI:2344-2346
Westinghouse, VI:2358
Wilkes, VI:2382
Williams, VI:2396-2398
Wilson's *Patriotic Gore,* IX:4014
Wise, VI:2401
Zeppelin, IX:4108, 4109
See also Reconstruction era
United States Constitution. *See* Constitution, U.S.
United States Exploring Expedition of 1838-1842.
    See Wilkes Expedition
United States Geological Survey of Territories,
    V:1072-1074; VI:1812, 1813, 2328

United States-Japan Security Treaty,
  VIII:1809, 1810
United States Lawn Tennis Association,
  IX:3989, 3990
United States Marine Corps, VI:1686; VII:1388;
  IX:3466, 3467
United States National Park System, VI:1608-1610
United States Navy
  Byrd, VII:534-536
  Decatur, V:634-636
  Dewey, V:656-658
  Farragut, V:772-774
  Halsey, VIII:1525-1528
  Holland, V:1123-1125
  Jones, IV:738, 740-742
  Kennedy, VIII:1928
  Lodge, VIII:2220
  Nimitz, VIII:2750-2752
  Peary, IX:2941, 2944, 2945
  Perot, IX:2973
  Perry, Matthew C., VI:1760-1763
  Perry, Oliver Hazard, VI:1764-1766
  prison system, IX:2853
  Rickover, IX:3173-3176
  Steichen's photography, IX:3503
  Stevenson, IX:3523
  Washington Conference on Naval Disarmament,
    VIII:1767
  Westinghouse, VI:2358
  Wilkes, VI:2381-2383
  women, IX:3446
  Wright brothers, IX:4067
United States Open
  golf, VIII:1874, 1876, 1877; IX:3041,
    3042, 4049
  tennis, VII:1112, 1363, 1364; VIII:1968
United States Sanitary Commission, V:1146
United States Signal Corps, VII:102; VIII:2554
United States Steel Corporation, VI:1582;
  VIII:2480
United States Supreme Court. See Supreme
  Court, U.S.
United States v. Lopez, IX:3144
United Steel Workers, VIII:2172
United We Stand America, IX:2973, 2974
Unity Building, V:56
Universal Christian Conference on Life and Work,
  IX:3456, 3457
Universal Declaration of Human Rights,
  VII:610-612, 1110; IX:3220
Universal Negro Improvement Association,
  VII:668, 1311

Universal Peace Union, VI:1408
Universal Private Telegraph Company, V:558
Uranus, IX:3700, 3701
Urban II, II:928-931
Urey, Harold C., IX:3787-3790
  Planets, The, IX:3789
Urianghad Mongols, II:1022
Urizen, IV:140
Urraca, II:268
Uruk, I:361
Usen, V:915
Utagawa Kunisada, V:1118
U Thant, VIII:2695
Utilitarianism
  Bentham, IV:108, 109
  Bradley, V:291
  Chadwick, V:457-460
  Condillac, IV:346
  Godkin, VIII:1400
  Hobbes, IV:665
  Holmes, VIII:1721
  Mill, James, VI:1557, 1558
  Mill, John Stuart, VI:1559, 1560, 1562, 1563
  Place, VI:1787
  Sidgwick, VI:2063, 2064
Utrecht, Maria von, III:574
Utrecht, Treaty of, IV:53, 157, 158, 161
Utrecht, Union of, III:575

vaccination
  Behring, V:182-184
  Pasteur, VI:1747
  polio, IX:3305-3307
  smallpox, IV:721-723
  tuberculosis, VII:546-548
  veterinary medicine, IX:3451, 3452
Vaché, Jacques, VII:448
Vagabond King, The, III:766
Vaillant, Édouard, V:1222
Val-de-Grâce, church of the, IV:899, 900
Valdemar I, II:932
Valdemar II, II:932-934
Valentinian I, I:44
Valentinian II, I:44, 870
Valentinian III, I:343
Valentinus, I:911-914
Valéry, Paul, IX:3791-3793
  "Fileuse, Le," IX:3791
  "Graveyard by the Sea, The," IX:3792
  "Introduction to the Method of Leonardo da
    Vinci," IX:3791
  Jeune Parque, La, IX:3792

My Faust, IX:3793
"Narcisse parle," IX:3791
Val-ès-Dunes, Battle of, II:997
Val-Kill, IX:3218
Valla, Lorenzo, **III:739-742**
    Adnotationes in Novum Testamentum, III:741
    De professione religiosorum, III:740
    Dialecticae disputationes, III:740
    Elegantiae linguae latinae, III:740
    On Free Will, III:739, 740
    On Pleasure, III:739
    Treatise on the Domination of Constantine, The,
      III:740
Valley Forge, Battle of, IV:678, 1405
Valley of the Kings, I:904-906
Vanbrugh, Sir John, IV:635-637, **1351-1354**
    Relapse, The, IV:1352
    Provok'd Wife, The, IV:1352
Van Buren, Martin, **VI:2292-2295**
    Bancroft, V:127
    Burr, V:371, 372
    Clay, V:509
    Clinton, V:519
    Polk, VI:1802
Vance, Vivian, VII:178
Vancouver, George, **IV:1355-1357;** VI:1257
    Voyage of Discovery to the North Pacific Ocean
      and Round the World, IV:1356
Vandals, I:342-344, 825; II:215
Vanderbilt, Cornelius, **VI:2296-2298**
Vanderbilt, Gloria, IX:3970
Van Dieman, Antony, IV:1313-1315
Vane, Sir Henry, IV:688
Van Gogh, Vincent. *See* Gogh, Vincent van
Vanzetti, Bartolomeo, VII:1212; IX:2885, 3060,
    3281-3283
Vanity Fair magazine, VII:809; IX:2884
Vanucci, Domenico Francesco, IV:147
Varangians, II:803, 804, 953
Varazdat, I:780
Vardhamāna, **I:915-917**
Varèse, Edgard, **IX:3794-3797,** 4076
    Amériques, IX:3795
    Bourgogne, IX:3794
    Deserts, IX:3796
    Hyperprism, IX:3795
    Ionisation, IX:3795
    L'Éspace, IX:3795
    musique concréte, IX:3795, 3796
    Offrandes, IX:3795
    Poème électronique, IX:3796
Varius, Lucius, I:927, 928

Varley, Samuel Alfred, VI:2068
Varro, Marcus Terentius, I:335, 659, **918-921**
    Antiquitates rerum humanarum et divinarum
      libri XLI, I:920
    Disciplinarum libri IX, I:920
    Imagines, I:920
    Menippean Satires, I:919, 920
    On Agriculture, I:920
    On the Latin Language, I:920; III:671
Varus, Publius Quintilius, I:134
Vasa Dynasty, IV:290-292
Vasari, Giorgio, **III:743-746**
    Lives of the Most Eminent Painters, Sculptors,
      and Architects, II:272, 273; III:743-745
Vasily II, III:381
Vasvár, Treaty of, IV:839
Vatican II. *See* Second Vatican Council
Vatican Council, VI:1783, 1784
Vaughan Williams, Ralph, **IX:3798-3800,**
    3874, 3875
    Fantasia on a Theme by Tallis, IX:3798
    Pastoral Symphony, IX:3799
    Sea Symphony, A, IX:3799
Vaux, Calvert, VI:1691, 1692
Vauxcelles, Louis, VII:431
Vaux-le-Vicomte, IV:834, 835
Vavilov, Nikolai Ivanovich, VII:224;
    IX:3801-3804
Veblen, Thorstein, **IX:3805-3807**
    Engineers and the Price System, The, IX:3806
    Imperial Germany and the Industrial Revolution,
      IX:3806
    Inquiry into the Nature of Peace and the Terms
      of Its Perpetuation, An, IX:3806
    Theory of Business Enterprise, The, IX:3806
    Theory of the Leisure Class, The, IX:3806
Vecellio, Tiziano. *See* Titian
Vedas, II:89
Vega Carpio, Lope de, IV:235, **1361-1363**
    Arcadia, La, IV:1362
    Gardener's Dog, The, IV:1362
    Justice Without Revenge, IV:1362
    Lady Nit-Wit, The, IV:1362
    New Art of Writing Plays, The, IV:1361
    Sheep-Well, The, IV:1362
Velázquez, Diego, IV:570; **1364-1367;** VI:1837
    Bloody Cloak of Joseph, The, IV:1366
    Meninas, Las, IV:1366
    Surrender of Breda, The, IV:1366
Velbuzd, Battle of, II:843
Velia. *See* Elea
Vendôme, Place, IV:902

Vendôme Column, V:567

Venette, Jean de, **II:935-937**

    Chronicle of Jean de Venette, The, II:935

Venice, Republic of

    Bayezid II, III:51, 52

    Bellini, III:58-61

    Canaletto, IV:242-244

    Dandolo, II:282, 284

    Sansovino, III:664-666

    Veronese, III:747, 748

    Villehardouin, II:944

Venice, Treaty of, II:284

Venizélos, Eleuthérios, **IX:3808-3810**

Ventose, Laws of, IV:1207

Vercingetorix, **I:922-925**

Verdi, Giusseppe, **VI:2299-2302;** IX:3096

    Aïda, VI:2300, 2301; IX:3083, 3093

    ballo in maschera, Un, VI:2300

    Don Carlos, VI:2300

    Falstaff, VI:2300, 2301; IX:3081

    forza del destino, La, VI:2300

    giorno di regno, Un, VI:2299

    I Lombardi alla prima crociata, VI:2299

    I masnadieri, VI:2299

    Il traviata, La, VI:2300, 2301

    Il trovatore, VI:2300, 2301

    Macbeth, VI:2299

    Nabucco, VI:2299

    Oberto, conte di San Bonifacio, VI:2299

    Otello, VI:2300, 2301

    Requiem Mass, VI:1484, 2300, 2301

    Rigoletto, VI:2300, 2301; VII:599

    Simone Boccanegra, VI:2300

Verdun, Treaty of, II:229, 600, 740

Verein fur Raumschiffahrt, VII:2778

Vergara, Convention of, V:414

Vergil, I:287, 512, 520, 521, 585, 587, **926-929;**

    II:288

    Aeneid, I:926-928; IV:318; V:205; VII:1250

    Eclogues, I:926

    Georgics, I:926, 928; IV:566

Vergil, Polydore, III:652

Vergine, Guglielmo, VII:598

Verkade, Jan, VII:910

Verlaine, Paul, VI:1886, 1887

Verlet, Raoul, VIII:2199

Vermeer, Jan, IV:827, **1368-1371**

    Allegory of Painting, The, IV:1369

    Astronomer, The, IV:1369

    Christ in the House of Martha and Mary,

        IV:1368

    Diana and Her Companions, IV:1368

    Geographer, The, IV:1369

    Guitar Player, The, IV:1369

    Love Letter, The, IV:1369

    Procuress, The, IV:1368

    View of Delft, IV:1369

Verne, Jules, VI:1532, **2303-2306**

    Antarctic Mystery, An, VI:2305

    Around the World in Eighty Days,

        VI:2304, 2305

    Begum's Fortune, The, VI:2304

    Discovery of the Earth, The, VI:2303

    Five Weeks in a Balloon, VI:2303

    For the Flag, VI:2304

    From the Earth to the Moon, VI:2304, 2305

    Journey to the Centre of the Earth, VI:2304, 2305

    Master of the World, VI:2305

    Mysterious Island, The, VI:2304, 2305

    Twenty Thousand Leagues Under the Sea,

        VI:2304, 2305; VII:180

Vernet, Carle, V:910

Vernet, Joseph, IV:1376

Veronese, Paolo, **III:747-749**

    Feast in the House of Levi, The, III:748

    Triumph of Mordecai, III:747

    Triumph of Venice, III:747

Verres, Gaius, I:195

Verrius Flaccus, Marcus, **I:930-932**

    De verborum significatu, I:930

Verrocchio, Andrea del, **III:750-753**

    Baptism of Christ, III:751

    Beheading of Saint John the Baptist, The, III:751

    Christ and Saint Thomas, III:751, 752

    David, III:750

    Equestrian Statue of Colleoni, III:751, 752

    Madonna Enthroned with Saints John the Baptist

        and Donatus, III:751

    Portrait of a Woman, III:751

    Putto with a Dolphin, III:750

Versailles, Treaty of

    Angell, VII:76

    Bordon, VII:366

    Botha, VII:378

    Clemenceau, VII:705

    Czechoslovakia, VIII:2442

    Erzberger, VII:1102

    Hitler, VIII:1694, 1695

    Keynes, VIII:1952, 1955

    La Follette, VIII:2048

    Laval, VIII:2105

    Law, VIII:2113

    New Zealand, VIII:2445

    Poincaré, IX:3044, 3045

Stresemann, IX:3564, 3565
Wilson, IX:4022
Verus, Lucius Aurelius, I:339, 340, 523
Verwey, Jock, IX:3040
Vesalius, Andreas, **III:754-757**
   Bloodletting Letter of 1539, The, III:754
   De fabrica, III:754
   Institutiones anatomicae, III:754
   Six Anatomical Tables, III:754, 755
Vespasian, I:472, 483, 484, 663, **933-935**
Vespucci, Amerigo, **III:758-762**
   First Four Voyages, The, III:759, 761
   Mondus Novus, III:761
Vézère Valley finds, VII:456
Viardot, Pauline, V:968
vice presidency, U.S.
   Adams, IV:18
   Bush, VII:520, 521
   Ferraro, VII:1153-1155
   Ford, VII:1181
   Garfield, V:78
   Gore, VIII:1431-1433
   Johnson, VIII:1867, 1868
   Nixon, VIII:2758-2760
   Tyler, V:509; VI:2288-2291
   Van Buren, VI:2293
Vicksburg, Battle of, V:976
Vico, Giambattista, **IV:1372-1375**
   New Science, The, IV:1372-1374; VI:1548
   On the Study Methods of Our Times, IV:1372
   Selected Writings, IV:1372
Victor III, II:928
Victor IV, II:48, 49, 359
Victor Emmanuel, V:447, 448, 881
Victor Emmanuel III, VIII:2668
Victoria, Queen, **VI:2307-2311**
   Edward VII:1020, 1021
   George III, IV:543
   Melbourne, VI:1518, 1519
   Palmerston, VI:1721
Victoria, Tómas Luis de, III:107, 108
Victorius of Aquitaine, II:298
Videla, González, VIII:2717
Vien, Joseph, V:610
Vienna
   Freud, VII:1224
   Haydn, IV:639
   Mahler, VIII:2359
Vienna, Concordat of, III:559
Vienna, Congress of
   Alexander I, V:44-46
   Castlereagh, V:441

Hardenberg, V:1033-1035
Metternich, VI:1545, 1546
Palmerston, VI:1720
Stein, VI:2116
Talleyrand, VI:2187
Vienna, Siege of, IV:840
Vienna Psychoanalytical Association, VII:1225
Viet Cong, VIII:1701; IX:3823
Viète, François, I:274
Viet Minh, VIII:1698-1701; IX:3821-3823
Vietnam Veterans Memorial, VIII:2185-2187
Vietnam War
   Acheson, VII:18
   Black, VII:322, 323
   Calder, VII:540
   Chomsky, VII:674, 675
   Ford, VII:1181, 1182
   Gore, VIII:1431
   Greene, VIII:1469
   Harriman, VIII:1562, 1563
   Hayslip, VIII:1593-1595
   Humphrey, VIII:1784, 1785
   Johnson, VIII:1867
   Kennedy, John F., VIII:1931
   Kennedy, Robert F., VIII:1934
   King, VIII:1974
   Kissinger, VIII:2000
   Lippmann, VIII:2205
   McCarthy, VIII:2306
   Mailer, VIII:2366
   Marcos, VIII:2421
   Nixon, VIII:2758, 2759
   O'Neill, IX:2825
   Perot, IX:2973
   Powell, IX:3070
   Rankin, IX:3119
   Sihanouk, IX:3417, 3419
   Smith, IX:3448
   Terry, IX:3643
   Vo Nguyen Giap, IX:3821-3823
   Washington Post, VIII:1452, 1453
Vigée-Lebrun, Élisabeth, **IV:1376-1379**
   Marie Antoinette and Her Children,
     IV:1376, 1378
   Peace Bringing Back Plenty, IV:1376
Vigilance Society, V:777
Vigilius, II:892
Vikings
   Alfred the Great, II:59, 60
   Canute the Great, II:201-204
   Charles the Bald, II:239
   Edward the Elder, II:319-321

Ethelred II, the Unready, II:344-346
  Olaf I, II:688-690
  Olaf, Saint, II:691-693
  Rollo, II:793-795
  Rurik, II:804
Villa, Pancho, IX:2782, 2984, **3811-3814,** 4106
Villa Dei, Alexander de, II:757
Village Voice, The, VIII:2365
Villahermosa, VI:1761, 1762
Villa-Lobos, Heitor, **IX:3815-3817**
  Bachianas brasileiras, IX:3815
  choros, IX:3816
  Guia Pratico, IX:3816
  Indian Symphony, The, IX:3816
  New York Skyline, The, IX:3816
  Rudepoema, IX:3816
Villa Mairea, VII:2
Villani, Giovanni, **II:938-941**
  Chronicle, II:938, 940, 941
Villani, Matteo, II:940
Villanova, Arnold of. *See* Arnold of Villanova
Villehardouin, Geoffroi de, **II:942-945**
  Conquête de Constantinople, La, II:943, 944
Villeneuve, Michel de. *See* Servetus, Michael
Villiers, George. *See* Buckingham, First Duke of
Villon, François, **III:763-767**
  "Ballade of the Hanged," III:764
  Great Testament, The, III:764, 766
  Legacy, The, III:763, 764
Vincennes, IV:312, 314
Vincent de Paul, Saint, **IV:1380-1382**
Vincentians. *See* Mission, Congregation of the
Vincent of Beauvais, **II:946-948**
  De morali principis institutiones, II:947
  Doctrinale, II:946, 947
  Historiale, II:946
  Naturale, II:946
  Speculum majus, II:946, 947
Vincent of Lérins, Saint, **I:936-938**
  Commonitory of Vincent of Lérins, The,
    I:937, 938
Viner, Charles, IV:129
Vines, Ellsworth, IX:2981
Vining, Elizabeth Gray, VII:41
Viollet-le-Duc, Eugène, IX:2976
violin
  Corelli, IV:360-362
  Paganini, VI:1711-1714
  Stradivari, IV:1281-1283
  Vivaldi, IV:1383
Viracocha Inca, III:577
Virchow, Rudolf, **VI:2312-2315**

Virgil. *See* Vergil
Virginia
  Bacon, IV:80-82
  Brown, V:324
  Grenville, III:316, 317
  Henry, IV:647-649
  Jefferson, IV:716, 718
  Lee, VI:1338, 1340
  Madison, IV:886
  Mason, IV:926-928
  Monroe, VI:1571
  Powhatan, IV:1122
  Smith, IV:1253-1255
Virginia Company, IV:189, 462, 1106-1108
Virginia Declaration of Rights, IV:926
Virgin Lands Program, VII:459; VIII:1962
Virgin Mary, **I:939-942**
  Immaculate Conception, II:310, 311; V:10
Visconti, Luchino, **IX:3818-3820**
  Damned, The, IX:3820
  Death in Venice, IX:3820
  Leopard, The, IX:3819
  Risorgimento, IX:3819
  Rocco and His Brothers, IX:3819
  Rosalinda, IX:3819
  Terra Trema, La, IX:3818, 3819
  Wanton Contessa, The, IX:3819
Visigoths
  Alaric, I:342
  Attila, I:126
  Clovis, II:276
  Isidore of Seville, II:518-520
  Stilicho, I:826
  Theodosius the Great, I:868-871
  Ulfilas, I:908-910
Vitellius, I:642
Vitoria, Francisco de, **III:768-770**
  De Indis, III:769
  Reflectiones theologicae, III:769
Vitruvius, I:76, 77; IV:153
Vitry, Phillippe de, **II:949-951**
  Ars Nova, II:660, 661, 949, 950
  Roman de Fauvel, II:950
Vivaldi, Antonio, III:285; **IV:1383-1386**
  cetra, La, IV:1384
  cimento dell'armonia e dell' inventione, Il,
    IV:1384
  estro armonico, L', IV:1383
  Four Seasons, The, IV:1384, 1385
Vivarium, II:215, 216
Vladimir I, **II:952-954**
Vladimir-Suzdal, Grand Duchy of, II:52

Vlad Tepes, III:500
Vogue magazine, IX:2884
Volcker, Paul A., VIII:1472
Volger, Georg Joseph, VI:2340
Volkogonov, Dimitri, VIII:1684
Vollard, Ambroise, IX:3252
Voloshin, Max, IX:3753
Voloshinov, Valentin Nikolayevich, VII:152, 153
Volta, Alessandro, IV:523-525, **1387-1391**
Voltaire, **IV:1392-1395**
   Age of Louis XIV, IV:1394
   Alembert, IV:32
   Boswell, IV:175
   Candide, IV:832, 1392, 1394, 1395
   Discourses in Verse on Man, IV:1394
   Elements of Sir Issac Newton's Philosophy, The,
     IV:344
   Frederick the Great, IV:506
   Henriad, IV:1392
   History of Charles XII, The, IV:1392
   Letters Concerning the English Nation, IV:1392
   Montagu, IV:984
   Oedipus, IV:1392
   Philosophical Dictionary for the Pocket, A,
     IV:1394
   Poem on the Lisbon Earthquake, IV:1394
   Zadig, IV:1394
Vo Nguyen Giap, **IX:3821-3825**
Voragine, Jacobus de, I:180
Vortigern, I:378, 379
Voting Rights Act of 1965, VIII:1868, 1974
Vuillard, Édouard, VII:362; **IX:3826-3828**
Vyrheid, VII:376
Vytautas, II:1001, 1002

WAAC. *See* Women's Auxiliary Army Corps
Wabash Confederacy, IV:314
Wach, Joachim, **IX:3829-3832**
Wadsworth, Charles, V:669, 670
Wafd Party, IX:4093-4095
Waffen SS, VIII:1668
Wagner, Honus, VII:719
Wagner, Richard, **VI:2316-2320**
   Ban on Love, The, VI:2316
   Bruckner, V:332
   chromaticism, VII:272
   Ehrenfels, VII:1027
   Faust Overture, VI:2316
   Flying Dutchman, The, VI:2316
   Liszt, VI:1393
   Lohengrin, VI:2317, 2319
   Love Feast of the Apostles, The, VI:2317

   Mahler, VIII:2362, 2363
   Mastersingers of Nuremberg, The, VI:2317, 2319
   Nietzsche, VI:1662
   Parsifal, V:1162; VI:1664, 2319; VII:389
   Puccini, IX:3096
   Ravel, IX:3129
   Rheingold, Das, VI:2319
   Rienzi, VI:2316
   Ring of the Nibelungs, VI:2316, 2317
   Schopenhauer, VI:1986
   Schumann, VI:1993
   Shaw, IX:3399
   Siegfried, VI:2319
   Tannhäuser, VI:2317; VIII:2059
   Thomas, VI:2232
   Toscanini, IX:3707
   Tristan und Isolde, VI:2316, 2317
   Twilight of the Gods, The, VI:2319
   Verdi, VI:2301
Wagner Labor Relations Act, VIII:1768
Wagoner, Porter, IX:2896
Wagram, Battle of, V:475
Wainwright Building, VI:2167
Waitangi, Treaty of, V:380
Wakefield, Battle of, III:647
Wakefield, Edward Gibbon, V:722; **VI:2321-2323**
   Letters from Sydney, VI:2321
Waksman, Selman Abraham, **IX:3833-3836**
Walcott, Jersey Joe, VIII:2412, 2413
Wald, Lillian D., **IX:3837-3840**
Walden, Herwarth, VIII:2013
Waldheim, Kurt, IX:2957, **3841-3843,** 3986
Waldrada, II:674
Waldseemüller, Martin, III:761
Wales, Council of, III:235
Walesa, Lech, **IX:3844-3848**
Walker, Alice, VIII:1789; **IX:3849-3852**
   Color Purple, The, IX:3850, 4030
   In Love and Trouble, IX:3850
   In Search of Our Mother's Gardens, IX:3850
   Living by the Word, IX:3850
   Meridian, IX:3850
   Possessing the Secret of Joy, IX:3851
   Revolutionary Petunias, IX:3850
   Temple of My Familiar, The, IX:3850
   Third Life of Grange Copeland, The, IX:3849
   You Can't Keep a Good Woman Down, IX:3850
Walker, Madam C.J., **IX:3853-3856**
Walker, George, V:450
Walker, James J., VIII:2055
Walker, John G., VIII:1435
Walker, William Hall, VII:996

Wallace, Alfred Russell, VI:1421
Wallace, Frank, IX:3949, 3951
Wallace George C., VIII:1785; **IX:3857-3859**
Wallace, Henry A., IX:3662, **3860-3864**
Wallace, Henry C., VIII:1552
Wallace, Sir William, II:185, **955-958**
Wallach, Meier Moiseevich. *See* Litvinov, Maksim Maksimovich
Wallenstein, Albrecht Wenzel von, IV:451, 452, 590, 591, **1396-1399**
Waller, Augustus Volney, VII:1040
Wall Street. *See* Dow Jones Industrial Average; New York Stock Exchange
Walo, V:763
Walpole, Horace, III:652; IV:204, 206
  Castle of Otranto, The, V:139
Walpole, Sir Robert, **IV:1400-1404**
  Bolingbroke, IV:157-159, 161
  Fielding, IV:469, 470
  George I, IV:531, 532
  George II, IV:535-538
  Montagu, IV:984
  Pelham, IV:1074-1076
  Pitt the Elder, IV:1098
  Stanhope, IV:1277-1280
Walras, Léon, **IX:3865-3868**
  Elements of Pure Economics, IX:3865, 3866
Walsh, Raoul, IX:3901
Walsingham, Francis, IV:46
Walsingham, Thomas, III:471, 472
Walter, John, II, **VI:2324-2327**
Walters, Barbara, **IX:3868-3871**
Walther, Balthasar, IV:154
Walther, Johann Gottfried, IV:77
Walther von der Vogelweide, **II:959-961**
  "I Was Sitting upon a Rock," II:961
  "What is Loving?," II:960
  "When the Flowers Spring out of the Grass," II:960
Walton, Sir William, **IX:3872-3876**
  Belshazzar's Feast, IX:3873, 3874
  Façade, IX:3872, 3874
  Spitfire Prelude and Fugue, IX:3874
  Troilus and Cressida, IX:3874
Walworth, Sir Thomas, II:922
Wampanoag Indians, IV:930-933, 954-956
Wamsutta, IV:931, 932, 954
Wang An-shih, II:840, 841, 855-857, 866, **962-964**
Wang Chin, II:967
Wang Ching-wei, **IX:3877-3880**
Wang Ch'ung, **I:943-945**
  Cheng-wu, I:943

Chi-su chieh-yi, I:943
Lun-hêng, I:943, 944
Wanghia, Treaty of, V:582
Wang Hsi-chih, **I:946-948**
  Lan t'ing hsu, I:947, 948
Wang Mang, I:590
Wang Pi, **I:949-951**
Wang Wei, I:841; **II:965-968**
Wang Yang-ming, **III:771-773**
  Instructions for Practical Living, III:772
Wankel, Felix, **IX:3881-3883**
Warbeck, Perkin, III:346
Ward, Joshua, IV:1182
Ward, Lester Frank, **VI:2328-2330**
  Dynamic Sociology, VI:2329
  Psychic Factors of Civilization, The, VI:2329
Ward, Montgomery, **VI:2331-2334**
Ward, Nancy, VIII:2389
Wardenclyffe, VI:2220
Wardley, James and Jane, IV:817, 818
Ware, Henry, V:470
Warens, Madame de, IV:1194
Warhol, Andy, IX:3828, **3884-3887**
  Andy Warhol's Dracula, IX:3886
  Andy Warhol's Frankenstein, IX:3886
  Campbell's Soup Can, IX:3885
  Flesh, IX:3886
  Liz, IX:3885
  Lonesome Cowboy, IX:3886
  Marilyn Monroe, IX:3885
  Trash, IX:3886
Warner, Pop, IX:3674
Warner Brothers, IX:4100
War of 1812. *See* 1812, War of
Warren, Earl, VII:509; **IX:3888-3892**
Warren, John Collins, VI:1597
Warren, Robert Penn, **IX:3893-3896**
  All the King's Men, IX:3894, 3895
  Approach to Literature, An, IX:3894
  At Heaven's Gate, IX:3894
  Band of Angels, IX:3894
  Brother to Dragons, IX:3894
  Cave, The, IX:3894
  John Brown, IX:3894
  Meet Me in the Green Glen, IX:3894
  Night Rider, IX:3894
  Segregation, IX:3894
  Understanding Poetry, IX:3894, 3895
  Who Speaks for the Negro?, IX:3894
  Wilderness, IX:3894
  World Enough and Time, IX:3894
Warren Commission, IX:3890

Warsaw Pact, VII:969; VIII:1530, 1961
Warsaw Uprising, VIII:1561
Warwick, Earl of, **III:774-777**
    Edward IV, III:234
    Henry VI, III:342, 343
    Henry VII, III:345, 346
    Richard III, III:647, 649
Washington, Booker T., **VI:2335-2339;** VII:964
Washington, George, **IV:1405-1408**
    Adams, IV:18, 19
    André, IV:44
    Arnold, IV:66
    Cornwallis, IV:367
    Fitch, IV:476, 477
    Greene, IV:574-577
    Hamilton, IV:608
    Heth, V:135
    Jay, IV:713
    Jefferson, IV:718, 719
    McGillivray, IV:876
    Marshall, VI:1488
    Monroe, VI:1571
    Peale, IV:1070, 1072
    Rochambeau, IV:1174-1176
    Ross, IV:1191-1193
    Stuart's portrait, IV:1289, 1291, 1292
    Wilson, IV:1458
    Witherspoon, IV:1469
    Wood's paintings, IX:4047, 4048
Washington Conference on Naval Disarmament,
    VIII:1767
Washington Monument, V:80
Washington Post, The, VIII:1451-1453, 2205
Washkansky, Louis, VII:195, 197
Watergate affair
    Bush, VII:521
    Ford, VII:1181
    Jordan, VIII:1888
    Nixon, VIII:2758, 2760
    Washington Post, VIII:1453
Waterloo, Battle of, V:942; VI:1617, 1647, 2353
Watson, James D., VII:797; IX:2927, **3897-3900,**
    3996, 3997
    Double Helix, The, VII:797, IX: 3898
Watson, John C., V:631
Watson, Thomas, III:472
Watson, Thomas A., V:185, 186
Watt, James, **IV:1409-1412**
    Arkwright, IV:62
    Boulton, IV:182-184
    Cavendish, IV:262
    Murdock, IV:1008-1010

    Roebuck, IV:1184, 1185
    Trevithick, VI:2251
    Wilkinson, IV:1443, 1444
Watteau, Antoine, **IV:1413-1416**
    Gersaint's Shopsign, IV:1415
    Gilles, IV:1415
    Pilgrimage to Cythera, IV:1414
    Venetian Pleasures, IV:1415
Watts, George Frederick, VI:2215, 2216
    Choosing, VI:2215
    Ellen Terry, VI:2215
    Ophelia, VI:2215
    Sisters, The, VI:2215
Waugh, Edith, V:1170
Waugh, Fanny, V:1170
Wayne, John, **IX:3901-3904**
    Alamo, The, IX:3903
    Big Trail, The, IX:3901
    Fort Apache, IX:3902
    Green Berets, The, IX:3903
    Man Who Shot Liberty Valance, The, IX:3903
    Quiet Man, The, IX:3903
    Red River, IX:3902, 3903
    Rio Grande, IX:3902, 3903
    Rooster Cogburn, IX:3903
    Salute, IX:3901
    Sands of Iwo Jima, IX:3903
    Searchers, The, IX:3902, 3903
    Seven Sinners, VII:932
    Shepherd of the Hills, The, IX:3902
    She Wore a Yellow Ribbon, IX:3902
    Shootist, The, IX:3903
    Stagecoach, IX:3902
    True Grit, IX:3902, 3903
WCTU. *See* Women's Christian Temperance
    Union
Webb, Beatrice, VII:308; **IX:3905-3909,** 3939
    History of Trade Unionism, The, IX:3907
    Industrial Democracy, IX:3907
    My Apprenticeship, IX:3908
    Our Partnership, IX:3908
    Soviet Communism: A New Civilisation?,
        IX:3908
Webb, Chick, VII:1157
Webb, James Watson, V:191
Webb, John, IV:736
Webb, Sidney, **IX:3905-3909,** 3939
    History of Trade Unionism, The, IX:3907
    Industrial Democracy, IX:3907
    Soviet Communism: A New Civilisation?,
        IX:3908
Webber, Andrew Lloyd, VII:1060

Weber, Carl Maria von, **VI:2340-2343**
  Abu Hassan, VI:2340
  Euryanthe, VI:2342
  Freischütz, VI:2341, 2342
  Konzerstück, VI:2341
  Oberon, VI:2342
  Peter Schmoll und seine Nachbarn, VI:2340
Weber, Ernst Heinrich, V:781
Weber, Max, IX:3723, **3910-3913**
  Economy and Society, IX:3911
  Protestant Ethic and the Spirit of Capitalism,
    IX:3911
Weber, Wilhelm Eduard, V:895
Webern, Anton von, VII:386, 387, 389; IX:3359,
  3542, **3914-3917**
  Passacaglia Op. 1, IX:3914, 3915
Webster, Daniel, VI:1772, 2075, **2344-2347**, 2375
Webster, John
  Duchess of Malfi, The, I:772
Webster, Noah, **IV:1417-1420**
  American Dictionary of the English Language,
    An, IV:1419
  Dissertations on the English Language, IV:1419
  Grammatical Institute of the English Language,
    A, IV:1417
  Little Reader's Assistant, The, IV:1417
  New England Primer, The, IV:1417
  Sketches of American Policy, IV:1419, 1420
Weddington, Sarah, IX:3170
Wedgwood, Josiah, **IV:1421-1425**
  Address on the Subject of Entering into Service
    of Foreign Manufacturers, An, IV:1423
  Address to the Young Inhabitants of the Pottery,
    An, IV:1423
Weed, Thurlow, V:792, 793, 984, 985; VI:2037,
  2038
Wegener, Alfred, **IX:3918-3921**
  Origin of Continents and Oceans, IX:3919
Wei, Lady, I:946
Wei Cheng, II:877, 879
Weigel, Helene, VII:444
Wei Jingsheng, VII:906
Weil, Simone, **IX:3922-3925**
  Condition ouvrière, La, IX:3922
  Écrits de Londres et dernières lettres, IX:3924
  Need for Roots, The, IX:3925
  Notebooks, IX:3924
Weill, Al, VIII:2412, 2413
Weill, Kurt, **IX:3926-3929**
  Down in the Valley, IX:3928
  Eternal Road, The, IX:3928
  Firebrand of Florence, The, IX:3928

  Happy End, IX:3927
  Johnny Johnson, IX:3928
  Knickerbocker Holiday, IX:3928
  Lady in the Dark, IX:3928
  Lost in the Stars, IX:3928
  Love Life, IX:3928
  "Mack the Knife," IX:3929
  Mahagonny Songspiel, IX:3927
  One Touch of Venus, IX:3928
  Protagonist, Der, IX:3927
  Rise and Fall of the City of Mahagonny, The,
    IX:3927
  Seven Deadly Sins of the Petit Bourgeois, The,
    IX:3928
  Sinfonia Sacra Op. 6; *Frauenatz*, IX:3926
  Street Scene, IX:3928
  Tale of Love and Death of Cornet Christopher
    Rilke, The, IX:3926
  Threepenny Opera, The, IX:3927, 3929
Weimar Republic
  Hindenburg, VIII:1674-1676
  Hitler, VIII:1694
  Niemöller, VIII:2742
Weismann, August, **VI:2348-2350**
Weiss, Carl Austin, VIII:2229
Weiss, Johannes, VII:498
Weizmann, Chaim, VII:252; VIII:2768;
  IX:3930-3933
Welcome House, VII:488, 489
welfare state
  England, VII:530; VIII:2094; IX:3908
  New Zealand, VI:2017-2019
  Stevens, VI:2137
  Sweden, VIII:2671-2673
Welfs, II:466, 468, 932
Welles, Orson, VIII:1597; **IX:3934-3937**
  Chimes at Midnight, IX:3935
  Citizen Kane, VIII:1604; IX:3935
  F for Fake, IX:3935
  Macbeth, IX:3934-3936
  Magnificent Ambersons, The, IX:3935
  Othello, IX:3935
  Shadow, The, IX:3934
  Touch of Evil, IX:3935
  Trial, The, IX:3935
  War of the Worlds, IX:3934
Wellesley, Arthur. *See* Wellington, Duke of
Wellington, Duke of, V:995; VI:1681, 1720,
  2351-2354, 2393
Wells, H.G., VI:2304; **IX:3938-3940**
  Ann Veronica, IX:3938
  Anticipations, IX:3939

Experiment in Autobiography, IX:3940
Future in America, The, IX:3939
God, the Invisible King, IX:3939
History of Mr. Polly, The, IX:3939
Invisible Man, The, IX:3939
Island of Doctor Moreau, The, IX:3939
Kipps, IX:3939
Modern Utopia, A, IX:3939
Mr. Britling Sees It Through, IX:3939
New Machiavelli, The, IX:3939
Outline of History, The, IX:3939, 3940
Passionate Friends, The, IX:3938
This Misery of Boots, IX:3939
Time Machine, The, IX:3938, 3940
Tono-Bungay, IX:3939
Wonderful Visit, The, IX:3939
Wells-Barnett, Ida B., **IX:3941-3944**
Welt, Die, V:1104; VII:484
Wenceslaus, **II:969-972,** 1030
Wen-ti, I:431
Wentworth, Lady, IV:765
Wentworth, Thomas. *See* Strafford, First Earl of
Wentworth, W.C., **VI:2355-2357**
Wert, Giaches de, IV:990, 991
Wertheimer, Max, **IX:3945-3948**
Wertheimer, Pierre, VII:651
Wesley, John, **IV:1426-1430,** 1490
Wessex, Godwin, Earl of, II:315, 316, 426
West, Benjamin
    Copley, IV:357
    Fulton, V:854
    Kauffmann, IV:765, 767
    Morse, VI:1592
    Peale, IV:1070
    Stuart, IV:1289, 1290
West, Mae, VII:829; **IX:3949-3952**
    Belle of the Nineties, IX:3950
    Catherine Was Great, IX:3950, 3951
    Come on Up, IX:3950
    Constant Sinner, The, IX:3949
    Diamond Lil, IX:3949, 3950
    Drag, The, IX:3949
    Heat's On, The, IX:3950
    I'm No Angel, IX:3950
    My Little Chickadee, IX:3950
    Myra Breckenridge, IX:3951
    Night After Night, IX:3950
    Pleasure Man, The, IX:3949, 3951
    Sextette, IX:3951
    She Done Him Wrong, IX:3950
    Wicked Age, The, IX:3949
West African Frontier Force, VIII:2269

Western Electric Company, VIII:2623
Western Federation of Miners, V:280
Western Female Institute, V:171
Western Pacific Railroad, VI:2098
Western Reserve Eclectic Institute, V:875, 876
Westinghouse, George, VI:2219, **2358-2362**
Westinghouse Electric Corporation, VI:2360; IX:4125
Westminster, Statute of, VIII:1982
Westminster Abbey
    Blake, IV:137
    Caxton, III:144
    Henry III, II:455
    Purcell, IV:1137-1139
    Scott, VI:2003
    Sharp, IV:1238
Westminster Bridge, IV:243
Westminster Confession, IV:99
Westminster Review, IV:109; V:751
Weston, Edward, VII:809
Westphalia, Treaty of, III:493; IV:304, 305, 342, 508; 644, 946, 1053; VI:2187
West Point, U.S. Military Academy at
    André, IV:43, 44
    Arnold, IV:66
    Bradley, VII:403
    Eisenhower, VII:1043
    Goethals, VIII:1410
    MacArthur, VIII:2295, 2296
    Patton, IX:2911
    Pershing, IX:2983-2985
    Thayer, VI:2223-2225
Wexler, Jerry, VII:1217
Weyden, Rogier van der, **III:778-780**
    Descent from the Cross, III:778, 779
    Portrait of a Woman, III:779
    Entombment, III:779
    Madonna with Four Saints, III:779
Whampoa Military Academy, VII:664, 676
Wharton, Edith, VII:1130; **IX:3953-3956**
    Age of Innocence, The, VIII:2175; IX:3954
    Buccaneers, The, IX:3954
    Bunner Sisters, The, IX:3954
    Custom of the Country, The, IX:3954
    Descent of Man, The, IX:3953
    Ethan Frome, IX:3954, 3955
    Fruit of the Tree, The, IX:3954
    Ghosts, IX:3954
    Glimpses of the Moon, IX:3954
    Gods Arrive, The, IX:3954
    House of Mirth, The, IX:3953, 3954
    Hudson River Bracketed, IX:3955

Madame de Treymes, IX:3954
Old New York, IX:3954
Reef, The, IX:3954
Sanctuary, IX:3953
Valley of Decision, The, IX:3953
Wheaton, Henry
    History of the Law of Nations, IV:581
Wheatstone, Charles, **V:555-559;** VI:2068;
    VII:1040
Wheeler, Ralph, IV:196
Wheelwright, John, IV:688
Whewell, William, VI:2063
Whig Party (England)
    Addison, IV:26
    Anne, IV:52, 53
    Bolingbroke, IV:158-161
    Brougham, V:314-316
    Burke, IV:222
    Canning, V:405
    Catholic emancipation, VI:1681
    Chadwick, V:457, 459
    Charles II, IV:285
    Cromwell, IV:381
    Defoe, IV:401
    Derby, V:653
    Disraeli, V:677
    Durham, V:721, 722
    Fielding, IV:470
    Fox, IV:479, 481-483
    George I, IV:531-533
    George II, IV:535
    George IV, V:902, 904
    Gladstone, VIII:2091
    Grey, V:994
    Jeffrey, V:1224-1226
    Kidd, IV:777, 779, 780
    Macaulay, VI:1427-1429
    Melbourne, VI:1517-1519
    Monmouth, IV:981
    Oates, IV:1039
    Palmerston, VI:1720
    Pelham, IV:1074, 1075
    Reynolds, IV:1162
    Russell, VI:1930-1932
    Seward, VI:2037-2039
    Shaftesbury, IV:1228, 1230, 1231
    Swift, IV:1307
    Vanbrugh, IV:1352
    Walpole, IV:1400-1403
Whig Party (U.S.)
    Blaine, V:255
    Clay, V:509, 510

    Crockett, V:578, 579
    Cushing, V:581, 582
    Fillmore, V:792-794
    Greeley, V:984
    Harrison, V:1062
    Lincoln, VI:1382
    Massachusetts, V:125
    Polk, VI:1803
    Scott, VI:2011, 2012
    Stephens, VI:2129
    Stevens, VI:2136
    Tyler, VI:2289, 2290
    Van Buren, VI:2294
    Webster, VI:2345
Whipple, George Hoyt, **IX:3957-3960**
Whiskey Rebellion, IV:611, 719
Whistler, James McNeill, **VI:2363-2367**
    *Arrangement in Grey and Black, No. 1: The
        Artist's Mother,* VI:2364
    Harmony in Blue and Gold, VI:2364
    Whistler v. Ruskin, VI:2364
Whitaker, Alexander, IV:1106, 1107
White, Stanford, VI:1941
White, Walter, **IX:3961-3964**
    Fire in the Flint, IX:3962
    Flight, IX:3962
    Rope and Faggot, IX:3962
Whitefield, George, IV:429, 1426, 1427
White Friars. *See* Carmelites
White Ghibellines. *See* Ghibellines
Whitehead, Alfred North, **IX:3965-3968**
    Adventures of Ideas, IX:3967
    Introduction to Mathematics, An, IX:3967
    Modes of Thought, IX:3968
    Principia Mathematica, VIII:2725;
        IX:3966, 3967
    Process and Reality, IX:3967
    Science and the Modern World, IX:3967
    Treatise on Universal Mathematics, A, IX:3966
White Lotus Sect, IV:302
Whitewater Development Corporation, VII:715
Whitman, Walt, **VI:2368-2373;** VII:263, 791;
    IX:3308, 3309
    "Child's Reminiscence, A," VI:2370
    "Crossing Brooklyn Ferry," VI:2370
    Democratic Vistas, VI:2371
    Drum Taps, VI:2371
    Franklin Evans, VI:2368
    Leaves of Grass, V:758; VI:2370, 2371
    "O Captain! My Captain!," VI:2371
    "Out of the Cradle Endlessly Rocking," VI:2370
    Passage to India, VI:2371

Specimen Days and Collect, VI:2371
"When Lilacs Last in the Dooryard Bloom'd,"
   VI:2371; VIII:1672
Whitney, Eli, **IV:1431-1434;** VI:2075, 2076
Whitney, Gertrude Vanderbilt, **IX:3969-3971**
   Fountain of El Dorado, IX:3970
   Paganism Immortal, IX:3969
   Spirit of Flight, The, IX:3971
   Titanic Memorial, IX:3970
Whitney Museum of American Art, IX:3969-3971
Whitney v. California, VII:422
Whittaker, James, IV:818, 819
Whittier, John Greenleaf, V:883; **VI:2374-2376**
   "Barefoot Boy, The," VI:2375
   "Bridal of Pennacock, The," VI:2375
   "Christian Slave, The," VI:2375
   "Exile's Departure, The," VI:2374
   "Farewell of a Virginia Slave Mother, The,"
     VI:2375
   Home Ballads and Other Poems, VI:2376
   "Ichabod," VI:2375
   Justice and Expediency, VI:2374
   Lays of My Home and Other Poems, VI:2375
   Legends of New England, VI:2374
   "Massachusetts to Virginia," VI:2375
   "Merrimack, The," VI:2375
   "New Wife and the Old, The," VI:2375
   "Skipper Ireson's Ride," VI:2376
   "Slave Ships, The," VI:2375
   Snow-Bound: A Winter Idyl, VI:2376
   "Telling the Bees," VI:2376
   "Toussaint L'Ouverture," VI:2374
   "Within the Gate," V:491
Whittle, Sir Frank, **IX:3972-3975**
Widukind, **II:973-975**
Wieland, Christopher Martin, VI:1294
Wiener, Norbert, **IX:3976-3979**
Wiesel, Elie, **IX:3980-3983**
   Accident, The, IX:3980
   Beggar in Jerusalem, A, IX:3982
   Dawn, IX:3980
   Gates of the Forest, The, IX:3980
   Jews of Silence, The, IX:3980
   Night, IX:3980
   Oath, The, IX:3982
   Town Beyond the Wall, The, IX:3980
   Zalmen, IX:3982
Wiesenthal, Simon, **IX:3984-3988**
Wightman, Hazel Hotchkiss, **IX:3989-3991**
   Better Tennis, IX:3991
Wightman Cup, IX:3990, 3991
Wilberforce, William, **IV:1435-1428;** V:378, 379

Wild, Richard, VI:1786
Wilde, Oscar, VI:1750, **2377-2380;**
   VII:1088, 1367
   Guido Ferranti, VI:2379
   Happy Prince and Other Tales, The, VI:2379;
     VII:371
   Importance of Being Earnest, The,
     VI:2377, 2379
   Intentions, VI:2379
   Picture of Dorian Gray, The, VI:2379
   Poems, VI:2377
   Salomé, V:163
Wilder, Laura Ingalls, **IX:3992-3994**
   By the Shores of Silver Lake, IX:3993
   Farmer Boy, IX:3993
   First Four Years, The, IX:3993
   Let the Hurricanes Roar, IX:3993
   Little House in the Big Woods, IX:3992, 3993
   Little House on the Prairie, IX:3992
   Long Winter, The, IX:3992
   On the Banks of Plum Creek, IX:3992
   On The Way Home, IX:3992
   These Happy Golden Years, IX:3992
   West From Home, IX:3993
Wilkes, Charles, **VI:2381-2383**
Wilkes, John, IV:176, 908, 1099, **1439-1442**
   Essay on Woman, IV:1440
   North Briton, The, IV:1439, 1440, 1441
Wilkins, Sir George Hubert, **IX:3999-4002**
   Flying the Artic, IX:4000
   Undiscovered Australia, IX:4000
Wilkins, Maurice H.F., VII:797, 798; IX:3897,
   3898, **3995-3998**
Wilkinson, James, IV:1094, 1096
Wilkinson, John, **IV:1443-1446**
Willard, Emma, **VI:2384-2387**
   Address Proposing a Plan for Improving Female
     Education, An, VI:2385
   Universal Peace, VI:2386
Willard, Frances, **VI:2388-2391**
Willard, Jess, VII:902
Willard, Samuel, IV:1225
William I, II:28, 29
William II, VII:494-496; IX:3689, **4003-4006**
William III, **IV:1447-1450**
   Anne, IV:50, 52
   Defoe, IV:399
   Godolphin, IV:553
   Kidd, IV:777
   Leeds, IV:823
   Locke, IV:857, 858
   Marlborough, IV:922-924

Mather, IV:940
Popish Plot, IV:1040
William IV, V:722, 995; VI:2307, 2308, **2392-2395**
William IX, II:336
William X, II:336
William of Auvergne, **II:976-980**
De Universo, II:978
Magisterium divinale sive sapientale, II:978
William of Auxerre, **II:981-984**
Summa aurea, II:982, 983
William of Champeaux, II:10
William of Moerbeke, **II:985, 986**
William of Newburgh, II:293
William of Normandy, II:317, 428, 429
William of Orange. *See* William III
William of Rubrouck, **II:987-989**
William of Saint-Amour, **II:990-993**
Collectiones catholicae et canonicae scripturae,
II:992
De periculis novissimorum temporum, II:992
William of Saint-Thierry, **II:994-996**
Enigma of Faith, The, II:995
Expositions on the Song of Songs, II:995
Golden Epistle, The, II:994
Meditations, The, II:995
Mirror of Faith, The, II:995
On Contemplating God, II:994
On the Nature and Dignity of Love, II:994
On the Sacrament of the Altar, II:994
Saint Bernard of Clairvaux, II:994, 995
William of Tyre, II:70
William Rufus, II:73
Williams, Eric, VII:760
Williams, George Washington, **VI:2396-2399**
History of the Negro Race in America, VI:2397
History of the Negro Troops in the War of the
Rebellion, 1861-1865, VI:2397
Open Letter to His Serene Majesty, Leopold II,
An, VI:2398
Williams, Roger, IV:371, 930-932, **1451-1454,**
1464; IX:2893
Bloody Tenent of Persecution, for Cause of
Conscience, Discussed, IV:1451
Bloody Tenent Yet More Bloody, The, IV:1452
Examiner Defended, The, IV:1452
Fourth Paper Presented by Major Butler, The,
IV:1452
George Fox Digg'd out of His Burrows, IV:1453
Hireling Ministry None of Christs, The, IV:1452
Mr. Cottons Letter Lately Printed, Examined,
and Answered, IV:1451
Queries of Highest Consideration, IV:1451

Williams, Tennessee, VII:795; VIII:2310; IX:3885,
4007-4011
American Blues, IX:4009
Battle of Angels, IX:4009
Camino Real, IX:4010
Glass Menagerie, The, IX:4007, 4009
Orpheus Descending, IX:4009, 4010
Streetcar Named Desire, A, VII:425; IX:4010
Suddenly Last Summer, IX:4009, 4010
Summer and Smoke, IX:4010
Williams, William Carlos, III:766
William the Conqueror, II:72, 443, 794, **997-1000**
William the Silent, III:574, 575, 600, **781-784**
Willibald, II:167, 168
Willibrord, Saint, II:167, 824, 825
Willich, August, V:761
Willkie, Wendell, VIII:2256
Wilmot Proviso, VI:1803
Wilson, Alexander
American Ornithology, V:86
Wilson, Edmund, VII:1161, 1163; VIII:2304;
IX:4012-4015
Axel's Castle, IX:4012-4014
I Thought of Daisy, IX:4013
"Man Who Shot Snapping Turtles, The," IX:4013
Memoirs of Hecate County, IX:4013
Patriotic Gore, IX:4014, 4015
"Princess with the Golden Hair," IX:4013
To the Finland Station, IX:4014
Travels in Two Democracies, IX:4012
Wound and the Bow, The, IX:4014
Wilson, Sir Harold, **IX:4016-4019**
Heath, VIII:1607, 1608
Wilson, Sir Horace, VII:645
Wilson, James, **IV:1455-1459**
Wilson, John, IV:688
Wilson, Robert T.
Black Phalanx, VI:2397
Wilson, Woodrow, **IX:4020-4024**
Balch, VII:161
Benes, VII:260
Brandeis, VII:421
Bryan, VII:481
Guggenheim, VIII:1500
Hoover, VIII:1727
Hughes, VIII:1777
Hull, VIII:1779
La Follette, VIII:2048
Lippmann, VIII:2204
Lodge, VIII:2221
Mexican Revolution, IX:3813
Mott, VIII:2639

neutrality declaration, VIII:1396
Roosevelt, IX:3229, 3231
Sargent, VI:1964
Shaw, VI:2046
Stimson, IX:3538
Washington, VI:2337
Wimbledon (tennis tournament)
 Borg, VII:368, 369
 Evert, VII:1113
 Gibson, VII:1364
 King, VIII:1968
 Laver, VIII:2109, 2110
 Navratilova, VIII:2703
 Perry, IX:2979, 2981, 2982
Winchester, Statutes of, II:322
Winchester, Treaty of, II:849
Winckelmann, Johann Joachim, IV:408, 410,
 1460-1462
 History of Ancient Art, IV:1460, 1461
 *Reflections on the Paintings and Sculpture of the
 Greeks,* IV:1460, 1461
Windsor, Duke of, **IX:4025-4028**
Windsor, House of, VII:1340
Winfrey, Oprah, **IX:4029-4032**
 Beloved, IX:4031
 Color Purple, The, IX:4030
 Native Son, IX:4030
 Oprah Winfrey Show, The, IX:4029-4031
 Women of Brewster Place, The, IX:4031
Wingolf Society, IX:3685
Winkler, Paula, VII:484
Winter, Thomas, III:258, 259
Winterfeld, Carl von, III:286
Winter War, VIII:2397, 2398
Winthrop, John, IV:688, **1463-1466**
 "Modell of Christian Charity, A," IV:1465
Winthrop, Robert, VI:1772
Wise, Issac Mayer, **VI:2400-2402**
 Minhag America, VI:2401
Wise, Stephen Samuel, **IX:4033-4035**
Wister, Owen, V:52
witchcraft trials. *See* Salem witchcraft trials
Witherspoon, John, **IV:1467-1470**
 Ecclesiastical Characteristics, IV:1457
Witmer, Lightner, IX:4070
Witt, Jan de, IV:1447
Witta, I:378
Wittel, Gaspar van, IV:242
Wittenberg Concord of 1536, III:102
Wittgenstein, Ludwig, VIII:2607; **IX:4036-4038**
 Philosophical Investigations, IX:4037
 Tractatus, IX:4036, 4037

Wladyslaw II Jagiello, **II:1001-1004**
Wladyslaw III, III:374, 375
Woffington, Peg, IV:527, 528
Wofford, Chloe Anthony. *See* Morrison, Toni
Wöhler, Friedrich, **VI:2403-2405;** VIII:2713
Wojtyla, Karol Jozef. *See* John Paul II
Wolf, Hugo, V:1163
Wolf, Max, **IX:4039-4040**
Wolfe, Harry Kirke, IX:4070
Wolfe, James, IV:37, 38, 676, **1471-1474**
Wolfe, Thomas, **IX:4041-4044**
 Face of a Nation, The, IX:4043
 Hills Beyond, The, IX:4043
 Look Homeward, Angel, IX:4041-4043
 Mannerhouse, IX:4043
 Of Time and the River, IX:4042
 Stone, a Leaf, a Door, A, IX:4043
 Story of a Novel, The, IX:4042
 Web and the Rock, The, IX:4041, 4042
 Western Journal, A, IX:4043
 You Can't Go Home Again, IX:4042
Wolff, Christian von, IV:832
Wolfram von Eschenbach, **II:1005-1007**
 Parzifal, II:393, 1005
 Schionatulander and Sigune, II:1007
 Willehalm, II:1007
Wolfsohn, Leopold, VII:766
Wolie, Ras Gugsa, VIII:1519
Wollman, Elie, VIII:1828
Wollstonecraft, Mary, IV:555-558, **1475-1479;**
 VI:2048, 2051
 *Historical and Moral View of the Origin and
 Progress of the French Revolution,* IV:1477
 Maria, IV:1477
 Mary, a Fiction, IV:1475
 Original Stories from Real Life, IV:138
 Thoughts on the Education of Daughters,
 IV:1475
 Vindication of the Rights of Men, A, IV:1477
 Vindication of the Rights of Women, A, IV:1477;
 VI:1600
Wolsey, Cardinal Thomas, **III:785-787**
 Boleyn, III:66, 68
 Catherine of Aragon, III:138
 Cromwell, III:208
 Fisher, III:264
 Gardiner, III:291
 Henry VIII, III:349, 351
 More, III:534, 535
Woman's Committee of the Council of National
 Defense, VI:2046
Woman's Journal, VI:2145, 2146

Woman's Peace Party, VII:23

Woman's State Temperance Society of New York, V:61; VI:2111

Women's Armed Services Integration Act of 1948, IX:3446

Women's Auxiliary Army Corps, VIII:1703-1705

Women's Christian Temperance Union, VI:1630, 1631, 2044, 2045, 2388-2390

Women's International League for Peace and Freedom, VII:161, 162, 354

Women's International of Socialists and Labour Organizations, VII:354

women's liberation movement, VII:231; VIII:2536

women's magazines, V:1022-1024; VII:1231

Women's Medical College of the New York Infirmary, V:252

Women's Rights, Declaration of, V:61

Women's Rights Convention, VI:1601, 2257

Women's Social and Political Union, V:778; IX:2871, 2873, 2874

Women's Strike for Equality, VII:1233

women's suffrage
    Addams, VII:23
    Alcott, V:42
    Anthony, V:61-64
    Argentina, IX:2966
    Catt, VII:627-629
    Bondfield, VII:354
    Fawcett, V:776-779
    Hale, V:1024
    Hardie, V:1037
    Higginson, V:1111, 1112
    Howe, V:1145, 1146, 1148
    Lockwood, VI:1407
    Mott, VI:1601
    New Zealand, VI:2018
    Oakley, VI:1679
    Pankhurst, IX:2871, 2873, 2874
    Paul, IX:2919, 2920, 2922
    Rankin, IX:3117-3119
    Shaw, VI:2044-2046
    Stanton, VI:2110-2113
    Stone, VI:2143, 2145, 2146
    Truth, VI:2258
    Turkey, VII:134
    Willard, VI:2388-2390
    Wyoming, IX:3243

Women's Tennis Association, VII:1114; VIII:1969

Women's Trade Union League, VII:160, 353-356

Wood, Grant, **IX:4045-4048**
    American Gothic, IX:4047
    Appraisal, IX:4047

Daughters of Revolution, IX:4047

Midnight Ride of Paul Revere, IX:4047

Parson Weems' Fable, IX:4047

Stone City, Iowa, IX:4047

Woman with Plants, IX:4047

Wood, Leonard, IX:3233

Wood, Sidney, IX:2979

Wood, Thelma, VII:201

Woodhull, Victoria, VI:1407

Woods, Frank, VIII:2232

Woods, Tiger, **IX:4049-4051**

Woodstock Music and Art Fair, VIII:1884

Woodville, Elizabeth, III:649, 650

Woodward, Robert Burns, **IX:4052-4055**

Woolf, Virginia, V:330; VII:1193, 1254; VIII:2626; **IX:4056-4059**
    Between the Acts, IX:4058
    Common Reader, The, IX:4058
    Flush: A Biography, IX:4058
    Jacob's Room, IX:4056
    Mrs. Dalloway, IX:4056
    Room of One's Own, A, IX:4058
    Three Guineas, IX:4058
    To the Lighthouse, IX:4056
    Waves, The, IX:4058
    Years, The, IX:4058

Woolner, Thomas, V:1170

Worcester, Battle of, IV:1310

Worcester v. Georgia, VI:2149

Wordsworth, William, V:69, 75; **VI:2406-2409**
    Descriptive Sketches, VI:2406
    Evening Walk, An, VI:2406
    Excursion, The, VI:2407
    Lyrical Ballads, VI:2406-2408
    Michael, IV:566
    Ode: Intimations of Immortality, VI:2407, 2408
    "Ode to Duty," VI:2407
    Prelude: Or, The Growth of a Poet's Mind, The, VI:2406-2408
    River Duddon, The, VI:2407

Workingmen's Concert Association, VII:607

Workman, Fanny Bullock, **VI:2410-2413**
    Algerian Memories, VI:2411
    In the Ice World of the Himálayas, VI:2411
    Sketches Awheel in Modern Iberia, VI:2411
    Through Town and Jungle, VI:2411

Workman, William Hunter, VI:2410, 2412

Works Progress Administration, VII:985; VIII:1736, 1737, 1783, 2023; IX:3224

World Columbian Exposition. *See* World's Columbian Exposition

World Congress for Labor Palestine, VII:252

World Council of Churches, VIII:2743, 2744;
    IX:3776
World Cup soccer, IX:2950-2952
World Exhibition of 1867, VII:268
World Jewish Congress, IX:3842, 4034
World Missionary Conference, VIII:2639
World's Columbian Exposition
    Burnham, V:367
    Stone, VI:2146
    Sullivan, VI:2168
    Tesla, VI:2220
    Thomas, VI:2232
    Wells-Barnett, IX:3943
    Westinghouse, VI:2360
    Wright, IX:4060
World's Fair of 1893. *See* World's Columbian
    Exposition
World's Fair of 1937, IX:3252
World's Student Christian Federation, VIII:2638
World's Woman's Party, IX:2920
World War I
    Addams, VII:23, 24
    Allenby, VII:58-61
    All Quiet on the Western Front, IX:3150-3152
    American Expeditionary Forces, VIII:1437,
        2555; IX:2893-2895
    Angell, VII:75-77
    Army Air Service, VIII:2554, 2555
    Army Medical Corps, VIII:1436, 1437
    Asquith, VII:122, 123
    Balfour Declaration, VII:174
    Banting, VII:187
    Barth, VII:204
    battlefield injuries, VII:219
    Berlin, Irving, VII:288
    Bernstein, VII:292, 293
    Beust, V:224
    Bondfield, VII:354
    Borah, V:280
    Bryan, VII:481
    Byrd, VII:534
    Canada, VII:365, 366
    Cassin, VII:610
    Catholic Center Party, VII:1102-1104
    Chaplin, VII:653
    chemical weapons, VIII:1510, 1514
    Clausewitz, V:505
    Clemenceau, VII:704
    Conant, VII:749
    conscription, VII:882; VIII:2103; IX:3584, 3585
    Curie, VII:812
    Czechoslovakia, VII:260; VIII:2441, 2442

Eden, VII:1015
Edison, V:746
Faisal I, VII:1122, 1124, 1125
Fawcett, V:778
Francis Ferdinand, VII:1197-1199; IX:4005
German aircraft, VIII:1614
German High Seas Fleet, IX:3688-3690
German music ban, IX:3130
Giraudoux, VII:1379
Girl Scouts, VIII:2247
Goethals, VIII:1409
Goldman, VIII:1413
Gompers, V:958
Göring, VIII:1438
Gorky's propaganda, VIII:1444
Gramsci, VIII:1460
Greece, IX:3809
Grey, VIII:1475-1477
Gropius's architecture, VIII:1486
Haile Selassie, VIII:1519
Harmsworths, VIII:1555
Hindenburg, VIII:1674-1676
Hitler, VIII:1692, 1694
Hobhouse, VIII:1709
Hoover, VIII:1727, 1729
Hughes, VIII:1775-1777
Hull, VIII:1779
India, VIII:1847
John XXIII, VIII:1858, 1860
John Bull, VII:384
Kitchener, VIII:2003, 2004
Kokoschka, VIII:2013
La Follette, VIII:2048
Laval, VIII:2105
Lawrence, D.H., VIII:2117
Lawrence, T.E., VIII:2125
Léger, VIII:2155
Lippmann, VIII:2204
Lloyd George, VIII:2216, 2217
Ludendorff, VIII:2265-2267
Luxemburg, VIII:2286
MacArthur, VIII:2295
Macmillan, VIII:2340
Mannix, VI:1480
Marc, VIII:2405, 2406
Marne, Battle of the, VIII:1851-1853
Marshall, VIII:2429
Mott, VIII:2639
Mountbatten, VIII:2641
munitions industry, VII:695
Mussolini, VIII:2667, 2668
Nash, VIII:2689, 2690

National Catholic War Council, V:922
National Research Council Fellowships, VII:745
New Zealand, VIII:2445
Oakley, VI:1679
Olympic Games, VII:775
Ottoman Empire, VII:133
Papen, VII:2876
Patton, IX:2911
Pétain, IX:2987-2989
Poincaré, IX:3044-3046
Reith, IX:3146
reparation policies, VII:1104; VIII:1767, 1768;
  IX:3045, 3046
rocketry, VIII:1396, 1397
Rolls-Royce, IX:3210
Rommel, IX:3213
Sargent, VI:1963
Scheler, IX:3347, 3348
Scotland, VIII:2323
Seeckt, IX:3380-3382
Stimson, IX:3538
Stone, IX:3546, 3547
submarines, IX:3279
Turkey, VII:1078, 1079; VIII:1523
Weber, IX:3911
Whitney's memorial sculpture, IX:3970
William II, IX:4003-4005
Wilson, IX:4021, 4022
Wright brothers, IX:4066
zeppelins, VII:1012; IX:4110
World War II
  African Intelligence Department, VIII:2146
  Akihito, VII:41
  Alanbrooke, VII:45-47
  Angell, VII:77
  Astor, VII:130, 131
  atom bombs, VII:464, 747; VIII:1515, 1801,
    2040, 2122, 2337, 2725, 2726; IX:2833-2835,
    3376, 3492, 3742
  Australia, VII:816-818
  Balch, VII:162
  Baldwin, VII:170
  Beard, VII:224
  Blum, VII:337
  Bradley, VII:403, 404
  Bragg, VII:412
  Braudel, VII:436
  Britain, Battle of, VII:236
  British Fourteenth Army, IX:3435-3437
  Burmese Independence Army, IX:3647
  Bush, VII:520
  Cartier-Bresson, VII:595

Catt, VII:629
Chamberlain, VII:645, 646
Chinese-Japanese War, VII:665
Churchill, VII:693
Czechoslovakia, VII:261, 561
de Gaulle, VII:866, 867
documentary films, VII:1329
Dole, VII:947
Eden, VII:1016
Eisenhower, VII:1043
Franco, VII:1201, 1202
French Resistance, VII:239, 360, 553, 867, 1076;
  VIII:1872, 2106, 2558; IX:3329, 3330
George VI, VII:1343-1346
German missile program, VII:2777, 2779
Halsey, VIII:1525-1528
Harriman, VIII:1560, 1561
Hatoyama Ichiro, VIII:1575
Heinkel's aircraft, VIII:1615
Hemingway, VIII:1626
Hirohito, VIII:1678, 1680, 1681
Hopkins, VIII:1737
Hull, VIII:1781
India, VII:1283
Ireland, VII:878
Jacob, VIII:1827
Japanese American relocation and internment,
  VIII:2084, 2085, 2206; IX:3889
John XXIII, VIII:1858
John Paul II, VIII:1862, 1863
Johnson, VIII:1867
Joliot-Curies, VIII:1872
Kawabata, VIII:1914
Keynes, VIII:1954
Kissinger, VIII:1998
Laval, VIII:2105-2107
Libya, IX:3098, 3099
Lindbergh, VIII:2194
Lippmann, VIII:2205
Litvinov, VIII:2210, 2211
Louis, VIII:2243
MacArthur, VIII:2297, 2298
Malraux, VIII:2381
Manchurian takeover, VI:1365
Marshall Plan, VII:315; VIII:1529, 1562, 1696,
  2205, 2258, 2431; IX:3862
Matsushita Electric Company, VIII:2458
Mendès-France, VIII:2491
Menzies, VIII:2497
Messiaen, VIII:2503
Milne, VIII:2544
Mitterrand, VIII:2558

Monnet, VIII:2583, 2585
Montgomery, VIII:2602, 2603
Mountbatten, VIII:2643-2645
Murrow, VIII:2664
music business, VIII:1420, 1748
Nimitz, VIII:2750-2752
Palestine, VII:244, 252
Paris Opéra, VIII:2184
Patton, IX:2913
Pearl Harbor attack, VIII:1525, 2172
Pershing, IX:2985
Pétain, IX:2988, 2989
Philippines, VIII:2420
Pius XI, IX:3027, 3028
Pius XII, IX:3030-3032
Rankin, IX:3119
refugees, IX:3017
rocketry, VII:440-442; VIII:1397
Rolls-Royce, IX:3211
Romania, VII:1055
Roosevelt, IX:3225, 3226
Sandburg, IX:3311
Solzhenitsyn, IX:3460
South Africa, IX:3454
Steichen's combat photography, IX:3503
Stevenson, IX:3523
submarines, IX:3174
Tito, IX:3692, 3693
Truman, IX:3742
Turkey, VIII:1813
United Nations Commission on Human Rights,
    VII:611
War Information, Office of, VII:257
Welcome House, VII:488, 489
Whittle, IX:3974
Women's Auxiliary Army Corps,
    VIII:1703-1705
Yugoslav Revolution, VII:944, 945
Zhukov, IX:4116-4118
See also Nazi Party
World Zionist Organization, VII:252;
    VIII:2766-2768; IX:3930-3933
Worlidge, John
    Systema Agriculturae, IV:1346
Worms, Colloquy of, III:101, 102
Worms, Concordat of, II:74, 357
Worms, Diet of, III:492
Worms, Edict of, III:445
Wounded Knee, Battle at, VI:2072, 2073
WPA. See Works Progress Administration
Wren, Sir Christopher, **IV:1480-1483**
    Hawksmoor, IV:635, 636

Mansart, IV:900
Vanbrugh, IV:1354
Wright, Frank Lloyd, VI:2168; VII:325;
    VIII:2488, 2522; **IX:4060-4063**
Wright, Orville and Wilbur, **IX:4064-4068**
    Cayley, V:452
    Dunbar, V:714
    Heinkel, VIII:1614
    Langley, VI:1314
    Mitchell, VIII:2554
    Otto, VI:1703
Wright, Richard, VII:164; VIII:1788; IX:4030
WSPU. See Women's Social and Political
    Union
Wu, Emperor, I:817, 819, 820
Wu Ch'eng-en, II:485
Wundt, Wilhelm, IX:3946, 3947, **4069-4071**
    Outlines of Psychology, IX:4070
    Principles of Physiological Psychology,
        IX:4069, 4070
    Völkerpsychologie, IX:4070
Württemberg, Duke of, VI:2340
Wu San-kuei, IV:421, 422
Wyatt's Rebellion, III:320, 480
Wyclif, John, II:487-489, 971, 992,
    1009-1011, 1030
    De civili dominio, II:1010
Wye River Agreement, VII:93
Wyeth, Andrew, **IX:4072-4074**
    Christina's World, IX:4073
    Christmas Morning, IX:4073
    Hunter, The, IX:4073
    Karl, IX:4073
    Northern Point, IX:4073
    Pantry, The, IX:4073
    Public Sale, IX:4072
    Revenant, The, IX:4073
    Seed Corn, IX:4073
    Spring Beauty, IX:4073
    Spring Freshet, IX:4073
    Thin Ice, IX:4073, 4074
    Wind from the Sea, IX:4073
    Winter, IX:4072
Wyeth, Newell Convers, IX:4072, 4073
Wyler, William, VIII:1417
Wyndham, Sir William, IV:159
Wynfrith. See Boniface, Saint
Wyoming
    Calamity Jane, V:390
    fur trade, VI:2077, 2078
    Ross, IX:3243, 3244
    women's suffrage, IX:3243

Wythe, George, V:507
Wyttenbach, Thomas, III:791

Xanthippe, **I:952-954**
Xanthippos, I:740
Xanthus, I:13
Xavier, Saint Francis, III:438, **788-790**
Xenakis, Iannis, **IX:4075-4078**
   Akrata, IX:4077
   Atrées, IX:4077
   Bohor 1, IX:4077
   Cendrées, IX:4077
   Concret PA, IX:4076
   Diomorphoses, IX:4076
   Duel, IX:4077
   Eonta, IX:4077
   Kraanerg, IX:4077
   Métastasis, IX:4075, 4077
   Pithopratka, IX:4076
   Polytope de Montréal, IX:4077
   ST/4, IX:4077
   ST/48, IX:4077
   ST/10, IX:4077
   Stratégie, IX:4077
   Terretektorh, IX:4077
   Vamos Gamma, IX:4077
Xeniades, I:270
Xenophanes, I:596, **955-957**
   Peri phuseos, I:956
Xenophon, I:457, **958-961**
   Anabasis, I:959
   Banquet, The, I:958
   Cyropaedia, I:233
   Defense of Socrates, The, I:958
   Hellenica, I:960
   Institution and Life of Cyrus, The,
     I:959
   Ways and Means, I:960
Xerox, VII:579, 580
Xerxes I, I:47, 238, 501, 502, 705, **962-966**
X-rays
   Becquerel, V:167
   Bothe, VII:379
   Bragg, VII:410-413
   Broglie, VII:472
   Hertz, VIII:1647
   Hevesy, VIII:1655, 1656
   Hounsfield, VIII:1751-1753
   Lawrence, VIII:2121
   Pauling, IX:2926
   Popov, VI:1806, 1808
   radiation genetics, VIII:2651-2653

Watson, IX:3897, 3898
Wilkins, IX:3995-3997

Yaddo, IX:2785, 3061
Yale, Frank, VII:563, 564
Yale University
   Benèt, VII:263
   Boswell, IV:177
   Farrand, VII:1131
   Gibbs, V:923
   Hindemith, VIII:1672
   Hutchins, VIII:1800
   Ives, VIII:1820
   Lin, VIII:2187
   Mather, IV:935, 936
   Sherman, IV:1244
Yalta Conference, IX:3225
Yamani, Ahmad Zaki, **IX:4079-4081**
Yamato clan, II:826
Yamoussoukro, VIII:1756
Yamuna, II:770
Yanayev, Gennady, IX:4087
Yaqut, II:148, **1013-1014**
   Kitab mu'jam al-buldan, II:1013, 1014
   Yaqut's Dictionary of Learned Men, II:1013,
     1014
Yaroslav the Wise, II:953
Yates, Robert, IV:609
Yathrib. *See* Medina
Yeats, William Butler, IV:141; VI:1750;
     VIII:2683; **IX:4082-4085**
   "Among School Children," IX:4083
   At the Hawk's Well, IX:4083
   "Circus Animals Desertion, The," IX:4083, 4085
   "Coat, A," IX:4082
   "Cold Heaven, The," IX:4082
   Countess Cathleen, The, IX:4083
   "Deep-Sworn Vow, A," IX:4083
   "Easter 1916," IX:4083
   "In Memory of Major Robert Gregory," IX:4083
   "Irish Airman Foresees Death, An," IX:4083
   Last Poems and Plays, IX:4083
   Michael Robartes and the Dancer, IX:4083
   "Paudeen," IX:4082
   Responsibilities, IX:4082
   Rose, The, IX:4082
   "Sailing to Byzantium," IX:4083
   "Soldier, Scholar, Horseman," IX:4083
   "To a Shade," IX:4082
   "To a Wealthy Man," IX:4082
   Tower, The, IX:4083
   Vision, A, IX:4083

"Wanderings of Oisin, The," IX:4082
Wild Swans at Coole, The, IX:4083
Winding Stair and Other Poems, The, IX:4083
Yellow Book, The, V:162
yellow journalism
    Borden, V:285
    Eddy, V:741
    Hearst, VIII:1601, 1603-1605
    McKinley, VI:1454, 1455
    Oakley, VI:1678
    Pulitzer, VI:1826
Yellowstone National Park, V:1072-1074
Yeltsin, Boris N., VIII:2010; **IX:4086-4089**
Yen-an Way, VIII:2190
Yen Li-pen, **II:1015-1017**
    Eighteen Scholars at the Palace of Ch'in, II:1015
    Scroll of the Emperors, II:1015
Yen Li-te, II:1015, 1016
Yen Wu, II:919
Yepes y Álvarez, Juan de. *See* John of the Cross, Saint
Yiddish Scientific Institute, VII:847, 848
YMCA. *See* Young Men's Christian Association
Yo Fei, **II:1018-1020**
Yohai, Simon bar, II:649
Yohannes IV, VI:1537, 1538
Yomiuri Giants, IX:2796-2798
Yom Kippur War, VII:856, 1002; VIII:2474, 2475; IX:3289, 3290
York, Duke of, III:341-343, 345, 346, 657, 774, 775
Yorktown, Battle of, IV:323, 368, 608, 1000, 1174-1176, 1406
Yosemite National Park, VI:1609, 1692
Yoshida, Shigeru, VIII:1575; IX:3336
Young, Brigham, V:840; **VI:2414-2416**
Young, Charles, VI:1262
Young, Lester, VIII:1717, 1718
Young Contemporaries Exhibition, VIII:1711
Young England movement, V:677
Young Germany movement, V:1087
Young Irelanders movement, VI:1682
Young Italy movement, V:932; VI:1514
Young Men's Christian Association, V:711, 712; VI:1575, 1579; VII:477; VIII:2637-2639; IX:3127
Young Turks
    Atatürk, VII:133, 134
    Enver Pasha, VII:1078-1081
    Halide Edib Adivar, VIII:1522-1524
    İnönü, VIII:1812
Ypsilanti, Alexander, **VI:2417-2419**

Ypsilanti, Demetrios, **VI:2417-2419**
Yuan Ch'ung-huan, IV:2
Yüan Dynasty, II:566-568, 1021
Yüan Shih-k'ai, VII:687
Yüan Shu, II:841
Yueh-chi, I:494
Yugoslav Communist Party, VII:944; IX:3692, 3693
Yukawa, Hidecki, **IX:4090-4092**
Yung-lo, II:253, 254, **1021-1024**
Yunnan, II:253
Yverdon, VI:1768, 1769

Zaccaro, John, VII:1153-1155
Zacharias, II:824
Zachow, Friedrich, IV:619
Zadar, II:284
Zaghlul, Sa'd, **IX:4093-4095**
Zaharias, "Babe" Didrikson, **IX:4096-4099**
Zahir-ud-Din Muhammad. *See* Babur
Zaïmis, Alexandros, IX:3808
Zalinski, Edmund L., V:1124
Zama, Battle of, I:536, 761
Zambezi River, VI:1399, 1400
ZANLA. *See* Zimbabwe African National Liberation Army
ZANU. *See* Zimbabwe African National Union
Zanuck, Darryl F., XIII:1630; **IX:4100-4103**
    Cleopatra, IX:4101
    Grapes of Wrath, The, IX:4101
    How Green Was My Valley, IX:4101
    Jazz Singer, The, IX:4100
    Longest Day, The, IX:4101
    Public Enemy, The, IX:4101
Zanuck, Richard, IX:4101
Zapata, Emiliano, IX:2782, **4104-4107**
ZAPU. *See* Zimbabwe African People's Union
Zeami Motokiyo, **II:1025-1029**
    Kintosho, II:1027
    Nogaku koten: Zeami jorokubushu, II:1027
    Tochu Zeami nijusambushu, II:1027
Zecca, III:665
Zeckendorf, William, IX:2946
Zedekiah, I:460
Zeeman, Pieter, VIII:2235
Zeffirelli, Franco, IX:3083
Zegzard, Count, II:851
Zemlinksy, Alexander von, IX:3357
Zen Buddhism, II:666, 1028; VIII:1745, 2754, 2755
Zenger, John Peter, **IV:1484-1487**
    Brief Narrative of the Case and Tryal of John Peter Zenger, A, IV:1486

Zeno of Citium, I:68, **967-971**
  Politeia, I:967, 969
Zeno of Elea, I:597, **972-974**
Zentralschule Laban, VIII:2059
Zephyrinus, I:416
Zeppelin, Ferdinand von, VII:1011; **IX:4108-4111**
Zetkin, Clara, **IX:4112-4115**
  Working Women and the Contemporary Woman Question, IX:4112
Zeyer, Julius, VIII:1836
Zhao Ziyang, VIII:2178, 2179
Zhdanov, Andrei, VIII:2377, 2378; IX:3409
Zhemchuzhina, Polina, VIII:2572
Zhukov, Georgy Konstantinovich, VIII:1962; **IX:4116-4120**
Zhukovsky, Nikolay Yegorovich, IX:3764
Zhukovsky, Vasily Andreyevich, V:48
Ziegfeld Follies, IX:3205, 3206
Ziegler, Karl, VIII:2699
Zimbabwe African National Liberation Army, VIII:2647
Zimbabwe African National Union, VIII:2318, 2647-2649
Zimbabwe African People's Union, VIII:2647-2649
Zimri-Lim, I:361, 362
Zincke, Theodor, VIII:1513
Zinj, VIII:2147
Zinzendorf, Graf von, IV:1488
Zionism
  Arendt, VII:99, 100
  Baeck, VII:150
  Balfour Declaration, VII:174
  Begin, VII:243
  Ben-Gurion, VII:251-254
  Brandeis, VII:419, 421
  Buber, VII:484, 485
  Cassin, VII:610
  Eban, VII:1000
  Faisal, VIII:1118, 1120
  Herzl, V:1102, 1104, 1105
  Meir, VIII:2472-2475
  Nordau, VIII:2766-2768
  Palestine, Conference on, VIII:1118
  Weizmann, IX:3930-3933
  Wise, VI:2402; IX:4033-4035

Zizka, Count Jan, **II:1030-1032**
Znanya, VII:64
Zoffany, Johann, IV:529
Zola, Émile, **VI:2420-2424**; VII:703
  Assommoir, L', VI:2421
  Claude's Confession, VI:2420, 2421
  Experimental Novel, The, VI:2420, 2421; VIII:2134
  Germinal, VI:2421
  Madeleine Férat, VI:2420
  Nana, VI:2421; VII:119; IX:3157
  Quatre Evangiles, Les, VI:2423
  Rougon-Macquart Novels, The, VI:2420
  Soirées de Medan, Les, VI:2421
  Stories for Ninon, VI:2420
  Thérèse Raquin, VI:2420
  Three Cities, The, VI:2421
Zons, Michael, VI:1702
Zorin, Valerian, IX:3525
Zorn, Anders, VII:1300
Zoroaster, **I:975-977**
  See also Zoroastrianism
Zoroastrianism, I:237, 238, 781
Zoser, I:443, **978-980**
Zukor, Adolph, VII:897; VIII:1415, 1417; IX:3006
Zuni, III:181
Zwide, VI:2041, 2042
Zwilich, Ellen Taaffe, **IX:4121-4124**
  Cello Symphony, IX:4122
  Chamber Symphony, IX:4122
  Clarino Quartet, IX:4122
  Double Quartet, IX:4122
  Einsame Nicht, IX:4121
  Fantasy for Harpsicord, IX:4122
  Passages, IX:4122
  Piano Concerto, IX:4123
  String Quartet, IX:4122
  Symbalom, IX:4123
  Symphony No.3, IX:4123
  Symposium for Orchestra, IX:4122
  Tanzspiel, IX:4123
  Three Movements for Orchestra, IX:4122
Zwingli, Huldrych, III:101, 102, 103, **791-794**
  Artikel, III:793
  De vera ac falsa religione, III:793
Zworykin, Vladimir, **IX:4125-4128**